Introduction to Management Accounting

A USER PERSPECTIVE

CANADIAN EDITION

Kumen H. Jones
Arizona State University (Retired)

Michael L. Werner
University of Miami

Katherene P. Terrell
University of Central Oklahoma

Robert L. Terrell
University of Central Oklahoma

Peter Norwoord
Langara College

Prentice Hall

Toronto

To Helen.

National Library of Canada Cataloguing in Publication

Introduction to management accounting : a user perspective / Kumen H. Jones ... [et al.]. — Canadian ed.

Includes index.
ISBN 0-13-039097-6

1. Managerial accounting. I. Jones, Kumen H.

HF5657.4.I69 2003   658.15′11   C2002-904030-2

ISBN 0-13-039097-6

Vice President, Editorial Director: Michael J. Young
Senior Acquisitions Editor: Samantha Scully
Executive Marketing Manager: Cas Shields
Senior Developmental Editor: Suzanne Schaan
Production Editor: Judith Scott
Copy Editor: Anita Smale
Production Coordinator: Andrea Falkenberg
Page Layout: Heidi Palfrey
Art Director: Mary Opper
Interior Design: Jennifer Federico
Cover Design: Alex Li
Cover Image: © Walter Hodges/CORBIS

8 9 10   10 09 08

Printed and bound in Canada

Contents

GLOSSARY OF ACCOUNTING TERMS 424

INDEX 431

Preface

*N*ow that we have entered the twenty-first century, we who are involved in accounting education have reassessed the way we prepare our students for the business world. Technology changes more quickly than most of us can comprehend, complicating accounting education. Yet one constant remains: Business people must be prepared to perform tasks that only people can perform—in particular, communicating, thinking, and making decisions. Decision making is *the* critical skill in today's business world, and *Introduction to Management Accounting: A User Perspective* helps students to better use accounting information and improve their decision-making skills.

This text provides an introduction to accounting within the context of business and business decisions. Readers will explore accounting information's role in the decision-making process, and learn how to use accounting information in a variety of management decision situations. Seeing how accounting information can be used to make better business decisions will benefit all students, regardless of their major course of study or chosen career.

Introduction to Management Accounting: A User Perspective was written as a companion text to *Introduction to Financial Accounting: A User Perspective*. Obviously, we hope you will adopt and use both texts. We believe strongly, however, that this text can be effectively used in the second course of the introductory accounting sequence irrespective of what financial accounting text you use.

As you work with this text, you will find it focuses heavily on the uses of accounting information rather than the preparation of the information. This, however, is only one characteristic which distinguishes *Introduction to Management Accounting: A User Perspective* from other texts you may have used in the past.

SUPPORT FOR THE INTERACTIVE CLASSROOM

We believe this text provides tools to actively involve students in their learning processes. The conversational tone of the text, its user perspective, and the logical presentation of topics all contribute to the ability of this text to meet that goal. However, several features are particularly important in developing a classroom atmosphere in which students share ideas, ask questions, and relate their learning to the world around them.

Throughout each chapter of the text, you will find Discussion Questions (DQs) that challenge students to reach beyond the surface of the written text to determine answers. Far from typical review questions, for which the students can scan a few pages of the text to locate an answer, many of the DQs provide relevant learning by relating students' personal experiences to the knowledge they gain through the text.

The DQs provide a variety of classroom experiences:

- Many DQs provide the basis for lively classroom discussions, requiring students to think about issues and formulate or defend their opinions.
- Some DQs are springboards for group assignments (in or out of the classroom) to put cooperative learning into practice.
- DQs may be assigned as individual writing assignments to allow students to practice and develop their writing skills.
- Combining individually written DQ responses with follow-up group discussions leading to group consensus can spark lively debate!
- Having students keep a journal of their responses to all DQs (regardless if they are used in another way) encourages solitary pondering of accounting concepts.

The DQs comprise a critically important part of the text's pedagogy designed to emphasize important points that students may skim across in their initial reading. Even if they are not formally part of the required work for your course, students will gain a greater understanding of the concepts discussed when they take time to consider each question as part of the text.

Students get enthused about accounting when they can relate it to real-world situations. This presents a challenge in presenting management accounting concepts because (a) many companies modify and tailor management accounting concepts to their individual needs, and (b) management accounting concepts often involve proprietary company policies and processes, so many companies guard their application of these concepts. When possible, however, we have tried to include as many real-world examples as we could. In addition to these features that help to foster an open, interactive environment in the classroom, a major distinction of this text is its total separation of the use of accounting and its preparation.

SEPARATION OF ACCOUNTING AND BOOKKEEPING

This text approaches accounting from the user perspective. The chapters contain no bookkeeping. Although we feel that a knowledge of bookkeeping is valuable, we feel that it is difficult for beginning accounting students to digest the uses of accounting information and the details of bookkeeping simultaneously.

Separating accounting and bookkeeping makes both subjects easier to grasp and more enjoyable to learn. To facilitate the separation of accounting and bookkeeping, accounting procedures are covered in appendices to selected chapters. This approach allows instructors and institutions to determine when and to what degree bookkeeping procedures are covered in their programs. Some schools choose to have all students learn basic recording procedures; others may only require accounting majors to acquire these skills.

Management accounting by its nature has less bookkeeping procedure than financial accounting. However, in Chapters 2, 3, and 9 we have included appendices that cover the bookkeeping procedures required to record the topics presented.

In addition to the decision to focus on the uses of accounting information rather than the details of accounting procedures, in this text we have made several other deliberate and important choices about topical coverage.

TOPICS COVERED

We carefully considered the inclusion or exclusion of topics from this text consistent with our pedagogical goals of building foundations that support effective student learning. Because our focus introduces students to accounting information and its uses in decision making, we could not simply follow the traditional coverage of topics. As we considered individual topics, we continually explored whether their inclusion would enhance a student's ability to interpret and use accounting information throughout his or her personal and professional life. Based on our own experiences in industry and conversations we have had with both operations and accounting managers from many companies, we believe that *Introduction to Management Accounting: A User Perspective* covers those topics that every introductory accounting student should leave the course understanding well. In short, we sought quality of learning, not quantity of minutiae.

For example, in our coverage of the separation of a mixed cost into its variable and fixed components, we discuss regression analysis, but do not include any calculations using this method. By limiting the coverage of detailed calculations, we have the opportunity to focus on the concept of cost separation without losing students in computations.

Another example of building foundations to learning is the introduction to the operating budget. Instead of sending students straight into the preparation of the budgets included in the operating budget, we present all the budgets conceptually first, and then walk them through budget preparation.

We also include some topics that traditional books omit. Chapter 7 includes not only information on how to budget for capital expenditures, but where capital budgeting fits in a company's overall planning and control process. This chapter also discusses frankly some of the dysfunctional management behaviour caused by inappropriate use of the capital budgeting process. Likewise, Chapter 8 includes a forthright discussion of appropriate and inappropriate uses of the operating budget. Finally, Chapter 10 provides a discussion on some recent trends in management accounting and business, such as nonfinancial performance measurement and ISO certification.

From our classroom experience with this text, we believe that the content is appropriate for students to embrace and take forward to additional courses. The carefully chosen sequence of topics helps to make them more understandable by establishing firm conceptual foundations.

SEQUENCE OF COVERAGE

To effectively present the user perspective, we developed a logical flow of topics so that each chapter builds on what the student has already learned. Students can easily understand how the topics fit together logically and how they are used together to make good decisions. Moreover, students can see that accounting and the information it provides is not merely something that exists unto itself, but rather it is something developed in response to the needs of economic decision makers.

A short tour through the material covered in each chapter will show you how we have structured our presentation of the topics to maximize student learning.

Chapter 1 provides a brief overview of the environment and future of management accounting. We have included not only a description of how management accounting compares and contrasts with financial accounting, but also the historical forces that have led to the development of management accounting techniques. Further, we discuss the state of management accounting today and what kinds of management accounting information will be needed in the future.

Chapter 2 presents an introduction to various cost classifications used in management accounting situations. We cover the concepts of cost objects, direct and indirect costs, and product and period costs. Students are introduced to the differences in product cost for a merchandiser and a manufacturer and learn the components of the costs included in each of the three types of inventory in a manufacturing operation. Finally, we explore the calculation of cost of goods manufactured and cost of goods sold for a manufacturer and cost of services for a service type firm. The chapter appendix presents the journal entries associated with the information presented in the chapter.

Chapter 3 introduces students to how manufacturers determine the cost of manufactured product. We present the documents used to help control the costs of manufactured products and cover how overhead costs are allocated to products using both traditional overhead allocation and activity-based costing. We walk students through the steps required to determine the cost of manufactured product using job order and process costing. The chapter appendix presents the journal entries associated with process costing and job order costing.

Chapter 4 explores the subject of cost behaviour. We explain the differences between fixed costs and variable costs, and how to classify costs by cost behaviour. We also cover the concept of the relevant range and its effect on cost behaviour information. We then present the characteristics of a mixed cost and discuss how to separate a mixed cost into its fixed and variable components using the engineering approach, the scatter graph, the high-low method, and regression analysis.

Chapter 5 extends the topic introduced in Chapter 4 by using cost behaviour information to make business decisions. In this chapter we present the functional income statement and contribution income statement and the differences between them. We cover the calculation of per unit amounts for sales, variable cost, and contribution margin, as well as the contribution margin ratio and its importance as a management tool. We present the contribution margin income statement for a merchandiser and introduce the concept of cost-volume-profit analysis, which we use to determine the amount of sales required to break even or to earn a targeted profit in both single-product and multiple-product situations. Finally, we use CVP to perform sensitivity analysis to changes in selling price, variable cost, and fixed cost.

Chapter 6 presents the topic of isolating and using relevant cost information in decision making. Included is a discussion of the characteristics of relevant and irrelevant costs, and a consideration of qualitative factors that should be considered when making business decisions. The specific decision situations covered in the chapter are equipment replacement, whether to accept or reject a special order, and the effects of fixed costs and opportunity costs on a make or buy decision.

Chapter 7 provides an in-depth look at the capital budget. The overall business planning process is discussed and where the capital budget fits in that process. The four shared characteristics of all capital projects are presented, as well as the cost of capital and the concept of scarce resources. Students learn how to identify the information relevant to the capital budgeting decision. We present four techniques used to evaluate proposed capital projects including net present value, internal rate of return, payback, and accounting rate of return. We briefly introduce the tax impact of capital budgeting decisions in Canada, as the result of capital cost allowances. There is an appendix to this chapter which presents the concept of the time value of money and all the calculations students need to compute net present values and internal rates of return.

Chapter 8 presents the operating budget, its benefits, preparation, and uses. First, we introduce and discuss all the budgets included in the operating budget from a conceptual standpoint. Then we present various approaches to budgeting, including perpetual, incremental, zero-based, top-down, bottom-up, imposed, and participative approaches. Next we discuss and stress the importance of the sales forecast in the budgeting process. Finally, we walk students through the preparation of all the budgets, and then discuss appropriate and inappropriate uses of the operating budget in the management process.

Chapter 9 presents the procedures involved in standard costing. We explore what standard costing is and why it can be an effective tool for managers. We cover management by exception, ideal and practical standards, and the weaknesses of standard costing. We compare standard costing, actual costing, and normal costing and introduce students to methods used to set standards for a manufacturing company. Finally, we walk students through the calculations of standard cost variances for direct material, direct labour, variable manufacturing overhead, and fixed manufacturing overhead. The chapter appendix presents the journal entries used to record all the procedures described in the chapter.

Chapter 10 introduces students to various methods of evaluating performance. We discuss centralized and decentralized management styles, business segments, and the problems associated with determining segment costs. We present the segment income statement and how it is used to evaluate segment performance. We also discuss transfer pricing and its effect on performance evaluation. We introduce students to return on investment, residual income and economic value added as methods used to evaluate performance. We also discuss some nonfinancial performance measures including quality, customer satisfaction, employee morale, employee safety, efficiency, the balanced scorecard, and just-in-time.

Other Important Features of This Text

In addition to the Discussion Questions discussed in detail above, our text offers other features that will enhance the learning process.

- Learning Objectives—Previewing each chapter with these objectives allows students to see what direction the chapter is taking, which makes the journey through the material a bit easier.
- A User's View—This boxed feature provides examples of how some of the techniques described are used by real small or medium-sized businesses.
- Marginal Glossary—Students often find the process of learning accounting terminology to be a challenge. As each new key word is introduced in the text, it is shown in bold and also defined in the margin. This feature offers students an easy way to review the key terms and locate their introduction in the text.
- Summary—This concise summary of each chapter provides an overview of the main points.
- Key Terms—At the end of each chapter, a list of the new key words directs students to the page on which the key word or phrase was introduced.
- Review the Facts—Students can use these basic, definitional questions to review the key points of each chapter. The questions are in a sequence reflecting the coverage of topics in the chapter.
- Apply What You Have Learned—Our end-of-chapter assignment materials include a mix of traditional types of homework problems and assignments requiring critical thinking and writing. You will find matching problems, short essay questions, and calculations. Assignments dealing directly with

the use of financial statements are also included. Many of these applications also work well as group assignments.
- Glossary of Accounting Terms—An alphabetical listing of all the key terms provides definitions and lists the page on which the term first appears.

Instructor Supplements

Instructor's Manual
This comprehensive resource includes chapter overviews that identify the chapter concepts, explain the chapter rationale and philosophy, and review the significant topics and points of the chapter. Also included are chapter outlines organized by objectives, lecture suggestions, teaching tips, chapter quizzes, transparency masters, group activities derived from the textbook Discussion Questions (DQs) as well as the Solutions to the DQs, communication exercises, and suggested readings.

Solutions Manual and Transparencies
Solutions are provided for all the end-of-chapter assignments. The Solutions Manual is also available in acetate form and on disk to adopters.

Test Item File
The Test Item File includes test items that can be used as quiz and/or exam material. Each chapter contains multiple-choice questions (both conceptual and quantitative), problems, exercises, and critical thinking problems. Each question will identify the difficulty level, page reference, and the corresponding learning objective(s).

Pearson TestGen
The Pearson TestGen is a special computerized version of the Test Item File that enables instructors to view and edit the existing questions, add questions, generate tests, and print the tests in a variety of formats. Powerful search and sort functions make it easy to locate questions and arrange them in any order desired. TestGen also enables instructors to administer tests on a local area network, have the tests graded electronically, and have the results prepared in electronic or printed reports. Issued on a CD-ROM, the Pearson TestGen is compatible with IBM or Macintosh systems.

PowerPoint Presentations
PowerPoint presentations are available for each chapter of the text. Each presentation allows instructors to offer a more interactive presentation using colourful graphics, outlines of chapter material, additional examples, and graphical explanations of difficult topics. Instructors have the flexibility to add slides and/or modify the existing slides to meet the course needs. Each presentation can also be downloaded from our Instructor Central website (see below).

Online Supplements
Some of the ancillary materials that accompany this text are available for download at www.pearsoned.ca/instructor, Pearson Education Canada's protected instructor's resource site. The texts on Instructor Central are organized by discipline. To access your supplements, click first on the link to the appropriate discipline, then on the link to the text you are using.

The following supplements for *Introduction to Management Accounting*, are available on Instructor Central, posted in the Accounting discipline area:

- Instructor's Manual (including Transparency Masters)
- PowerPoint Presentations

Online Learning Solutions

Pearson Education Canada supports instructors interested in using online course management systems. We provide text-related content in WebCT, Blackboard, and our own private label version of Blackboard called CourseCompass. To find out more about creating an online course using Pearson content in one of these platforms, contact your local Pearson Education Canada representative.

Student Supplement

Accounting Central

Visit AccountingCentral, Pearson Education Canada's accounting website, at www.pearsoned.ca/accounting. The goal of this site is to provide students and instructors with a springboard to online accounting resources. It gives you easy access to both Canadian and international links designed to heighten your awareness of the world of accounting, including information on careers, accounting software, taxation and various accounting organizations and resources. The site also acts as a portal to Companion Websites for some of Pearson's accounting texts.

ACKNOWLEDGMENTS

This project would not have happened without the support and encouragement of a number of people, the faith of Pearson Education Canada, and the suggestions for improvement from various colleagues.

The publishers and author would like to acknowledge the instructors who contributed to the project through their reviews of the American edition of the text and/or manuscript for the Canadian edition:

Mike Barrette, St. Lawrence College
Maria Bélanger, Algonquin College
Angela Davis, University of Winnipeg
Johan de Rooy, University of British Columbia
Richard Hudson, Mount Allison University
Pamela Quon, Athabasca University
Nancy Tait, Sir Sanford Fleming College
J. Roderick Tilley, Mount Saint Vincent University
Brian Winter, Southern Alberta Institute of Technology

The first Canadian edition of this book is due, in large part, to the efforts of Samantha Scully, the acquisitions editor. Suzanne Schaan kept the project moving as the developmental editor. Without their efforts, a Canadian edition would not have been possible. I would also like to thank Anita Smale, Judith Scott, Betty Robinson, and Eleanor MacKay for their contributions and dedication to this project.

Peter Norwood

Management Accounting: Its Environment and Future

"*I*n this era of rapid change, it is impossible to predict the future with certainty. Yet one thing is certain—the unwillingness or inability to manage change is a prescription for failure in the marketplace of the 21st century.

A wired, interconnected marketplace has emerged with breathtaking speed. Trade barriers have been eliminated and national borders have virtually disappeared, creating a truly global economy. Organizations of all sizes and in all sectors of the global economy are confronting new market realities that are driving fundamental changes in the creation, production, and distribution of goods and services....

The demands of the new business organization have created a need for a new type of business professional. As organizations address new market realties and competitive challenges, they need leaders who bring vision, imagination, and broad-based strategic management capabilities...."[1]

The role of the manager has changed over the past few years. Managers used to be concerned primarily with cost control. However, their role has expanded from using accounting information for cost control to using information for strategic business decisions. A manager must respond quickly to market conditions and competitive initiatives that were not present a decade ago. Their companies, in many different industries, have had to change their business operations to remain competitive and to respond to global market forces. In order to be successful, a manager needs information to make the future-oriented decisions that will substantially impact an organization's fortunes.

---

[1] Excerpted from "CMA Canada's Strategic Direction" from The Society of Management Accountants of Canada's (CMA-Canada) web site, www.cma-canada.org/ (accessed July 22, 2002). Used with permission.

Our focus will be not on the specific changes that managers have to make in responding to these new realities but rather on the way these changes have affected managers' accounting needs and how accounting information has responded. ■

LEARNING OBJECTIVES

After completing your work on this chapter, you should be able to do the following:

1. Describe management accounting and contrast it with financial accounting.
2. Explain major historical developments that have affected management accounting.
3. Discuss what may have led to the stagnation in the development of management accounting.
4. Describe how changes in management accounting affect today's businesses.
5. Explain how business people use management accounting information and skills.

WHAT IS MANAGEMENT ACCOUNTING?

Over the past two decades, the Canadian economy has changed. Competition in every industrial sector has intensified with both domestic and international companies competing for business. The service sector has grown in stature and importance in the economy. Technology has created management systems that supply more comprehensive information for managers. Business decisions need to be made quickly, in an ethical manner, that will maximize the return to shareholders. Accounting plays an important role in the decision making that takes place in companies.

There are two branches in accounting. Financial accounting is the branch of accounting that provides information to external decision makers—to people outside the company. **Management accounting,** in contrast, provides information to internal decision makers, or managers. It is most commonly defined as the process of identification, measurement, accumulation, analysis, preparation, interpretation, and communication of financial information used by management to plan, evaluate, and control an organization.

Management accounting is sometimes referred to as **managerial accounting** or **cost accounting.** Management accounting and managerial accounting mean exactly the same thing. We will use the term *management accounting* throughout our discussions of the subject. Cost accounting is a narrow application of management accounting. It deals specifically with procedures designed to determine how much a particular item costs.

Exhibit 1-1 contrasts financial accounting and management accounting by listing some of the many external and internal users of a company's accounting information.

management accounting
The branch of accounting designed to provide information to internal economic decision makers (managers).

managerial accounting
Another name for *management accounting.*

cost accounting   A narrow application of management accounting dealing specifically with procedures designed to determine how much a particular item (usually a unit of manufactured product) costs.

Exhibit 1–1
External and Internal
Decision Makers

External	Internal
• Shareholders (present and potential)	• Marketing managers
• Bankers and other lending institutions	• Salespersons
• Bondholders (present and potential)	• Production managers
• Suppliers	• Production supervisors
• Customers	• Strategic planners
• Competitors	• Company president
	• Engineers

 Discussion Questions

1–1. For each of the external parties listed in Exhibit 1–1, suggest one economic decision they might make regarding a company.

1–2. Name two external parties in addition to those listed in Exhibit 1–1, and provide an example of an economic decision each might make regarding a company.

1–3. For each of the internal parties listed in Exhibit 1–1, describe one economic decision they might make regarding their company.

1–4. Name two more internal parties in addition to those listed in Exhibit 1–1, and give an example of an economic decision each might make regarding the company.

Discussion Questions 1–1 through 1–4 highlight the different nature of the decisions made by external and internal parties. If you review your answers to these questions, you will discover that the decisions external parties make focus on the company as a whole, whereas the decisions internal parties make usually centre on some *part* of the company. Because people use financial accounting information and management accounting information differently, the nature of the two differs.

Accounting Rules

Financial accounting information must be prepared in accordance with rules known as Generally Accepted Accounting Principles (GAAP). No such rules apply to management accounting. Because management accounting information is prepared for use by those working within the company, its users can question the content, meaning, level of detail, and validity of the accounting information they receive. They can also determine the format of the information. As discussed later, in addition to accountants, managers may also gather and prepare management accounting information. In sum, internal decision makers can generally make certain the information they receive is exactly what they want. External decision makers must accept the financial accounting information they receive, like it or not.

Level of Detail

In contrast to the general-purpose nature of financial accounting information, firms prepare management accounting information to address specific company issues. Therefore, it is often much more detailed than financial accounting information. For example, it may be fine for a potential investor to know that IBM's sales were $82,000,000,000 last year, but this information would be nearly useless to the national sales manager for IBM ThinkPads™, the company's line of notebook computers, who needs to know that product's sales numbers for last year.

 Discussion Questions

1–5. In addition to sales information, what other accounting information would you want if you were the national sales manager for IBM ThinkPads™?

In addition to preparing general-purpose financial statements for the public, a company's accountants also prepare management accounting information for the managers or employees who need it. For a given internal decision, a user may need specific information from a division, product line, product, or department. The company's accountants should be able to customize information to fit the needs of the user.

For example, Molson Breweries Inc. has facilities in various locations across Canada. These facilities require various types of maintenance, including mowing the lawn and weeding the flower beds outside the buildings. This maintenance costs money. The amount spent for grounds maintenance at any facility is totally irrelevant to external parties. The maintenance supervisors at these facilities, however, would find that amount quite relevant. Molson's accountants should be able to customize a report providing the supervisors with pertinent cost information.

Timeliness

Timeliness is important to both financial and management accounting information users. Regardless of whether the user is external or internal, accounting information is useful only if it is available in time to help the decision maker.

Because it has become customary, users of financial accounting information expect that financial results will be available quarterly. However, managers making frequent decisions need information much more often. They need information monthly, weekly, or even daily, so they can make informed decisions. Because of the fast pace of business decision making, sometimes it is better to forfeit precision in favour of speed. Management accountants must strike a balance between information accuracy and timeliness to provide managers with information that is accurate enough to make good decisions, and yet timely enough to make a difference.

Future Orientation

Although financial accounting information should have predictive value, it primarily depicts historical results. In contrast, management accounting has a forward-looking orientation. Management accounting focuses on estimating future revenues, costs, and other measures to forecast future activities and their results. Firms use these forecasts to plan their course of action toward future goals.

As you can see, because of the fundamental differences between the information needs of external and internal parties, financial and management accounting differ. Exhibit 1–2 summarizes the differences we have discussed.

Exhibit 1–2
Contrast of Financial
and Management
Accounting

Feature	Financial Accounting	Management Accounting
• Principal users	External parties	Internal parties
• Rules and regulations	Governed by GAAP	No rules
• Level of detail	Deals with the company as a whole	Deals with various parts of the company
• Timeliness	Quarterly and annually	As users need
• Orientation	The past	The future

WHERE ACCOUNTING FITS IN A COMPANY

treasurer The corporate officer who is responsible for cash and credit management and for planning activities, such as investment in long-lived property, plant, and equipment.

controller A company's chief accountant, who is responsible for the preparation of accounting reports for both external and internal decision makers.

Exhibit 1–3 presents a typical corporate organizational structure. Note where financial and management accounting fit within a company.

The accounting function centres around the treasurer and the controller. Generally, the **treasurer** is responsible for managing cash and credit including the management of foreign currency, and for planning activities, such as investment in long-lived property, factory, and equipment. The **controller** is a company's chief accountant. This person is responsible for preparing accounting reports for both external and internal decision makers.

In a large company, such as Bombardier Inc. or Magna International Inc., the treasurer and controller are both likely to have large staffs reporting to them. At a midsized company, one or two people may perform all the duties of the treasurer and controller. In small firms, one person may perform all the functions.

Exhibit 1–3
Corporate Organization
Structure

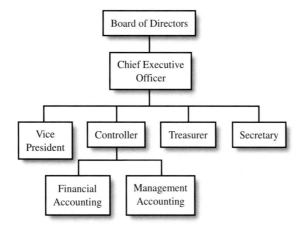

 Discussion Question

1–6. What possible problems may arise when the same accountants prepare reports for both external parties and internal parties?

The Origin and Evolution of Management Accounting

Accounting and accounting records have existed since the dawn of civilization. Indeed, formal accounting systems have been in use for thousands of years. The need for accounting information for management decision-making purposes, however, did not exist until the early 19th century. Before that time almost all businesses were proprietorships or small partnerships. Businesses had no permanent employees to speak of and no management as we know it today. Management usually consisted of the proprietor or partners and immediate family members. Because businesses had no management, they had no need for management accounting information. Virtually all transactions were between the company and parties outside the company. Transactions with external parties such as suppliers, contract labour, and customers were easy to measure and evaluate: A company was successful if it collected more cash from its customers than it paid to suppliers and contract labourers.

In the hundred years between 1825 and 1925, however, four significant changes took place in business operation and organization: the emergence of permanent employees, the Industrial Revolution, the rise of scientific management, and diversification. These changes altered the nature of management accounting.

Emergence of Permanent Employees

For the most part, businesses had no employees before the 1880s. Businesses purchased labour with a piece rate contract and hired independent contractors to complete all their production functions. A chair manufacturer, for example, purchased wood at a certain price per board foot. Then the company contracted someone to turn the wood into legs, arms, seats, and backs at some specified rate per item. When the pieces were produced and paid for, the company contracted someone else to assemble the chairs, and paid that person some specified amount per chair assembled. Determining the cost of a chair produced was very simple—the sum of the wood cost, the amount paid per component piece (arm, leg, and so on), and the cost of assembling it. The company was not terribly interested in how long it took any of these contractors to complete their tasks, so long as they met the needs of the company.

Then companies began hiring permanent employees to fill the role of the independent contractors. Why the switch to permanent employees happened and whether it was positive or negative has been hotly debated by scholars for over 100 years. From the company's standpoint, moving from a contract system to a wage system gave the firm greater control of the production process and, in fact, created what we now know as the factory. From the labourer's standpoint, the change was likely an exchange of freedom for security.

 ## Discussion Questions

1-7. In what ways do you think hiring permanent employees gives a company greater control of the production process?

1-8. What kinds of freedom do you think permanent employees exchange for security?

When we see the word *factory*, we tend to think of the huge factories of the 20th century. Actually, early factories were still small businesses. Management accounting did not develop because of the size or complexity of the organization. Rather, it developed because the accounting systems then in existence did not provide business people with enough information to determine the cost of a manufactured product.

 ## Discussion Question

1–9. Why do you think the emergence of the factory (even a small one) made it more difficult to determine the cost of a manufactured product?

The Industrial Revolution

Industrial Revolution
A term used to describe the transition in North America from an agricultural-based economy to a manufacturing-based economy.

The **Industrial Revolution** was the 19th-century transition in North America from an agricultural-based economy to a manufacturing-based economy. From 1825 to 1925 businesses greatly increased their investment in property, plant, and equipment, and began to rely more on machines instead of human labour to produce products. As companies grew in size and complexity, owners found it impossible to be in all places at all times. They were forced to create hierarchical levels of management for their organizations. These managers sought needed information to control costs and production processes. Over time, businesses developed methods to measure the conversion of raw materials into units of finished product. These methods were the foundation for present-day management accounting. Their focus was on the effectiveness and efficiency of various internal processes, rather than on the overall profitability of the company.

Scientific Management

scientific management A management philosophy based on the notion that factories were run by machines—some mechanical and some human. Scientific management experts believed they could improve production efficiency by establishing standards of performance for workers.

The scientific management movement began near the end of the 19th century and had a tremendous influence on business management and management accounting. **Scientific management** was a philosophy based on the notion that factories were run by machines—some mechanical and some human. You may think it insensitive to treat employees as nothing more than machines plugged into the production process. Nonetheless, scientific management took this view. Experts in this area believed they could improve production efficiency by establishing standards of performance for workers. In a tool-manufacturing company, for instance, experts conducted time-and-motion studies to set a standard for the time workers should take to convert a given amount of resources into a finished product, such as a hammer.

These standards of performance were quickly adapted to accounting for the purpose of determining how much it *should* cost to manufacture a product. The experts, often engineers, determined how much material, labour, and other resources a business needed to manufacture a single unit of product. This information served as a benchmark to measure whether resources were used efficiently or squandered during the production process. Such standards were the beginning of what is referred to as *standard costing*, one of the most important developments in management accounting. We will discuss standard costing in greater detail in Chapter 9.

Discussion Questions

Assume a company manufactures tables. Scientific management studies show that each tabletop requires 1.5 square metres of wood, and it takes a worker 45 minutes to convert the wood into a tabletop.

1-10. If the wood costs the company $4.00 per square metre and the company's workers are paid $15.00 per hour, how much does each tabletop cost to produce?

1-11. What other costs should be considered in the calculation of the cost to produce the tabletop? Explain.

Diversification

During the first two decades of the 20th century, companies began to diversify. Before this time, virtually all companies undertook only one activity, for example, railroad companies were strictly in the railroad business and steel companies were strictly in the steel business. The primary investment decision for these single-activity companies was whether to expand. The emergence of diversified, multi-activity companies changed the nature of decision making.

 Discussion Question

1-12. Why do you think companies began to diversify in the early years of the 20th century?

Owners of diversified companies could not directly manage all the various business operations. Instead, they relied on others to manage operations that they could not personally oversee; and they obtained additional management accounting information from the various parts of the business so they could plan, control, and evaluate performance. Company accountants tailored reports to meet the needs of managers at each level of the organization. Lower-level managers, such as production supervisors, received reports that focused on production efficiencies. Higher-level managers received reports that focused on product profits.

Development Stops (or at least dramatically slows)

The Society of Management Accountants of Canada (CMA-Canada) A professional association of management accountants comparable to the professional association of financial accountants (Canadian Institute of Chartered Accountants).

In 1920, the Canadian Society of Cost Accountants was incorporated and offered courses in cost accounting and business organization. In order to ensure that a standard of competence could be maintained and recognized, the Society decided to issue a qualifying designation. Thus, starting in 1941, provincial societies were incorporated and the Registered Industrial Accountant (RIA) designation came into being. As the field of management changed, the Society changed its name to **The Society of Management Accountants of Canada (CMA-Canada)** and changed the name of the designation to Certified Management Accountant (CMA). CMAs are certified under provincial guidelines, but the standards and the education process are national in scope. CMA-Canada provided the same sort of professional status for management accountants as the Canadian Institute of Chartered Accountants (CICA) did for financial accountants.

The evolution of management accounting in Canada has been cyclical, to say the least. Many of the management accounting tools used today were developed in the early part of the last century. New techniques were practically nonexistent in the middle part of the century. However, in the past 20 years, new methods have emerged as the economy has started to shift to include services as well as manufacturers. The advent of technology has allowed for more sophisticated accounting systems.

But why did the changes in management accounting take so long? In the following section, we examine possible causes of the stagnation.

Dominance of Financial Accounting

The growth of publicly held corporations, the stock market crash, and the Great Depression led to the establishment of Generally Accepted Accounting Principles (GAAP) and provincial securities commissions. The new rules and regulations governed financial reporting to external parties and required that corporations file audited financial statements with the provincial securities commissions that were prepared in accordance with GAAP. The rules and regulations led to the design of accounting systems that could provide financial information and reports to outsiders. These financial accounting systems, however, ignored (or at least underrepresented) information managers could use to make decisions about the internal processes of their companies.

Companies could have maintained two systems—one that generated and gathered information to meet external reporting requirements, and another that generated the information managers needed to manage and control the operation of the company. Or, a common system could collect data for both purposes and then customize the information to conform to the informational requests and needs of users. The cost of creating and maintaining a dual-purpose system, however, would have been prohibitive before computers, which is when GAAP and the securities commissions came into being.

Today, a high percentage of management accountants have a financial accounting background. It stands to reason that those who bring that type of background into a management accounting setting will tend to approach management accounting from a financial accounting perspective.

Consider also the legal environment existing in the 1930s after the creation of the securities commissions. If a company failed to have an accounting system designed to produce financial accounting information for external parties in accordance with GAAP, there would be serious legal consequences. If a company's accounting system did not produce management accounting information, however, there were no legal consequences. Given this situation, it is not surprising that, at that time, financial accounting requirements drove the creation and use of accounting information.

 Discussion Question

> **1–13.** What possible problems do you think arise when a company's single accounting system is designed to produce financial accounting information? Explain.

Accounting Education

Prior to 1900, universities and colleges did not teach accounting. As a result, no uniform methods for gathering and distributing management accounting information were developed. Accountants gathered and distributed management accounting information as needed to suit management's needs. After the development of GAAP, companies needed accountants trained to provide financial accounting information. In response, universities and colleges began to offer accounting courses that focused on financial accounting information preparation.

As college-trained accountants became available, businesses began to rely on them for more than their expertise in providing information to outsiders. Managers also began to rely on accountants to specify *what* management accounting information should be gathered and *how* it should be presented. In the late 1800s, for instance, owners and company engineers developed product costing methods to make reasonable product cost estimates and better pricing decisions. In the early 1900s, trained accountants adapted established accounting methods of product costing to provide information to managers. In short, managers began relying on product costing methods their accountants learned in school instead of newly developed techniques tailored specifically to the needs of the company.

Focus on Financial Profits

Another possible reason for the slowdown in the development of management accounting is that we usually focus on financial profits in the performance evaluation of managers. Virtually all measures used to evaluate managers in Canadian companies are short-term financial accounting measures. Managers are bright people. In no time they determine how to manipulate the financial results of operations to maximize a short-run performance measure. It seems reasonable to expect managers to focus on short-term financial accounting measures if their compensation and career advancement rely on these items.

Bonus programs that motivate key managers to perform better seem reasonable, except that most bonuses are heavily weighted in favour of short-term, not long-term performance. This trend can be seen in the weighting between salary and bonuses paid to top executives. For example, the chairman of the Bank of Montreal received a salary of $900,000 in 2001 and also received a bonus of $1,400,000! The bonus was based on financial results for the fiscal year.

These incentives encourage managers to focus on improving financial statement measures rather than on improving productivity and efficiency measures. Preoccupation with financial accounting income has diminished their interest in demanding new management accounting techniques.

The problem of the short-term view is compounded by the mobility of management. In the early part of the century, managers stayed in their jobs longer than they do today. It was not uncommon for a manager to occupy the same position for 10 or even 20 years. For such managers, taking actions that would result in an impressive short-term performance at the expense of the long run made no sense. Today, however, many managers believe they will stay in a particular position for only a few years, so their objective is often to maximize short-term measures and not worry about what will happen in five or ten years.

Lack of Competitive Pressure

Canada's largest trading partner has always been, and continues to be, the United States. In fact, many U.S. corporations operate in Canada through subsidiary companies. Until the 1970s, there was little competition in the North American market from foreign competitors. The lack of competition allowed North American companies to flourish, despite their managements' short-run views. If satisfactory decisions could be made without sophisticated accounting information, then why would management even recognize that improvements were needed? Even business executives who were aware of the weaknesses in management accounting systems did not believe changes were worth making because they felt they were no worse off than their competition.

By the early 1980s, foreign competition became commonplace. Foreign companies relied on more sophisticated management accounting systems, which forced North American companies to pay closer attention to management accounting information in both their short-term and long-term business decisions.

Who or What Should We Blame?

Which factor or factors should we blame for the slowdown in the development of management accounting techniques—the preoccupation of accountants with financial accounting, formal accounting education, management focus on financial results, or the lack of competition? It is difficult to say, but even if we cannot determine precisely why management accounting development slowed, business leaders and accounting academics now recognize a need for better management accounting information for today's business leaders. Even if we could determine who or what caused the problem, what would be the point? An old adage applies well to the situation in the mid-1980s:

Let's fix problems, not blame.

The first step in solving a problem is to recognize that you have a problem. By the mid-1980s, Canadian companies had certainly recognized that they had a problem, and since then have made great strides toward solving that problem.

CHALLENGES AND TRENDS IN MANAGEMENT ACCOUNTING

As we move forward in this new century, businesses face many challenges. Global competition is one we have discussed already. Another is a basic consideration of what kind of economy is going to exist in Canada in the future. Many business analysts believe that we are moving away from the traditional manufacturing-based economy toward a service-based economy. If so, management accounting techniques must adapt to such a change.

A New Era

Heightened global competition has spurred changes in business operations and management accounting in Canada.

First, businesses began using production and management techniques that were initiated in other countries, most notably Japan and the former West Germany. Second, companies became more innovative. Automobile manufacturers in North America are much more efficient in their production processes than they were a decade ago. In the area of inventory control alone, North American auto manufacturers have drastically reduced the level of inventories on hand, using Just-in-time systems, thereby reducing their annual inventory holding cost by hundreds of millions of dollars. This reduced cost translates into cars that are cheaper to manufacture.

As businesses examined and reorganized their operations to become more competitive, they also examined the way managers use accounting information to make decisions. Managers and accountants are making or considering many changes in management accounting as a result.

The question really is, what kind of changes must be made in management accounting techniques and procedures to cope with a dynamic business environment? Opinions about which "old" management accounting techniques still apply and what "new" techniques should be developed are sharply divided. Next, we present three alternative perspectives on what is and what should be happening in management accounting to respond to these fundamental changes taking place in business.

Out with the Old, in with the New

The first perspective contends that virtually all the management accounting techniques and practices used before the mid-1980s are obsolete and do not apply to the new business environment. Advocates of this perspective urge businesses to develop entirely new management accounting techniques and to shed past methods. A few of the techniques they categorize as "new" include Just-in-time (JIT) inventory systems, Activity Based Management (ABM), Activity Based Costing (ABC), design for manufacturing (DFM), and Process Value Added (PVA).

Keep the Status Quo

The second perspective does not advocate any change in management accounting methods. Supporters of this view perceive business problems as unrelated to accounting. They believe that as new business practices are developed, management accounting methods of the past can and will provide managers with the information they need to operate their companies. Advocates believe that many of the management accounting techniques developed over the past ten years are simply variations of traditional techniques that have only been renamed.

Don't Change Just for the Sake of Change

The third perspective lies somewhere between the first two. Those who hold this view believe that there are serious flaws in the management accounting techniques of the past and that some of them probably have no place in the new business environment. They warn, however, not to change just to change. Supporters of this view advocate caution in abandoning old ways and embracing new ones. They believe that many of the techniques developed over the past 15 years lack universal application—they may greatly benefit some companies, some industries, or some circumstances but should not be hailed as cures for all problems facing all businesses.

The debate over the future of management accounting show no signs of waning. No matter what happens over the next several years, you will have begun your business careers before the debate is settled. The majority of firms today still employ traditional management accounting techniques and practices, and they likely will for many years. Some companies, however, have embraced new techniques.

We discuss both traditional and new management accounting techniques throughout the following chapters.

CONSUMERS OF MANAGEMENT ACCOUNTING INFORMATION

To make effective decisions, business managers must understand the firm's management accounting system, know whether the information is reliable, and recognize that no system will provide perfect information. Decision making by its very nature is forward-looking, and the future always contains an element of uncertainty. Managers should look for ways to reduce the amount of that uncertainty.

Every decision results in an outcome, and even good decisions can lead to bad outcomes. For example, suppose you are about to get in the checkout line at the grocery store. You evaluate the lines leading to open cash registers and, after counting the number of people in line and eyeballing the amount of groceries each customer is about to buy, you select what appears to be the shortest line. Your decision is sound and based on the information available. Well, just as the person ahead of you is about to pay with a debit card, shopping disaster strikes. The store's debit-card system goes down and the customer does not have enough cash to pay for the groceries. The entire order has to be voided before the cashier can help you. Quickly you look to see whether you can jump to another line, but it is too late: The other lines are now too long, and you must wait it out. Did you make a poor decision? No, you made the best decision you could with the available information. Your good decision simply led to a poor outcome.

Regardless of your career, at some point you will probably use accounting information to make a decision. If you are studying marketing, you may start as an assistant who helps prepare and implement marketing programs. As you advance in the firm, you may manage a staff of people who handle marketing programs, so you will need the accounting tools to make well-informed decisions. When you are responsible for the well-being of a company, department, division, or management team, you will face decisions that depend on your using management accounting information. The following chapters will teach you to be a careful consumer of accounting information.

 A User's View

As explained in this chapter, the roots of management accounting are in the manufacturing sector. Historically, large corporations like General Motors and Dupont were considered leaders in developing analytical tools for decision-making purposes.

The economy has changed. The Canadian economy is largely diversified, with merchandisers, the service sector, and the public sector all being large contributors to economic growth. These different sectors also need tools for decision-making purposes. Throughout this textbook, we will discuss the role of management accounting in Canadian small and medium-sized businesses operating in the manufacturing and service sectors, to give "a user's view" of the management accounting concepts discussed in the chapter.

SUMMARY

Management accounting is the process of identifying, measuring, and communicating financial information used by managers to plan, evaluate, and control their organization.

Financial accounting, which is intended for use by external parties, is subject to Generally Accepted Accounting Principles (GAAP). No such rules apply to management accounting, which is intended for use by internal parties. The general-purpose financial statements produced by financial accounting focus on past results. Reports produced by management accounting are much more detailed and focus on the future of the organization.

Although accounting and accounting records have existed since the dawn of civilization, the need for accounting information for use by management did not exist prior to the early 19th century. The emergence of permanent employees, the Industrial Revolution, scientific management, and the diversification by businesses all contributed to significant development of management accounting techniques between 1825 and 1925.

Around the year 1925, there was a dramatic slowdown in the development of new management accounting techniques. Some of the contributing factors often cited for this slowdown are the dominance of financial accounting, weaknesses in accounting education, a focus by many companies on short-term financial results, and the lack of competitive pressure on North American businesses. However, great strides have been made in the past 15 years toward developing improved management accounting techniques.

Canadian companies face significant competitive challenges as we move forward in this new century, and the role of management accounting information in helping these companies will be critical.

KEY TERMS

controller, p. 5
cost accounting, p. 2
Industrial Revolution, p. 7
management accounting, p. 2
managerial accounting, p. 2

scientific management, p. 7
The Society of Management
   Accountants of Canada
   (CMA-Canada), p. 8
treasurer, p. 5

REVIEW THE FACTS

1. What are the differences among management accounting, managerial accounting, and cost accounting?
2. What is the purpose of management accounting?
3. What are the primary differences between financial accounting and management accounting?
4. Financial accounting information must be prepared in conformity with GAAP. Why are there no such rules for management accounting?
5. List four significant changes in business that led to the development of management accounting.

6. What is The Society of Management Accountants of Canada (CMA-Canada) and what is its purpose?
7. Describe four factors that possibly led to the stagnation of management accounting development.
8. Explain the difference between a good decision and a good outcome.
9. Why is an understanding of management accounting an important ingredient for success in your career?

APPLY WHAT YOU HAVE LEARNED

LO 1: Contrast Management Accounting and Financial Accounting

1. Following are certain characteristics of either financial accounting information or management accounting information.

    1. __f__ Must conform to GAAP.
    2. __M__ Tends to be quite detailed.
    3. __f__ Generally limited to presenting historical information.
    4. __M__ Need not conform to a formal set of rules and standards.
    5. __f__ Information prepared primarily for external users.
    6. __f__ Tends to include only a limited amount of detail.
    7. __f__ Information prepared on a quarterly or yearly basis.
    8. __m__ Information prepared on a monthly, weekly, or daily basis.
    9. __M__ Information often includes future projections.
    10. __f/m__ Information prepared for use by internal parties.

REQUIRED:
Designate each of the characteristics as pertaining to (a) financial accounting information or (b) management accounting information.

LO 1: Describe Management Accounting

2. Is management accounting important for not-for-profit organizations as well as for-profit organizations? Explain.

LO 1: Describe Management Accounting

3. If you were the manager of a Blockbuster Video store, what accounting information would you desire to help you do your job better?

LO 3: Stagnation in Development of Management Accounting

4. Explain why managers tend to focus on improving short-term financial results.

LO 4: Changes in Management Accounting

5. Explain why there has been a renewed emphasis on the development of management accounting in Canada in the last decade.

LO 1: Contrast Management Accounting and Financial Accounting

6. Following are examples of users of financial accounting information and users of management accounting information.

1. _____ Sales supervisor
2. _____ Salespersons
3. _____ Financial analyst
4. _____ Suppliers
5. _____ Current shareholders
6. _____ Potential shareholders
7. _____ Personnel manager
8. _____ Maintenance supervisor
9. _____ Maintenance worker
10. _____ Loan officer at a company's bank

REQUIRED:

Designate each of the users of accounting information as either (a) an external party or (b) an internal party.

Classifying Costs

*S*uppose for a moment that your boss has asked you to organize a consumer catalogue of all the toys in the world. You need to classify the toys in several ways so users of your catalogue will be able to find information easily. After thinking about your task for a while, you start a list of toy classifications—toys organized by age or gender of user, by price, or by design. Your initial list of categories may look like the following:

Classification

By Age of User:
Toys for infants
Toys for toddlers ages one to three
Toys for children ages three to five
Toys for children ages five to nine
Toys for children ages ten and older

By Gender of User:
Toys designed for girls
Toys designed for boys
Toys for all children

By Price:
Toys under $10
Toys for $10 to $50
Toys for $51 to $100
Toys over $100

By Design:
Electronic toys vs. nonelectronic toys
Toys with wheels vs. toys without wheels
Breakable vs. unbreakable toys

Your boss now wants you to pick only one or two categories, to make your job easier. You scan your list to see which classifications will be most useful. You realize that the catalogue must have each classification to be as useful as possible, because purchasers may need different information for different decisions.

For instance, if purchasers are choosing toys to donate to the annual toy drive for underprivileged children, they may want to focus on price so they can donate several toys. In this case, the price classification would be most helpful. Further, those same purchasers may want to use the gender classification to find toys for all children because they would not know in advance whether the child receiving the toy is a girl or a boy.

If buyers are shopping for a birthday gift intended for a two-year-old relative, they would use the age classification to find appropriate toys. They might also want to use the price category to help them decide how much to spend. As these examples show, even in making just one decision, more than one classification may provide useful information.

Like our hypothetical toy purchasers, managers must have information to make effective planning and controlling decisions. Cost information is one of the key components of financial decision making; but what exactly is a cost? In accounting, a cost is how much we have to give up to get something. Put more formally, a **cost** is the resources forfeited to receive some goods or services. Note that cost is different from price. Price is what we charge; cost is what we pay.

cost The resources forfeited to receive some goods or services.

Business managers classify costs in many different ways because, just like the vast array of toys, there are many types of costs. Each classification can provide managers with useful information. In this chapter, we explore several different cost classifications that managers use to make decisions. ■

LEARNING OBJECTIVES

After completing your work on this chapter, you should be able to do the following:

1. Classify costs by cost objects, and distinguish between direct and indirect costs.
2. Distinguish between product costs and period costs, and contrast their accounting treatment.
3. Explain the differences between product cost for a merchandiser and for a manufacturer.
4. Describe the components of the costs included in each of the three types of inventory in a manufacturing operation.
5. Calculate cost of goods manufactured and cost of goods sold.
6. Describe the components of the cost of services provided by a service firm.

MAJOR COST CLASSIFICATIONS

Businesses incur many different costs as they operate and there are many useful ways to classify these costs. As managers make each internal business decision, they must determine what cost classifications will help them most. We will first identify important cost terms and investigate several cost classifications.

Assigning Costs to Cost Objects

cost object Any activity or item for which a separate cost measurement is desired.

One of the most useful classifications of cost is by cost object. A **cost object** is any activity or item for which we desire a separate cost measurement. Think of any noun associated with business and you have a potential cost object. Exhibit 2–1 lists some cost objects commonly used by companies.

Exhibit 2–1
Common Cost Object Designations

Cost Object	Examples
• Activity	• Repairing equipment, testing manufactured products for quality
• Product	• Paper towels, personal computers, automobiles (These can be either purchased or manufactured products.)
• Service	• Performing accounting work, legal work, consulting services
• Project	• Constructing a bridge, designing a house
• Geographic region	• A province, a city, a county
• Department	• Marketing department, accounting department

We identify a cost object to determine the cost of that particular object. Such classification can provide useful information. For example, a manufacturer may need information about the cost of the products it manufactures. In this case, the individual products are the cost objects. All costs associated with a particular product are grouped to determine the full cost of that product. Managers may also want to determine the cost associated with a group of products, such as a fleet of delivery trucks. When we assign costs to cost objects, we classify costs as direct or indirect.

direct cost A cost that can be easily traced to an individual cost object.

indirect cost A cost that supports more than one cost object.

common cost Another name for *indirect cost.*

A cost that is easily traced to individual cost objects is a **direct cost.** Many times, however, a cost may benefit more than one cost object, so tracing that cost to individual cost objects becomes difficult or even impossible. A cost that supports more than one cost object is an **indirect cost.** An indirect cost may also be called a **common cost,** because it is common to more than one cost object.

To illustrate the difference between direct and indirect costs, consider 12 The Bay stores in British Columbia. Each store has a manager who is responsible for the day-to-day operation of that store. The Bay also has a general manager who is responsible for the operation of all stores in the province. If we define each of the 12 stores as cost objects, the salary of each store manager would be considered a direct cost to his or her store. The salary of the general manager is not incurred to support any one of the 12 stores. Rather, it supports all 12 stores. Therefore, the general manager's salary would be considered an indirect cost of each cost object (the individual stores).

Discussion Questions

Assume that instead of defining each individual The Bay store as a cost object, we define the entire The Bay operation in British Columbia as a cost object.

2–1. In this case, would the salaries of the 12 store managers be considered direct or indirect costs? Explain your reasoning.

2–2. Would the salary of the general manager be considered a direct or an indirect cost? Explain your reasoning.

2–3. Why do you think managers at various levels in a company would find it useful to classify costs as direct or indirect?

Product Cost

product cost The cost of the various products a company sells.

When you see inventory on store shelves, you know the store did not get the inventory for free. Rather, each unit of product had some cost. The cost of the various products that a company sells is called **product cost.** More specifically, product costs are the costs associated with making the products available and ready to sell. For a bookstore, such as Chapters, product cost is the cost of the books purchased for resale, the freight to get the books to the store (also known as freight-in), and other costs involved in getting the books ready to sell.

inventoriable cost Another name for *product cost.*

Product costs are also known as **inventoriable costs**—product costs become part of a company's inventory until the goods associated with the costs are sold. Because product held for sale is considered an asset, its cost is shown on the balance sheet (inventory) until the product is actually sold. When the goods are sold, the product cost is converted from an asset on the balance sheet to an expense (cost of goods sold) on the income statement.

For example, when Payless Shoe Source buys shoes to sell, the cost of the shoes is a product cost and is added to inventory on the balance sheet. The cost remains in inventory on the balance sheet until the shoes are sold. When the shoes are sold, the reality of the reduced inventory caused by the sale is reflected in the company's accounting records by reducing inventory on the balance sheet and increasing cost of goods sold on the income statement.

Period Cost

period cost All costs incurred by a company that are not considered product cost. Includes selling and administrative cost.

Period costs are all the costs that a company incurs which are not considered product costs. They include selling and administrative expenses, but not any costs associated with acquiring product or getting it ready to sell.

selling cost The cost of locating customers, attracting customers, convincing customers to buy, and the cost of necessary paperwork to document and record sales.

Selling Cost **Selling cost** includes the cost of locating customers, attracting them, convincing them to buy, and the cost of necessary paperwork to document and record sales. Examples of selling cost include salaries paid to members of the sales force, sales commissions, and advertising.

Two selling costs are less obvious: the cost of delivering product to customers (also known as freight-out) and the cost of storing merchandise inventory. The reason delivery cost is considered a selling cost is that companies probably would not provide delivery unless it helped sell more product. If customers would buy with or without free delivery, the seller would probably not offer it.

Do not confuse freight-out (period cost) with freight-in (product cost). The key to keeping the two straight is to think about when they are incurred. Freight-in is a cost incurred before the product is ready to sell and is therefore considered a product cost. Freight-out is incurred after the product is ready for sale and is therefore classified as a period cost.

The cost of storing merchandise inventory is also classified as a selling cost, because merchandise in stock enhances its sales potential. Businesses cannot easily sell what they do not have. For example, if you went to your local music shop to buy a compact disc and the salesperson told you, "We don't keep that CD in stock, but we'll be glad to order it for you," then you would probably walk out and find another store that carries a better-stocked inventory of compact discs rather than wait. Because both delivery and merchandise inventory enhance sales, these items are considered selling costs.

administrative cost All costs incurred by a company that are not product costs or selling costs. Includes the cost of accounting, finance, employee relations, and executive functions.

Administrative Cost Administrative cost includes all costs that are not product or selling cost. These costs are typically associated with support functions—areas that offer support to the product and selling areas, such as accounting, finance, human resources, and executive functions.

Generally, period costs are shown as operating expenses (selling and administrative expenses) on the income statement. Most period costs—administrators' salaries, for example—are presented as expenses when the expenditure is made. When long-lived, or fixed, assets that will be used for selling or administrative functions are purchased, a slightly different treatment is necessary. At the time they are purchased, the cost of long-lived assets is shown on the balance sheet. As time passes, the amortization expense associated with these assets becomes part of selling and administrative expense.

 Discussion Questions

Assume that you are using a felt-tip highlighter to mark this book as you read it. Assume further that you purchased the marker at a bookstore.

2–4. What costs associated with the marker do you think the bookstore would consider to be product costs? Explain your reasoning for each cost you included.

2–5. What costs associated with operating the bookstore do you think would be considered period costs (selling and administrative)? Explain your reasoning for each cost you included.

Comparing Product and Period Costs

The distinction between product cost and period cost is based on whether the cost in question benefits the process of getting products ready for sale (product cost), or the selling and administrative functions (period cost). Let us look at some examples to make sure you understand the distinction. The cost of a factory security guard is a product cost because it benefits the factory. Conversely, the cost of a security guard in the sales office is a selling expense, which is a period cost. Note that the classification depends on the company function that benefits from the cost.

What about the salary of the vice president of manufacturing? Even though vice president of manufacturing may sound like an administrative position, the cost of it benefits the manufacturing function, so it is a product cost. Further, all costs associated with that position, including the amortization on the vice president's desk, the cost of his or her support personnel, travel costs, and all other costs associated with this position, would be classified as a product cost. Likewise, the vice president of marketing would be an example of selling expense, which is a period cost. The amortization on a company sales representative's car would be a selling expense, because it benefits the sales area of the company.

Next, we examine how manufacturing, merchandising, and service firms identify their product costs.

PRODUCT COST IDENTIFICATION FOR MERCHANDISING FIRMS

Merchandising firms, whether wholesale or retail, purchase products ready to sell, add a markup, and resell the goods. They generate profits by selling merchandise for a price that is higher than their cost. Wholesalers generally buy products from manufacturers (or other wholesalers) and then sell them to retailers. Retailers buy from manufacturers or the wholesalers and sell their products to the final consumers.

In this section we explore how a merchandising company identifies product costs and how those product costs flow through the balance sheet and income statement.

For a merchandising firm, product cost includes the cost of the merchandise itself, freight costs to obtain the merchandise, and any other costs incurred to get the product ready to sell. Because merchandisers buy goods for resale, often the cost of getting products ready to sell is minor or nonexistent. Product cost does not include any cost incurred after the product is in place and ready to sell.

Product cost is often the most significant of all costs for a merchandiser. It is not uncommon for merchandising companies to have cost of goods sold as high as 80 percent of the selling price of the product sold, indicating of course that they have a gross profit as low as 20 percent. Besides increasing sales, managers are always interested in reducing expenses, which is impossible without an understanding of what items are included in product cost. Efforts to reduce total cost of goods sold may focus on any component of that expense; that is, any component of product cost.

The Flow of Product Cost—Merchandising Company

If you were responsible for the profitability of a product or group of products, not only would you want to know total product cost, but you would also want to know and understand the various components of each product's cost. With this understanding, you could analyze reports detailing these products' cost components and work to isolate costs that could be reduced or eliminated. Exhibit 2–2 illustrates the flow of costs in a merchandising operation.

The diagram indicates that as goods are purchased, their cost is classified as merchandise inventory. In fact, all product costs are originally shown, like those in Exhibit 2–2, as an asset on the balance sheet. Typically, a merchandising firm has only one inventory classification, which is usually referred to as *merchandise inventory* or, simply, *inventory*. As the units of product are sold, their cost is converted to an expense and shown on the income statement as the cost of goods sold.

Exhibit 2–2
Flow of Product Costs—
Merchandising
Company

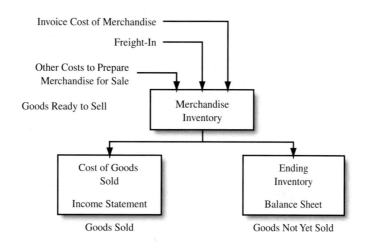

Cost of Goods Sold

Exhibit 2–3 is a cost of goods sold schedule for Jason's Supply Company. As the exhibit shows, we add purchases to the inventory on hand at the beginning of the period to arrive at the goods available for sale. Generally, one of two things can happen to the goods available for sale: They are either sold or remain on hand at the end of the period and are reflected as ending inventory. Thus, when ending inventory is subtracted from the goods available for sale, we can determine the cost associated with the products that have been sold—that is, we can determine the cost of goods sold.

The January 1, 2003, beginning inventory amount shown in Exhibit 2–3 is actually the ending inventory from Jason's Supply Company's balance sheet at December 31, 2002, and the ending inventory amount shown is from Jason's Supply Company's balance sheet at December 31, 2003. The cost of goods sold amount is included as an expense item on the company's income statement for the year ending December 31, 2003.

Exhibit 2–3
Cost of Goods Sold
Schedule

JASON'S SUPPLY COMPANY	
Cost of Goods Sold Schedule	
For the Year Ending December 31, 2003	
Beginning Inventory at January 1, 2003	$ 23,000
+ Purchases during 2003	300,000
= Goods Available for Sale in 2003	323,000
− Ending Inventory at December 31, 2003	(30,000)
= Cost of Goods Sold for 2003	$293,000

 Discussion Question

2–6. Accounting for the flow of product cost for a merchandiser seems to be a lot of bother. If all merchandise inventory will eventually be sold anyway, why not just record it as an expense (cost of goods sold) on the income statement when it is purchased?

Any company that sells tangible, physical product must sell its product for more than the product costs or it will eventually go bankrupt. This may seem very obvious, and in fact, good business managers are well aware of this necessity. Understanding the need is one thing; making sure it happens is another. Competitive pressures exist in most industries that cause companies to sell their products for less than desired. Managers of these businesses must have a solid understanding of the relationship between the selling price of their products and the cost of those products, or they may actually sell product for less than it costs.

 ## A User's View

Rick Montgomery is the vice-president and general manager of West Coast Alloys and Metals Ltd., located in Richmond, British Columbia. The company provides stainless piping, primarily for the forest products industry. The company also has expanded into fabrication, or custom manufacturing, and has expanded its product line to include valves and fittings. It has also expanded its customer base in an effort to diversify away from forest products.

In the different aspects of his business, it is important for Rick to know costs. His business is highly competitive. West Coast Alloys and Metals Ltd. competes against some very large companies, which means that profit margins are very low.

"In order to ensure that we will be profitable, I have to understand the cost of my product. That includes the cost of the material and the cost of the labour to prepare it for delivery. But I also need to know the cost of running my office so that I can ensure that when I bid for a job, I price it to recover all of my direct costs and have some money left over to pay for the overhead. Otherwise, I can't stay in business.

"As a manager of a medium-sized business, I know my operation inside out. Still, the first thing I do every morning is check the margin on the sales from the day before. If I didn't know how to classify costs, I couldn't manage the business."

PRODUCT COST IDENTIFICATION FOR MANUFACTURING FIRMS

Virtually all the products that consumers purchase have undergone some manufacturing process. In this section we explore how a manufacturing company identifies product costs and how those product costs flow through the balance sheet and income statement. As in merchandising firms, product cost for a manufacturer includes all costs associated with acquiring the product and getting it ready to sell. For manufacturers, however, getting the product ready to sell is usually an extensive process requiring the use of factory facilities such as production machinery and factory workers.

For a manufacturer, units of product are normally considered cost objects and their cost encompasses three distinct elements. We will introduce them briefly here and then discuss each of them in more detail a bit later. As we present each of the elements, think back to our discussion earlier in the chapter about cost objects and direct versus indirect costs.

direct materials cost The cost of all raw materials that can be traced directly to a unit of manufactured product.

direct labour cost The cost of all production labour that can be traced directly to a unit of manufactured product.

manufacturing overhead cost All costs associated with the operation of the manufacturing facility besides direct materials cost and direct labour cost. It is composed entirely of indirect manufacturing cost incurred to support multiple cost objects.

1. **Direct materials cost.** Direct materials cost is the cost of all raw materials that can be traced directly to a single unit of manufactured product, or the cost incurred for only one cost object. Note that direct materials cost is not the cost of all materials used in the manufacture of the product. In most manufacturing operations some materials costs are incurred for multiple cost objects. These costs are indirect materials cost, which we consider a part of manufacturing overhead.
2. **Direct labour cost.** Direct labour cost is the cost of all production labour that can be traced directly to a unit of manufactured product. Note that direct labour cost is not the cost of all labour incurred in the manufacture of product. In most manufacturing operations some labour costs are incurred for multiple cost objects. That type of cost is indirect labour cost, which we consider a part of manufacturing overhead, discussed next.
3. **Manufacturing overhead cost.** Manufacturing overhead is all the costs associated with the operation of the manufacturing facility other than direct materials cost and direct labour cost. It is composed entirely of indirect manufacturing cost—that is, manufacturing cost incurred to support multiple cost objects. Among others, manufacturing overhead includes indirect materials and indirect labour as discussed in items 1 and 2.

Inventory Classifications

As with merchandising firms, product costs for a manufacturer are inventoriable costs. However most manufacturing companies have not just one, but three types of inventory: raw materials, work in process, and finished goods. Note that these three types of inventory are not the same as the three elements of manufactured product we just introduced. Rather, these inventory classifications specify where manufactured product is at any given time in the production process.

As we discuss the three inventory classifications used by manufacturers, consider the following thoughts. First, our discussion in this chapter is intended to serve only as a broad introduction to the flow of product cost through a manufacturing company. The following chapter deals with specific methods used to accumulate product cost for a manufacturer. Second, there is a difference between reality and the measurement of reality. Reality is physical units of product moving through the production process, separate from our attempt to measure that reality.

raw materials inventory Materials that have been purchased but have not yet entered the production process.

material stores Another name for *raw materials inventory*.

Raw materials inventory, sometimes called **material stores,** consists of materials that have been purchased but have not yet entered the production process. Included in raw materials inventory are those materials that will eventually be accounted for as either direct or indirect materials. For example, Steelcase, Inc. manufactures metal desks, filing cabinets, and other metal office furniture. Raw materials inventory for Steelcase would consist of the sheet metal, screws, paint, and glue it has on hand with which to make metal office furniture. It would not include any of the material in the office furniture the company has begun to manufacture but has not yet finished, nor would it include the material in the office furniture that has been completed. Until raw materials actually enter the production process, the cost associated with those materials is classified as raw materials inventory on the balance sheet.

work-in-process inventory Products that have entered the production process but have not yet been completed.

Work-in-process inventory consists of products that have entered the production process but have not yet been completed—those units currently on the production line or in the production process. In our Steelcase example, work-in-process inventory at any given time would consist of the desks, filing cabinets, and other metal office furniture that have been started but are not yet finished. The reality is partially completed desks, filing cabinets, and other metal office furniture. The measurement of reality counts the costs associated with these partially completed units of product and classifies them as work-in-process inventory on the balance sheet. These costs include the cost of the materials associated with these units, the labour cost incurred so far in the production process, and some amount of manufacturing overhead applied to each of the partially completed units of product.

Work-in-process inventory does not include the cost of raw materials that have not yet entered the production process, nor does it include the cost associated with products that have been completed.

finished goods inventory
Products that have been completed and are ready to sell.

As you might imagine, **finished goods inventory** consists of products that have been completed and are ready to sell. With respect to Steelcase, finished goods inventory would be the pieces of metal office furniture completed but not yet sold. Remember, these are real units of finished product: They are reality. They have completed the production process and are sitting in a warehouse somewhere waiting to be sold. The measurement of that reality is a classification of inventory on the balance sheet called finished goods inventory. Included in that amount are all the materials, labour, and manufacturing overhead costs accumulated for those units completed, but not yet sold.

 Discussion Question

2-7. Why do you think managers of a manufacturing firm would find it beneficial to separate the amount and cost of inventory items into raw materials, work in process, and finished goods?

If managers in manufacturing businesses are to make prudent production decisions, they must have relevant information. The decisions they must make include how much and what type of materials they need to purchase, how many production workers are needed, what skill level these workers must possess, and whether production capacity is sufficient to produce the product required. The information that managers need to help them make these and many other production decisions includes the amount and cost of raw materials on hand, the composition of the labour force, the capacity and cost of production facilities, and the amount and cost of both work-in-process and finished goods inventory.

Although much of the relevant information managers need to make these decisions is provided by nonaccountants, such as marketing and sales personnel, accountants provide vital information concerning the cost of raw materials, work in process, and finished goods. All three classifications of inventory have one or more of the product cost elements introduced earlier: direct material, direct labour, and manufacturing overhead. We will now discuss each of those elements in more detail.

Direct Material

direct material The raw material that becomes a part of the final product and can be easily traced to the individual units produced.

Direct material is the raw material that becomes part of the final product and can be easily traced to the individual units produced. Obviously, direct materials cost is the cost of these raw materials. Examples of direct materials used in the manufacture of automobiles are sheet metal, plastic, and window glass. In the manufacture of computers, direct materials include circuit boards, cathode ray tubes, and other items. At Steelcase, Inc., direct materials would include the sheet metal used to manufacture the desks, filing cabinets, and other metal office furniture.

Often, the final product of one company is purchased by another to be used as part of its raw material in the manufacturing process. For example, direct materials used in the manufacture of Cessna aircraft include aluminum, wheels, tires, cables, and engines. The tires that Cessna uses as raw materials in the manufacture of its aircraft are the finished product of one of the company's suppliers, Goodyear Tire and Rubber Company.

 Discussion Questions

2-8. In addition to the tires supplied by Goodyear, what other finished products do you think Cessna uses in its production of small aircraft? What companies might produce these products?

2-9. Name three additional pairs of manufacturing companies that have a supplier-buyer relationship—that is, the finished product of one company becomes the raw material of another company.

When materials are purchased for use in the manufacture of products, their cost at first is added to raw materials inventory. Once the material has entered the production process (reality), its cost is removed from raw materials inventory and added to work-in-process inventory (measurement of reality). Thus, in our Steelcase example, as sheet metal is purchased, its cost is added to raw materials. Once the metal has been used to make a desk or other piece of office furniture, its cost is removed from raw materials inventory and becomes part of work-in-process inventory.

Direct Labour

direct labour hours The time spent by production workers as they transform raw materials into units of finished products.

Direct labour hours are defined as the time spent by production workers as they transform raw materials into units of finished products. Direct labour costs are the salaries and wages paid to these workers, which can be easily traced to the products the workers produce.

Think about some article of clothing, say a pair of pants, you are wearing at this moment. Certainly there is material in the pants. But how did the pants become pants? Well, you may not know all the steps, but you do know that somewhere, someone sat at a sewing machine and stitched the cut material into a pair of pants. The money paid to that person, whether in Taiwan, Korea, or Alberta, is considered direct labour, because her or his efforts (and therefore cost) can easily be traced to that single cost object (the pair of pants).

The accounting treatment of direct labour cost may surprise you. In financial accounting, employees' wages are classified as wages expense, salaries expense, or some similar expense. However, direct labour needed to get products ready to sell is a product cost that enhances the value of direct material. Because product costs are inventoriable costs, direct labour cost is added to the value of work-in-process inventory, along with direct material. Why? Because the work of production-line personnel increases the value of material as it is fabricated, assembled, painted, or processed. As a result, the cost of production-line labour should increase the value of inventory, shown as an asset on the balance sheet and ultimately as cost of goods sold on the income statement. In our Steelcase example, then, wages paid to workers who actually make the desks, filing cabinets, and other metal office furniture would be considered direct labour and added to work-in-process inventory.

Thus far we have explored two elements of product costs for a manufacturing firm: direct material and direct labour. Next, we consider the third and last element of manufacturers' product costs—manufacturing overhead.

Manufacturing Overhead

manufacturing overhead
All activities involved in the manufacture of products besides direct materials or direct labour.

factory overhead Another name for *manufacturing overhead cost.*

factory burden Another name for *manufacturing overhead cost.*

overhead In a manufacturing company, another name for manufacturing overhead cost; in a service type business, the indirect service cost.

indirect materials Materials consumed in support of multiple cost objects.

Manufacturing overhead is defined as all activities involved in the manufacture of products besides direct materials or direct labour. Manufacturing overhead cost, then, is the cost of these indirect manufacturing activities. It is also referred to as **factory overhead, factory burden,** or simply **overhead.** In recent years, manufacturing companies have begun to call the cost of manufacturing overhead *indirect manufacturing cost,* which is certainly more descriptive than any of its other names. Old habits die hard, however, so we will call it manufacturing overhead because this term has been and remains universally understood in business.

To be considered part of manufacturing overhead, the cost must be associated with the manufacturing facility, not some other aspect of the company such as selling or administrative functions. Manufacturing overhead includes three groups of costs: indirect materials, indirect labour, and other indirect manufacturing costs.

Indirect Material **Indirect materials** are those consumed in a manufacturing facility in support of multiple cost objects. There are two types of indirect material costs in manufacturing. The first is the cost of raw materials so insignificant that the added benefit of physically tracing these materials to individual products is not worth the effort. Examples include glue, rivets, solder, small nails, and caulking. In fact, businesses could physically trace all material cost to their products, but in the case of indirect materials, the effort required to trace the cost outweighs the benefit of the additional information. The second type of indirect material is factory supplies. These are materials used in the manufacturing facility but not incorporated into the product. Examples include paper towels, janitorial supplies, and lubricants for production machinery. The cost of all indirect materials, whether the materials actually become part of manufactured product, is added to the cost of the product as part of manufacturing overhead.

indirect labour The labour incurred in support of multiple cost objects.

Indirect Labour **Indirect labour** is labour incurred in a manufacturing facility in support of multiple cost objects. As was the case with indirect material costs, there are two types of indirect labour in manufacturing. The first is the cost associated with factory workers who are neither on the production line nor directly involved in the manufacturing process. Examples include the cost of materials handlers, production supervisors, plant security personnel, plant janitorial personnel, factory secretarial and clerical personnel, and the vice president of manufacturing. Although the effort of these workers is important to the production process, their labour costs are not easily traceable to products. They are therefore classified as indirect labour.

The second type of indirect labour is the cost of wages paid to direct labour employees when they are doing something other than working on the product they produce. These activities might include setting up equipment for production runs or sweeping up at the end of a shift. The idea is that direct labour should include only the cost of direct labour personnel when they are actually working on the product. The cost of all indirect labour is added to the cost of the product as part of manufacturing overhead.

As automation has become commonplace in the manufacturing process, many companies in Canada now consider *all* labour as indirect labour. In some types of operations, the direct labour element of a manufactured product is as low as 4 percent of the total manufacturing cost. If managers believe labour cost is insignificant, they may choose not to separate it into direct and indirect labour cost and may instead classify all labour costs as indirect.

Other Overhead Costs   In addition to indirect material and indirect labour, manufacturing overhead includes other costs associated with the production facility. Examples include amortization on the factory building, rent paid for production equipment, factory insurance, property taxes for the factory, and telephone service for the factory. All the costs in this category are associated with the operation of the production facility.

We have seen that manufacturing overhead is the sum of all indirect material, indirect labour, and other overhead costs. Manufacturing overhead costs are necessary costs to produce products and enhance the value of the goods being manufactured. Accordingly, as products are being manufactured, manufacturing overhead costs are added to work-in-process inventory.

 Discussion Question

2–10. The textbook you are reading was published (manufactured) by Pearson Education Canada Inc. What costs of manufacturing this book do you think Pearson Education Canada Inc. would include as

  a. direct materials?

  b. direct labour?

  c. manufacturing overhead?

The Flow of Product Cost—Manufacturing Company

In a manufacturing environment, just as in merchandising operations, managers must understand the flow of product costs to successfully control and plan for them. Product cost information is also an essential element of the information needed when making pricing and sales decisions. How could a business price a product if none of its managers knew how much the product cost to produce? Having the information is not enough, though. Managers must also understand the components of product cost and the way these costs will affect the company's assets as reported on the balance sheet and the profits as reported on the income statement. Exhibit 2–4 shows the flow of product costs through a manufacturing operation.

The exhibit looks more complicated than it really is. In fact, this exhibit summarizes our entire discussion of product cost identification for a manufacturer. Let's take some time to walk through the diagram.

Exhibit 2–4
The Flow of Product Costs—Manufacturing Company

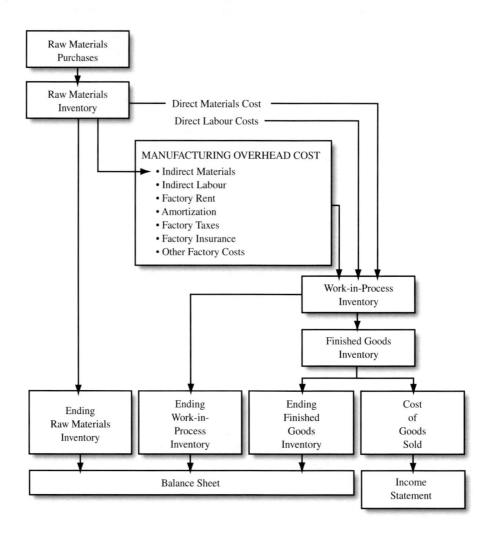

As raw materials are purchased, they become part of raw materials inventory (a).

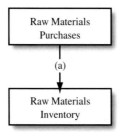

When materials actually enter the production process, their cost is classified as either direct materials (b, on the facing page) or indirect materials (c) depending on the type of material. The cost of any raw materials still on hand at the end of the production period is classified as ending raw materials inventory on the balance sheet at the end of the period (d).

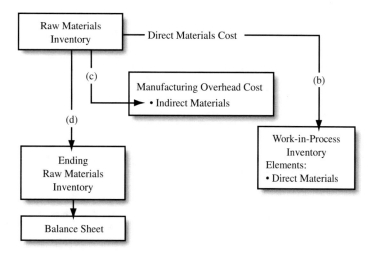

Note that the cost of direct materials is added to work-in-process inventory at this point, whereas the cost of indirect materials is classified as manufacturing overhead. We will return to manufacturing overhead in a moment.

We now have one of the three elements of product cost in work-in-process inventory (direct materials). The next element added is labour. Note that direct labour (e) is added directly to work-in-process inventory, whereas indirect labour (f) is classified as manufacturing overhead.

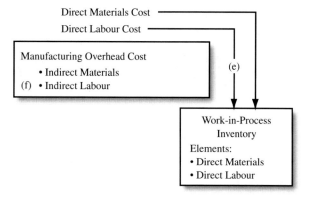

We now have two of the three elements of product cost in work-in-process inventory (direct materials and direct labour). The last element added is manufacturing overhead. In addition to indirect materials and indirect labour (which we classified as manufacturing overhead earlier), all other indirect manufacturing costs are classified as manufacturing overhead (g, next page). The ones we have provided in Exhibit 2–4 are representative only. In reality, the list is almost endless.

Once the manufacturing overhead items and amounts have been accumulated, the cost of manufacturing overhead is added to work in process (h).

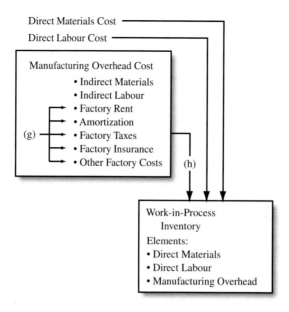

Work-in-process inventory, then, consists of the direct material, direct labour, and manufacturing overhead cost associated with goods that are currently in production. As units are completed, the cost associated with these units is transferred from work-in-process inventory to finished goods inventory (i, below). The cost of product still in production at the end of the production period is classified as ending work-in-process inventory on the balance sheet at the end of the period (j).

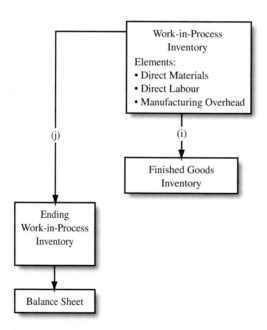

Once finished units of product (and their cost) have been transferred to finished goods inventory, usually only one of two things will happen to the actual units: Either they will be sold by the end of the accounting period or they will not be sold. If they are sold, we transfer the cost associated with them to cost of goods sold (k, facing page). We classify the cost of finished product still on hand at the end of the accounting period as ending finished goods inventory on the balance sheet at the end of the period (l).

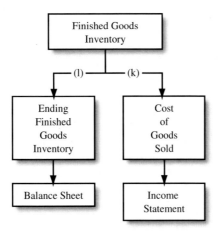

For most manufacturers, inventory is a sizeable asset requiring considerable financial resources. A walk through a manufacturing facility would make you aware of the significance of inventory, because you would be able to see stacks of it sitting there. Raw materials, work in process, and finished goods are all important assets of a manufacturer. Proper measurement of these assets is crucial if managers are to make good decisions about inventory management. For this reason, business people should understand the component costs of each type of inventory.

Cost of Goods Manufactured

We have seen that a manufacturer's product cost consists of direct material, direct labour, and manufacturing overhead. These three product classifications are summarized on the cost of goods manufactured schedule. You will find a typical presentation of this schedule for Lowell Manufacturing, Inc. in Exhibit 2–5.

Exhibit 2–5
Cost of Goods
Manufactured Schedule

LOWELL MANUFACTURING, INC.
Cost of Goods Manufactured Schedule
For the Year Ending December 31, 2003

Direct Materials:		
Beginning Direct Material Inventory	$ 13,000	
+ Purchases during 2003	400,000	
= Materials Available during 2003	413,000	
− Ending Direct Material Inventory	(20,000)	
= Direct Materials Used during 2003		$ 393,000
Direct Labour during 2003		220,000
Manufacturing Overhead Cost:		
Indirect Materials	$ 5,000	
Indirect Labour	20,000	
Factory Rent	144,000	
Amortization of Equipment	250,000	
Repairs and Maintenance on Equipment	40,000	
Utilities	39,000	
Property Taxes	15,000	
Total Manufacturing Overhead Cost during 2003		513,000
Manufacturing Cost for Current Period		1,126,000
+ Beginning Work-in-Process Inventory (January 1, 2003)		41,000
= Cost of Goods Available to be Finished during 2003		1,167,000
− Ending Work-in-Process Inventory (December 31, 2003)		(65,000)
= Cost of Goods Manufactured during 2003		$1,102,000

Although this schedule looks quite involved, it consists of four relatively simple parts.

1. **Direct materials section.** This section is similar in format to the cost of goods sold section of the income statement. In both cases, we deal with costs stored in inventory to determine the cost of the inventory that has been used.

LOWELL MANUFACTURING, INC.
Cost of Goods Manufactured Schedule
Direct Materials Section
For the Year Ending December 31, 2003

Direct Materials:		
Beginning Direct Material Inventory	$ 13,000	
+ Purchases during 2003	400,000	
= Materials Available during 2003	413,000	
− Ending Direct Material Inventory	(20,000)	
= Direct Materials Used during 2003		$393,000

2. **Direct labour section.** We see that the direct labour section of Lowell Manufacturing, Inc.'s cost of goods manufactured schedule consists of only one line, which is a common way to present this information. Remember, direct labour represents the cost of employees directly involved in the production process.

LOWELL MANUFACTURING, INC.
Cost of Goods Manufactured Schedule
Direct Labour Section
For the Year Ending December 31, 2003

Direct Labour during 2003	$220,000

3. **The manufacturing overhead section.** This section lists manufacturing overhead costs by functional description. Depending on the level of detail desired, this section can be as short as one line, which depicts total manufacturing overhead. Lowell's cost of goods manufactured schedule provides several lines detailing the various components of manufacturing overhead.

LOWELL MANUFACTURING, INC.
Cost of Goods Manufactured Schedule
Manufacturing Overhead Section
For the Year Ending December 31, 2003

Manufacturing Overhead Cost:		
Indirect Materials	$ 5,000	
Indirect Labour	20,000	
Factory Rent	144,000	
Amortization of Equipment	250,000	
Repairs and Maintenance on Equipment	40,000	
Utilities	39,000	
Property Taxes	15,000	
Total Manufacturing Overhead Cost during 2003		$513,000

4. **Cost summary and work-in-process section.** The last section of the cost of goods manufactured schedule summarizes the current period's product cost and incorporates the beginning and ending work-in-process inventory balances. Note that as in a cost of goods sold schedule, beginning inventory is added and ending inventory is subtracted to arrive at inventory used.

LOWELL MANUFACTURING, INC.
Cost of Goods Manufactured Schedule
Cost Summary and Work-in-Process Section
For the Year Ending December 31, 2003

	Manufacturing Cost for Current Period	$1,126,000
+	Beginning Work-in-Process Inventory (January 1, 2003)	41,000
=	Cost of Goods Available to be Finished during 2003	1,167,000
−	Ending Work-in-Process Inventory (December 31, 2003)	(65,000)
=	Cost of Goods Manufactured during 2003	$1,102,000

Using the information from the cost of goods manufactured schedule, we can prepare a cost of goods sold schedule, such as the one for Lowell Manufacturing, Inc. shown in Exhibit 2–6.

Exhibit 2–6
Cost of Goods Sold
Schedule

LOWELL MANUFACTURING, INC.
Cost of Goods Sold Schedule
For the Year Ending December 31, 2003

	Beginning Finished Goods Inventory	$ 70,000
+	Cost of Goods Manufactured during 2003	1,102,000
=	Goods Available for Sale in 2003	1,172,000
−	Ending Finished Goods Inventory	(28,000)
=	Cost of Goods Sold for 2003	$1,144,000

PRODUCT COST IDENTIFICATION FOR SERVICE FIRMS

In contrast to both merchandisers and manufacturers, service type businesses such as law firms, health care providers, airlines, and accounting firms do not sell tangible, physical products. Many service firms are huge. For example, Fairmont Hotels and Resorts Inc. is a diversified service company in the hospitality industry. The company reported revenues from hotel services of over $2,500,000,000 for 2001.

Service companies offer their customers a product just as real as those sold by merchandisers and manufacturers, but service products lack physical substance. Determining the cost of its product is as important for a service company as it is for merchandisers and manufacturers, but the procedures differ because service type businesses have no inventory.

Costs can be accumulated for almost any facet of a service company's operation. To illustrate, let us consider the Marston Veterinary Clinic. The three doctors at the clinic (Dr. Helen Marston and two of her veterinary school classmates) perform a variety of medical services on dogs and cats. The clinic performs routine check-ups, examinations in response to specific symptoms, immunizations, and surgery when necessary. Any one of these services could be designated as a cost object, and cost could be accumulated for a particular service provided to an individual animal. Likewise, costs can be accumulated for a particular category of procedure, for a department or a particular area of the veterinary practice, or for each of the three doctors or the five assistants.

The three broad cost classifications included in the cost of services provided are materials, labour, and indirect service cost (sometimes called overhead). The cost classifications for a service firm look almost exactly like the classifications used in costing manufactured products, with some important differences.

Materials

The materials used in performing services are normally incidental supplies. The cost of these materials is relatively insignificant compared to the direct materials used in the production of manufactured products. In the case of Marston Veterinary Clinic, materials would include items such as splints, the needles and serum used for immunizations, bandages, and so forth.

Some service companies separate material that is significant enough to trace to individual cost objects from insignificant material that is simply treated as indirect overhead cost. In many cases, however, the materials used in performing a service are actually more like the indirect materials used by a manufacturer. Whereas a manufacturer such as Steelcase might consider glue and screws to be indirect materials, a legal firm would probably consider legal pads, computer discs, and pens as indirect materials, and all costs of materials are treated as an indirect (overhead) cost.

Labour

Generally, service businesses are labour intensive, meaning that the largest component of product cost for service organizations is often labour cost. It includes costs of those people who perform part or all of the service. In the case of Marston Veterinary Clinic, labour cost would certainly include the salaries of the three doctors and the five assistants. It would not, however, include the amount paid to the receptionist or bookkeeper. Even though their work is important, these employees do not perform the veterinary care services provided by the clinic. The labour cost of the receptionist and bookkeeper, then, would be considered a period cost.

Overhead or Indirect Service Costs

The overhead costs in a service business are similar to those for a manufacturer. They are costs that are associated specifically with performing the services provided but that cannot easily be traced to one specific cost object. In the case of the Marston Veterinary Clinic, rent on the clinic building is an indirect cost of providing veterinary care—the building is necessary to provide veterinary services. However, its cost is hard to trace to one cost object, so it is considered an overhead cost.

 Discussion Question

2–11. Airline companies, such as Air Canada, often define the routes they fly as cost objects. Given that definition, consider a specific route from Vancouver to Toronto and describe the costs you believe Air Canada would include as

    a. materials

    b. labour

    c. overhead

The Flow of Service Cost—Service Company

Just as managers in manufacturing and merchandising operations must understand the flow of costs associated with products they sell, managers of service type businesses must understand the flow of service costs if they are to control and plan for them. Also, service cost information is an essential element of the information needed when making pricing and sales decisions. Having the information is not enough though. Managers must also understand how these costs will affect the company's assets reported on the balance sheet and profits reported on the income statement. The flow of costs through a typical service firm is shown in Exhibit 2–7.

Exhibit 2–7
The Flow of Service Costs—Service Company

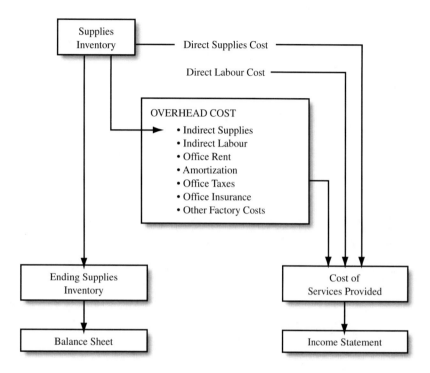

Cost of Services

As Exhibit 2–7 indicates, cost of services has three parts: direct labour, overhead, and supplies. With this in mind, we can easily create a schedule computing the cost of service products. As an example, the schedule in Exhibit 2–8 shows the computation of the cost of veterinary services for Marston Veterinary Clinic.

Exhibit 2–8
Cost of Services Schedule

MARSTON VETERINARY CLINIC		
Cost of Services Schedule		
For the Year Ending December 31, 2003		
Direct Labour Cost		$ 940,000
Overhead Cost:		
Indirect Supplies	$12,000	
Office Rent	24,000	
Amortization—Equipment	18,000	
Office Taxes	2,000	
Office Insurance	8,000	
Other Indirect Costs	6,000	
Total Overhead Cost		70,000
Direct Supplies Cost		20,000
Cost of Services Provided		$1,030,000

Exhibit 2–8 shows that the cost of services for Marston Veterinary Clinic was $1,030,000 for the year ended December 31, 2003. The total cost included the three components of service product cost: direct labour, overhead, and direct supplies.

We have examined how service firms identify product costs and how those costs flow through the firm. We now turn briefly to hybrid firms, which produce both goods and services.

HYBRID FIRMS

hybrid firms Companies that generate revenue from both providing services and selling products.

Some companies, called **hybrid firms,** generate revenue from both providing services and selling products. For example, although the majority of Blockbuster Video Canada Inc.'s revenue comes from its videotape rental service, the company also generates significant revenue from videotape product sales. In accounting for an operation that combines service and products, companies such as Blockbuster must incorporate techniques used by both service and merchandising firms. A single company, such as General Motors, might actually be a manufacturer (making cars and trucks), a merchandiser (selling floor mats and other accessories to GM dealers), and a service type business (offering GMAC Financing).

MERCHANDISING, MANUFACTURING, AND SERVICE FIRMS—A COMPARISON

Now that we have explored how merchandising, manufacturing, and service businesses identify their product costs and how those costs flow through each type of operation, we can see how merchandisers, manufacturers, and service businesses present product costs and period costs on their income statements. We begin with a merchandising operation, then we look at a manufacturer and a service business.

Exhibit 2–9
Product Costs and Period Costs on the Income Statement—Merchandiser

JASON'S SUPPLY COMPANY
Cost of Goods Sold Schedule
For the Year Ending December 31, 2003

Beginning Inventory at January 1, 2003	$ 23,000
+ Purchases during 2003	300,000
= Goods Available for Sale in 2003	323,000
− Ending Inventory at December 31, 2003	(30,000)
= Cost of Goods Sold for 2003	$293,000

JASON'S SUPPLY COMPANY
Income Statement
For the Year Ending December 31, 2003

Sales		$673,000
Cost of Goods Sold		293,000
Gross Profit		380,000
Operating Expenses:		
Selling Expense	$120,000	
Administrative Expense	80,000	
Total Operating Expenses		200,000
Operating Income		$180,000

Exhibit 2–9 illustrates how a merchandiser reports its product costs and period costs on an income statement. This exhibit shows the 2003 income statement for Jason's Supply Company and includes the cost of goods sold schedule we developed for Jason's Supply Company earlier in the chapter (presented as Exhibit 2–3 on page 23).

As Exhibit 2–9 indicates, the amount of product cost recognized as expense (cost of goods sold) on Jason's Supply Company's 2003 income statement ($293,000) is calculated in the cost of goods sold schedule. The period cost recognized is the total of the operating expenses ($200,000).

Exhibit 2–10 illustrates how a manufacturer reports its product costs and period costs on an income statement. This exhibit shows the 2003 income statement for

Exhibit 2–10
Product Costs and
Period Costs on the
Income Statement—
Manufacturer

LOWELL MANUFACTURING, INC.
Cost of Goods Manufactured Schedule
For the Year Ending December 31, 2003

Direct Materials:		
Beginning Direct Material Inventory	$ 13,000	
+ Purchases during 2003	400,000	
= Materials Available during 2003	413,000	
− Ending Direct Material Inventory	(20,000)	
= Direct Materials Used during 2003		$ 393,000
+ Direct Labour during 2003		220,000
+ Manufacturing Overhead Cost:		
Indirect Materials	$ 5,000	
Indirect Labour	20,000	
Factory Rent	144,000	
Amortization of Equipment	250,000	
Repairs and Maintenance on Equipment	40,000	
Utilities	39,000	
Property Taxes	15,000	
Total Manufacturing Overhead Cost during 2003		513,000
= Manufacturing Cost for Current Period		1,126,000
+ Beginning Work-in-Process Inventory (January 1, 2003)		41,000
= Cost of Goods Available to be Finished		1,167,000
− Ending Work-in-Process Inventory (December 31, 2003)		(65,000)
= Cost of Goods Manufactured during 2003		$1,102,000

Cost of Goods Sold Schedule
For the Year Ending December 31, 2003

Beginning Finished Goods Inventory	$ 70,000
+ Cost of Goods Manufactured during 2003	1,102,000
= Goods Available for Sale in 2003	1,172,000
− Ending Finished Goods Inventory	(28,000)
= Cost of Goods Sold for 2003	$1,144,000

Income Statement
For the Year Ending December 31, 2003

Sales		$1,884,000
Cost of Goods Sold		1,144,000
Gross Profit		740,000
Operating Expenses:		
Selling Expense	$250,000	
Administrative Expense	180,000	
Total Operating Expenses		430,000
Operating Income		$ 310,000

Lowell Manufacturing, Inc. and includes the cost of goods manufactured schedule (presented as Exhibit 2–5 on page 33) and cost of goods sold schedule (presented as Exhibit 2–6 on page 35) we developed for Lowell earlier in the chapter.

As Exhibit 2–10 indicates, the amount of product cost recognized as expense (cost of goods sold) on Lowell's 2003 income statement ($1,144,000) is calculated in the cost of goods manufactured schedule and the cost of goods sold schedule. The period cost recognized is the total of the operating expenses ($430,000).

Exhibit 2–11 illustrates how a service type company reports its cost of services and period costs on an income statement. This exhibit shows the 2003 income statement for Marston Veterinary Clinic and includes the cost of services schedule we developed for Marston earlier in the chapter (presented as Exhibit 2–8 on page 37).

As Exhibit 2–11 indicates, the amount of services cost recognized as expense (cost of services) on Marston's 2003 income statement ($1,030,000) is calculated in the cost of services schedule. The period cost recognized is the total of the operating expenses ($175,000).

Whether the costs are related to products purchased for sale, products manufactured for sale, or services provided, cost information is an important input in the decision-making process. Remember that management accounting information helps internal decision makers plan and control the firm's future. In the chapters that follow, you will see how the cost classifications and cost flows you learned about in this chapter will help you understand and apply management accounting decision-making techniques.

Exhibit 2–11
Cost of Services and Period Costs on the Income Statement— Service Type Company

MARSTON VETERINARY CLINIC
Cost of Services Schedule
For the Year Ending December 31, 2003

Direct Labour Cost		$ 940,000
Overhead Cost:		
Indirect Supplies	$12,000	
Office Rent	24,000	
Amortization—Equipment	18,000	
Office Taxes	2,000	
Office Insurance	8,000	
Other Indirect Costs	6,000	
Total Overhead Cost		70,000
Direct Supplies Cost		20,000
Cost of Services Provided		$1,030,000

MARSTON VETERINARY CLINIC
Income Statement
For the Year Ending December 31, 2003

Service Revenue		$1,260,000
Cost of Services		1,030,000
Gross Margin on Services		230,000
Operating Expenses:		
Selling Expense	$ 45,000	
Administrative Expense	130,000	
Total Operating Expenses		175,000
Operating Income		$ 55,000

SUMMARY

Businesses incur many different costs as they operate in the modern business world. These costs can be classified in many different ways and managers must determine what cost classifications will be most helpful if they are to make effective planning and control decisions.

Costs can be accumulated by cost object, which is any activity or item for which we desire a separate cost measurement. Some of the costs associated with a cost object can be traced directly to that cost object. These are called direct costs. Other costs incurred to support multiple cost objects are known as indirect costs.

The classification of costs as either product cost or period cost is very important because it determines how costs are reported on a company's income statement. Product cost is the sum of all costs required to make the products available and ready to sell, and is reported on the income statement as cost of goods sold. Period costs are all costs a company incurs that are not classified as product cost. Period costs are divided into selling and administrative costs, and are reported on the income statement as expenses.

There are significant differences in the way product cost is determined for merchandising companies and for manufacturing companies. For a merchandiser, product cost includes the cost of the merchandise itself and freight costs to obtain the merchandise. For a manufacturer, product cost includes the direct materials, direct labour, and manufacturing overhead required to produce finished units of product.

Manufacturing companies have additional cost classification challenges because they have three distinct types of inventory: raw materials that have been purchased but have not yet entered the production process; work-in-process units that have begun the production process but are not yet complete; and units that have been completed and are ready for sale.

Cost of services performed for a service type business is similar in many ways to product cost for a manufacturer. It includes the cost of materials, labour, and overhead required to perform services.

APPENDIX—RECORDING BASIC MANUFACTURING COSTS

This appendix is intended to provide a basic overview of how costs are accumulated in the accounting records of a manufacturer. To keep the example simple, we assume that the factory makes only one product and manufacturing overhead is attributed directly to work in process. The technical aspects of the application of manufacturing overhead to production will be covered in the next chapter.

After completing your work in this appendix, you should be able to record the following types of entries:

1. The purchase of raw material
2. The three main components of manufacturing cost
   a. Direct material
   b. Direct labour
   c. Manufacturing overhead
3. The transfer of the cost of completed units from work in process to finished goods
4. The sale of completed units

The following accounts will be used for the entries in this appendix:

1. Cash
2. Accounts receivable
3. Raw materials inventory
4. Work-in-process inventory
5. Finished goods inventory
6. Accounts payable
7. Sales
8. Cost of goods sold

Recall that debits increase assets, expenses, and losses, while credits increase liabilities, equity, revenues, and gains. The dollar amount of the debits must equal that of the credits in each journal entry.

1. $90,000 of raw material was purchased on account on January 2, 2003:

2003
Jan. 2	Raw materials inventory	90,000	
	Accounts payable		90,000
	To record the purchase of raw material.		

2. **a.** $70,000 of direct material was transferred to production on January 3, 2003:

2003
Jan. 3	Work-in-process inventory	70,000	
	Raw materials inventory		70,000
	To record the transfer of direct material to production.		

2. **b.** $80,000 of direct labour cost was incurred during January 2003.

2003
Jan. 31	Work-in-process inventory	80,000	
	Cash		80,000
	To record wages paid for direct labour in January.		

2. **c.** Paid for various factory overhead items totaling $110,000 during January 2003. To keep the example simple, manufacturing overhead is attributed *directly* to production. As you will see in the next chapter, manufacturing overhead is generally *allocated* to production, which necessitates the use of more complicated accounting procedures.

2003
Jan. 31	Work-in-process inventory	110,000	
	Cash		110,000
	To record manufacturing overhead for January.		

After the above entries have been posted, the balance in the work-in-process inventory account is $260,000 as shown in the t-account below.

Work-in-Process Inventory

70,000	
80,000	
110,000	
260,000	

3. At January 31, a physical count of the goods in production revealed that $230,000 or all but $30,000 of the goods were completed and transferred to finished goods inventory. The amount transferred from work-in-process inventory to finished goods inventory must equal the cost of goods manufactured.

2003
Jan. 31 Finished goods inventory   230,000
                  Work-in-process inventory   230,000
          To transfer completed goods from
          production to finished goods inventory.

After the $230,000 is transferred to finished goods inventory, the work-in-process inventory account and finished goods inventory account have balances of $30,000 and $230,000, respectively, as shown below.

Work-in-Process Inventory

70,000	230,000
80,000	
110,000	
260,000	230,000
30,000	

Finished Goods Inventory

230,000	

4. Goods that cost $210,000 to manufacture were sold on account for $300,000. This transaction is recorded in two parts. First the sale on account is recorded:

2003
Jan. 31 Accounts receivable   300,000
                  Sales   300,000

Next the reduction in finished goods inventory and increase in cost of goods sold is recorded:

2003
Jan. 31 Cost of goods sold   210,000
                  Finished goods inventory   210,000

The following t-accounts depict balances after recording the $300,000 sale.

Work-in-Process Inventory

70,000	230,000
80,000	
110,000	
260,000	230,000
30,000	

Finished Goods Inventory

230,000	210,000
20,000	

Accounts Receivable

300,000	

Sales

	300,000

Cost of Goods Sold

210,000	

APPENDIX SUMMARY

Recording basic manufacturing entries involves eight accounts: cash, accounts receivable, accounts payable, raw materials inventory, work-in-process inventory, finished goods inventory, cost of goods sold, and sales. The basic flow through the accounts is depicted in Exhibit 2–A1. The purchase of raw material is recorded with a debit to raw materials. Work-in-process inventory is debited to record the transfer of direct materials to production and the incurrence of direct labour and manufacturing overhead costs. When goods are completed, work-in-process inventory is credited and finished goods inventory is debited for the amount of the cost of the goods manufactured. When the finished goods are sold, separate entries are made to reflect the sale and to reflect the decrease in finished goods inventory and increase in cost of goods sold.

Exhibit 2–A1
Basic Flow of Costs Through Manufacturing Accounts

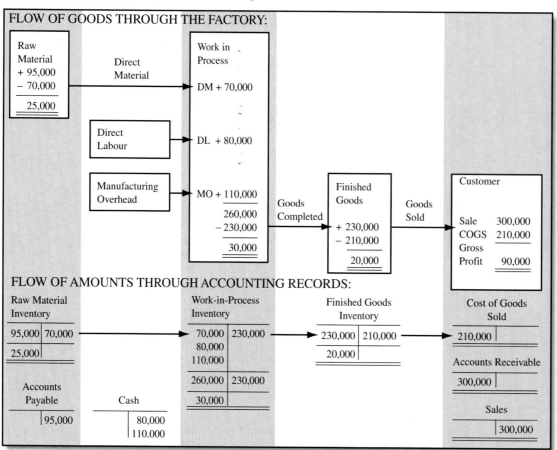

KEY TERMS

administrative cost, p. 21
common cost, p. 19
cost, p. 18
cost object, p. 19
direct cost, p. 19
direct labour cost, p. 25
direct labour hours, p. 27
direct material, p. 26
direct materials cost, p. 25
factory burden, p. 28
factory overhead, p. 28
finished goods inventory, p. 26
hybrid firms, p. 38

indirect cost, p. 19
indirect labour, p. 28
indirect materials, p. 28
inventoriable cost, p. 20
manufacturing overhead, p. 28
manufacturing overhead cost, p. 25
material stores, p. 25
overhead, p. 28
period cost, p. 20
product cost, p. 20
raw materials inventory, p. 25
selling cost, p. 20
work-in-process inventory, p. 25

REVIEW THE FACTS

1. What is a cost object?
2. What is the difference between a direct cost and an indirect cost?
3. What is product cost?
4. What is period cost?
5. Why is the cost of delivering merchandise to customers included in selling expense?
6. Why is the cost of storing inventory that is ready to sell included in selling expense?
7. What classification includes costs that are neither product costs nor costs directly associated with selling activities?
8. Why are product costs called inventoriable costs?
9. Describe the difference between the accounting treatment for product costs and period costs.
10. Describe the flow of inventory costs for a merchandising operation as goods are bought and then sold.
11. What are the inventory classifications for a manufacturing type firm?
12. What are the three main cost components included in product cost for a manufacturing type firm?
13. What is the difference between direct material and indirect material?
14. What is the difference between direct labour and indirect labour?
15. In which product cost classification would you most likely find indirect material and indirect labour?
16. With respect to the cost of goods sold section of an income statement, what is the similarity between purchases for a merchandising type company and cost of goods manufactured for a manufacturing type company?
17. What is included in the cost of services provided for a service type firm?

LO 1: Distinguish between Direct and Indirect Costs

1. Brittany operates a small chain of five children's shoe stores called Baby Feet. She employs a store manager and two sales clerks for each store. In addition, she rents office space that houses her office, the personnel department, and the accounting department for the chain.

Brittany has collected the following information regarding the stores and has asked you to determine which costs are direct and which costs are indirect.

REQUIRED:

For each of the following items, indicate which would describe a direct cost (D) for the store at the corner of Elm Street and Main and which would describe an indirect cost (I) for an individual store.

1. **I** Rent for the office space
2. **D** Rent for the store
3. **I** Brittany's salary
4. **D** The store manager's salary
5. **I** The company personnel manager's salary
6. **I** Accountant's salary
7. **D** Maintenance cost for the store
8. **D** Amortization on sales equipment
9. **I** Amortization on the accounting computer
10. **D** Sales clerks' salaries
11. **D** Cost of shoes
12. **I** Advertising cost for the chain

LO 1: Distinguish between Direct and Indirect Costs

2. Sue Lee is the president of Baby Care. The company operates a chain of four child care centres in Alberta. In addition to the four Baby Care locations, the company rents office space that is used by the company's accountant and Sue Lee.

REQUIRED:

a. List four costs that would be considered direct costs of one of the four child care centres.

b. List four costs that would be considered indirect costs of one of the four child care centres.

LO 1: Distinguish between Direct and Indirect Costs

3. Blue Water Travel operates a chain of travel agent offices in eastern Canada. Blue Water Travel's home office is in Halifax. There are six sales offices and a district office located in New Brunswick.

REQUIRED:

If the cost object is one of the sales offices in New Brunswick, indicate which of the following would describe a direct cost (D) and which would describe an indirect cost (I).

1. _____ Rent for the New Brunswick district office building
2. _____ Rent for the home office building in Halifax
3. _____ Rent for the sales office
4. _____ The company president's salary

5. _____ The salary of the vice president in charge of the New Brunswick division
6. _____ The salary of a sales office manager
7. _____ The salary of a sales associate

LO 2: Types of Cost for a Manufacturer

DM, DL, MO } product costs

period costs { S, A

4. Following are several representative costs incurred in a typical manufacturing company. For each of the costs, indicate in the space provided whether the cost is a direct material (DM), direct labour (DL), manufacturing overhead (MO), selling (S), or administrative (A) cost.

1. __DM__ Material incorporated into products
2. __S__ Sales supplies
3. __MO__ Supplies used in the factory
4. __MO__ Wages of the factory security guard
5. __S__ Wages of security guard for the sales office
6. __MO__ Amortization on a file cabinet used in the factory
7. __A__ Amortization on a file cabinet used in the general accounting office
8. __A__ President's salary
9. __A__ President's assistant's salary
10. __MO__ Manufacturing vice president's salary
11. __MO__ Salary of the manufacturing vice president's assistant
12. __DL__ Wages paid to production-line workers
13. __MO__ Factory rent
14. __A__ Accounting office rent
15. __S__ Amortization on a copy machine used in the sales department
16. __MO__ Amortization on a copy machine used to copy work orders in the factory
17. __MO__ Salary of the factory supervisor

LO 2: Types of Cost for a Manufacturer

5. Following are several representative costs incurred in a typical manufacturing company. For each of the costs, indicate in the space provided whether the cost is a product cost (PR) or a period cost (PE).

1. __PR__ Material incorporated into products
2. __PE__ Sales supplies
3. __PR__ Supplies used in the factory
4. __PR__ Wages of the factory security guard
5. __PE__ Wages of security guard for the sales office
6. __PR__ Amortization on a file cabinet used in the factory
7. __PE__ Amortization on a file cabinet used in the general accounting office
8. __PE__ President's salary
9. __PE__ President's assistant's salary
10. __PR__ Manufacturing vice president's salary
11. __PR__ Salary of the manufacturing vice president's assistant
12. __PR__ Wages paid to production-line workers
13. __PR__ Factory rent
14. __PE__ Accounting office rent
15. __PE__ Amortization on a copy machine used in the sales department
16. __PR__ Amortization on a copy machine used to copy work orders in the factory
17. __PR__ Salary of the factory supervisor

LO 5: Calculate Costs for a Manufacturer, No Inventories

6. The following data pertain to the Anderson Table Manufacturing Company for January 2003. The company made 1,000 tables during January, and there are no beginning or ending inventories.

Wood used in production	$25,000
Cleaning supplies used in the factory	300
Machine lubricants used in the factory	100
Factory rent	2,000
Rent on the sales office	3,000
Sales salaries	20,000
Production-line labour cost	50,000
Factory security guard cost	1,200
Factory supervision	2,500
Office supervision	3,000
Amortization on production equipment	4,000
Amortization on office equipment	1,000

REQUIRED:

a. What is the cost of direct material used in production during January 2003?
b. What is the cost of direct labour for January 2003?
c. What is the cost of manufacturing overhead for January 2003?
d. What is the total cost of tables manufactured in January 2003?
e. What is the cost of each table manufactured in January 2003?
f. Do you think the cost per table is valuable information for Carole Anderson, the company's owner? How might she use this information?

LO 5: Calculate Ending Inventory

7. Steinmann Window Corporation makes aluminum window units. At the beginning of November, the company's direct material inventory included 300 square metres of window glass. During November Steinmann purchased another 4,000 square metres of glass. Each completed window unit requires 3 square metres of glass. During November, 3,300 square metres of glass was transferred to the production line.

REQUIRED:
How many square metres of glass remain in the ending direct material inventory?

LO 4: Analyzing Inventory

8. Van Kirk Manufacturing Company has been in business for many years. Dottie Van Kirk, the company president, is concerned that the cost of raw material is skyrocketing. The production supervisor assured Van Kirk that the use of direct material actually dropped in 2004.

Van Kirk has engaged your services to provide insight into what she thinks may be a sizable problem. Not only does it seem that the cost of direct material is increasing, but it also seems that her production supervisor is being less than honest with her.

The following information is available:

VAN KIRK MANUFACTURING COMPANY
Direct Materials Schedule
For the Year Ending December 31, 2003

Beginning Direct Material Inventory	$ 25,000
Purchases during 2003	435,000
Materials Available during 2003	460,000
Ending Direct Material Inventory	(30,000)
Direct Materials Used during 2003	$430,000

VAN KIRK MANUFACTURING COMPANY
Direct Materials Schedule
For the Year Ending December 31, 2004

Beginning Direct Material Inventory	$ 30,000
Purchases during 2004	501,000
Materials Available during 2004	531,000
Ending Direct Material Inventory	(103,000)
Direct Materials Used during 2004	$428,000

REQUIRED:

Examine the information presented and write a brief report to Dottie Van Kirk detailing your findings and addressing her concerns.

LO 3: Analyze Costs of a Merchandiser

9. Ralph Brito opened Brito Auto Sales Inc. several years ago. Since then, the company has grown and sales have steadily increased. In the last year, however, income has declined despite successful efforts to increase sales. In addition, the company is forced to borrow more and more money from the bank to finance the operation.

The following information is available:

BRITO AUTO SALES INC.
Income Statement
For the Year Ending December 31, 2003

Sales		$758,000
Cost of Goods Sold		
Beginning Inventory	$ 66,000	
+ Cost of Goods Purchased	639,000	
= Goods Available for Sale	705,000	
− Ending Inventory	(85,000)	
= Cost of Goods Sold		620,000
Gross Profit		138,000
Operating Expenses:		
Selling Expense	55,000	
Administrative Expense	60,000	115,000
Operating Income		$ 23,000

BRITO AUTO SALES INC.
Income Statement
For the Year Ending December 31, 2004

Sales		$890,000
Cost of Goods Sold		
Beginning Inventory	$ 85,000	
+ Cost of Goods Purchased	799,000	
= Goods Available for Sale	884,000	
− Ending Inventory	(123,000)	
= Cost of Goods Sold		761,000
Gross Profit		129,000
Operating Expenses:		
Selling Expense	66,000	
Administrative Expense	60,000	126,000
Operating Income		$ 3,000

REQUIRED:
Assume that you are hired by Mr. Brito as a consultant. Review the Brito income statement and write a report to Mr. Brito that addresses his concerns.

LO 4: Calculate Ending Direct Material Inventory for a Manufacturer

10. Matheis Designs Inc. manufactures swimming suits. At the beginning of October 2003, the company had $1,450 worth of cloth on hand that was included in its direct material inventory. During October, Matheis purchased cloth costing $12,360 and used cloth costing $12,750 in production.

REQUIRED:
What is the cost of the ending direct material inventory of cloth for Matheis Designs Inc.?

LO 4: Calculate Direct Material Used

11. The following information relates to Penny Manufacturing Company.

Beginning direct material inventory	$ 540,000
Ending direct material inventory	$ 480,000
Direct material purchased	$4,680,000

REQUIRED:
    a. Compute the cost of direct material used in production.
    b. Appendix: Prepare a journal entry to record the use of direct material in production.

LO 4: Calculate Direct Material Used

12. The following information relates to Montoya Manufacturing Inc.

Beginning direct material inventory	$ 40,000
Ending direct material inventory	$ 48,000
Direct material purchased	$437,000

REQUIRED:
    a. Compute the cost of direct material used in production.
    b. Appendix: Prepare a journal entry to record the use of direct material in production.

LO 4: Calculate the Cost of Supplies Used

13. The following information relates to Pons Maintenance Service.

Maintenance supplies at January 1, 2004	$ 4,210
Maintenance supplies at December 31, 2004	$ 3,840
Maintenance supplies purchased during 2004	$27,530

REQUIRED:
What was the cost of maintenance supplies consumed by Pons Maintenance Service during 2004?

LO 6: Calculate Cost of Materials Used by a Service Company

14. On January 1, 2004, Bowden Auto Repair had $3,560 worth of auto parts on hand. During the year, Bowden purchased auto parts costing $286,000. At the end of 2004, the company had parts on hand amounting to $4,260.

REQUIRED:
What was the cost of the auto parts used by Bowden Auto Repair during 2004?

LO 3: Calculate the Cost of Goods Sold for a Merchandiser

15. On January 1, 2005, the cost of merchandise on hand at Margaret's Fashions was $56,530. Purchases during the month amounted to $488,668 and the cost of merchandise on hand at the end of January was $52,849.

REQUIRED:
Determine January's cost of goods sold for Margaret's Fashions.

LO 5: Inventory and Production Costs for a Manufacturer

16. The following data pertain to Hudik Manufacturing Corporation for the year ended December 31, 2004. The company made 115,000 light fixtures during 2004. There are no beginning or ending inventories.

Metal used in production	$750,000
Wire used in production	40,000
Factory supplies	5,200
Amortization on the factory	48,000
Amortization on the sales office	3,000
Sales salaries	90,000
Assembly-line labour cost	960,000
Factory security guard cost	8,200
Factory supervision	62,500
General accounting cost	43,000
Amortization on production equipment	454,850
Amortization on office equipment	9,200

REQUIRED:
a. What is the cost of direct material used during 2004?
b. What is the cost of direct labour during 2004?
c. What is the cost of manufacturing overhead during 2004?
d. What is the total product cost for 2004 production?
e. What is the cost per light fixture for 2004?

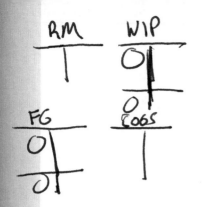

RM, FG, WIP - Balance sheet

COGS - income sheet

LO 5: Inventory and Production Costs Including Cost of Goods Manufactured and Cost of Goods Sold, No Inventories

17. The following data pertain to Elsea Manufacturing Company for the year ended December 31, 2003. The company made 60,000 SW20 switching units during 2003.

Beginning direct material inventory	$ 42,000
Ending direct material inventory	48,000
Beginning work-in-process inventory	84,000
Ending work-in-process inventory	93,000
Beginning finished goods inventory	124,000
Ending finished goods inventory	133,000
Direct material purchased	850,000
Indirect material used in production	4,000
Factory supplies	6,200
Amortization on the factory	60,000
Amortization on the sales office	4,000
Amortization on the administrative office	3,000
Sales salaries	120,000
Assembly-line labour cost	820,000
Factory security guard cost	12,000
Factory supervision	82,600
Amortization on production equipment	560,000
Amortization on office equipment	22,200

REQUIRED:

a. What is the cost of direct material used during 2003?
b. What is the cost of direct labour during 2003?
c. What is the cost of manufacturing overhead for 2003?
d. What is total manufacturing cost incurred during 2003?
e. What is the cost of goods manufactured for 2003?
f. What is the cost of goods sold for 2003?

LO 5: Inventory and Production Costs Including Cost of Goods Manufactured and Cost of Goods Sold

18. The following data pertain to Milton Manufacturing Corporation for the year ended December 31, 2005.

Beginning finished goods inventory	$ 255,000
Ending finished goods inventory	270,000
Beginning direct material inventory	82,000
Ending direct material inventory	98,000
Beginning work-in-process inventory	164,000
Ending work-in-process inventory	184,000
Direct material purchased	1,740,000
Indirect material used in production	3,000
Factory supplies	12,500
Amortization on the factory	134,000
Amortization on the sales office	14,000
Amortization on the administrative office	9,000
Sales salaries	350,000
Assembly-line labour cost	2,120,000
Factory security guard cost	22,000
Factory supervision	183,500
Amortization on production equipment	1,340,000
Amortization on office equipment	52,200

REQUIRED:

a. What is the cost of direct material used during 2005?
b. What is the cost of direct labour during 2005?
c. What is the cost of manufacturing overhead for 2005?
d. What is total manufacturing cost incurred during 2005?
e. What is the cost of goods manufactured for 2005?
f. What is the cost of goods sold for 2005?

LO 5: Inventory and Production Costs Including Cost of Goods Manufactured and Cost of Goods Sold

19. The following data pertain to Mini Manufacturing Company for the year ended December 31, 2003.

Beginning direct material inventory	$ 2,000
Ending direct material inventory	3,000
Beginning work-in-process inventory	4,000
Ending work-in-process inventory	5,000
Beginning finished goods inventory	9,500
Ending finished goods inventory	8,000
Direct material purchased	22,000
Factory supplies	12,500
Amortization on the factory	34,000
Assembly-line labour cost	120,000
Amortization on production equipment	42,000
Other indirect factory costs	12,000

REQUIRED:

a. What is the cost of direct material used during 2003?
b. What is the cost of direct labour during 2003?
c. What is the cost of manufacturing overhead for 2003?
d. What is total manufacturing cost incurred during 2003?
e. What is the cost of goods manufactured for 2003?
f. What is the cost of goods sold for 2003?

LO 5: Inventory and Production Costs Including Cost of Goods Manufactured and Cost of Goods Sold

20. The following data pertain to Ace Manufacturing Inc. for the year ended December 31, 2004.

Beginning direct material inventory	$ 22,000
Ending direct material inventory	28,000
Beginning finished goods inventory	30,000
Ending finished goods inventory	28,000
Beginning work-in-process inventory	16,000
Ending work-in-process inventory	15,000
Direct material purchased	280,000
Production worker labour cost	290,000
Amortization on production equipment	80,000
Factory rent	24,000
Other indirect factory costs	36,000

REQUIRED:

a. What is the cost of direct material used during 2004?
b. What is the cost of direct labour during 2004?
c. What is the cost of manufacturing overhead for 2004?
d. What is total manufacturing cost incurred during 2004?
e. What is the cost of goods manufactured for 2004?
f. What is the cost of goods sold for 2004?

LO 5: Preparation of Cost of Goods Manufactured and Cost of Goods Sold Schedules

21. The following data pertain to Adler Manufacturing Company for the year ended December 31, 2005.

Beginning direct material inventory	$ 12,000
Ending direct material inventory	13,000
Beginning work-in-process inventory	24,000
Ending work-in-process inventory	25,000
Beginning finished goods inventory	29,500
Ending finished goods inventory	28,000
Direct material purchased	122,000
Factory utilities	2,500
Rent on the factory	64,000
Assembly worker labour cost	86,000
Amortization on production equipment	92,000
Other indirect factory costs	22,000

REQUIRED:

a. Prepare a cost of goods manufactured schedule for 2005.
b. Prepare a cost of goods sold schedule for 2005.

LO 5: Preparation of Cost of Goods Manufactured and Cost of Goods Sold Schedules

22. The following data pertain to Clifford Manufacturing Corp. for the year ended December 31, 2003.

Beginning direct material inventory	$ 2,300
Ending direct material inventory	3,400
Beginning work-in-process inventory	5,500
Ending work-in-process inventory	4,100
Beginning finished goods inventory	6,500
Ending finished goods inventory	5,100
Direct material purchased	12,300
Factory supplies used	500
Amortization on the factory	22,000
Assembly-line labour cost	48,600
Amortization on production equipment	12,000
Other indirect factory costs	4,700

REQUIRED:

a. Prepare a cost of goods manufactured schedule for 2003.
b. Prepare a cost of goods sold schedule for 2003.

LO 5: Preparation of Cost of Goods Manufactured Schedule, Cost of Goods Sold Schedule, and Multistep Income Statement

23. The following data pertain to Ryder Manufacturing Company for the year ended December 31, 2004.

Sales	$1,267,000
Beginning direct material inventory	40,000
Ending direct material inventory	50,000
Beginning work-in-process inventory	70,000
Ending work-in-process inventory	60,000
Beginning finished goods inventory	90,000
Ending finished goods inventory	80,000
Direct material purchased	350,000
Indirect material used in production	24,000
Factory supplies used	6,000
Amortization on the factory	90,000
Amortization on the sales office	24,000
Amortization on the administrative office	36,000
Sales salaries	110,000
Assembly-line labour cost	220,000
Factory security guard cost	22,000
Factory supervision	42,000
Amortization on production equipment	160,000
Amortization on office equipment	16,000

REQUIRED:

a. Prepare a cost of goods manufactured schedule for 2004.
b. Prepare a cost of goods sold schedule for 2004.
c. Prepare a multistep income statement for 2004.

LO 5: Preparation of Cost of Goods Manufactured Schedule, Cost of Goods Sold Schedule, and Multistep Income Statement

24. The following data pertain to Dhaliwal Manufacturing Company for the year ended December 31, 2005.

Sales	$1,302,000
Beginning finished goods inventory	93,000
Ending finished goods inventory	86,000
Beginning direct material inventory	45,000
Ending direct material inventory	56,000
Beginning work-in-process inventory	72,000
Ending work-in-process inventory	77,000
Direct material purchased	370,000
Indirect material used in production	34,000
Amortization on production equipment	145,000
Amortization on office equipment	19,000
Factory supplies used	8,000
Amortization on the factory	96,000
Amortization on the sales office	34,000
Amortization on the administrative office	30,000
Sales salaries	122,000
Assembly-line labour cost	240,000
Factory security guard cost	32,000
Factory supervision	48,000

REQUIRED:
a. Prepare a cost of goods manufactured schedule for 2005.
b. Prepare a cost of goods sold schedule for 2005.
c. Prepare a multistep income statement for 2005.

LO 5: Preparation of Cost of Goods Manufactured Schedule, Cost of Goods Sold Schedule, and Multistep Income Statement

25. The following data pertain to Wong Manufacturing Corporation for the year ended December 31, 2003.

Sales	$1,124,000
Beginning direct material inventory	55,000
Ending direct material inventory	56,000
Beginning finished goods inventory	83,000
Ending finished goods inventory	96,000
Beginning work-in-process inventory	62,000
Ending work-in-process inventory	67,000
Direct material purchased	290,000
Direct labour cost	220,000
Manufacturing overhead	286,000
Selling expense	122,000
Administrative expense	140,000

REQUIRED:
a. Prepare a cost of goods manufactured schedule for 2003.
b. Prepare a cost of goods sold schedule for 2003.
c. Prepare a multistep income statement for 2003.

LO 5: Preparation of Cost of Goods Manufactured Schedule, Cost of Goods Sold Schedule, and Multistep Income Statement

26. The following data pertain to Fraser Manufacturing Limited for the year ended December 31, 2004.

Sales	$333,000
Beginning direct material inventory	5,000
Ending direct material inventory	4,000
Beginning work-in-process inventory	6,000
Ending work-in-process inventory	7,000
Beginning finished goods inventory	8,000
Ending finished goods inventory	10,000
Direct material purchased	56,000
Direct labour cost	96,000
Manufacturing overhead	86,000
Selling expense	46,000
Administrative expense	34,000

REQUIRED:
a. Prepare a cost of goods manufactured schedule for 2004.
b. Prepare a cost of goods sold schedule for 2004.
c. Prepare a multistep income statement for 2004.

LO 5: Preparation of Cost of Goods Manufactured Schedule

27. The following information is for Megan Hat Manufacturing Company.

Inventory information:

	January 1, 2005	December 31, 2005
Raw materials inventory	$ 9,000	$11,000
Work-in-process inventory	22,000	18,000
Finished goods inventory	42,000	38,000

Other information:

Direct materials purchases	$120,000
Direct labour cost	250,000
Manufacturing overhead	140,000

REQUIRED:

a. What is the cost of direct material used in production?
b. Prepare a cost of goods manufactured schedule for 2005.
c. Prepare a cost of goods sold schedule.
d. Appendix: Prepare journal entries to record the following:
    1. The purchase of direct material
    2. The use of direct material in production
    3. Direct labour cost
    4. Manufacturing overhead cost (Use "Various accounts" for the credit side of the entry.)
    5. The cost of goods manufactured
    6. The sale of finished goods assuming the sale price was $600,000

LO 5: Preparation of Cost of Goods Manufactured Schedule

28. The following information is for Friedman Shelving Manufacturing Company.

Inventory information:

	January 1, 2003	December 31, 2003
Raw materials inventory	$22,000	$24,000
Work-in-process inventory	42,000	43,000
Finished goods inventory	82,000	78,000

Other information:

Direct materials purchases	$280,000
Direct labour cost	540,000
Manufacturing overhead	240,000

REQUIRED:

a. What is the cost of direct material used in production?
b. Prepare a cost of goods manufactured schedule for 2003.
c. Prepare a cost of goods sold schedule.
d. Appendix: Prepare journal entries to record the following:
    1. The purchase of direct material
    2. The use of direct material in production
    3. Direct labour cost
    4. Manufacturing overhead cost (Use "Various accounts" for the credit side of the entry.)
    5. The cost of goods manufactured
    6. The sale of finished goods assuming the sale price was $1,400,000

LO 5:   Preparation of Cost of Goods Manufactured Schedule

29. The following information is for Tatum Manufacturing Corporation.

Inventory information:

	January 1, 2004	December 31, 2004
Raw materials inventory	$2,000	$4,000
Work-in-process inventory	4,000	3,000
Finished goods inventory	8,000	6,000

Other information:

Direct materials purchases	$ 8,000
Direct labour cost	12,000
Manufacturing overhead	9,000

REQUIRED:
  a. Prepare a cost of goods manufactured schedule for 2004.
  b. Appendix: Prepare journal entries to record the following:
     1. The purchase of direct material
     2. The use of direct material in production
     3. Direct labour cost
     4. Manufacturing overhead cost (Use "Various accounts" for the credit side of the entry.)
     5. The cost of goods manufactured
     6. The sale of finished goods assuming the sale price was $40,000

LO 5:   Preparation of Cost of Goods Manufactured Schedule

30. The following information is for Munter Manufacturing Company.

Inventory information:

	January 1, 2005	December 31, 2005
Raw materials inventory	$6,000	$5,000
Work-in-process inventory	3,000	4,000
Finished goods inventory	7,000	9,000

Other information:

Direct materials purchases	$ 9,000
Direct labour cost	10,000
Manufacturing overhead	11,000

REQUIRED:
  a. Prepare a cost of goods manufactured schedule for 2005.
  b. Appendix: Prepare journal entries to record the following:
     1. The purchase of direct material
     2. The use of direct material in production
     3. Direct labour cost
     4. Manufacturing overhead cost (Use "Various accounts" for the credit side of the entry.)
     5. The cost of goods manufactured
     6. The sale of finished goods assuming the sale price was $39,000

LO 5: Preparation of Cost of Goods Manufactured Schedule and Multistep Income Statement

31. The following information is for Chan Manufacturing Inc.

Inventory information:

	January 1, 2003	December 31, 2003
Raw materials inventory	$16,000	$14,000
Work-in-process inventory	23,000	25,000
Finished goods inventory	33,000	36,000

Other information:

Sales	$760,000
Direct materials purchases	159,000
Direct labour cost	110,000
Manufacturing overhead	221,000
Selling expense	62,000
Administrative expense	47,000

REQUIRED:

a. Prepare a cost of goods manufactured schedule for 2003.

b. Prepare a multistep income statement for 2003.

LO 5: Preparation of Cost of Goods Manufactured Schedule and Multistep Income Statement

32. The following information is for Richard Manufacturing Company.

Inventory information:

	January 1, 2004	December 31, 2004
Raw materials inventory	$14,000	$16,000
Work-in-process inventory	25,000	28,000
Finished goods inventory	32,000	36,000

Other information:

Sales	$790,000
Direct materials purchases	162,000
Direct labour cost	140,000
Manufacturing overhead	234,000
Selling expense	72,000
Administrative expense	57,000

REQUIRED:

a. Prepare a cost of goods manufactured schedule for 2004.

b. Prepare a multistep income statement for 2004.

LO 3: Preparation of a Multistep Income Statement for a Manufacturer

33. Bonnie's Pet Cage Company has the following information for 2005:

Sales	$300,000
Cost of goods manufactured	200,000
Selling expense	30,000
Administrative expense	25,000
Beginning finished goods inventory	21,000
Ending finished goods inventory	28,000

REQUIRED:

Prepare a multistep income statement for Bonnie's Pet Cage Company.

LO 3: Preparation of a Multistep Income Statement for a Manufacturer

34. Albert's Manufacturing Corporation has the following information for 2003:

Beginning finished goods inventory	$ 41,000
Ending finished goods inventory	58,000
Sales	600,000
Cost of goods manufactured	400,000
Selling expense	90,000
Administrative expense	60,000

REQUIRED:

Prepare a multistep income statement for Albert's Manufacturing Corporation for 2003.

LO 5: Preparation of Cost of a Multistep Income Statement for a Merchandiser

35. Phillips Merchandising Company has the following information for 2004:

Sales	$400,000
Cost of merchandise purchased	300,000
Selling expense	30,000
Administrative expense	20,000
Beginning finished goods inventory	40,000
Ending finished goods inventory	50,000

REQUIRED:

Prepare a multistep income statement for Phillips Merchandising Company for 2004.

LO 5: Preparation of Cost of a Multistep Income Statement for a Merchandiser

36. Bally Merchandising Limited has the following information for 2005:

Beginning finished goods inventory	$ 60,000
Ending finished goods inventory	50,000
Sales	840,000
Cost of merchandise purchased	630,000
Selling expense	90,000
Administrative expense	40,000

REQUIRED:

Prepare a multistep income statement for Bally Merchandising Limited for 2005.

LO 6: Determine the Cost of Services Provided and Preparation of a Single-Step Income Statement for a Service Company

37. Butterfield's Bookkeeping Service began operations on January 1, 2003. The following information is taken from its accounting records as of December 31, 2003.

Bookkeeping service revenue	$80,000
Bookkeeping salaries	42,000
Bookkeeping office rent	12,000
Amortization on computer equipment	2,000
Bookkeeping supplies used	700
Advertising	800

REQUIRED:

a. What is the cost of services provided?

b. Prepare a single-step income statement for Butterfield's Bookkeeping Service. (A single-step income statement groups all expenses together as operating expenses to determine operating income.)

LO 6: Determine the Cost of Services Provided and Preparation of a Single-Step Income Statement for a Service Company

38. Tony's Film Delivery Service began operations on January 1, 2004. The following information is taken from its accounting records as of December 31, 2004.

Delivery revenue	$40,000
Driver wages	22,000
Amortization on truck	4,000
Fuel cost	2,700
Advertising	800
Bookkeeping cost	240

REQUIRED:

a. What is the cost of services provided?

b. Prepare a single-step income statement for Tony's Film Delivery Service. (A single-step income statement groups all expenses together as operating expenses to determine operating income.)

LO 3: Preparation of a Multistep Income Statement for a Merchandiser

39. Cam's Swimsuit Shop provided the following information for 2005:

Merchandise inventory, January 1, 2005	$ 16,000
Merchandise inventory, December 31, 2005	19,000
Sales	190,000
Advertising	1,200
Store rent	2,400
Purchases of merchandise	82,000
Sales salaries	22,000
Store utilities	3,600
Sales supplies used during 2005	1,000
Sales supplies on hand, December 31, 2005	500
Office rent	800
Administrative salaries	18,000

REQUIRED:

Prepare a multistep income statement for Cam's Swimsuit Shop for 2005.

LO 3: Preparation of a Multistep Income Statement for a Merchandiser

40. Leroy's Auto Parts Inc. provided the following information for 2003:

Merchandise inventory, January 1, 2003	$ 19,000
Merchandise inventory, December 31, 2003	21,000
Sales	280,000
Advertising	2,200
Amortization on the store	18,000
Purchases of merchandise	182,000
Sales salaries	21,000
Store utilities	1,200
Amortization on office building	4,000
Administrative salaries	15,000
Office utilities	600

REQUIRED:

Prepare a multistep income statement for Leroy's Auto Parts Inc. for 2003.

LO 6: Preparation of a Single-Step Income Statement for a Service Company

41. Dan's Security Service Limited provided the following information for 2004:

Security revenue	$480,000
Advertising	12,000
Amortization on the home office building	12,000
Security guard wages	362,000
Administrative salaries	21,000
Sales salaries	24,000
Utilities	1,200

REQUIRED:

Prepare a single-step income statement for Dan's Security Service Limited for 2004. (A single-step income statement groups all expenses together as operating expenses to determine operating income.)

LO 3: Preparation of a Multistep Income Statement for a Merchandiser

42. Margaret's Flower Shop provided the following information for 2005:

Merchandise inventory, January 1, 2005	$ 1,000
Merchandise inventory, December 31, 2005	1,200
Sales	42,400
Advertising	3,200
Store rent	1,200
Purchases of merchandise	18,000
Sales salaries	21,000
Utilities	1,300
Sales supplies used during 2005	9,000
Sales supplies on hand, December 31, 2005	300

REQUIRED:

Prepare a multistep income statement for Margaret's Flower Shop for 2005.

LO 2, 3, & 4: Understanding Cost of Goods Sold

43. The management of Diversified Incorporated is concerned that few of its employees understand cost of goods sold. The company president has decided that a series of presentations will be made focusing on cost of goods sold.

Assume that the company has formed two teams, Team A and Team B. You and several of your classmates have been assigned to Team B.

Team A is given the responsibility of preparing a presentation detailing the cost of goods sold pertaining to a subsidiary that operates a chain of hardware stores. Team B, your team, has been given the responsibility of preparing a presentation detailing the cost of goods sold of a subsidiary that manufactures electronic calculators.

In short order, Team A has completed its assignment and is ready to make its presentation. Your team, however, is still working. Company executives question why Team A is so far ahead of your team's progress.

REQUIRED:
Working as a group, develop a response to the concerns relating to your team's slow progress. Explain why Team A could complete its assignment so quickly and why your team will have to work longer.

LO 6: Understanding Service Company Costs

44. Assume that you are the manager of an accounting practice. You are concerned about billing your clients so that the company covers all costs and makes a reasonable profit.

REQUIRED:
a. What information might you desire to help develop a method of billing clients?
b. How would you use the information to ensure that costs are covered and profits result?

LO 1, 2, & 4: Understanding Inventory Cost Classifications

45. The inventory of a manufacturer is typically grouped into one of three classifications—raw material inventory, work-in-process inventory, and finished goods inventory.

REQUIRED:
Discuss why it provides more useful information to use three classifications of inventory rather than one for a manufacturer.

LO 1, 2, & 4: Understanding Inventory Costs

46. Assume that you work for the Acme Wire Manufacturing Company. Some employees in the company are unsure of which costs should be included in inventories and which costs should not. There is also some confusion regarding the logic of including some items while excluding others.

You have been assigned to a group that is responsible for making a presentation on which of Acme's costs would properly be classified as inventory costs and which would not.

REQUIRED:

Prepare a presentation describing the type of items that would be included in inventories and those that would not. Comment on the logic of including some cost items in inventory while excluding others.

LO 1, 2, & 3: General Inventory and Cost Analysis

47. One year ago, Herb Smith quit his job at Adcox Medical, where he earned $28,000 a year as a health care technician, to start the Super CD Store. He invested almost his entire life's savings in the venture and is now concerned. He notes that, when his money was in the bank, he earned about 4% interest. Now, when he compares his company profits to the amount invested in the store, the profits seem lower than what he could have earned if he had simply left the money in the bank. The following information is available for the company's first year of business:

Annual sales	$600,000
Cost of goods sold	450,000
Selling expense	90,000
Administrative expense	50,000
Inventory	300,000
Other assets	30,000
Total liabilities	50,000

The administrative expense includes $30,000 received by Herb in the form of salary. Herb's friend Bill has suggested that a simple $5,000 computer might help with company record keeping and ordering inventory. Herb has indicated that he does not mind the added work or ordering the merchandise without a computer. In fact, when it comes to ordering product, he seems quite proud of the job he is doing as he almost always has the CDs his customers want.

Herb has engaged your services as a consultant to determine whether his feelings are correct about the low earnings of the company and to suggest some possibilities to improve the situation. Also, Herb would like some input regarding the computer.

REQUIRED:

Prepare a report for Herb addressing each of his concerns.

LO 1, 2, & 3: General Inventory and Cost Analysis

48. Alberto Manufacturing Company has been in business for many years. Toward the end of 2004, management began to notice that the company had to rely more and more on borrowing to support the cash flow needs of the operation. Although sales increased in 2005, profits declined and the cash flow problem worsened. The company president is very concerned that the cash shortfall is caused by mismanagement of the daily operation of the factory. Managers argue that the company's operations are quite satisfactory. They cite that expenses have increased only slightly as sales have risen, and that production levels have been dictated by customer demand.

The president has hired your team of consultants to review the situation and comment on the possible problems that exist. The following information is available for 2004 and 2005.

ALBERTO MANUFACTURING COMPANY
Schedule of Cost of Goods Manufactured
For the Year Ending December 31, 2004

Direct Materials:		
Beginning Direct Material Inventory	$ 15,000	
Purchases during 2004	420,000	
Materials Available during 2004	435,000	
Ending Direct Material Inventory	(45,000)	
Direct Materials Used during 2004		$ 390,000
Direct Labour during 2004		225,000
Total Manufacturing Overhead Cost during 2004		415,000
Manufacturing Cost for Current Period		1,030,000
Beginning Work-in-Process Inventory, January 1, 2004		40,000
Cost of Goods Available to be Finished		1,070,000
Ending Work-in-Process Inventory, December 31, 2004		(82,000)
Cost of Goods Manufactured during 2004		$ 988,000

ALBERTO MANUFACTURING COMPANY
Income Statement
For the Year Ending December 31, 2004

Sales		$1,758,000
Cost of Goods Sold		
Beginning Finished Goods Inventory	$ 65,000	
+ Cost of Goods Manufactured	988,000	
= Goods Available for Sale in 2004	1,053,000	
− Ending Finished Goods Inventory	(75,000)	
= Cost of Goods Sold for 2004		978,000
Gross Profit		780,000
Operating Expenses:		
Selling Expense	355,000	
Administrative Expense	190,000	545,000
Operating Income		$ 235,000

ALBERTO MANUFACTURING COMPANY
Schedule of Cost of Goods Manufactured
For the Year Ending December 31, 2005

Direct Materials:		
Beginning Direct Material Inventory	$ 45,000	
Purchases during 2005	457,000	
Materials Available during 2005	502,000	
Ending Direct Material Inventory	(73,000)	
Direct Materials Used during 2005		$ 429,000
Direct Labour during 2005		263,000
Total Manufacturing Overhead Cost during 2005		450,000
Manufacturing Cost for Current Period		1,142,000
Beginning Work-in-Process Inventory, January 1, 2005		82,000
Cost of Goods Available to be Finished		1,224,000
Ending Work-in-Process Inventory, December 31, 2005		(154,000)
Cost of Goods Manufactured during 2005		$1,070,000

ALBERTO MANUFACTURING COMPANY
Income Statement
For the Year Ending December 31, 2005

Sales		$1,772,000
Cost of Goods Sold		
Beginning Finished Goods Inventory	$ 75,000	
+ Cost of Goods Manufactured during 2005	1,070,000	
= Goods Available for Sale in 2005	1,143,000	
− Ending Finished Goods Inventory	(91,000)	
= Cost of Goods Sold for 2005		1,052,000
Gross Profit		720,000
Operating Expenses:		
Selling Expense	365,000	
Administrative Expense	228,000	593,000
Operating Income		$ 127,000

REQUIRED:

Your team should review the provided information and comment on problems that exist. It may help to segment the statements into sections and assign group members to a particular area. For example, a group member might be assigned to review the purchase and use of direct material, another member might be assigned the direct labour and manufacturing overhead areas, and so forth. Each group member should comment on his or her assigned area as it pertains to cash flow and income.

3

Determining Costs of Products

"*T*ime was when Ford Motor's giant River Rouge plant in Dearborn, Michigan was the pinnacle of industrial achievement. Barges of iron ore docked at one end, new Fords rolled out the other.

But that was half a century ago, an eternity at Internet speed. Today's model is no longer Ford's assembly line but the quick assembly techniques made famous by Dell Computers...."[1]

The world of manufacturing is changing. As technology brings about continuous improvement in the way products are manufactured, companies are able to change their approach to manufacturing. Ford and General Motors anticipate that, in the near future, they will be able to produce a car to a customer's specifications within a very short period of time. The advantage to the customer is obvious—a car will be customized with the options you want. For the auto manufacturers, guessing what colours and options to include in a particular car will become a thing of the past. The assembly process will be much more efficient, which will reduce the cost of manufacturing the car and reduce the amount of inventory that will be produced. The auto manufacturers can then pass the savings on to their customers.

Regardless of the method used to produce a product, companies need to determine the costs of the products they manufacture. If you are the sales manager for Dell Computers, you must be sure that the selling price of a computer is high enough to earn a profit. To ensure the selling price of the computer exceeds its cost, you need accurate product cost information.

---

[1]Fred Andrews, "Dell, It Turns Out, Has a Better Idea Than Ford," January 26, 2000, from *The New York Times'* web site, www.nytimes.com (accessed August 1, 2002).

Besides the product pricing decision are several other applications of information about product cost. First, a company must determine the cost of products to compute cost of goods sold on its income statement for a particular period. Second, a company must have product cost information to determine the value of inventories shown on its balance sheet. Third, product cost information helps managers evaluate the efficiency and productivity of a company's manufacturing facility.

In Chapter 2 we stated that the three elements of product cost for a manufacturer are direct material, direct labour, and manufacturing overhead. We also presented an overview of the product costing process. In this chapter, we will delve more deeply into the job order costing and process costing methods that manufacturers use to determine the cost of the individual units of product they produce. ■

LEARNING OBJECTIVES

After completing your work on this chapter, you should be able to do the following:

1. Compare and contrast process costing with job order costing.
2. Describe how process costing and job order costing work.
3. Describe the documents used to help control the costs of manufacturing products.
4. Describe how overhead costs are allocated to products.
5. Determine the cost of products using job order costing.
6. Determine the cost of products using process costing.

ACCUMULATING PRODUCT COST—COST ACCOUNTING

The process of assigning manufacturing costs to manufactured products is called *cost accounting.* When we first introduced this term in Chapter 1, we said that it is often used interchangeably with the terms *management accounting* and *managerial accounting,* but that cost accounting is a narrow application of management accounting dealing with costing products. Cost accounting information can help managers plan and control their operations; make decisions about investments in property, plant, and equipment; establish selling prices; and determine the value of inventories on the balance sheet. Cost accounting information also affects reported net income on the income statement, because the cost of the products sold during the income statement period is reported as cost of goods sold.

UNITS OF PRODUCT AS COST OBJECTS

Recall from Chapter 2 that a cost object is any activity or item for which a separate cost measurement is desired. For our purposes in this chapter, we will consider a unit of manufactured product as the cost object. As we said earlier, the cost of a unit of manufactured product includes the cost of the direct material, direct labour, and manufacturing overhead required to produce that unit of product. The amount of direct material included in each unit of production can actually be traced to finished products. Assigning the cost of direct material to production is relatively simple, as long as the company keeps track of the amount of material used to produce each unit of product. Similarly, if a company keeps track of the amount of direct labour used to produce each unit of product, it can readily assess the cost of direct labour used to produce each unit. Unlike direct material and direct labour, however, the amount of manufacturing overhead cost associated with particular units of production is quite abstract.

Manufacturing overhead cost includes all manufacturing cost except direct material or direct labour costs. Accordingly, it includes a wide assortment of factory-related items. Some examples are production design setup, factory security, supervisory salaries, raw materials storage, building maintenance, and factory supplies.

Even though their cost cannot easily be traced to individual units of production, the manufacturing overhead activities mentioned (and many others) are all necessary to produce products, and their cost should be included in the cost of products produced. The problem, of course, is that the cost of these activities cannot be traced directly to the units of product produced. Their cost, therefore, must be allocated to the units. Consider the cost of factory lighting, for example. The production facility has lights turned on so that those who are working on the product can see what they are doing. As units of product make their way through the production process the lights shine on them and lighting cost is incurred. Because the purpose of the lights is to enhance the production process, a certain amount of the cost of lighting should be included in the cost of each unit of product manufactured. Unfortunately, when the power company sends the bill at the end of the month, there is no breakdown as to how much lighting cost is to be included in each unit. The bill only shows the total cost of electricity used, say $10,000. The manufacturer has to determine how to assign some portion of the lighting cost to each unit produced. **Manufacturing overhead allocation** is a process of assigning or allotting an amount of manufacturing overhead cost to each unit of product produced based on some reasonable basis of distribution. This allocation has traditionally been a two-stage process.

manufacturing overhead allocation The process of assigning or allotting an amount of manufacturing overhead cost to each unit of product produced based on some reasonable basis of distribution.

TRADITIONAL MANUFACTURING OVERHEAD ALLOCATION

cost pool An accumulation of the costs associated with a specific cost object.

The first stage in the process of assigning manufacturing overhead costs to products is to gather overhead cost into a cost pool. A **cost pool** is an accumulation of the costs associated with a specific cost object. Traditionally, the cost of manufacturing overhead was gathered into one large cost pool, including all manufacturing costs except for direct material and direct labour.

The second stage is to assign the manufacturing overhead cost gathered in the pool to units of product manufactured. Manufacturers attempt to allocate the amount of manufacturing overhead cost that corresponds to the overhead resources consumed to make the product. In other words, if it seems likely that $1,000 worth of manufacturing overhead resources were consumed to manufacture a pool table, then $1,000 should be allocated to that pool table for overhead. Because it is impractical, if not impossible, for managers to estimate the amount of overhead associated with each unit of individual product produced, an equitable basis for cost allocation must be determined.

allocation base An amount associated with cost objects that can be used to proportionately distribute manufacturing overhead costs to each cost object.

An **allocation base** is an amount associated with cost objects that can be used to proportionately distribute manufacturing overhead costs to each cost object. The traditional approach to allocating manufacturing overhead cost to units produced is to identify some other cost or item to serve as an indicator of the relative amounts of indirect factory resources used to make each unit of production. This other cost or item is then used as the allocation base. Direct labour hours, direct labour cost, and machine hours are common traditional allocation bases.

It seems logical that a larger unit of production would require the use of more factory resources than a smaller unit of production, which may mean more direct labour, direct materials, machine time, or some combination of these. The idea behind using an allocation base such as direct labour dollars is that if a unit of product requires a large amount of direct labour cost, it follows that its manufacture would also consume a large amount of overhead resources.

As an example, assume Buck Slade Company uses direct labour cost as the allocation base for manufacturing overhead. Assume manufacturing overhead was $1,000,000 and direct labour cost totaled $100,000 for July 2003. The company can express the relationship between these two costs by dividing the $1,000,000 manufacturing overhead by the $100,000 direct labour cost. Notice that we are dividing the cost we wish to allocate (the $1,000,000 manufacturing overhead) by the allocation base (the $100,000 direct labour cost). The result is the company's overhead application rate. Buck Slade Company will allocate overhead cost to the units of manufactured product at a rate of $10 per direct labour dollar.

What this means is that every time $1 of direct labour cost is added to a unit of product, $10 of manufacturing overhead cost will be added to the product's cost as well. A product that requires little direct labour will receive a small allocation for manufacturing overhead. The total direct material cost, direct labour cost, and the total allocated manufacturing overhead cost are then added together to determine the cost of the manufactured product.

For example, assume that Buck Slade Company produces a batch of 15,000 precision cutters. If 15,000 cutters required a total of 80 direct labour hours at $10 per hour, the manufacturing overhead allocation would be $8,000, calculated as follows:

Direct Labour Hours		Direct Labour Rate		Direct Labour Cost
80	×	$10	=	$800

Direct Labour Cost		Overhead Allocation Rate		Total Overhead Allocation
$800	×	$10	=	$8,000

This method uses a single manufacturing overhead cost pool and a single, factory-wide application rate. Virtually all manufacturers used this method until the mid-1980s, and many still do today.

During the mid-1980s, some companies realized that a factory-wide application rate has significant weaknesses. Whereas some manufacturing overhead costs may relate to the allocation base, many others do not. Manufacturing overhead costs are typically caused by (or related to) many different activities—the activity that drives one cost may be totally different from the activity that drives another cost. To use one activity (such as direct labour) as the allocation base for applying all manufacturing overhead cost to product will likely cause some products to be overcosted and others to be undercosted. For example, assume that a company uses direct labour hours to allocate all manufacturing overhead cost, and its factory has five machines, two of which use significant amounts of water for cooling. In this situation, the overhead cost per direct labour hour will include an amount for cooling water. The amount will be allocated to products whether they are produced on a machine that requires cooling water or not. Therefore, products that are produced on machines that do not require cooling water will be overcosted and, because some of the cost of cooling water is allocated to products produced on machines that do not require cooling water, products produced on machines that do require cooling water will be undercosted.

In the past decade, many companies have begun to study the cost incurred in their operations and are attempting to determine the activities that cause those costs. Great strides have been made and the result has been the development of a new costing method that provides more realistic and reasonable cost for units of manufactured product. This new method is activity-based costing.

MANUFACTURING OVERHEAD ALLOCATION USING ACTIVITY-BASED COSTING

activity-based costing
Allocating cost to products based on the activities that caused the cost to happen.

One way to increase the accuracy of product cost is to trace the cost of overhead activities to products based on activities that cause the cost. Allocating cost to products based on the activities that cause the cost is called **activity-based costing.**

This allocation process improves on traditional overhead allocation in two ways. First, an analysis of what causes cost to happen may result in the reclassification of certain costs from manufacturing overhead to direct material, direct labour, or some other direct cost classification. That is, some costs traditionally viewed as indirect can actually be traced directly to units of product and need not be allocated. This in and of itself contributes to a more accurate unit cost because less cost remains to be allocated.

Second, rather than using one giant cost pool and a single allocation base resulting in one factory-wide application rate, activity-based costing uses multiple cost pools to develop multiple application rates. Adding manufacturing overhead cost to the units of production based on the various activities that drive the costs leads to more accurate unit product cost.

For example, say Buck Slade Company has analyzed its $1,000,000 of manufacturing overhead cost and has classified the activities that cause that cost to happen. This analysis has led the company to reclassify $220,000 from manufacturing overhead to direct cost because it found that, using modern technology, it could readily trace those costs directly into units of product as they are produced. The remaining $780,000 manufacturing overhead cost consists of the items listed in Exhibit 3–1.

Exhibit 3–1
Remaining Overhead
for Buck Slade
Company

Materials purchasing and handling cost	$ 75,000
Production engineering and design	60,000
Production machine setup	40,000
Production machine amortization	300,000
Production machine maintenance	50,000
Quality testing	100,000
Factory security	25,000
Factory supervision	70,000
Building maintenance	10,000
Factory supplies	20,000
Factory insurance	30,000
Total manufacturing overhead	$780,000

To implement activity-based costing, we begin by reviewing overhead to identify specific overhead activities and their cost. Once identified, the costs of a given overhead activity are removed from the general overhead pool and grouped together in a separate pool. This action results in costs being accumulated in several small cost pools, within practical limits, instead of a single large pool. For example, separate pools might be established for the cost of setup, materials handling, quality inspection, and so forth.

The second stage of manufacturing overhead allocation is to assign the cost accumulated in the pool to products. Manufacturers hope to find an activity associated with products that causes the cost and that can also be used as an allocation base. **cost driver** A cost cause that is used as a cost allocation base. This cause is a **cost driver**. It differs from a traditional allocation base in that it actually *causes* the cost. Traditional allocation bases such as direct labour hours, direct labour cost, and machine hours do not cause cost. Rather, they are cost correlates that have historically been viewed as good indicators of the amount of overhead associated with particular products. The lack of a causal relationship between the cost and the allocation base is a significant weakness of traditional overhead allocation.

The estimated activities for the Buck Slade Company are listed in Exhibit 3–2. Buck Slade Company has separated the large $780,000 pool into various small pools and used cost drivers to allocate the manufacturing overhead to products. In other words, Buck Slade Company allocates manufacturing overhead cost to products based on activities that cause the cost.

Exhibit 3–2
Estimated Activities
for Buck Slade
Company

Number of parts	750,000
Number of production runs	25
Number of machine hours	2,000
Number of components tested	25,000
Number of direct labour hours	10,000

Buck Slade Company has separated the $780,000 manufacturing overhead pool into five smaller pools to be allocated as follows:

Pool 1—Materials purchasing and handling, allocated using the number of parts as the cost driver.

Pool 2—Production engineering and design cost, and production machine setup cost, allocated using the number of production runs as the cost driver.

Pool 3—Production machine amortization and production machine maintenance, allocated using the number of machine hours as the cost driver.

Pool 4—Quality testing, allocated using the number of components tested as the cost driver.

Pool 5—Remaining manufacturing overhead costs. Because Buck Slade Company is unable to determine cost drivers, or because it is impractical to determine cost drivers for these remaining costs, a traditional allocation base—direct labour hours—will be used.

To calculate the application rate, we divide the estimated cost from the cost pool by the estimated number of occurrences of the cost driver.

$$\frac{\text{Estimated Overhead Cost}}{\text{Cost Driver}} = \text{Overhead Application Rate}$$

Buck Slade Company has developed the following applications rates:

Manufacturing Overhead Pool	Cost Driver (Allocation Base)	Application Based on Occurrence of the Cost Driver
Pool 1		
• Materials purchasing and handling cost	Number of parts	$75,000 ÷ 750,000 = $0.10 per part
Pool 2		
• Production engineering and design	Number of production runs	$100,000 ÷ 25 = $4,000 per prod. run
• Production machine setup		
Pool 3		
• Production machine amortization	Number of machine hours	$350,000 ÷ 2,000 = $175 per machine hour
• Production machine maintenance		
Pool 4		
• Quality testing	Number of components tested	$100,000 ÷ 25,000 = $4 per comp. tested
Pool 5		
• Factory security	Number of direct labour hours	$155,000 ÷ 10,000 = $15.50 per direct labour hour
• Factory supervision		
• Building maintenance		
• Factory supplies		
• Factory insurance		

For every part added to a unit of product, $0.10 of manufacturing overhead cost is added to the product as well (Pool 1). Every time a production run is made, $4,000 is added to the cost of the products in that production run (Pool 2). For every machine hour devoted to the unit of product, $175 of manufacturing overhead is added (Pool 3); and for every component tested, $4 of manufacturing overhead is added (Pool 4). For every hour of direct labour, $15.50 of manufacturing overhead is added to the cost of the product (Pool 5). The total direct material cost, direct labour cost, and total allocated manufacturing overhead cost are then added together to determine the cost of the product.

As an example, take another look at Buck Slade Company's production run of 15,000 precision cutters. Each cutter is made of three parts. In addition, it takes 16 machine hours and 80 direct labour hours to produce the 15,000 cutters. Finally, during production, samples totaling 1,000 cutters are tested for sharpness. The manufacturing overhead cost for the cutters is calculated as follows:

Manufacturing Overhead Pool	Cost Allocation
Pool 1	
• Materials purchasing and handling cost	15,000 × 3 × $0.10 = $ 4,500
Pool 2	
• Production engineering and design	1 × $4,000 = $ 4,000
• Production machine setup	
Pool 3	
• Production machine amortization	16 × $175 = $ 2,800
• Production machine maintenance	
Pool 4	
• Quality testing	1,000 × $4 = $ 4,000
Pool 5	
• Factory security	80 × $15.50 = $ 1,240
• Factory supervision	
• Building maintenance	
• Factory supplies	
• Factory insurance	
Total manufacturing overhead for the 15,000 cutters	$16,540
Manufacturing overhead per cutter ($16,540 ÷ 15,000)	$ 1.103

Notice that the $16,540 of overhead allocated to the precision cutters when activity-based costing is used is more than double the $8,000 allocated when a traditional allocation method is used. The cutters are not more expensive to make when activity-based costing is used; rather, the amount of overhead allocated to the cutters under activity-based costing is a more accurate representation of the cost attributable to the products produced.

PRODUCT COSTING METHODS

To make informed decisions about which products should be produced and what selling price should be charged, managers need accurate product cost information.

Users of accounting information generally rely on one of two methods for determining the cost of products, the job order cost method and the process cost method. Although both methods are used, they are not interchangeable. A company must select the method best suited to the type of products being made and to the manufacturing process itself.

Job Order Costing Basics

job order costing A costing method that accumulates cost by a single unit, or batch of units.

Job order costing is a method that accumulates the cost of production for each job, each individual unit of production, each order, or each product. This method is used to accumulate the cost of one-of-a-kind and custom-made goods such as custom furniture or custom cabinets, ships, airplanes, bridges, buildings, and advertising posters. For instance, when Bombardier Aerospace manufactured two Q400 aircraft for Hydro-Québec in 2002, the airplane manufacturer used job order costing to determine how much each plane cost.

The key consideration for choosing between process costing and job order costing is whether the goods produced consumed similar enough amounts of factory resources (direct material, direct labour, and manufacturing overhead) that an average cost per unit would be an accurate reflection of the product's cost. If the units consumed very different amounts of factory resources, an average cost per unit is meaningless, and job order costing should be used.

Under job order costing, managers keep close track of the material and labour associated with each job. The "job" may consist of a single unit or a batch of units. For example, a job for Bombardier would consist of a single airplane. For Quebecor Inc., a printing company, however, a job would consist of a batch of 20,000 advertising posters. In either case, the costs of direct material, direct labour, and overhead are accumulated and totaled for each job (see page 75).

Process Costing Basics

process costing A method of allocating manufacturing cost to products to determine an average cost per unit.

Process costing is a method of allocating manufacturing cost to products to determine an average cost per unit. Process costing is used when units of production are identical, or nearly so, and each unit of production receives the same manufacturing input as the next. Examples of such products are milk, soft drinks, canned goods, breakfast cereal, household cleaners, motor oil, and gasoline. For example, Molson Inc. uses process costing to determine the cost of the beer it produces.

When process costing is used, total manufacturing cost is divided by the number of units produced to arrive at a cost per unit. For example, if a toothbrush factory makes 2,000,000 toothbrushes and the total production cost is $400,000, then the cost per tooth brush is $0.20, computed as follows:

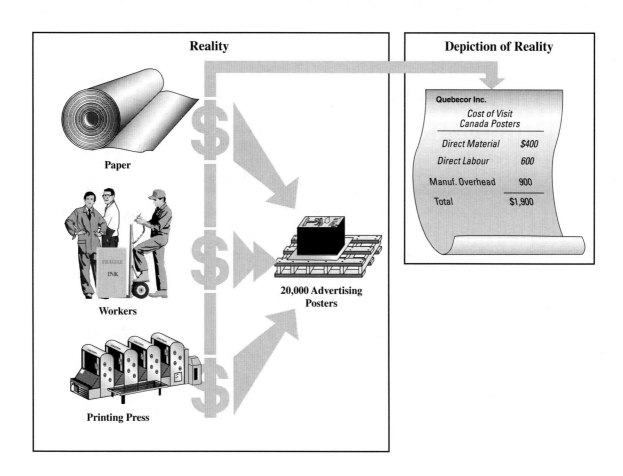

Reality		Depiction of Reality

Paper

Workers

Printing Press

20,000 Advertising Posters

Quebecor Inc.
Cost of Visit Canada Posters

Direct Material	$400
Direct Labour	600
Manuf. Overhead	900
Total	$1,900

$$\frac{\text{Total Production Cost}}{\text{Number of Units Produced}} = \text{Cost Per Unit}$$

$$\frac{\$400,000}{2,000,000 \text{ Units Produced}} = \$0.20 \text{ Per Unit}$$

The reason this simple method is adequate for a product such as toothbrushes is that each toothbrush is identical to, and consumes the same amount of resources as, the next. Accordingly, an average cost per toothbrush provides an accurate indication of each unit's cost.

 Discussion Questions

3–1. Name four products (other than those mentioned in the text) for which process costing would be appropriate.

3–2. Name four products (other than those mentioned in the text) for which job order costing would be appropriate.

3–3. Are any products difficult to classify? List some and explain the difficulty.

The first product costing method we will explore in detail is job order costing. As we cover job order costing, we will also look at the documents manufacturers use to control factory resources and accumulate the cost of products.

Job Order Costing

We have seen that in job order costing the job may be the production of a single unit, or a batch of units. The key is that the units produced for one job are dissimilar from the units produced for another job, and that cost information is gathered for each individual production job.

Keeping track of product cost is not as challenging as it may seem. Particular documents help keep track of the direct material, direct labour, and manufacturing overhead associated with each production job.

For example, a company that makes custom boats would keep a list of the direct material cost, direct labour hours, and direct labour cost used to make a boat. It would also need to keep track of the manufacturing overhead associated with each boat made. The company would total the direct material, direct labour, and manufacturing overhead to determine the boat's cost.

Managers use a system of documents to track the cost of units produced and to control the costs incurred in the factory. We will review these documents—a critical part of a job order cost method—and explore the process of job order costing in the following sections.

The manufacturer in our example, Ocean Extreme Boats Inc. (Ocean Extreme), is a top-quality, custom boat manufacturer located in North Vancouver. In contrast to production-line boats—boats made in large quantities that are nearly identical—Ocean Extreme's boats are manufactured to the specifications of each customer. Customers select the boat style, interior, engines, construction material, and paint scheme they want. No two boats are alike. Let's look at how Ocean Extreme calculates the cost of one boat.

Documentation Relating to Job Order Costing

job cost sheet   A document that tracks the costs of products, and organizes and summarizes the cost information for each job.

When job order costing is used, a document called a **job cost sheet** simplifies tracking the costs of products because it organizes and summarizes the cost information for each job. An example of a job cost sheet is shown in Exhibit 3–3.

This job cost sheet will list the manufacturing costs for job 97384. An entry will be made on the job cost sheet each time direct material, direct labour, and manufacturing overhead costs are incurred in connection with the job. Managers can refer to a job cost sheet any time they need information about the cost of producing a particular boat.

A job cost sheet is prepared for each individual unit produced. In Ocean Extreme's case, the costs for each boat are placed on a separate job cost sheet. In Exhibit 3–3, job 97384 is for a 12-metre Open Fisherman. At any time, the manager can review the job cost sheet for job 97384 to determine its cost.

Job cost sheets not only help managers keep track of the costs of current production, but they also provide historical information that can help managers estimate the cost of future production. For example, if an order is received for a boat similar to one that Ocean Extreme has made in the past, the estimator can look at the first boat's job cost sheet to help estimate how much the next boat will cost.

Let's now look at how these costs are monitored and measured. We begin with an analysis of direct material.

Cost Information for Raw Material   Manufacturers such as Ocean Extreme generally keep close track of raw material costs because it is such an expensive part of the manufacturing process. The raw materials needed at Ocean Extreme to build power boats include fibreglass cloth, polyester resin, wood, plastic, aluminum, engines, and much more. Because these materials are so costly, Ocean

Exhibit 3–3
Job Cost Sheet for
Ocean Extreme
Boats Inc.

Job Cost Sheet

Job #: _97384_

Date Promised: _July 11, 2003_

Customer: _Bill Hudik_

Date Started: _June 2, 2003_

Product Description: _12 m Open Fisherman_

Direct Materials			Direct Labour		Manufacturing Overhead			Total
Date	Req #	Amount	Date	Amount	Base	Rate	Amount	Total
		$		$			$	$
Total		$		$			$	$

Date Completed: _____

Extreme, like other manufacturers, does not allow just any employee to buy raw material on behalf of the company. An unqualified employee might buy too much or too little, or he or she may buy the wrong raw material altogether. In most manufacturing companies, a request for material is made by the employee in charge of monitoring the raw material inventory levels. This person may be in charge of the materials store room or perhaps is the production supervisor. At Ocean Extreme Boats Inc., the stores manager monitors the amount of material on hand. When a component required in the manufacturing process runs low, the stores manager requests that more be purchased. This purchase request comes in the form of a purchase requisition.

purchase requisition
A request form that lists the quantity and description of the materials needed.

A **purchase requisition** is a request form that lists the quantity and description of the materials needed. This form helps to control and monitor all material requested to ensure that the company secures the right amount and quality. Copies of the completed purchase requisition are forwarded to Ocean Extreme's purchasing department and to the accounts payable clerk in charge of paying the company's bills. Exhibit 3–4 shows the completed materials requisition for Ocean Extreme Boats Inc.

purchasing department
A specialized department that purchases all the goods required by a company.

The **purchasing department** is a specialized department that purchases all the goods required by the company. In the purchasing department, trained individuals called purchasing agents contact several competing vendors or suppliers to obtain the highest-quality material at the lowest price.

purchase order A formal document used to order material from a vendor.

Once the purchasing agent has selected a vendor, the agent issues a **purchase order,** a formal document created to order material from a vendor. The purchase order specifies the quantity, type, and cost of the materials, payment terms, and method of delivery. Copies of the purchase order are distributed to the receiving

Exhibit 3–4
Purchase Requisition
for Ocean Extreme
Boats Inc.

Ocean Extreme Boats Inc.
Purchase Requisition

Number: 1001

Date: _June 4, 2003_

Name: _Carl Bevans, Stores Manager_

Department: _Production Material Stores_

Quantity	Description
400 litres	Polyester Resin

Signature: _Carl Bevans_

department, the accounts payable department, and the vendor. A sample purchase order for Ocean Extreme Boats Inc. is shown in Exhibit 3–5.

When Ocean Extreme's receiving department receives the material from the supplier, the receiving clerk compares the material received to the purchase order and completes a receiving report. The **receiving report** is a document that indicates the quantity of each item received. It is used to note any differences between the goods ordered and the goods received. Ocean Extreme's receiving clerk completes a receiving report for each delivery received as shown in Exhibit 3–6.

receiving report A document that indicates the quantity of each item received.

A copy of the receiving report is sent to the accounts payable department. Ocean Extreme's accounts payable clerk now has three documents related to the purchase: (1) the purchase requisition, (2) the purchase order, and (3) the receiving report. When the accounts payable clerk receives the vendor's invoice for the materials, information on the invoice is matched to the other three documents. If everything is correct, the invoice is paid according to the payment terms.

Discussion Question

3–4. The accounts payable department verifies that the information on the vendor's invoice matches the purchase requisition, the purchase order, and the receiving report. What would a discrepancy show if the information on the following documents conflicted?

a. The receiving report conflicts with the vendor's invoice.

b. The purchase order conflicts with the receiving report.

c. The purchase requisition conflicts with the purchase order.

Exhibit 3–5
Purchase Order for
Ocean Extreme
Boats Inc.

Purchase Order

PO #: _06059702_

Vendor: _Pitman Sales Company_	**Order Date:** _June 5, 2003_
Address: _8650 Venables_	**Delivery Date:** _June 7, 2003_
Vancouver, BC V6A 2B5	
Phone: _604_ – _555_ – _9558_	

Purchase Requisition #: _1001_   **Department:** _Prod. Mat. Stores_

Quantity	Description	Unit Cost	Total Cost
400 litres	Polyester Resin	6.00	2,400.00

Purchasing Agent: _Bob Pass_

Once the materials have been checked in, they are stored in the materials stores warehouse until they are needed for production. Generally, such storage space is quite secure to protect the raw material from damage and theft.

When the material is needed for production, Ocean Extreme's production manager completes a materials requisition. The **materials requisition** is a formal request for material to be transferred from the raw materials storage area to production. The document lists the type of material and the quantity needed. To begin work on the 12-metre Open Fisherman boat for job 97384, fibreglass and polyester resin are needed, so the production manager has prepared the materials requisition shown in Exhibit 3–7 to transfer the polyester resin into production.

Keep in mind that a materials requisition is different from a purchase requisition. The purchase requisition is a request to purchase material, whereas the materials requisition is a request by manufacturing personnel to transfer previously purchased material from the materials stores warehouse to production.

materials requisition
A formal request for material to be transferred from the raw materials storage area to production.

Exhibit 3–6
Receiving Report for
Ocean Extreme
Boats Inc.

Receiving Report

Vendor: _Pitman Sales Company_

Purchase Order #: _06059702_   Date Received: _June 7, 2003_

Quantity	Description
400 litres	Polyester Resin

Receiving Clerk: _Lauren Elsea_

Exhibit 3–7
Materials Requisition
for Ocean Extreme
Boats Inc.

Materials Requisition

Req #: 2002

Job #: _97384_

Date: _June 16, 2003_

Quantity	Item #	Description	Unit Cost	Total Cost
200 litres	PR55X	Polyester Resin	6.00	1,200.00

Issued By: _Carl Bevans_

Received By: _Kevin Dunn_

The materials requisition is a useful tool for accumulating the cost of products. Materials requisitions show how much material is being used, for what purpose, and at what cost. The information from the materials requisitions is transferred to the job cost sheets to show the quantity and cost of material used for each job.

For instance, Exhibit 3–8 shows how the accounting department at Ocean Extreme Boats Inc. transfers information from the materials requisition to the job cost sheet for job 97384.

Materials requisitions are also valuable tools for controlling the movement of materials in the factory. Because the movement is documented, it is easier to monitor employees' use of material. This record helps prevent theft, waste, or other inappropriate use of material.

Exhibit 3–8
Transfer of Information from a Materials Requisition Form to a Job Cost Sheet

Cost Information for Direct Labour Once raw material enters the production process, factory workers begin working with it, converting the material into finished product. Remember from Chapter 2 that the value of the goods in work-in-process inventory is enhanced by the cost of the raw material incorporated into the product and by the labour of production workers. Therefore, in accounting records, work-in-process inventory is increased not only by the cost of direct material, but also by the cost of direct labour.

labour time ticket A document used to track the amount of time each employee works on a particular production job or a particular task in the factory.

A **labour time ticket** is used to track the amount of time each employee works on a particular production job or a particular task in the factory. Exhibit 3–9 shows a sample labour time ticket for Ocean Extreme Boats Inc.

Exhibit 3–9
Labour Time Ticket for Ocean Extreme Boats Inc.

Labour Time Ticket								
Employee: Edward Clark								
Employee Number: 127					Week Ending: June 8, 2003			
Job #	M	T	W	T	F	S	S	Total
97384	8	8	4		8			28
97383			4	8				12
Supervisor: MLW				Receiving Clerk: E.C.				

Labour time tickets include a wealth of information regarding the amount of direct labour associated with each production job. As was the case with the materials requisitions, cost information is transferred from the labour time tickets to the job cost sheet for each job. Exhibit 3–10 shows how information is transferred from the labour time tickets to the job cost sheet for job number 97384 at Ocean Extreme Boats Inc.

Most companies now use computer technology to make entries on labour time tickets. Employees are issued identification cards that are scanned by a card reader. The employees then enter codes to indicate the duties they are performing and the job to which these duties relate. Information from the electronic labour time tickets is stored in a computer file and transferred electronically to electronic job cost sheets.

Manufacturing Overhead

The information from the materials requisitions and labour time tickets makes it easy to trace direct material cost and direct labour cost to individual jobs. Tracing manufacturing overhead is not quite as straightforward.

As discussed, the cost of manufacturing overhead must be allocated to production. Accurate allocation is often difficult to achieve because the benefit of manufacturing overhead expenditures is difficult to trace to individual jobs or units of production. Manufacturing overhead generally benefits the factory as a whole and therefore all units produced. Because it cannot be traced to individual units,

Exhibit 3–10
Transfer of Information from Labour Time Tickets to a Job Cost Sheet at Ocean Extreme Boats Inc.

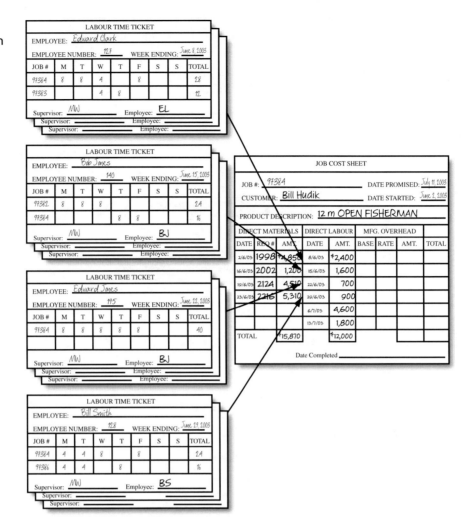

manufacturing overhead must be allocated to the individual units produced. As seen in Exhibit 3–11, generally the cost to be allocated is divided by the total allocation base to determine the amount to allocate per occurrence of the allocation base.

Exhibit 3–11
General Formula to Allocate a Cost

$$\frac{\text{Cost to Be Allocated}}{\text{Total Occurrences of the Allocation Base}} = \text{Cost Per Occurrence of the Allocation Base}$$

When manufacturing overhead is allocated to production, the first step in the process is selecting an allocation base. One alternative is to use the number of units produced as the allocation base.

If we use the number of units produced as an allocation base, we divide the manufacturing overhead by the number of units to arrive at an amount of overhead per unit. This method of allocation provides an equal amount of manufacturing overhead cost for each unit of production. When the products produced are

Exhibit 3–12
Allocating
Manufacturing
Overhead Based on
the Number of Units
Produced

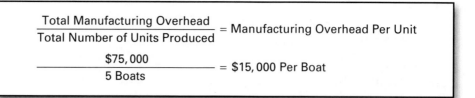

$$\frac{\text{Total Manufacturing Overhead}}{\text{Total Number of Units Produced}} = \text{Manufacturing Overhead Per Unit}$$

$$\frac{\$75,000}{5 \text{ Boats}} = \$15,000 \text{ Per Boat}$$

Manufacturing overhead cost

$15,000

$15,000

$15,000

$15,000

$15,000

different from one another, such as Ocean Extreme's, a uniform cost per unit is generally inadequate for job order costing.

For instance, if the overhead for Ocean Extreme Boats Inc. is $75,000, and the company makes five boats, the overhead per boat would be $15,000 for each boat produced, as calculated in Exhibit 3–12.

However, this allocation of $15,000 per boat seems unfair because the boats are so different from one another. It stands to reason that a large boat would consume more factory resources and should receive a higher overhead cost allocation than a small boat. It would be more accurate to allocate according to the resources consumed instead of allocating the exact same manufacturing overhead cost to each boat produced.

In selecting an allocation base, we should strive to find one that will distribute cost fairly. The best allocation base would be one that causes the cost that is to be allocated; but, when a single cost pool is used for manufacturing overhead, it is impossible to find a single allocation base that causes all the cost in the pool. Instead, we attempt to find an allocation base that has the second-best attribute for cost allocation, an allocation base that is correlated to the incurrence of cost. Thus, we should try to find an allocation base that is correlated to the amount of manufacturing overhead resources consumed by each unit produced.

Taking a closer look at our boat company example, we note that no two boats are identical, and manufacturing a larger or more complicated boat would, in all likelihood, consume more overhead than a smaller or less complicated boat. As a start, we should find an allocation base that would apportion more overhead to a larger or more complicated boat and less to a smaller, less complicated boat. To do this, the allocation base must increase as boat size or complexity increases.

It seems logical that the amount of factory resources consumed to make a large boat would be more than those consumed to make a small boat. It also seems reasonable that a correlation exists between the number of direct labour hours and the amount of manufacturing overhead resources consumed to make each boat.

As an example, let's use direct labour cost for Ocean Extreme Boats Inc. as the allocation base for manufacturing overhead.

When we calculate product cost using actual amounts for direct material, direct labour, and manufacturing overhead, the system is called an actual cost system. Manufacturing overhead is allocated to production based on actual manufacturing overhead cost and the actual amount of the allocation base. For example, we use actual direct labour to allocate actual manufacturing overhead.

Unfortunately, when we do this, several problems emerge. First, managers must wait until the end of the accounting period for actual cost information to be known. Another problem with using actual amounts to allocate overhead is that the overhead application rate fluctuates as actual overhead and direct labour fluctuate. The overhead application rate will be different for each period if it is calculated using these fluctuating actual amounts. This will result in identical products having different cost amounts unless they were made during the same months.

To eliminate these problems, we estimate annual amounts. In this approach, called a **normal cost system,** product cost reflects actual direct material cost, actual direct labour cost, and estimated overhead costs. Estimated annual manufacturing overhead cost and the annual estimated amount for the allocation base are used to calculate a **predetermined overhead application rate.**

Ocean Extreme Boats Inc. allocates overhead using a normal cost system. Suppose, for example, that the estimated annual overhead for Ocean Extreme is $1,000,000 and estimated annual direct labour cost is $1,250,000. In this case, the predetermined overhead application rate is 80 percent ($1,000,000/$1,250,000) of direct labour cost. To determine the overhead cost for the 12-metre Open Fisherman boat for job 97384, we must know the direct labour cost. According to the job cost sheet in Exhibit 3–10, the direct labour cost for this job is $12,000. Using the predetermined overhead application rate of 80 percent of direct labour cost, we calculate the manufacturing overhead associated with job 97384 as follows: $12,000 × 80% = $9,600.

The total cost for job 97384 is $15,870 for direct material, $12,000 for direct labour, and $9,600 for manufacturing overhead. These costs are summarized in the job cost sheet in Exhibit 3–13.

A normal cost system generally is superior to an actual cost system because it smoothes out the fluctuations in product cost due to monthly differences in overhead cost and the allocation base. In addition, because the predetermined application rate is calculated at the very beginning of the year, there is no need to wait until month's end when actual overhead cost information is available to determine product cost.

Activity-Based Costing

As we have explained, companies allocate indirect costs to cost objects using average allocation rates. The larger the indirect cost pool used in the numerator of the allocation rate formula and the broader the allocation base used in the denominator, the less accurate the resulting cost allocation. As the proportion of indirect costs gets larger compared to the direct costs, the cost information provided becomes less useful to managers.

normal cost system
System in which product cost reflects actual direct material cost, actual direct labour cost, and estimated overhead costs.

predetermined overhead application rate An overhead allocation rate calculated using estimated annual manufacturing overhead cost and the annual estimated amount for the allocation base.

Exhibit 3–13

Completed Job Cost
Sheet for Job 97384

Job Cost Sheet

Job #:	97384						Date Promised:	July 11, 2003
Customer:	Bill Hudik						Date Started:	June 2, 2003
Product Description:	12 m Open Fisherman							

Direct Materials			Direct Labour		Manufacturing Overhead			
Date	Req #	Amount	Date	Amount	Base	Rate	Amount	Total
June 2/03	1998	$ 4,850	June 8/03	$ 2,400	DL$	80%	$ 1,920	$
June 16/03	2002	1,200	June 15/03	1,600	DL$	80%	1,280	
June 19/03	2124	4,510	June 22/03	700	DL$	80%	560	
June 23/03	2216	5,310	June 29/03	900	DL$	80%	720	
			July 6/03	4,600	DL$	80%	3,680	
			July 13/03	1,800	DL$	80%	1,440	
Total		$ 15,870		$ 12,000			$ 9,600	$ 37,470

Date Completed: July 11, 2003

One method of overcoming this cost allocation dilemma is to introduce activity-based costing. Activity-based costing (ABC) focuses on activities as the fundamental cost objects. The costs of those activities become building blocks for compiling costs, since ABC links costs to the activities that cause these costs. ABC can be used with job order costing or process costing, and it is used by service sector companies, such as banks and hospitals, as well as by manufacturers.

Let's explore how activity-based costing works by revisiting our Ocean Extreme Boats Inc. example. Ocean Extreme boats are made of fibreglass and plastic resin formed in moulds. A series of moulds is used to make the necessary components of each boat. Before a mould can be used, it must be cleaned and waxed to keep the fibreglass and plastic resin from sticking. The process of preparing production equipment to produce a particular product, in this case preparing moulds to make a boat, is called setup.

When activity-based costing is used, the cost of each manufacturing activity is accumulated in a dedicated cost pool. In the case of Ocean Extreme, overhead costs are examined and all costs associated with setup are separated out and grouped in a cost pool. Now setup cost can be allocated to products separately from other overhead costs. Assume the annual setup cost at Ocean Extreme is $117,000.

Next a cost driver must be selected to allocate setup cost. Assume that Ocean Extreme has decided to use the number of moulds used as the cost driver. Preparing a single mould for use causes additional setup cost to occur. The number of moulds required to make a single boat varies depending on each boat design. As shown in Exhibit 3–14, a basic Open Fisherman boat requires the use of ten moulds, but a basic sport boat requires the use of only five moulds. The actual number of moulds used to make a boat varies depending on the customer's specifications.

Exhibit 3–14
Number of Moulds
Used for Each Basic
Boat Design

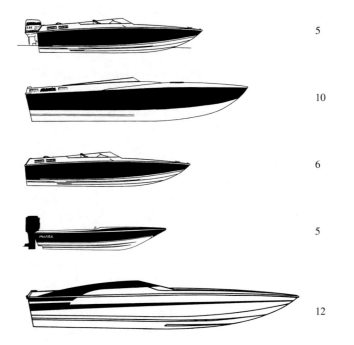

	5
	10
	6
	5
	12

The effort and cost of setup varies from boat to boat depending on the number of moulds required. By using the number of moulds as the cost driver, we can reflect the differing amounts of setup effort in the costs of each boat produced. For example, the setup cost for a boat that requires 12 moulds will be twice as much as the setup cost for a boat that requires six moulds.

The calculations for allocating an overhead cost pool using a cost driver are similar to the calculations using a traditional allocation base. The total estimated annual cost for the cost pool is divided by the estimated annual activity of the cost driver to arrive at an application rate per occurrence of the cost driver. The general formula is as follows:

$$\frac{\text{Total Cost to Be Allocated}}{\text{Total Occurrences of the Cost Driver}} = \text{Cost Per Occurrence of the Cost Driver}$$

Based on past experience, Ocean Extreme estimates that it will need 360 mould preparations this year to produce 45 boats. Recall that Ocean Extreme's estimated total annual setup cost is $117,000. With those two numbers, we can find Ocean Extreme's application rate for setup. Ocean Extreme divides the estimated total setup cost by the estimated number of mould preparations for the year to determine the application rate for setup cost.

$$\frac{\text{Total Setup Cost}}{\text{Total Number of Mould Preparations}} = \text{Cost Per Mould Preparation}$$

$$\frac{\$117,000}{360 \text{ Mould Preparations}} = \$325 \text{ Per Mould Preparation}$$

We find that with an estimated annual setup cost of $117,000 and a total number of mould preparations of 360, the application rate is $325 per mould used.

Discussion Questions

3–5. If you owned a factory, would you prefer that employees spend time setting up production equipment or producing product?

3–6. If the production manager was able to use one less mould when making a boat, would the cost allocated to that boat be less? Is it likely that the company's actual setup cost would also be less?

Using the activity-based costing application rate, we can now allocate setup cost to each boat based on the number of moulds required. For example, boat 1 requires the use of five moulds, so its setup cost would be $1,625 (5 × $325 = $1,625). The setup cost allocated to boat 2 would be $3,250 based on the use of 10 moulds (10 × $325 = $3,250). The more moulds required to make a boat, the higher the allocation for setup cost.

In a traditional cost system, a manager can reduce manufacturing overhead cost associated with a given product by reducing the allocation base used to allocate the cost. For example, if manufacturing overhead is allocated using machine hours, a manager could reduce the overhead allocated to his or her product by reducing the amount of machine time it takes to make the product. This process would reduce the manufacturing overhead cost allocated to the given product, but it would generally not affect the various overhead costs actually incurred by the company. Reducing machine hours has no significant effect on the amount the company spends for manufacturing overhead items such as property taxes, factory insurance, factory security, indirect material, indirect labour, and so forth. Even though accounting records would indicate a lower cost for that product's manufacturing overhead, the reduced machine hours would have little effect on the dollars the company spent for manufacturing overhead.

When activity-based costing is used to reduce the setup cost of a particular boat, a manager would try to decrease the number of moulds used. For instance, if the number of moulds used to make boat 2 were reduced by one mould, the cost allocated to that boat would be reduced by $325. With this cost reduction technique, the decrease in the allocation base (the cost driver) actually reduces the amount of cost incurred by the company. That is, reducing the number of moulds used actually reduces the amount of work that must be done to make a boat. In general, this reduction in work contributes to true cost savings for the company.

We have seen how well job order costing works for custom-made, one-of-a-kind products, but tracking the cost of each unit would be impractical if hundreds or thousands of identical products are made on a dedicated production line. In such a case, a process costing method is preferred.

Activity-Based Management

activity-based management (ABM) The process of using activity-based costing information to make decisions that increase profits while satisfying customers' needs.

Activity-based management (ABM) is the process of using activity-based costing information to make decisions that increase profits while satisfying customers' needs. ABM can be used for making three kinds of decisions:

1. Pricing and product mix decisions
2. Cost-reduction decisions
3. Routine planning and control decisions

We will briefly examine each decision.

Let's return to West Coast Alloys and Metals Ltd. from Chapter 2. As part of its operation, West Coast operates a fabrication shop that allows it to customize products for customers in the forest products industry. How does the company keep track of costs?

"Each job we do in our fabrication shop is different," Rick Montgomery, vice-president and general manager, explains, "So we follow a job order costing system. The cost of all material related to the job is recorded as it is taken from inventory. The employees working on the job keep accurate records of the time spent. From a direct cost perspective, we know our costs.

"Because we have to bid or compete for this type of work, we have to estimate a charge for manufacturing overhead and for our mark-up to cover administrative costs. We use a budgeted rate based on labour hours, but we are not as accurate as I would like us to be.

"The competitive nature of the business does not leave a lot of room for error. After the job is completed, I review the job cost sheet. The price has already been negotiated with the customer, so our efficiency determines our profitability. A mistake or two along the way can really affect our profit."

1. Pricing and Product Mix Decisions Activity-based costing (ABC) assigns costs previously considered to be indirect to cost objects in a more direct, meaningful manner. Thus, a more accurate costing of a cost object, such as a product, becomes available. Companies can then determine if the product, at its current selling price, provides enough profit. If not, ABM can be used to find ways to cut costs. If costs cannot be cut, the company may need to raise the product's selling price. Or the company may decide to stop producing the product.

The key point to remember is that ABC gives a company the ability to better analyze a product's costs. The company can then make better pricing and product mix decisions. We will examine this issue again in Chapter 6.

value engineering The process of systematically evaluating activities in an effort to reduce costs while satisfying customers' needs.

2. Cost-Reduction Decisions Managers often find that they reap substantial benefits by using ABM to pinpoint opportunities to cut costs. With an ABC system in place, companies can use value engineering to reduce costs. **Value engineering** is the process of systematically evaluating activities in an effort to reduce costs while satisfying customers' needs.

3. Routine Planning and Control Decisions Companies using ABC can carry out activity-based budgeting, where managers budget costs of individual activities to build up indirect cost schedules in a master budget (this will be discussed fully in Chapter 8). Companies can also perform variance analysis on the activities identified to help control costs. Variance analysis will be discussed more thoroughly in Chapter 9.

PROCESS COSTING

Recall that with process costing we allocate cost to products by dividing the total manufacturing cost of the period by the number of units produced to arrive at an average per unit cost. The basic method is simple—just total direct materials, direct labour, and manufacturing overhead; then divide by the number of units produced.

For example, to determine the cost of each tube of toothpaste made in a toothpaste factory, we first determine the total manufacturing cost and divide it by the number of units produced. Assume that the total manufacturing cost for toothpaste is $100,000 and the total number of units produced is 1,000,000. The cost per tube is 10 cents per tube ($100,000 / 1,000,000 = $0.10). Because each tube of toothpaste is identical to the next, the 10 cents per unit would be a reasonably accurate measure of the cost of each unit. This method only works well if all the units produced are the same—if each unit of production is identical to the next, with the exception of minor variations such as colour.

Process costing presents some challenges, however, because some units are only partially completed at the end of the accounting period. To reflect reasonably accurate cost amounts, process costing calculations must accommodate situations when some units are only partially completed.

Like job order costing, process costing is simply a method to help managers determine the cost of products. It provides several key items of information:

1. The number of equivalent units of production
2. The cost per unit
3. The cost of the completed units
4. The cost of the units that remain in ending work-in-process inventory

An understanding of the basics of process costing is a necessary foundation to using product cost information wisely. Let's take a closer look at process costing and the complexities related to beginning and ending work-in-process inventories.

Assume that a company makes decorative pink flamingos. The process to make the decoration is simple. A two-part mould is pressed together and the inside coated with hot plastic. After the plastic has cooled and hardened, the mould is pulled apart and the animal figure drops out. It is finished except for painting the eyes and beaks and adding the legs.

Equivalent Units

The number of units produced must be established before a cost per unit can be determined. In our example, assume that 10,000 flamingos were completed and another 1,000 are still in production. The 1,000 units in production comprise the work-in-process inventory. Obviously the 10,000 units completed should be included in the number of units produced, but what about the other 1,000 units? By definition, units in ending work-in-process inventory are incomplete. Thus, it would be inaccurate to assign the same cost per unit to these units as to the completed units. However, they required expenditures for direct material, direct labour, and manufacturing overhead to bring them to their present state of completion. Thus, some cost should be assigned to these units. Let's see how we arrive at a cost.

The 1,000 flamingos in work-in-process inventory are at various stages of completion. It would be impractical to determine the percentage of completeness for each individual unit of production, so we use an average. In our example, on average, the flamingos in work-in-process inventory are approximately 40 percent complete.

Because the flamingos are only 40 percent complete, we should not include the entire 1,000 units in the number of units produced. Instead, we proportion the number of units by multiplying the number of units by their average completion percentage. Because the 1,000 flamingos are on average 40 percent complete, they are the equivalent of 400 completed flamingos (1,000 × 40% = 400 equivalent units).

Theoretically, if we had started only 400 flamingos into the production process, we could have concentrated our efforts on those 400 units and possibly completed them. However, we started 1,000 units into the production process, and we ended up with 1,000 units that were 40 percent complete, which is equivalent to 400 completed units.

equivalent units The number of units that would have been completed if all production efforts resulted in only completed units.

In process costing, **equivalent units** are the number of units that would have been completed if all production efforts resulted in only completed units. The number of equivalent units is calculated by adding the number of completed units to the number of units in ending work-in-process inventory times their percentage complete. In our example the calculations for the number of equivalent units of production—10,400 units—is as follows:

	Number of Raw Units		Percent Complete		Equivalent Units
Units completed	10,000	×	100	=	10,000
Ending work in process	1,000	×	40	=	400
Total equivalent units					10,400

It is likely that the percentage of completion for direct material is different from that of direct labour or manufacturing overhead. Product costs would be more accurate if we used separate completion percentages for direct material, direct labour, and manufacturing overhead. Although necessary in practice, such precise calculations greatly complicate process costing. To keep our example simple and understandable, we will use a single percentage to represent the degree of completion for direct material, direct labour, and manufacturing overhead.

Cost Per Equivalent Unit

In our example, we also assume that the manufacturer uses the average inventory cost flow method. Generally acceptable accounting principals allow companies to use the first in first out (FIFO), last in first out (LIFO), or the average cost flow method. In process costing, the FIFO and average cost flow methods are popular.

The FIFO cost flow method assumes that the cost of the first units added to inventory is the first cost removed from inventory. Thus, the cost of units must be tracked through the inventory records so the first cost in is the first cost out. As you might expect, this complicates process costing calculations. To keep our example simple, we assume the average cost flow method is used.

Now let us examine the cost associated with producing the 10,400 equivalent units in our flamingo factory. Assume the production costs are $5,408 as summarized in Exhibit 3–15.

Exhibit 3–15
Summary of
Production Cost

Cost of beginning work in process	$ 0
Current month's cost	5,408
Total	$5,408

To compute cost per unit when the average cost flow method is used in process costing, we divide the total production cost by the number of equivalent units as follows:

$$\frac{\text{Total Production Cost}}{\text{Equivalent Units}} = \text{Cost Per Equivalent Unit}$$

$$\frac{\$5,408}{10,400 \text{ Equivalent Units}} = \$0.52 \text{ Per Equivalent Unit}$$

In our example we see that the cost per flamingo is $0.52. Now that we know the cost of each unit produced, we can determine the cost of the ending work-in-process inventory and the cost of the units completed. Barring theft or other losses, units of production are either completed and transferred to finished goods inventory, or they remain in ending work-in-process inventory. Therefore, it stands to reason that production costs are associated either with completed units or with units in ending work-in-process inventory.

Cost of Ending Work-in-Process Inventory

The cost of ending work-in-process inventory is shown as an asset on manufacturers' balance sheets. To determine this cost, the number of equivalent units (not raw units) in ending work-in-process inventory is multiplied by the cost per unit. For our flamingo example, 400 equivalent units are in ending work-in-process inventory and the cost per unit is $0.52. Therefore, the cost of the ending work-in-process inventory is $208 as follows:

Number of Equivalent Units		Cost Per Unit		Cost of Ending Work-in-Process Inventory
400	×	$0.52	=	$208

Cost of Completed Units

To determine the cost of completed units, we multiply the number of completed units by the cost per unit. For our flamingo example, 10,000 completed units is multiplied by the $0.52 cost per unit. The cost of the completed units then is $5,200, calculated as follows:

Number of Units		Per Unit Cost		Cost of Units Completed and Transferred to Finished Goods Inventory
10,000	×	$0.52	=	$5,200

The cost of completed units is important because initially it becomes part of finished goods inventory. Then, as products are sold, the cost of sold units becomes part of cost of goods sold on the income statement.

Assuming no units are spoiled, stolen, or otherwise lost, the cost of production is either transferred to finished goods inventory or remains as the cost of ending work-in-process inventory. In our example the total manufacturing cost was $5,408. If no units are lost or spoiled during production, the actual units are either completed and physically transferred to finished goods or they remain in ending work-in-process inventory. As we see in Exhibit 3–16, part of the $5,408 total manufacturing cost is transferred to finished goods inventory, and the remainder reflects the cost of the units that remain in ending work-in-process inventory.

As stated at the beginning of this chapter, Ford and General Motors are anticipating a huge change in their production processes in the near future. These auto manufacturers currently produce an inventory of cars and use *process costing* to track the cost of the cars produced. But as the production process changes to customization, the auto manufacturers will change the way they track costs and use a *job order costing* approach.

Exhibit 3-16
Flow of
Manufacturing Cost

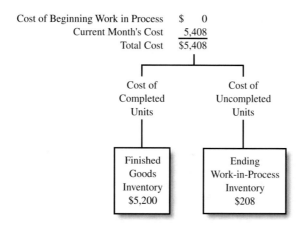

As was also stated at the beginning of this chapter, it is important for managers, such as the sales manager for Dell Computers, to know how much products cost. Otherwise, how could managers know which products are profitable and which are not? Whether it is being used to determine the company's cost of goods sold, the cost of inventories shown on the balance sheet, or to help set selling prices and determine the profitability of individual products, accurate product cost information is essential.

SUMMARY

As Canadian manufacturing companies experience increasing competition, both domestic and foreign, accurate costing of the products they produce becomes ever more important. Information about the cost of manufactured product is useful in establishing a selling price for the products, determining cost of goods sold on the income statement, and valuing inventories on the balance sheet.

The cost of a manufactured product is composed of the cost of direct materials, direct labour, and manufacturing overhead associated with the units of product produced. Although accounting for the cost of direct materials and direct labour is relatively straightforward, determining the amount of manufacturing overhead that should be included in a unit of manufactured product is more difficult because these costs must be allocated to the units of product produced.

The traditional method of allocating manufacturing overhead to product uses a factory-wide application rate based on a single allocation base. Manufacturing overhead allocation using activity-based costing uses multiple application rates based on the various activities that cause costs to be incurred.

Job order costing is one of two main methods used to accumulate product costs and is most appropriate when units or batches of production are unique. Under this method, cost information is gathered for each production job. The second of the two main product costing methods is called process costing and is most appropriate when units of production are identical and each unit of production receives the same manufacturing input as the next.

Regardless of whether the job order costing method or the process costing method is used, the overall purpose of accumulating product costs is to provide managers with the information they need to make many of the decisions necessary to plan and control their operations.

APPENDIX—RECORDING MANUFACTURING COSTS AND THE ALLOCATION OF MANUFACTURING OVERHEAD

This appendix is intended to provide a basic overview of how costs are recorded for manufactured products.

After completing your work in this appendix, you should be able to record the following types of entries:

1. The use of direct material in production
2. The use of direct labour for production
3. The accumulation of manufacturing overhead
4. The allocation of manufacturing overhead to production
5. The transfer of the cost of a completed job to finished goods
6. The entry to close overapplied or underapplied manufacturing overhead
7. The transfer of the cost of completed products to finished goods when process costing is used

The following accounts will be used for the entries in this appendix:

1. Cash
2. Raw materials inventory
3. Work-in-process inventory
4. Manufacturing overhead incurred
5. Manufacturing overhead applied
6. Finished goods inventory
7. Accumulated amortization
8. Utilities payable
9. Cost of goods sold

Recall that debits increase assets, expenses, and losses, while credits increase liabilities, equity, revenues, and gains. The dollar amount of the debits must equal that of the credits in each journal entry.

We will use the job cost sheet in Exhibit 3–13 for the 12 m Open Fisherman job 97384 to provide information for the entries that follow. In practice, separate entries are made for each transfer of material, each payment of wages, and each application of manufacturing overhead. To simplify our example, we will make entries that summarize the amounts for each cost category.

1. The following entry records the $15,870 of direct material used to manufacture job 97384.

Work-in-process inventory	15,870	
Raw materials inventory		15,870
To record the transfer of direct		
material to production for job 97384.		

2. The following entry records the $12,000 of direct labour cost incurred to manufacture job 97384.

Work-in-process inventory	12,000	
Cash		12,000
To record direct labour for job 97384.		

3. The Extreme Ocean Boats Inc. example indicates that the actual manufacturing overhead for the month is $75,000. We will assume that the manufacturing overhead is composed of the following items:

Factory rent	$33,000
Factory utilities	11,000
Factory supervision	23,000
Amortization for production equipment	8,000
Total	$75,000

We will record the actual manufacturing overhead costs listed above in an account called Manufacturing Overhead Incurred. Sometimes this account is called Actual Manufacturing Overhead or simply Manufacturing Overhead.

The following entries would be made to record the actual overhead costs listed previously:

Manufacturing overhead incurred	33,000	
Cash		33,000
To record factory rent for June 2003.		

Manufacturing overhead incurred	11,000	
Cash (or Utilities payable)		11,000
To record factory utilities for June 2003.		

Manufacturing overhead incurred	23,000	
Cash		23,000
To record factory supervision for June 2003.		

Manufacturing overhead incurred	8,000	
Accumulated amortization		8,000
To record amortization of production equipment June 2003.		

After the above entries have been posted, the Manufacturing Overhead Incurred account has a balance of 75,000 as shown in the following t-account:

**Manufacturing
Overhead
Incurred**

33,000
11,000
23,000
8,000
75,000

4. As you recall from the chapter, the actual costs of manufacturing overhead items are not generally assigned directly to particular products being manufactured. Rather, a predetermined overhead application rate is used to allocate manufacturing overhead to production. In our example, the overhead is allocated at 80 percent of direct labour cost. Therefore job 97384 was allocated overhead of $9,600.

Work-in-process inventory	9,600	
Manufacturing overhead applied		9,600
To apply manufacturing overhead to job 97384.		

Note that the account used to record the *application* of manufacturing overhead to production is different from the one used to record the *actual* manufacturing overhead costs. The use of different accounts allows managers and accountants to keep track of both the actual overhead costs incurred and the overhead applied to production.

5. When job 97384 is completed, its cost is transferred to finished goods as follows:

Finished goods inventory	37,470	
Work-in-process inventory		37,470
To transfer the completed job from production		
to finished goods.		

6. As you might imagine, the actual amount of manufacturing overhead cost incurred will be different than the amount applied to production. In a given month, the actual amount of overhead may be more than the amount applied and in another month it may be less. The hope is that the differences will nearly balance out during the year. If the amount applied to production exceeds the actual overhead amount, overhead is overapplied. If the amount applied to production is less than the actual overhead amount, overhead is underapplied. The underapplication or overapplication of overhead is monitored during the year but generally no accounting entries are made to dispense with the amount until the end of the year. In most cases, an accounting entry is made at year end to close the manufacturing overhead incurred, and manufacturing overhead is applied to cost of goods sold. Because the amount of underapplied or overapplied overhead is generally relatively small, and most product cost ends up in cost of goods sold by year end, closing the overhead accounts to cost of goods sold is adequate for most companies.

Assume that the year end balances in the manufacturing overhead incurred and manufacturing overhead applied accounts are as follows:

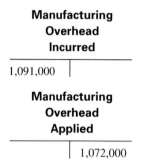

**Manufacturing
Overhead
Incurred**

1,091,000

**Manufacturing
Overhead
Applied**

1,072,000

In this case, manufacturing overhead is $19,000 underapplied. The following entry closes the manufacturing overhead accounts to cost of goods sold.

Cost of goods sold	1,091,000	
Manufacturing overhead incurred		1,091,000
To close manufacturing overhead incurred to cost of goods sold.		

Manufacturing overhead applied	1,072,000	
Cost of goods sold		1,072,000
To close manufacturing overhead applied to cost of goods sold.		

7. The next entry is to transfer of the cost of completed products to finished goods when process costing is used.

You have already learned to record direct material, direct labour, and manufacturing overhead in the work-in-process inventory account. Those entries are basically the same for job order and process costing. The purpose of the next section is to emphasize the fact that the cost calculated for the units completed in process costing is the same amount transferred from work-in-process inventory to finished goods inventory.

According to the information presented in the flamingo example, goods costing $5,200 were completed and transferred to finished goods inventory. The entry to record this transaction is as follows:

Finished goods inventory	5,200	
Work-in-process inventory		5,200

To transfer completed goods from production to
finished goods inventory.

The above entry is significant in arriving at appropriate ending balances in
the inventory accounts. After the $5,200 is transferred to finished goods
inventory, the work-in-process inventory account and finished goods
inventory have balances of $208 and $5,200, respectively, as shown below.

Work-in-Process Inventory

5,408	5,200
5,408	5,200
208	

Finished Goods Inventory

5,200	

Appendix Summary

Work-in-process inventory is debited to record the transfer of direct material to production and the incurrence of direct labour. Manufacturing overhead incurred is
debited to record the actual amount of manufacturing overhead cost incurred. To
apply manufacturing overhead to production, work-in-process inventory is debited
and manufacturing overhead applied is credited. If the amount applied to production exceeds the actual overhead amount, overhead is overapplied. If the amount
applied to production is less than the actual overhead amount, overhead is underapplied. Manufacturers generally make an accounting entry at year end to close the
manufacturing overhead incurred and manufacturing overhead applied accounts
to cost of goods sold. When products are completed, finished goods inventory is
debited and work-in-process inventory is credited for the cost of those products.

Key Terms

activity-based costing, p. 71
activity-based management
  (ABM), p. 88
allocation base, p. 69
cost driver, p. 72
cost pool, p. 69
equivalent units, p. 91
job cost sheet, p. 76
job order costing, p. 74
labour time ticket, p. 82
manufacturing overhead
  allocation, p. 69

materials requisition, p. 79
normal cost system, p. 85
predetermined overhead
  application rate, p. 85
process costing, p. 74
purchase order, p. 77
purchase requisition, p. 77
purchasing department, p. 77
receiving report, p. 78
value engineering, p. 89

REVIEW THE FACTS

1. Describe a manufacturing overhead cost pool.
2. What are the two stages of assigning manufacturing overhead cost to products?
3. List three traditional manufacturing overhead allocation bases.
4. What is the significant weakness of a factory-wide allocation base?
5. What is activity-based costing?
6. In what two ways does activity-based costing improve upon the traditional approach to manufacturing overhead allocation?
7. Describe a cost driver.
8. What is activity-based management (ABM)? What are the three kinds of decisions ABM can be used to make?
9. What are the general characteristics of products for which process costing would be used?
10. What are the general characteristics of products for which job order costing would be used?
11. What is the purpose of a job cost sheet?
12. Which form is sent to a vendor to order materials and supplies?
13. What is the purpose of a receiving report?
14. What is the difference between a purchase requisition and a materials requisition?
15. Which type of form is used to track the amount of labour associated with various jobs?
16. List the four key items of information provided by process costing.
17. Define the term *equivalent units* as used in process costing.

APPLY WHAT YOU HAVE LEARNED

LO 1:   Compare Process Costing with Job Order Costing

1. Following is a list of several products.

   1. _____ Commercial jetliners

   2. _____ Hair spray

   3. _____ Oil tankers

   4. _____ Breakfast cereal

   5. _____ Office buildings

   6. _____ Aspirin

   7. _____ Dog food

   8. _____ Advertising posters

   9. _____ Custom kitchen cabinets

   10. _____ Gasoline

REQUIRED:
For each item, indicate whether job order costing (J) or process costing (P) would be the preferred costing method.

LO 4: Calculate and Describe How Overhead Costs Are Allocated to Products

2. Arbutus Company manufactures playground equipment. For 2004, estimated manufacturing overhead is $240,000. Estimated direct labour is 30,000 hours at a cost of $400,000. Estimated machine hours are 12,500.

REQUIRED:

a. When production begins on January 1, 2004, would it be a good idea for the managers to determine the cost of the manufacturing overhead associated with each swing set produced, or should managers wait for this information until actual overhead cost amounts are available at the end of the year?

b. If we assume that managers need to know the manufacturing overhead cost associated with the playground equipment as soon as the equipment is manufactured, would *actual* overhead cost information be available when the first few swing sets are made in January?

c. If we assume managers need to know the overhead cost associated with the playground equipment as soon as the equipment is made, and it is too early in the year to have actual overhead cost information, what overhead cost information must be used to allocate overhead cost to playground equipment produced by the company?

d. Determine the overhead application rates based on the following:
   (1) Direct labour hours
   (2) Direct labour cost
   (3) Machine hours

e. If you were asked to help select an allocation base for Arbutus Company, which of the three used in (d) would you recommend? Which would you not recommend? Why?

LO 4: Calculate Traditional Overhead Allocation

3. Adamson Company allocates manufacturing overhead to production based on direct labour hours. The following information is available for Adamson Company:

Estimated manufacturing overhead	$403,200
Actual manufacturing overhead	$378,000
Estimated direct labour hours	21,000
Actual direct labour hours	20,000

REQUIRED:

a. Compute Adamson Company's budgeted overhead application rate.

b. Regardless of your answer to Part a, assume that Adamson Company's overhead application rate is $19. Calculate the amount of overhead that should be allocated to production.

c. Appendix: Prepare the following journal entries:
   (1) Record the actual manufacturing overhead. (Use "Various accounts" for the credit side of the entry.)
   (2) Assuming that Adamson Company's overhead application rate is $19, record the overhead allocated to production.
   (3) Close the overapplication or underapplication of overhead.

LO 4:   Calculate Traditional Overhead Allocation

4. Khalil Company (Khalil) allocates manufacturing overhead to production based on machine hours. The following information is available for Khalil:

Estimated manufacturing overhead	$2,000,000
Actual manufacturing overhead	$2,100,000
Estimated machine hours	125,000
Actual machine hours	140,000

REQUIRED:

a. Compute Khalil's budgeted overhead application rate.
b. Regardless of your answer to Part a, assume that Khalil's overhead application rate is $16. Calculate the amount of overhead that should be allocated to production.
c. Appendix: Prepare the following journal entries:
   (1) Record the actual manufacturing overhead. (Use "Various accounts" for the credit side of the entry.)
   (2) Assuming that Khalil's overhead application rate is $16, record the overhead allocated to production.
   (3) Close the overapplication or underapplication of overhead.

LO 4:   Calculate Traditional and ABC Overhead Allocation

5. The president of Creston Products Inc. is attending a management seminar and has just heard about activity-based costing. He wonders whether it would help his company.

Creston Products Inc. uses common machinery to manufacture two simple products. Each year, there are two production runs for each product requiring similar setup effort. Manufacturing overhead includes setup cost of $50,400 per year. Total overhead for the company including the setup cost is $198,000 annually and direct labour hours are expected to total 18,000 for the year.

The following information is available for Products A and B.

	Product A	Product B
Units produced	1,000	8,000
Direct material cost per unit	$14	$14
Direct labour cost per unit	$24	$24
Machine hours per unit	1	1
Direct labour hours per unit	2	2

REQUIRED:

a. Calculate the cost per unit for each product using an overhead allocation rate based on direct labour hours.
b. Calculate the cost per unit for each product using activity-based costing.
c. Do you believe activity-based costing would benefit Creston Products Inc.? Explain your answer.

LO 4:   Calculate Traditional and ABC Overhead Allocation

6. The president of Wilson Products Inc. is attending a management seminar and has just heard about activity-based costing. She wonders whether it would help her company.

Wilson Products Inc. uses common machinery to manufacture two complex products. Each year, there are two production runs for each product requiring similar setup effort. Manufacturing overhead includes setup cost totaling $52,000. To maintain a competitive edge, these products are updated periodically to conform to the latest technological advancements. These engineering changes are considered part of manufacturing overhead and cost $26,000 per year. Total overhead for the company including the cost of setup and engineering changes is $175,000 per year. Direct labour hours total 7,000 for the year.

The following information is available for Products C and D.

	Product C	Product D
Units produced	1,000	1,000
Direct material cost per unit	$24	$24
Direct labour cost per unit	$36	$48
Machine hours per unit	6	8
Direct labour hours	3	4
Engineering changes per year	6	2

REQUIRED:
a. Calculate the cost per unit for each product using an overhead allocation rate based on direct labour hours.
b. Calculate the cost per unit for each product using activity-based costing.
c. Do you believe activity-based costing would benefit Wilson Products Inc.? Explain your answer.

LO 4: Calculate Traditional and ABC Overhead Allocation

7. The following estimates are available for Dunstin Manufacturing Inc. for 2004.

DUNSTIN MANUFACTURING INC.
Estimated Manufacturing Overhead
For the Year Ended December 31, 2004

Materials handling cost	$ 50,000
Product engineering	110,000
Production machine setup	200,000
Production machine amortization	450,000
Quality testing	100,000
Other overhead cost	250,000
Total manufacturing overhead	$1,160,000

DUNSTIN MANUFACTURING INC.
Estimated Overhead Activities
For the Year Ended December 31, 2004

Number of material movements	200,000
Number of product engineering hours	4,400
Number of machine setups	100
Number of machine hours	18,000
Number of tests performed	125,000
Number of direct labour hours	25,000

The following information is available for production runs of two products, the FP111 and the FP222:

	FP111	FP222
Selling price	$ 23	$ 26
Number of units produced	5000	500
Direct material cost	$60,000	$6,000
Direct labour cost	$14,400	$1,440
Number of material movements	10,000	1,000
Number of product engineering hours	100	100
Number of machine setups	1	1
Number of machine hours	200	20
Number of tests performed	1,250	125
Number of direct labour hours	800	80

Dunstin Manufacturing Inc. uses a traditional overhead allocation system. Manufacturing overhead is allocated based on direct labour hours.

Dunstin Manufacturing Inc.'s sales manager has submitted a proposal that would shift the marketing focus to low-volume products such as the FP222. The proposal is prompted by the higher markups that can be charged for these products without customer complaint. The company president is concerned that the company's cost per unit may be sending the wrong message. He recently learned of activity-based costing and wonders if it might help.

Assume that you are part of a group that has been assigned to review the situation.

REQUIRED:

a. Determine the per unit cost for FP111 and FP222 using direct labour hours as the allocation base for all manufacturing overhead cost.
b. Determine the per unit cost for FP111 and FP222 using activity-based costing to allocate manufacturing overhead cost. (Note: Allocate Other Overhead Cost based on direct labour hours.)
c. Discuss the marketing manager's proposal in light of your findings. Discuss what would happen if the marketing manager's sales strategy was adopted.

LO 4: Calculate Traditional and ABC Overhead Allocation

8. The following estimates are available for Olfort Manufacturing Inc. for 2003.

OLFORT MANUFACTURING INC.
Estimated Manufacturing Overhead
For the Year Ended December 31, 2003

Production machine setup	$ 75,000
Production machine amortization	240,000
Quality testing	25,000
Other overhead cost	150,000
Total manufacturing overhead	$490,000

OLFORT MANUFACTURING INC.
Estimated Overhead Activities
For the Year Ended December 31, 2003

Number of machine setups	100
Number of machine hours	3,200
Number of tests performed	50,000
Number of direct labour hours	16,000

The following information is available for production of two products, the AA1 and the BB2:

	AA1	BB2
Selling price	$ 2.40	$3.25
Number of units produced	10,000	500
Direct material cost	$ 5,000	$ 250
Direct labour cost	$ 6,400	$ 320
Number of machine setups	1	1
Number of machine hours	100	5
Number of tests performed	100	50
Number of direct labour hours	400	20

Olfort Manufacturing Inc. uses a traditional overhead allocation system. Manufacturing overhead is allocated based on direct labour hours. Olfort Manufacturing Inc.'s sales manager has submitted a proposal that would shift the marketing focus to low-volume products such as the BB2. The proposal is prompted by the higher markups and lack of competition, even at high selling prices.

The company president is concerned that the company's cost per unit may be sending the wrong message. He recently learned of activity-based costing and wonders if it might help.

Assume that you are a member of a work team that has been assigned to review the situation.

REQUIRED:
a. Determine the per unit cost for AA1 and BB2 using direct labour hours as the allocation base for all manufacturing overhead cost.
b. Determine the per unit cost for AA1 and BB2 using activity-based costing to allocate manufacturing overhead cost. (Note: Allocate Other Overhead Cost based on direct labour hours.)
c. Discuss the marketing manager's proposal in light of your findings. Discuss what would happen if the marketing manager's sales strategy was adopted.

LO 4: Calculate Traditional Overhead Allocation

9. Letourneau Company allocates manufacturing overhead to production based on cost of direct labour. The following information is available for Letourneau Company:

Estimated manufacturing overhead	$3,500,000
Actual manufacturing overhead	$3,485,000
Estimated cost of direct labour	$1,750,000
Actual cost of direct labour	$1,700,000

REQUIRED:
a. Compute the estimated overhead application rate for Letourneau Company.
b. Regardless of your answer to Part a, assume that the overhead application rate for Letourneau Company is 190%. Calculate the amount of overhead that should be allocated to production.

LO 4 & 5: Calculate Traditional Overhead Allocation and Determine the Cost of Products Using Job Order Costing

10. Bridgeport Custom Truck Bodies Ltd. makes aluminum truck bodies for medium and large trucks. The estimated manufacturing overhead for 2004 is $40,000, and the estimated direct labour cost is $60,000. Manufacturing overhead is applied to production based on direct labour cost.

The following information pertains to truck bodies manufactured during February 2004.

Beginning work-in-process inventory:

Job 101	Direct material	$1,000
	Direct labour	2,000
Job 102	Direct material	750
	Direct labour	1,200

Cost for current month:

Direct material	Job 101	$ 500
	Job 102	1,100
	Job 103	2,300
Direct labour	Job 101	$ 800
	Job 102	1,300
	Job 103	3,200

Job 101 was completed and sold in February and Job 102 was completed, but has not been sold. Job 103 remains in production.

REQUIRED:

a. What is the cost of Bridgeport's beginning work-in-process inventory for February 2004?

b. What is the cost of Bridgeport's ending work-in-process inventory for February 2004?

c. **(1)** What is the cost of Job 101?
   (2) How would Job 101 appear on Bridgeport's financial statements?

d. **(1)** What is the cost of Job 102?
   (2) How would Job 102 appear on Bridgeports financial statements?

LO 4 & 5: Calculate Traditional Overhead Allocation and Determine the Cost of Products Using Job Order Costing

11. Beaulieu Company began operations in June 2003. During that month, two jobs were started. The following costs were incurred:

	Job 101	Job 202
Direct material	$3,000	$4,000
Direct labour	6,000	7,000

Manufacturing overhead is applied at 60% of direct labour cost. During the month, Job 101 was completed but not sold. Job 202 is yet to be completed.

REQUIRED:

a. Calculate the cost of the ending work-in-process inventory as of June 30, 2003.

b. Calculate the cost of the finished goods inventory as of June 30, 2003.

LO 4 & 5:   Calculate Traditional Overhead Allocation and Determine the Cost of Products Using Job Order Costing

12. Wong Manufacturing began operations in August 2004. During that month, two jobs were started. The following costs were incurred:

	Job 1	Job 2
Direct material	$5,400	$8,900
Direct labour	6,500	9,000

Factory overhead is applied at 50% of direct labour cost. During the month, Job 1 was completed but not sold. Job 2 has not been completed.

REQUIRED:
a. Calculate the cost of the ending work-in-process inventory as of August 31, 2004.
b. Calculate the cost of the finished goods inventory as of August 31, 2004.

LO 4 & 5:   Calculate Traditional Overhead Allocation and Determine the Cost of Products Using Job Order Costing

13. Dhuri Manufacturing began operations in September 2004. During that month, two jobs were started. The following costs were incurred:

	Job A	Job B
Direct material	$2,500	$5,000
Direct labour	7,000	9,500

Factory overhead is applied at 120% of direct labour cost. During the month, Job A was completed but not sold. Job B has not been completed.

REQUIRED:
a. Calculate the cost of the ending work-in-process inventory as of September 30, 2004.
b. Calculate the cost of the finished goods inventory as of September 30, 2004.
c. Appendix: Prepare the following journal entries:
   (1) Record direct materials for each job.
   (2) Record direct labour for each job.
   (3) Record the allocation of manufacturing overhead for each job.
   (4) Record the transfer to finished goods inventory of Job A.

LO 4 & 5:   Calculate Traditional Overhead Allocation and Determine the Cost of Products Using Job Order Costing

14. Pacific Manufacturing Inc. began two jobs during the month of January 2005. There was no beginning inventory. The following costs were incurred:

	Job A	Job B
Direct material	$2,000	$3,000
Direct labour	4,000	5,000

Estimated manufacturing overhead for 2005 is $117,000, and the estimated direct labour cost is $90,000. Pacific applies overhead to production based on direct labour cost. During the month, Job A was completed but not sold. Job B has not been completed.

REQUIRED:
a. Calculate the cost of the ending work-in-process inventory as of January 31, 2005.
b. Calculate the cost of the finished goods inventory as of January 31, 2005.
c. Appendix: Prepare the following journal entries:
   (1) Record direct materials for each job.
   (2) Record direct labour for each job.
   (3) Record the allocation of manufacturing overhead for each job.
   (4) Record the transfer to finished goods inventory of Job A.

LO 4 & 5:   Calculate Traditional Overhead Allocation and Determine the Cost of Products Using Job Order Costing

15. Booth Industries Inc. makes custom optical glass equipment. The company began two jobs during January 2003. There was no beginning inventory. The following information is available:

	Job 7	Job 8
Direct material cost	$7,250	$3,640
Direct labour cost	$4,251	$5,125
Direct labour hours	212	234

Booth's estimated manufacturing overhead for 2003 is $110,400, and the company estimates that the labour force will work 9,200 direct labour hours. Booth applies overhead to production based on direct labour hours.

REQUIRED:
a. Calculate the cost of Job 7.
b. Calculate the cost of Job 8.

LO 4 & 5:   Calculate Traditional Overhead Allocation and Determine the Cost of Products Using Job Order Costing

16. Ontario Cleaning Equipment Ltd. began two jobs during March 2004. There was no beginning inventory. The following information is available:

	Job 10	Job 15
Direct material cost	$14,350	$23,530
Direct labour cost	$ 7,231	$15,125
Machine hours	124	236

The company estimated manufacturing overhead for 2004 is $307,200, and the company estimates that 4,800 machine hours will be used during the year. Ontario Cleaning Equipment Ltd. applies overhead to production based on machine hours.

REQUIRED:
a. Calculate the cost of Job 10.
b. Calculate the cost of Job 15.

LO 5: Determine the Cost of Products Using Job Order Costing

17. Atlantic Automotive Security Ltd. converts regular automobiles to armoured cars. Each car is custom made to conform to the needs of each individual customer. Modifications may be as minor as the addition of bullet-resistant windows or as extravagant as full armour. The following information is presented for March 2003.

Beginning work-in-process inventory:

Job 2727	Direct material	$24,000
	Direct labour	9,000
	Manufacturing overhead	5,400

Cost for current month:

	Direct Material	Direct Labour	Manufacturing Overhead
Job 2727	$ 8,000	$4,000	$2,400
Job 2728	11,000	6,000	3,600

Job 2727 was completed and sold in March, and Job 2728 was not complete as of March 31.

REQUIRED:

a. What is the cost of the beginning work-in-process inventory for March 2003?
b. What is the cost of the ending work-in-process inventory for March 2003?
c. **(1)** What is the cost of Job 2727?
   (2) How would Job 2727 appear on the financial statements?

LO 4 & 5: Calculate Traditional Overhead Allocation and Determine the Cost of Products Using Job Order Costing

18. Johnson Brothers Equipment Company began two jobs during March 2004. At the beginning of March, Job 303 was the only job in work-in-process inventory. There was no finished goods inventory. The cost in beginning work-in-process inventory for Job 303 consisted of $5,450 in direct material cost, $8,825 in direct labour cost, and manufacturing overhead cost of $7,354. The following information is available for costs added during March:

	Job 303	Job 304	Job 305
Direct material cost	$ 4,350	$12,650	$11,300
Direct labour cost	$ 8,400	$ 8,125	$ 6,750
Direct labour hours	560	520	480

Job 303 was completed and sold during March. Job 304 was completed but has yet to be sold, and Job 305 remains in production.

Johnson's estimated manufacturing overhead for 2004 is $225,000, and the company estimates that the labour force will work 18,000 hours during the year. Johnson applies overhead to production based on direct labour hours.

REQUIRED:

a. Calculate the cost of the ending work-in-process inventory as of March 31, 2004.
b. Calculate the cost of the finished goods inventory as of March 31, 2004.
c. Calculate the cost of goods sold for March.

LO 4 & 5: Calculate Traditional Overhead Allocation and Determine the Cost of Products Using Job Order Costing

19. Greenberg and Son Manufacturing began two jobs during July 2005. At the beginning of July, Job 227 was the only job in work-in-process inventory. There was no finished goods inventory. The cost in beginning work-in-process inventory for Job 227 consisted of $1,500 in direct material cost, $2,000 in direct labour cost, and manufacturing overhead cost of $4,500. Total manufacturing overhead for the month was $16,054. The following information is available for costs added during July:

	Job 227	Job 228	Job 229
Direct material cost	$ 935	$2,850	$1,300
Direct labour cost	$1,840	$3,225	$1,975
Direct labour hours	184	310	204

Job 227 was completed and sold during July. Job 228 was completed but has yet to be sold, and Job 229 remains in production.

Greenberg's estimated manufacturing overhead for 2005 is $180,000, and the company estimates that the labour force will work 8,000 hours during the year. Greenberg applies overhead to production based on direct labour hours.

REQUIRED:
a. Calculate the cost of the ending work-in-process inventory as of July 31, 2005.
b. Calculate the cost of the finished goods inventory as of July 31, 2005.
c. Calculate the cost of goods sold for July 2005.

LO 4 & 5: Calculate Traditional Overhead Allocation and Determine the Cost of Products Using Job Order Costing

20. Chen Manufacturing Inc. began two jobs during May 2003. At the beginning of May, Job 411 was the only job in work-in-process inventory. There was no finished goods inventory. The cost in beginning work-in-process inventory for Job 411 consisted of $4,000 in direct material cost, $6,000 in direct labour cost, and manufacturing overhead cost of $8,000. Total manufacturing overhead for the month was $22,050. The following information is available for costs added during May:

	Job 411	Job 412	Job 413
Direct material cost	$2,000	$4,000	$6,000
Direct labour cost	$2,500	$6,500	$8,500
Direct labour hours	224	572	780

Job 411 was completed and sold during May. Job 412 was completed but has yet to be sold, and Job 413 remains in production.

Chen's estimated manufacturing overhead for 2003 is $277,875, and the company estimates that the labour force will work 19,500 hours during the year. Chen applies overhead to production based on direct labour hours.

REQUIRED:
a. Calculate the cost of the ending work-in-process inventory as of May 31, 2003.
b. Calculate the cost of the finished goods inventory as of May 31, 2003.
c. Calculate the cost of goods sold for May 2003.

LO 4 & 5: Calculate Traditional and ABC Overhead Allocation and Determine the Cost of Products Using Job Order Costing

21. Stuart Equipment Company began the following jobs during March 2004:

	Job 303	Job 304
Direct material cost	$2,000	$2,000
Direct labour cost	$3,120	$6,240
Direct labour hours	260	520
Machine hours Machine A	5	30
Machine hours Machine B	20	0
Machine setups	2	1
Engineering changes	22	9

Estimated overhead cost for 2004:

Amortization Machine A	$ 100,000
Amortization Machine B	500,000
Machine setup cost	50,000
Engineering cost	200,000
Other overhead cost	150,000
Total	$1,000,000

Estimated activities for 2004:

Machine hours Machine A	1,000
Machine hours Machine B	1,000
Number of setups	80
Number of engineering changes	800
Number of direct labour hours	20,000

REQUIRED:

a. Calculate the cost of each job using direct labour hours as the allocation base for all overhead.

b. Calculate the cost of each job using activity-based costing. Use direct labour hours as the allocation base for "other overhead cost."

LO 4 & 5: Calculate Traditional and ABC Overhead Allocation and Determine the Cost of Products Using Job Order Costing

22. Duskin Equipment Company began the following jobs during August 2005:

	Job 500	Job 600
Direct material cost	$1,000	$1,000
Direct labour cost	$1,800	$3,000
Direct labour hours	120	200
Machine hours Machine A	10	50
Machine hours Machine B	50	0
Machine setups	2	1
Material movements	200	75

Estimated overhead cost for 2005:

Amortization Machine A	$ 50,000
Amortization Machine B	300,000
Machine setup cost	75,000
Material handling cost	100,000
Other overhead cost	80,000
Total	$605,000

Machine hours Machine A	500
Machine hours Machine B	500
Number of setups	75
Number of material movements	5,000
Number of direct labour hours	10,000

REQUIRED:

a. Calculate the cost of each job using total machine hours as the allocation base for all overhead.

b. Calculate the cost of each job using activity-based costing. Use total machine hours as the allocation base for "other overhead cost."

LO 4 & 5: Calculate Traditional and ABC Overhead Allocation and Determine the Cost of Products Using Job Order Costing

23. Landry Manufacturing Company began the following jobs during July 2003:

	Job 901	Job 922
Direct material cost	$3,000	$3,000
Direct labour cost	$1,800	$3,000
Direct labour hours	250	100
Machine hours Machine A	20	12
Machine hours Machine B	0	8
Machine setups	1	2
Material movements	90	300

Estimated overhead cost for 2003:

Amortization Machine A	$ 150,500
Amortization Machine B	599,900
Machine setup cost	175,000
Material handling cost	150,000
Other overhead cost	180,000
Total	$1,255,400

Estimated activities for 2003:

Machine hours Machine A	700
Machine hours Machine B	700
Number of setups	100
Number of material movements	5,000
Number of direct labour hours	10,000

REQUIRED:

a. Calculate the cost of each job using direct labour hours as the allocation base for all overhead.

b. Calculate the cost of each job using activity-based costing. Use direct labour hours as the allocation base for "other overhead cost."

LO 6:   Determine the Cost of Products Using Process Costing—No Beginning or Ending Inventory

24. Daysi's Specialty Food Company makes canned chili. The following cost information is available for March 2004:

Units produced	25,000
Direct material cost	$8,000
Direct labour cost	$3,000
Manufacturing overhead costs	$2,000

There were no beginning or ending inventories.

REQUIRED:
a. What is the total production cost for Daysi's Specialty Food Company?
b. What is the cost per unit?
c. If the chili sold for $0.82 per can, what is the gross profit for the company?

LO 6:   Determine the Cost of Products Using Process Costing—With Beginning Inventory

25. Dunn Electronic Manufacturing Corp. makes low-cost calculators. The following information is available for January 2005:

	Units	Percent Complete	Cost
Beginning work-in-process inventory	700	40	$224
Ending work-in-process inventory	900	60	?
Units completed	12,000	100	

Manufacturing cost for January 2005 is $10,659.

REQUIRED:
a. What is the number of equivalent units of production for January 2005?
b. What is the cost per equivalent unit?
c. What is the cost of the 900 calculators in the ending work-in-process inventory?
d. What is the cost of the calculators that were completed during January?
e. If 11,000 of the completed calculators were sold for $1.12 each, what is the gross profit for Dunn Electronic Manufacturing Corp.?
f. (1) Do you think there is a benefit for Dunn's managers to know the cost of the calculators that are in ending work-in-process inventory? Explain.
   (2) Where would the cost of the ending inventory appear on the financial statements?
   (3) Do you think there is a benefit for Dunn's managers to know the cost of the calculators completed during January? Explain.
   (4) Where would the cost of the 11,000 sold calculators be found on the financial statements?
   (5) Where would the cost of the calculators that were completed, but not yet sold be found on the financial statements?

LO 6: Determine the Cost of Products Using Process Costing—With Beginning Inventory

26. The following information is for Brown Volleyball Manufacturing Corporation for February 2003:

	Units	Percent Complete	Cost
Beginning work-in-process inventory	2,400	80	$2,304
Ending work-in-process inventory	3,200	50	

64,000 volleyballs were completed in February. Manufacturing cost for February is $88,560.

REQUIRED:

a. What is the number of equivalent units of production for February?
b. What is the cost per equivalent unit for February?
c. What is the cost of the 3,200 volleyballs in the ending work-in-process inventory for February?
d. What is the cost of the volleyballs that were completed during February?
e. If 50,000 of the completed volleyballs were sold for $1.80 each, what is the gross profit for Brown Volleyball Manufacturing Corporation?

LO 6: Determine the Cost of Products Using Process Costing—No Beginning Inventory

27. Kerry's Manufacturing makes candy. During 2004, the company's first year of operations, the company completed 200,000 boxes of candy and incurred direct material cost of $160,800, direct labour cost of $40,200, and manufacturing overhead cost of $60,300. There were 2,000 boxes of candy that were 50% complete in the production process at the end of the year.

REQUIRED:

a. What is the number of equivalent units of production for 2004?
b. What is the cost per equivalent unit of production for 2004?
c. What is the cost of the 2004 ending work-in-process inventory?
d. What is the cost of the boxes of candy that were completed in 2004?

LO 6: Determine the Number of Equivalent Units

28. The following information relates to Collins Company for 2005:

	Units	Percent Complete
Work in process at January 1	10,000	75
Units started into production	145,000	
Units completed	138,000	
Work in process at December 31	17,000	50

REQUIRED:

Calculate the number of equivalent units of production.

LO 6:   Determine the Number of Equivalent Units

29. The following information relates to Munter Corp. for June 2003:

	Units	Percent Complete
Work in process at June 1	115,000	60
Units started into production	1,800,000	
Units completed	1,850,000	
Work in process at June 30	65,000	30

REQUIRED:
Calculate the number of equivalent units of production.

LO 6:   Determine the Number of Equivalent Units

30. The following information relates to Holder Company for July 2004:

	Units	Percent Complete
Work in process at July 1	5,000	90
Units started into production	70,000	
Units completed	72,000	
Work in process at July 31	3,000	20

REQUIRED:
Calculate the number of equivalent units of production.

LO 6:   Determine the Number of Equivalent Units
with Missing Information

31. The following information relates to Mayber Limited for May 2005:

	Units	Percent Complete
Work in process at May 1	5,000	45
Units started into production	77,000	
Work in process at May 31	12,000	35

REQUIRED:
a. Assuming no units of production were lost or spoiled, how many units were completed during May?
b. Calculate the number of equivalent units of production.

LO 6:   Determine the Number of Equivalent Units
with Missing Information

32. The following information relates to Strayform Company for August 2003:

	Units	Percent Complete
Work in process at August 1	7,000	95
Units started into production	87,000	
Work in process at August 31	6,500	25

REQUIRED:

a. Assuming no units of production were lost or spoiled, how many units were completed during August?

b. Calculate the number of equivalent units of production.

LO 6: Determine the Number of Equivalent Units with Missing Information

33. The following information relates to Golden Company for February 2004:

	Units	Percent Complete
Work in process at February 1	22,500	80
Units started into production	185,000	
Work in process at February 29	14,500	25

REQUIRED:

a. Assuming no units of production were lost or spoiled, how many units were completed during February?

b. Calculate the number of equivalent units of production.

LO 6: Determine the Cost of Products Using Process Costing— With Beginning Inventory

34. The following information relates to Smithfield Corporation for July 2005:

	Units	Percent Complete
Work in process at July 1	19,500	50
Units started into production	220,000	
Units completed in July	231,000	
Work in process at July 31	8,500	40
Cost of the beginning work in process	$ 7,020	
Current month's production cost	$166,436	

REQUIRED:

a. Calculate the number of equivalent units of production.

b. Calculate the cost per equivalent unit of production.

c. Calculate the cost of the ending work-in-process inventory.

d. Calculate the cost of the completed units.

LO 6: Determine the Cost of Products Using Process Costing— With Beginning Inventory

35. The following information relates to Richard Renick Company for 2003:

	Units	Percent Complete
Work in process at January 1	42,000	50
Units started into production	420,000	
Units completed in 2003	390,000	
Work in process at December 31	72,000	20
Cost of the beginning work in process	$ 14,280	
Current year's production cost	$248,580	

REQUIRED:

a. Calculate the number of equivalent units of production.
b. Calculate the cost per equivalent unit of production.
c. Calculate the cost of the ending work-in-process inventory.
d. Calculate the cost of the completed units.

LO 6: Determine the Cost of Products Using Process Costing— With Beginning Inventory

36. The following information relates to Robert Lewis Manufacturing Company for 2004:

	Units	Percent Complete
Work in process at January 1	120,000	25
Units started into production	1,300,000	
Units completed in 2004	1,290,000	
Work in process at December 31	130,000	70
Cost of the beginning work in process		$ 40,200
Current year's production cost		$1,768,910

REQUIRED:

a. Calculate the number of equivalent units of production.
b. Calculate the cost per equivalent unit of production.
c. Calculate the cost of the ending work-in-process inventory.
d. Calculate the cost of the completed units.

LO 6: Determine the Cost of Products Using Process Costing— With Beginning Inventory

37. The cost of the work-in-process inventory at January 1 for Robinson Manufacturing Inc. was $7,420, consisting of 10,000 units that were 35% complete. An additional 130,000 units were started into production during the year. The cost of material, labour, and overhead added during the year amounted to $280,680. The units completed and transferred to finished goods inventory totaled 125,000. The ending work-in-process inventory consisted of 15,000 units that were 60% complete.

REQUIRED:

a. Calculate the number of equivalent units of production.
b. Calculate the cost per equivalent unit of production.
c. Calculate the cost of the ending work-in-process inventory.
d. Calculate the cost of the completed units.

LO 6: Determine the Cost of Products Using Process Costing— With Beginning Inventory

38. The cost of the work-in-process inventory at January 1 for Mays Manufacturing Inc. was $61,875, consisting of 11,000 units that were 45% complete. An additional 150,000 units were started into production during the year. The cost of material, labour, and overhead added during the year amounted to $1,872,855. The units completed and transferred to finished goods inventory totaled 145,000. The ending work-in-process inventory consisted of 16,000 units that were 65% complete.

REQUIRED:

  a. Calculate the number of equivalent units of production.
  b. Calculate the cost per equivalent unit of production.
  c. Calculate the cost of the ending work-in-process inventory.
  d. Calculate the cost of the completed units.

LO 6:   Determine the Cost of Products Using Process Costing— With Beginning Inventory

39. The cost of the work-in-process inventory at January 1 for Hanamura Manufacturing was $119,805, consisting of 112,500 units that were 30% complete. An additional 750,000 units were started into production during the year. The cost of material, labour, and overhead added during the year amounted to $2,627,820. The units completed and transferred to finished goods inventory totaled 790,000. The ending work-in-process inventory consisted of 72,500 units that were 25% complete.

REQUIRED:

  a. Calculate the number of equivalent units of production.
  b. Calculate the cost per equivalent unit of production.
  c. Calculate the cost of the ending work-in-process inventory.
  d. Calculate the cost of the completed units.
  e. Appendix: Prepare a journal entry to transfer the cost of completed goods from work-in-process inventory.

LO 6:   Determine the Cost of Products Using Process Costing— With Beginning Inventory and Missing Information

40. The following information relates to Lewis Manufacturing Company for 2003:

	Units	Cost
Work in process at January 1	18,500	$ 35,668
Units started into production	190,000	
Units completed in 2003	187,000	
Current production cost		$1,873,052

The beginning work-in-process inventory was 20% complete and the ending work-in-process inventory is 55% complete.

REQUIRED:

  a. Calculate the number of equivalent units of production.
  b. Calculate the cost per equivalent unit of production.
  c. Calculate the cost of the ending work-in-process inventory.
  d. Calculate the cost of the completed units.
  e. Appendix: Prepare a journal entry to transfer the cost of completed goods from work-in-process inventory.

LO 6: Determine the Cost of Products Using Process Costing— With Beginning Inventory and Missing Information

41. The following information relates to Mathias Manufacturing Inc. for 2004:

	Units	Cost
Work in process at January 1	77,000	$ 107,415
Units started into production	602,500	
Work in process at December 31	92,000	
Current production cost		$2,979,922

The beginning work-in-process inventory was 30% complete and the ending work-in-process inventory is 80% complete.

REQUIRED:
a. Calculate the number of equivalent units of production.
b. Calculate the cost per equivalent unit of production.
c. Calculate the cost of the ending work-in-process inventory.
d. Calculate the cost of the completed units.
e. Appendix: Prepare a journal entry to transfer the cost of completed goods from work-in-process inventory.

LO 6: Determine the Cost of Products Using Process Costing— With Beginning Inventory and Missing Information

42. The following information relates to Heromi Manufacturing Company for 2005:

	Units	Cost
Work in process at January 1	13,000	$ 4,368
Units started into production	83,500	
Work in process at December 31	7,500	
Current production cost		$37,262

The beginning work-in-process inventory was 70% complete and the ending work-in-process inventory is 20% complete.

REQUIRED:
a. Calculate the number of equivalent units of production.
b. Calculate the cost per equivalent unit of production.
c. Calculate the cost of the ending work-in-process inventory.
d. Calculate the cost of the completed units.
e. Appendix: Prepare a journal entry to transfer the cost of completed goods from work-in-process inventory.

4

Cost Behaviour

*L*aura Jorgensen is the newly elected social chairperson of her mountain climbing club. Her first duty is to plan the club's big kickoff party for the upcoming year. Of course funds are limited, so she must plan well and estimate costs carefully.

Laura's first step in estimating the total cost of the party is to identify the individual costs involved. As she begins the planning process, she identifies two major costs:

1. Entertainment—A live band is a must.
2. Food and drinks—Large amounts are essential.

When Laura checks the records of last year's social chairperson, she discovers he spent $3,650 on these two items for last year's party ($525 for entertainment and $3,125 for food and drinks). Assuming the prices for entertainment and food and drinks have remained the same, the club should be able to have this year's party for $3,650. In fact, Laura has money to spare because the spending limit for this year's event is $5,500.

But wait. . . . The mountain climbing club has grown, so about 175 guests are expected to attend this year's party, compared to 125 last year. Laura must estimate the party's cost for 175 guests, not 125. How should she begin?

To determine the total expected cost of the party, Laura needs to know which costs are and which costs are not affected by the number of guests attending. Let's examine Laura's two major costs for the party:

1. Entertainment: Will the band charge more if more guests attend? No.

$y = a + bx$

y = estimated total cost

x = expected or actual activity level

a = estimated fixed cost per period

b = estimated variable cost per unit of activity

2. Food and drinks: Will the caterer charge more if the number of guests increases? Yes.

How should Laura determine the cost of this year's party when the number of people attending is 175 rather than 125? Clearly, she knows her cost for the item that is unaffected by the activity level (the band), but what about the cost that is affected by a change in activity level (food and drinks)? This chapter will demonstrate how to determine these amounts.

As managers plan for business success, they must know which costs will vary with changes in business activity and which will remain constant. That is, managers must determine cost behaviour. **Cost behaviour** is the reaction of costs to changes in levels of business activity. ■

cost behaviour   The reaction of costs to changes in levels of business activity.

LEARNING OBJECTIVES

After completing your work on this chapter, you should be able to do the following:

1. Describe the differences between fixed costs and variable costs.
2. Classify costs by cost behaviour.
3. Explain the concept of relevant range and its effect on cost behaviour information.
4. Describe the characteristics of a mixed cost and the four basic approaches to separating a mixed cost into its fixed and variable components.
5. Determine the fixed and variable components of a mixed cost using scatter graphs and the high-low method.

COMMON COST BEHAVIOUR PATTERNS

Costs may react in various ways to changes in activity levels, creating many different cost behaviour patterns. In this chapter we describe and compare the two most common patterns: fixed and variable.

Fixed Costs

fixed cost   A cost that remains constant in total regardless of the level of activity.

Fixed costs are costs that remain constant *in total* regardless of the level of activity. In our chapter-opening example, the entertainment cost is a fixed cost. As the number of guests increases, this cost does not change. The band will cost $525 for the night, regardless of how many guests attend the club's party.

Suppose Laura is interested in determining the fixed cost *per guest*. Would the fixed cost amount change per guest as the number of guests changes? Let's take a look.

	125 Guests	175 Guests
Total fixed cost	$525	$525
Cost per guest	$525 ÷ 125 = $4.20	$525 ÷ 175 = $3.00

As you can see, the fixed cost *per unit* (in this case, the entertainment cost per guest) changes as the activity level changes. A fixed cost, then, is a cost that remains constant in total, but changes per unit as the activity level changes. Fixed cost per unit decreases as activity increases.

 ## Discussion Question

4-1. Consider the costs involved in operating a fast-food restaurant such as McDonald's. What are three examples of fixed costs?

Variable Costs

variable cost A cost that changes in total proportionately with changes in the level of activity.

Variable costs are costs that change *in total* proportionately with changes in the level of activity. As activity increases, total variable cost also increases. In our party example, the variable cost is the catering cost of $25 per guest. We know this because the total cost for food and drinks last year was $3,125 for 125 guests, and $3,125 ÷ 125 = $25. For each additional guest added to the party, the total cost for food and drinks will increase by $25.

If 175 guests attend, the total catering cost is as follows:

175 guests × $25 = $4,375

Variable cost *per unit* stays the same as activity changes. In our example, the catering cost per guest remains constant. Variable cost is a cost that increases in total, but remains constant per unit as activity increases.

 ## Discussion Question

4-2. Consider the costs involved in operating a fast-food restaurant such as McDonald's. What are three examples of variable costs and the activity or activities that cause them to change?

Comparison of Cost Behaviours

Cost and activity can be plotted on a graph to yield a visual representation of cost behaviour. When doing so, the activity is plotted on the horizontal axis (called the *x*-axis). The type of cost is plotted on the vertical axis (called the *y*-axis). You may recall from past math classes that *x* is the independent variable, and *y* is the dependent variable, which means that the item depicted on the *x*-axis (activity) affects the item shown on the *y*-axis (cost).

A graphical representation of a fixed cost is as follows:

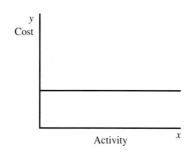

Examples of activities and fixed costs are shown in Exhibit 4–1. Notice that each example in Exhibit 4–1 suggests a cost that remains constant even if the level of the activity changes.

Exhibit 4–1
Examples of Fixed Costs

Activity	Fixed Cost
Production	Rent on the factory building
Production	Production supervisor's salary
Sales	Salary of vice president of sales
Delivery	Vehicle insurance

From our party example, we can graph the cost of the band as an example of a fixed cost, as shown in Exhibit 4–2.

Exhibit 4–2
Graph of Fixed Cost Behaviour Pattern of Entertainment at the Climbing Club Party

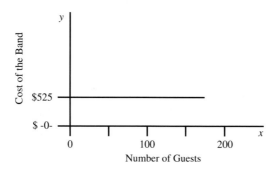

The horizontal line on the graph in Exhibit 4–2 shows that the fixed cost of entertainment stays constant no matter how the number of guests changes.

A graphical representation of variable cost is as follows:

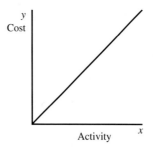

Examples of activities and variable costs are shown in Exhibit 4–3. Notice that for each example in Exhibit 4–3, a change in the level of the activity results in a change in the total cost.

Exhibit 4–3
Examples of Variable
Costs

Activity	Variable Cost
Production	Direct material
Production	Direct labour
Sales	Sales commissions
Delivery	Gasoline

The cost of catering is a variable cost and can be graphically depicted as shown in Exhibit 4–4. The upward sloping line in Exhibit 4–4 shows us that as the number of guests increases from 125 to 175, the catering cost increases proportionately.

Exhibit 4–4
Graph of Variable Cost
Behaviour Pattern for
Catering Cost at the
Climbing Club Party

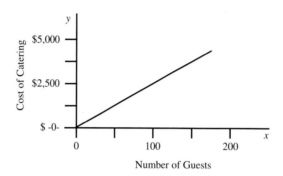

Discussion Question

4–3. Identify four additional costs of hosting the mountain climbing club party and describe the cost behaviour of each if the number of guests changes.

In this section, we defined and compared the two most common types of cost behaviour. Next, we see how to estimate the total cost of an activity.

Determining Total Cost

Once managers classify costs according to cost behaviour, they can determine the total cost of an activity. The formula for finding total cost is as follows:

Total Cost = Fixed Cost + Variable Cost

Recall from our example that we have $525 of fixed cost for the band, and $4,375 of variable cost for the food and drinks (based on 175 guests). Using this information, Laura can calculate the total cost of the party as $4,900, as follows:

$4,900 = $525 + $4,375

The total cost of the party is shown on the graph in Exhibit 4–5.

Exhibit 4–5
Graph of Total Climbing
Party Cost

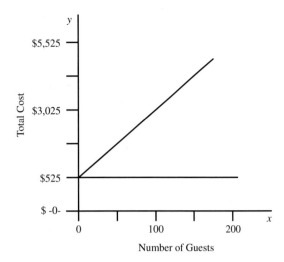

The graph in Exhibit 4–5 shows both the horizontal line depicting the fixed cost of the band and the upward sloping line representing the fixed cost plus the variable cost of the food and drinks. Exhibit 4–5, then, is actually a combination of the graphs in Exhibits 4–2 and 4–4. These graphs are consistent with the statement that total cost is equal to fixed cost plus variable cost.

Since the budget for the event was $5,500, and Laura plans to spend only $4,900, she must have planned well, right? Not necessarily. Keep in mind that the numbers only tell part of the story. As a decision maker, Laura must not be lulled into thinking that she has made the most effective spending choices just because she failed to spend every budgeted dollar. Is it wise to spend nearly $5,000 on one event? Could some costs be reduced? To make strong decisions, managers must consider all issues—not just whether the budget has been met. In this chapter, we examine cost behaviours to equip you with a cost estimation tool. Remember, however, that when making decisions the numbers tell part, not all, of a story.

 Discussion Question

4–4. The total cost of $4,900 covers the cost of 175 guests. Based on the cost behaviour information available, what is the largest possible number of guests that could attend the party within the $5,500 budget?

RELEVANT RANGE

Are there any situations when a cost behaviour might change? Let's reexamine the cost of entertainment in the party example to answer this question. We assumed the cost of the band would remain fixed if the number of guests attending the party increased; however, if the number of guests increased well outside normal expectations to 500 or 1,000, the guests could not be entertained with a single band. At least two bands would be needed. Once the number of guests exceeds a certain range, the entertainment cost does not remain fixed at $525.

The range of activity within which cost behaviour assumptions are valid is the **relevant range.** In the party example, the relevant range might be up to 250 guests. If more than 250 guests attend, another band will be needed. For a business, relevant range is usually considered to be the normal range of activity for the company.

Activity that is outside the relevant range can affect costs in a business setting. For example, in Exhibit 4–1, we described rent for a factory building as a fixed cost relative to production. This fixed cost behaviour holds true only within the relevant range. On the one hand, if production dropped to two units there would be no point in having a factory. Work could be contracted to an outside party. Conversely, if the factory building provided just enough space to produce 1,000 units per month, and production requirements increased to 1,500 units per month, a second factory would be needed. If the activity level were higher than the relevant range, factory rent would no longer be fixed at the original cost level.

Variable costs also have a relevant range. To illustrate, we return to the catering costs for the party example. The caterer charged the club $25 per guest for food and drinks for a party with 125 to 175 guests. Would the caterer offer the same service for $25 per guest if the event were a private evening with only six people attending? Probably not. The caterer's fee is based on a relatively large number of guests. Conversely, the caterer might be willing to provide food and drinks for a cost of less than $25 per guest if the crowd were significantly larger. For example, the caterer might offer a $25 per guest charge for groups of 50 to 200, and a $20 per guest charge for groups of more than 200. In such a case, the relevant range of the variable cost behaviour would be from 50 to 200 guests.

In business settings, similar types of quantity discounts exist. For example, if IBM were to purchase just enough electrical wire to manufacture one computer, it would likely pay a higher price for the wire than if it were buying enough to make 1,000 computers. Buying enough electrical wire to make 1,000 computers allows IBM to get quantity discounts that would be unavailable otherwise. At the other extreme, if IBM were to make such a large number of computers that it outstripped its normal source for wire and had to resort to secondary, more expensive suppliers, the cost for electrical wire per computer could actually increase as production increased.

With these examples in mind, how can fixed cost be described as a cost that remains constant in total, and variable cost be described as a cost that remains constant per unit regardless of activity? For most decision situations, the fixed and variable cost information provided to managers assumes activity will be within the relevant range, that is, the normal operating range for the company. The relevant range can be depicted graphically as shown in Exhibit 4–6.

Exhibit 4–6
Relevant Ranges of
Fixed and Variable
Costs

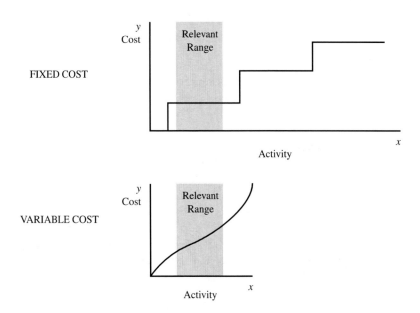

As shown in Exhibit 4–6, the fixed cost remains constant in total and the variable cost is constant per unit within the relevant range.

Decision makers usually assume activity levels will be within a company's relevant range. Activity levels may exceed or fall below the relevant range, such as when growth in production activity is significant. However, unless some evidence suggests the contrary, you should assume in our text discussion that the activity levels will be within the relevant range.

MIXED COSTS

The costs we have looked at thus far have been either completely fixed (the cost of entertainment at the party) or completely variable (the cost of food and drinks at the party). Some costs, however, are actually a combination of fixed and variable cost, and are known as mixed costs. A **mixed cost** is an individual cost that has elements of both fixed and variable costs.

mixed cost An individual cost that has both a fixed cost and a variable cost component. It also describes a company's total cost structure.

For decision-making purposes, it is useful to identify the fixed and variable components of a mixed cost. For example, consider the cost of electricity consumed in a manufacturing facility. When production lines are completely shut down on weekends, production is zero. Even without any production, however, the facility will still require minimal electricity to operate water heaters, refrigerators, and security lighting. This minimum cost of keeping the factory ready for use is the fixed portion of electricity cost. When production begins and production machinery cranks up, much more electric power is used. This incremental cost, which is driven by the actual use of the manufacturing facility, is the variable portion of electricity cost. Exhibit 4–7 shows a graph of a mixed cost.

Exhibit 4–7
Graph of a Mixed Cost

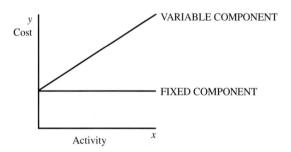

 Discussion Questions

4-5. Consider the costs involved in operating a fast-food restaurant such as McDonald's. What are three examples of activities that would have mixed costs?

Assume you are the sales manager for Hinds Wholesale Supply Company, and you are trying to estimate the cost of operating the fleet of delivery vehicles for the coming year. The only information you have is that $110,000 was spent last year to operate the fleet.

4-6. Would it help you to know which delivery vehicle costs are fixed and which are variable? Why?

4-7. What other information would you need to gather before being able to estimate next year's costs?

4-8. Why would the sales manager at Hinds Wholesale Supply Company be concerned about the cost of delivery vehicles?

Exhibit 4–7 shows that even when the activity level is at zero (the intercept of the *x*-axis and the *y*-axis), cost is incurred. This cost is the fixed element of the mixed cost. As activity increases, the cost rises from that initial point. This cost is the variable component of the mixed cost.

You may have observed that the graph in Exhibit 4–7 is quite similar to that in Exhibit 4–5 depicting the total cost of the climbing club party. This similarity occurs because total cost (which is composed of its fixed costs and its variable costs) could be described as one giant mixed cost.

 A User's View

Alan Raffan is the vice-president of finance for AFM Hospitality Inc. The company has its headquarters in Toronto and has an administrative office in Vancouver. The company works in the hospitality industry, particularly in hotels. It acts as the franchise holder for several different international hotel chains, including Ramada and Park Plaza hotels in Canada; it also manages hotels for a variety of clients.

"Our profitability is based on our ability to control costs," Raffan says. "We break our hotel business into different components (hotel rooms, food and beverage, and ancillary services). The types of costs vary from department to department, and we have to keep a close eye on them. For example, our costs of renting a room are mainly variable—the cost of the housekeeping services. But our front desk costs (reservations, registration, and checkout) tend to be fixed. The breakdown of these costs is very important to us."

We will see how AFM Hospitality Inc. uses this knowledge of cost behaviour in Chapter 5.

IDENTIFYING THE FIXED AND VARIABLE ELEMENTS OF A MIXED COST

We often know that a cost has behavioural characteristics of both fixed and variable costs, but we have no information to tell us how much of the cost is unaffected by the level of activity (fixed) and how much of it will increase as activity increases (variable). Mixed cost information is much more useful for cost control, planning, and decision-making purposes if the manager can determine which part of the mixed cost is fixed and which is variable. In this section we will discuss four methods commonly used to identify the fixed and variable elements of a mixed cost: the engineering approach, scatter graphing, the high-low method, and regression analysis.

The Engineering Approach

engineering approach
A method used to separate a mixed cost into its fixed and variable components using experts who are familiar with the technical aspects of the activity and associated cost.

The **engineering approach** relies on engineers or other professionals who are familiar with the technical aspect of the activity and the associated cost to analyze the situation and determine which costs are fixed and which are variable. This approach may employ time-and-motion studies or other aspects of scientific management.

For example, experts in the field of aviation and aircraft operations could analyze the cost of operating a corporate aircraft to determine which portion of the operating cost increases as aircraft usage increases and which portion of the cost remains constant. Based on the experts' industry experience and evaluations, they would then separate the fixed and variable components of this mixed cost.

Analysts would be likely to use flying time as the activity level base because hours of use will affect costs. They would then classify the cost of insurance and of renting hangar space in which to store the plane as fixed costs. Why? The insurance and rental costs are unaffected by the number of hours the plane may be flown. The cost of the airplane's battery will likely be classified as a fixed cost because the deterioration of this item and the need for replacement are affected more by the passing of time and very little by the number of flight hours.

Aviation experts would probably classify fuel costs and expected maintenance and repair costs as variable costs, as both depend on usage. For example, experts may estimate that a plane's engines require an overhaul every 2,000 hours of flight time.

 ## Discussion Questions

Again assume you are a sales manager for Hinds Wholesale Supply Company trying to estimate the cost of operating the fleet of delivery vehicles for the coming year.

4–9. Would you engage the services of an automotive expert to help separate costs into fixed and variable? Why or why not?

4–10. List four costs you (or the automotive expert) would identify as part of the cost of operating the fleet of delivery trucks. Classify each by its cost behaviour and the activity to which it relates.

4–11. If an expert determined that the fixed cost of operating each vehicle is $3,000 per year and the variable cost is $0.20 per kilometre, what would be the expected cost of operating the fleet? (Assume there are eight trucks, and they are driven an average of 40,000 kilometres each.)

The engineering approach to separating mixed cost relies on an expert's experience and judgment to classify costs as fixed or variable. It is often used when the company has no past experience concerning a cost's reaction to activity. In contrast, the other three methods we examine use historical data and mathematical computations to approximate the fixed and variable components of mixed cost.

Scatter Graphing

scatter graphing A method used to separate a mixed cost into its fixed and variable components by plotting historical activity and cost data to see how a cost relates to various levels of activity.

Scatter graphing plots historical activity and cost data on a graph to see how a cost relates to various levels of activity. The analyst places a straight line through the *visual centre* of the points plotted on the graph, so roughly half the dots are above the line and half are below the line, as shown in Exhibit 4–8.

With some simple calculations, an analyst can now approximate the fixed and variable elements of the cost being analyzed.

Exhibit 4–8
A Scatter Graph

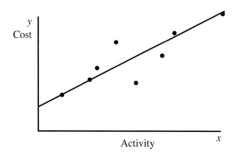

To demonstrate how scatter graphing is used, imagine you are again the sales manager for Hinds Wholesale Supply Company with the task of estimating the expected delivery vehicle maintenance cost for 2004. Your first step is to obtain relevant historical cost data. At your request, the accounting department provides you with the following maintenance cost information about the company's delivery vehicles for 2003:

Truck Number	Maintenance Cost
202	$2,000
204	1,600
205	2,200
301	2,400
422	2,600
460	2,200
520	2,000

You now ask yourself a couple of questions. First, is vehicle maintenance cost a fixed cost? Clearly it is not a fixed cost, because the cost is not the same for all trucks. Second, is this cost a variable cost? Well, if it is a variable cost, it varies based on some activity. After careful consideration, you determine that activity might be either (1) the number of kilometres driven or (2) the number of packages delivered. On request, the accounting department provides you with the following expanded data for 2003:

Truck Number	Maintenance Cost	Kilometres Driven	Packages Delivered
202	$2,000	15,000	1,200
204	1,600	11,000	1,000
205	2,200	24,000	1,500
301	2,400	30,000	1,500
422	2,600	31,000	500
460	2,200	26,000	1,000
520	2,000	20,000	2,000

Remember, if a cost is truly variable, it changes proportionately as activity changes. Let's consider kilometres driven first and see whether there is a proportional change in total vehicle maintenance cost as activity changes. Compare trucks 202 and 301. The kilometres driven for truck 301 are exactly twice as many as for truck 202. If vehicle maintenance cost is variable based on kilometres driven, then the cost for truck 301 should be twice the cost for truck 202, but it is not.

Now we look at packages delivered as the activity. Compare truck 204 with truck 422. Truck 204 delivered twice as many packages as truck 422. If vehicle maintenance cost is variable based on the number of packages delivered, the cost for truck 204 should be exactly twice the cost for truck 422. Again, it is not.

If a cost is neither fixed nor variable, then it is mixed, meaning it has both a fixed element and a variable element. This is the case with Hinds' delivery vehicle maintenance cost. Therefore, you must find a way to estimate the amount of fixed and variable costs associated with the maintenance cost if you are to reasonably predict the vehicle maintenance cost for 2004.

You have decided to use the scatter graph method to determine the fixed and variable elements of the vehicle maintenance cost. The first step is to plot the information for each observation (in this case, each delivery vehicle) on a graph. Remember, the vertical axis on a graph is the y-axis (total cost), and the horizontal axis is the x-axis (activity). Recall also that the independent variable, shown as the x-axis, is not affected by a change in y. However, the dependent variable value, shown on the y-axis, depends on the numerical value of the x variable. The assumption is that a change in x will lead to a change in y.

If a truck driver travels 1,000 kilometres, for example, Hinds must spend money on gasoline. In our case, driving is the independent (x) variable and the company's gasoline cost is the dependent (y) variable. Driving affects the company's gasoline cost; however, the reverse does not hold true. The mere purchase of gasoline, which increases the dependent (y) variable, will not cause a change in the number of kilometres driven.

For mixed cost calculations, the y variable is the cost affected by the activity and it is the cost you are trying to estimate. The x variable represents the activity you believe will affect the cost behaviour. Do not fall into the trap of thinking that the dependent variable (y) will be measured in dollars and the independent variable (x) will not. It is possible to predict a cost such as sales commissions, expressed in dollars, based on an activity such as sales, also expressed in dollars.

Recall the Hinds Wholesale Supply Company example. The data provided by the company's accounting department show two possible activity-cost pairs. The first pair is the number of kilometres driven and vehicle maintenance cost. The second pair is the number of packages delivered and vehicle maintenance cost.

We begin by graphing maintenance cost and kilometres driven. When we plot the data on a graph, we plot each observation as a pair of values. The maintenance cost for a particular vehicle, the dependent variable, is plotted using the index on the y-axis. The kilometres driven for the same vehicle, the independent variable, are plotted using the index on the x-axis. The position on the graph occupied by the plotted pair of numbers is called a *coordinate*. As the graph in Exhibit 4–9 indicates, each observation is represented by a dot.

Exhibit 4–9
Partial Scatter Graph for Hinds Company Vehicle Maintenance Cost and Kilometres Driven

DATA:

Truck Number	Maintenance Cost	Kilometres Driven
202	$2,000	15,000
204	1,600	11,000
205	2,200	24,000
301	2,400	30,000
422	2,600	31,000
460	2,200	26,000
520	2,000	20,000

The next step is to place a straight line through the visual centre of the plotted coordinates, which we have done in Exhibit 4–10.

In this exhibit it is easy to place the straight line through the points on the graph because they seem to line up in a nearly straight line on their own. This straight line effect occurs when the relationship of the two variables is relatively constant, or linear. The graph in Exhibit 4–10 suggests a relatively constant relationship between the kilometres driven (x) and maintenance cost (y). The straight line represents the behaviour of maintenance cost as it relates to the number of kilometres driven.

Exhibit 4–10
Completed Scatter Graph for Vehicle Maintenance Cost and Kilometres Driven

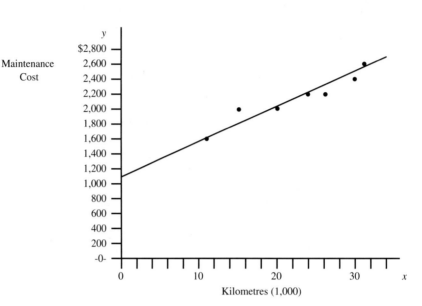

Now that we have a completed scatter graph for Hinds' vehicle maintenance cost, we can employ some simple calculations to approximate the fixed and variable portion of that cost. As you recall from earlier in the chapter:

Total Cost = Fixed Cost + Variable Cost

For total mixed costs we can modify the equation slightly as follows:

Total Mixed Cost = Fixed Cost Element + Variable Cost Element

When using the scatter graph method, we identify the fixed element of the maintenance cost first. Note that in Exhibit 4–10 the straight line that indicates the relationship of kilometres driven and maintenance cost intercepts the y-axis at $1,100. At this point, the x variable (kilometres) is zero, which suggests that when activity is zero, maintenance cost will still be $1,100. That $1,100 represents fixed cost. In the scatter graph method, fixed cost is determined simply by noting where the straight line intercepts the y-axis. Thus, in our example we now know the following information:

Total Mixed Cost = $1,100 + Variable Cost Element

Next, we find the variable cost per kilometre using simple mathematics. First we choose two points along the scatter graph line to determine the effect of the x variable on the y variable. Note: We select two points on the *scatter graph line,* not two points as plotted to represent our original data. Any two positions on the line are fine, but it is better to select points that are somewhat separated. That way, the error caused by our visual estimation in reading the graph will be small relative to the numerical difference between the two points selected.

As one coordinate for our variable cost per unit calculations, we select the point at which activity is zero and cost is $1,100. We then choose as our second point the coordinate at which the activity level is 34,000 kilometres and cost is $2,700. As the graph in Exhibit 4–11 indicates, we determined that coordinate by choosing a position on the line and following the lines to the *x*-axis and the *y*-axis. The locations on these axes indicate the cost and activity level represented by that position on the line.

The next step is to determine the mathematical difference between the two coordinates.

Exhibit 4–11
Scatter Graph with
Activity Points Selected

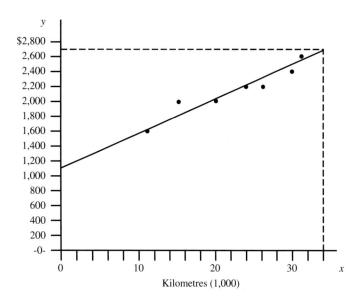

Kilometres	Cost
34,000	$2,700
(0)	(1,100)
34,000	$1,600

We can see from our calculations that the maintenance cost at 34,000 kilometres is $1,600 higher than it is for zero kilometres. What do you think caused the $1,600 difference? We assume it is the change in the activity level that causes changes in the cost. That is, it cost an additional $1,600 in maintenance cost to drive the 34,000 extra kilometres.

Now we can calculate the average amount of maintenance cost per kilometre caused by the additional activity. We do this by dividing the 34,000 kilometre difference into the $1,600 increased maintenance cost:

$1,600 ÷ 34,000 = $0.047059, or about 4.7 cents per kilometre

The calculations show that each additional kilometre of driving causes maintenance cost to rise by $0.047. If we add this information to the fixed cost information determined earlier, we can create a cost formula for vehicle maintenance cost:

Vehicle Maintenance Cost = $1,100 + ($0.047 per kilometre driven)

We have now used scatter graphing to separate maintenance cost into its fixed and variable components. With this information, we can project maintenance cost at any level of activity. To do this, we add the fixed cost to the activity multiplied by the cost per unit of activity. For example, the estimated maintenance cost for a single delivery truck that is to be driven 28,000 kilometres is $2,416, calculated as follows:

$1,100 + ($0.047 × 28,000) = $2,416

4-12. Based on the information obtained from the scatter graph, what would be the maintenance cost of operating one delivery truck if we expected the truck to be driven 25,000 kilometres next year?

4-13. Based on the information obtained from the scatter graph, what would be the maintenance cost of operating a fleet of delivery trucks? (Assume there are eight trucks, and they are driven an average of 25,000 kilometres each.)

Now we turn to the information the accounting department provided about the number of packages delivered. Then we use the scatter graphing method to plot maintenance cost as the dependent (y) variable and packages delivered as the independent (x) variable. Exhibit 4–12 shows a partial scatter graph of the maintenance cost and packages delivered.

We draw a straight line through the points depicted by the observations, as in Exhibit 4–13.

Note in Exhibit 4–13 that placing a straight line through the points on this graph is considerably more challenging than in the previous scatter graph. This is because a straight line could take any one of several paths through the points on the graph. Each of the lines seems to depict the relationship between maintenance cost and packages delivered, but none does a very good job. The reason for the difficulty is that the relationship between the variables is not linear. The question is, how do we use this method if the data do not have a clear linear relationship? The answer is, we don't. Before we employ the scatter graph method, we must be sure the activity

Exhibit 4–12
Partial Scatter Graph for Vehicle Maintenance Cost and Packages Delivered

DATA:

Truck Number	Maintenance Cost	Packages Delivered
202	$2,000	1,200
204	1,600	1,000
205	2,200	1,500
301	2,400	1,500
422	2,600	500
460	2,200	1,000
520	2,000	2,000

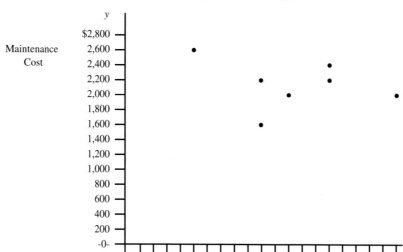

Exhibit 4–13
Completed Scatter
Graph for Vehicle
Maintenance Cost and
Packages Delivered

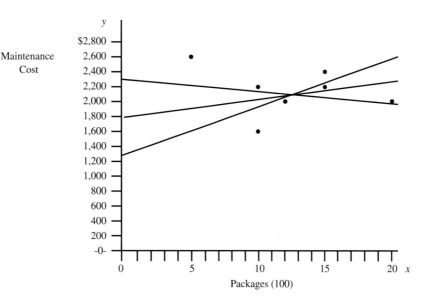

we have chosen has a relatively linear relationship with the cost in question. If we plot points on a graph and the coordinates resemble a random pattern with little linearity, the data do not indicate a constant relationship between the activity and the cost. In the case of a random pattern, any conclusions drawn from the data will be useless for predicting future cost, and may cause trouble if used. Once we see that random pattern, then, we should not use the packages delivered data to estimate the fixed and variable elements of vehicle maintenance cost.

Even if a scatter graph appears to represent a linear relationship between an activity and a cost, we must be cautious to not imply relationships that do not exist. For instance, if we tried to determine cost behaviour of vehicle maintenance cost by relating it to an activity such as the number of direct labour hours worked, we might possibly get mathematically reasonable results. However, common sense tells us that no relationship exists between direct labour hours and vehicle maintenance cost, so the results would be meaningless. A random guess would provide as good or better information. The activity and cost should have a clear, common sense relationship.

The High-Low Method

high-low method A method used to separate a mixed cost into its fixed and variable components using the mathematical differences between the highest and lowest levels of activity and cost.

Like the scatter graph approach, the **high-low method** uses historical data and mathematical computations to approximate the fixed and variable components of mixed cost. To illustrate the steps required by the high-low method, we review the following vehicle maintenance cost and activity data gathered for the Hinds Wholesale Supply Company:

Truck Number	Maintenance Cost	Kilometres Driven	
202	$2,000	15,000	
204	1,600	11,000	Low
205	2,200	24,000	
301	2,400	30,000	
422	2,600	31,000	High
460	2,200	26,000	
520	2,000	20,000	

The high-low method focuses on the mathematical differences between the highest and lowest observations. If we examine the data list, we see that the highest observation is 31,000 kilometres with a maintenance cost of $2,600. The lowest observation is 11,000 kilometres with a maintenance cost of $1,600.

Remember, our purpose is to find the amount of the fixed and variable elements of a mixed cost. With the high-low method, we focus on determining the variable component of the cost first. The calculations to determine variable cost per unit are similar to those used in scatter graphing. By comparing the differences in activity and cost between the highest observation and the lowest observation, we can calculate a per unit cost that describes the relationship shown by these differences as follows:

	Kilometres	Cost
High	31,000	$2,600
Low	(11,000)	(1,600)
Difference	20,000	$1,000

Notice the kilometre difference of 20,000 kilometres is accompanied by a cost difference of $1,000. So, to drive the extra 20,000 kilometres, the company spent $1,000 more in maintenance cost. We assume that the $1,000 increase in maintenance cost was caused exclusively by the increase in the number of kilometres from 11,000 to 31,000 kilometres. The cost per kilometre, then, is simply the $1,000 increased cost divided by the 20,000 additional kilometres as shown here:

$$\$1,000 \div 20,000 = \$0.05, \text{ or 5 cents per kilometre}$$

Before we calculate the fixed cost element, recall that total mixed cost is total fixed cost plus total variable cost (Total Mixed Cost = Fixed Cost Element + Variable Cost Element). The variable cost element can be calculated by multiplying the variable cost per unit by the activity. In this case we multiply the variable cost per kilometre by the number of kilometres. With what we have determined thus far, we can begin to construct a cost formula for vehicle maintenance cost as follows:

Total Mixed Cost = Fixed Cost Element + ($0.05 per kilometre driven)

For each of our observations (high and low), we know the total mixed cost and variable cost element. Therefore, we can easily determine the fixed cost element with simple calculations. Let's determine the fixed cost element associated with the high observation used in our example.

Total Mixed Cost = Fixed Cost Element + ($0.05 per kilometre driven)
$2,600 = ? + ($0.05 × 31,000)
$2,600 = ? + $1,550

To solve the equation, the fixed cost element must be $2,600 − $1,550, or $1,050, shown as follows:

Total Mixed Cost = Fixed Cost Element + ($0.05 per kilometre driven)
$2,600 = $1,050 + $1,550

We now know both the variable cost per kilometre and the total fixed cost of operating one of the delivery vehicles. To check our math, we can do the same calculation for the low observation, as follows:

Total Mixed Cost = Fixed Cost Element + ($0.05 per kilometre driven)
$1,600 = ? + ($0.05 × 11,000)
$1,600 = ? + $550

For the low observation, to solve the equation, fixed cost must be $1,600 − $550, or $1,050, as we see next.

Total Mixed Cost = Fixed Cost Element + ($0.05 per kilometre driven)
$1,600 = $1,050 + $550

The high-low method yields a fixed cost for maintenance of $1,050, and a variable cost of 5 cents per kilometre. As with scatter graphing, to estimate the mixed cost at a particular level of activity, we add the fixed cost to the activity multiplied by the cost per unit of activity. For example, the estimated maintenance cost for a single delivery truck that is to be driven 28,000 kilometres is $2,450, calculated as follows:

$$\$1,050 + (\$0.05 \times 28,000) = \$2,450$$

 ## Discussion Questions

4-14. Using the high-low method and the data from our example, what would be the maintenance cost for operating one of the delivery trucks if we expected the truck to be driven 25,000 kilometres next year?

4-15. Using the high-low method and the information from our Hinds Company example, what would be the maintenance cost for operating the fleet of eight trucks, if each is to be driven 25,000 kilometres on average?

When we compare the scatter graph method with the high-low method, we find that the fixed and variable cost results are somewhat different. If you were going to present your cost estimates to the vice president of marketing, which method would you use? Which provides the most dependable information? The scatter graph method is based on visual estimation whereas the high-low method is based on hard mathematics with no visual estimation. Does that make the high-low method better? No, because the high-low method considers only two observations. What if these two observations are not representative of the data in general? Then the cost behaviour conclusions will be flawed and possibly misleading.

Another drawback to the high-low method is that users cannot assess whether the data items have a linear relationship, which is necessary to find meaningful results. Because the scatter graph method considers all observations and indicates whether the data items have a linear relationship, practitioners regard it as superior to the high-low method, despite the fact that it is more time consuming to use and it is based on visual estimation.

Regression Analysis

regression analysis A method used to separate a mixed cost into its fixed and variable components using complex mathematical formulas.

least-squares method Another name for *regression analysis*.

linear regression analysis Another name for *regression analysis*.

Regression analysis, also called the **least-squares method** or **linear regression analysis,** is a mathematical approach to determining fixed and variable cost with statistical accuracy. The mathematical computations are complex and beyond the scope of this text; however, it is important to note that regression is a more reliable estimation technique than either the scatter graph method or the high-low method. Regression analysis uses the information contained in all the observations in a data set. That thoroughness makes it superior to the high-low method. Because it considers all these points of observation mathematically, rather than visually, regression analysis is also superior to the scatter graph method.

The basic mathematical equation for regression analysis follows:

$$Y = a + bX$$

When applying regression analysis to find the fixed and variable elements of a mixed cost, the variables in the regression equation are defined as follows:

$$Y = \text{total cost}$$
$$a = \text{fixed cost}$$
$$b = \text{unit variable cost}$$
$$X = \text{activity level}$$

Results of regression analysis would provide answers to the same questions that we posed for the scatter graph and the high-low methods. In fact, the results of regression analysis allow us to determine total cost, Y, for any given level of activity, X. Reexamine the basic regression analysis formula and compare it with the total cost equation.

$$Y = a + bX$$

Where: $Y = \text{total cost}$
$a = \text{fixed cost}$
$b = \text{unit variable cost}$
$X = \text{activity level}$

When we rewrite the equation, we see that it translates directly to our earlier total cost equation, as follows:

$$\text{Total Cost} = \text{Fixed Cost} + (\text{Unit Variable Cost} \times \text{Activity Level})$$

Although regression analysis is difficult to compute manually, most spreadsheet software packages provide easy-to-use regression functions. Also, almost all business calculators are programmed to compute linear regression problems. By reading your calculator's instruction manual, and practising a little, you can easily determine fixed and variable cost components of a mixed cost using linear regression.

No matter which of the methods a company uses to separate mixed costs into fixed and variable elements, the outcome of the mixed cost analysis is useful information for controlling costs, setting prices, and assessing profitability. Indeed, a variety of internal users of accounting information, from marketing managers to production managers, will want access to such cost behaviour information.

Whether large or small, simple or complex, managers of all companies must understand cost behaviour. Production managers at companies as diverse as Finning Ltd. and Campbell Soup Company need this information to plan and control their operations. Marketing managers at companies as different as General Motors and Gerber Baby Foods must know how costs react to activity if they are to do their jobs properly.

Once a determination has been made as to a cost's behaviour, an appropriate notation can be made in the accounting records to designate it as fixed, variable, or mixed. Then, the accounting system can produce reports sorted by cost behaviour. Internal reports providing cost behaviour information are valuable in a variety of decision-making settings. We will explore several of these settings in more detail in the next chapter.

SUMMARY

If managers are to plan and control their operations effectively, they must understand cost behaviour. Cost behaviour is the reaction of costs to changes in levels of business activity.

The most common cost behaviour patterns are fixed cost, variable cost, and mixed cost. A fixed cost is a cost that remains constant in total regardless of the level of activity within the relevant range. A variable cost is a cost that changes in total proportionately with changes in the level of activity within the relevant range. The relevant range is the range of activity within which fixed and variable cost assumptions are valid. A mixed cost is a cost that has both a fixed cost element and a variable cost element.

Over the years, several methods have been developed to separate a mixed cost into its fixed and variable components. The most commonly used methods are the engineering approach, scatter graphing, the high-low method, and regression analysis.

The engineering approach to separating a mixed cost into its fixed and variable components uses experts who are familiar with the technical aspects of the activity and associated cost. Scatter graphing separates a mixed cost into its fixed and variable components by plotting historical activity and cost data to see how a cost relates to various levels of activity. The high-low method uses the mathematical differences between the highest and lowest levels of activity and cost. Regression analysis uses complex mathematical formulas, but the results are more mathematically precise than those of the scatter graph or high-low method.

Regardless of the method that managers choose to separate mixed costs into fixed and variable elements, the analysis provides useful information for a myriad of business decisions.

KEY TERMS

cost behaviour, p. 119
engineering approach, p. 126
fixed cost, p. 119
high-low method, p. 133
least-squares method, p. 135
linear regression analysis, p. 135

mixed cost, p. 125
regression analysis, p. 135
relevant range, p. 124
scatter graphing, p. 127
variable cost, p. 120

REVIEW THE FACTS

1. What is cost behaviour?
2. For fixed costs, what happens to total cost as activity increases?
3. For fixed costs, what happens to the cost per unit as activity increases?
4. For variable cost, what happens to total cost as activity increases?
5. For variable cost, what happens to the cost per unit as activity increases?
6. With respect to cost behaviour, what is the relevant range?
7. Does the relevant range pertain to fixed costs, variable costs, or both fixed and variable costs?
8. What are the two elements of a mixed cost?
9. What are the four methods of separating a mixed cost into its two cost components?
10. Compare the high-low method to the scatter graph method. Which provides the more dependable information?
11. What is the major limitation of the high-low method?
12. What is another name for regression analysis?
13. If you desired the reliability of the regression analysis method but did not want to suffer through the difficulty of doing the mathematics manually, what would you do?

LO 2: Classifying Cost by Cost Behaviour

1. Indicate whether the following costs are more likely to be fixed (F), variable (V), or mixed (M) with respect to the number of units produced.

1. __V__ Direct material
2. __V__ Direct labour
3. __VM__ Cost of factory security guard
4. __F__ Straight line amortization on production equipment
5. __M__ Maintenance on production equipment
6. __M__ Maintenance on factory building
7. __V__ Cost of cleaning supplies used in the factory
8. __F__ Rent on the factory building
9. __F__ Salary for the two factory supervisors
10. __F__ Vice president of manufacturing's salary
11. __M__ Cost of electricity used in the factory
12. __V__ Cost of production machine lubricants

LO 2: Classifying Cost by Cost Behaviour

2. Assume that you are trying to analyze the costs associated with driving your car. Indicate whether the following costs are more likely to be fixed (F), variable (V), or mixed (M) with respect to the number of kilometres driven.

1. __F__ Cost of the car
2. __F__ Insurance cost
3. __V__ Maintenance cost
4. __V__ Cost of gasoline
5. __F__ The cost of a college parking permit
6. __F__ CAA membership

LO 2: Classifying Cost by Cost Behaviour

3. Assume that you are planning a large party. As you are trying to figure out how much the party will cost, you decide to separate the costs according to cost behaviour. Indicate whether the following costs are more likely to be fixed (F), variable (V), or mixed (M) with respect to the number of guests attending the party.

1. _____ Rent for the party hall
2. _____ Cost of the band
3. _____ Cost of cold drinks
4. _____ Cost of food
5. _____ Cost of party decorations
6. _____ Cost of renting tables and chairs

LO 2: Classifying Cost by Cost Behaviour

4. Assume that you have been assigned to analyze the costs associated with operating the law firm of Moore & Moore and Company. The law firm just moved into a new, large office building that it purchased last year. Indicate whether the following costs are more likely to be fixed (F), variable (V), or mixed (M) with respect to the number of lawyers working for the firm.

1. _____ Cost of the new office building
2. _____ Basic telephone service
3. _____ Cost of lawyers' salaries
4. _____ Cost of the receptionist's wages

LO 2: Classifying Cost by Cost Behaviour

5. Assume that you have been assigned to analyze the costs of a retail merchandiser, Auto Parts City. Indicate whether the following costs are more likely fixed (F), variable (V), or mixed (M) with respect to the dollar amount of sales.

1. _____ Cost of store rent
2. _____ Basic telephone service
3. _____ Cost of salaries for the two salespeople
4. _____ Cost of advertising
5. _____ Cost of store displays
6. _____ Cost of electricity
7. _____ Cost of merchandise sold

LO 4: Evaluating a Mixed Cost Situation

6. Assume that you work for Brier Manufacturing Company and have been asked to review the cost of delivery truck maintenance. The company president, Wilma Hudik, is dissatisfied with the accounting department's reluctance to calculate the fixed and variable cost of truck maintenance as it pertains to the number of units produced in the factory.

   The accounting department prepared the following scatter graph:

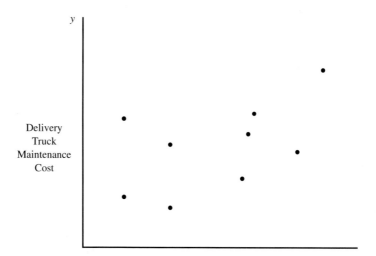

The accounting department personnel seem unable to use the graph to determine fixed and variable cost. The company president knows that regression analysis will provide mathematically accurate amounts for the fixed and variable truck maintenance cost, but no one in the accounting department seems to know how to do it.

REQUIRED:
Prepare a short memo to the president that details the feasibility of using the scatter graph and regression analysis to determine the fixed and variable components of delivery truck maintenance relative to the amount of factory production. In addition, your memo should recommend an alternative approach that could be used to evaluate the cost and cost behaviour of truck maintenance.

LO 5:   Use of a Scatter Graph for Separating Mixed Cost

7. Consider the following scatter graphs:

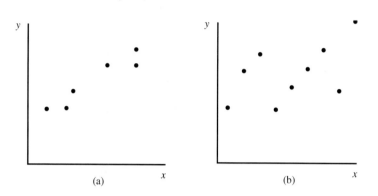

(a)   (b)

REQUIRED:
Which of the scatter graphs (a or b) do you think would be more appropriate for determining the fixed and variable portions of a mixed cost? Explain your reasoning.

LO 5:   Separating Mixed Cost Using the High-Low Method

8. The following information pertains to Prairie Sales Inc.:

2003	Information:	
	Sales	$2,300,000
	Selling expense	$ 347,000
2004	Information:	
	Sales	$2,860,000
	Selling expense	$ 369,400

REQUIRED:
Using the high-low method, determine the following:
a. The variable cost element for selling expense
b. The fixed selling expense
c. The selling expense that can be expected if sales are $2,500,000

LO 5:   Separating Mixed Cost Using the High-Low Method

9. The following information pertains to Dunn Manufacturing Company:

2003	Information:	
	Units packaged	14,500
	Packaging cost	$32,567
2004	Information:	
	Units packaged	15,300
	Packaging cost	$33,191

REQUIRED:

Using the high-low method, determine the following:
a. The variable cost element for packaging cost
b. The fixed packaging cost
c. The packaging cost that can be expected if 15,000 units are packaged

LO 5: Separating Mixed Cost Using the High-Low Method

10. The inspection department at Timmins Corporation inspects every third unit produced. The following information is available for the inspection department:

2003	Information:	
	Number of inspections	41,950
	Inspection cost	$77,273

2004	Information:	
	Number of inspections	48,600
	Inspection cost	$83,790

REQUIRED:

Using the high-low method, determine the following:
a. The variable cost element for inspection cost
b. The fixed inspection cost
c. The inspection cost that can be expected if 45,000 units are inspected

LO 5: Separating Mixed Cost Using the High-Low Method

11. The factory manager has asked you to analyze the cost of electricity used in the manufacturing facility. Information for 2003 and 2004 follows:

	2003	2004
Machine hours	100,000	120,000
Cost of electricity	$188,000	$221,600

REQUIRED:

a. Determine the variable rate for electricity per machine hour.
b. Determine the total fixed cost of electricity.
c. Determine the estimated cost of electricity for next year if machine hours are expected to be 122,500.

LO 5: Separating Mixed Cost Using the High-Low Method

12. The office manager has asked you to analyze the cost of service and supplies for the office copy machines. Information for 2002 and 2003 follows:

	2002	2003
Number of copies produced	52,550	77,800
Cost of service and supplies	$1,961.57	$2,592.82

REQUIRED:

a. Determine the variable cost per copy.
b. Determine the total fixed cost for service and supplies for the copy machines.
c. Determine the estimated cost of service and supplies for next year if 75,000 copies are expected to be made.

LO 5:   Separating Mixed Cost Using the High-Low Method

13. The production manager has asked you to analyze the cost of materials handling. Information for 2003 and 2004 follows:

	2003	2004
Number of parts handled	154,300	185,400
Materials handling cost	$9,244.77	$10,675.37

REQUIRED:

a. Determine the variable cost per part handled.
b. Determine the total fixed cost for materials handling.
c. Determine the estimated cost of materials handling if 160,000 parts are handled next year.

LO 5:   Separating Mixed Cost Using the High-Low Method

14. The sales manager has asked you to estimate the shipping cost that can be expected for 2005. Following is information for 2003 and 2004:

	2003	2004
Sales in units	15,000	18,000
Shipping cost	$30,000	$35,400

REQUIRED:

Estimate 2005 shipping cost assuming sales of 16,500 units.

LO 5:   Separating Mixed Cost Using the High-Low Method

15. The transportation manager has asked you to estimate the operating cost that can be expected for the company jet for 2004. Following is information for 2002 and 2003:

	2002	2003
Flight time in hours	1,250	1,875
Aircraft operating cost	$1,563,750	$2,148,125

REQUIRED:

Estimate the cost of operating the company jet for 2004 assuming that flight time will be 1,500 hours.

LO 5:   Separating Mixed Cost Using the High-Low Method

16. Tom Robinson is the owner of Robinson Fishing Guide Service. He is trying to estimate the cost of operating his fishing service next year. He expects to have 185 charters during 2005. The following information is available:

	2003	2004
Number of charters	150	190
Operating cost	$7,741	$8,601

REQUIRED:

Determine the estimated operating cost for 2005.

LO 5: Separating Mixed Cost Using the High-Low Method

17. The following information pertains to Yeung Manufacturing Inc. for 2003:

	Number of Purchase Orders Issued	Cost of Operating the Purchasing Department
Fourth quarter of 2002	2,500	$130,000
First quarter of 2003	1,000	80,000
Second quarter of 2003	1,500	110,000
Third quarter of 2003	2,000	115,000
Fourth quarter of 2003	3,000	140,000

REQUIRED:

Using the high-low method, determine the following:
a. The variable cost per purchase order
b. The fixed cost of operating the purchasing department for one quarter
c. The estimated cost of operating the purchasing department in 2004 assuming that 7,000 purchase orders will be issued. (Hint: Remember that the fixed cost for one year is four times the amount of fixed cost for one quarter.)

LO 5: Separating Mixed Cost Using the Scatter Graph Method

18. Refer to the information from problem 17.

REQUIRED:

Using the scatter graph method, determine the following:
a. The variable cost per purchase order
b. The fixed cost of operating the purchasing department for one quarter
c. The estimated cost of operating the purchasing department in 2004 assuming that 7,000 purchase orders will be issued. (Hint: Remember that the fixed cost for one year is four times the amount of fixed cost for one quarter.)

LO 5: Separating Mixed Cost Using the High-Low Method

19. The following information pertains to Lake Erie Bottled Spring Water Inc.:

	Number of Sales Invoices Processed	Cost of Operating the Invoicing Department
Fourth quarter of 2002	10,500	$50,574.65
First quarter of 2003	11,000	52,711.12
Second quarter of 2003	15,000	58,231.51
Third quarter of 2003	12,000	59,439.73
Fourth quarter of 2003	9,000	46,297.51

REQUIRED:

Using the high-low method, determine the following:
a. The variable cost per invoice processed
b. The fixed cost of operating the invoicing department for one quarter
c. The estimated cost of operating the invoicing department in 2004 assuming that 45,000 invoices will be processed. (Hint: Remember that the fixed cost for one year is four times the amount of fixed cost for one quarter.)

LO 5: Separating Mixed Cost Using the High-Low Method

20. The following information pertains to Jillian Munter & Associates:

	Number of Computers Repaired	Cost of Operating the Repair Department
Fourth quarter of 2001	125	$26,100.91
First quarter of 2002	130	26,529.16
Second quarter of 2002	110	25,400.65
Third quarter of 2002	105	25,212.91
Fourth quarter of 2002	115	25,799.88

REQUIRED:

Using the high-low method, determine the following:
a. The variable cost per computer repair
b. The fixed cost of operating the repair department for one quarter
c. The estimated cost of operating the repair department in 2003 assuming that 450 invoices will be processed. (Hint: Remember that the fixed cost for one year is four times the amount of fixed cost for one quarter.)

LO 5: Separating Mixed Cost Using the High-Low Method

21. The following information is taken from Manitoba Broom Manufacturing Company:

	Number of Brooms Produced	Total Production Cost
January	9,800	$17,100
February	7,000	14,992
March	8,000	16,000
April	7,500	15,500
May	10,100	17,200
June	9,000	17,000
July	10,500	19,000
August	11,600	20,000
September	10,600	18,200
October	8,500	16,800
November	12,100	20,500
December	11,000	18,000

REQUIRED:

Using the high-low method, determine the following:
a. The variable production cost per unit
b. The total fixed production cost
c. The expected production cost to produce 12,000 brooms

LO 5: Separating Mixed Cost Using the Scatter Graph Method

22. Refer to the information in problem 21.

REQUIRED:

Using the scatter graph method, determine the following:
a. The variable production cost per unit
b. The total fixed production cost
c. The expected production cost to produce 12,000 brooms

LO 5: Separating Mixed Cost Using the High-Low Method

23. Rolland Computer Training offers short computer courses. The number of course sessions offered depends on student demand. The following information pertains to 2004:

	Number of Sessions	Cost
First quarter	30	$ 75,000
Second quarter	35	78,000
Third quarter	15	42,000
Fourth quarter	20	48,000
Total	100	$243,000

REQUIRED:
Using the high-low method, determine the following:
a. The variable cost per session
b. The total fixed cost of operating the company
c. The expected cost for a quarter if 25 sessions are offered

LO 5: Separating Mixed Cost Using the Scatter Graph Method

24. Refer to the information in problem 23.

REQUIRED:
Using the scatter graph method, determine the following:
a. The variable cost per session
b. The total fixed cost of operating the company
c. The expected cost for a quarter if 25 sessions are offered

LO 5: Separating Mixed Cost Using the High-Low Method

25. The following information is taken from Edmonton Avionics Testing Service:

	Number of Tests Performed	Total Cost of Testing
January	61,000	$1,420,000
February	55,000	1,340,000
March	50,000	1,290,000
April	72,000	1,430,000
May	78,000	1,440,000
June	81,000	1,540,000
July	90,000	1,590,000
August	108,000	1,610,000
September	111,000	1,700,000
October	128,000	1,720,000
November	140,000	1,860,000
December	132,000	1,810,000

REQUIRED:
Using the high-low method, determine the following:
a. The variable cost per test
b. The total fixed cost of operating the testing facility
c. The expected cost for a month if 125,000 tests are performed

LO 5: Separating Mixed Cost Using the Scatter Graph Method

26. Refer to the information in problem 25.

REQUIRED:
Using the scatter graph method, determine the following:
  a. The variable cost per test
  b. The total fixed cost of operating the testing facility
  c. The expected cost for a month if 125,000 tests are performed

LO 5: Separating Mixed Cost Using the High-Low Method

27. The following information is for the Dhalia Supply Company:

	2002	2003
Sales	$1,000,000	$1,150,000
Costs:		
Cost of goods sold	$ 800,000	$ 920,000
Sales commissions	15,000	17,250
Store rent	3,000	3,000
Amortization	20,000	20,000
Maintenance cost	3,800	4,100
Office salaries	34,000	35,500

REQUIRED:
Assuming sales is the activity base, use the high-low method to determine the variable cost element and the fixed cost component of each of the costs just listed.

LO 5: Separating Mixed Cost Using the High-Low Method

28. The following information is for Brontford Production Company:

	2003	2004
Units produced	257,000	326,000
Costs:		
Direct material	$ 611,660	$ 775,880
Direct labour	1,662,790	2,109,220
Manufacturing overhead	1,781,820	1,868,760

REQUIRED:
Assuming units produced is the activity base, use the high-low method to determine the variable cost element and fixed cost component of each of the costs just listed.

LO 5: Separating Mixed Cost Using the High-Low Method

29. The following information is for the Steveston Gift Shop:

	2003	2004
Sales	$100,000	$150,000
Costs:		
Cost of goods sold	$ 75,000	$112,500
Sales commissions	5,000	7,500
Store rent	1,000	1,000
Amortization	500	500
Maintenance cost	200	250
Office salaries	5,000	6,000

REQUIRED:

a. Assuming sales is the activity base, use the high-low method to determine the variable cost element and the fixed cost component of each of the costs just listed.

b. Why is it useful to know the information requested in requirement a?

LO 4: Components of Mixed Cost

30. Consider the following mathematical formula:

$$Y = a + bX$$

REQUIRED:

Match the variables to the correct descriptions. Some variables have two correct matches.

1.	Y _____	a.	Independent variable
		b.	Variable cost per unit
2.	a _____	c.	Dependent variable
		d.	Total fixed cost
3.	b _____	e.	Activity
		f.	Total cost
4.	X _____		

LO 4: Describing the Methods of Separating Mixed Cost

31. Besides the engineering approach, this chapter discussed three methods of separating a mixed cost into its variable and fixed components.

REQUIRED:

Write a brief memo outlining the relative advantages and disadvantages of the high-low method, the scatter graph method, and regression analysis in estimating the variable and fixed portions of a mixed cost.

LO 4: Describing the Methods of Separating Mixed Cost

32. Mr. Robinson, the director of Medical Diagnostics Clinic, is preparing a presentation to the clinic's board of directors about the fee charged for thallium stress tests. Part of the presentation will include information about the variable cost element and fixed costs associated with the tests. The accounting department has provided the director with a report that details the monthly costs associated with the thallium stress tests and the number of tests performed each month. Mr. Robinson is contemplating whether to use the scatter graph method, the high-low method, or regression analysis to separate the cost into its variable cost element and fixed cost. The director has asked your help in choosing an appropriate method.

REQUIRED:

Prepare a short report to Mr. Robinson providing insight into the strengths and weaknesses of the scatter graph method, the high-low method, and regression analysis. Your report should conclude with support for a final recommendation of one of the methods of separating mixed cost.

LO 1, 2, 4, and 5: Analyzing a Situation Using Cost Behaviour

33. Sznadel Furniture Company has been in business for two years. When the business began, Sznadel established a delivery department with a small fleet of trucks. The delivery department was designed to be able to handle the substantial future growth of the company. As expected, sales for the first two years of business were low and activity in the delivery department was minimal.

In an effort to control costs, Sznadel Furniture Company's store manager is considering a proposal from a delivery company to deliver the furniture sold by Sznadel for a flat fee of $30 per delivery.

The following information is available regarding the cost of operating Sznadel's delivery department during its first two years of business.

	2002	2003
Number of deliveries	600	700
Cost of operating the delivery department	$25,480	$26,480

Sales and the number of deliveries are expected to increase greatly in the coming years. For example, sales next year will require an estimated 1,250 deliveries, while in 2005, it is expected that 1,775 deliveries will be required.

Due to the high growth rate, the store manager is concerned that the delivery cost will grow out of hand unless the proposal is accepted. He states that the cost per delivery was about $42.47 ($25,480/600) in 2002 and $37.83 ($26,480/700) in 2003. Even at the lower cost of $37.83, it seems the company can save about $7.83 ($30.00 − $37.83) per delivery. For 2005, the store manager believes the proposal can save the company about $13,898.25 (1,775 × $7.83).

REQUIRED:

Assume that you have been assigned to a group that has been formed to analyze the delivery cost of Sznadel Furniture Company. Your group should prepare a report and presentation that indicates the advantage or disadvantage of accepting the proposed delivery contract. Your report and presentation should not only include calculations to support your recommended course of action, but should also address the nonmonetary considerations of contracting with an outside source for delivery services.

LO 1, 2, 3, and 4: Addressing a Situation Using Cost Behaviour Concepts

34. John Reed is considering starting his own business. He has worked for a large corporation all his life and desires a change of pace. He is most interested in retail merchandising, but does not know what products his new business should sell. Mr. Reed is unsure about how to proceed with this major change in his life and has hired a consulting firm to help.

Assume that you have been assigned to the consulting group that will advise Mr. Reed.

REQUIRED:

Your group is to prepare a report that recommends a particular product line for Mr. Reed's new retail merchandising business. In addition, your report should recommend ways for Mr. Reed to gather information about the various costs associated with the merchandising business you have recommended. Finally, your report should explain how costs are classified as variable, fixed, and mixed costs, and why such classification by cost behaviour is important.

LO 1, 2, and 4: Analyzing a Situation Using Cost Behaviour

35. Sturgeon Bowling Inc. operates a small chain of bowling alleys in northern Alberta. Sturgeon's president, Al Palmer, is considering adding a supervised playground facility to each of the bowling alley properties. The playgrounds would require that a small addition be built onto each of the bowling alley buildings. Each playground would include a swing, a slide, climbing bars, and some other small-scale playground equipment. Each child would be charged an admission fee to use the facility. It is expected that parents will stay at the bowling alleys longer while their children are occupied in the playground area.

Mr. Palmer is interested in obtaining cost information relative to the proposed playground project. He understands that the more hours each playground area is open for business, the higher the cost of operating the playground will be. Beyond that, he knows nothing of cost behaviour patterns.

REQUIRED:

Prepare a memorandum to Mr. Palmer that describes the following:
a. The various variable, fixed, and mixed costs that are likely to be associated with the new playground facilities
b. The concept of fixed costs, variable costs, and mixed costs
c. Why an understanding of the methods available for estimating cost behaviour patterns will help him to better plan and control his operations

5

Business Decisions Using Cost Behaviour

Megan Cameron is the owner of Steveston T-Shirt Shop Company, one of many souvenir shops located on the pier in Steveston, British Columbia. The store sold 3,000 T-shirts during 2001 (the company's first year of operation), and Megan's accountant prepared the following multistep income statement for the year.

STEVESTON T-SHIRT SHOP COMPANY
Income Statement
For the Year Ended December 31, 2001

Sales		$60,000
Cost of Goods Sold		36,000
Gross Profit		$24,000
Operating Expenses:		
Selling Expenses	$18,000	
Administrative Expense	13,000	(31,000)
Operating Income (Loss)		$ (7,000)

Frankly, Megan was quite pleased with the results for 2001 because she did not expect the store to be profitable in its first year. As Megan planned for 2002, she figured she needed to increase sales by only 875 T-shirts to break even for the year. Her reasoning was based on the fact that each T-shirt cost $12.00 and sold for $20, resulting in $8 gross profit on each T-shirt ($20 − $12 = $8). If the shop sold 3,875 T-shirts, it would earn a gross profit of $31,000 (3,875 × $8), which would be exactly enough to cover the selling and administrative expenses of $31,000. If Megan met her sales goal, the store would break even in only its second year of operation.

As luck would have it, Steveston T-Shirt Shop Company sold exactly 3,875 T-shirts during the year ended December 31, 2002. Each T-shirt sold for exactly $20 and cost the company exactly $8.

Confident that the shop had broken even for the year, Megan excitedly opened the envelope from her accountant and found the following multistep income statement for 2002.

STEVESTON T-SHIRT SHOP COMPANY
Income Statement
For the Year Ended December 31, 2002

Sales		$77,500
Cost of Goods Sold		46,500
Gross Profit		$31,000
Operating Expenses:		
Selling Expense	$19,100	
Administrative Expense	13,525	(32,625)
Operating Income (Loss)		$(1,625)

Megan was disappointed and discouraged when she saw an operating loss of $1,625 for the year. She rechecked the arithmetic and her assumptions about what it would take to break even for 2002 and could not understand why the store had an operating loss.

Megan may not understand what happened, but after having studied Chapter 4 and its discussion of cost behaviour, you should understand the problem. Megan failed to consider that some costs are affected by changes in activity level and others are not. In this chapter, we explore cost-volume-profit analysis and see how business people use an understanding of this analytical technique to predict financial performance effectively. ■

LEARNING OBJECTIVES

After completing your work on this chapter, you should be able to do the following:

1. Describe the differences between a functional income statement and a contribution income statement.
2. Determine per unit amounts for sales, variable cost, and the contribution margin.
3. Determine the contribution margin ratio and explain its importance as a management tool.
4. Prepare and analyze a contribution income statement for a merchandising firm.
5. Describe cost-volume-profit (CVP) analysis and explain its importance as a management tool.
6. Use CVP analysis to determine the amount of sales required to break even or to earn a targeted profit.
7. Use CVP to perform sensitivity analysis.

THE CONTRIBUTION INCOME STATEMENT

As discussed in Chapter 4, separating costs by means of cost behaviour provides managers insight about forecasting cost at different levels of business activity. This valuable cost behaviour information, however, is not presented in either the multistep or the single-step income statement used for financial reporting. The traditional income statement prepared for external parties separates costs (expenses) as either product costs or period costs.

functional income statement An income statement that classifies cost by function (product cost and period cost).

An income statement that separates product and period costs is called a **functional income statement.** Management accountants have developed a special income statement format for internal use that categorizes costs by behaviour (fixed cost and variable cost) rather than by function (product cost and period cost). An income statement that classifies costs by behaviour is a **contribution income statement.** Now, do not be alarmed, as this new format is no more complicated than the income statements you studied in financial accounting. The main difference between the two is that the contribution income statements list variable costs first, followed by fixed costs. Note that the contribution income statement cannot be used for financial accounting information prepared for external decision makers; it is only used for internal decision-making purposes.

contribution income statement An income statement that classifies cost by behaviour (fixed cost and variable cost).

Purpose of the Contribution Income Statement

Let's return to the Steveston T-Shirt Shop Company example to see how a contribution income statement could have helped Megan better predict the future profitability of her merchandising company. The two income statements presented for Steveston (2001 and 2002) were functional income statements. Steveston's 2001 functional income statement is reproduced as Exhibit 5–1.

Exhibit 5–1
Steveston T-Shirt Shop Company's 2001 Functional Income Statement

STEVESTON T-SHIRT SHOP COMPANY
Functional Income Statement
For the Year Ended December 31, 2001

Sales		$ 60,000
Product Cost → Cost of Goods Sold		36,000
Gross Profit		$ 24,000
Operating Expenses:		
Period Cost → Selling Expense	$18,000	
Administrative Expense	13,000	(31,000)
Operating Income (Loss)		$ (7,000)

We see that the cost information in Exhibit 5–1 is separated into product cost (cost of goods sold) and period cost (selling expenses and administrative expenses). Next we will examine how Megan can convert her functional income statement into a contribution income statement.

First, Megan needs additional information about the cost behaviour of the expenses in Steveston's 2001 functional income statement. On request, Megan's accountant provides the following information:

Cost of goods sold	All variable
Selling expense	40% variable, so 60% must be fixed
Administrative expense	$11,200 fixed, so $1,800 must be variable

Discussion Question

5–1. With the cost behaviour information just presented, can you help Megan determine how much her profit will change if she sells 5,000 shirts in 2003? (Remember to look at the 2002 income statement shown at the beginning of the chapter.)

Now that she has Steveston's cost behaviour information, Megan can prepare a contribution income statement for 2001. The contribution income statement lists sales first, as does the functional income statement, with variable costs listed next. These costs are subtracted from sales to arrive at the contribution margin. **Contribution margin** is defined as the amount remaining after all variable costs have been deducted from sales revenue. The contribution margin is an important piece of information for managers, because it tells them how much of their company's original sales dollars remain after deduction of variable costs. This remaining portion of the sales dollars contributes to fixed costs and, once fixed costs have been covered, to profit. The contribution margin, then, is the amount available to contribute to covering fixed costs and ultimately toward profits for the income statement period.

contribution margin The amount remaining after all variable costs have been deducted from sales revenue.

Steveston's 2001 contribution income statement (through the contribution margin) is presented as Exhibit 5–2.

Exhibit 5–2
Steveston's Partial 2001 Contribution Income Statement

STEVESTON T-SHIRT SHOP COMPANY		
Partial Contribution Income Statement		
For the Year Ended December 31, 2001		
Sales		$60,000
Variable Cost:		
Cost of Goods Sold	$36,000	
Variable Selling Expense ($18,000 × 40%)	7,200	
Variable Administrative		
Expense ($13,000 – $11,200)	1,800	
Total Variable Cost		(45,000)
Contribution Margin (Sales Less Total Variable Cost)		$15,000

Finally, fixed costs are listed and subtracted from the contribution margin to arrive at operating income, as shown in Exhibit 5–3.

Like a functional income statement, the contribution income statement can be detailed or condensed depending on the needs of the information users. It can also be prepared showing the per unit costs and percentage of sales calculations. A condensed version of Steveston's 2001 contribution income statement, including per unit and percentage of sales figures, is presented as Exhibit 5–4.

Throughout the rest of the chapter we will use a condensed version of the contribution income statement.

Exhibit 5–3
Steveston's Completed
2001 Contribution
Income Statement

STEVESTON T-SHIRT SHOP COMPANY
Contribution Income Statement
For the Year Ended December 31, 2001

Sales		$60,000
Variable Cost:		
Cost of Goods Sold	$36,000	
Variable Selling Expense ($18,000 × 40%)	7,200	
Variable Administrative		
Expense ($13,000 – $11,200)	1,800	
Total Variable Cost		(45,000)
Contribution Margin (Sales Less Total Variable Cost)		$15,000
Fixed Cost:		
Fixed Selling Expense ($18,000 × 60%)	$10,800	
Fixed Administrative		
Expense	11,200	
Total Fixed Cost		(22,000)
Operating Income (Loss)		$ (7,000)

Discussion Questions

5–2. Why is the gross margin found on the functional income statement different from the contribution margin found on the contribution income statement?

5–3. Why is the operating loss shown on Steveston's 2001 contribution income statement exactly the same as the operating loss shown on the company's 2001 functional income statement?

Looking at the per unit column in Exhibit 5–4, we note that the contribution margin per unit is $5. We calculate this by dividing the total contribution margin of $15,000 by the number of units sold—in this case 3,000 ($15,000 / 3,000 = $5). The $5 per unit contribution margin means that for every T-shirt sold, the sale generates $5 to contribute toward fixed costs. Then, once fixed costs have been covered, $5 per T-shirt sold contributes to profit. That is, if Steveston sells one more shirt for $20, then the $20 selling price less the $15 variable cost leaves $5. The contribution margin contributes toward fixed cost first, then to profits.

Exhibit 5–4
Steveston's Condensed
2001 Contribution
Income Statement

STEVESTON T-SHIRT SHOP COMPANY
Contribution Income Statement
For the Year Ended December 31, 2001

	Total	Per Unit	Sales (%)
Sales in Units	3,000	1	
Sales	$60,000	$20	100
Variable Cost	45,000	15	75
Contribution Margin	$15,000	$ 5	25
Fixed Cost	22,000		
Operating Income (Loss)	$ (7,000)		

contribution margin ratio
The contribution margin
expressed as a percentage
of sales.

Note in the percentage column of Exhibit 5–4 that the contribution margin is 25 percent of sales. When the contribution margin is expressed as a percentage of sales, it is called the **contribution margin ratio.**

The contribution margin ratio is calculated by dividing the total contribution margin by total sales, or by dividing the per unit contribution margin by per unit selling price, as follows:

$$\frac{\text{Total Contribution Margin}}{\text{Total Sales}} = \text{Contribution Margin Ratio}$$

or

$$\frac{\text{Per Unit Contribution Margin}}{\text{Per Unit Selling Price}} = \text{Contribution Margin Ratio}$$

In the case of Steveston T-Shirt Shop Company, the calculations are as follows:

$$\frac{\$15,000}{\$60,000} = 25\%$$

or

$$\frac{\$5}{\$20} = 25\%$$

The contribution margin ratio is the same whether it is computed using total figures or per unit figures, because the contribution margin is based on sales minus only variable costs. Thus, the variable costs and contribution margin change in direct proportion to sales. This proportional relationship holds true whether we are using per unit amounts or amounts in total.

In our example, the 25 percent contribution margin ratio means that, of each sales dollar, 25 percent (or 25 cents) is available to contribute toward fixed cost and then toward profit.

 Discussion Question

5–4. If Steveston's sales increase by $20,000, and the contribution margin ratio is 25%, by how much will profits increase?

The contribution income statement is a wonderful management tool because it allows managers to see clearly the amounts of fixed and variable costs incurred by the company. Understanding which costs are variable and which are fixed is essential if managers are to reasonably predict future costs. More importantly, a solid understanding of the contribution income statement approach and the concept of the contribution margin and contribution margin ratio is the backbone of another important decision-making tool: cost-volume-profit analysis.

COST-VOLUME-PROFIT ANALYSIS

cost-volume-profit (CVP) analysis The analysis of the relationship between cost and volume and the effect of these relationships on profit.

As its name implies, **cost-volume-profit (CVP) analysis** is the analysis of the relationships between cost and volume (the level of sales), and the effect of those relationships on profit. In this section, we examine how managers can use CVP concepts to predict sales levels at which a firm will break even or attain target profits. CVP analysis is a useful tool for managers, business owners, and potential business owners for determining the profit potential of a new company or the profit impact of changes in selling price, cost, or volume on current businesses.

Thousands of businesses are started every day. Unfortunately, most of them fail a short time later, and the people who start these businesses suffer significant financial and emotional hardship. Such hardships might be avoided if new business owners used CVP analysis to evaluate the potential profit of their business ventures. With CVP analysis, a new business owner can discover potential disaster before starting the business, thereby preserving savings that could be used more productively elsewhere.

Breakeven

breakeven Occurs when a company generates neither a profit nor a loss.

break-even point The sales required to achieve breakeven. This can be expressed either in sales dollars or in the number of units sold.

We begin our coverage of CVP analysis with a discussion of breakeven. **Breakeven** occurs when a company generates neither a profit nor a loss. The sales volume required to achieve breakeven is called the **break-even point.** Because most businesses exist to earn a profit, why would managers be interested in calculating a break-even point? In at least two situations this kind of information is valuable. First, the break-even point will show a company how far product sales can decline before the company will incur a loss. This information could provide the encouragement to continue in business, or may provide an early warning of impending business failure. Second, owners and managers may use break-even analysis when starting a business, just as Megan did with the Steveston T-Shirt Shop Company. Recall that Steveston experienced a $7,000 operating loss in its first year of operation, but Megan expected the loss because she understood most businesses are not profitable in their first year. Her break-even prediction for Steveston's second year, however, failed to allow for certain cost increases as sales increased.

With our understanding of cost behaviour and the contribution income statement, we can predict the level of sales that Steveston will need to break even for the year.

Let's look again at the 2001 contribution income statement for Steveston T-Shirt Shop Company, reproduced in Exhibit 5–5.

Exhibit 5–5
Steveston's Condensed 2001 Contribution Income Statement

STEVESTON'S T-SHIRT SHOP COMPANY
Contribution Income Statement
For the Year Ended December 31, 2001

	Total	Per Unit	Sales (%)
Sales in Units	3,000	1	
Sales	$60,000	$20	100
Variable Cost	45,000	15	75
Contribution Margin	$15,000	$ 5	25
Fixed Cost	22,000		
Operating Income (Loss)	$ (7,000)		

Managers who use CVP analysis must apply simple formulas to obtain useful information. Understanding and applying these formulas during this course should be relatively simple, but remembering them when you are actually working as a manager may be difficult. To make these formulas easier to remember, we will relate them to the most basic math used in an income statement, beginning with sales minus cost equals profit. Next, recall that cost can be broken down into variable and fixed cost. We use this information to derive a basic CVP equation, as shown in Exhibit 5–6.

Exhibit 5–6

Basic CVP Equation

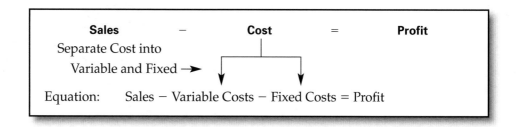

| Sales | − | Cost | = | Profit |

Separate Cost into
Variable and Fixed →

Equation: Sales − Variable Costs − Fixed Costs = Profit

The basic equation for CVP analysis in Exhibit 5–6 requires that the costs be identified as fixed or variable, and that any mixed cost be separated into its fixed and variable components. In the examples that follow, we assume costs have been properly classified as fixed or variable.

Managers can calculate the break-even point based either on units or on sales dollars. We will demonstrate the process in units first, and then in sales dollars.

Break-Even Point in Units   To illustrate how to find the break-even point in units, we examine the Steveston T-Shirt Shop Company example. As shown in Exhibit 5–5, the selling price per T-shirt is $20, the variable cost is $15 per shirt, the contribution margin is $5 per T-shirt, and fixed costs total $22,000 per year. With this information, we can determine the number of T-shirts Steveston must sell to achieve a break-even point by dividing the contribution margin per unit into the total fixed cost, as shown in the following CVP formula:

CVP Formula 1—Break-Even Point in Units

$$\frac{\text{Total Fixed Cost}}{\text{Contribution Margin Per Unit}} = \text{Break-Even Point in Units}$$

Using the information from Steveston, we calculate the following:

$$\frac{\$22,000}{\$5} = 4,400 \text{ T-shirts}$$

By using this simple formula (and our knowledge of the cost behaviour patterns associated with Steveston T-Shirt Shop Company), we see that if Steveston had sold exactly 4,400 T-shirts in 2002, the company would have broken even for the year. We can prove this fact if we use the equation from Exhibit 5–6 and the information from Steveston as follows:

Sales	−	Variable Costs	−	Fixed Costs	=	Profit
(4,400 × $20)	−	(4,400 × $15)	−	$22,000	=	Profit
$88,000	−	$66,000	−	$22,000	=	$ 0

We can also prove it by preparing a contribution income statement based on the results of our calculation, as shown in Exhibit 5–7.

Break-Even Point in Sales Dollars   Because business performance is measured in total dollar sales and in the number of units of product sold, managers also find it useful to have breakeven presented in both sales dollars and unit sales. To demonstrate the calculation of the break-even point in sales dollars, we once again use the information provided by Steveston T-Shirt Shop Company's contribution income statement in Exhibit 5–5.

When calculating the break-even point in sales dollars, we divide the contribution margin ratio into total fixed cost, as shown in the second of the CVP formulas.

Exhibit 5–7
Steveston's Condensed
2002 Contribution
Income Statement

STEVESTON T-SHIRT SHOP COMPANY
Projected Contribution Income Statement
For the Year Ended December 31, 2002

	Total	Per Unit	Sales (%)
Sales in Units	4,400	1	
Sales	$88,000	$20	100
Variable Cost	66,000	15	75
Contribution Margin	$22,000	$ 5	25
Fixed Cost	22,000		
Operating Income	$ 0		

CVP Formula 2—Break-Even Point in Sales Dollars

$$\frac{\text{Total Fixed Cost}}{\text{Contribution Margin Ratio}} = \text{Break-Even Point in Sales Dollars}$$

Using the information from Steveston's contribution income statement, we know that total fixed cost is $22,000 and the contribution margin ratio is 25 percent. The break-even point calculation is

$$\frac{\$22,000}{25\%} = \$88,000 \text{ Sales Dollars}$$

A quick review of the contribution income statement in Exhibit 5–7 shows that our calculation of $88,000 sales at the break-even point is correct.

We have examined the calculation of a break-even point in required units and in sales dollars. As stated earlier, however, companies are not in business to break even. Rather, they are usually interested in earning profits. In the next section, we discuss how the break-even calculations are modified to predict a company's profitability.

Predicting Profits Using CVP Analysis

Megan Cameron now knows that her T-shirt business must sell 4,400 T-shirts to break even, assuming of course that the T-shirt selling price and the variable and fixed costs remain unchanged. Megan can also use CVP analysis to predict Steveston's profit for any given level of sales above the break-even point. Assume, for example, that Steveston expects to sell 7,500 shirts in 2003. Megan can quickly predict the expected profit at that sales level by preparing a contribution income statement, such as that in Exhibit 5–8.

STEVESTON T-SHIRT SHOP COMPANY
Projected Contribution Income Statement
For the Year Ended December 31, 2003

	Total	Per Unit	Sales (%)
Sales in Units	7,500	1	
Sales	$150,000	$20	100
Variable Cost	112,500	15	75
Contribution Margin	$ 37,500	$ 5	25
Fixed Cost	22,000		
Operating Income	$ 15,500		

If we did not want to take the time required to construct an actual contribution income statement, we could calculate the same operating income using the following basic CVP equation shown in Exhibit 5–6.

Sales	–	Variable Costs	–	Fixed Costs	=	Profit
(7,500 × $20)	–	(7,500 × $15)	–	$22,000	=	Profit
$150,000	–	$112,500	–	$22,000	=	$15,500

The sales figure in this calculation is the number of T-shirts multiplied by the selling price per unit (7,500 × $20 = $150,000). Variable cost is the number of T-shirts sold multiplied by the variable cost per unit (7,500 × $15 = $12,500). The fixed cost of $22,000 remains the same in total. With these three figures in place, simple arithmetic gave us the expected profit of $15,500 if 7,500 T-shirts are sold.

Projecting Sales Needed to Meet Target Profits Using CVP Analysis

Using CVP analysis to project profits at a given level of sales is only one application of this technique. Next we explore how to use CVP analysis when price and cost information are known, and a manager wants to determine the sales required to meet a specific target profit objective. As with the break-even point, we can apply CVP analysis to determine the sales needed to meet target profits in either units or sales dollars.

Projecting Required Sales in Units   Assume Megan targets $27,000 as Steveston's profit for 2003. By making a simple addition to the formula we used to calculate the break-even point, Megan can determine how many T-shirts Steveston must sell to earn that target profit. The modified formula is as follows:

CVP Formula 3—Unit Sales Required to Achieve Target Profits

$$\frac{\left(\text{Total Fixed Cost + Target Profit}\right)}{\text{Contribution Margin Per Unit}} = \text{Required Unit Sales}$$

Recall that the contribution margin is the amount available to contribute to covering fixed cost first, and then profits. When considering the break-even point, we calculated the number of units required simply to cover the fixed cost. In our present discussion, we are looking for the number of units required not only to cover the fixed cost, but also to achieve a specific target profit. As shown in CVP formula 3, we simply add the target profit to the total fixed cost and then divide the sum by the contribution margin per unit. This equation will tell us how many units must be sold to cover all the fixed cost and to attain the target profit. Using the information from Steveston, the calculation is as follows:

$$\frac{\left(\$22,000 + \$27,000\right)}{\$5} = \text{Required Unit Sales}$$

or

$$\frac{\$49,000}{\$5} = 9,800 \text{ T-Shirts}$$

We see, then, that with a fixed cost of $22,000 and a contribution margin per unit of $5, Steveston will need to sell 9,800 T-shirts to earn $27,000 profit.

Discussion Question

5–5. How would you prove to Megan that 9,800 T-shirts must be sold to earn a $27,000 profit?

Projecting Required Sales in Dollars To demonstrate the calculation of the sales dollars required to attain target profits, we once again use the information provided by Steveston T-Shirt Shop Company's contribution income statement in Exhibit 5–5.

We use the contribution margin ratio as the denominator in the CVP formula, instead of the unit contribution margin, as follows:

CVP Formula 4—Sales Dollars Required to Achieve Target Profits

$$\frac{\left(\text{Total Fixed Cost} + \text{Target Profit}\right)}{\text{Contribution Margin Ratio}} = \text{Required Sales Dollars}$$

With the information from Steveston, the calculation is as follows:

$$\frac{\left(\$22,000 + \$27,000\right)}{25\%} = \text{Required Sales Dollars}$$

or

$$\frac{\$49,000}{25\%} = \$196,000 \text{ in Sales}$$

 Discussion Question

5–6. How would you prove to Megan that sales must total $196,000 to earn a $27,000 profit?

In this section we introduced you to four cost-volume-profit formulas, as summarized in Exhibit 5–9.

Exhibit 5–9
Cost-Volume-Profit
Formulas

Formula	Calculation	Purpose
CVP Formula 1	$\dfrac{\text{Total Fixed Cost}}{\text{Contribution Margin Per Unit}}$	To determine the break-even point in units
CVP Formula 2	$\dfrac{\text{Total Fixed Cost}}{\text{Contribution Margin Ratio}}$	To determine the break-even point in sales dollars
CVP Formula 3	$\dfrac{\left(\text{Total Fixed Cost} + \text{Target Profit}\right)}{\text{Contribution Margin Per Unit}}$	To determine the unit sales required to achieve a target profit
CVP Formula 4	$\dfrac{\left(\text{Total Fixed Cost} + \text{Target Profit}\right)}{\text{Contribution Margin Ratio}}$	To determine the sales dollars required to achieve a target profit

These formulas are used daily by managers of manufacturing, merchandising, and service type companies as they attempt to predict the future performance of their firms. Regardless of the career you choose, if it involves business you will see these formulas again and will be using them much sooner than you might think.

Cost-Volume-Profit Graph

In addition to the calculations we have been studying, CVP analysis can also be depicted graphically. The graph used to present CVP analysis is similar to those used in the discussion of cost behaviour in Chapter 4. A CVP graph for Steveston T-Shirt Shop Company is presented as Exhibit 5–10.

Exhibit 5–10
CVP Graph—Steveston
T-Shirt Shop Company

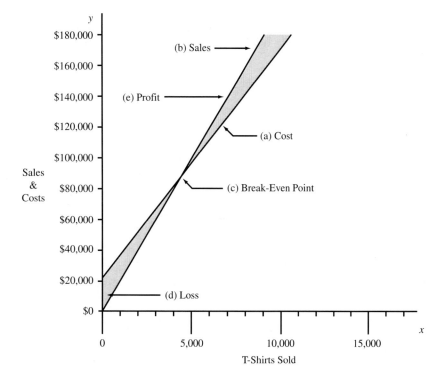

The main difference between the graph in Exhibit 5–10 and those in Chapter 4 is the graph in Exhibit 5–10 shows sales in addition to variable and fixed costs. The cost line (a) on the graph is exactly like those in Chapter 4. Note that this line intercepts the y-axis at $22,000, the total fixed cost for Steveston T-Shirt Shop Company. Thus, Steveston incurs $22,000 fixed cost even if the company sells no T-shirts. The cost line slopes upward at $15 for each T-shirt sold (variable cost).

Now consider the sales line (b) on the graph. If Steveston sells no T-shirts, there would obviously be no sales dollars, which explains why the sales line intercepts the y-axis at zero. The line slopes upward at $20 for every T-shirt sold. The point at which the cost line and the sales line cross (c) is Steveston's break-even point, which we know from our calculations in this chapter to be 4,400 T-shirts, or $88,000 in sales revenue. The loss area (d) on the graph and the profit area (e) represent a loss and profit, respectively, for Steveston. Thus, if Steveston sells fewer than 4,400 T-shirts, the company will experience a loss. If it sells more than 4,400 T-shirts, the company will earn a profit.

Discussion Question

5-7. Using the CVP graph in Exhibit 5–10, can you plot the level of sales (in units and dollars) where Steveston will earn a profit of
  a. $10,500?
  b. $27,000?

The CVP graph is a useful management tool. Although it should not take the place of the calculations we have demonstrated thus far in this chapter, it has a distinct advantage over the calculations in that it allows managers to view the entire cost-volume-profit picture. Megan Cameron can, for example, assess Steveston's profit potential at any level of business within the relevant range of activity.

 Discussion Question

5-8. If Megan is faced with competition from a new T-shirt shop in town, and is forced to lower her selling price to $18 per T-shirt, how much profit can she expect in 2002? (Assume that Megan expects to sell 9,800 shirts and the cost information stays the same.)

To demonstrate the basics of CVP analysis, we have assumed that the selling price per unit, variable costs per unit, and total fixed cost all remained unchanged. Businesses, however, experience daily pressures that can cause each of these items to change. CVP analysis can adapt to any such change.

Now that we have covered the basics, we are ready to put CVP to perhaps its greatest use: sensitivity analysis.

Sensitivity Analysis—What If?

sensitivity analysis A technique used to determine the effect on cost-volume-profit when changes are made in the selling price, cost structure (variable and/or fixed), and volume used in the CVP calculations. Also called "what if" analysis.

Sensitivity analysis is a technique used to determine the effect on CVP when changes are made in the selling price, cost structure (variable and/or fixed), and volume used in the calculations. Sensitivity analysis is also called "what if?" analysis. Managers are often looking for answers to the following types of questions, in terms of the effect on projected profits: "What if we raised (or lowered) the selling price per unit?" "What if variable cost per unit increased (or decreased)?" and "What if fixed cost increased (or decreased)?" Sensitivity analysis can provide those answers.

One other item to note before we proceed with the discussion of sensitivity analysis is that we will be using only CVP formula 3 and CVP formula 4. Although sensitivity analysis can certainly be used to assess the effect of changes in selling price, variable cost, and fixed cost on breakeven, all our examples will include target profits.

To demonstrate how sensitivity analysis is used, we return to Megan Cameron and the Steveston T-Shirt Shop Company. Assume 2003 has now ended. Steveston's contribution income statement for the year is presented as Exhibit 5–11.

Exhibit 5–11
Steveston's Condensed
2003 Contribution
Income Statement

STEVESTON T-SHIRT SHOP COMPANY
Contribution Income Statement
For the Year Ended December 31, 2003

	Total	Per Unit	Sales (%)
Sales in Units	9,500	1	
Sales	$190,000	$20	100
Variable Cost	142,500	15	75
Contribution Margin	47,500	$ 5	25
Fixed Cost	22,000		
Operating Income	$ 25,500		

Megan is quite pleased with the $25,500 profit Steveston earned in 2003 and is aiming for a target profit of $27,000 in 2004 (the same target profit as 2003). The problem is that a new T-shirt shop just opened three doors from Steveston. Megan feels she must lower her selling price to $18 due to competitive pressure and wants to know how many T-shirts Steveston must now sell to attain the $27,000 target profit. Megan can use CVP analysis to determine the required sales level to achieve a targeted profit even if she changes her selling price.

Change in Selling Price

If the selling price changes but variable cost does not, the number of units required to attain a target profit is determined using CVP formula 3 and a recalculated contribution margin based on the new selling price. In the case of Steveston T-Shirt Shop Company, the new contribution margin is $3 (new selling price of $18 − variable cost of $15). We now apply this contribution margin to the formula. (Remember, the fixed cost is unchanged.)

$$\frac{(\$22,000 + \$27,000)}{\$3} = \text{Required Unit Sales}$$

or

$$\frac{\$49,000}{\$3} = 16,334 \text{ T-shirts}$$

Our calculations show that with a lower selling price, as reflected in the revised contribution margin per unit, Steveston must sell 16,334 T-shirts to attain the target profit of $27,000.

 Discussion Question

5-9. How would you prove to Megan that 16,334 T-shirts must be sold to earn a $27,000 profit if she reduces the selling price per T-shirt from $20 to $18?

We can also calculate the sales dollars required to attain the target profit of $27,000. To do this, we first calculate a new contribution margin ratio and then use CVP formula 4 to determine the sales dollars needed to earn the target profit. The new contribution margin ratio is 16.67 percent (rounded), which is calculated by dividing the new selling price ($18) into the new contribution margin ($3). We now apply this new information to CVP formula 4.

$$\frac{(\$22{,}000 + \$27{,}000)}{16.67\% \text{ (rounded)}} = \text{Required Sales Dollars}$$

or

$$\frac{\$49{,}000}{16.67\% \text{ (rounded)}} = \$293{,}941 \text{ Sales Dollars (rounded)}$$

By applying the revised contribution margin ratio to CVP formula 4, we see that Steveston will need $293,941 in sales to achieve the target profit of $27,000.

Discussion Questions

5–10. How would you prove to Megan that sales must total $293,941 to earn a $27,000 profit if she reduces the selling price per T-shirt from $20 to $18?

5–11. Why must we calculate a new contribution margin ratio when the per unit selling price changes?

5–12. Under what other circumstances must we calculate a new contribution margin ratio?

If Megan reduces her selling price to $18, then Steveston must sell 16,334 T-shirts in 2004 to earn the target profit of $27,000. Megan believes it would be impossible to sell that many shirts, so she begins to consider alternative ways to earn a $27,000 profit in a competitive environment.

Notice that Megan was able to determine by CVP analysis that her business may be in trouble. The analysis itself, however, does nothing whatever to solve the problem—that is up to Megan. Management accounting can provide the informational tools to help managers and business owners spot problems, but it is ultimately up to the manager or owner to make the decisions and solve the problems.

Discussion Question

5–13. If Megan must lower her selling price to $18 per shirt to be competitive, and it would be impossible to sell 16,334 T-shirts, what are some of the alternatives she might consider to attain the $27,000 profit?

Change in Variable Cost and Fixed Cost

Alternatives to changing the selling price include changing variable cost or fixed cost. Because Megan believes the selling price per T-shirt must be $18, either the variable cost per unit or the total fixed cost must be reduced. We start with an analysis of possible changes in variable cost.

First, we must analyze how Steveston determined its original variable cost. We determine per unit variable cost by dividing the total variable cost by the number of units sold. Recall from the earlier discussion and Exhibit 5–4 that Steveston sold 3,000 T-shirts during 2001, and total variable cost was $45,000. Therefore, the variable cost per unit was calculated as $15 ($45,000 variable cost / 3,000 units sold).

To analyze how a change in variable cost will affect the variable cost per unit of $15, we must look at the three components of per unit variable cost: the cost of each T-shirt, the variable selling expenses, and the variable administrative expenses. We need to know what portion of the $15 variable unit cost relates to each component. We can determine these portions by dividing the 3,000 units sold into each of the three cost components. We use 3,000 because that number of units caused these costs to be incurred. We find the cost of each variable cost component in the contribution income statement presented in Exhibit 5–3. The cost and per unit calculation for each component are presented in Exhibit 5–12.

Exhibit 5–12
Analysis of Steveston's Variable Cost Components

	Total Cost		Units Sold		Unit Cost
Cost of Goods Sold (T-shirts)	$36,000	÷	3,000	=	$12.00
Variable Selling Expenses	7,200	÷	3,000	=	2.40
Variable Administrative Expenses	1,800	÷	3,000	=	0.60
Variable Cost	$45,000 Total				$15.00 Per Unit

Megan does not believe any change can be made in either the variable selling expenses or the variable administrative expenses. Any possible reduction in variable cost, then, must be in the cost of the T-shirts. Our calculations in Exhibit 5–12 show that the per unit cost of each T-shirt is $12.00.

Assume Megan has contacted her shirt supplier which has agreed to lower its price from $12.00 to $9.50 per T-shirt. This reduction of $2.50 ($12.00 − $9.50 = $2.50) will reduce Steveston's variable cost from $15.00 per shirt to $12.50 per shirt ($15.00 − $2.50 = $12.50). The new contribution margin is $5.50 ($18.00 selling price − $12.50 variable cost = $5.50), and the new contribution margin ratio is 30.556 percent ($5.50 contribution margin / $18 selling price = 0.30556 or 30.556 percent rounded).

Now consider a change in Steveston's fixed cost. Recall that Steveston's total fixed cost is $22,000. Assume that Megan has agreed to provide fellow business-woman Susan Williams with space in her shop to sell bathing suits to Megan's customers. Susan has agreed to pay Megan $250 per month as rent on the space she will use. The $250 per month works out to be $3,000 per year ($250 per month × 12 months = $3,000). Thus, Steveston's total fixed cost decreases from $22,000 to $19,000.

With these proposed changes in Steveston T-Shirt Shop Company's variable cost and fixed cost, we can now do sensitivity analysis. Let's see what effect these changes would have on Megan's company. To do this, again, we will use CVP formulas 3 and 4. We simply need to plug the new cost structures (variable and fixed) into the formulas as follows:

CVP Formula 3—Unit Sales Required to Achieve Target Profits

$$\frac{\left(\text{Total Fixed Cost} + \text{Target Profit}\right)}{\text{Contribution Margin Per Unit}} = \text{Required Unit Sales}$$

$$\frac{\left(\$19,000 + \$27,000\right)}{\$5.50} = 8,364 \text{ T-shirts (rounded up)}$$

By using CVP formula 3 (and Steveston's new variable and fixed cost structure), we found that if Steveston sells 8,364 T-shirts in 2004, the company will earn a profit of $27,000.

To calculate the sales dollars required to attain Steveston's target profit of $27,000, we use the company's new contribution ratio and CVP formula 4:

CVP Formula 4—Sales Dollars Required to Achieve Target Profits

$$\frac{\left(\text{Total Fixed Cost } + \text{ Target Profit}\right)}{\text{Contribution Margin Ratio}} = \text{Required Sales Dollars}$$

$$\frac{\left(\$19,000 + \$27,000\right)}{30.556\% \text{ (rounded)}} = \$150,543 \text{ in Sales (rounded)}$$

With the changes in cost structure Megan has negotiated, she will be able to earn $27,000 profit in 2004 even if her sales drop to 8,364 T-shirts.

 Discussion Questions

5–14. How would you prove to Megan that sales must total $150,543 (8,364 T-shirts) to earn a $27,000 profit if she reduces the cost per T-shirt from $12.00 to $9.50 and reduces total fixed cost from $22,000 to $19,000?

5–15. If Megan is more successful than anticipated in 2004 and sells 10,000 T-shirts by reducing her selling price to $18, and she also implements the variable and fixed cost changes described earlier, what will be Steveston's profits for 2004?

5–16. What complications do you foresee in using CVP analysis if Megan begins selling a deluxe line of T-shirts that cost $22.00 each and sell for $34.00?

 A User's View

Alan Raffan was poring over the latest management reports for one of the hotels managed by AFM hospitality Inc. The monthly reports break down the hotel's operations by department and Alan was a little concerned about the food and beverage department.

"Our room occupancy for the month was better than we had planned and our variable costs associated with maintaining the rooms were very good. Unfortunately, though, in the food and beverage department, the food costs and the labour costs were higher than we had anticipated. These costs are primarily variable, in that they will vary as the volume of meals produced changes, but the per unit cost should stay about the same. This month we were 2 percent higher than we thought we would be."

Alan's understanding of variable costs allows him to better manage his business. Margins are small and food costs that are 2 percent above what was anticipated must be investigated.

"We also use our knowledge of how costs behave in the hotel industry to forecast," Raffan says. "We set our profit target and determine the number of rooms we need to fill in order to achieve it. We can then use that information in the determination of our budget and staffing requirements for the year."

Multiple Products and CVP

In reality, most companies sell more than one product. Companies that sell multiple products often have information about total variable cost and total sales for a given income statement period, but have no one variable cost and selling price that can be easily determined and used for CVP.

When a company sells multiple products, managers may still use CVP analysis, but they must apply CVP formula 2 for break-even analysis and CVP formula 4 to determine the required level of sales to attain target profits. CVP formulas 1 and 3 are useless in a multiproduct situation if the various products sold have different unit contribution margins.

To demonstrate how managers use CVP analysis in a multiproduct situation when per unit information is unavailable, let's consider the example of Century Frame Factory Ltd.

Century Frame Factory Ltd. makes and sells picture frames of various size and quality. Exhibit 5–13 presents Century's condensed contribution income statement for 2000.

There is a per unit variable cost and selling price for each of the frame models Century manufactures and sells, but they are not included in Exhibit 5–13. All we have are the totals. The $185,000 contribution margin comes from the sale of several different products, each with its own contribution margin. The 37 percent contribution margin ratio, then, is an average contribution margin ratio based on the sales mix of these different products. Even with this limited information, however, we can use CVP analysis to both calculate a break-even point and predict target profits.

Exhibit 5–13
Century's Condensed 2000 Contribution Income Statement

CENTURY FRAME FACTORY LTD.
Contribution Income Statement
For the Year Ended December 31, 2000

	Total	% of Sales
Sales	$500,000	100%
Variable Cost	315,000	63%
Contribution Margin	185,000	37%
Fixed Cost	143,000	
Operating Income	$ 42,000	

Break-Even Point in a Multiproduct Situation

To calculate the break-even point in a multiproduct situation, we use CVP formula 2.

CVP Formula 2—Break-Even Point in Sales Dollars

$$\frac{\text{Total Fixed Cost}}{\text{Contribution Margin Ratio}} = \text{Break-Even Point in Sales Dollars}$$

Using the information from Century, the calculation is as follows:

$$\frac{\$143,000}{37\%} = \$386,486 \text{ Sales Dollars (rounded)}$$

We know that Century is well above the break-even point because the company earned a profit of $42,000 in 2000. The break-even calculation is still valuable to company management because it reveals the margin of safety. The margin of safety shows how far sales could decline before the company would experience a loss. In this example, sales could decline by $113,514 ($500,000 2000 sales − $386,486 break-even point = $113,514 decline) before Century would experience a loss.

Projecting Required Sales in a Multiproduct Situation

Assume that Century is interested in increasing profits to $80,000 in 2001. Based on the information contained in the 2000 contribution income statement presented in Exhibit 5–13, what would be the required sales to earn this target profit of $80,000? To find out, we use CVP formula 4:

CVP Formula 4—Sales Dollars Required to Achieve Target Profits

$$\frac{\left(\text{Total Fixed Cost} + \text{Target Profit}\right)}{\text{Contribution Margin Ratio}} = \text{Required Sales Dollars}$$

Using the information from Century Frame Factory Ltd.'s contribution income statement, we know that total fixed cost is $143,000, the target profit is $80,000, and the contribution margin ratio is 37 percent. The calculation of the required sales dollars is as follows:

$$\frac{\$143,000 + \$80,000}{37\%} = \$602,703 \text{ in Sales (rounded)}$$

Our calculations indicate that Century Frame Factory Ltd. will need $602,703 in sales to attain a target profit of $80,000, assuming a constant sales mix.

 Discussion Question

5–17. How would you prove to Century that sales must total $602,703 to earn an $80,000 profit?

We have demonstrated how CVP analysis can provide useful information about how changes in selling price, variable cost, and fixed cost affect a company's break-even point. Managers can also use CVP analysis to see what sales (in either units or dollars) the company needs to attain target profits.

CVP analysis is highly adaptable. It works equally well when managers are trying to determine profit potential, whether of a small segment of a large business or of an entire company. Before a company expands an existing business market or makes the decision to enter new markets, management should invest some time in gathering revenue and cost data, separating the cost-by-cost behaviour, developing a contribution income statement, and applying these simple CVP procedures.

CVP Assumptions

CVP analysis is a great "what if?" management tool because it is used by managers to estimate a company's profit performance under a variety of different scenarios. It is, however, an estimation technique only, and the following assumptions are made when this type of analysis is used.

1. All costs can be classified as either fixed or variable. Implicit in this assumption is that a mixed cost can be separated into its fixed and variable components.
2. Fixed costs remain fixed throughout the range of activity.
3. Variable cost per unit remains the same throughout the range of activity.
4. Selling price per unit remains the same throughout the range of activity.
5. The average contribution margin ratio in a multiproduct company remains the same throughout the range of activity.

These assumptions rarely, if ever, match reality. Market pressures, inflation, and a myriad of other factors cause revenue and cost structures to change in ways that place limitations on CVP analysis. Notwithstanding these limitations, however, CVP helps managers make more realistic estimates of future profit potential. It is a technique used every day by managers of large and small companies worldwide as they attempt to better manage their businesses.

SUMMARY

The functional income statement, which separates the costs shown into product cost and period cost, is limited in its usefulness to managers as they attempt to plan and control their operations. It does not take into account that some costs change as volume changes, and some do not. The contribution income statement is more useful to managers as a planning tool because it separates the costs presented into fixed costs and variable costs rather than into product costs and period costs.

An integral part of the contribution income statement is the contribution margin, which is the amount remaining after all variable costs have been deducted from sales revenue. When the contribution margin is presented as a percentage of sales, it is called the contribution margin ratio. Both the contribution margin and the contribution margin ratio are used in cost-volume-profit analysis.

Cost-volume-profit (CVP) analysis is the analysis of the relationships between cost and volume, and the effect of those relationships on profit. The first application of CVP analysis is the calculation of breakeven, which is the sales level resulting in neither a profit nor a loss. Breakeven can be calculated either in sales dollars or in the number of units of product that must be sold.

Cost-volume-profit analysis can also be used to calculate the sales level required to achieve a target profit. As was the case with breakeven, the sales level required to achieve a target profit can be calculated in both sales dollars and the number of units of product that must be sold.

Cost-volume-profit analysis can also be used to perform sensitivity analysis, which is a technique used to determine the effect on CVP when changes are made in the selling price, cost structure (variable and/or fixed), and volume used in the calculations.

Although CVP analysis is easier to perform in a single-product situation, it can also be used to calculate breakeven and sales required to achieve target profits in a multiple product situation.

KEY TERMS

breakeven, p. 156
break-even point, p. 156
contribution income statement, p. 152
contribution margin, p. 153
contribution margin ratio, p. 155

cost-volume-profit (CVP) analysis, p. 155
functional income statement, p. 152
sensitivity analysis, p. 162

REVIEW THE FACTS

1. What is the difference between a contribution income statement and a functional income statement?
2. What is the contribution margin?
3. What does the contribution margin "contribute toward"?
4. How does total contribution margin differ from contribution margin per unit?
5. What is the contribution margin ratio and how does it differ from the contribution margin?
6. What is cost-volume-profit (CVP) analysis?
7. What does the term *break-even point* mean?
8. In what ways does the calculation of the break-even point in units differ from the calculation of the break-even point in sales dollars?
9. How would you calculate the required sales in units to attain a target profit?
10. How would you calculate the required sales in dollars to attain a target profit?
11. What does the term *sensitivity analysis* mean in the context of CVP analysis?
12. What does the term *average contribution margin ratio* mean for a company that sells multiple products?
13. Which two of the four CVP formulas are used to calculate breakeven and sales required to attain target profits for a multiproduct company?
14. Why are two of the CVP formulas useless in a multiproduct situation when contribution margins for individual products are unknown?

APPLY WHAT YOU HAVE LEARNED

LO 4: Prepare a Contribution Income Statement

1. Fresh Baked Cookie Company sells cookies in a large shopping mall. The following multistep income statement was prepared for the year ending December 31, 2003.

FRESH BAKED COOKIE COMPANY
Income Statement
For the Year Ended December 31, 2003

Sales		$36,000
Cost of Goods Sold		4,000
Gross Profit		32,000
Operating Expenses:		
Selling Expense	$18,000	
Administrative Expense	10,000	28,000
Operating Income		$ 4,000

Cost of goods sold is a variable cost. Selling expense is 20% variable and 80% fixed, and administrative expense is 5% variable and 95% fixed.

REQUIRED:

Prepare a contribution income statement for Fresh Baked Cookie Company.

LO 4: Prepare a Contribution Income Statement

2. The following multistep income statement was prepared for Steinmann's Bait Shop Ltd. for the year ending December 31, 2004.

STEINMANN'S BAIT SHOP LTD.
Income Statement
For the Year Ended December 31, 2004

Sales		$98,000
Cost of Goods Sold		22,000
Gross Profit		76,000
Operating Expenses:		
Selling Expense	$27,000	
Administrative Expense	36,000	63,000
Operating Income		$13,000

Cost of goods sold is a variable cost. Selling expense is 30% variable and 70% fixed, and administrative expense is 10% variable and 90% fixed.

REQUIRED:

Prepare a contribution income statement for Steinmann's Bait Shop Ltd.

LO 4: Prepare a Contribution Income Statement

3. Quality Fishing Gear Company sells high-quality fibreglass fishing rods to retailers. The following multistep income statement was prepared for the year ending December 31, 2003.

QUALITY FISHING GEAR COMPANY
Income Statement
For the Year Ended December 31, 2003

Sales		$540,000
Cost of Goods Sold		360,000
Gross Profit		180,000
Operating Expenses:		
Selling Expense	$88,000	
Administrative Expense	72,000	160,000
Operating Income		$ 20,000

Cost of goods sold is a variable cost. Selling expense is 65% variable and 35% fixed, and administrative expense is 25% variable and 75% fixed.

REQUIRED:

Prepare a contribution income statement for Quality Fishing Gear Company.

LO 4: Prepare a Contribution Income Statement

4. Ray Placid is considering opening a greeting card shop in a local mall. Ray contacted the mall manager and determined that the store rent will be $550 per month. In addition, he called the telephone company and based on the information from the telephone company representative, he estimates that the cost of telephone service will be about $95 per month. Based on the size of the store, Ray believes that cost of electricity will average about $200 per month. Ray will be able to buy the greeting cards for $0.50 each and plans to sell them for $2 each. Salaries are expected to be $1,200 per month regardless of the number of cards sold. Ray estimates that other miscellaneous fixed costs will total $150 per month and miscellaneous variable cost will be $0.10 per card. Ray anticipates that he will be able to sell about 3,000 greeting cards per month. If Ray opens the store, his first month of business will be November 2004.

REQUIRED:
Prepare a projected contribution approach income statement for November 2004.

LO 4:   Prepare a Contribution Income Statement

5. Joe's Pretzel Stand is located near Commonwealth Stadium and sells pretzels before sporting events. The following information is available:

- Selling price per pretzel $2.00
- Cost of each pretzel $0.25
- Cost of renting the pretzel stand is $12,000 per year.
- Instead of an hourly wage, Joe pays college students $0.20 per pretzel sold to run the pretzel stand.

REQUIRED:
Prepare a contribution income statement for 2004 assuming that 8,000 pretzels are sold.

LO 4:   Prepare a Contribution Income Statement

6. The following information is available for Blaire's Hot Dog Stand:

- Selling price per hot dog $2.50
- Cost of each hot dog $0.30
- Rent paid for the stand, at a local flea market, is $2,400 per year.
- Instead of an hourly wage, Blaire's pays high school students $0.40 per hot dog sold.

REQUIRED:
Prepare a contribution income statement for 2003 assuming that 6,000 hot dogs are sold.

LO 4:   Prepare a Condensed Contribution Income Statement

7. The following is the contribution income statement for The Bevens Company:

THE BEVENS COMPANY
Contribution Income Statement
For the Year Ended December 31, 2004

Sales		$800,000
Variable Cost:		
Cost of Goods Sold	$420,000	
Variable Selling Expense	75,000	
Variable Administrative Expense	33,000	
Total Variable Cost		528,000
Contribution Margin		272,000
Fixed Cost:		
Fixed Selling Expense	128,000	
Fixed Administrative Expense	53,000	
Total Fixed Cost		181,000
Operating Income		$ 91,000

REQUIRED:
Based on the contribution income statement for The Bevens Company, prepare a condensed contribution income statement.

LO 1: Prepare a Multistep Income Statement

8. Refer to the information presented in problem 7.

REQUIRED:

Prepare a multistep income statement for The Bevens Company.

LO 4: Prepare a Condensed Contribution Income Statement

9. Following is the contribution income statement for Transalta Distributors Ltd.:

TRANSALTA DISTRIBUTORS LTD.
Contribution Income Statement
For the Year Ended December 31, 2003

Sales		$4,800,000
Variable Cost:		
Cost of Goods Sold	$2,320,000	
Variable Selling Expense	265,000	
Variable Administrative Expense	484,000	
Total Variable Cost		3,069,000
Contribution Margin		1,731,000
Fixed Cost:		
Fixed Selling Expense	648,000	
Fixed Administrative Expense	973,000	
Total Fixed Cost		1,621,000
Operating Income		$ 110,000

REQUIRED:

Based on Transalta Distributors Ltd.'s contribution income statement, prepare a condensed contribution income statement.

LO 1: Prepare a Multistep Income Statement

10. Refer to the information presented in problem 9.

REQUIRED:

Prepare a multistep income statement for Transalta Distributors Ltd.

LO 4: Prepare a Condensed Contribution Income Statement

11. The following is the contribution income statement for All Season Athletic Shops Ltd.:

ALL SEASON ATHLETIC SHOPS LTD.
Contribution Income Statement
For the Year Ended December 31, 2004

Sales		$422,000
Variable Cost:		
Cost of Goods Sold	$205,000	
Variable Selling Expense	55,000	
Variable Administrative Expense	22,000	
Total Variable Cost		282,000
Contribution Margin		140,000
Fixed Cost:		
Fixed Selling Expense	75,000	
Fixed Administrative Expense	34,000	
Total Fixed Cost		109,000
Operating Income		$ 31,000

REQUIRED:
Based on this contribution income statement, prepare a condensed contribution income statement for All Season Athletic Shops Ltd.

LO 1: Prepare a Multistep Income Statement

12. Refer to the information presented in problem 11.

REQUIRED:
Prepare a multistep income statement for All Season Athletic Shops Ltd.

LO 4: Prepare a Contribution Income Statement

13. Paradise Manufacturing Inc. makes weight-lifting equipment. During 2003, the following costs were incurred:

	Amount	Percent Fixed	Percent Variable
Direct material	$680,000	–	100
Direct labour	420,000	–	100
Variable manufacturing overhead	130,000	–	100
Fixed manufacturing overhead	900,000	100	–
Selling cost	300,000	20	80
Administrative cost	220,000	10	90

Sales for 2003 totaled $2,780,000 and there were no beginning or ending inventories.

REQUIRED:
Prepare a contribution income statement for the year ended December 31, 2003.

LO 4: Prepare a Contribution Income Statement

14. The following information is available for Western Toy Manufacturing Company for 2004:

	Amount	Percent Fixed	Percent Variable
Direct material	$440,000	–	100
Direct labour	90,000	–	100
Variable manufacturing overhead	70,000	–	100
Fixed manufacturing overhead	800,000	100	–
Selling cost	950,000	45	55
Administrative cost	570,000	85	15

Sales for 2004 totaled $3,164,000 and there were no beginning or ending inventories.

REQUIRED:
Prepare a contribution income statement for the year ended December 31, 2004.

LO 4: Prepare a Contribution Income Statement

15. The following information is available for Zenith Watch Company for 2005:

	Amount	Percent Fixed	Percent Variable
Direct material	$534,000	–	100
Direct labour	129,000	–	100
Variable manufacturing overhead	397,000	–	100
Fixed manufacturing overhead	998,000	100	–
Selling cost	196,000	33	67
Administrative cost	243,000	78	22

Sales for 2005 totaled $2,745,000 and there were no beginning or ending inventories.

REQUIRED:
Prepare a contribution income statement for the year ended December 31, 2005.

LO 4: Prepare a Contribution Income Statement

16. Alumacraft Manufacturing Inc. makes aluminum serving carts for use in commercial jetliners. During 2003, the following costs were incurred:

	Amount	Percent Fixed	Percent Variable
Direct material	$2,600,000	–	100
Direct labour	1,820,000	–	100
Variable manufacturing overhead	540,000	–	100
Fixed manufacturing overhead	1,900,000	100	–
Selling cost	380,000	15	85
Administrative cost	230,000	5	95

Sales for 2003 totaled $7,900,000 and there were no beginning or ending inventories.

REQUIRED:
Prepare a contribution income statement for the year ended December 31, 2003.

LO 6: Determine Breakeven and Sales Required to Earn Target Profit Using Per Unit Amounts

17. The following information is available for Spectrum Testing Corporation.

Amount charged for each test performed	$90
Annual fixed cost	$200,000
Variable cost per test	$25

REQUIRED:
a. Calculate how many tests Spectrum Testing Corporation must perform each year to break even.
b. Calculate how many tests Spectrum Testing Corporation must perform each year to earn a profit of $25,000.

LO 6: Determine Breakeven and Sales Required to Earn Target Profit Using Per Unit Amounts

18. The following information is available for Smitty's Donut Shop Ltd.

Amount charged per dozen doughnuts	$0.99
Annual fixed cost	$385,000.00
Variable cost per dozen doughnuts	$0.22

REQUIRED:

a. Calculate how many dozen doughnuts Smitty's must sell each year to break even.

b. Calculate how many dozen doughnuts Smitty's must sell each year to earn a profit of $35,000.

LO 6: Determine Breakeven and Sales Required to Earn Target Profit Using Per Unit Amounts

19. You are considering starting a small company to paint driveways. The following information is available.

Amount charged per square metre painted	$5
Annual fixed cost	$3,000
Variable cost per square metre painted	$2

REQUIRED:

a. Calculate how many square metres of driveway you must paint each year to break even.

b. Calculate how many square metres of driveway you must paint each year to earn a profit of $5,000.

LO 6: Determine Breakeven and Sales Required to Earn Target Profit Using Per Unit Amounts

20. Carbonnel Calendar Company is considering adding a new calendar design to its line. The following information is available.

Selling price	$3.97
Additional annual fixed cost	$4,558.00
Variable cost per calendar	$3.11

REQUIRED:

a. Calculate how many calendars must be sold each year to break even.

b. Calculate how many calendars must be sold each year to earn a profit of $2,580.

LO 3 & 6: Use Ratios to Determine Breakeven and Sales Required to Earn Target Profit

21. Melissa Valdez is planning to expand her clothing business by opening another store. In planning for the new store, Melissa believes that selling prices and costs of the various merchandise sold will be similar to those of the existing store. In fact, she thinks that variable and fixed costs for the new store will be similar to those of the existing store, except that rent for the new store will be $300 per month more than the rent paid for the existing store.

The following information is available for the existing store for the year ended December 31, 2004:

Sales	$200,000
Variable cost	130,000
Fixed cost	48,000

REQUIRED:
a. Determine the sales required for the new store to break even.
b. Determine the sales required for the new store to earn a profit of $20,000 per year. (Hint: Keep in mind that the $300 increase in rent is a monthly amount and the fixed cost of $48,000 is an annual amount.)

LO 3 & 6: Use Ratios to Determine Breakeven and Sales Required to Earn Target Profit

22. PetCare Inc. is considering opening a new pet store. The sales and costs of the new store will be similar to those of the existing store. The only exception is that the annual fixed cost for the new store is expected to be $75,000 more than that of the existing store.

The following information is available for PetCare Inc.'s existing store for 2005:

Revenue	$1,250,000
Variable cost	600,000
Fixed cost	420,000

REQUIRED:
a. Determine the revenues required for the new store to break even.
b. Determine the revenues required for the new store to earn a profit of $120,000 per year.

LO 3 & 6: Use Ratios to Determine Breakeven and Sales Required to Earn Target Profit

23. The law firm of Baynes and Wood is considering opening a second office in a suburban area. The annual fixed cost of the new office is expected to be $500,000 per year.

The following information is available for the firm's main office for 2003.

Revenue	$3,650,000
Variable cost	1,387,000

The firm expects that the relationship between variable costs and revenue will be the same in the suburban office.

REQUIRED:
a. Based on this information, what is the required revenue for the suburban office to break even?
b. Based on this information, what is the required revenue for the suburban office to earn a profit of $150,000?

LO 2, 4, & 6: Use Per Unit Amounts to Determine Breakeven and Sales Required to Earn Target Profit and Prepare a Contribution Income Statement

24. Richard Davenport owns a clothing store and is considering renting a soft-drink vending machine for his store. He can rent the soft-drink machine for $125.00 per month. Richard would supply the soft drinks for the machine, which he can buy for $3.00 per dozen. Richard plans to charge $0.75 per can.

REQUIRED:
a. List the fixed costs for renting and stocking the soft-drink machine.
b. List the variable costs for renting and stocking the soft-drink machine.
c. Calculate the contribution margin per can of soft drink.
d. (1) Calculate how many cans of soft drinks Richard must sell each month to break even.
   (2) Prepare a contribution income statement that proves the answer you just calculated.
e. (1) Calculate how many cans of soft drinks Richard must sell each month to earn a profit of $50.00.
   (2) Prepare a contribution income statement that proves your answer to the previous requirement.

LO 2, 4, & 6: Use Per Unit Amounts to Determine Breakeven and Sales Required to Earn Target Profit and Prepare a Contribution Income Statement

25. Erich Traebeecke owns the Kenpo Karate School in Toronto. He is considering renting a candy vending machine for his school lobby. He can rent the candy machine for $100.00 per month. Erich would supply the candy bars for the machine. He can buy a box of eight candy bars for $3.20 per box. Erich plans to sell each candy bar for $1.00.

REQUIRED:
a. List the fixed costs of renting and stocking the candy machine.
b. List the variable costs of renting and stocking the candy machine.
c. Calculate the contribution margin per candy bar.
d. (1) Calculate how many candy bars must be sold each month to break even.
   (2) Prepare a contribution income statement that proves the answer you just calculated.
e. (1) Calculate how many candy bars must be sold each month to earn a profit of $180.00
   (2) Prepare a contribution income statement that proves your answer to the previous requirement.

LO 2, 4, and 6: Use Per Unit Amounts to Determine Breakeven and Sales Required to Earn Target Profit and Prepare a Contribution Income Statement

26. Monica Llobet owns Cornwall School of Dance. She is considering installing a cappuccino machine in the school's dance studio. Monica can rent the cappuccino machine for $48.88 per month. Coffee and supplies would cost about $0.12 per cup of cappuccino. Monica plans to sell each cup of cappuccino for $2.00.

REQUIRED:

a. List the fixed costs of renting and stocking the cappuccino machine.
b. List the variable costs of renting and stocking the cappuccino machine.
c. Calculate the contribution margin per cup of cappuccino.
d. (1) Calculate how many cups of cappuccino must be sold each month to break even.
   (2) Prepare a contribution income statement that proves the answer you just calculated.
e. (1) Calculate how many cups of cappuccino must be sold each month to earn a profit of $100.00 (Round your answer to the nearest unit.)
   (2) Prepare a contribution income statement that proves your answer to the previous requirement.

LO 2 & 6:   Use Per Unit Amounts to Determine Breakeven and Sales Required to Earn Target Profit

27. Lee Chan is interested in selling pin-on buttons at various school events. The button machine will cost $200, and the material to produce each button costs $0.15. In exchange for the right to sell the buttons, Lee has agreed to donate $300.00 per year and $0.20 per button to the school's scholarship fund. Lee plans to sell the buttons for $1.00 each and to operate the service for four years. By then it will be time to graduate, and the button machine will be worn out.

REQUIRED:

a. Assuming the button machine will be able to produce buttons for four years, calculate the cost per year for the button machine.
b. Calculate the total fixed cost per year for Lee's button business.
c. Calculate the variable cost per button.
d. Calculate the annual break-even point
   (1) in units.
   (2) in dollars.
e. Calculate how many buttons must be sold to earn an annual profit of $800.00.
f. Calculate the sales in dollars required to earn an annual profit of $800.00.

LO 2 & 6:   Use Per Unit Amounts to Determine Breakeven and Sales Required to Earn Target Profit

28. Andrea Craig is interested in setting up a kiosk to sell Mylar helium balloons at a local mall. The stand would cost $250.00, and the material for each balloon would cost $0.75. In exchange for the right to sell the balloons, Andrea has agreed to pay $300.00 per month and $0.50 per balloon to the mall's owner. Andrea plans to sell the balloons for $3.00 each. Andrea thinks the kiosk will last four years.

REQUIRED:

a. Assuming the balloon kiosk has an estimated useful life of four years, with no salvage value, calculate the cost per year for the balloon kiosk.
b. Calculate the total fixed cost per year for Andrea's balloon business.
c. Calculate the variable cost per balloon.
d. Calculate the annual break-even point
   (1) in units.
   (2) in dollars.
e. Calculate how many balloons must be sold to earn an annual profit of $20,000.
f. Calculate the sales in dollars required to earn an annual profit of $20,000.

LO 2 & 6:   Use Per Unit Amounts to Determine Breakeven and Sales Required to Earn Target Profit

29. Bill Smith is interested in selling ice cream bars at school events. The vendor stand will cost $800.00, and the ice cream bars cost $0.65. In exchange for the right to sell the ice cream bars, Bill has agreed to donate $600.00 per year and $0.25 per ice cream bar to the school's library. Bill plans to sell the ice cream bars for $1.50 each. Bill intends to sell the ice cream bars and run the stand for four years. By then it will be time to graduate, and the vendor stand will be worn out.

REQUIRED:

a. Assuming the vendor stand can be used for four years, calculate the cost per year for the vendor stand.
b. Calculate the total fixed cost per year for Bill's ice cream business.
c. Calculate the variable cost per ice cream bar.
d. Calculate the annual break-even point
   (1) in units.
   (2) in dollars.
e. Calculate how many ice cream bars must be sold to earn an annual profit of $3,000.
f. Calculate the sales in dollars required to earn an annual profit of $3,000.
g. Calculate Bill's profit if sales were $8,000 for this year.

LO 3 & 6:   Determine the Contribution Margin Ratio and Determine Breakeven and Sales Required to Earn Target Profit

30. Amanda is considering opening a gift shop. She has collected the following information:

Monthly rent	$2,800
Monthly sales salaries	1,200

In addition to the sales salaries, Amanda intends to pay sales commissions of 5% of sales to her sales staff. The cost of the merchandise sold is expected to be 40% of sales.

REQUIRED:

a. Determine the following:
   (1) Amanda's break-even point in monthly sales dollars
   (2) The monthly sales dollars required to earn a profit of $2,000 per month
   (3) Amanda's break-even point if she is able to reduce rent by $200
b. Assume that Amanda has negotiated a 10% discount on all merchandise purchases. The new cost of merchandise will not change the selling price of the product. Determine the following:
   (1) The new contribution margin ratio
   (2) The new break-even point in monthly sales dollars, assuming monthly rent is $2,800.

LO 3 & 6:   Determine the Contribution Margin Ratio and Determine Breakeven and Sales Required to Earn Target Profit

31. Noelle is considering opening a bookstore. She has collected the following information:

Monthly rent	$3,286
Monthly sales salaries	4,200

In addition to the sales salaries, Noelle intends to pay sales commissions of 10% of sales to her sales staff. The cost of the merchandise sold is expected to be 30% of sales.

REQUIRED:
a. Determine the following:
   (1) Noelle's break-even point in monthly sales dollars
   (2) The monthly sales dollars required to earn a profit of $1,500 per month
   (3) Noelle's break-even point if she is able to reduce rent by $300
b. Assume that Noelle has negotiated a 5% discount on all merchandise purchases. The new cost of merchandise will not change the selling price of product. Determine the following:
   (1) The new contribution margin ratio
   (2) The new break-even point in monthly sales dollars

LO 2 & 6:   Use Per Unit Amounts to Determine Breakeven and Sales Required to Earn Target Profit

32. Clarice is considering buying a video rental business. If she finances the entire purchase price, the payments will be $2,900 per month. Store rent would be $2,000 per month and cost of sales clerks, replacement tapes, and other expenses would be $1,200 per month. Clarice plans to rent the tapes for $4.00 each.

REQUIRED:
a. Calculate the variable cost (if any) per tape rental.
b. Calculate the total fixed cost per month.
c. Determine how many tapes Clarice must rent each month to break even.
d. Determine how many tapes Clarice must rent each month to earn a profit of $1,000 per month.

LO 3 & 6:   Determine the Contribution Margin Ratio and Determine Breakeven and Sales Required to Earn Target Profit

33. Margaret Pitman is considering opening a gift shop. She has collected the following information:

Monthly rent	$1,800
Monthly sales salaries	1,200

The cost of the merchandise sold is expected to be 55% of sales.

REQUIRED:
a. What is the annual rent cost?
b. What is the annual sales salaries cost?
c. What is the contribution margin ratio?

d. What is the break-even point in dollars?

e. Determine the amount of sales needed to earn a profit of $12,000 for the year.

LO 3 & 6: Determine the Contribution Margin Ratio and Determine Breakeven and Sales Required to Earn Target Profit

34. Carol Jean is considering opening a frame shop. She has collected the following information:

Monthly rent	$ 600
Monthly sales salaries	1,100

The cost of the merchandise sold is expected to be 45% of sales.

REQUIRED:

a. What is the annual rent cost?

b. What is the annual sales salaries cost?

c. What is the contribution margin ratio?

d. What is the break-even point in dollars?

e. Determine the amount of sales needed to earn a profit of $18,000 for the year.

LO 3 & 6: Determine the Contribution Margin Ratio and Determine Breakeven and Sales Required to Earn Target Profit

35. Terry Thibert is considering opening a beauty supply store. She has collected the following information:

Monthly rent	$3,400
Monthly sales salaries	2,800

The cost of the merchandise sold is expected to be 68% of sales.

REQUIRED:

a. What is the annual rent cost?

b. What is the annual sales salaries cost?

c. What is the contribution margin ratio?

d. What is the break-even point in dollars?

e. Determine the amount of sales needed to earn a profit of $36,000 for the year.

LO 3 & 6: Determine the Contribution Margin Ratio and Determine Breakeven and Sales Required to Earn Target Profit

36. Chris Nixon is considering opening a music store. He has collected the following information:

Monthly rent	$1,400
Monthly sales salaries	1,700

The cost of the merchandise sold is expected to be 52% of sales.

REQUIRED:

a. What is the annual rent cost?

b. What is the annual sales salaries cost?

c. What is the contribution margin ratio?

d. What is the break-even point in dollars?

e. Determine the amount of sales needed to earn a profit of $36,000 for the year.

LO 2, 3, 4, & 5: Analyze a Situation Using CVP

37. Quality Instrument Company manufactures various industrial thermometers. Last year the company sold 600 model QI-22 thermometers for $129 each. Managers are concerned that the profits from the QI-22 were only $7,740 last year. Fixed costs for this product are $50,000 per year. In an effort to increase profits, the company raised the price of the QI-22 to $148. Based on annual sales of 600 units, managers are confident that profits from the QI-22 will be increased to $19,140 next year.

     The sales manager is concerned about the price increase. He believes the company should move a little more slowly in making the pricing decision and has suggested that a group be formed to explore the ramifications of such a pricing move.

REQUIRED:

Assume that you have been assigned to the group who will evaluate the proposed price change. The group is to create a report discussing the various ramifications of the price increase including its effect on projected sales and profits. Your report should make recommendations that are supported by calculations similar to those found in this chapter.

LO 2, 3, 4, & 5: Analyze a Situation Using CVP

38. The Sliding Glass Door Company manufactured and sold 1,000 model SD4896 doors for $88 each. Managers are concerned that the profits from the SD4896 doors were only $8,000 last year. In an effort to increase profits, the company raised the price of the SD4896 to $106. Based on annual sales of 1,000 units, managers are confident that profits from the SD4896 will increase to $26,000 next year. Fixed costs of $40,000 are allocated to the SD4896 based on the number of units produced.

     The sales manager is concerned about the price increase. He believes the company should move a little more slowly in making the pricing decision and has suggested that a group be formed to explore the ramifications of such a pricing move.

REQUIRED:

Assume that you have been assigned to the group who will evaluate the proposed price change. The group is to create a report discussing the various ramifications of the price increase including its effect on projected sales and profits. Your report should make recommendations that are supported by calculations similar to those found in this chapter.

LO 2, 3, 4, & 5: Analyze a Situation Using CVP

39. Carol Juriet is considering the purchase of a hot dog vending cart to sell hot dogs in a busy parking lot. The city of Moncton requires that the cart be licensed at a cost of $500 per year.

REQUIRED:

a. (1) How would Carol determine the cost to rent a small space in the parking lot to operate the hot dog cart?

   (2) How much do you think the monthly rent would be?

   (3) How much do you think the hourly wage would be for an employee to operate the stand?

   (4) How many hours per day do you think the stand should be open?

      (5) Based on your answers to questions 3 and 4, what would you estimate monthly wage cost to be for the hot dog stand?

      (6) How much do you think Carol should charge for each hot dog?

  b. Answer the following questions using your answers to question 1.

      (1) What is the variable cost per hot dog?

      (2) What is the monthly fixed cost for operating the hot dog stand?

      (3) What is the contribution margin per hot dog?

      (4) What is the contribution ratio?

      (5) What is the variable cost ratio?

      (6) **a)** How many hot dogs must Carol sell each month to break even?

         b) Prepare a contribution income statement that proves your answer.

      (7) **a)** How many hot dogs must Carol sell each month to earn a profit of $300?

         b) Prepare a contribution income statement that proves your answer.

6

Making Decisions Using Relevant Information

$\mathcal{F}$inancial accounting information provided to external decision makers must be relevant to be useful. Not surprisingly, management accounting information provided to internal decision makers must also possess the characteristic of relevance. It is critically important that managers make their decisions based on relevant information and that they disregard all irrelevant information. To be relevant, the information must be pertinent to the decision at hand. In accounting, **relevant costing** is the process of determining which dollar inflows and outflows pertain to a particular management decision.

Determining which costs are relevant is not always an easy job. For instance, consider an actual example about a couple that went to Disney World with their three-year-old daughter, Jessica. The family stayed at a Disney hotel to be close to the Disney attractions, and to take advantage of the hotel's staff of baby-sitters. The baby-sitting service required payment of a four-hour minimum at $11 per hour, or $44. Users must cancel three hours in advance to avoid the $44 minimum fee. Jessica's parents planned to take her to the Magic Kingdom early in the day and then leave her with a sitter in the late afternoon while they visited EPCOT on their own.

Jessica and her parents went to Disney's Magic Kingdom as they had planned and were having a wonderful time. As the day progressed, Jessica enjoyed the amusement park so much that Jessica's parents were having second thoughts about leaving her with the sitter. They had to make a decision: Should they take Jessica to EPCOT or leave her with the sitter as planned?

relevant costing The process of determining which dollar inflows and outflows pertain to a particular management decision.

Because the family's admission tickets permitted them to enter all the Disney parks, the main issue was the minimum $44 charge for the sitter, because it was too late to cancel. As Jessica's parents discussed the pros and cons of each alternative, they realized the $44 charge would have to be paid whether they took Jessica to EPCOT or not. The baby-sitter's fee, then, was an irrelevant cost in this decision, because Jessica's parents would have to pay the baby-sitting fee no matter which alternative they chose. Once Jessica's parents determined that the fee was irrelevant, they dismissed the sitter and Jessica was off to EPCOT with them.

In business, the issue of what is relevant often confuses even the most seasoned business executive. To make the best possible decisions, decision makers must learn to consider only relevant information. ■

LEARNING OBJECTIVES

After completing your work on this chapter, you should be able to do the following:

1. Identify the characteristics of a relevant cost.
2. Explain why sunk costs and costs that do not differ between alternatives are irrelevant costs.
3. Describe the qualitative factors that should be considered when making a business decision.
4. Use accounting information and determine the relevant cost of various decisions.
5. Explain the effects of fixed costs and opportunity costs on outsourcing decisions.

RELEVANT COSTS

relevant cost A dollar inflow or outflow that pertains to a particular management decision in that it has a bearing on which decision alternative is preferable.

sunk cost A past cost that cannot be changed by current or future actions.

You may wonder why an entire chapter of this text is devoted to determining which costs are relevant. Isn't it understood that decision makers should disregard superfluous information and concentrate on the facts that relate to the decision at hand? Yes, but with so many cost considerations to muddy the water, determining what information is relevant is not always as easy as it might seem.

A **relevant cost** is a cost that is pertinent to a particular decision in that it has a bearing on which decision alternative is preferable. A relevant cost possesses two important characteristics: (1) The cost must be a future cost, and (2) the cost must differ between decision alternatives.

A relevant cost must be a future cost because current decisions can have no effect on past expenditures. Expenditures that have already occurred are called **sunk costs** and they cannot be changed by current or future actions. Because sunk costs are unaffected by current decisions, they are irrelevant and should not be considered when evaluating current decision alternatives. For example, if your firm was deciding whether to replace an old printing press with a new, labour-saving model, the cost of the old press would be irrelevant. Why? The firm already bought the old press. The purchase of the new printing press would not lessen or change the amount paid for the old press. Whether the company purchases the new press or not, the cost of the old press is a sunk cost: Nothing we can do now can change it. Sunk costs include both amounts paid in the past and past commitments to pay. That is, once there is a binding commitment to pay cash or otherwise transfer resources, the cost associated with that commitment is a sunk cost.

A relevant cost must differ between decision alternatives. If a cost remains the same regardless of the alternative we choose, it is irrelevant. Again, focus on the decision to buy a new printing press or to keep the old one. If the new printing press will use the same quantity and type of ink as the old one, the cost of ink is irrelevant, no matter how large the dollar figure.

 Discussion Questions

6-1. Refer back to the decision faced by Jessica's parents in Disney World. Which criteria of relevance did the $44 baby-sitting cost fail to meet? Explain your reasoning.

6-2. Have you ever made a decision and later found that you mistakenly let irrelevant factors sway your choice? Explain.

The term *relevant cost* is something of a misnomer. Perhaps a better description of this topic would be *relevant factors*. The reason for this is that the term relevant cost is used to describe not only changes in cost, but also changes in revenue. These cost and revenue changes often result in inflows of resources rather than outflows.

quantitative factors
Factors that can be measured by numbers.

qualitative factors Factors that cannot be measured by numbers—they must be described in words.

Quantitative factors are those that can be represented by numbers. Almost all accounting information is quantitative, including relevant cost. However, managers often consider additional factors that cannot be quantified. **Qualitative factors** are factors that cannot be measured numerically—they must be described in words. Examples include customer satisfaction, product quality, employee morale, and customer perceptions.

In addition to their financial impact, business decisions affect a multitude of nonfinancial areas. For example, closing an outdated factory may reduce production cost, but it will also adversely impact employee morale. The employees that remain after the factory closing may believe that the company's loyalty is to profits, not their well-being. Lower employee morale is likely to lead to less productivity. Qualitative factors should also be considered in smaller, routine decisions. For example, a furniture store manager considering a proposal to switch from company owned and operated delivery trucks to a delivery service should consider her lack of control if the delivery service is used. Even though it may be less expensive to use a delivery service, the furniture store's manager may not want to lose the ability to select the most responsible truck drivers and to schedule deliveries exactly as desired. When making a decision, managers should evaluate all relevant quantitative and qualitative factors.

Discussion Questions

Assume you are planning a trip from Montreal to Halifax to visit some friends. You have a job, but your boss will let you take off as many days as you wish for the trip. Your car is unreliable, so you compare two alternatives—take a bus or take an airplane.

6-3. What are the relevant quantitative factors you should consider in making your decision?

6-4. What are the relevant qualitative factors you should consider in making your decision?

Decision makers must question the relevance of accounting information. As discussed in Chapter 1, managers and engineers no longer specify accounting information requirements. Instead, accountants provide information to managers based on accepted accounting techniques, so its relevance to management decision makers has diminished. Although some businesses have taken steps to make management accounting information more relevant to internal decision makers, managers should be able to determine for themselves what is relevant so they can make sound, well-informed decisions (see Exhibit 6–1).

Exhibit 6–1
Determining
Relevant Cost

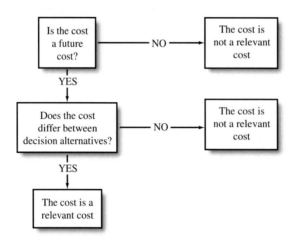

Throughout the remainder of this chapter, we will explore several common business situations to demonstrate how to determine relevant cost and its importance to good decision making. For each example, we will gather all costs associated with the decision. Next, we will determine the relevant cost of each decision alternative. Finally, we will compare the relevant costs of the alternative and determine the preferred alternative. The first example we will explore is an equipment replacement decision.

EQUIPMENT REPLACEMENT

To apply the concepts of relevant costing, we examine a proposed equipment replacement project. Our example highlights the treatment of amortization, sunk costs, and costs that do not differ between alternatives.

Naxon and Lewis, a local law firm, purchased and installed a sophisticated computer system recently at a cost of $35,500. A client notices the new system. He remarks that it is too bad the system is not the latest and quickest because, if it were, the data input time could be cut in half. The client suggests that the firm consider updating. The partners respond, "We can't buy a new system. We just bought this one two weeks ago." The client advises the firm to take a closer look before deciding.

Gather All Costs Associated with the Decision

The partners turn to you for advice. They explain that the recently installed computer system cost $35,500 to purchase, has an estimated useful life of five years, with a residual value of $500. The partners note that the firm plans to use straight-line amortization, so it will recognize $7,000 amortization per year. The cost of operating the recently installed system, which we will call the "old" system, includes two operators at $30,000 per year, and a maintenance contract at $1,000 per year. The maintenance agreement, however, can be cancelled at any time. After calling around, the controller informs you that he can sell the old system now, but he will get only $10,000 for it (everyone wants the new model). The new model would cost $76,000 and also has an estimated useful life of five years, with a $1,000 residual value. Using the straight-line method, annual amortization would be $15,000. Because data entry is twice as fast, the new computer system would require only one operator at $30,000 per year. The maintenance contract on the new machine would cost $1,000 per year and would be cancellable at any time.

A summary of the cost of each system is shown in Exhibit 6–2. These costs are generally classified as start-up costs, operating costs, and shutdown costs.

Exhibit 6–2
Computer System
Replacement
Cost Summary

	Old System	Replacement System
Start-up costs:		
Cost of system	$ 35,500	$76,000
Operating costs:		
Annual amortization	$ 7,000	$15,000
Total amortization	35,000	75,000
Annual labour cost	60,000	30,000
Total labour cost	300,000	150,000
Annual maintenance cost	1,000	1,000
Total maintenance cost	5,000	5,000
Shutdown costs:		
Residual value of system	$ 500	$ 1,000
Current sale price of old system	10,000	

To help the partners make a wise decision about the new computer system, you must first look at each cost and determine whether it is relevant. To make an informed decision, a manager must consider the total cost of each alternative, including all the costs incurred over the life of the alternative. For our computer replacement decision, the annual costs associated with each system are multiplied by the number of years the system will be used to determine the total cost of the system over its lifetime.

Determine the Relevant Cost of Each Alternative

Next we determine the relevant cost of each decision alternative. As you consider each cost, try to determine whether it is relevant to the equipment replacement decision. Ask yourself the following two questions: (1) Is the cost a future cost? and (2) Does the cost differ between alternatives? We will examine the cost associated with the old computer system first.

Relevant Cost of the Old Computer System   The $35,500 cost of the old system is not relevant because it is a sunk cost. The firm's decision to purchase or not to purchase the new computer system cannot change the past expenditure for the old one.

Although it may appear that amortization is a future cost, it is nothing more than an allocation of an asset's original cost. The cost of an asset purchased in the past is a sunk cost, and, therefore, amortization simply allocates this sunk cost. If amortization expense relates to an asset purchased in the past, it is irrelevant. In this situation, the amortization for the old computer system is not relevant because the amortization is an allocation of the purchase price, which is a sunk cost.

The total cost of $300,000 to pay for two operators is relevant, because it is a future cost and it differs between alternatives. The old system requires two operators, each costing $30,000 per year. Over the five-year expected life of the old system, that totals $300,000 (2 operators × $30,000 × 5 years).

The $5,000 total cost of the maintenance contract for the old system is irrelevant, because it does not differ between decision alternatives. The cost of the maintenance contract for the old system is the same as that for the new one. Therefore, although this is a future cost, it is irrelevant because it does not differ between alternatives.

The $500 residual value of the old system is relevant because it is a future cost and it differs between alternatives. If the firm stays with the old computer system, it will be able to sell the old system at the end of its useful life for $500. If, however, the firm buys the new one, it will sell the old one now for $10,000, and therefore will be unable to sell it for its residual value in five years.

The $10,000 that the firm could get if it sells the old system now is a future cost that differs between alternatives, and therefore it is relevant. If the firm buys the new computer system, it can sell the old one for $10,000, but if the firm does not buy the new system, it will need the old one so it would not sell it.

Relevant Costs of the Replacement System   Next, we will analyze the start-up, operating, and shutdown costs of the replacement computer system. The only start-up cost for the replacement system is the $76,000 to purchase and install it. This cost is relevant because it is a future cost and it differs between alternatives.

The $75,000 in total amortization on the new computer system is an allocation of the replacement system's cost. Because we have already considered the cost of the new computer system, we avoid double-counting by excluding its amortization expense from our analysis of relevant costs.

The $150,000 ($30,000 × 5 years) total labour cost for the replacement system's one operator is relevant because it is a future cost that differs between alternatives. The labour cost for the old system is $300,000, whereas the labour cost for the replacement system is $150,000.

The total cost of the maintenance contract on the replacement system is $5,000. As it happens, the maintenance cost of the old system is also $5,000. In this situation, although maintenance cost is a future cost, it is irrelevant because it does not differ between alternatives.

The $1,000 residual value for the new computer system is relevant because it is a future cost that differs between alternatives. If the firm replaces its current system with a new one, then it can sell the new system for $1,000 at the end of its useful life (in the future). If the firm does not buy the new one, it obviously cannot sell the old system.

Compare the Relevant Costs and Select an Alternative

Now that you have determined which costs are relevant, you compare them to see which alternative is best for the law firm. It is important to differentiate between inflows and outflows. In Exhibit 6–3 we use parentheses to identify outflows.

Exhibit 6–3
Relevant Cost Comparison for Naxon and Lewis

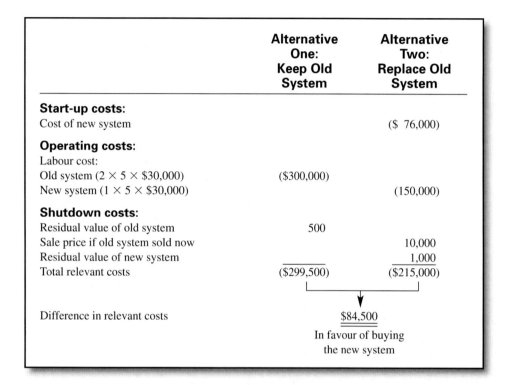

	Alternative One: Keep Old System	Alternative Two: Replace Old System
Start-up costs:		
Cost of new system		($ 76,000)
Operating costs:		
Labour cost:		
Old system (2 × 5 × $30,000)	($300,000)	
New system (1 × 5 × $30,000)		(150,000)
Shutdown costs:		
Residual value of old system	500	
Sale price if old system sold now		10,000
Residual value of new system		1,000
Total relevant costs	($299,500)	($215,000)
Difference in relevant costs		$84,500

In favour of buying
the new system

As this analysis shows, the firm would save $84,500 over the next five years by buying the new computer system. So the firm should buy the new system to save money, right? From a purely monetary point of view, it should. However, can the firm? The replacement system is not cheap. Often business decision makers determine the best alternative, only to learn the business does not have enough available cash to take advantage of a course of action that would save money in the long run. Considering only relevant costs in decision making will lead to better business decisions, but it will not necessarily enable a company to take advantage of what can be learned in the process.

 ## Discussion Questions

6-5. Assuming all purchases and sales of computer systems are cash transactions, how much cash would the firm need to buy the new system?

6-6. Now that we know the relevant cost associated with the computer replacement, what qualitative factors should the law firm consider before it makes its final decision?

Interest—The Time Value of Money

New equipment purchase decisions generally have long-term effects. Because of the long life of the equipment, the associated cash inflows and outflows will occur for many years. Therefore, decision makers should consider the interest-earning potential of the cash flows associated with equipment acquisitions. The interest-earning potential of cash is sometimes called the **time value of money.** Chapter 7 covers special techniques developed to incorporate the effect of interest and the timing of cash flows.

time value of money
The interest-earning potential of cash.

SPECIAL ORDERS

special order An order that is outside a company's normal scope of business activity.

Manufacturing businesses must often consider whether to accept a **special order**— an order that is outside its normal scope of business activity. As we will see, proper treatment of fixed cost is critical in making sound special-order decisions.

Assume that your company, Alumafloat, makes small aluminum boats. Alumafloat has been in operation for almost ten years and sells boats to marine supply stores in Canada. One day, a Canadian Tire Corporation, Limited representative approaches you with an interesting proposition. Canadian Tire is interested in purchasing 1,000 of your boats for $125 each. The largest order your company has received to date was for 100 boats, so obviously, this huge order requires special consideration.

Gather All Costs Associated with the Decision

The $125 offer from Canadian Tire is considerably less than Alumafloat's normal selling price of $160 per boat. In fact, the boats cost $130 each to produce, so the company would lose $5 per boat if it accepts the $125 offer.

As you discuss the order with the representative from Canadian Tire, you tell her that you would be willing to sell the boats to Canadian Tire at a discounted price of $140 each because of the large quantity of boats they need. Canadian Tire refuses your offer. The company will only pay $125 per boat, and the representative expects you to accept or reject the order within five days.

You gather all the information necessary to make a wise decision. First, you meet with your company's cost accountant, who confirms that your cost per unit is $130. You also request a report detailing production cost so you can see how the cost per unit figure was calculated. Using expected total sales (excluding the special order from Canadian Tire) and production costs for the year, the cost accountant prepares the report shown in Exhibit 6–4.

We must determine the potential effect on Alumafloat's revenues and expenses of accepting the order. Which costs shown in Exhibit 6–4 would be affected by the decision to accept the special order from Canadian Tire? To determine which costs are relevant, we will again ask the following two questions: (1) Is the cost a future cost? and (2) Does the cost differ between alternatives?

Determine the Relevant Cost of Each Alternative

Next you must determine which costs are relevant. In this situation, the alternatives are to accept the order or reject it. Generally speaking, because no cost is associated with rejecting the order, our analysis focuses on the alternative to accept.

Exhibit 6–4
Per Unit Cost Report
for Alumafloat

	Per Unit	Total
Expected sales (5,500 units at $160 each)		$880,000
Less: Cost of goods sold (see detail below)		(715,000)
Expected gross margin		$165,000

Detailed calculation for cost of goods sold:

	Per Unit	Total
Number of units	1	5,500
Direct material costs	$ 50	$275,000
Direct labour costs	55	302,500
Variable production costs	10	55,000
Fixed production costs	15	82,500
Total cost of goods sold	$130	$715,000

If the order is accepted, sales will increase by $125,000 (1,000 boats × $125 per boat). The increase in sales due to the special order is relevant, because it is something that will happen in the future and it differs between alternatives.

All variable costs are relevant because they are future costs that differ between alternatives. If the special order is accepted, variable costs will be incurred to produce the 1,000 boats. In this example, variable cost includes direct material, direct labour, and variable production costs.

Depending on the decision situation, fixed cost may or may not be relevant. Often fixed production costs are not relevant costs because total fixed cost for the company will be unaffected by the increase in production volume. This fact holds true unless specific fixed cost increases occur due to the special order, or the order is so substantial that production would exceed the relevant range if the company accepts the order. As the report in Exhibit 6–4 indicates, the company expects total fixed costs to be $82,500. Assume in our example that the decision to accept or reject the special order from Canadian Tire would not affect total fixed cost. Therefore, in this case, fixed cost does not differ between alternatives and is irrelevant to the special order decision.

Compare the Relevant Costs and Select an Alternative

Armed with information about relevant cost, you can make an informed decision about the Canadian Tire order. Exhibit 6–5 presents a schedule of relevant costs for this special order. The schedule excludes fixed costs because they are irrelevant.

Exhibit 6–5
Relevant Costs for
Special Order of
1,000 Boats

	Per Unit	Total
Sales from special order	$125	$125,000
Direct material costs	(50)	(50,000)
Direct labour costs	(55)	(55,000)
Variable production costs	(10)	(10,000)
Total relevant production costs	(115)	(115,000)
Total increase in income	$ 10	$ 10,000

Alumafloat's income would increase by $10,000 if it accepted the special order.

The reasoning in the Alumafloat example may seem logical, but companies often reject special orders that would increase profits, because managers do not understand the concept of relevant cost as it pertains to fixed cost. To avoid making poor decisions, managers must carefully consider how a special order will affect fixed cost.

An accountant for a large, well-known manufacturing company once remarked, "I can't believe that the product sales manager is selling below cost. He is disregarding fixed cost as he sets prices to move old stock." In fact, the manager may have made a good decision about the price of the product, depending on whether the fixed costs are relevant to the pricing decision. As a manager, you should know that routinely prepared accounting information cannot be relevant to every decision. Accounting information must be tailored, sometimes by the information user, to provide information that is relevant to the decision at hand.

 Discussion Questions

6–7. What would happen if you treated every order as a special order and routinely disregarded fixed cost considerations from your pricing decisions?

6–8. Assume that the production manager at Alumafloat reminds you that four years ago sales skyrocketed for a while. Demand was so great that production increased to the limit of the company's capacity. Alumafloat produced 6,950 boats in a 12-month period. What implications does this information have on your decision to accept the special order from Canadian Tire?

6–9. What qualitative factors should you consider regarding accepting an order to sell Canadian Tire the boats for less than the price you charge your regular customers? For example, what would your regular customers think if they found that Canadian Tire was selling the same style boat they buy from you?

OUTSOURCING: THE MAKE-OR-BUY DECISION

outsourcing Buying services, products, or components of products instead of producing them.

Often companies purchase subcomponents used to manufacture their products instead of making them in their in-house manufacturing facilities. Buying services, products, or components of products from outside vendors instead of producing them is called **outsourcing**. Decision makers considering a make-or-buy decision must pay close attention to fixed costs and opportunity costs.

Assume you are a product manager at Microbake, a factory that manufactures microwave ovens. A vendor has approached you about supplying the timer assemblies for your ovens for $12 each. Currently, Microbake makes the timers in its own subassembly department. The subassembly department makes many of the small component parts for the various products manufactured at the factory. When you review the cost sheets for the timers, you discover that the company uses 80,000 timers each year and they cost $14 each to produce in-house.

Gather All Costs Associated with the Decision

You call a meeting with Microbake's cost accounting department to discuss the situation and confirm that the $14 in-house manufacturing cost is correct. Even when pressed, the cost accountants are confident their cost figures are carefully prepared and accurate. In fact, they are surprised the company can buy the timers from the outside vendor for only $12 each. At your request, the cost accounting department prepares the cost breakdown for the timers shown in Exhibit 6–6.

Exhibit 6–6
Cost of Producing Oven Timers In-House

Number of timers produced each year		80,000
	Per Unit	Total
Direct material	$ 5	$ 400,000
Direct labour	4	320,000
Variable manufacturing overhead	1	80,000
Fixed manufacturing overhead	4	320,000
Total	$14	$1,120,000

Determine the Relevant Cost of Each Alternative

Once again we assess whether each cost is relevant by asking the following questions: (1) Is the cost a future cost? and (2) Does the cost differ between alternatives? The answers appear in Exhibit 6–7.

Exhibit 6–7
Selecting Relevant Costs of Producing Oven Timers

	Future?	Differs?	Relevant?
Direct material:	yes	yes	yes
Direct labour:	yes	yes	yes
Variable manufacturing overhead:	yes	yes	yes
Fixed manufacturing overhead:	yes	**no**	**no**

By definition, *fixed* manufacturing overhead remains constant in total regardless of the level of activity (in this case "activity" is the number of units produced). The fixed cost presented by the cost accountants is an allocation of the total fixed overhead cost of the whole factory, or possibly of the subassembly department. If the company stops making the timers, the subassembly department will not go away and neither will its fixed cost, because the company needs the subassembly department to produce other components. Unless fixed cost changes based on management's decision to buy the timers, it is irrelevant.

Compare the Relevant Costs and Select an Alternative

We compare the relevant costs of the make-or-buy decision in Exhibit 6–8. As the exhibit indicates, once we have screened out the irrelevant fixed costs it becomes apparent that Microbake can save $160,000 per year by making the timers rather than buying them. Based on this relevant cost comparison, you decide to not purchase the timer assemblies from the outside vendor.

In a final effort to get the sale, the vendor contacts several people at Microbake informing them that you are squandering your company's money. The vendor points out to other Microbake managers that its price is $2 per unit less than your in-house production cost as determined by Microbake's highly trained cost accountants. Other managers are pressing to accept the outside vendor's proposal.

Exhibit 6–8
Relevant Cost of Make-or-Buy Decision for Oven Timers

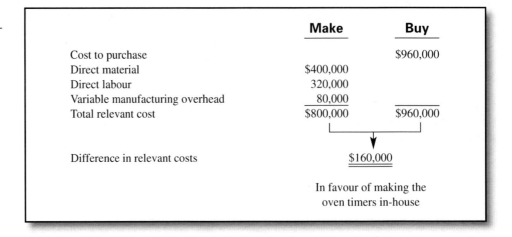

	Make	Buy
Cost to purchase		$960,000
Direct material	$400,000	
Direct labour	320,000	
Variable manufacturing overhead	80,000	
Total relevant cost	$800,000	$960,000
Difference in relevant costs		$160,000

In favour of making the
oven timers in-house

To settle the issue, you call a meeting of the managers and present your relevant cost findings. Several managers comment that your information disregards fixed manufacturing overhead. You explain that the fixed manufacturing overhead is irrelevant. The other managers argue that fixed manufacturing overhead is a very real part of business cost and that it should be included in your presentation. As it happens, this presents little problem. Including fixed manufacturing overhead, although irrelevant, may highlight how fixed costs are affected (or in this case, unaffected) by changes in production. You must demonstrate, however, that if the units are manufactured in-house, fixed manufacturing overhead cost will happen; and that if the units are purchased from the outside vendor, the fixed manufacturing overhead will still occur. The relevant cost comparison can include the irrelevant fixed cost as shown in Exhibit 6–9.

Exhibit 6–9
Relevant Cost of Make-or-Buy Decision for Oven Timers with Fixed Costs Shown

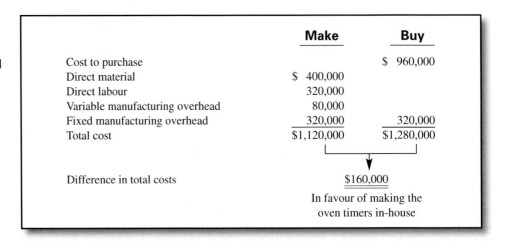

	Make	Buy
Cost to purchase		$ 960,000
Direct material	$ 400,000	
Direct labour	320,000	
Variable manufacturing overhead	80,000	
Fixed manufacturing overhead	320,000	320,000
Total cost	$1,120,000	$1,280,000
Difference in total costs		$160,000

In favour of making the
oven timers in-house

As Exhibit 6–9 shows, because fixed manufacturing overhead is the same for the two alternatives, the outcome of the comparison is the same as that in Exhibit 6–8. Microbake can save $160,000 by making the timers instead of buying them.

 ## Discussion Question

6–10. What will happen to the cost of producing other Microbake products if your decision is overturned and the company outsources the timer assemblies?

Special Relevant Cost Considerations for Fixed Costs

In some situations, fixed costs are affected by the alternative selected. For example, suppose Microbake could eliminate an entire eight-hour production shift if it no longer made the timers. Eliminating that shift thus eliminates one line supervisor whose annual salary is $45,000 per year and reduces other fixed costs by $150,000. Therefore, fixed manufacturing overhead would decrease by $195,000 ($45,000 + $150,000). Exhibit 6–10 shows the relevant cost of the make-or-buy decision when the alternative to buy the timers enables the company to eliminate a production shift.

Exhibit 6–10
Relevant Cost of the Make-or-Buy Decision for Oven Timers with Relevant Fixed Costs

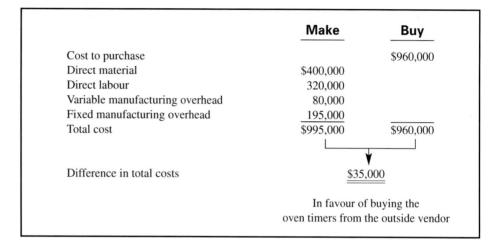

	Make	Buy
Cost to purchase		$960,000
Direct material	$400,000	
Direct labour	320,000	
Variable manufacturing overhead	80,000	
Fixed manufacturing overhead	195,000	
Total cost	$995,000	$960,000
Difference in total costs		$35,000

In favour of buying the oven timers from the outside vendor

Exhibit 6–10 shows that the savings in fixed manufacturing overhead alters the cost comparison such that Microbake should opt to buy the timers. If the $195,000 reduction in fixed costs were realized, Microbake would save $35,000 by purchasing the timer assemblies from the vendor instead of making them.

Discussion Question

6–11. What qualitative factors should managers at Microbake consider with respect to their outsourcing decision?

Considering Opportunity Costs

opportunity cost The benefit foregone (given up) because one alternative is chosen over another.

Recall that an **opportunity cost** is the value of what is foregone (given up) because one alternative is chosen over another. For example, the opportunity cost of attending college rather than working full-time is what you could have earned by working instead of going to college.

If Microbake buys the timer assemblies from an outside vendor, it may have an alternative use for the production capacity or assets used to make the timers—it may have an opportunity to enhance its earnings through an alternative use of the facilities. Assume that Microbake can use the production capacity freed up by purchasing the timers to make electronic alarm clocks. Assume further that the electronic alarm clocks would provide an annual contribution margin of $200,000 with no significant changes to fixed cost. If Microbake continues to make the timer assembles, it would forego the opportunity to earn the $200,000. The foregone $200,000 contribution margin on the electronic alarm clocks is an opportunity cost.

Rick Montgomery was reviewing the monthly financial statements for West Coast Alloys and Metals Ltd. One expense category caught him by surprise.

"Our delivery charges for last month were significantly higher than we thought they would be," Rick says. "As we have gained more market share and diversified out of the forest products industry, the number of deliveries we have to make is going up."

Rick decided to review his alternatives. He decided there were three choices. First, he could continue with the current delivery service; second, he could have other delivery companies bid for the company's business; or third, he could buy a truck, hire a driver, and West Coast could do the deliveries itself.

Rick then evaluated these options. He was happy with the current delivery service and was quite sure that the current delivery company was as efficient and cost-effective as any of its competitors. So his decision came down to whether to bring the delivery cost in-house.

Rick reviewed the relevant costs involved in the two alternatives. He estimated the number of deliveries that would be required and the cost per delivery as quoted by the current delivery company. He then determined the costs if West Coast did the deliveries itself. These costs included the cost of the delivery truck, the cost of operating and maintaining it, and the cost of the driver. Rick compared the costs and decided to stay with the outside service.

"The decision was not only based on the quantitative analysis," Rick says. "I thought about some factors that I could not necessarily quantify but that were important, such as the effect of a downturn in business. If I buy the truck, the costs become fixed, and I have to pay a lot of them whether we are busy or not. Under the current system, the cost is variable to me and I only pay when a delivery is required."

Because opportunity cost is the cost of *not* doing something, it is not reflected in the accounting records of a business and is not reported in the company's external financial statements or internal management reports. This does not mean an opportunity cost is not real—remember, reality and the measurement of reality are not the same thing. Opportunity cost is an economic reality. Although it is not generally part of financial accounting measures, opportunity cost is a relevant consideration in business decisions.

Returning to the Microbake timer example, the relevant costs of making or buying the 80,000 timers, including the $200,000 opportunity, is presented in Exhibit 6–11, which suggests that if the $200,000 contribution margin from the production of alarm clocks could be realized, Microbake should buy the timer assemblies from the outside vendor. The production capacity no longer needed to produce the timers could then be used to produce the alarm clocks, resulting in a $40,000 difference in the relevant cost in favour of buying the timers.

Microbake's outsourcing problem is an example of a very real business dilemma. Managers cannot rely solely on the cost information from accountants. They themselves must have enough accounting knowledge to determine the relevant cost of each decision alternative.

Although we have explored relevant cost using only three examples, you should understand that relevant cost concepts apply to almost every business decision.

Exhibit 6–11
Relevant Cost of Make-or-Buy Decision for Oven Timers with Opportunity Cost

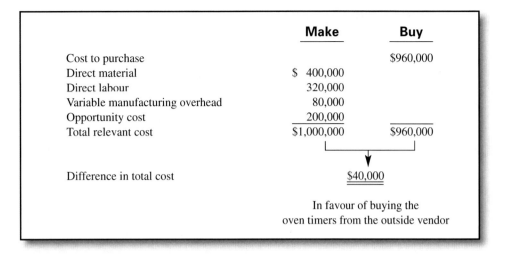

	Make	Buy
Cost to purchase		$960,000
Direct material	$ 400,000	
Direct labour	320,000	
Variable manufacturing overhead	80,000	
Opportunity cost	200,000	
Total relevant cost	$1,000,000	$960,000
Difference in total cost	$40,000	

In favour of buying the oven timers from the outside vendor

Relevant costing is even helpful with personal decisions such as whether to attend summer school at a local university or enroll in a student exchange program and study abroad. Business situations and life in general provide an array of quantitative and qualitative considerations for every decision alternative. As a decision maker, you must be able to seek out the relevant considerations and disregard the irrelevant ones.

SUMMARY

All management decision making entails choosing between or among alternatives. If managers are to have any chance of making the best decision in a given situation, they must attempt to consider only relevant information.

A relevant cost is a cost that makes a difference in a given decision situation. What is relevant in one situation may not be relevant in another. Relevant costs are also always future costs, because past costs cannot be changed by any current or future actions. Further, a future cost must differ between or among the alternatives to be considered relevant. Opportunity costs are often relevant and should be considered by managers making decisions. An opportunity cost is the value of benefits foregone because one alternative is chosen over another.

In addition to the quantitative information managers must consider in making decisions, qualitative information such as customer satisfaction, product quality, and employee morale must also be considered. Oftentimes the qualitative considerations should outweigh purely quantitative considerations.

There are many applications of relevant costing in management decision making. Careful application of relevant costing techniques can help managers to make appropriate decisions in various business situations.

KEY TERMS

opportunity cost, p. 197
outsourcing, p. 194
qualitative factors, p. 187
quantitative factors, p. 187
relevant cost, p. 186

relevant costing, p. 186
special order, p. 192
sunk cost, p. 186
time value of money, p. 192

REVIEW THE FACTS

1. What is relevant costing?
2. What is a relevant cost?
3. What two important characteristics do all relevant costs possess?
4. What is a sunk cost?
5. Describe the difference between qualitative and quantitative factors.
6. When trying to determine whether a cost is relevant, what are the two questions the decision maker should ask?
7. Why is the amortization for existing assets considered irrelevant for equipment replacement decisions?
8. What is the time value of money?
9. Why is the time value of money important for decisions involving the purchase of long-lived assets?
10. What would cause a fixed cost to be relevant for a special-order decision?
11. What is outsourcing?
12. Define opportunity cost.
13. The concepts of relevant costing apply to what types of decisions?

APPLY WHAT YOU HAVE LEARNED

LO 1: Determine Which Costs Are Relevant

1. The production manager at Atlantic Manufacturing Inc. is contemplating whether he should upgrade some old production equipment. He is considering the following factors:

   1. __I__ The cost of the old equipment
   2. __R__ The cost of the new equipment
   3. __I__ Amortization on the old equipment
   4. _____ Amortization on the new equipment
   5. _____ Trade-in value of the old equipment
   6. _____ Residual value of the old equipment
   7. _____ Residual value of the new equipment

REQUIRED:
For each item listed, indicate whether it is relevant (R) or irrelevant (I).

LO 3: Quantitative and Qualitative Considerations

2. Tom Robinson is thinking about buying a laptop computer. He has a computer at home, but the laptop computer would allow him to work during his frequent business trips. Tom is trying to convince his boss that the computer would save the company some money. Tom hopes that his company will pay at least part of the computer's purchase price and the monthly fee for an e-mail service and Internet connection.

   Tom has asked a group of friends to help him think of all the advantages of buying the computer. Assume you are part of the group.

REQUIRED:

a. Prepare an informal schedule of the costs associated with the computer purchase.

b. List as many quantitative benefits as you can that the company will gain if Tom buys the laptop computer.

c. List as many quantitative benefits as you can that Tom will gain if he buys the laptop computer.

d. List as many qualitative benefits as you can that the company will gain if Tom buys the laptop computer.

e. List as many qualitative benefits as you can that Tom will gain if he buys the laptop computer.

f. How much of the computer's cost do you think Tom should pay? How much should Tom's employer pay?

LO 3 & 4: Determine Relevant Cost Schedule and Qualitative Factors

3. Tina Alberts is thinking about trading her car for a new one. Her present car is only three years old, completely paid for, but out of warranty. The car's original cost was $22,000. Lately, the car has been somewhat undependable and the repair bills have been quite high. In the last three months, Tina paid over $1,200 for repairs. Tina intends to use her trade-in as the down payment and then finance the balance. She is looking at a new Nissan that she can get for about $23,000, less her trade.

   Tina has asked a group of close friends to help her think of all the relevant advantages and disadvantages of getting the new car. Assume you are part of this group.

REQUIRED:

a. Prepare an informal schedule listing the relevant quantitative factors that Tina should consider. Do not limit your answer to the items found in the problem. Include all the factors you can think of. When possible, try to include estimated dollar amounts in your schedule.

b. Prepare an informal schedule listing the relevant qualitative factors that Tina should consider.

c. From a quantitative point of view, do you think Tina should buy the new car?

d. Considering both quantitative and qualitative factors, do you think Tina should buy the new car?

LO 1: Determine Which Costs Are Relevant

4. Jean Parks is a salesperson for Quality Food Products Inc. She is considering a 250-kilometre trip to visit a potential customer, ByLots. Following are the factors she is pondering.

   1. _____ The cost of traveling the 250 kilometres to ByLots
   2. _____ The time she will spend on the road
   3. _____ The time she will spend visiting with ByLots's executives
   4. _____ The amount of time already devoted to ByLots
   5. _____ The revenue potential from ByLots
   6. _____ The cost of her last visit to ByLots
   7. _____ The probability that her visit will result in new sales
   8. _____ The cost of lunch for herself if she visits ByLots
   9. _____ The cost of the lunch she would buy for ByLots's executives

REQUIRED:

For each item listed, indicate whether it is relevant (R) or irrelevant (I).

LO 3:   Determine Quantitative and Qualitative Factors

5. This question is based on the same situation as problem 4. Jean Parks is a salesperson for Quality Food Products Inc. She is considering a 250-kilometre trip to visit a potential customer, ByLots. Following are the factors she is pondering.

1. _____ The cost of traveling the 250 kilometres to ByLots
2. _____ The time she will spend on the road
3. _____ The time she will spend visiting with ByLots's executives
4. _____ The amount of time already devoted to ByLots
5. _____ The revenue potential from ByLots
6. _____ The cost of her last visit to ByLots
7. _____ The probability that her visit will result in new sales
8. _____ The cost of lunch for herself if she visits ByLots
9. _____ The cost of the lunch she would buy for ByLots's executives

REQUIRED:

For each item listed, indicate whether it is quantitative (A) or qualitative (B).

LO 3:   Determine Quantitative and Qualitative Factors

6. Managers at Poulin Manufacturing Inc. are considering upgrading some production equipment. They are considering the following factors:

1. _____ Maintenance cost
2. _____ Changes in product quality
3. _____ Residual value of the old equipment
4. _____ Cost of new equipment
5. _____ Difficulty of training employees to use new equipment
6. _____ Residual value of the new equipment
7. _____ The ill feelings due to the possible reduction in the labour force

REQUIRED:

For each item listed, indicate whether it is quantitative (A) or qualitative (B).

LO 1, 2, 3, & 5:   List All Costs, Indicate Relevant Costs, Indicate Qualitative Factors

7. Assume that you are deciding whether to live in a campus residence or an off-campus apartment.

REQUIRED:

a. List all the costs that come to mind as you think about this decision.
b. Review your list and indicate which costs are relevant and which are irrelevant to the decision.
c. What are some qualitative factors that you should consider when making this decision?

LO 1, 2, 3, & 5:   List Costs, Indicate Relevant Costs, Indicate Qualitative Factors

8. Assume that you are deciding what to do next summer. You are considering two alternatives: Go to summer school, or tour Europe.

REQUIRED:

a. List all the costs that come to mind as you think about this decision.
b. Review your list and indicate which costs are relevant and which are irrelevant to your decision.
c. What are some qualitative factors that you should consider when making this decision?

LO 1, 2, 3, & 5:   List Costs, Indicate Relevant Costs, Indicate Qualitative Factors

9. George Binkley's car is seven years old. The car is no longer under warranty and requires frequent repairs. George is trying to decide whether to buy a new car. He has asked you what you think about his idea.

REQUIRED:

a. List all the costs that come to mind as you think about his decision.
b. Review your list and indicate which costs are relevant and which are irrelevant to the decision.
c. What are some qualitative factors that he should consider when making this decision?

LO 4:   Determine Relevant Cost for Equipment Replacement

10. The managers at Gooderich Manufacturing Company are considering replacing the industrial mixer used in the company's factory.

Information about the old mixer:

Cost	$28,000
Estimated useful life	10 years
Estimated residual value	$0
Current age	5 years
Estimated current fair value	$8,000
Annual operating cost	$15,000

Information about the new mixer:

Cost	$34,000
Estimated useful life	5 years
Estimated residual value	$0
Annual operating cost	$12,000

REQUIRED:

Prepare a relevant cost schedule showing the benefit of keeping the old mixer or buying the new one.

LO 4:   Determine Relevant Cost for Equipment Replacement

11. The managers at Prairie Manufacturing Company are considering replacing the industrial lathe used in the company's factory.

Information about the old lathe:

Cost	$57,000
Estimated useful life	8 years
Estimated residual value	$0
Current age	2 years
Estimated current fair value	$32,000
Annual operating cost	$32,000

Information about the new lathe:

Cost	$61,000
Estimated useful life	6 years
Estimated residual value	$0
Annual operating cost	$24,000

REQUIRED:

Prepare a relevant cost schedule showing the benefit of keeping the old lathe or buying the new one.

LO 4: Determine Relevant Cost for Equipment Replacement

12. Randy Allen, president of Allen Boat Hauling, is considering replacing the company's industrial lift used to haul boats. The new lift would allow the company to lift larger boats out of the water.

Information about the old lift:

Cost	$94,000
Estimated useful life	12 years
Estimated residual value	$10,000
Current age	4 years
Estimated current fair value	$48,000
Annual contribution margin	$50,000

Information about the new lift:

Cost	$128,000
Estimated useful life	8 years
Estimated residual value	$ 25,000
Annual contribution margin	$ 65,000

REQUIRED:

Prepare a relevant cost schedule showing the benefit of keeping the old lift or buying the new one.

LO 4: Determine Relevant Cost for Equipment Replacement

13. The managers at North Coast Manufacturing are considering replacing a printing press with a new, high-speed model.

Information about the old printing press:

Cost	$255,000
Estimated useful life	10 years
Estimated residual value	$ 25,000
Annual amortization	$ 23,000
Current age	3 years
Accumulated amortization to date	$184,000
Estimated current fair value	$150,000
Annual contribution margin	$110,000

Information about the new printing press:

Cost	$535,000
Estimated useful life	7 years
Estimated residual value	$ 45,000
Annual amortization	$ 70,000
Annual contribution margin	$150,000

REQUIRED:

Prepare a relevant cost schedule showing the benefit of keeping the old printing press or buying the new one.

LO 4: Determine Relevant Cost for New Business Segment

14. Photo Express operates a small camera store in St. Andrew by the Sea, New Brunswick. The store has two departments, camera sales and photo finishing. Rent, utilities, and other operating expenses are allocated to the departments based on the square metres occupied by the department. Currently, the camera sales department occupies 600 square metres and the photo finishing department occupies 400 square metres.

The Photo Express president, Judith Dunstra, is thinking about buying a computer system to produce poster prints. The poster print system would occupy 40 square metres of the store's floor space.

Budgeted monthly information for the store:

Store rent	$ 5,000
Salaries and wages	10,500
Utilities	750
Other operating expenses	3,000
Sales	125,000
Cost of goods sold	95,000

Information about the poster print system:

Cost of the poster system	$25,700
Estimated useful life	5 years
Estimated residual value	$500
Floor space required	40 square metres
Monthly cost of additional electricity used by poster system	$50
Budgeted monthly amounts:	
Poster sales revenue	$1,200
Poster supplies	200
Wages for poster operation	250
Store rent	200
Utilities	30
Other operating expenses	120

Dunstra believes the company should not buy the poster system because it will show a loss every month. Because she is not sure, she has contacted a small consulting group to seek advice. Assume you are part of the consulting group.

REQUIRED:

a. Would the poster system show a loss every month as Judith suggests? Prepare a schedule to substantiate your answer.

b. Would the company's overall monthly profits increase or decrease as a result of buying the poster system? Prepare a schedule to substantiate your answer.

c. Prepare a relevant cost schedule showing the advantage or disadvantage of buying the poster system.

LO 4: Determine Relevant Cost for New Business Segment

15. The Canmore Gift Hut operates a small souvenir shop in Canmore, Alberta. The shop has two departments, retail sales and mail order. Rent, utilities, and other operating expenses are allocated to the departments based on the square metres occupied by the department. Currently, the retail sales department occupies 1,000 square metres and the mail order department occupies 200 square metres.

Canmore's president, Frank Sillars, is thinking about buying a silk screen machine to make souvenir T-shirts. The silk screen machine would occupy 100 square metres of the souvenir shop's floor space.

Budgeted monthly information for the store:

Store rent	$ 5,100
Salaries and wages	8,500
Utilities	1,000
Other operating expenses	3,000
Sales	80,000
Cost of goods sold	57,000

Information about the silk screen machine:

Cost of the silk screen machine	$9,640
Estimated useful life	5 years
Estimated residual value	$400
Floor space required	100 square metres
Monthly cost of additional electricity used by silk screen machine	$20
Budgeted monthly amounts:	
T-shirt sales revenue	$1,700
Cost of T-shirts	450
Cost of T-shirt supplies	100
Wages for the T-shirt operation (additional)	250
Store rent	425
Utilities	83
Other operating expenses	250

Sillars believes the company should not buy the silk screen machine because it will show a loss every month. Because he is not sure, he has contacted a small consulting group to seek advice. Assume you are part of the consulting group.

REQUIRED:

a. Would the silk screen machine show a loss every month as Sillars suggests? Prepare a schedule to substantiate your answer.

b. Would the company's overall monthly profits increase or decrease as a result of buying the silk screen machine? Prepare a schedule to substantiate your answer.

c. Prepare a relevant cost schedule showing the advantage or disadvantage of buying the silk screen machine.

LO 4: Determine Relevant Cost for Equipment Replacement

16. Fraser Marine Service purchased a forklift five years ago for $16,000. When it was purchased the forklift had an estimated useful life of ten years and a residual value of $4,000. The forklift can be sold now for $6,000. The operating cost for the forklift is $4,500 per year.

Fraser Marine is thinking about buying a newer forklift for $17,000. The newer model would have an estimated useful life of five years and a residual value of $7,000. The operating cost for the newer forklift would be $3,000 per year.

REQUIRED:

a. What are the relevant costs associated with the decision to replace the forklift?

b. Prepare a relevant cost schedule showing the advantage or disadvantage of buying the forklift.

LO 4: Determine Relevant Cost for Equipment Replacement

17. Al Hart of Hart Engineering Inc. is considering whether to purchase a new copy machine. He purchased the old machine two years ago for $8,500. When purchased, the old machine had an estimated useful life of eight years and a residual value of $500. The operating cost of the old machine is $3,000 per year. The old machine can be sold today for $2,000. A new machine can be bought today for $10,000 and would have an estimated useful life of six years with a residual value of $1,000. The operating cost of the new copy machine is expected to be $1,500 per year.

REQUIRED:

a. Prepare a schedule showing all the costs associated with the current copy machine.

b. Prepare a schedule showing all the costs associated with the new copy machine.

c. Prepare a schedule showing the relevant cost of the copy machine replacement decision and the favoured alternative.

d. Discuss the qualitative factors that Hart should consider.

e. Would you buy the newer copy machine?

LO 4: Determine Relevant Cost for Equipment Replacement

18. Mike Thomlinson is considering whether to replace one of his delivery trucks. He purchased the current delivery truck four years ago for $24,000, and it came with a three-year, 60,000-kilometre warranty. When purchased, the current truck had an estimated useful life of five years and a residual value of $2,000. Thomlinson uses the straight-line method for amortization. The new truck would be identical to the current truck, except it would be new and would have the new 60,000-kilometre warranty. The operating cost for the current truck is $4,000 for fuel, $23,200 for the driver's salary, and maintenance cost is about $5,000 per year. If Thomlinson keeps the old truck, it will last another five years, but would require $5,000 in maintenance each year. The current truck can be sold now for $4,000, or it can be sold in five years for $1,000. The new truck would cost $25,500, has an estimated useful life of five years, and can be sold at the end of the five years for $4,000. At the end of the warranty period, the new truck will require maintenance of $5,000 per year.

REQUIRED:

a. Prepare a schedule showing all the costs associated with the current truck.

b. Prepare a schedule showing all the costs associated with the new truck.

c. Prepare a schedule showing the relevant cost of the truck replacement decision and the favoured alternative.

d. Discuss the qualitative factors that Thomlinson should consider.

e. If the old truck had an estimated useful life of five years when it was purchased, and it has already been used for four years, discuss the ramifications of using the truck for another five years.

f. Would you buy the new truck? Why or why not?

LO 4: Determine Relevant Cost for Equipment Replacement

19. Conlin Engineering Inc. is considering whether to replace a piece of production equipment with a new model. The new machine would cost $170,000, have an eight-year life, and have no residual value. The variable cost of operating the machine would be $180,000 per year. The present machine was purchased one year ago, and could be used for the next eight years. When it was purchased, the present machine had an estimated useful life of nine years and a residual value of zero. The present machine can be sold now for $28,000, but will have no salvage value in eight years. The variable cost of operating the present machine is $200,000 per year.

REQUIRED:

a. Prepare a schedule showing the costs associated with the present machine.

b. Prepare a schedule showing the costs associated with the new machine.

c. Prepare a schedule showing the relevant cost of the equipment replacement decision and the favoured alternative.

d. Discuss the qualitative factors that the company should consider.

LO 3 & 4: Determine the Relevant Cost of Buying a House and List Qualitative Factors

20. Jeremy Chang is in the process of buying a house. He is interested in two houses. One house is three kilometres from his work, the other is on the outskirts of town, 55 kilometres from work. Surprisingly, the two houses are nearly identical, except the closer house is much more expensive. The house that is three kilometres from Jeremy's work is $207,000, whereas the other house is only $189,000. Maintenance, taxes, insurance, and other costs would be the same for both houses.

Jeremy goes to work about 250 days each year. He has just traded his old car for a new one. Each time his car reaches 120,000 kilometres, he trades it for a new model. Generally, he expects to pay about $30,000 when he trades for a new car. His cars usually get about 10 kilometres per litre of regular, $0.70-per-litre gasoline. Maintenance on his car runs about $0.03 per litre on average. Other than driving to and from work, Jeremy drives about 25,000 kilometres each year.

Regardless of which house Jeremy buys, he expects to be transferred to another area of the country in five years.

Jeremy is about to buy the less expensive house when he asks your advice.

REQUIRED:

a. Which house should Jeremy buy?

b. How much will Jeremy save if he follows your advice? (Disregard the time value of money.)

c. What qualitative factors should Jeremy consider?

LO 4:   Relevant Cost of a Make-or-Buy Decision

21. Microline Ltd. is considering buying computer cabinets from an outside vendor. Currently, Microline makes the cabinets in its own manufacturing facility. Microline can buy the cabinets for $15 each. The company uses 15,000 cabinets each year. Information about Microline's cost to manufacture the 15,000 cabinets follows:

	Per Unit	Total
Direct material	$ 4	$ 60,000
Direct labour	6	90,000
Variable overhead	7	105,000
Fixed overhead	5	75,000
Total	$22	$330,000

Fixed cost for Microline would not change if the company stopped making the cabinets.

REQUIRED:
Prepare a relevant cost schedule that indicates whether Microline Ltd. should buy the cabinets or continue to make them.

LO 4:   Relevant Cost of a Make-or-Buy Decision

22. Gem Products Ltd. is considering buying the casters it uses in the manufacture of office chairs from an outside vendor. Currently, Gem Products Ltd. makes the casters in its own manufacturing facility. Gem Products can buy the casters for $1.15 each. The company uses 450,000 casters each year.

Information about Gem Products Ltd.'s cost to manufacture the 450,000 casters follows:

	Per Unit	Total
Direct material	$0.50	$225,000
Direct labour	0.10	45,000
Variable overhead	0.40	180,000
Fixed overhead	0.25	112,500
Total	$1.25	$562,500

Fixed cost for Gem Products Ltd. would not change if the company stopped making the casters.

REQUIRED:
Prepare a relevant cost schedule that indicates whether Gem Products Ltd. should buy the casters or continue to make them.

LO 4:   Relevant Cost of a Make-or-Buy Decision

23. Richards Manufacturing Inc. is considering buying the mounting brackets it uses to make its fire extinguishers from an outside supplier. Currently, Richards Manufacturing Inc. makes the brackets in its own manufacturing facility. Richards Manufacturing Inc. can buy the brackets for $0.75 each. The company uses 700,000 brackets each year.

Information about Richards Manufacturing Inc.'s cost to manufacture the 700,000 brackets follows:

	Per Unit	Total
Direct material	$0.30	$210,000
Direct labour	0.10	70,000
Variable overhead	0.40	280,000
Fixed overhead	0.14	98,000
Total	$0.94	$658,000

Fixed cost for Richards Manufacturing Inc. would not change if the company stopped making the brackets.

REQUIRED:
Prepare a relevant cost schedule that indicates whether Richards Manufacturing Inc. should buy the brackets or continue to make them.

LO 4:   Relevant Cost of an Outsourcing Decision

24. Jumbo Chinese Restaurant Ltd. operates a small laundry facility to launder the uniforms, tablecloths, and other linens used by its restaurant chain. Jumbo's laundry operation occupies space in an industrial area close to the company's home office and its largest restaurant. Jumbo is considering using a laundry service to perform the laundering needed by the company.

    Jumbo's $180,000 administrative expense is allocated based on the number of employees. Jumbo employs 90 people.

    Information about the laundry facilities follows:

Direct cost information:	
Wages for two employees	$38,000
Cost of equipment	$7,500
Original estimated useful life of equipment	5 years
Estimated remaining useful life of equipment	1 year
Building rent per year	$3,000
Utilities	$2,000
Miscellaneous cost	$1,500
Indirect cost information:	
Administrative expense	$4,000

An outside laundry service has offered to provide Jumbo's laundering services for $50,000 per year. The fee is guaranteed for one year. If the offer is accepted, Jumbo will scrap the laundry equipment and close down its laundry operation completely.

REQUIRED:
The president of Jumbo has asked you to prepare a report that details the qualitative and quantitative factors that should be considered in making the decision about whether to close the laundry operation. Your report should discuss the relevant qualitative and quantitative factors for each alternative and include a relevant cost schedule. Your report should conclude with a well-supported recommended course of action.

LO 4:   Relevant Cost of an Outsourcing Decision

25. Fast Track Delivery Service Ltd. operates a small auto repair facility to service its fleet of 35 delivery vehicles. Fast Track's repair facility occupies space in an industrial area close to the company's home office. Fast Track is considering using a local repair shop to service its vehicles. Fast Track's $120,000 administrative expense is allocated based on the number of employees. Fast Track employs 50 people.

Information about the repair facility follows:

Direct cost information:	
Wages for three employees	$64,000
Cost of equipment used	$33,500
Original estimated useful life of equipment	12 years
Estimated remaining useful life of equipment	9 years
Building rent per year	$6,000
Utilities	$2,000
Cost of automobile parts	$30,000
Miscellaneous cost	$1,500
Indirect cost information:	
Administrative expense	$7,200

A dependable automotive service centre has offered to provide maintenance contracts of $3,000 per vehicle. If Fast Track accepts the offer it would close the maintenance facility. The company estimates that it can sell the maintenance equipment for $10,000.

REQUIRED:

The president of Fast Track has asked you to prepare a report that details the qualitative and quantitative factors that should be considered in making the decision about whether to close the maintenance facility. Your report should discuss the relevant qualitative and quantitative factors for each alternative and include a relevant cost schedule. Your report should conclude with a well-supported recommendation.

LO 3 & 4: Relevant Cost and Qualitative Factors of a Special-Order Decision

26. Abraham Manufacturing Corp. produces 22,000 rubber engine mounts each year for use in its electric cart manufacturing factory. Abraham's engine mounts have an excellent reputation for strength and durability. At a production level of 22,000, the cost per unit is as follows:

Direct material	$0.53
Direct labour	1.45
Variable overhead	0.92
Fixed overhead	1.27
Total	$4.17

A competitor, Jenkins Cart Company, is interested in purchasing 14,000 rubber engine mounts from Abraham. Jenkins has offered to pay $4.17 each for the engine mounts. Abraham Manufacturing Corp. has the capacity and can easily manufacture the engine mounts for Jenkins.

Several managers at Abraham are concerned that there would be no financial benefit whatsoever for Abraham if the engine mounts are sold at cost.

REQUIRED:

a. Prepare a schedule that details the advantage or disadvantage of selling the 14,000 engine mounts to Jenkins.
b. Discuss the qualitative aspects of selling the parts to Jenkins.

LO 3 & 4: Relevant Cost and Qualitative Factors of a Special-Order Decision

27. Camrose Gas Grill Company produces 200,000 RV22 propane gas regulator and valve assemblies each year for use in its gas grill factory. Camrose's gas grills are known for quality and have a reputation of lasting a lifetime.

At 200,000 units per year, the cost per unit is as follows:

Direct material	$ 3.02
Direct labour	2.44
Variable overhead	1.20
Fixed overhead	5.60
Total	$12.26

A competitor, Econo Grill Inc., is interested in purchasing 80,000 RV22 assemblies from Camrose. Econo Grill has offered to pay $12.30 per unit. Camrose has the capacity and can easily manufacture the parts for Econo Grill.

Several managers at Camrose are concerned that there would be almost no financial benefit if the RV22 assemblies are sold for $12.30 each.

REQUIRED:
a. Prepare a schedule that details the advantage or disadvantage of selling the 80,000 RV22 assemblies to Econo Grill.
b. Discuss the qualitative aspects of selling the parts to Econo Grill.

LO 3 & 4: Relevant Cost and Qualitative Factors of a Special-Order Decision

28. Summerside Marine Cable Company produces 400,000 metres of SS316 cable each year. At 400,000 metres per year, the cost per metre is as follows:

Direct material	$0.32
Direct labour	0.14
Variable overhead	0.08
Fixed overhead	0.73
Total	$1.27

A competitor, Moncton Marine Inc., is interested in purchasing 175,000 metres of SS316 cable from Summerside. Moncton has offered to pay $0.92 per metre for the cable. Summerside has the capacity and can easily manufacture the cable for Moncton Marine.

Frank Layton, president of Summerside Marine Cable Company, is concerned that there is no financial benefit for the company if it sells the cable for only $0.92 per metre.

REQUIRED:
a. Prepare a schedule that details the advantage or disadvantage of selling the 175,000 metres of cable to Moncton Marine.
b. Discuss the qualitative aspects of selling the cable to Moncton.

LO 3 & 4: Relevant Cost and Qualitative Factors of a Special-Order Decision

29. Timberline Corporation manufactures camping equipment. One of Timberline's most popular products is its T1012 tent, which the company sells for $28 each. Timberline sells about 9,000 T1012 tents each year through its mail-order business. Another camping equipment company, TreeClimb Corporation, has approached Timberline about purchasing 2,000 T1012 tents. The tents would be the same as the T1012 except they would bear the TreeClimb brand. TreeClimb is willing to pay $20 per tent. Although Timberline has plenty of factory capacity to produce the additional 2,000 tents, the company's manufacturing cost is $23 per unit, or $3 more per tent than TreeClimb is willing to pay.

The following per unit information pertains to Timberline's cost to produce 9,000 T1012 tents.

Direct material	$ 9
Direct labour	4
Variable manufacturing overhead	2
Fixed manufacturing overhead	8
Total	$23

REQUIRED:
a. By what amount would Timberline's operating income increase or decrease if the company accepts the special order?
b. Discuss the qualitative aspects of this special-order decision.

LO 3 & 4: Relevant Cost and Qualitative Factors of a Special-Order Decision

30. Refer to problem 29. Assume that Timberline Corporation would have to purchase an additional sewing machine to accept the special order from TreeClimb. The cost of the new sewing machine is $2,500.

REQUIRED:
a. By what amount would Timberline's operating income increase or decrease if the company accepts the special order under these circumstances?
b. Discuss the qualitative aspects of this special-order decision.

LO 4: Relevant Cost of a Special-Order Decision

31. Kootenay Cast Corporation manufactures fishing rods. Part of Kootenay's sales success comes from a patented material, tuflex, used to make the fishing rods. Tuflex allows the fishing rods to be very flexible, yet nearly unbreakable. Kootenay sells about 150,000 fishing rods annually to wholesalers for $18 each. A major department store chain, CanMart, is interested in purchasing 30,000 fishing rods that would bear CanMart's brand name. CanMart is willing to pay only $9 per fishing rod, considerably less than Kootenay's normal selling price. Although Kootenay has plenty of factory capacity available to make the additional 30,000 fishing rods, the company's manufacturing cost is $11 per fishing rod, or $2 more per rod than CanMart is willing to pay. CanMart has indicated that the 30,000 fishing rods do not have to be as flexible and tough as the regular Kootenay rods.

The following per unit information pertains to Kootenay's cost to produce 150,000 fishing rods.

Direct material:	
Tuflex	$4
Other material	1
Direct labour	3
Variable manufacturing overhead	1
Fixed manufacturing overhead	2
Total	$11

If fibreglass is used in place of tuflex, the direct material cost can be reduced by $2 per rod.

REQUIRED:

By what amount would Kootenay's operating income increase or decrease if the company accepts the special order?

LO 3 & 4: Relevant Cost and Qualitative Factors of an Outsourcing Decision

32. Andrie Equipment Company makes high-pressure pumps. Andrie makes 10,000 V1 valve assembles per year for use in production. The manufacturing facilities used to make the V1 valves are also used to produce a variety of other subassemblies and products. Accordingly, no special production equipment is needed to make the V1 valves.

The production cost for V1 valve assembles is as follows:

Direct material	$ 55,000
Direct labour	140,000
Variable manufacturing overhead	70,000
Fixed manufacturing overhead	210,000
Total	$475,000

Sure Flow Valve Company has offered to supply the V1 valve assemblies to Andrie for $32 each.

REQUIRED:

a. Prepare a schedule that shows whether Andrie should buy the valves from Sure Flow or continue to make them.

b. Discuss the qualitative factors that Andrie should consider in this make-or-buy decision.

LO 3 & 4: Relevant Cost and Qualitative Factors of an Outsourcing Decision

33. Refer to problem 32. Assume Andrie could use the manufacturing facilities that are no longer needed to make the V1 valves to produce a new line of small pumps. The small pumps would provide a contribution margin of $60,000.

REQUIRED:

a. Prepare a schedule that shows whether Andrie should buy the valves from Sure Flow or continue to make them.

b. Discuss the qualitative factors that Andrie should consider in this make-or-buy decision.

LO 3 & 4:   Relevant Cost and Qualitative Factors of an Outsourcing Decision

34. Jackson Manufacturing Company makes residential aluminum windows. A company has offered to supply Jackson with the window crank assembly it needs for $3.50 each. Jackson uses 50,000 crank assemblies each year. The machinery used to make the window cranks is used to produce a variety of other subassemblies and products.

The production cost for the window crank assemblies is as follows:

Direct material	$ 70,000
Direct labour	40,000
Variable manufacturing overhead	55,000
Fixed manufacturing overhead	35,000
Total	$200,000

REQUIRED:

a. Prepare a schedule that shows the relevant cost and the preferred alternative of this make-or-buy decision.

b. Discuss the qualitative factors that Jackson should consider when deciding whether to buy the window cranks from the outside supplier.

LO 3 & 4:   Relevant Cost and Qualitative Factors of an Outsourcing Decision

35. Mowatt Electric Inc. produces electric fans. Mowatt manufactures 19,000 small electric fan motors each year. Delta Motor Company has offered to supply Mowatt with the small electric motors for $12.50 each. The facilities that Mowatt uses to make the small motors is used to make larger motors and other components.

Mowatt's production cost for the small electric fan motors is as follows:

Direct material	$132,000
Direct labour	26,500
Variable manufacturing overhead	43,500
Fixed manufacturing overhead	77,500
Total	$279,500

REQUIRED:

a. Prepare a schedule that shows whether Mowatt Electric Inc. should buy the electric fans or continue to make them.

b. Discuss the qualitative factors that Mowatt should consider when making this make-or-buy decision.

LO 3 & 4:   Relevant Cost and Qualitative Factors of an Outsourcing Decision

36. Refer to problem 35. Assume that Mowatt Electric Inc. can use the facilities freed up by purchasing the electric motors from Delta Motor Company to produce a new model fan that would have a contribution margin of $95,000.

REQUIRED:

a. Prepare a relevant cost schedule that shows whether Mowatt Electric Inc. should buy the electric fans or continue to make them.

b. Discuss the qualitative factors that Mowatt should consider when making this make-or-buy decision.

LO 3 & 4: Relevant Cost and Qualitative Factors of an Outsourcing Decision

37. Morishita Inc. requires 12,000 units of part X45 per year. At the current level of production, the cost per unit is as follows:

Direct material	$ 3
Direct labour	1
Variable overhead	2
Fixed overhead	4
Total	$10

JLW Inc. has offered to sell Morishita 12,000 units of X45 for $8 each. If Morishita is no longer required to produce the X45s, a supervisor can be eliminated. The supervisor's salary of $30,000 is part of fixed overhead cost. Other fixed overhead costs would remain the same.

REQUIRED:

a. Prepare a schedule that details the advantage or disadvantage of buying the 12,000 units of X45 from JLW Inc.

b. Discuss the qualitative aspects of purchasing the parts from JLW Inc.

LO 3 & 4: Relevant Cost and Qualitative Factors of an Outsourcing Decision

38. Cox Inc. requires 3,000 spindles per year. At the current level of production, the cost per unit is as follows:

Direct material	$ 38
Direct labour	12
Variable overhead	14
Fixed overhead	44
Total	$108

AMW Inc. has offered to sell Cox the 3,000 spindles for $100 each. If Cox is no longer required to produce the spindles, a supervisor can be eliminated. The supervisor's salary of $36,000 is part of fixed overhead cost. Other fixed overhead costs would remain the same.

REQUIRED:

a. Prepare a schedule that details the advantage or disadvantage of buying the 3,000 spindles from AMW Inc.

b. Discuss the qualitative aspects of purchasing the parts from AMW Inc.

LO 3 & 4: Relevant Cost and Qualitative Factors of an Outsourcing Decision

39. Vacca Inc. requires 4,000 switch assemblies per year. At the current level of production, the cost per unit is as follows:

Direct material	$ 3
Direct labour	3
Variable overhead	2
Fixed overhead	2
Total	$10

Camron Inc. has offered to sell Vacca Inc. the 4,000 switch assemblies for $9 each. If Vacca is no longer required to produce the switch assemblies, part of the building can be leased to another company for $10,000 per year. Other fixed overhead costs would remain the same.

REQUIRED:

a. Prepare a schedule that details the advantage or disadvantage of buying the 4,000 switch assemblies from Camron Inc.

b. Discuss the qualitative aspects of purchasing the parts from Camron Inc.

LO 1, 2, & 4: Prepare a Report for an Equipment Replacement Decision

40. The Wong Manufacturing Co. operates a chain of Chinese restaurants. Restaurant managers are paid bonuses based on the financial profits of their restaurants.

Last year, the manager of the Ottawa Wong Restaurant installed a new oven that cost $5,000. At the time, the oven had an estimated useful life of five years with no residual value. Annual repair and maintenance on the oven is $900, and the cost of electricity used by the oven is $3,400 per year. The old oven can be sold now for $1,500.

A salesperson is trying to convince the store manager to replace the oven purchased last year with a new, energy-efficient model. The salesperson says the new oven will increase company profits. The new oven can be purchased for $6,000, and has an estimated useful life of four years with a salvage value of $1,000. The annual repair and maintenance would be the same as the old oven, or $900 per year, but the annual cost of electricity used by the oven would drop to $1,800.

The manager is not convinced by the salesperson. "If I buy this new oven, my financial income will drop and I'll never get my bonus. The loss in the first year will make me look like a fool!"

REQUIRED:

a. Prepare a report showing the relevant cost of keeping the old oven versus buying the new one.

b. Based on your report, what do you think of the restaurant manager's comments?

7

The Capital Budget: Evaluating Capital Expenditures

"2001 marked the completion of several key projects which accounted for approximately $200 million in capital expenditures. These projects included completing construction of Dofasco de Mexico's tube mill, and the completion of Hamilton's Hot Mill Improvement and Tin Mill Upgrade programs. Dofasco has invested almost $1 billion in capital expenditures in the last five years"[1]

Dofasco Inc. is a steelmaker located in Hamilton, Ontario. The company has been very successful and has been profitable even through economic downturns that have adversely affected its industry. Like most companies, Dofasco has had to acquire and upgrade operating assets, such as its mills and factories, in order to stay competitive. These assets can be extremely expensive, and the future success of a company is greatly influenced by its decision to invest in such assets.

Business expenditures for acquiring expensive assets that will be used for more than one year are called **capital investments**. Because of the cost and extended useful life of these assets, companies devote tremendous time and energy to evaluating potential capital investments. For example, as was mentioned above, Dofasco Inc. has invested approximately $1,000,000,000 in capital expenditures in the last five years. Certainly, this magnitude of investment required serious analysis on the part of this company before it committed to the various projects represented by those dollars.

Generally, capital investments, also known as **capital projects**, are investments in property, plant, and equipment. Examples include investments in computer equipment, production equipment, another

---

[1]Dofasco Inc. 2001 Annual Report.

capital investments
Business expenditures in acquiring expensive assets that will be used for more than one year.

capital projects Another name for capital investments.

capital budgeting The planning and decision process for making investments in capital projects.

factory, a new wing of a hospital, or a new campus residence. **Capital budgeting** is the planning and decision process for making investments in capital projects. Although we focus on business firms in our discussion, all types of organizations can use capital budgeting techniques: for-profit, nonprofit, and social organizations.

In this chapter, we explain how firms make capital budgeting decisions. Capital budgeting, however, is only part of a much more involved planning process, which we also discuss in this chapter.

Two of the evaluation techniques used to evaluate potential capital projects rely heavily on a knowledge of the time value of money. For this reason, we have included an appendix to the chapter that details the time value of money. ∎

LEARNING OBJECTIVES

After completing your work on this chapter, you should be able to do the following:

1. Describe the overall business planning process and where the capital budget fits in that process.
2. Explain in your own words the process of capital budgeting.
3. Discuss the four shared characteristics of all capital projects.
4. Describe the cost of capital and the concept of scarce resources.
5. Determine the information relevant to the capital budgeting decision.
6. Evaluate potential capital investments using four capital budgeting decision models: net present value, internal rate of return, payback period method, and accounting rate of return.
7. Determine present and future values using present value tables and future value tables (chapter appendix).

THE BUSINESS PLANNING PROCESS

Managers use accounting information for two main types of business decisions, planning and control. In this section, we give an overview of how organizations plan for the future. We discuss the *why,* the *what,* the *how,* and the *who* of business planning. Though management accounting information is used in all steps in the planning process, it is especially important to the *what, how,* and *who* decisions.

Company Goals: The Why

People form an organization to accomplish a purpose or purposes—the organization's goals. These goals define why the organization exists. Setting goals, then, is the *why* of the business.

organizational goals The core beliefs and values of the company. They outline why the organization exists and are a combination of financial and nonfinancial goals.

Organizational goals constitute the core beliefs and values of the company, so those goals should not be subject to short-term economic pressures. Examples of some organizational goals might be to maximize profitability, to save lives, or to improve communication among employees. Most companies' goals are stated in general terms that are not easily quantified, which means that although progress toward fulfillment can be measured, it is not really possible to determine when the goals have been attained. For instance, a firm with the goal of maximizing profitability usually does not specify exactly how much profit it must earn to meet its goal.

The goals of a business organization are usually a combination of nonfinancial and financial aspirations. Whether nonfinancial or financial, however, almost all goals have either a direct or indirect effect on the company's financial well-being. Does this sound strange? The next section explains why almost all goals can affect the financial health of a business.

Nonfinancial Goals

Typically, nonfinancial goals do not mention profitability. Rather, they refer to activities that may or may not result in profits. A hospital's nonfinancial goals, for instance, might be to provide the best health care possible to its patients; to recruit and employ highly qualified workers; to provide a safe, pleasant environment for its employees and patients; and to create an atmosphere of caring for both the physical and the emotional concerns of its patients.

 Discussion Questions

7-1. Consider the hospital's nonfinancial goals. What financial effect will occur if the hospital *does* work toward those goals?

7-2. What financial effect will result if the hospital *does not* work toward those goals?

7-3. Review the hospital's nonfinancial goals. How would you determine when those goals have been reached?

Note that the nonfinancial goals for the hospital are stated in very general language. More than specific results, these goals represent standards of conduct and performance toward which the hospital should always be striving. They are stated in such a way that it is very difficult, if not impossible, to determine when the goals have been attained.

Financial Goals

For most business organizations, the primary financial goal is to earn a profit. What this really means, of course, is that the goal is to earn a return on investment for the business owner or owners. This goal may be worded as "achieving superior financial performance," "earning a reasonable return for the shareholders," "maximizing shareholder value," or similar language. As was the case with the nonfinancial goals, it is difficult to determine when these financial goals have been attained.

Goal Awareness

mission statement A summary of the main goals of the organization.

Once goals have been set, the company should communicate them to every person in the organization. This communication maximizes the likelihood that a business will achieve its goals. Many companies use a **mission statement**—a summary of the main goals of the organization—to communicate the firm's goals to all employees. Exhibit 7-1 is a sample mission statement from The Forzani Group Ltd. This company is the largest sporting good retailer in Canada, operating retail stores under various brand names, including SportChek.

Exhibit 7-1
The Forzani Group Ltd.
Used with permission.

Our vision is to provide the BEST customer shopping experience; to have the BIGGEST market share and procurement leverage; to always remain the LOWEST COST competitor in any retail business that we exploit; and to offer branded and private labels in a manner that is UNIQUE, maintaining our company's continued position as the MOST PROFITABLE sports/lifestyle retailer in Canada.

To do so, we will embrace the following core values:

1. Aim for bold performance targets.
2. Ensure that all areas of our business are constantly reevaluated in a bid to continually improve what we do.
3. Encourage individual initiatives and risk taking in an environment that is forgiving of mistakes.
4. Invest in our people, place them constantly outside of their "comfort zone" so that they and our company may progress faster.

SOURCE: "Corporate Overview" from The Forzani Group Ltd. web site, www.forzani group.com/wwwenglish/overview/values.html (accessed August 7, 2002).

Merely stating lofty goals in a mission statement is not enough to reach the goals. Businesses must act consistently with their goals to ensure progress. Consider the following two examples. In 1982 Johnson & Johnson demonstrated the company's commitment to its goals after two fatalities occurred in the Chicago area when someone injected cyanide into six bottles of Tylenol. Once aware of these events, Johnson & Johnson immediately responded by recalling all Tylenol bottles. The company also instituted a nationwide advertising campaign advising consumers *not* to use Tylenol and provided full disclosure about the situation. In short, the company responded in a manner consistent with its goals.

Compare Johnson & Johnson's actions to Ford Motor Company's response to faulty ignition systems in some of its cars. These faulty ignition systems caught fire without warning and created a dangerous and potentially fatal situation. Ford's response was to wait for the federal government to tell the company which cars it had to recall. Legal? Certainly. A smart way to conduct business? In the short run, it cost Ford less than a total recall of the affected vehicles. In the long run, however, the company may not be conducting its business in a way consistent with its stated goal of total quality.

strategic plan A long-range plan that sets forth the actions a company will take to attain its organizational goals.

Once a business has set its goals, the firm must then create a **strategic plan**—a long-range plan that sets forth the actions the firm will take to attain its goals. In the following section, we explore briefly how firms develop strategic plans.

Strategic Plan: The What

The steps outlined in the strategic plan, sometimes referred to as a long-range budget, are the *what* of doing business. The actions specified in the strategic plan describe what actions a business must take to implement its goals. To be effective, then, strategic plans should support—not conflict with—the company's goals.

Companies make long-range plans so they are well positioned to reach their goals and benefit as the future unfolds. For example, it can take Dofasco five years or longer to build and upgrade a production facility, so Dofasco managers must anticipate product demand accurately in advance, in order to build a factory of the appropriate size in time to produce enough to meet consumer demand.

A company's strategic plan tends to have objectives that are quantifiable, and a time frame for attainment of the objectives. A company might specify, for instance, that it plans to replace its four least-efficient production facilities over the next five years, reduce customer complaints by 20 percent over the next three years, or increase market share for its newest product by 25 percent within ten years. As you can readily see, a firm can determine exactly when it has met all these objectives.

After an organization has developed a strategic plan that specifies the actions it will take to reach its goals, the company then decides how to allocate its monetary resources to implement its strategies, and who will be responsible for the day-to-day activities of the business. This step in the planning process is the preparation of budgets.

Preparation of the Capital Budget: The How

capital budget The budget that outlines how a company intends to allocate its scarce resources over a five-year, ten-year, or even longer time period.

The capital budget is the *how* of the planning process. The **capital budget** is the budget that outlines how a firm intends to allocate its scarce resources over a five-year, ten-year, or even longer time period.

The capital budget lays out plans for the acquisition and replacement of long-lived assets such as land, buildings, machinery, and equipment. During the capital budgeting process, companies decide whether and what items should be purchased, how much should be spent, and how much profit can be generated from the items. In sum, capital budgeting decisions should further the strategic plan and goals of the business.

Operating Budget: The Who

operating budget The budget that plans a company's routine day-to-day business activities for one to five years.

Companies not only must budget for long-term activities, they also must plan and budget for day-to-day business activities. The budget that pertains to routine company operations for one to five years in the future is called the **operating budget.** The operating budget establishes who is responsible for the day-to-day operation of the organization, so we refer to it as the *who* of the planning process. The operating budget will be our focus in Chapter 8.

An important thing to understand about the planning process is the interrelationship among goals, strategic plan, capital budget, and operating budget. Exhibit 7–2 demonstrates that interrelationship.

Exhibit 7–2
Interrelationship among the Planning Elements

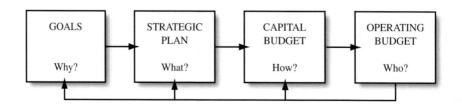

The overall function of management accounting is to provide a substantial portion of the information that company management needs not only to achieve the *what*, the *how*, and the *who*, but also to ensure that these functions are achieved within the context of the *why*.

THE CAPITAL BUDGET: WHAT IS IT?

capital assets Long-lived expensive items such as land, buildings, machinery, and equipment.

The capital budget plans for the acquisition and replacement of long-lived expensive items such as land, buildings, machinery, and equipment. These long-lived items are called **capital assets.** The capital budget focuses on the long-term operations of the company to determine how an organization intends to allocate its scarce resources over the next five, ten, or even 20 years. Thus, we refer to this part of the planning process as the *how* of being in business and doing business.

During the capital budgeting process, companies decide whether items should be purchased, how much should be spent, and how much profit the items promise to generate. No decisions made in the capital budgeting process, however, should conflict with the company's strategic plan or organizational goals.

Capitalizing Assets

Capital budgeting deals with decisions regarding investments that will benefit the company for many years, so most companies do not use capital budgeting techniques for small purchases or those that provide benefits for only the current year.

When an expenditure is made, the cost of the item purchased will be reflected either as an expense on the company's income statement for the year of purchase, or as an increase in the company's assets on its balance sheet. Theoretically, the distinction lies in whether the item purchased will provide economic value to the company beyond the year of purchase. If a purchased item is expected to provide economic benefits beyond the year in which it was purchased, it should be capitalized, which means that its cost has been recorded as an increase in long-term assets and will be amortized (converted from asset to expense) over the item's estimated useful life. Conversely, if a purchased item is not expected to provide economic benefit to the company beyond the year of purchase, its cost should be reflected as an expense on the income statement for that year.

To illustrate, the cost of a delivery truck should be reflected as an increase in assets because the truck will likely be used for several years. In contrast, the cost of last month's lawn service does not provide any future value and therefore should be reflected as an expense immediately.

Judgment plays an important role in determining whether a purchased item should be capitalized or expensed. For example, how should the cost of a $3 wastebasket with an estimated useful life of three years be recorded? Because the wastebasket will be used for several years, the item should theoretically be capitalized—its cost should be added to long-term assets and amortized over the wastebasket's estimated useful life.

From a practical standpoint, it is senseless to expend the additional accounting effort to capitalize and then amortize the wastebasket. Why? Because, whether or not the wastebasket is capitalized and amortized over its estimated useful life or expensed immediately, the effect on a company's financial statements would be so minimal that no economic decision maker will be influenced by the alternative selected. Thus, the cost of the wastebasket is immaterial. Due to the modifying convention of materiality discussed in financial accounting courses, the wastebasket is expensed when purchased.

Capitalization Amount

Generally, companies set a cost threshold that helps determine the appropriate accounting treatment for capitalizing long-lived items. For example, a company might say that any long-lived item costing less than $3,000 will be expensed when purchased, while those costing $3,000 or more will be capitalized. There are no hard and fast rules for setting the capitalization threshold, but most businesses choose an amount between $500 and $5,000 as their capitalization amount.

Characteristics of Capital Projects

Capital budgeting deals with planning for purchases of items that will be capitalized, meaning they will be classified as assets when purchased and then amortized over their estimated useful lives. While the capitalization amount and the evaluation process for capital projects vary from company to company, all capital projects share certain characteristics. The four main shared characteristics include

1. **Long lives.** Capital projects are expected to benefit the company for at least two years, which is the whole idea behind capitalizing the cost of a purchased item. As discussed in the previous section, if a purchased item will benefit the company only in the year of purchase, the cost of the item is expensed immediately. If the item purchased is likely to benefit a company in years beyond the year of purchase, the cost of that item is capitalized. Usually the kinds of purchases discussed in this chapter benefit the company longer than two years, perhaps five, ten, or an even greater number of years.

2. **High cost.** Technically, the purchase of any long-lived item for which the cost exceeds a company's capitalization amount is considered a capital project. As stated earlier, this may be as low as $500 for some firms. As a practical matter, however, the capital budgeting techniques we consider in this chapter are used to evaluate high-cost projects. A good example is the cost of a new factory built by Bombardier Inc. or IPSCO Inc., the Regina-based steel producer. Such a factory may cost $200,000,000 or more. Another example is the decision by Canadian Tire Corporation Limited or The Bay to open a new store in a particular location. Many millions of dollars are involved in opening a store for these companies.

3. **Quickly sunk costs.** Costs that cannot be recovered are called sunk costs. A capital project usually requires a firm to incur substantial cost in the early stages of the project. As new information about market size, technology, and so on becomes available, the company's management may decide the project should be abandoned. Unfortunately, much of the cost already incurred may not be able to be recouped. For example, consider the case of a manufacturer that begins construction on a new factory with an estimated cost of $500,000,000. After spending $200,000,000 on construction, the company decides the new factory is not needed because the product it planned to manufacture in the facility has become obsolete. The company cannot sell the partially completed factory and has no other use for it. The $200,000,000 is a sunk cost because it cannot be recovered.

4. **High degree of risk.** Capital projects have a high degree of business risk because they involve the future, which always entails uncertainty. Because of the long lives, high costs, and sunk costs of capital projects, companies must try to estimate the returns from those projects in future years. These characteristics increase the likelihood of erroneous estimates. The uncertainty of the future coupled with the high initial investment make capital projects quite risky.

Discussion Question

Consider these questions: "Will I be paid?" "How much will I be paid?" and "When will I be paid?"

7–4. Why do you think these questions were extremely difficult for Microsoft to answer as the company considered the development of Windows ME as a potential capital project?

THE COST OF CAPITAL AND THE CONCEPT OF SCARCE RESOURCES

When you put money into a savings account, you expect to earn interest. This interest is the return on your investment. Like most people, you would like the return to be as high as possible. If you were going to deposit $5,000 in a savings account, you would probably shop for a secure bank, with a return as high as or higher than that of competing banks.

Businesses shop for capital projects the same way you would shop for a bank in which to deposit your $5,000. If it appears that a capital project will be profitable, how does a company determine whether it will be profitable enough to warrant investing its money? A proposed project should promise a return that is equal to or exceeds the firm's cost of capital.

In evaluating potential capital projects, a company must determine a benchmark rate of return to help select which capital project or projects it will undertake. The benchmark return rate for selecting projects is usually the company's **cost of capital,** which is the cost of obtaining financing from all available financing sources. Cost of capital is also referred to as the **cost of capital rate,** the **required rate of return,** or the **hurdle rate.** For the sake of consistency, we use cost of capital throughout all our discussions in this chapter.

As you may recall from financial accounting courses, companies can obtain financing from two sources, borrowing from creditors (debt financing) and investments by owners (equity financing). When a company invests in a capital project, the money must come from one or both of these sources. Both creditors and owners require a return on the funding they provide to the company, and the company must seek investments that provide a return at least equal to the cost of obtaining funding from debt and equity sources. If a company borrows funds at an interest rate of 9 percent, then the expected return on a capital project must be at least 9 percent. Similarly, if a company's owners provide the financing and expect a return of 20 percent on their investment, then the expected return from a capital project should be at least 20 percent to be acceptable.

cost of capital The cost of obtaining financing from all available financing sources.

cost of capital rate Another name for *cost of capital.*

required rate of return Another name for *cost of capital.*

hurdle rate Another name for *cost of capital.*

Weighted-Average Cost of Capital

The funding for a company's capital projects usually comes from a combination of debt and equity financing. The combined cost of debt and equity financing is called the **weighted-average cost of capital.** The rate for the weighted-average cost of capital represents the combined rate of the cost of both debt and equity financing.

The **cost of debt capital** is the interest a company pays to its creditors. The interest rate, say 8 percent, is agreed upon when a company borrows from either the

weighted-average cost of capital The combined cost of debt financing and equity financing.

cost of debt capital The interest a company pays to its creditors.

bank or the bond market. The amount of interest a company pays is easy to determine because it is reported on the company's income statement as interest expense.

The cost of a company's equity financing is more challenging to determine than the cost of its debt financing, because the **cost of equity capital** is what equity investors relinquish when they invest in one company rather than another. To illustrate, assume Elizabeth Todd has $5,000 to invest and she is considering the purchase of either Boardman Corporation stock or Emry Limited stock. The question is, what does Elizabeth give up if she invests her $5,000 in Boardman? She relinquishes what she would have earned had she invested in Emry. That is, she lost the opportunity to earn whatever she would have earned had she purchased Emry's stock rather than Boardman's.

The amount an equity investor earns is a combination of dividends received and the appreciation in the market value of the stock the investor owns. In Elizabeth's case, the amount earned if she buys the Boardman Corporation stock is a combination of the dividends she receives from Boardman, plus any increase in the market value of the Boardman stock she owns.

cost of equity capital
What equity investors give up when they invest in one company rather than another.

 Discussion Question

Assume Elizabeth buys the Boardman stock and consistently earns an 8% return on her investment (dividends plus appreciation of the Boardman stock).

7–5. If Elizabeth could earn a 17% return on an investment in Emry Limited stock (or some other company), what would you advise her to do? Explain your reasoning.

It's all well and good for us to discuss this topic from the investor's point of view (in this case Elizabeth Todd), but what has this to do with the cost of equity capital for Boardman Corporation? Well, if Boardman wants to keep Elizabeth as a shareholder, it must return to her an amount at least as great as she could earn by investing her money somewhere else. If Elizabeth can earn 17 percent from an investment in Emry, Boardman must give her that kind of return or she may sell her Boardman stock and invest in Emry (or some other company). Boardman, then, would use 17 percent as the cost of the equity capital it received from Elizabeth, because that is what she could earn elsewhere. In other words, that is what she gave up by investing in Boardman.

In a real-world situation, Boardman Corporation would not know about the alternatives being considered by Elizabeth Todd and her $5,000. Therefore, the company cannot determine the specific percentage return Elizabeth must earn to keep her happy. What Boardman must do is try to determine what percentage return equity investors can generally expect on their investments and use that percentage as the cost of equity capital.

Unlike debt financing costs (interest expense), the cost of equity financing is not reported in financial statements in its entirety. Firms do report profit distributions to shareholders in the form of dividends, but the larger part of the cost of equity capital is the appreciation in the market value of shareholders' ownership interest. This market value is not reported on financial statements.

To determine the full cost of equity capital, we must examine how stocks appreciate in value. We assume first that rational investors would desire a return on an investment in an individual company at least equal to the return they could receive from investing in other, similar publicly traded companies.

Exhibit 7–3
Returns Provided by
the Stock Market

| HIGH RETURN COMPANIES 25% of Firms |
| MEDIUM RETURN COMPANIES 50% of Firms |
| LOW RETURN COMPANIES 25% of Firms |

If all companies whose stocks are traded on recognized stock markets (TSX, TSX Venture Exchange, NYSE, NASDAQ, and so on) were separated based on the percentage return they provide their shareholders, the breakdown would appear as shown in Exhibit 7–3.

The high return companies in Exhibit 7–3 represent one-fourth of all the companies whose stock is publicly traded. The medium return companies comprise one-half of the companies, and the low return companies represent one-fourth of the total.

 Discussion Question

7–6. If you owned shares in a publicly traded company, in which group of companies in Exhibit 7–3 would you want your company to be?

Most equity investors desire to own stock in high return companies because they naturally want their investment to earn the highest possible return. Many high return companies in the stock market yield as high as 17 percent to 20 percent annually to their shareholders in the form of dividends and appreciation in share value.

 Discussion Questions

Assume you own shares in a publicly traded company and you consistently earn an 8% return on your investment (dividends plus appreciation of the company's shares).

7–7. If you are certain you could earn a 20% return on an investment in some other company's shares, what would you do? Explain your reasoning.

7–8. Because a publicly traded company receives money only when its shares are originally issued, why do you think it would care about the share's market value in the stock market?

It is important to note here that the issue is not whether investors can, in fact, earn a 20 percent return by selling their shares in one company and investing in another. They only need to *think* they can earn the higher return.

If enough of a company's shareholders begin selling their shares, the market price of the shares will drop—the economic law of supply and demand at work. As the share price drops, more shareholders may decide to sell their share before the price drops even lower. This, of course, makes the share price drop further.

 Discussion Question

7–9. What would you think about a company whose shares were selling for $50 a share in January and $12 a share in December?

Stock analysts, customers, suppliers, and many other parties have a tendency to gauge a company's health by the market value of its stock. For this reason, companies have a vested interest in making sure the market value of their shares does not begin a downward spiral.

Because the investors in the stock market think they can earn a 17 to 20 percent return by investing in the top performing companies, a company must return 17 to 20 percent annual return to its shareholders to be considered one of the high performing companies. Publicly traded companies usually consider their cost of equity financing to be as high as 20 percent. This percentage is commonly used to compute the company's weighted-average cost of capital.

To illustrate the calculation of the weighted-average cost of capital, we consider the case of Adler Enterprises, which has $2,000,000 in assets. A total of $1,200,000 (60 percent) of these assets was obtained using debt financing with an interest rate of 7.5 percent. The remaining $800,000 (40 percent) was financed through equity capital and the company uses a 20 percent cost of equity financing. We find the weighted-average cost of capital for Adler Enterprises using the following calculation:

Method of Financing	Proportion of Financing Provided		Cost of Financing		Weighted Cost of Financing
Debt	60%	×	7.5%	=	4.5%
Equity	40%	×	20.0%	=	8.0%
	Weighted-Average Cost of Capital				12.5%

We see that Adler's weighted cost of debt financing is the proportion of debt financing (60 percent) multiplied by the cost of that financing (7.5 percent). The company's weighted cost of equity financing is the proportion of equity financing (40 percent) times the cost of the equity financing (20 percent). Its weighted-average cost of capital is the sum of the weighted cost of each type of financing—12.5 percent.

Firms use their weighted-average cost of capital as a benchmark rate of return to evaluate capital projects. For example, suppose Adler Enterprises is considering a capital project that requires an investment of $200,000. If Adler decides to undertake this project, it must obtain $200,000 to fund it. Recall that Adler's weighted-average cost of capital is 12.5 percent. Unless the expected rate of return on the project is 12.5 percent or higher, Adler's management will probably reject the project. Otherwise, it would cost more to fund the project than the project could earn.

Discussion Questions

7-10. When you consider that companies are generally in business to earn a profit, why might it be acceptable to select a capital project that promises a return that is just equal to the weighted-average cost of capital?

7-11. Under what circumstances do you think a company might accept one capital project over another even though the project selected promises a lower return?

7-12. Do you think there would ever be a situation when a company should proceed with a capital project even though the project promises a return lower than the cost of capital? Explain your reasoning.

7-13. What do you think might cause a company to reject a proposed capital project even though it promises a return significantly higher than the cost of capital?

Capital Rationing

capital rationing A term describing the allocation of the limited amount of money a company has to invest in capital projects and operations.

In our personal lives, what we buy is usually not limited by how much we want, but rather by how much money we have available to spend. Well, what is true for individuals is also true for businesses. The number and size of capital projects a company undertakes is not limited by a lack of viable alternative projects. What limits companies is that they simply do not have access to enough financial resources. Companies also have to understand that financial resources are required for operating-budget decisions as well as capital-budgeting decisions. Companies thus follow **capital rationing,** the allocation of the limited amount of money a company has to invest in capital projects and operations. Even huge multinational companies must select only investments they consider most favourable from a virtually unlimited pool of possible investment opportunities, because firms do not have access to enough money to invest in every good project that comes along. Managers must carefully evaluate the alternative capital projects available to their companies so they can select the projects that promise the highest return (as long as the projects are consistent with the company's goals and strategies).

EVALUATING POTENTIAL CAPITAL PROJECTS

Because capital projects are usually long lived, costly, and high risk, managers must carefully evaluate capital expenditure decisions, especially in light of their financial limitations. The evaluation process generally includes the following four steps.

1. Identifying possible capital projects
2. Determining the relevant cash flows for alternative projects
3. Selecting a method of evaluating the alternatives
4. Evaluating the alternatives and selecting the capital project or projects to be funded

Let's investigate each of these steps from the manager's point of view.

Identifying Possible Capital Projects

Businesses usually make capital expenditures to maximize profits by either increasing revenue, reducing costs, or creating a combination of the two. A project that satisfies the company's desire to maximize profits will be identified as a potential capital expenditure.

Firms often generate revenue increases by investing in projects that increase capacity or draw more customers. For a hotel chain, an increase in available rooms might increase revenue. For a restaurant, revenue might be enhanced by investing in cooking equipment that prepares food more rapidly.

To reduce operating costs a manufacturer might upgrade production equipment so less direct labour or less electricity is required. An airline catering company could invest in more energy-efficient ovens to reduce food preparation cost. Reducing cost has exactly the same effect as increasing revenue. As Benjamin Franklin said, "A penny saved is a penny earned." If you think about it, this really makes sense. If a company saves $1 by reducing costs by $1, the cost reduction has the same impact on profits as increasing selling price to increase revenue by $1.

Although the majority of potential capital projects are intended to either increase revenue or reduce costs, in certain instances a company must make a capital expenditure that will result in neither. These projects are usually concerned with safety or environmental issues and may come as a result of governmental regulation requirements; or, a company may simply determine such an expenditure is necessary given its goal of worker safety or good corporate citizenship.

In any event, capital projects that are deemed necessary but do not promise either to increase revenue or reduce costs are usually not evaluated using the same criteria as those projects that do promise increased profits. In this chapter, we restrict ourselves to the evaluation of potential capital projects that promise to either increase revenue or reduce costs.

As the need for increasing revenue or reducing costs presents itself, all alternative courses of action should be explored. Brainstorming sessions and input from multiple sources both within and outside a firm can help generate ideas for alternative options.

Determining Relevant Cash Flows for Alternative Projects

Throughout our discussion of capital budgeting, we have discussed capital projects that promise to increase a company's profits by either increasing revenue or reducing costs (expenses). Recall, however, that under accrual accounting, revenue is not the same as cash inflow and expense is not the same as cash outflow in the short run. Recall also that in the long run, revenue and expenses measured using accrual accounting *are* the same as cash inflow and cash outflow.

Because capital projects usually are long lived, most business managers believe it is appropriate to analyze an alternative using cash inflow and cash outflow over the life of the project. They do this by determining the **net cash flow** of a project—the project's expected cash inflows minus its cash outflows for a specific time period. For example, if a manager estimates that investing in a new production machine will yield $40,000 in cash inflows during the useful life of the machine but will require spending $30,000 for the same period, the net cash flow would be $10,000 ($40,000 − $30,000).

net cash flow Cash inflow less cash outflow.

Only relevant net cash flows should be considered in a capital budgeting decision. **Relevant net cash flows** are future cash flows that differ between or among alternatives. Thus, a relevant cash flow must be one that will occur in the future, not one that has already occurred, and it must be affected by the investment decision. Past cash flows, or cash flows that will not change as a result of the investment decision, are irrelevant and should not be considered in the decision process.

relevant net cash flows Future net cash flows that differ between or among the alternatives being considered.

This concept should seem familiar because it follows the same reasoning as our discussion of relevant costs, the subject of Chapter 6.

Once a company obtains and assesses the relevant cash flows for each alternative project, the next step is to choose a method to measure the value of each project.

Selecting a Method of Evaluating the Alternatives

Over time, many capital budgeting decision methods have been developed to evaluate potential capital projects. In this chapter, we present four methods:

- Net present value
- Internal rate of return
- Payback period method
- Accounting rate of return

Each of these methods offers a different way to measure a project's value, and sometimes the different methods render conflicting rankings. In such a case, managers should be aware of the strengths and weaknesses of each capital budgeting method. In the next section we discuss each of the four methods and the advantages and disadvantages of each.

Selecting Capital Budgeting Projects

To select a capital budgeting project, firms decide first whether to accept or reject a project using one or more capital budgeting techniques to measure the project's value. If the project does not generate an acceptable rate of return, it will probably be rejected. Furthermore, any proposed capital project that is inconsistent with a company's goals and strategic plan should be rejected, even if the promised return on that project is higher than some other potential project.

Once a project has been accepted as viable, the project can then be ranked with other acceptable projects based on expected performance.

CAPITAL BUDGETING DECISION METHODS

In this section, we explain four capital budgeting methods: net present value, internal rate of return, payback period method, and accounting rate of return. The first two methods, which are discounted cash flow methods, are used more frequently in business because they include the concept of the time value of money.

A dollar received at some point in the future does not have the same value as a dollar received today. The reason for the difference in value is that if cash is available now, it can be invested now and earn a return as time passes. This increase in the value of cash over time due to investment income is referred to as the **time value of money.** The concept of the time value of money is used to determine either the future value of money invested today or the present value of money to be received at some point in the future.

time value of money The increase in the value of cash over time due to investment income.

In the following discussion of net present value and internal rate of return, we assume you have a working knowledge of the time value of money, discussed in detail in the appendix to this chapter. Refer to it now if you need to refresh your understanding.

discounting cash flows Determining the present value of cash to be received in the future.

Capital projects deal with cash flows that begin in the present and extend into the future, sometimes for many years. Therefore, the evaluation of these kinds of projects uses the concept of present value. Determining the present value of cash to be received in future periods is called **discounting cash flows.**

Discounted Cash Flow Methods

Business managers use two discounted cash flow methods to evaluate potential capital projects: net present value and internal rate of return.

Net Present Value The **net present value (NPV)** of a proposed capital project is the present value of cash inflows minus the present value of cash outflows associated with a capital budgeting project. Note that the net present value is different from the present value. The former is the difference between the present value of a capital project's net cash flows. The latter is the amount a future payment or series of payments is in today's dollars evaluated at the appropriate discount rate. This discount rate is normally the weighted-average cost of capital. However, in some instances, a different rate may be used if the risk of the project is different from the normal risk associated with other capital projects. For purposes of our discussion, we will assume that the weighted-average cost of capital is the appropriate rate. The net present value method is used to determine whether a proposed capital project provides a return higher or lower than the discount rate.

A company calculates the NPV of a capital project by discounting the net cash flows for all years of the project using the company's weighted-average cost of capital as the discount rate. A positive net present value indicates that the expected return on a proposed project is higher than the company's cost of capital. A negative net present value indicates that the expected return on a proposed project is lower than the company's cost of capital. A net present value of zero shows that the expected return on a project is exactly equal to the company's cost of capital.

To illustrate the net present value calculations, assume CanCo Manufacturing Inc. is considering a computer hardware upgrade that would require an investment of $100,000. Assume further that the enhanced speed of the computer is expected to save $31,000 annually in operator salaries. Remember, this reduction of cash outflow is a cash inflow in net present value analysis. The computer has an estimated useful life of five years with no residual value.

The cash flows associated with the computer upgrade are shown in Exhibit 7–4.

Exhibit 7–4
Expected Cash Flows for CanCo Manufacturing Inc.'s Computer Upgrade

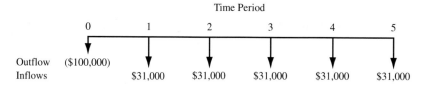

Notice in Exhibit 7–4 that the initial cash outlay of $100,000 occurs at "time 0." When working with present values, time 0 is considered today, or the present. Unless otherwise specified, we assume all other cash flows for this project will occur at the end of each period.[2]

CanCo Manufacturing Inc. has a 14 percent weighted-average cost of capital, so we use 14 percent as the discount rate to evaluate whether the company should accept the computer upgrade project; that is, we use a 14 percent discount rate to calculate the present value of the project's cash outflows and cash inflows. In this case, the project's $100,000 cash outflow occurs today (time 0), so that amount is already stated in present value terms.

Next, we must find the present value of the project's cash inflows, which occur at the end of each of the next five years. Because the stream of $31,000 positive

---

[2]We also ignore amortization in our analysis because amortization is a noncash expense under accrual accounting and the NPV method focuses on cash flow rather than accrual operating income.

cash flows constitutes an annuity, we use the *Present Value of an Annuity of $1 Table,* found in the chapter appendix in Exhibit A7–10, to find the present value factor of a five-year annuity, with a discount rate of 14 percent. We have reproduced a portion of the table as Exhibit 7–5. As you can see from the highlighted portion in this exhibit, the factor for five years with a discount rate of 14 percent is 3.433.

Exhibit 7-5

Present Value of Annuity of $1

Period	4%	5%	6%	7%	8%	10%	12%	14%	16%
1	0.962	0.952	0.943	0.935	0.926	0.909	0.893	0.877	0.862
2	1.886	1.859	1.833	1.808	1.783	1.736	1.690	1.647	1.605
3	2.775	2.723	2.673	2.624	2.577	2.487	2.402	2.322	2.246
4	3.630	3.546	3.465	3.387	3.312	3.170	3.037	2.914	2.798
5	4.452	4.329	4.212	4.100	3.993	3.791	3.605	3.433	3.274
6	5.242	5.076	4.917	4.767	4.623	4.355	4.111	3.889	3.685
7	6.002	5.786	5.582	5.389	5.206	4.868	4.564	4.288	4.039

We multiply $31,000, the amount of the annuity, by the 3.433 present value factor and find that the present value of the annuity is $106,423 ($31,000 × 3.433 = $106,423). Finally, we find the net present value of the project by subtracting the present value of cash outflows from the present value of cash inflows. In our example, the net present value calculations are presented in Exhibit 7–6.

Exhibit 7-6
Net Present
Value Calculations

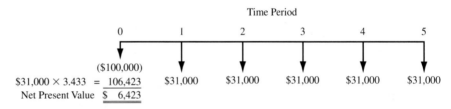

$31,000 × 3.433 = 106,423
Net Present Value $ 6,423

NPV = PV of project's expected returns − initial cash outlay

NPV = $106,423 − $100,000

NPV = $6,423

As Exhibit 7–6 shows, the positive net present value of $6,423 indicates that the project's expected return exceeds CanCo Manufacturing Inc.'s 14 percent weighted-average cost of capital.

A word of caution here. A net present value of $6,423 does not mean that the project's return is only $6,423. Rather, it means that the project's return *exceeds* the company's 14 percent cost of capital by $6,423.

 Discussion Questions

7-14. How would you explain the difference between present value and net present value?

7-15. Should a business accept or reject a project with an NPV of zero? Explain your reasoning.

The CanCo Manufacturing Inc. example was relatively easy to calculate because the project's expected cash flows were the same each year (an annuity). When the expected cash flows are uneven, we find the present value of each year's cash flow and then add those amounts. To demonstrate, assume that CanCo's computer upgrade has expected annual returns of $31,000, but in year 3 the computer system will require $12,000 in maintenance fees (a cash outflow), and at the end of year 5, the system can be sold for $6,000 (a cash inflow). A time line depicting these additional cash flows is shown in Exhibit 7–7.

Exhibit 7–7
Uneven Expected Cash Flows for CanCo Manufacturing Inc.'s Computer Upgrade

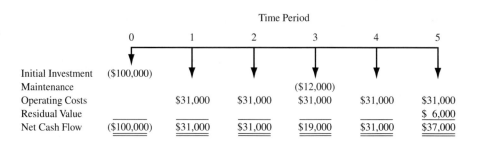

Each of the amounts for the five years shown in Exhibit 7–7 can be discounted to present value using the *Present Value of $1 Table*, found in the chapter appendix in Exhibit A7–5, a portion of which is reproduced as Exhibit 7–8.

Exhibit 7–8

Present Value of $1

Period	4%	5%	6%	7%	8%	10%	12%	14%	16%
1	0.962	0.952	0.943	0.935	0.926	0.909	0.893	0.877	0.862
2	0.925	0.907	0.890	0.873	0.857	0.826	0.797	0.769	0.743
3	0.889	0.864	0.840	0.816	0.794	0.751	0.712	0.675	0.641
4	0.855	0.823	0.792	0.763	0.735	0.683	0.636	0.592	0.552
5	0.882	0.784	0.747	0.713	0.681	0.621	0.567	0.519	0.476
6	0.790	0.746	0.705	0.666	0.630	0.564	0.507	0.456	0.410
7	0.760	0.711	0.665	0.623	0.583	0.513	0.452	0.400	0.354

The calculations of the present values, using the highlighted factors in the 14 percent discount rate column, are shown in Exhibit 7–9.

As Exhibit 7–9 demonstrates, the positive $1,406 net present value indicates that the computer upgrade exceeds the 14 percent weighted-average cost of capital for CanCo Manufacturing Inc. This positive NPV indicates that the project is acceptable for the company.

Although the net present value method indicates whether a proposed capital project is acceptable, it does have limitations as a ranking method to compare competing projects. A direct comparison of the net present values of various projects may lead to poor decisions regarding project selection, because NPV is measured in dollars rather than percentages. For example, assume that management intends to select one of two projects, Project A and Project B. Calculations indicate that the NPV of Project A is $5,000, whereas the NPV of Project B is $6,000.

Exhibit 7–9
Net Present Value
Calculations with
Uneven Cash Flows

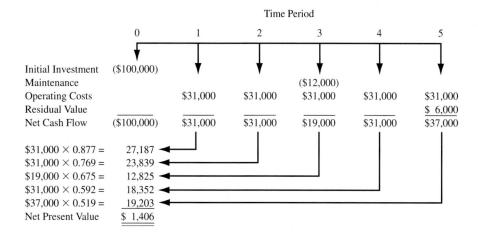

An important part of the capital-budgeting decision is the impact of Canadian income taxes. The annual cash flows would be subject to income tax using the same rates and rules as those used to determine net income. Additionally, the Canadian Income Tax Act allows companies to amortize the cost of the investment. For income tax purposes, this deduction is referred to as a capital cost allowance.

The steps involved in determining the present value of the tax savings on a company's investment is beyond the scope of this text. However, be aware that the impact of the income tax effects can be significant and is an important component in the capital budgeting decision.

Although choosing the project with the higher NPV seems wise, this is not always a good choice because NPV analysis does not consider the relative investments required by the projects. In our example, for instance, say the present value of Project A's cash inflows was $105,000 and the present value of its cash outflows was $100,000. Then suppose that the present value of Project B's cash inflows was $206,000 and the present value of its cash outflows was $200,000. We see that Project A requires an investment of $100,000, whereas Project B requires double that investment amount. In firms with scarce funds, the relatively small increase in the NPV from $5,000 to $6,000 may not justify selecting a project that requires double the amount of investment. How then can the net present value method be used when ranking various projects? The problem of selecting among projects is solved by using a profitability index.

profitability index A method used to rank acceptable proposed capital projects.

Profitability Index The **profitability index** is an index of the values of alternative but acceptable capital budgeting projects, whose index values are calculated by dividing the present value of the project's cash inflows by the present value of its cash outflows. To illustrate, we return to our example. We know that both Projects A and B have positive NPVs and are acceptable projects. Suppose, however, we want to rank the projects in order of preference.

We find that the profitability index for Project A is 1.05 ($105,000/$100,000 = 1.05). The profitability index for Project B is 1.03 ($206,000/$200,000 = 1.03). We would rank Project A higher than Project B because Project A's index value is 1.05 compared to Project B's lower index value of 1.03. We see, then, how the profitability index is a tool that allows firms to rank competing projects.

Although the NPV method indicates whether a project's return is lower or higher than the required rate of return, it does not show the project's expected percentage return. Many managers find it helpful to know the expected rate of return of projects when making capital budgeting decisions. The internal rate of return method, discussed in the following section, is a capital budgeting method that provides this information.

internal rate of return (IRR)
The calculated expected
percentage return promised by
a proposed capital project.

real rate of return Another
name for *internal rate of return.*

time-adjusted rate of return
Another name for *internal rate
of return.*

Internal Rate of Return

The **internal rate of return (IRR)** of a proposed capital project is the calculated expected percentage return promised by the project. Just like the net present value method, the internal rate of return method considers all cash flows for a proposed project and adjusts for the time value of money. However, the IRR results are expressed as a percentage, not a dollar amount. This method, also known as the **real rate of return,** or the **time-adjusted rate of return,** determines the discount rate that makes the present value of a project's cash inflows and the present value of a project's outflows exactly the same.

To calculate a project's IRR, we use the same present value tables we use to calculate net present value, but we interpret them differently. In this application, we consult the tables to determine a discount rate (a percentage), rather than present value amounts (expressed in dollars).

As an example, assume that Project C requires an initial investment of $300,000 and will provide cash inflows of $56,232 per year for eight years. Because this project is an annuity, to determine the IRR we use the *Present Value of an Annuity of $1 Table* found in the chapter appendix in Exhibit A7–10, a portion of which is reproduced as Exhibit 7–10.

First we calculate the present value factor for the project as follows:

$$\frac{\text{Initial Investment}}{\text{Expected Annual Return}} = \text{Present Value Factor}$$

In the case of Project C, the present value factor is

$$\frac{\$300,000 \text{ Initial Investment}}{\$56,232 \text{ Expected Annual Return}} = 5.335 \text{ Present Value Factor}$$

Now that we know the present value factor, we can find Project C's internal rate of return by moving down the time period column on the table in Exhibit 7–10 to eight periods, as that is the life of the project. Next we follow across the row corresponding to eight periods until we find a factor that is close to the one we calculated (5.335). As we follow across the row for eight periods, we find a factor that is not just close but matches exactly. The factor of 5.335 is in the 10 percent column, which indicates the internal rate of return for Project C is 10 percent. Thus, the actual rate of return promised by Project C is 10 percent.

Exhibit 7–10
Partial Present Value of an Annuity of $1 Table

Present Value of Annuity of $1

Period	4%	5%	6%	7%	8%	10%	12%
1	0.962	0.952	0.943	.935	0.926	0.909	0.893
2	1.886	1.859	1.833	1.808	1.783	1.736	1.690
3	2.775	2.723	2.673	2.624	2.577	2.487	2.402
4	3.630	3.546	3.465	3.387	3.312	3.170	3.037
5	4.452	4.329	4.212	4.100	3.993	3.791	3.605
6	5.242	5.076	4.917	4.767	4.623	4.355	4.111
7	6.002	5.786	5.582	5.389	5.206	4.868	4.564
8	6.733	6.463	6.210	5.971	5.747	5.335	4.968
9	7.435	7.108	6.802	6.515	6.247	5.759	5.328
10	8.111	7.722	7.360	7.024	6.710	6.145	5.650
11	8.760	8.306	7.877	7.499	7.139	6.495	5.938
12	9.382	8.863	8.384	7.943	7.536	6.814	6.194

Once determined, the internal rate of return is compared to the cost of capital to gauge the project's acceptability. An internal rate of return that exceeds the firm's cost of capital indicates an acceptable project. For example, if the company's cost of capital is 9 percent, Project C's 10 percent internal rate of return shows that the firm would find the project acceptable.

In the example for Project C, we contrived the dollar amounts so that the factor we calculated exactly equaled one of the factors in the present value table. In a real-life situation, the calculated factor will usually fall between two factors on the present value table. For example, assume Project D would require an investment of $330,000 and would generate estimated annual returns of $64,900 for eight years. The present value factor for this project is 5.085, determined as follows:

$$\frac{\$330,000 \text{ Initial Investment}}{\$64,900 \text{ Annual Returns}} = 5.085 \text{ Present Value Factor}$$

Returning to the table in Exhibit 7–10 and following across the year 8 row, we find that our calculated 5.085 factor is between the factors 5.335 (the 10 percent column) and 4.968 (the 12 percent column), but is much closer to 4.968. Therefore, the project's return would fall between 10 and 12 percent, but would be much closer to 12 percent. We then estimate that the internal rate of return for Project D is slightly less than 12 percent.

Comparing Projects Using the IRR Method Managers can use the internal rate of return method to rank projects. For example, the internal rate of return of Project C (10 percent) can be compared to the approximate internal rate of return of Project D (almost 12 percent). Assuming both projects were acceptable, Project D would be ranked higher than Project C because it promises a higher IRR.

Comparing the NPV and IRR Methods Both the net present value method and the internal rate of return method are well-respected techniques used to determine the acceptability of a proposed capital project for two reasons. First, they are based on cash flows, not accounting income. Second, both methods consider the time value of money.

The net present value method is used to determine whether the promised return from a proposed capital project meets the minimum acceptable return requirements (cost of capital). A drawback of this method is that the calculated net present value is stated in dollars rather than percentages. Thus, comparison between projects is difficult. The profitability index overcomes this difficulty.

The internal rate of return method is used to calculate a proposed capital project's actual expected rate of return. Because this method is calculated using percentages rather than dollars, it can be used as a direct comparison of various proposed projects.

Nondiscounted Cash Flow Methods

The net present value and internal rate of return methods are generally considered the most reliable techniques available because they utilize the time value of money in their evaluation of potential capital projects. Other methods that ignore the time value of money exist, however, and are used to some degree by many companies. We now discuss two of them—the payback period method and the accounting rate of return method.

Payback Period Method As its name implies, the **payback period method** is a capital budgeting technique that measures the length of time a capital project must generate positive net cash flows that equal, or "pay back," the original investment in the project. For instance, assume that a project's estimated initial outlay is $40,000. Assume further that the project is expected to generate a net cash inflow of $12,500 per year. When net cash inflows are equal from one year to the next, we determine the payback period by dividing the required initial investment by the annual cash inflows. In our example, we find that the payback period is 3.2 years. The calculations follow:

$$\frac{\text{Required Initial Investment}}{\text{Annual Net Cash Inflow}} = \text{Payback Period in Years}$$

$$\frac{\$40,000}{\$12,500} = 3.2 \text{ Years}$$

If a project has uneven cash flows, we can determine the payback period by adding the cash inflows year by year until the total equals the required initial investment. For example, suppose a project requires an initial investment of $50,000 and is expected to generate the following net cash inflows:

2003	$12,000
2004	$15,000
2005	$18,000
2006	$15,000
2007	$12,000

We find the payback period by totaling the net cash inflows until we reach $50,000 as shown in Exhibit 7–11.

Exhibit 7–11
Payback Period with Uneven Cash Flows

Year	Cash Received in Prior Years		Cash Received in Current Year		Accumulated Cash Received
1	0	+	$12,000	=	$12,000
2	$12,000	+	$15,000	=	$27,000
3	$27,000	+	$18,000	=	$45,000
4	$45,000	+	$15,000	=	$60,000
5	$60,000	+	$12,000	=	$72,000

As Exhibit 7–11 shows, the initial investment will be "paid back" after the third year, but before the end of the fourth year. At the end of the third year, it is anticipated that $45,000, or all but $5,000 of the initial $50,000 investment will be recouped. The remaining $5,000 will be received during the fourth year as part of the $15,000 net cash inflows anticipated for that year. It will take about 1/3 ($5,000/$15,000) of the fourth year to collect the final $5,000 to make up the $50,000 needed to pay back the initial investment. Therefore the payback period is 3 1/3 years.

The payback period method highlights the liquidity of an investment and can be used as a screening device to reject projects with unreasonably low cash flow expectations. This method is simple to use, is easily understood, and offers some limited insight into a project's liquidity.

The payback period method is not often used to make final capital investment decisions because it does not consider three crucial elements: (1) the expected returns of a project after the payback period, (2) how the returns will compare to the firm's cost of capital, and (3) the time value of money.

Because the payback method ignores the firm's cost of capital, total cash flow, and time value of money concerns, managers do not normally accept or reject a project based solely on the payback period method. If used at all, the payback period method is usually a screening device only to eliminate potential projects from further evaluation. Companies often establish a maximum payback period for potential projects. If a proposed capital project promises a payback of longer than the established maximum period, that project would be eliminated from further consideration. For example, assume a company has established a maximum payback period of three years. Using this standard, the project presented in Exhibit 7–11 would be rejected because its payback period is longer than three years.

Accounting Rate of Return Method In our discussion so far, we have emphasized that the focus in capital budgeting decisions should be on cash flows. Over time, however, the net cash flow associated with a capital project should approximate operating income as determined using accrual accounting revenue and expense recognition. The accounting rate of return method uses accrual accounting operating income, rather than net cash flow, as the basis for evaluating alternative capital budgeting projects.

accounting rate of return
The rate of return for a capital project based on the anticipated increase in accounting operating income due to the project, relative to the amount of capital investment required.

The **accounting rate of return** is the rate of return for a capital project based on the anticipated increase in accounting operating income due to the project, relative to the amount of capital investment required.

This method focuses on how the project changes a company's operating income and the company's required investment. As an example, we reexamine the computer hardware upgrade project for CanCo Manufacturing Inc. discussed earlier in the chapter. As you recall, the computer hardware upgrade required an initial investment of $100,000. Additionally, the upgrade would reduce operating expenses by $31,000 per year for five years. The computer has an estimated useful life of five years with no residual value. Accounting operating income would be affected in two ways by the computer upgrade. First, the reduced operating expenses would increase operating income by $31,000 each year. Second, amortization for the computer upgrade would decrease operating income by $20,000 each year ($100,000/5 years). With this information, we can calculate the accounting rate of return as follows:

$$\frac{\text{Increase in Operating Income}}{\text{Required Investment}} = \text{Accounting Rate of Return}$$

$$\frac{\$31,000 - \$20,000}{\$100,000} = 11\% \text{ Accounting Rate of Return}$$

The accounting rate of return is simple to calculate and provides some measure of a project's profitability; however, it has two major drawbacks. First, the accounting rate of return method focuses on accounting income rather than cash flow. In capital budgeting it is generally believed that a focus on cash flow is preferred to a focus on accounting income. Second, like the payback method, the accounting rate of return does not consider the time value of money.

The accounting rate of return method is generally considered to be superior to the payback period method because it offers at least a limited measure of a proposed capital project's rate of return. As with the payback period method, however, managers should not accept or reject a project based solely on the accounting rate of return. Both of these methods should be used only as screening devices or in conjunction with discounted cash flow methods of evaluating capital project alternatives.

FACTORS LEADING TO POOR CAPITAL PROJECT SELECTION

The process of determining which capital projects to select is serious business for any company. We mentioned earlier in the chapter that Dofasco reported investment in capital projects of $1,000,000,000 in the past five years. If managers do not treat capital budgeting with the seriousness it deserves, they run the risk of making poor decisions as to the capital projects selected. At the very least, selecting the wrong capital projects is enormously costly. At worst, investing in the wrong projects can lead to financial ruin for any company, regardless of its size or past performance. The two main factors leading to poor capital project selection are natural optimism on the part of managers and the tendency of some managers to turn the capital project evaluation process into a game.

Natural Optimism

Human beings are essentially optimistic. As managers they estimate both the cash inflows and outflows associated with a proposed project they are sponsoring with an overly optimistic outlook. This means they will likely overstate the estimated cash inflows and understate the estimated cash outflows. At the very minimum, this natural optimism limits the effectiveness of any of the evaluation techniques we have discussed in this chapter, because all of them use inflow and outflow estimates as the basis of evaluation.

There is nothing wrong with thinking positively. Optimism is, in fact, a desirable trait. Managers must understand, however, that such optimism can cloud their judgment as they assess potential capital projects. Good managers attempt to be as realistic as possible as they prepare proposals for the evaluation of potential capital projects.

Capital Budgeting Games

The managers who propose potential capital projects understand that there is usually not enough money available to fund all projects, even if they all promise a return greater than the cost of capital. A manager who proposes a capital project is, in fact, competing with other managers' projects for a limited number of capital investment dollars. For this reason, the capital project evaluation process is sometimes treated like a game with little consideration of the potentially disastrous consequences. Some managers manipulate the estimates of cash inflow and cash outflow to get "pet" projects approved, often at the expense of other, more deserving projects. Do not confuse this idea with the natural optimism we discussed a moment ago. The manipulation we are talking about here is an additional factor that can lead to selecting the wrong capital projects.

For example, consider the Electronics Division of Monolith Enterprises. This division has established a limit of $3,000,000 for capital projects in 2004. Mary and Fred are the only two managers within the division who have potential capital projects to propose to division upper management. Both the potential projects will require an initial investment of $2,000,000, so only one of them is going to be approved.

Mary is in her office late one night putting the finishing touches on her proposal. She is reviewing the cash inflow and cash outflow estimates she has made for her project. As she goes over the estimates one last time, she is feeling a little guilty because she knows she has purposely overstated the inflows and understated the outflows to make her project look more favourable. She is convinced, however, that if she is totally realistic in her estimates, her project will stand no chance of being approved. Why? Because she knows Fred is in his office down the hall putting the finishing touches on his proposal, and she is sure he has manipulated the inflow and outflow estimates on his project to make it look better. To have any chance of approval, then, Mary must "play the game." The sad part of this situation is that Fred is down the hall in his office thinking exactly the same thing about Mary. He is certain she has manipulated her estimates, so he must also, or his project has no chance of being approved. Now we introduce one more person to our scenario—Bill, the division controller. Bill is the person who will evaluate the proposed projects submitted by Mary and Fred and will decide which of the two projects will be funded. He knows that both Mary and Fred have manipulated their estimates, so when he receives them, he compensates by arbitrarily revising their proposals or by using a higher cost of capital percentage in the NPV and IRR evaluations.

Does this seem to you to be an intelligent way to run a business? No, but this kind of game is played every day in many companies by otherwise bright and honest managers.

 ## Discussion Question

Assume you have been hired as a consultant by Monolith Enterprises to help the company improve its capital project evaluation process.

    7-16. What suggestions would you make to help Monolith eliminate the kind of "game" being played by Mary, Fred, and Bill?

How does a company make its capital project evaluation process more cooperative and less competitive? This question is difficult, if not impossible, to answer. What we do know, however, is that the global nature of business will not allow these kinds of budget games to continue. If firms are to compete in this worldwide market, they must eliminate dysfunctional business practices. The stakes are simply too high for managers of these companies to continue this approach to capital budgeting.

In a very short time, you will occupy the positions held by Mary, Fred, or Bill. Not at Monolith, of course, because it is a fictitious company. The company that employs you, however, may approach capital budgeting the same way Monolith does. If so, you must do all you can to help the company find a better, more constructive capital budgeting process.

SUMMARY

There are four elements in the overall planning process for any organization. These elements include the establishing of goals, the formulation of a strategic plan, the preparation of the capital budget, and the preparation of the operating budget.

The capital budgeting process has been described as the *how* of being in business and doing business, which means that the capital budget outlines how a company will allocate its scarce resources over the next five, ten, or even 20 years.

All capital projects have at least four shared characteristics. Such projects are usually long lived, carry with them high costs, have costs associated with the project that usually become sunk almost immediately, and usually involve a high degree of risk.

In the long run, the capital projects a company undertakes must cover at least the cost of the company's capital. The cost of capital is the cost of obtaining financing from both debt and equity sources. The combination of the cost of debt financing and equity financing is referred to as the weighted-average cost of capital. If the capital project being considered does not at least cover the cost of capital, it makes no sense, from a purely financial standpoint, to undertake it.

Over time, several methods have been developed to evaluate potential capital projects. Among these are the net present value (NPV) method, the internal rate of return (IRR) method, the payback period method, and the accounting rate of return. Each of these four methods has certain advantages and disadvantages relative to the other methods. The NPV and IRR methods are generally considered to be superior to the payback and accounting rate of return methods because they incorporate the time value of money in their approach to evaluating potential capital projects.

APPENDIX: THE TIME VALUE OF MONEY

The Time Value of Money—The Concept of Interest

A dollar received at some point in the future does not have the same value as a dollar received today. If you were asked why this is so, you might think the change in value is due to inflation. Even if inflation did not exist, a dollar received in the future would not have the same value as a dollar received today. The reason for the difference in value is that if cash is available now, it can be invested now and earn a return as time passes. This increase in the value of cash over time, due to investment income, is referred to as the *time value of money*. The concept of the time value of money is used to determine either the future value of money invested today or the present value of money to be received at some point in the future.

After completing your work in the appendix to this chapter, you should be able to do the following:

1. Explain the concepts of simple interest and compound interest.
2. Determine the future value of a single amount invested today using a future value table.
3. Determine the present value of a single amount to be received at some point in the future using a present value table.
4. Describe the concept of an annuity.
5. Determine the future value of an annuity using a future value table.
6. Determine the present value of an annuity using a present value table.

Future Value

future value The value of a payment, or series of payments, at some future point in time calculated at some interest rate.

Future value is the value of a payment, or series of payments, at some future point in time calculated at some interest rate. For example, if you were to invest $2,000 at an annual interest rate of 10 percent, your investment would grow to $2,200 in one year. How? The amount of the increase is calculated by multiplying the principal—the original investment—by the interest rate. In our case the principal is $2,000, the interest rate is 10 percent, so the total return on your investment is $200. The $200 is added to the $2,000 investment for a total of $2,200. So far, so good. But suppose you left the investment untouched for three years. What would be its total value at the end of the three years? The answer depends on whether the interest is calculated as simple interest or compound interest.

simple interest Interest calculated on the original principal amount invested only.

Simple interest is interest calculated only on the original principal. A calculation of interest earned at 10 percent per year for three years on a $2,000 principal using simple interest is presented in Exhibit A7–1.

Exhibit A7–1
Simple Interest
Calculation

	Year 1	Year 2	Year 3
Principal	$2,000	$2,000	$2,000
Times the interest rate	× 10%	× 10%	× 10%
Equals interest earned	$ 200	$ 200	$ 200

Note in Exhibit A7–1 that interest for each of the three years is calculated only on the original investment of $2,000. At the end of three years you would receive your $2,000 (return of your principal) and $600 interest (return on your investment).

compound interest Interest calculated on the original principal amount invested plus all previously earned interest.

Compound interest is interest calculated on the investment principal *plus* all previously earned interest. Continuing with our example, a principal of $2,000 that earns a compounded rate of 10 percent interest per year for three years is shown in Exhibit A7–2.

Note in Exhibit A7–2 that interest for each of the three years is calculated not only on the original investment of $2,000, but also on the interest earned in previous years. At the end of three years you would receive your $2,000 back (return of principal) and $662 interest (return on your investment). The difference of $62 between the interest earned using compound interest ($662) and the interest earned using simple interest ($600) is interest earned on your previously earned interest.

Exhibit A7–2
Compound Interest
Calculations

	Year 1	Year 2	Year 3
Principal + Previously earned interest	$2,000	$2,200*	$2,420**
Times the interest rate	× 10%	× 10%	× 10%
Equals interest earned	$ 200	$ 220	$ 242

* Principal ($2,000) plus the interest earned in year 1 ($200) becomes the amount earning interest in year 2.

** Principal ($2,000) plus the interest earned in year 1 ($200) and the interest earned in year 2 ($220) becomes the amount earning interest in year 3.

The power of compounding is tremendous. To demonstrate, let's extend our example of the $2,000 investment. Suppose Dick Gustufson invests $2,000 at 10 percent annual interest when he is 18 years old and leaves it untouched until he is 38 years old. Using the simple interest calculation, Dick's investment will earn interest of $4,000 ($2,000 × 10% × 20 years). If, however, the interest over that same 20 years is compounded, the total interest earned would be $11,454. The $7,454 difference in interest earned is due entirely to interest earning interest on previously earned interest.

We could calculate the amount of compound interest on Dick's investment by extending the three-year example presented in Exhibit A7–2 for another 17 years. This, however, would be cumbersome, time consuming, and tiresome. Fortunately, future value tables greatly simplify the calculation of compound interest.

Future value tables are previously calculated values of $1 at various rates of interest and time periods. The tables are used to determine either the future value of a single payment or the future value of an annuity—that is, a stream of equal payments made at equal intervals.

The *Future Value of $1 Table* (Exhibit A7–3) is used to determine the future value of a single amount deposited today. With this information, we can quickly determine the future value of Dick Gustufson's $2,000 investment at a 10 percent interest rate compounded annually.

As we see in Exhibit A7–3, by moving across the interest rate column headings to the 10 percent column, and then down the time period row to the 20 time periods row, we find a number on the table at the point where the row and column intersect, at a value of 6.727. This number is called a future value factor. Because we are using the *Future Value of $1 Table*, the 6.727 factor tells us that the value of a single dollar 20 years into the future is $6.727, or about $6.73. That is to say that if $1 is invested today at 10 percent, it will be worth $6.73 in 20 years.

But Dick invested $2,000, not $1. To determine the future value of $2,000, we multiply $2,000 by the factor of 6.727 to determine that $2,000 invested today at 10 percent will be worth $13,454 after 20 years ($2,000 × 6.727 = $13,454). If you subtract his initial investment of $2,000, the amount of interest he will earn is $11,454.

A *Future Value of an Annuity of $1 Table*, presented as Exhibit A7–4, is used to determine the future value of a stream of cash flows when the stream of cash flows constitutes an annuity. An **annuity** is a stream of cash flows where the dollar amount of each payment and the time interval between each payment are uniform.

annuity A stream of equal periodic cash flows.

To see how the table in Exhibit A7–4 is used, assume Susan King intends to deposit $2,000 in an account at the end of each year for four years at a compound interest rate of 12 percent per year. Using the *Future Value of an Annuity of $1 Table* we determine that the factor for 4 years at 12 percent is 4.779. Accordingly, if Susan deposits $2,000 at the end of each year for four years at 12 percent, the account balance will be approximately $9,558 ($2,000 × 4.779).

Exhibit A7–3
Future Value of $1 Table

Future Value of $1

Period	4%	5%	6%	7%	8%	9%	10%	12%	14%	16%
1	1.040	1.050	1.060	1.070	1.080	1.090	1.100	1.120	1.140	1.160
2	1.082	1.103	1.124	1.145	1.166	1.188	1.210	1.254	1.300	1.346
3	1.125	1.158	1.191	1.225	1.260	1.295	1.331	1.405	1.482	1.561
4	1.170	1.216	1.262	1.311	1.360	1.412	1.464	1.574	1.689	1.811
5	1.217	1.276	1.338	1.403	1.469	1.539	1.611	1.762	1.925	2.100
6	1.265	1.340	1.419	1.501	1.587	1.677	1.772	1.974	2.195	2.436
7	1.316	1.407	1.501	1.606	1.714	1.828	1.949	2.211	2.502	2.826
8	1.369	1.477	1.594	1.718	1.851	1.993	2.144	2.476	2.853	3.278
9	1.423	1.551	1.689	1.838	1.999	2.172	2.358	2.773	3.252	3.803
10	1.480	1.629	1.791	1.967	2.159	2.367	2.594	3.106	3.707	4.411
11	1.539	1.710	1.898	2.105	2.332	2.580	2.853	3.479	4.226	5.117
12	1.601	1.796	2.012	2.252	2.518	2.813	3.138	3.896	4.818	5.936
13	1.665	1.886	2.133	2.410	2.720	3.066	3.452	4.363	5.492	6.886
14	1.732	1.980	2.261	2.579	2.937	3.342	3.797	4.887	6.261	7.988
15	1.801	2.079	2.397	2.759	3.172	3.642	4.177	5.474	7.138	9.266
16	1.873	2.183	2.540	2.952	3.426	3.970	4.595	6.130	8.137	10.748
17	1.948	2.292	2.693	3.159	3.700	4.328	5.054	6.866	9.276	12.468
18	2.026	2.407	2.854	3.380	3.996	4.717	5.560	7.690	10.575	14.463
19	2.107	2.527	3.026	3.617	4.316	5.142	6.116	8.613	12.056	16.777
20	2.191	2.653	3.207	3.870	4.661	5.604	6.727	9.646	13.743	19.461

Exhibit A7–4
Future Value of an Annuity of $1 Table

Future Value of Annuity of $1

Period	4%	5%	6%	7%	8%	9%	10%	12%	14%	16%
1	1.000	1.000	1.000	1.000	1.000	1.000	1.000	1.000	1.000	1.000
2	2.040	2.050	2.060	2.070	2.080	2.090	2.100	2.120	2.140	2.160
3	3.122	3.153	3.184	3.215	3.246	3.278	3.310	3.374	3.440	3.506
4	4.246	4.310	4.375	4.440	4.506	4.573	4.641	4.779	4.921	5.006
5	5.416	5.526	5.637	5.751	5.867	5.985	6.105	6.353	6.610	6.877
6	6.633	6.802	6.975	7.153	7.336	7.523	7.716	8.115	8.536	8.977
7	7.898	8.142	8.394	8.654	8.923	9.200	9.487	10.089	10.730	11.414
8	9.214	9.549	9.897	10.260	10.637	11.028	11.436	12.300	13.233	14.240
9	10.583	11.027	11.491	11.978	12.488	13.021	13.579	14.776	16.085	17.519
10	12.006	12.578	13.181	13.816	14.487	15.193	15.937	17.549	19.337	21.321
11	13.486	14.207	14.972	15.784	16.645	17.560	18.531	20.665	23.045	25.733
12	15.026	15.917	16.870	17.888	18.977	20.141	21.384	24.133	27.271	30.850
13	16.627	17.713	18.882	20.141	21.495	22.953	24.523	28.029	32.089	36.786
14	18.292	19.599	21.015	22.550	24.215	26.019	27.975	32.393	37.581	43.672
15	20.024	21.579	23.276	25.129	27.152	29.361	31.772	37.280	43.842	51.660
16	21.825	23.657	25.673	27.888	30.324	33.003	35.950	42.753	50.980	60.925
17	23.698	25.840	28.213	30.840	33.750	36.974	40.545	48.884	59.118	71.673
18	25.645	28.132	30.906	33.999	37.450	41.301	45.599	55.750	68.394	84.141
19	27.671	30.539	33.760	37.379	41.446	46.018	51.159	63.440	78.969	98.603
20	29.778	33.066	36.786	40.995	45.762	51.160	57.275	72.052	91.025	115.380

Present Value (Discounting)

The basic premise of the present value of money is that it is more valuable to receive cash today (so it can be invested to receive interest) than to receive the cash later. The question is, just *how* valuable is it to receive cash sooner rather than later?

If we know the expected rate of return, it is possible to actually calculate the value of receiving cash sooner rather than later. For example, if you are offered the option of receiving $1,000 today or $1,000 one year from now, how much more valuable is it to receive the $1,000 today? If the $1,000 received today can be invested in a savings account earning 6 percent interest, then it will grow by $60 during the year. At the end of one year, it will be worth $1,060 and you would be $60 richer than if you had opted to receive the $1,000 one year from now. The $60 growth in value over time exemplifies the time value of money. Clearly, if money is available and invested, it grows as time passes.

If cash can be invested at 6 percent, $1,000 received today is equivalent to receiving $1,060 one year from now. The amount a future cash flow or stream of cash flows is worth today evaluated at the appropriate interest rate is the cash flow's **present value.** Determining the present value of an amount of cash to be received in the future is called *discounting*.

present value The amount future cash flows are worth today based on an appropriate interest rate.

Present value tables greatly simplify the calculation of discounting to find the present value of a single amount or an annuity. Present value tables are previously calculated values of $1 at various interest rates and time periods. The tables are used to determine either the present value of a single amount or the present value of an annuity.

A *Present Value of $1 Table,* presented as Exhibit A7–5, is used to determine the present value of a single amount to be received at some point in the future.

To see how we use the *Present Value of $1 Table,* suppose you visited your rich Aunt Hattie and helped her wash her dog. Your aunt was so touched by your kindness, she offers to give you a gift of $1,000. You are excited and hold out your hand for the money, but she informs you that she is not going to give you the money now. Rather she intends to give you the money one year from now. Her only request is that you tell her how much to deposit in a 6 percent savings account today so that the account will equal $1,000 one year from now.

In this case, you know that the future value of the amount is $1,000 one year from now. The amount your Aunt Hattie wants to know is the present value, the amount that must be deposited today at 6 percent so that the account will be worth $1,000 in one year. To find out how much Aunt Hattie must deposit, we use the *Present Value of $1 Table* in Exhibit A7–5. We quickly scan the table to find the point of intersection between the 6 percent interest rate column and the number of time periods row, which is 1. The point of intersection, the present value factor, is 0.943. This factor indicates that the present value of one dollar discounted at 6 percent is $0.943, or about 94 cents. Thus, if $0.943 is invested today at 6 percent, it will be worth $1 one year from now.

But Aunt Hattie is going to give you $1,000, not $1. To determine the present value of $1,000, we simply multiply $1,000 by the factor of 0.943 to determine that $943 invested today at 6 percent will be worth $1,000 in one year, as shown by the time line presentation in Exhibit A7–6.

Exhibit A7–6 shows that to earn $1,000 a year from now, given an expected rate of interest of 6 percent per year, Aunt Hattie must deposit $943. So, the present value of $1,000 to be received one year from now at 6 percent is $943. The $943 will grow in value as it accumulates interest. This growth is the time value of money. You immediately inform your Aunt Hattie that she must deposit $943 today at 6 percent to have the $1,000 gift ready for you one year from now.

Aunt Hattie is so happy with your quick response that she offers you an additional $1,000 gift. The second $1,000 gift, however, will be given two years from now, which means you will receive the first $1,000 gift at the end of year 1, and the

Exhibit A7–5
Present Value of $1 Table

Present Value of $1

Period	4%	5%	6%	7%	8%	10%	12%	14%	16%
1	0.962	0.952	0.943	0.935	0.926	0.909	0.893	0.877	0.862
2	0.925	0.907	0.890	0.873	0.857	0.826	0.797	0.769	0.743
3	0.889	0.864	0.840	0.816	0.794	0.751	0.712	0.675	0.641
4	0.855	0.823	0.792	0.763	0.735	0.683	0.636	0.592	0.552
5	0.882	0.784	0.747	0.713	0.681	0.621	0.567	0.519	0.476
6	0.790	0.746	0.705	0.666	0.630	0.564	0.507	0.456	0.410
7	0.760	0.711	0.665	0.623	0.583	0.513	0.452	0.400	0.354
8	0.731	0.677	0.627	0.582	0.540	0.467	0.404	0.351	0.305
9	0.703	0.645	0.592	0.544	0.500	0.424	0.361	0.308	0.263
10	0.676	0.614	0.558	0.508	0.463	0.386	0.322	0.270	0.227
11	0.650	0.585	0.527	0.475	0.429	0.350	0.287	0.237	0.195
12	0.625	0.557	0.497	0.444	0.397	0.319	0.257	0.208	0.168
13	0.601	0.530	0.469	0.415	0.368	0.290	0.229	0.182	0.145
14	0.557	0.505	0.442	0.388	0.340	0.263	0.205	0.160	0.125
15	0.555	0.481	0.417	0.362	0.315	0.239	0.183	0.140	0.108
16	0.534	0.458	0.394	0.339	0.292	0.218	0.163	0.123	0.093
17	0.513	0.436	0.371	0.317	0.270	0.198	0.146	0.108	0.080
18	0.494	0.416	0.350	0.296	0.250	0.180	0.130	0.095	0.069
19	0.475	0.396	0.331	0.277	0.232	0.164	0.116	0.083	0.060
20	0.456	0.377	0.312	0.258	0.215	0.149	0.104	0.073	0.051

Exhibit A7–6
Time Line Presentation
of Present Value of $1

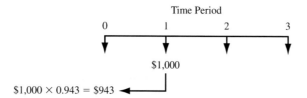

second $1,000 gift at the end of year 2. You are thrilled, but again, your Aunt Hattie requests that you tell her exactly how much she must deposit today at 6 percent to have the additional $1,000 in two years. We use the *Present Value of $1 Table* in Exhibit A7–5 to find that the present value factor for a time period of 2 and an interest rate of 6 percent is 0.890. Accordingly, the present value of $1,000 to be received two years from now is $890 ($1,000 × 0.890). You quickly inform your aunt that she must deposit a total of $1,833 ($943 + $890) today to pay both the $1,000 at the end of year 1, and the $1,000 at the end of year 2. The time line and calculations are shown in Exhibit A7–7.

Exhibit A7–7
Time Line Presentation

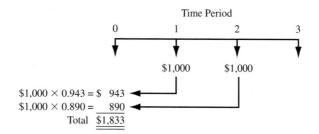

Now suppose your Aunt Hattie planned to give you a gift of $1,000 per year for the next three years. We could rely on the *Present Value of $1 Table* and add the totals for each year as shown in Exhibit A7–8.

Exhibit A7–8
Time Line Presentation

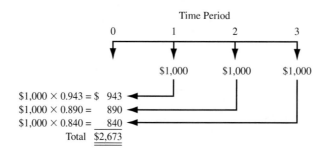

We can simplify the calculations, however, by multiplying the $1,000 by the sum of the three present value factors, which is 2.673. Accordingly, instead of multiplying $1,000 by 0.943, then $1,000 by 0.890, then $1,000 by 0.840, and summing the total, we simply multiply the $1,000 by the sum of the factors as shown in Exhibit A7–9.

Exhibit A7–9
Time Line Presentation

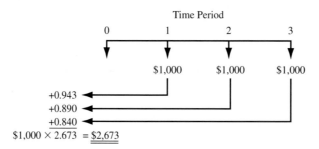

Because the stream of cash flows in our example is an annuity—three equal payments made at regular intervals of one year—we can use the *Present Value of an Annuity of $1 Table*, presented as Exhibit A7–10.

By examining the table in Exhibit A7–10, we find that the present value factor of an annuity for three periods at 6 percent is 2.673. Notice that the 2.673 equals the sum of the individual present value of $1 factors for each of the three years in Exhibit A7–9. Next, we multiply the $1,000 by the 2.673 factor to find that the present value of Aunt Hattie's $1,000, three-year annuity paid yearly is $2,673.

As you use the future value and present value tables provided in this book, note that the number of interest rates and time periods is limited. Although these smaller tables are useful for learning the basics, in business practice future value and present value tables include a much larger number of interest rates and time periods. If needed, comprehensive tables are available at bookstores and office supply stores.

As an alternative to using future and present value tables, we can compute future value and present value using nothing more than a somewhat sophisticated business handheld calculator. (It must be a business calculator. Engineering and scientific calculators generally do not have present value and future value functions.) In the business world, most managers rely on calculators and computers to calculate future and present values.

Most computers can also be used to solve present value and future value problems. Many software packages now include modules that can handle simple and advanced calculations dealing with the time value of money.

Exhibit A7–10
Present Value of an Annuity of $1 Table

Present Value of Annuity of $1

Period	4%	5%	6%	7%	8%	10%	12%	14%	16%
1	0.962	0.952	0.943	0.935	0.926	0.909	0.893	0.877	0.862
2	1.886	1.859	1.833	1.808	1.783	1.736	1.690	1.647	1.605
3	2.775	2.723	2.673	2.624	2.577	2.487	2.402	2.322	2.246
4	3.630	3.546	3.465	3.387	3.312	3.170	3.037	2.914	2.798
5	4.452	4.329	4.212	4.100	3.993	3.791	3.605	3.433	3.274
6	5.242	5.076	4.917	4.767	4.623	4.355	4.111	3.889	3.685
7	6.002	5.786	5.582	5.389	5.206	4.868	4.564	4.288	4.039
8	6.733	6.463	6.210	5.971	5.747	5.335	4.968	4.639	4.344
9	7.435	7.108	6.802	6.515	6.247	5.759	5.328	4.946	4.607
10	8.111	7.722	7.360	7.024	6.710	6.145	5.650	5.216	4.833
11	8.760	8.306	7.877	7.499	7.139	6.495	5.938	5.453	5.029
12	9.382	8.863	8.384	7.943	7.536	6.814	6.194	5.660	5.179
13	9.986	9.394	8.853	8.358	7.904	7.103	6.424	5.842	5.342
14	10.563	9.899	9.295	8.745	8.244	7.367	6.628	6.002	5.468
15	11.118	10.380	9.712	9.108	8.559	7.606	6.811	6.142	5.575
16	11.652	10.838	10.106	9.447	8.851	7.824	6.974	6.265	5.669
17	12.166	11.274	10.477	9.763	9.122	8.022	7.120	6.373	5.749
18	12.659	11.690	10.828	10.059	9.372	8.201	7.250	6.467	5.818
19	13.134	12.085	11.158	10.336	9.604	8.365	7.366	6.550	5.877
20	13.590	12.462	11.470	10.594	9.818	8.514	7.469	6.623	5.929

A working knowledge of present and future value concepts will be extremely important to you not only in your course work but also in your professional career. Whether the task is the evaluation of potential capital projects, as in this chapter, or any of its many other applications, you will find these concepts invaluable throughout your life.

KEY TERMS

accounting rate of return, p. 239
annuity, p. 244
capital assets, p. 223
capital budget, p. 222
capital budgeting, p. 219
capital investments, p. 219
capital projects, p. 219
capital rationing, p. 229
compound interest, p. 243
cost of capital, p. 225
cost of capital rate, p. 225
cost of debt capital, p. 225
cost of equity capital, p. 225
discounting cash flows, p. 231
future value, p. 243
hurdle rate, p. 225
internal rate of return (IRR), p. 236

mission statement, p. 221
net cash flow, p. 230
net present value (NPV), p. 232
operating budget, p. 222
organizational goals, p. 220
payback period method, p. 238
present value, p. 246
profitability index, p. 235
real rate of return, p. 236
relevant net cash flows, p. 230
required rate of return, p. 225
simple interest, p. 243
strategic plan, p. 221
time-adjusted rate of return, p. 236
time value of money, p. 231
weighted-average cost of capital, p. 225

Review the Facts

1. What constitutes a firm's goals?
2. What is a mission statement and how does it relate to a company's goals?
3. What is a strategic plan and how does it relate to a company's goals?
4. What is the purpose of a capital budget and how does it relate to the strategic plan and a company's goals?
5. What is the purpose of an operating budget and how does it relate to the capital budget, the strategic plan, and a company's goals?
6. What are capital investments?
7. What is the difference between a capital investment and a capital project?
8. What is the focus of the capital budget?
9. What does it mean when the cost of a purchased item is capitalized?
10. What does it mean when the cost of a purchased item is expensed?
11. What are the four shared characteristics of virtually all capital projects?
12. What are some other terms used to describe the cost of capital?
13. Describe what is meant by the net present value of an investment.
14. With respect to net present value calculations, what is the advantage of calculating the profitability index?
15. What is determined by the internal rate of return?
16. What is determined by the payback method?
17. What is the accounting rate of return?
18. What are two factors that can lead to poor capital project selection?
19. What is the basic difference between simple interest and compound interest? (Appendix)
20. What is an annuity? (Appendix)

Apply What You Have Learned

LO 1: Match Elements of Planning to Characteristics

1. Following are the elements of the planning process as discussed in this chapter, with some characteristics pertaining to those elements.

    a. Goals
    b. Strategic plan
    c. Capital budget
    d. Operating budget

    1. _____ Pertains to day-to-day activities
    2. _____ Pertains to the allocation of scarce resources
    3. _____ Consists of both financial and nonfinancial considerations
    4. _____ Stated in terms that are not easily quantified
    5. _____ Stated in terms that are easily quantified
    6. _____ Constitutes the *who* of business planning
    7. _____ Constitutes the *why* of business planning
    8. _____ Constitutes the *how* of business planning
    9. _____ Constitutes the *what* of business planning
    10. _____ Relates to long-lived, expensive assets

    REQUIRED:
    Match each element of the planning process with the appropriate characteristics. Each letter may be used more than once.

LO 4: Discuss and Calculate the Cost of Capital

2. Kelavna Distributors Inc. is in the process of determining a return rate to use for its cost of capital.

   Upon review of the financial statements, it was determined that the total interest-bearing debt is $1,400,000 and total shareholders' equity is $1,000,000. In addition, it was determined that the cost of debt financing is 8%, and the cost of equity financing is 18%.

REQUIRED:

a. What proportion of Kelavna Distributors Inc.'s total financing comes from debt?
b. What proportion of Kelavna Distributors Inc.'s total financing comes from equity?
c. Calculate Kelavna Distributors Inc.'s weighted-average cost of capital rate.

LO 4: Discuss and Calculate the Cost of Capital

3. The Byrne Company is in the process of determining a return rate to use for its cost of capital.

   Upon review of the financial statements, it was determined that the total interest-bearing debt is $4,800,000 and total shareholders' equity is $14,400,000. In addition, it was determined that the cost of debt financing is 7%, and the cost of equity financing is 22%.

REQUIRED:

a. What proportion of The Byrne Company's total financing comes from debt?
b. What proportion of The Byrne Company's total financing comes from equity?
c. Calculate The Byrne Company's weighted-average cost of capital rate.

LO 4: Discuss and Calculate the Cost of Capital

4. The Cunningham Company is in the process of determining a return rate to use for its cost of capital.

   Upon review of the financial statements, it was determined that the total interest-bearing debt is $800,000 and total shareholders' equity is $1,700,000. In addition, it was determined that the cost of debt financing is 9%, and the cost of equity financing is 20%.

REQUIRED:

a. What proportion of The Cunningham Company's total financing comes from debt?
b. What proportion of The Cunningham Company's total financing comes from equity?
c. Calculate The Cunningham Company's weighted-average cost of capital rate.

LO 2: Determine the Sequence of Evaluating Capital Expenditures

5. Following in random order are the five steps for evaluating a capital expenditure.

   a. _____ Identify alternative capital projects.
   b. _____ Identify the need for a capital expenditure.
   c. _____ Select a method for evaluating the alternatives.
   d. _____ Evaluate the alternatives and select the project or projects to be funded.
   e. _____ Determine relevant cash inflow and cash outflow information.

REQUIRED:

In the space provided, indicate a logical sequence of the steps for evaluating a capital expenditure.

LO 6 & 7: Determine Net Present Value, No Residual Value

6. Asacia Boyd owns Discount Fashions. She is contemplating the purchase of a drink machine that would be used to sell soft drinks to customers for $1.00 each. The following estimates are available.

Initial outlay	$3,500
Annual cash inflow	$1,000
Cost of capital	10%
Estimated life of the drink machine	5 years
Estimated residual value of the drink machine	$0

REQUIRED:

Determine the net present value of the drink machine purchase.

LO 6 & 7: Determine Net Present Value, No Residual Value

7. Brianna Chen is contemplating the purchase of an ice cream vending machine that would be used to sell ice cream to customers for $2 each. The following estimates are available.

Initial outlay	$4,000
Annual cash inflow	$1,200
Cost of capital	12%
Estimated life of the ice cream machine	5 years
Estimated residual value of the ice cream machine	$0

REQUIRED:

Determine the net present value of the ice cream machine purchase.

LO 6 & 7: Determine Net Present Value, No Residual Value

8. Asha Parmor is contemplating the purchase of a machine that will automate the production of baseball bats in her factory. The following estimates are available.

Initial outlay	$97,000
Annual reduction in manufacturing labour cost	$22,500
Cost of capital	14%
Estimated life of the baseball bat machine	8 years
Estimated residual value of the bat machine	$0

REQUIRED:

Determine the net present value of the baseball bat machine purchase.

LO 6 & 7: Determine Net Present Value, No Residual Value

9. Kristen Hohman is contemplating the purchase of a machine that will automate the production of hosiery in her factory. The following estimates are available.

Initial outlay	$112,000
Annual reduction in manufacturing labour cost	$22,500
Cost of capital	12%
Estimated life of the hosiery machine	8 years
Estimated residual value of the hosiery machine	$0

REQUIRED:
Determine the net present value of the hosiery machine purchase.

LO 6 & 7: Determine Net Present Value and Profitability Index, Various Rates, No Residual Value

10. Harrison Sporting Goods Ltd. is considering the purchase of a machine that is used to cut material to make baseball gloves. The cost of the machine is $265,000. The machine has an estimated useful life of eight years, with no residual value. Currently, the company leases a similar machine for $50,000 per year. If the new machine is purchased, the company's cost of labour would be reduced by $12,000 per year.

REQUIRED:
a. Determine the net present value of the machine under each of the following assumptions.
   1. The cost of capital is 12%
   2. The cost of capital is 14%
   3. The cost of capital is 16%
b. Determine the profitability index under each of the following assumptions.
   1. The cost of capital is 12%
   2. The cost of capital is 14%
   3. The cost of capital is 16%

LO 6 & 7: Determine Net Present Value and Profitability Index, Various Rates, No Residual Value

11. Brantford Manufacturing Inc. is considering the purchase of a computer-controlled manufacturing machine that is used in its factory. The cost of the machine is $3,600,000. The machine has an estimated useful life of ten years, with no residual value. If the new machine is purchased, the company's cost of labour would be reduced by $650,000 per year.

REQUIRED:
a. Determine the net present value of the machine under each of the following assumptions.
   1. The cost of capital is 10%
   2. The cost of capital is 12%
   3. The cost of capital is 14%
b. Determine the profitability index under each of the following assumptions.
   1. The cost of capital is 10%
   2. The cost of capital is 12%
   3. The cost of capital is 14%

LO 6 & 7:   Determine Net Present Value, No Residual Value

12. Tom Suto is considering the purchase of an engine lift for use in his marine repair business. He has determined that a used lift is available for $5,500. The engine lift has an estimated useful life of eight years and a residual value of zero. Currently, Frank rents engine lifts as needed. If the lift is purchased, annual rental payment of $1,400 would be saved. The cost of capital is 16%.

REQUIRED:
Calculate the net present value of the engine lift purchase.

LO 6 & 7:   Determine Net Present Value, No Residual Value

13. Michael Francis is considering the purchase of an industrial glass-cutting machine for use in his business. He has determined that a used glass cutter is available for $25,800. The cutter has an estimated useful life of ten years and a residual value of zero. Currently, Michael rents an industrial cutter for $4,400 annually. The cost of capital is 14%.

REQUIRED:
Calculate the net present value of the industrial glass cutter.

LO 6 & 7:   Determine Net Present Value, with Residual Value

14. The owner of Wynn Sports Cards is contemplating the purchase of a machine that will automate the production of baseball cards in her factory. The following estimates are available.

Initial outlay	$35,000
Annual reduction in manufacturing labour cost	$8,500
Cost of capital	14%
Estimated life of the card machine	5 years
Estimated residual value of the card machine	$2,000

REQUIRED:
Determine the net present value of the baseball card machine purchase.

LO 6 & 7:   Determine Net Present Value, with Residual Value

15. Kevin Petty owns Discount Auto Parts. He is contemplating the purchase of a brake lathe that could be used to refurbish brake parts for customers. The following estimates are available.

Initial outlay	$6,500
Annual cash inflow	$1,500
Cost of capital	16%
Estimated life of the brake lathe	6 years
Estimated residual value of the brake lathe	$1,000

REQUIRED:
Determine the net present value of the brake lathe purchase.

LO 6 & 7:   Determine Net Present Value, with Residual Value

16. Patty Gillan owns Gillan Skin Care Products. She is contemplating the purchase of an industrial mixer that would be used to mix cosmetics in her factory. The following estimates are available.

Initial outlay	$78,500
Annual cash inflow	$19,500
Cost of capital	16%
Estimated life of the mixer	7 years
Estimated residual value of the mixer	$4,000

REQUIRED:
Determine the net present value of the industrial mixer purchase.

LO 6 & 7:   Determine Net Present Value, with Residual Value

17. Elianne Vinas owns Vinas Shoe Company. She is contemplating the purchase of a cutting machine that would be used to make shoes in her factory. The following estimates are available.

Initial outlay	$58,000
Annual cash inflow from reduced labour cost	$11,500
Cost of capital	12%
Estimated life of the cutter	8 years
Estimated residual value of the cutter	$2,000

REQUIRED:
Determine the net present value of the cutting machine purchase.

LO 6 & 7:   Determine Net Present Value and Profitability Index, Various Rates, with Residual Value

18. Golden Construction Company is considering the purchase of a new road grader. The cost of the road grader is $68,000. The road grader has an estimated useful life of seven years and an estimated residual value of $5,000. Currently, the company rents road graders as needed. If the road grader is purchased, annual rental payments of $17,000 would be saved.

REQUIRED:
a. Determine the net present value of the grader purchase under each of the following assumptions.
  1. The cost of capital is 12%
  2. The cost of capital is 14%
  3. The cost of capital is 16%
b. Determine the profitability index under each of the following assumptions.
  1. The cost of capital is 12%
  2. The cost of capital is 14%
  3. The cost of capital is 16%

LO 6 & 7:   Determine Net Present Value and Profitability Index, Various Rates, with Residual Value

19. Parker Pencil Company is considering the purchase of a new machine to make pencils. The cost of the machine is $248,000. The pencil machine has an estimated useful life of ten years and an estimated residual value of $25,000. Currently, the company leases a similar machine for $45,000 per year.

REQUIRED:

a. Determine the net present value of the pencil machine purchase under each of the following assumptions.
    1. The cost of capital is 10%
    2. The cost of capital is 12%
    3. The cost of capital is 14%

b. Determine the profitability index under each of the following assumptions.
    1. The cost of capital is 10%
    2. The cost of capital is 12%
    3. The cost of capital is 14%

LO 6 & 7: Determine Net Present Value and Profitability Index, Various Rates, with Residual Value

20. Sylvain Charest's Catering Service is considering the purchase of new energy-efficient cooking equipment. The cost of the new equipment is $78,000. The equipment has an estimated useful life of eight years and an estimated residual value of $5,000. Currently, the company leases similar cooking equipment for $10,000 per year. If the new cooking equipment is purchased, the company's cost of electricity would be reduced by $8,000 per year.

REQUIRED:

a. Determine the net present value of the cooking equipment under each of the following assumptions.
    1. The cost of capital is 12%
    2. The cost of capital is 14%
    3. The cost of capital is 16%

b. Determine the profitability index under each of the following assumptions.
    1. The cost of capital is 12%
    2. The cost of capital is 14%
    3. The cost of capital is 16%

LO 6 & 7: Determine Internal Rate of Return, Various Rates, No Residual Value

21. Penny Nordelli is contemplating the purchase of a new computer system for her company, Nordelli Manufacturing Ltd. She has made the following estimates.

Initial outlay	$18,023.88
Annual cash savings	$5,000.00
Estimated life of the computer	5 years
Estimated residual value of the computer	$0

REQUIRED:

a. Determine the internal rate of return for the computer purchase.

b. Indicate whether the computer purchase should be accepted under each of the following assumptions.
    1. The cost of capital is 9%
    2. The cost of capital is 11%
    3. The cost of capital is 13%
    4. The cost of capital is 15%

LO 6 & 7:   Determine Internal Rate of Return, Various Rates, No Residual Value

22. Cornerbrook Moving and Storage is contemplating the purchase of a new delivery truck. The following estimates are available.

Initial outlay	$51,590
Annual cash flow from the new truck	$14,000
Estimated life of the truck	6 years
Estimated residual value of the truck	$0

REQUIRED:

a. Determine the internal rate of return for the truck purchase.

b. Indicate whether the truck purchase should be accepted under each of the following assumptions.
   1. The cost of capital is 14%
   2. The cost of capital is 16%
   3. The cost of capital is 18%

LO 6 & 7:   Determine Internal Rate of Return for Three Projects, Select Project, No Residual Value

23. Hank Mundt & Company is in the process of replacing its existing computer system. The following three proposals are being considered.

	System A	System B	System C
Initial outlay	$18,023.88	$22,744.72	$24,031.57
Annual cash savings	$5,000.00	$6,000.00	$7,000.00
Estimated useful life	5 years	5 years	5 years

The estimated residual value of all computer systems under consideration is zero.

REQUIRED:

a. Determine the internal rate of return for each of the proposed computer systems.

b. Which computer system would you recommend? Explain your reasoning.

LO 6 & 7:   Determine Internal Rate of Return for Three Projects, Select Project, No Residual Value

24. Markham Equipment Company is in the process of selecting some new manufacturing equipment. The following three proposals are being considered.

	Equipment A	Equipment B	Equipment C
Initial outlay	$14,902.92	$18,555.46	$26,674.63
Annual cash savings	$3,000.00	$4,000.00	$5,000.00
Estimated useful life	8 years	8 years	8 years

The estimated residual value of all equipment under consideration is zero.

REQUIRED:

a. Determine the internal rate of return for each of the proposed pieces of equipment.

b. Which piece of equipment would you recommend? Explain your reasoning.

LO 6 & 7: Determine Net Present Value, Profitability Index, and Internal Rate of Return, Various Rates, No Residual Value

25. Dunn Manufacturing Corporation is considering the purchase of a factory that makes valves. These valves would be used by Dunn to manufacture water pumps. The purchase would require an initial outlay of $1,449,968. The factory would have an estimated life of ten years and no residual value. Currently, the company buys 500,000 valves per year at a cost of $1.50 each. If the factory were purchased, the valves could be manufactured for $0.90 each.

REQUIRED:

a. Determine the net present value of the proposed project and whether it should be accepted under each of the following assumptions.
1. The cost of capital is 12%
2. The cost of capital is 14%
3. The cost of capital is 16%

b. Determine the profitability index under each of the following assumptions.
1. The cost of capital is 12%
2. The cost of capital is 14%
3. The cost of capital is 16%

c. Determine the internal rate of return of the proposed project and indicate whether it should be accepted under each of the following assumptions.
1. The cost of capital is 12%
2. The cost of capital is 14%
3. The cost of capital is 16%

LO 6: Determine Payback Period, Even Cash Flows

26. Discount Hardware is contemplating the purchase of a copy machine that would be used to make copies to sell to customers for $0.05 each. The following estimates are available.

Initial outlay	$4,500
Annual cash inflow	$1,800

REQUIRED:
Determine the payback period for the copy machine purchase.

LO 6: Determine Payback Period, Even Cash Flows

27. Magic Makers Manufacturing is contemplating the purchase of a machine that would be used to manufacture various products that would be sold to magic shops. The following estimates are available.

Initial outlay	$23,539.20
Annual cash inflow	$7,356.00

REQUIRED:
Determine the payback period for the machine purchase.

LO 6: Determine Payback Period, Even Cash Flows

28. Vargas Supplies Corp. is contemplating the purchase of a machine that would be used in its business. The following estimates are available.

Initial outlay	$5,826.50
Annual cash inflow	$1,355.00

REQUIRED:
Determine the payback period for the machine purchase.

LO 6: Determine Payback Period, Even Cash Flows

29. Nieto Manufacturing is contemplating the purchase of a machine that would be used in its business. The following estimates are available.

Initial outlay	$323,400
Annual cash inflow	$33,000

REQUIRED:
Determine the payback period for the machine purchase.

LO 6: Determine Payback Period, Uneven Cash Flows

30. Lim Distributing Ltd. is considering the purchase of a machine to produce a new product. The company believes the cash inflows will grow each year as the new product gains market acceptance. The company has made the following cash inflow estimates.

First year	$30,000
Second year	$45,000
Third and subsequent year	$50,000

The cost of the machine is $110,000.

REQUIRED:
Determine the payback period for the purchase of the machine.

LO 6: Determine Payback Period, Uneven Cash Flows

31. Vickki Chang is considering opening a ceramic studio. She has determined that it would require an investment of $14,000 to open the store. She believes that the cash inflows would grow each year as more and more people learn of the store. She has made the following cash inflow estimates.

First year	$2,000
Second year	$4,000
Third and subsequent years	$5,000

REQUIRED:
Determine the payback period for the ceramic studio.

LO 6: Determine Payback Period, Uneven Cash Flows

32. Karen Gallagher is considering adding a new style of gym shorts to her product line. She has determined that it would require an investment of $22,000 to add the new style of shorts. She believes that the cash inflows would grow each year as the new style becomes more popular. She has made the following cash inflow estimates.

First year	$ 4,000
Second year	$ 6,000
Third and subsequent years	$10,000

REQUIRED:
Determine the payback period for the new style of gym shorts.

LO 6: Determine Accounting Rate of Return

33. BRV Construction Company is contemplating the purchase of scaffolding at the cost of $32,000. Currently, the company rents similar scaffolding for use at each of its construction sites. The scaffolding has an estimated useful life of five years and an estimated residual value of $2,000. By purchasing the scaffolding, BRV could save rental fees of $11,760 per year.

REQUIRED:
Determine the accounting rate of return for BRV's investment in the scaffolding.

LO 6: Determine Accounting Rate of Return

34. Smith and Smith & Associates is contemplating the purchase of equipment that would cost $196,600. Currently, the company rents similar equipment for $45,076 per year. The proposed new equipment has an estimated useful life of eight years and an estimated residual value of $9,000.

REQUIRED:
Determine the accounting rate of return for Smith and Smith & Associates' investment in the new equipment.

LO 6: Determine Accounting Rate of Return

35. Condore & Company is contemplating the purchase of a machine that would cost $142,790. The machine would provide an annual contribution margin of $47,262.55 each year. The proposed new machine has an estimated useful life of five years and an estimated residual value of $10,000.

REQUIRED:
Determine the accounting rate of return for Condore & Company's investment in the new machine.

LO 5, 6, & 7: Determine Relevant Information, Net Present Value, Screen Project, with Residual Value

36. Mainland Marine Service purchased a forklift five years ago for $16,000. When it was purchased, the forklift had an estimated useful life of ten years and a residual value of $4,000. The forklift can be sold now for $6,000. The operating cost for the forklift is $4,500 per year.

The company is thinking about buying a newer forklift for $17,000. The newer forklift would have an estimated useful life of five years and a residual value of $7,000. The operating cost for the newer forklift would be $3,000 per year.

The company's cost of capital is 10%.

REQUIRED:
a. Prepare a relevant cost schedule showing the benefits of buying the new forklift. (For this requirement, ignore the time value of money.)
b. How much must the company invest today to replace the old forklift?
c. If the company replaces the old forklift, what is the increase in the company's annual contribution margin?

d. If the company sells the old forklift now to make room for the new one, it will not receive the $4,000 residual value at the end of its useful life. Instead, the company will receive the $7,000 residual value from the new forklift. With this in mind, if the company buys the forklift, what is the change in the residual value the company is to receive at the end of the five-year life of the equipment?

e. Calculate the net present value of replacing the old forklift.

f. Do you think the company should replace the old forklift?

LO 5, 6, & 7: Determine Relevant Information, Net Present Value, Screen Project, with Residual Value

37. Hart Engineering Company is considering the purchase of a new copy machine. The company purchased the old machine two years ago for $8,500. When it was purchased the old machine had an estimated useful life of eight years and a residual value of $500. The operating cost of the old machine is $3,000 per year. The old machine can be sold today for $2,000. A new machine can be purchased today for $10,000 and would have an estimated useful life of six years with a residual value of $1,000. The operating cost of the new copy machine is expected to be $1,500 per year.

The company's cost of capital is 8%.

REQUIRED:

a. Prepare a relevant cost schedule showing the benefit of buying the new copy machine. (For this requirement, ignore the time value of money.)

b. How much must the company invest today to replace the old copy machine?

c. If the company replaces the old copy machine, what is the increase in the company's annual contribution margin?

d. If the company sells the old copy machine now to make room for the new one, it will not receive the $500 residual value at the end of its useful life. Instead, the company will receive the $1,000 residual value from the new copy machine. With this in mind, if the company buys the copy machine, what is the change in the residual value the company is to receive at the end of the six-year life of the equipment?

e. Calculate the net present value of replacing the old copy machine.

f. Do you think the company should replace the old copy machine?

LO 5, 6, & 7: Determine Relevant Information, Net Present Value, Screen Project, No Residual Value

38. The managers at AAA Manufacturing Corp. are considering replacing an industrial mixer used in the company's factory. The company's cost of capital is 10%.

Information about the old mixer:

Cost	$28,000
Estimated useful life	10 years
Estimated salvage value	$0
Current age	5 years
Estimated current fair value	$8,000
Annual operating cost	$18,000

Information about the new mixer:

Cost	$34,000
Estimated useful life	5 years
Estimated residual value	$0
Annual operating cost	$12,000

REQUIRED:

a. Prepare a relevant cost schedule showing the benefit of buying the new mixer.
b. How much must the company invest today to replace the old mixer?
c. If the new mixer is purchased, how much would be saved in operating costs each year?
d. How much would the company receive at the end of the five-year useful life of the new mixer?
e. Calculate the net present value of replacing the old mixer.
f. Do you think the company should replace the old mixer?

LO 5, 6, & 7: Determine Relevant Information, Net Present Value, Screen Project, No Residual Value

39. The managers at Gardner Manufacturing Company are considering replacing the industrial lathe used in the company's factory. The company's cost of capital is 12%.

Information about the old lathe:

Cost	$57,000
Estimated useful life	8 years
Estimated residual value	$0
Current age	2 years
Estimated current fair value	$32,000
Annual operating cost	$32,000

Information about the new lathe:

Cost	$61,000
Estimated useful life	6 years
Estimated residual value	$0
Annual operating cost	$24,000

REQUIRED:

a. Prepare a relevant cost schedule showing the benefit of buying the new lathe. (For this requirement, ignore the time value of money.)
b. How much must the company invest today to replace the old lathe?
c. If the company replaces the old lathe, how much will be saved in operating costs each year?
d. Calculate the net present value of replacing the old lathe.
e. Do you think the company should replace the old lathe?

LO 5, 6, & 7: Determine Relevant Information, Net Present Value, Screen Project, with Residual Value

40. Island Marina Inc. is considering replacing the company's industrial lift used to haul boats. The new lift would allow the company to lift larger boats out of the water. The company's cost of capital is 14%.

Information about the old lift:

Cost	$94,000
Estimated useful life	12 years
Estimated residual value	$10,000
Current age	4 years
Estimated current fair value	$48,000
Annual contribution margin	$50,000

Information about the new lift:

Cost	$128,000
Estimated useful life	8 years
Estimated residual value	$25,000
Annual contribution margin	$70,000

REQUIRED:

a. Prepare a relevant cost schedule showing the benefit of buying the new lift. (For this requirement, ignore the time value of money.)

b. How much must the company invest today to replace the old lift?

c. If the company replaces the old lift, what is the increase in the company's annual contribution margin?

d. If the company sells the old lift now to make room for the new one, it will not receive the $10,000 residual value at the end of its useful life. Instead, the company will receive the $25,000 residual value from the new lift. With this in mind, if the company buys the new lift, what is the change in the residual value the company is to receive at the end of the eight-year life of the equipment?

e. Calculate the net present value of replacing the old lift.

f. Do you think the company should replace the old lift?

LO 5, 6, & 7: Determine Relevant Information, Net Present Value, Screen Project, with Residual Value

41. The managers at Erie Manufacturing Ltd. are considering replacing a printing press with a new, high-speed model. The company's cost of capital is 12%.

Information about the old printing press:

Cost	$255,000
Estimated useful life	10 years
Estimated residual value	$25,000
Annual amortization	$23,000
Current age	3 years
Accumulated amortization to date	$184,000
Estimated current fair value	$150,000
Annual contribution margin	$110,000

Information about the new printing press:

Cost	$335,000
Estimated useful life	7 years
Estimated residual value	$45,000
Annual amortization	$70,000
Annual contribution margin	$150,000

REQUIRED:

a. Prepare a relevant cost schedule showing the benefit of buying the new printing press. (For this requirement, ignore the time value of money.)

b. How much must the company invest today to replace the old printing press?
c. If the company replaces the old printing press, what is the increase in the company's annual contribution margin?
d. If the company sells the old printing press now to make room for the new one, it will not receive the $25,000 residual value at the end of its useful life. Instead, the company will receive the $45,000 residual value from the new printing press. With this in mind, if the company buys the new printing press, what is the change in the residual value the company is to receive at the end of the seven-year life of the equipment?
e. Calculate the net present value of replacing the old printing press.
f. Do you think the company should replace the old printing press?

APPENDIX

LO 7: Calculate Simple, Compound Interest, Full Years

42. Magog Marine borrowed $5,000 from National Bank on January 1, 2003.

REQUIRED:
a. Assuming 9% simple interest is charged, calculate interest for 2003, 2004, and 2005.
b. Assuming 9% compound interest is charged, calculate interest for 2003, 2004, and 2005.

LO 7: Calculate Simple, Compound Interest, Full Years

43. Gary borrowed $8,000 from Pacific Bank on January 1, 2003.

REQUIRED:
a. Assuming 8% simple interest is charged, calculate interest for 2003, 2004, and 2005.
b. Assuming 8% compound interest is charged, calculate interest for 2003, 2004, and 2005.

LO 7: Calculate Simple, Compound Interest, Full Years

44. Cam borrowed $2,000 from Bank of Toronto on January 1, 2003.

REQUIRED:
a. Assuming 6% simple interest is charged, calculate interest for 2003, 2004, and 2005.
b. Assuming 6% compound interest is charged, calculate interest for 2003, 2004, and 2005.

LO 7: Calculate Future Value, Single Cash Flow, Various Rates and Maturities

45. Susan Jones made the following investments on January 1, 2003:
1. $ 2,000 at 10% for 5 years
2. $12,000 at 4% for 8 years
3. $ 9,000 at 14% for 15 years

Assume the interest on each investment is compounded annually.

REQUIRED:

Calculate the future value of each of the investments listed above at their maturity.

LO 7: Calculate Future Value, Single Cash Flow, Various Rates and Maturities

46. Ivan Zhang made the following investments on January 1, 2004:

1. $3,000 at 8% for 6 years
2. $4,000 at 6% for 8 years
3. $5,000 at 10% for 5 years

Assume the interest on each investment is compounded annually.

REQUIRED:

Calculate the future value of each of the investments listed above at their maturity.

LO 7: Calculate Future Value, Single Cash Flow, Various Rates and Maturities

47. Natashiia Bone made the following investments on January 1, 2004:

1. $1,000 at 14% for 3 years
2. $2,000 at 10% for 5 years
3. $4,000 at 8% for 8 years

Assume the interest on each investment is compounded annually.

REQUIRED:

Calculate the future value of each of the investments listed above at their maturity.

LO 7: Calculate Future Value, Yearly Cash Flows, Various Rates and Maturities

48. Consider the following investments.

1. $2,000 at the end of each of the next 5 years at 10% interest compounded annually
2. $12,000 at the end of each of the next 8 years at 4% interest compounded annually
3. $9,000 at the end of each of the next 15 years at 14% interest compounded annually

REQUIRED:

Calculate the future value of each of the investments listed above at their maturity.

LO 7: Calculate Future Value, Yearly Cash Flows, Various Rates and Maturities

49. Consider the following investments.

1. $12,000 at the end of each of the next 3 years at 12% interest compounded annually
2. $16,000 at the end of each of the next 5 years at 10% interest compounded annually
3. $20,000 at the end of each of the next 10 years at 8% interest compounded annually

REQUIRED:

Calculate the future value of each of the investments listed above at their maturity.

LO 7: Calculate Future Value, Yearly Cash Flows, Various Rates and Maturities

50. Consider the following investments.

    1. $1,000 at the end of each of the next 5 years at 6% interest compounded annually

    2. $1,000 at the end of each of the next 5 years at 8% interest compounded annually

    3. $1,000 at the end of each of the next 5 years at 10% interest compounded annually

REQUIRED:
Calculate the future value of each of the investments listed above at their maturity.

LO 7: Calculate Present Value, Single Cash Flow, Single Rate

51. Jim Johnson is planning to buy a new car when he graduates in three years. He would like to invest a single amount now, in order to have the $24,000 he estimates the car will cost.

REQUIRED:
Calculate the amount Jim must invest today to have enough to buy the new car, assuming his investment will earn 4% compounded annually for the three-year investment.

LO 7: Calculate Present Value, Single Cash Flow, Single Rate

52. Cathy Johnson needs to have $50,000 at the end of five years. Cathy would like to invest a single amount now to have the $50,000 in five years.

REQUIRED:
Calculate the amount Cathy must invest today to have the amount of money she needs, assuming her investment will earn 8% compounded annually for the five-year investment.

LO 7: Calculate Present Value, Single Cash Flow, Single Rate

53. Lauren Elsea is planning to buy a condominium when she graduates. She would like to have $20,000 for the down payment. Lauren would like to invest a single amount now to have the $20,000 at the end of three years.

REQUIRED:
Calculate the amount Lauren must invest today to have the amount of money she needs, assuming her investment will earn 6% compounded annually for the three-year investment.

LO 7: Calculate Present Value, Yearly Cash Flows, Single Rate

54. Linda Chidister is planning to send her son, Edward, to university. While he is in university, Linda intends to give him $3,000 at the end of each year.

REQUIRED:
How much must Linda invest today so she will have enough to give Edward $3,000 at the end of each of the next four years, assuming the investment will earn 6% interest?

LO 7: Calculate Present Value, Yearly Cash Flows, Single Rate

55. Alex Malpin is planning to spend the next three years doing research in China. An Asian studies research institute has agreed to pay Alex $20,000 at the end of each of the three years he is in China.

REQUIRED:

How much must be invested today to have enough to pay Alex $20,000 at the end of each of the next three years assuming the investment will earn 10% interest?

LO 7: Calculate Present Value, Yearly Cash Flows, Single Rate

56. Photo Factory Inc. is planning to purchase some photo processing equipment from Ace Equipment Company. The equipment will provide cash flow of $15,000 at the end of each of the next eight years.

REQUIRED:

How much should Photo Factory Inc. pay for the equipment assuming it will provide cash flow of $15,000 at the end of each of the next eight years and Ace has promised that it will earn a return of exactly 14%?

8

The Operating Budget

*T*he 2001 annual report for Canadian Tire Corporation, Limited contained a letter to shareholders from the President and Chief Executive Officer, Wayne Sales, which stated in part:

"I consider setting targets and measuring our progress against them essential to our continuing improvement and ultimate success. In the strategic planning process, we established the following targets for the period 2001—2005:

- Compounded annual growth in revenue of greater than 10 percent;
- Comparable store sales growth of 3–4 percent;
- Compounded annual growth in earnings per share of 12–15 percent;
- Compounded annual growth in earnings before interest, income taxes, depreciation and amortization and minority interest of 10–15 percent;
- Return on invested capital of greater than 10 percent, after tax.[1]

As we saw in Chapter 7, the steps outlined in the strategic planning process are the "what" of doing business. As you can see from its annual report, Canadian Tire has established targets for performance over a five-year period. But how will Canadian Tire monitor its progress toward the goals that have been stated? Its managers must plan and budget for day-to-day activities, normally on an annual basis. This is called an operating budget and Canadian Tire can use this tool to plan

---

[1]Canadian Tire Corporation, Limited 2001 Annual Report, p. 5.

and control activities that need to be undertaken to achieve the targets listed in the strategic plan.

The **operating budget** is a budget for a specific time, usually one to five years, that establishes who is responsible for the day-to-day operation of the business during that time. This budget is also sometimes called the **master operating budget** or simply the **master budget**. For the sake of consistency, we will use the term *operating budget* throughout our discussions of this topic.

The operating budget will be an important part of your business life, regardless of your occupation or the type of company for which you choose to work. Whether the organization is profit or not for profit, and whether it is a service, merchandising, or manufacturing firm, budgeting has become increasingly more important in charting the success of today's organizations. Gone are the days when companies could succeed on simple luck and optimism. Gone, too, are the days when a select group of top managers prepared operating budgets with little input from others in the organization. Many companies today involve all managers and employees in the budgeting process. Large Canadian companies such as Petro-Canada, Inco, Air Canada, Bombardier, and others have recognized that better budgeting is achieved when they involve those who actually work in the area or function for which the budget is being prepared. As you read the pages that follow, we hope you remember that budgets will be an important ingredient in your personal business success and that you will very likely be involved in the budgeting process much earlier in your career than you may have expected.

The chapter is divided into two main parts. Part One contains an overview of the operating budget, its purpose, and where it fits into the overall management process. Part Two contains a detailed presentation of how the operating budget is actually prepared and how it should and should not be used by managers. ■

operating budget A budget for a specific period, usually one to five years, that establishes who is responsible for the day-to-day operation of a business during that time.

master operating budget Another name for *operating budget*.

master budget Another name for *operating budget*.

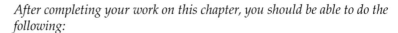

After completing your work on this chapter, you should be able to do the following:

1. Describe some of the benefits of the operating budget.
2. Describe the three budgeted financial statements contained in the operating budget and the other budgets that support the budgeted financial statements.
3. Compare and contrast various approaches to the preparation and use of the operating budget.
4. Describe the role of the sales forecast in the budgeting process.
5. Prepare the budgets included in the operating budget.
6. Describe the appropriate use of the operating budget in the overall management process.

PART ONE: AN OVERVIEW OF THE OPERATING BUDGET

The Operating Budget: What Is It?

What exactly *is* an operating budget? We know it is the plan for a company's operating activities for some period of time, but what is in that plan? The operating budget includes a set of estimated financial statements.

Recall that the three main financial statements are the balance sheet, the income statement, and the cash flow statement. Businesses prepare these statements at the end of a given time period to show the effects of past transactions and events. An operating budget contains those same three financial statements, except they are estimates—or forecasts—of future transactions and events. The forecasted financial statements in the operating budget are sometimes called pro forma financial statements. *Pro forma* is a Latin phrase meaning "provided in advance."

Because the operating budget is a set of estimated financial statements, much of what we will cover in this chapter will at least be familiar to you. The only difference between the financial statements businesses use to show the effects of past events and transactions, and the ones you will explore in this chapter, is that the budgeted financial statements are used to predict future events.

BENEFITS OF BUDGETING

A well-prepared operating budget can create many benefits for the company. In this section, we will explore four of them. First, budgeting serves as a guide. Second, it helps organizations allocate resources. Third, it encourages communication and coordination. Fourth, it sets performance standards, or *benchmarks*.

Serves as a Guide

The operating budget should serve as a guide for a company to follow during the budgeted period. What if economic or industry conditions change? The company will likely have to make adjustments given this new information. Thus, companies should adjust their budgets when desirable or necessary.

To illustrate, suppose the budget for Pam's Flower Shop forecasted sales revenue of $310,000 for the first three months of 2004. Business was better than expected and the flower shop had sales of $310,000 by the end of February. Should Pam close the flower shop until April 1 because she attained her budgeted sales figure for the quarter? Of course not. Or suppose Pam has the opportunity to purchase 20 dozen roses just before Valentine's Day at a discounted price. She can probably sell all of them for a whopping profit, but she didn't budget for this special purchase. What should she do? It may seem obvious that she should take advantage of this terrific opportunity, but a surprising number of businesses view the budget as "set in stone," so to speak, and meeting the budget becomes the primary business objective. An unwillingness to adjust a budget based on new information can be detrimental to a company because opportunities are missed and poor decisions made.

Assists in Resource Allocation

As discussed in Chapter 7, all organizations have scarce resources. No company can afford to do everything it desires, or even everything it needs to do within a given time period. A budget can help management decide where to allocate its limited resources.

The budgeting process may uncover potential bottlenecks and allow managers to address these issues in advance as the budget is being prepared, rather than as problems occur during the year. An example of a bottleneck in a manufacturing environment is presented for Montrose Manufacturing Corporation in Exhibit 8–1.

Exhibit 8–1
Example of Production
Bottleneck at Montrose
Manufacturing
Corporation

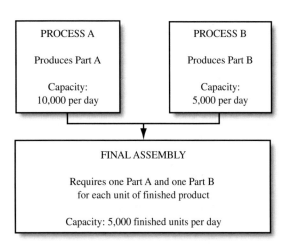

As you can see from Exhibit 8–1, each unit of finished product Montrose manufactures requires one Part A and one Part B. The maximum number of finished units of product the company can produce per day is 5,000. The limiting factor is Process B, which can produce only 5,000 parts per day. Montrose could increase the capacity of Process A from 10,000 parts per day to 100,000 parts per day and the company *still* could produce only 5,000 finished units per day because of the restriction caused by Process B. Process B is the bottleneck in this company's production process.

Assume Montrose Manufacturing Corporation moved some production machinery from Process A to Process B. This change reduces the capacity of Process A by 2,500 units per day, but the capacity of Process B was increased by 2,500 units per day as reflected in Exhibit 8–2.

Exhibit 8–2
Elimination of
Production Bottleneck
at Montrose
Manufacturing
Corporation

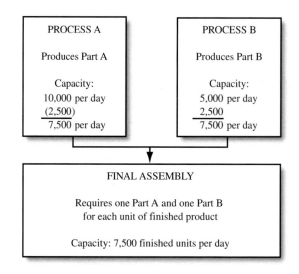

As you can see by looking at Exhibit 8–2, Montrose has increased its capacity to produce finished units by 50 percent (from 5,000 units to 7,500 units) without adding any additional machinery to its operation, which is a significant factor if you recall our discussion of capital expenditures in Chapter 7.

The issue of resource allocation is also important for a merchandising business. For example, February may be so busy for Pam's Flower Shop that Pam will need extra workers. If Pam knows this in advance, she will have time to hire the needed workers at the least cost so she can offer quality service and sell more flowers. In contrast, if Pam did not plan for the February rush, she would find herself understaffed and unable to provide quality, timely service. She might lose customers before she could hire more workers, and sales could drop. Budgeting, then, helps Pam make good decisions about how to allocate her resources.

Fosters Communication and Coordination

As managers from different functional areas in an organization work together to prepare the budget, they gain a better understanding of the entire business. When managers from all areas learn of difficulties facing others and spot duplication of effort, the firm can then solve problems and coordinate efforts more effectively. Our previous example of Montrose Manufacturing Corporation and its production bottleneck points out the possibilities of increased communication and coordination through the budgeting process. In working to solve this production problem, the managers of Process A, Process B, and Final Assembly had the opportunity to view the production process from a broader perspective. Rather than concentrating only on their own part of the process, they were better able to understand the problems facing managers in other areas of the company's operations. They were forced to communicate with one another and to better coordinate their efforts.

Even for a small company like Pam's Flower Shop, success can depend on coordinating many activities. For example, Pam expects sales to increase in February because of Valentine's Day. She anticipates she will need more flowers to sell, and more labour to sell them. The number of extra workers, however, may depend on the amount of additional flowers ordered. When she prepares the budget, Pam speaks to the inventory manager and the personnel manager about the February rush to better coordinate their activities. Then the managers will know in advance exactly what needs to be done.

Establishes Performance Standards

The operating budget also sets performance standards for an organization. As managers prepare budgets for their companies, they must estimate performance levels they both want and can attain. If a company's actual sales, for example, are less than its budgeted sales for a particular period, the sales manager will review the deficit and ask why. Once she has learned why, she will probably budget more effectively next time. Without a budget she might not notice the sales shortfall and therefore would not learn from it.

These performance standards become benchmarks against which firms can compare the actual results. Differences between the actual results and the budget can be explored and improvements made. The improvements may focus on performance, the budgeting process, or both.

 Discussion Question

> **8-1.** In what other ways do you think a company might benefit from preparing an operating budget?

CONTENTS OF THE OPERATING BUDGET

Many of us have had to prepare a personal cash budget, in which we compare the amount of cash coming in to the amount of cash going out. Because of this personal experience with budgeting, many people think that business budgeting focuses only on budgeting for cash inflows and outflows. This view, however, is far too narrow. Remember, the operating budget is a set of estimated financial statements that includes the balance sheet, income statement, and the cash flow statement, regardless of whether the business preparing the budget is a manufacturer, a merchandiser, or a service company.

Technically, the operating budget consists of only these three pro forma financial statements. In preparing the budget, however, several supporting schedules are included that, when completed, provide the information necessary to complete the three financial statements contained in the budget. These supporting schedules are also usually referred to as budgets, and we will refer to them as such in all our discussions.

Sales Budget

sales budget Details the expected sales revenue from a company's primary operating activities during a certain time period.

The sales budget is the first budget prepared and is based on a sales forecast. As the name implies, the **sales budget** details the expected sales revenue from a company's primary operating activities during a certain time period. Because manufacturers and merchandisers sell tangible, physical product, the sales budget is based on the number of units the firm expects to sell. The sales budget of a service business is based on the amount of services the firm expects to render.

Because sales revenue is an income statement item, the information provided by the sales budget is used to construct the budgeted income statement.

Production or Purchases Budget

For manufacturers, the budget that plans for the cost and number of units that must be manufactured to meet the sales forecast and the desired quantity of ending finished goods inventory is known as the **production budget.** Although merchandisers call this budget the **purchases budget,** the two are functionally equivalent. Their names reflect the source of the item sold: Manufacturers produce the products they sell, and merchandisers purchase the products they sell.

The production budget and the purchases budget are simply pro forma versions of the cost of goods manufactured schedule and the cost of purchases schedule, as discussed in Chapter 2. A production budget is usually more complicated than a purchases budget because, as discussed in Chapter 2, costing manufactured product is more complicated than costing purchased product. A production budget includes schedules for materials, labour, and manufacturing overhead. An operating budget for a service business does not include a production budget or purchases budget because a service company does not sell tangible, physical product.

Only some of the product scheduled to be produced by a manufacturer or purchased by a merchandiser is intended to be sold during the period covered by the budget. The product not projected to be sold is called *ending finished goods inventory* for a manufacturer and *ending merchandise inventory* for a merchandiser. In either case, this projected ending inventory is classified as an asset. Therefore, some of the information provided by the production budget or purchases budget is used to construct the budgeted balance sheet.

The product that is projected to be sold during the period covered by the budget is classified as an expense item and will be shown on the budgeted income statement. As you recall, this expense item is called cost of goods sold. The cost of goods sold information needed to construct the budgeted income statement comes from the cost of goods sold budget.

Cost of Goods Sold or Cost of Services Budget

A **cost of goods sold budget** calculates the total cost of all the product a company estimates it will sell during the period covered by the operating budget. This budget differs from the production (purchases) budget because of inventory requirements. Under accrual accounting, the cost of product is not recognized as an expense (cost of goods sold) on the income statement until it is sold. Until then, it is recorded as an asset (inventory) and is shown as such on the balance sheet. For a service type business, this budget is called the **cost of services budget.**

Whether we are talking about the cost of goods sold budget or the cost of services budget, they are similar to the schedules in Chapter 2 regarding the costing of products and services. The only difference is that the budgets discussed in this chapter pertain to the future.

Because cost of goods sold or cost of services is an income statement item, the information provided by the cost of goods sold budget or cost of services budget is used to construct the budgeted income statement.

Selling and Administrative Expense Budget

After a company makes its sales forecast and estimates its product (or service) cost, it can estimate all other costs needed to support that level of sales. A **selling and administrative expense budget** calculates all costs required to support a company's forecasted sales other than the cost of product or services. The kinds of items included in this budget are identical to those included in the income statements, as discussed throughout this text. They are what we described as period costs in Chapter 2 and include such items as advertising, administrative salaries, rent, and utilities.

production budget Details the cost and number of units that must be produced by a manufacturer to meet the sales forecast and the desired ending inventory.

purchases budget Details the cost and number of units that must be purchased by a merchandiser to meet the sales forecast and the desired ending inventory.

cost of goods sold budget Calculates the total cost of all the product a manufacturing or merchandising company estimates it will sell during the period covered by the budget.

cost of services budget Calculates the total cost of all the services a service type business estimates it will provide during the period covered by the budget.

selling and administrative expense budget Calculates all costs required to support a company's forecasted sales other than the cost of product or services.

Budgeted Income Statement

budgeted income statement
Shows the expected net income for the period covered by the operating budget.

A **budgeted income statement** shows the expected net income for the period covered by the operating budget. It subtracts all estimated product (or service) cost and period cost from estimated sales revenue. This budget is prepared using information from the sales budget, the cost of goods sold (or cost of services) budget, and the selling and administrative expense budget.

Cash Budget

cash budget Shows whether the expected amount of cash generated by operating activities will be sufficient to pay anticipated expenses during the period covered by the operating budget.

A **cash budget** shows whether the expected amount of cash generated by operating activities will be sufficient to pay anticipated expenses during the period covered by the operating budget. It also reveals whether a company should expect a need for short-term external financing during the budget period. Be careful not to confuse the cash budget with the budgeted cash flow statement, as discussed later in the chapter. The budgeted cash flow statement of cash flows is more comprehensive than a simple cash budget.

Budgeted Balance Sheet

budgeted balance sheet
A presentation of estimated assets, liabilities, and owners' (or shareholders') equity at the end of the budgeted period.

A **budgeted balance sheet** is a presentation of estimated assets, liabilities, and owners' (or shareholders') equity at the end of the budgeted period. It is created exactly the way a balance sheet based on actual historical results is prepared. At the start of the period being budgeted, a company has a balance sheet that presents its assets, liabilities, and owners' equity. Most (if not all) of the company's asset, liability, and equity items will be changed by the estimated results of operations (budgeted income statement). The result is an estimated balance sheet at the end of the budget period.

The budgeted balance sheet for a manufacturer or a merchandiser is prepared using information from the actual balance sheet at the beginning of the period covered by the budget, the production (purchases) budget, the budgeted income statement, and the cash budget. A service type company has no production or purchases budget, so the budgeted balance sheet is prepared using information from the actual balance sheet at the beginning of the budget period, the budgeted income statement, and the cash budget.

Budgeted Cash Flow Statement

budgeted cash flow statement A statement of a company's expected sources and uses of cash during the period covered by the operating budget.

A **budgeted cash flow statement** is a statement of a company's expected sources and uses of cash during the period covered by the operating budget. Manufacturers, merchandisers, and service companies create the budgeted cash flow statement in a manner similar to the way they create the budgeted balance sheet. At the start of the period being budgeted, they report their cash balance. Based on the estimated results of operations (budgeted income statement) and other business activities that either generate or use cash, they estimate the cash balance at the end of the budget period. The purpose of this statement is to explain how that change in cash is to happen.

 Discussion Question

8–2. In what ways do you think the cash budget described earlier differs from the budgeted cash flow statement?

Interrelationship among the Budgets

The budgets we have discussed are closely interrelated. A change in any one of them will cause a ripple effect throughout all the others. Exhibit 8–3 shows the extent of this interrelationship.

Exhibit 8–3
Interrelationship among the Budgets

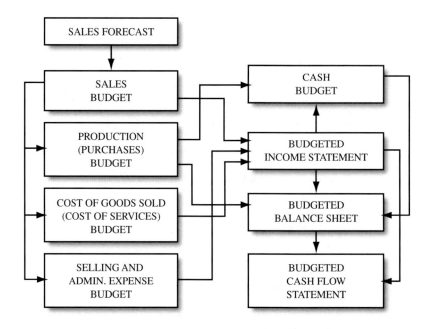

To demonstrate the interrelationship among the budgets, we return to Pam's Flower Shop for a moment. Because Pam's company is a merchandiser, the operating budget she prepares will include a sales budget, a purchases budget, a cost of goods sold budget, a selling and administrative expense budget, a cash budget, a budgeted income statement, a budgeted balance sheet, and a budgeted cash flow statement.

Pam prepared the various budgets described for the first three months of 2004 based on the following sales forecast.

PAM'S FLOWER SHOP
Sales Forecast
For the Three Months Ended March 31, 2004

	January	February	March	Total
Sales	$90,000	$120,000	$100,000	$310,000

 Discussion Question

8–3. From what you have learned so far about the operating budget, which of the budgets for Pam's Flower Shop will be affected by the amounts in this sales forecast? Explain how each is affected.

Now assume that a new flower shop opened just down the street from Pam's after she had prepared her operating budget. Pam believes that to be realistic in her planning, she needs to revise her sales forecast as follows:

PAM'S FLOWER SHOP
Revised Sales Forecast
For the Three Months Ended March 31, 2004

	January	February	March	Total
Sales	$75,000	$100,000	$90,000	$265,000

 ## Discussion Question

8–4. Which of the budgets for Pam's Flower Shop will be affected by the changes in her sales forecast? Explain how each is affected.

Because sales revenue is changed in Pam's revised sales forecast, the sales budget will be different. Even without any information about purchases, you should intuitively recognize that lower sales probably means fewer flowers sold; therefore, fewer flowers will need to be purchased, meaning that the purchases budget must be revised. The same holds true for the cost of goods sold budget. The selling and administrative expense budget may need to be revised based on the new forecast, because lower sales probably means fewer sales clerks, at least. The cash budget will need to be revised because lower sales means less cash collected and lower purchases means less cash spent. The budgeted income statement must surely be revised, because the sales budget, the cost of goods sold budget, and the selling and administrative expense budget are used to construct the budgeted income statement. If those budgets must be revised, the budgeted income statement must also be revised. If the budgeted income statement is affected, the budgeted balance sheet must be revised because the results from the income statement are reflected in the balance sheet. If cash is affected in any way (and we already determined it would be), the budgeted cash flow statement must be revised.

As you can see, a change in any of the budgets has a ripple effect throughout all the other budgets. Because the various budgets contained in the operating budget are so closely tied together, the preparation of the operating budget in most organizations is extremely time consuming and complicated. Depending on the size of the company, it may take several months to prepare the operating budget. For example, a manufacturer or merchandiser prepares a sales budget for each product the company sells. If the company sells 80 products, then 80 sales budgets must be prepared. If the company also has 80 sales territories, a whopping 6,400 sales budgets must be prepared (80 products × 80 sales territories). Companies must begin the budgeting process early enough to allow sufficient time for completion. If the budgeted period begins on January 1, 2004, for example, the budgeting process may begin in August or September 2003, or even earlier.

For some large, multinational companies, the process never ends. They work on the 2004 budget from January through December 2003. Then they turn right around in January 2004 and begin work on the 2005 budget, and so on. It takes so long to complete the process that by they time they finish one year, it is time to start again for the next year.

DIFFERENT APPROACHES TO BUDGETING

We now know what an operating budget is, but exactly how do businesses prepare one? The answer depends on the needs of the business and the approach it takes to the budgeting process. Next we investigate seven budgeting approaches: perpetual, incremental, zero-based, top-down, bottom-up, imposed, and participative approaches.

Firms may vary as to the maximum duration for the operating budget period. Because virtually all prepare it for at least one year, we focus on a one-year budget period in the following discussion.

Perpetual Budgeting

perpetual budgeting
The budgeting approach of updating the budget every month.

continual budgeting
Another name for *perpetual budgeting.*

Some companies continually update their operating budgets. As one month ends, another month's budget is added to the end of the budget. Therefore, at any given time, the budget projects 12 months into the future. This budgeting approach is called **perpetual budgeting,** or **continual budgeting.** Companies that use perpetual budgeting always budget 12 months in advance. At any given time, these companies have an operating budget that forecasts 12 months into the future.

The main advantage of perpetual budgeting is that it spreads the workload for budget preparation evenly over the year, which allows employees to incorporate the work required to prepare the budget into their routine work schedule. Another advantage of a perpetual budget is that the budget always extends 12 months into the future. In contrast, when perpetual budgeting is *not* used, the new operating budget is typically prepared when only a couple of months are left on the old budget. One disadvantage of perpetual budgeting may be that the budget preparation process becomes so routine that employees lose the motivation and creativity required to prepare an innovative operating budget. An important aspect of solid budgeting is looking for better ways to do things. Think back to the example we used earlier for Montrose Manufacturing Corporation, which was able to restructure its production process because its managers were serious about looking for a better way. If the preparation of the budget becomes routine (just another bunch of forms to fill out), managers may stop this critical evaluation and become satisfied with the status quo. Another disadvantage is that many managers believe they do not have sufficient time to do all that is asked of them in their regular day-to-day responsibilities. Adding the responsibility of preparing a perpetual budget to a heavy workload can lead to sloppy budgeting.

Incremental Budgeting

incremental budgeting
The process of using the prior year's budget or the company's actual results to build the new operating budget.

The process of using the prior year's budget or the company's actual results to build the new operating budget is called **incremental budgeting.** If, for example, a company's 2003 budget included $200,000 for maintenance and repairs on the machinery and equipment in its production facility, $200,000 becomes the starting point for this item in preparing the 2004 budget. The only question to be answered is whether the company needs to include more than $200,000 for repairs and maintenance in 2004. This budgeting approach is used by governmental entities such as the federal government and by many companies.

The trouble with the incremental budgeting approach is that if the prior year's budget includes unnecessary costs, or items that do not optimize performance, this waste may be simply rolled over into the next year's budget. The advantage to this approach is its simplicity. Some practitioners and many experts believe the disadvantages greatly outweigh the advantages.

Discussion Question

8–5. In what ways, if any, do you think the federal government's use of incremental budgeting contributes to the national debt?

Zero-Based Budgeting

zero-based budgeting
A process of budgeting in which managers start from scratch, or zero, when preparing a new budget.

An alternative to the incremental budgeting approach is zero-based budgeting. In **zero-based budgeting,** managers start from scratch, or zero, when preparing a new budget. Each item on the budget must be justified every year as though it were a new budget item. Zero-based budgeting is much more difficult and time consuming than incremental budgeting, but many organizations believe the results are worth that time and effort because managers are forced to reexamine the items included in the budget and justify their continuation.

Top-Down versus Bottom-Up Budgeting

Budgeted information can flow either from the upper levels of management in a company down to managers and employees at lower levels, or vice versa. For fairly obvious reasons, the former approach is known as the top-down approach and the latter as the bottom-up approach. Each has distinct advantages and disadvantages.

top-down budgeting
A budget prepared by top managers in a company.

Top-Down Budgeting When a budget is prepared by top managers in the company, the process is called **top-down budgeting.** The top executives prepare the budget, and lower-level managers and employees work to meet that budget.

The top-down approach has several advantages. First, a company's upper management is usually most knowledgeable about the company's overall operation. It makes sense (on the surface, at least) that upper managers be responsible for the information contained in the operating budget because they are the most experienced and knowledgeable individuals in the company. Second, top management is keenly aware of company goals, so they will prepare the budget with these goals in mind. Finally, the top-down budgeting approach involves fewer people, so it causes fewer disruptions, is more efficient, and is less time consuming than the bottom-up approach.

The top-down approach to budgeting has two major disadvantages. First, lower-level managers and employees are usually less accepting of budgets when they have no part in setting the standards. Second, top managers may be keenly aware of the big picture, but they do not have the working knowledge of daily activities needed to prepare the detailed budgets for all company activities.

Most large, publicly traded companies in North America use some form of top-down budgeting. Why? If you recall our discussion of the cost of equity capital in Chapter 7, you know that a firm's top management fully understands the need to maximize returns for shareholders. Most of that return is in the form of stock appreciation (increase in the market price of the stock), rather than dividends. The greatest influence on the selling price of a company's stock price is company profits. So, to ensure maximum stock appreciation, a company must be as profitable as possible. The top management of these publicly traded companies generally has a better sense than lower-level managers and employees of how much profit the company must have in a given year to maintain (or attain) a high return for shareholders. In top-down budgeting, the target profit figures become the starting point of the budgeting process.

imposed budget A budget in which upper management sets figures for all operating activities that the rest of the company rarely, if ever, can negotiate.

Traditionally, most firms that used top-down budgeting also used an imposed budgeting process. An **imposed budget** is a budget in which upper management sets figures for all operating activities that the rest of the company rarely, if ever, can negotiate. No matter how unreasonable the budget numbers, top management expects all other managers to "do whatever it takes to make it happen." This type of budgeting process can do more harm than good, because it can lead to business practices that conflict with the company's stated goals. Today, however, not all top-down budgets are imposed budgets, as we will see shortly.

bottom-up budgeting A budget initially prepared by lower-level managers and employees.

Bottom-Up Budgeting

In **bottom-up budgeting,** the budget is initially prepared by lower-level managers and employees. For example, members of the sales force prepare the sales schedule for their own sales territories. The sales manager then reviews these sales schedules, makes any necessary changes, and combines them to form the overall company sales schedule. Likewise, employees in the production facility prepare schedules for production, including schedules for direct material, direct labour, and manufacturing overhead.

Bottom-up budgeting has three main advantages. First, the budget may be more realistic. Those who work in a functional area are usually better informed about what should be included in the budget than upper managers. If lower-level managers and employees take the budgeting process seriously, they are likely to create an operating budget based on accurate, realistic information. Second, lower-level managers and employees are more likely to work toward budgeted performance standards because they helped to set those standards. Third, as employees prepare the budget, they learn to think about the company's goals, how various activities can affect the future, and how they personally will participate. In short, they begin to think about the work they will need to do in the coming year.

Bottom-up budgeting has two disadvantages. First, employees at every level must take time from their day-to-day responsibilities to work on the budget as it is prepared, reviewed, revised, and approved—all of which adds up to substantial time and effort. Second, some employees may be tempted to prepare a budget that is so generous they can effortlessly outperform it. For example, sales representatives may budget sales of $300,000, when they can achieve sales of $350,000 with little effort. Thus, their actual sales performance looks great compared with budgeted sales. Manipulating the budget to make certain that the actual performance exceeds budgeted performance is one example of a budget game. A *budget game* is the game of using the budget to do things it was never intended to do, such as ensuring a strong performance appraisal.

participative budget A budget in which managers and employees at many levels of the company are involved in setting the performance standards and preparing the budget.

Bottom-up budgeting is always a participative budgeting process. A **participative budget** is one in which managers and employees at many levels of the company are involved in setting the performance standards and preparing the budget. Recent developments have expanded the use of participative budgeting to top-down budgeting, so it is beneficial to discuss imposed and participative budget philosophies a little further.

Imposed versus Participative Budgets

A bottom-up budget will always be a participative budget. Managers and employees at all levels of the company participate in the preparation of a bottom-up budget. A top-down budget, however, can be either imposed or participative.

In recent years, companies have discovered that by allowing more participation, they empower their employees. To empower employees means to give employees the authority to make decisions concerning their job responsibilities, including decisions about items in the operating budget.

A company committed to both top-down budgeting and empowered employees must combine the top-down and bottom-up approaches to budgeting. Rather than having all budget information flow from the top of the company downward to lower levels, upper management provides profit targets to managers at lower levels. These lower level managers then prepare the operating budget for their functional areas, given the profit targets provided by upper management.

 Discussion Questions

8-6. What possible positive results do you think can come from more empowerment:
  a. for the company? Explain your reasoning.
  b. for managers and employees? Explain your reasoning.

8-7. What possible negative results do you think can come from more empowerment:
  a. for the company? Explain your reasoning.
  b. for managers and employees? Explain your reasoning.

As an example of combining the top-down and bottom-up approaches to budgeting, we look at QI Data Technology Inc. QI Data is a publicly traded company that wants to be one of the top-performing companies (in terms of dividends and share appreciation) in the stock market. Upper management has determined that the company must earn a profit of $1,000,000 in the upcoming year to reach that goal. The company has three divisions (A, B, and C), and each must earn some part of the targeted $1,000,000 profit. Division C is the smallest of the three, and corporate headquarters has assigned this division a target profit of $150,000 for the next year.

Now that Division C has received its target profit (this is the top-down part), the division manager, Joanne Moss, and her managers and employees set about to prepare the operating budget for the year (this is the participative part). When they have completed their budgeting process, the result in summary form is as follows:

Sales	$500,000
Expenses	(450,000)
Net Income	$150,000

Wait a minute! Something's wrong. The numbers just don't add up. Well, what we see is a conflict between the top-down target profit ($150,000) and what Joanne and her people at Division C think they can accomplish in the upcoming year ($500,000 in sales and $450,000 in expenses). What happens next will determine whether this budget is imposed or participative.

If the upper management of QI Data refuses to negotiate and compromise with Division C, the budget becomes imposed. Remember, there is little room for negotiation between upper management and the rest of the company as to the amounts included in an imposed operating budget. If, however, upper management is willing to yield somewhat on its profit targets, the budget becomes participative.

It is unrealistic to think QI Data will simply adjust its target from $150,000 to $50,000, which would certainly make the arithmetic in the budgeted income statement work. More than likely, QI Data's upper management will meet with Joanne and her staff to negotiate a compromise target profit. Let's say they did just that, and the negotiations led to a revised target profit of $90,000 for the division. The revised summary budgeted income statement, then, would be as follows:

Sales	$500,000
Expenses	(450,000)
Net Income	$ 90,000

The math still doesn't work! Management at the division level must now either forecast more sales or find some way to reduce expected expenses (or some combination of the two) to project an additional $40,000 in profit for the year.

The key to making a top-down budget a participative budget is the ability and willingness on the part of upper management to negotiate and compromise.

 Discussion Questions

8–8. If you were the chief executive officer of your company, would you prefer a top-down or bottom-up budgeting process? Why?

8–9. If you were in middle management, would you prefer a top-down or bottom-up budgeting process? Why?

8–10. If you were the company CEO, do you think it would be wise for you to spend time tending to the details of the various budgets, given all your other responsibilities?

The overall approach a company takes to preparing its operating budget may actually be a combination of several of the approaches we have discussed here. For example, one company may have a top-down, participative, zero-based budgeting approach. Another company may be committed to an incremental, participative, bottom-up, perpetual budgeting philosophy. The object is not to select a particular approach from a laundry list. Rather, managers must approach the preparation of the operating budget in a way that makes sense in the circumstances.

THE SALES FORECAST

sales forecast The prediction of sales for the period covered by the operating budget.

Although technological advances over the past 30 years have improved financial forecasting methods, predicting future sales still remains largely an educated guess. The prediction of sales for the period covered by the operating budget is called the **sales forecast.**

Cornerstone and Keystone of Budgeting

A solid, realistic sales forecast is perhaps the most critical feature of a solid, realistic operating budget. Why? Once the sales forecast has been developed, the business can prepare the sales budget, the production or purchases budget, the cost of goods sold or cost of services budget, the selling and administrative expense budget, the cash budget, and the three budgeted financial statements (income statement, balance sheet, and cash flow statement).

The sales forecast is often called the cornerstone of budgeting. In the construction of a building, the first brick or stone laid is called the cornerstone. The remainder of the entire building is built off this cornerstone. In the construction of the operating budget, the sales forecast is the first step; all the budgets are built from the sales forecast. The sales forecast, then, is the cornerstone of the budgeting process, as depicted in Exhibit 8–4.

Exhibit 8–4
The Sales Forecast as the Cornerstone of Budgeting

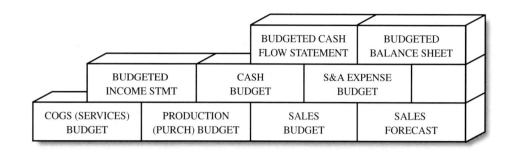

The sales forecast has also been called the keystone of budgeting. This description clearly reflects the importance of the forecast. In the building of a stone archway, the keystone is the stone placed at the exact centre at the top of the arch. If this stone is strong and placed properly, the arch will last. In fact, some arches built without mortar in the Middle Ages are still standing. They are held together solely from the strength of the keystone. If the keystone is weak, however, or is improperly set, the arch will collapse; and so it is with budgeting. The quality of the entire master budget depends on the quality and accuracy of the sales forecast as depicted in Exhibit 8–5.

As an archway made of stones depends on the keystone for its strength, the reliability of the operating budget depends on the strength of the sales forecast. If the sales forecast does not reasonably reflect the actual sales during the operating budget period, the budget will not reasonably estimate the actual results for the period. Thus, there will be differences between the actual income statement, balance sheet, and cash flow statement and the budgeted income statement, balance sheet, and cash flow statement.

Exhibit 8–5
The Sales Forecast as the Keystone of Budgeting

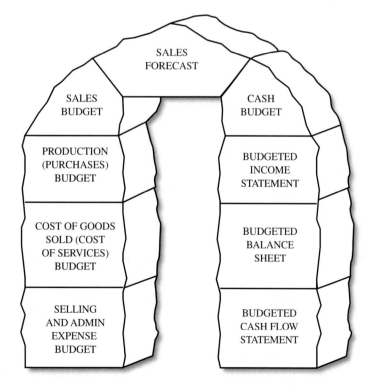

Factors Affecting the Accuracy of the Sales Forecast

Many factors influence the accuracy of the sales forecast. We have chosen four to discuss here: the economy, industry conditions, the competition, and technology.

General Economy If the economy goes into a recession, consumer saving and spending patterns change. Sales forecasts are usually affected as a result. The problem is, most economists estimate that the economy can be entering or moving out of a recession for at least six to nine months before we realize it. Thus, when a firm creates its sales forecast for the next year's budget, it may be unaware of what the actual state of the economy will be throughout the period covered by the operating budget.

Industry Conditions It is possible for the general economy to be healthy and a particular industry to be in a recession or for the economy to be unhealthy and the industry quite healthy.

Actions of Competitors All companies take great pains to keep information about their plans from their competitors. Therefore, all companies make their sales forecasts without information that has a tremendous impact on the accuracy of the forecast. For example, imagine Intel is about to launch a revolutionary product that could absolutely blow its competitors away. Motorola does not know this, so it creates a sales forecast that is inaccurate because it is unaware of Intel's planned actions.

Technological Developments Technological developments can greatly influence the quality of the sales forecast. It is possible that the market for a particular product may not be as strong—or may not even exist—when the time the period being budgeted for arrives. When Microsoft introduced its Windows ME program, the need for products compatible with Microsoft's old operating system sharply declined. Sales forecasts for software companies that did not expect the drop in demand for their products were rendered unreliable.

 Discussion Question

8–11. What other factors can you think of that would influence the accuracy of a company's sales forecast?

We cannot overemphasize the importance of the sales forecast in the budgeting process, despite the difficulty of being completely accurate. It is worth the time and effort. Managers, however, must prepare and use the operating budget with a solid understanding of its limitations.

PART TWO: PREPARING AND USING THE OPERATING BUDGET

Preparing a Master Operating Budget

Marcy's Board Shop Inc. is a retail store that sells only one product (snowboards) and deals in only one product model, which it will sell for $300. The company's fiscal year ends September 30. At Marcy's request, we will prepare the operating budget for the first quarter of the fiscal year ending September 30, 2005. Thus, we will be budgeting for the quarter ending December 31, 2004.

We start with Marcy's budgeted income statement and the budgets that provide information used to construct that budgeted financial statement. We will then prepare the budgeted balance sheet along with all other budgets required to prepare the budgeted balance sheet. Finally, we will prepare the budgeted cash flow statement.

Because we focus on a merchandising company rather than a manufacturer, we will work with a purchases budget rather than a production budget.

Budgeted Income Statement

To prepare the budgeted income statement, we need information about sales, cost of goods sold, and selling and administrative expenses for the period covered by the budget. Therefore, we must prepare a budget for each of those items before we can construct the budgeted income statement.

Sales Budget The first information we need to build the budgeted income statement is found in the sales budget. Our first task, then, is to request that Marcy's marketing and sales personnel provide a sales forecast. They tell us that they will be happy to do so, but are not sure how. Should we suggest they take last year's sales numbers and increase them by, say, 5 percent? This would be incremental budgeting, and—without a critical look at market factors that affect sales—it is a poor approach to budgeting. If simply increasing last year's amounts by a constant percentage were adequate, a computer could easily be programmed to do the job.

Before Marcy's Board Shop Inc. can forecast its sales realistically, sales management and the sales personnel must first consider the factors that influence market conditions. After much discussion, Marcy's staff decided to research the following items:

- Current customer spending patterns
- The ability to attract new customers through market promotions
- The introduction of any new products
- The discontinuation of any products
- The competition
- Price changes
- The general economy
- Technological changes

The sales department's recent customer satisfaction survey shows, for example, that 60 percent of past customers plan to buy another product in the next quarter and that price is the number one consideration in snowboard purchases. Any increase in price is therefore likely to have a negative impact on repeat business. The market research done by the company indicates that due to planned market promotions, Marcy's can expect a 20 percent growth in first-time customer purchases.

You see, then, that each of the items chosen for evaluation by the company is researched and the results examined in an attempt to make the forecasting of sales something more than just a guessing game.

Once the sales team considers all its research, it develops a forecast of unit sales for each month in the quarter. The sales team forecasts sales for Marcy's Snow Shop Inc. of 30 units in October, 50 units in November, and 40 units in December, shown as Exhibit 8–6.

Based on this forecast, we can prepare Marcy's sales budget for the quarter, as shown in Exhibit 8–7.

Exhibit 8–6
Sales Forecast for
Marcy's Board Shop Inc.

MARCY'S BOARD SHOP INC. Sales Forecast For the Quarter Ended December 31, 2004				
	October	November	December	Total
Forecasted Sales in Units	30	50	40	120

We simply used the sales forecast of unit sales and the projected selling price of $300 per snowboard to develop the sales budget.

A real sales budget for an actual company is no more complicated than this one. Of course, in our example, Marcy's sells only one product. Remember from our earlier discussion that if Marcy's sold 80 different products, the company would need to prepare 80 of these sales budgets. If Marcy's sold 80 different products in 80 different locations, the company would need to prepare 6,400 of these sales budgets (80 products × 80 locations).

Exhibit 8–7
Sales Budget for
Marcy's Board Shop Inc.

MARCY'S BOARD SHOP INC. Sales Budget For the Quarter Ended December 31, 2004				
	October	November	December	Total
Forecasted Unit Sales	30	50	40	120
× Forecasted Sales Price	$ 300	$ 300	$ 300	$ 300
= Budgeted Sales Dollars	$9,000	$15,000	$12,000	$36,000

Discussion Question

8–12. What factors should Marcy's management consider when setting the $300 budgeted selling price for its snowboards?

Cost of Goods Sold Budget Once we know how many units Marcy's Board Shop Inc. plans to sell, and the cost per unit, we can prepare a cost of goods sold budget. As its name implies, this budget is used to determine how much cost of goods sold should be based on forecasted sales. Preparing the cost of goods sold budget consists of multiplying forecasted unit sales by the cost per unit. The cost of goods sold budget for Marcy's Board Shop Inc. is presented in Exhibit 8–8.

The exhibit shows that Marcy's forecasted cost of goods sold for the quarter is $18,000 ($4,500 + $7,500 + $6,000 = $18,000). The cost of goods sold budget provides the forecasted product cost information that is used to prepare the budgeted income statement. This product cost information helps Marcy's management determine whether the company will be profitable based on its budget, or whether changes should be planned now to ensure profits in the budget period.

Exhibit 8–8
Cost of Goods Sold
Budget for Marcy's
Board Shop Inc.

MARCY'S BOARD SHOP INC.
Cost of Goods Sold Budget
For the Quarter Ended December 31, 2004

	October	November	December	Total
Forecasted Unit Sales	30	50	40	120
× Forecasted Unit Cost	$ 150	$ 150	$ 150	$ 150
= Budgeted COGS	$4,500	$7,500	$6,000	$18,000

 Discussion Questions

Compare the sales budget in Exhibit 8–7 with the cost of goods sold budget in Exhibit 8–8.

8–13. What are the similarities?

8–14. What are the differences?

Realistically, Marcy's will need to purchase more units of product than just the ones it expects to sell in October, November, and December. Thus, in addition to the budgets required to prepare the budgeted income statement, Marcy's will need to prepare a purchases budget. For our demonstration purposes, however, we will wait until after we have prepared the budgeted income statement to present the purchases budget. The only additional budget we need to prepare before we can prepare the budgeted income statement is the selling and administrative expense budget.

Selling and Administrative Expense Budget The various expenses associated with the selling and administrative functions are estimated and used to prepare this budget. Selling and administrative expenses include salaries, advertising, rent, utilities, etc. The selling and administrative expense budget for Marcy's Board Shop Inc. is presented in Exhibit 8–9.

Exhibit 8–9
Selling and
Administrative Expense
Budget for Marcy's
Board Shop Inc.

MARCY'S BOARD SHOP INC.
Selling and Administrative Expense Budget
For the Quarter Ended December 31, 2004

	October	November	December	Total
Salaries and Wages	$2,500	$3,000	$2,750	$ 8,250
Rent	500	500	500	1,500
Amortization	100	100	104	304
Others	800	1,000	900	2,700
Total	$3,900	$4,600	$4,254	$12,754

The types of items and the amounts included in the selling and administrative expense budget vary from company to company. As we said earlier, the items included in this budget are determined by what is required to support the level of sales in the sales budget.

 ## Discussion Questions

8-15. If you were preparing a selling and administrative expense budget, what are some of the things you would consider as you mapped out strategies to increase sales?

8-16. Besides those included in Exhibit 8–9, what are some other administrative costs you think would normally be included in a selling and administrative expense budget?

8-17. What do you think might explain the increase in anticipated amortization expense in December from $100 to $104?

Building the Budgeted Income Statement

To prepare the budgeted income statement, we use information from the sales, cost of goods sold, and selling and administrative expense budgets. The budgeted income statement depicts the amount of profit or loss a business can expect from its budgeted operating activities. First, we take the total forecasted sales revenue from the sales budget and subtract the forecasted cost of goods sold from the cost of goods sold budget. The result is a forecasted gross profit. We then subtract the total selling and administrative expense, which we get from the selling and administrative expense budget. The result is the company's budgeted net income for the period covered by the budget. The budgeted income statement for Marcy's Board Shop Inc. is presented in Exhibit 8–10.

Exhibit 8-10
Budgeted Income Statement for Marcy's Board Shop Inc.

MARCY'S BOARD SHOP INC.
Budgeted Income Statement
For the Quarter Ended December 31, 2004

	October	November	December	Total
Sales	$9,000	$15,000	$12,000	$36,000
− Cost of Goods Sold	4,500	7,500	6,000	18,000
= Gross Profit	4,500	7,500	6,000	18,000
− Selling and Admin. Expense	3,900	4,600	4,254	12,754
= Net Income	$ 600	$ 2,900	$ 1,746	$ 5,246

We see from Exhibit 8–10 that Marcy's Board Shop Inc. is projecting net income of $600 for October. In November Marcy's is projecting a net income of $2,900 and in December it is $1,746. The total net income for the quarter, then, is $5,246.

After the budgeted income statement has been prepared, Marcy's management team may want to change its plans so that it meets its profit goals more effectively. For instance, management may look at the budgeted income statement in

Exhibit 8–10 and find the $600 net income in October unacceptable. If so, it would review all the information used to build the budgeted income statement and either adjust its expectations or adjust the assumptions used to prepare the budget.

Whatever the outcome of this evaluation, Marcy's Board Shop Inc. has a better chance of planning for a successful future if management takes the budgeting process seriously. If budgets are used properly, managers will have an opportunity to see trouble spots in advance and make the required adjustments before it is too late.

Budgeted Balance Sheet

Now that we have prepared the budgeted income statement, we have much of the information we need to prepare the budgeted balance sheet. First, however, we must prepare two more budgets: the purchases budget, as mentioned when we were preparing the budgeted income statement, and the cash budget.

Purchases Budget

The cost of goods sold budget we prepared accounts only for the units projected to be sold during the period covered by the budget. If Marcy's planned to begin and end the period covered by the budget with no inventory on hand and planned to purchase only the amount of inventory during the budgeted period sufficient to support the level of projected sales, there would be no need for a separate purchases budget. Rather, the company could just use the information from the cost of goods sold budget. This plan is unrealistic, however, because a company like Marcy's must begin and end each period with a certain amount of merchandise on hand. These inventory requirements create the need for the purchases budget. Marcy's purchases budget for the three months ended December 31, 2004, is presented as Exhibit 8–11.

Exhibit 8–11
Purchases Budget for Marcy's Board Shop Inc.

		October	November	December	Total	
	MARCY'S BOARD SHOP INC. **Purchases Budget** **For the Quarter Ended December 31, 2004**					
	Forecasted Unit Sales	30	50	40	120	(a)
+	Desired Ending Inventory*	20	16	24	24	(b)
=	Total Units Needed	50	66	64	144	(c)
−	Beginning Inventory	(8)	(20)	(16)	(8)	(d)
=	Units to Be Purchased	42	46	48	136	(e)
×	Cost Per Unit	$ 150	$ 150	$ 150	$ 150	(f)
=	Cost of Purchases	$6,300	$6,900	$7,200	$20,400	(g)

*40% of the next month's sales requirements

As you can see by looking at Exhibit 8–11, the purchases budget, even for a small company like Marcy's Board Shop Inc., can seem rather complicated. A line-by-line analysis of this budget, however, reveals that much of the information it contains is already known, and the new information is basically straightforward.

(a) *Forecasted Unit Sales.* These numbers should look familiar to you because you have seen them three times already. They come directly from the sales forecast presented in Exhibit 8–6 and were used to construct the sales budget in Exhibit 8–7 and the cost of goods sold budget in Exhibit 8–8.

(b) *Desired Ending Inventory.* These numbers represent the number of units of product the company believes it needs on hand at the end of a given period to support sales in the early days of the next period. As the asterisk note in Exhibit 8–11 explains, Marcy's has decided it should have inventory of product on hand at the end of any given month equal to 40 percent of the next month's sales requirements. At the end of October, for example, Marcy's desires an ending inventory of 20 units, which is 40 percent of November's sales of 50 units (50 × 40% = 20 units).

The amount of desired ending inventory is determined by at least two factors. First, the company must consider how long it usually takes to get product from the company's supplier. This information is obtained from the purchasing records and discussions with the purchasing department. Second, the company must estimate the number of units of product it will sell in the early days of each month. This information comes from historical sales records and discussions with sales personnel.

The desired ending inventory amounts for October, November, and December will be important to us when we construct the budgeted balance sheet, but we will defer our discussion of how they are used until we actually prepare that budget.

 Discussion Question

8–18. Can you tell by looking at the purchases budget in Exhibit 8–11 how many snowboards Marcy's has forecasted it will sell in January? Explain your reasoning.

(c) *Total Units Needed.* This figure is the sum of (a) and (b).

(d) *Beginning Inventory.* Because the purpose of the purchases budget is to determine how many units of inventory must be purchased during each of the months included in the budget period, any inventory forecasted to be on hand at the beginning of each month must be subtracted from the total units needed to determine how many units must be purchased during the month.

The beginning inventory for any period is the ending inventory for the previous period. You will note in the purchases budget in Exhibit 8–11 that the beginning inventory for November (20 units) is the same as the desired ending inventory for October, and the beginning inventory for December (16 units) is the same as the desired ending inventory for November. You should also note that the beginning inventory in the total column (8 units) is the same as the beginning inventory for October, because the total column is for the entire quarter and the quarter begins in October.

(e) *Units to Be Purchased.* This figure is simply (c) minus (d) and tells us the number of snowboards that must be purchased in each of the three months of the budget period and the total for the quarter.

(f) *Cost Per Unit.* The cost per unit is what Marcy's must pay for each snowboard it purchases. Note that this cost is the same as the cost per unit used when we prepared the cost of goods sold budget presented in Exhibit 8–8.

Discussion Question

8-19. The purchases budget in Exhibit 8-11 indicates that Marcy's desires ending inventory equal to 40% of the next month's sales requirements. Because sales in October are expected to be 30 snowboards, the beginning inventory in October (which is the ending inventory for September) should be 12 units (30 × 40%). Why do you think the beginning inventory in October is only 8 snowboards?

(g) *Cost of Purchases.* This figure is simply (e) multiplied by (f) and tells us what the purchase of snowboards will cost Marcy's in each of the three months of the budget period and the total for the quarter.

Cash Budget

When a company uses accrual accounting, revenue is recognized when it is earned rather than when the cash associated with that revenue is collected, and expenses are recognized when the benefit is received rather than when the cash associated with the expenses is paid. This means, of course, that while the budgeted income statement (including the sales budget, cost of goods sold budget, and the selling and administrative expense budget) provides information about Marcy's projected earnings activities for the budget period, it does not provide direct information about what is projected to happen during that period in terms of cash. Also, unless Marcy's pays cash for its purchase of snowboards, the purchases budget suffers from the same limitation.

Before we can prepare the budgeted balance sheet, we must determine the effect on cash of the budgets we have prepared so far. We do that by preparing a cash budget, which is composed of a cash receipts schedule and a cash payments schedule.

cash receipts schedule
Presents the amount of cash a company expects to collect during the budget period.

Cash Receipts Schedule The **cash receipts schedule** presents the amount of cash a company expects to collect during the budget period from the sales of its product. Before we can prepare Marcy's cash receipts schedule, we must make certain estimates about the composition of the company's sales (cash or credit) and the pattern of collecting the accounts receivable created by the credit sales. We estimate that 25 percent of Marcy's sales are for cash and the remaining 75 percent are on account (credit sales). Of the sales on account, we estimate that 30 percent are collected in the month of the sale, 60 percent in the month following the sale, and 10 percent in the second month following the sale. Because of the lag between the time a credit sale is made and the time cash is collected, some of the cash for credit sales made in August and September will not have been collected by the end of September, which means that those amounts will be collected during the three months included in our budget period. Therefore, we need to know August credit sales were $4,500, and September credit sales were $6,000.

Using the credit sales figures from August and September, and our assumptions about when cash is collected, we can prepare Marcy's cash receipts schedule for the three months ended December 31, 2004 as shown in Exhibit 8-12.

Although the cash receipts schedule presented in Exhibit 8-12 seems quite complex, it is more straightforward than it first appears. It is broken into two major parts. The first presents the amount of cash collected from credit sales during the period covered by the schedule (a through c) and the second part presents the amount of cash collected from cash sales during the budget period (d).

Exhibit 8–12
Cash Receipts Schedule for Marcy's Board Shop Inc.

MARCY'S BOARD SHOP INC.
Cash Receipts Schedule
For the Quarter Ended December 31, 2004

	October	November	December	Total	
Credit Sales Collected:					
From Accounts Receivable at Sept. 30, 2004:					
August Credit Sales ($4,500)					
Collected in October (10%)	$ 450			$ 450	
September Credit Sales ($6,000)					(a)
Collected in October (60%)	3,600			3,600	
Collected in November (10%)		$ 600		600	
From New Credit Sales:					
October Credit Sales ($6,750)					
Collected in October (30%)	2,025			2,025	
Collected in November (60%)		4,050		4,050	
Collected in December (10%)			$ 675	675	
November Credit Sales ($11,250)					(b)
Collected in November (30%)		3,375		3,375	
Collected in December (60%)			6,750	6,750	
December Credit Sales ($9,000)					
Collected in December (30%)			2,700	2,700	
Budgeted Receipts from Credit Sales	$6,075	$8,025	$10,125	$24,225	(c)
Cash Sales:					
October Cash Sales	2,250			2,250	
November Cash Sales		3,750		3,750	(d)
December Cash Sales			3,000	3,000	
Budgeted Cash Receipts	$8,325	$11,775	$13,125	$33,225	(e)

Let's take a few minutes to examine this schedule and see where the numbers came from and what they mean.

(a) *From Accounts Receivable at September 30, 2004.* The accounts receivable balance at September 30, 2004 is composed of receivables arising from sales in August and September. August's credit sales were $4,500. Based on our collection assumption, 30 percent of that amount was collected in August and 60 percent in September. If 90 percent had been collected by the end of September, the remaining $450 ($4,500 × 10%) had not and was included in the balance of accounts receivable at September 30, 2004. Since October is the second month following the credit sales in August, the $450 balance is shown as a collection in October ($4,500 × 10%).

Credit sales in September totaled $6,000. Only $1,800 of that amount was collected in September ($6,000 × 30%). If 30 percent had been collected by the end of September, $4,200 ($6,000 × 70%) had not and was included in the balance of accounts receivable at September 30, 2004. Since October is the month following the credit sales in September, $3,600 is shown as a collection in October ($6,000 × 60%); and because November is the second month following the credit sales in September, the remaining $600 balance is shown as a collection in November ($6,000 × 10%).

(b) *From New Sales.* Recall from the sales budget in Exhibit 8–7 that budgeted sales for the three months covered by our budget example were $9,000 in October, $15,000 in November, and $12,000 in December. One of the assumptions we made as we began our discussion of the cash receipts schedule was that 75 percent of Marcy's sales were credit sales. Therefore, the amounts we are dealing with in this section of the schedule are $6,750 for October ($9,000 × 75%), $11,250 for November ($15,000 × 75%), and $9,000 for December ($12,000 × 75%).

The collection pattern for each of the three months is the same: 30 percent of credit sales are collected in the month of sale, 60 percent in the month following the sale, and 10 percent in the second month following the sale. So for October's credit sales, for example, the schedule shows $2,025 will be collected in October ($6,750 × 30%), $4,050 will be collected in November ($6,750 × 60%), and $675 ($6,750 × 10%) in November. The amounts projected to be collected for November and December credit sales are calculated exactly the same way.

(c) *Budgeted Receipts from Credit Sales.* This figure is simply the sum of (a) and (b). It presents the total amount of cash Marcy's expects to collect during the period covered by the schedule from credit sales.

(d) *Cash Sales.* This section is the least complicated of the schedule. For the three months included in the schedule it presents the portion of sales that will be cash sales. If 75 percent of the sales made in a given month are credit sales, then 25 percent will be cash sales. Therefore, in October the cash sales will be $2,250 ($9,000 × 25%) and that amount is shown as a cash receipt in October. The amount for November is $3,750 ($15,000 × 25%), and for October $3,000 ($12,000 × 25%).

(e) *Budgeted Cash Receipts.* This figure is simply the sum of (c) and (d). As the description indicates, it presents the total amount of cash Marcy's plans to collect from the accounts receivable balance at September 30, 2004, the credit sales it will have during the period covered by the schedule, and the cash sales made during the period.

cash payments schedule
Presents the amount of cash a company expects to pay out during the budget period.

Cash Payments Schedule

The **cash payments schedule** presents the amount of cash a company expects to pay out during the budget period. Before we can prepare Marcy's cash payments schedule, we must make certain assumptions about the company's pattern of cash payments. We assume that payment for the purchase of snowboards is made in the month following the purchase. Because of the lag time between the time a purchase is made and the time cash is paid, the purchases made in September will not have been paid by the end of September, which means that this amount will be paid in October, one of the months included in our budget period. Therefore, we need to know that purchases of merchandise in September totaled $5,200. All cash selling and administrative expenses are paid in the month incurred.

Using these assumptions about when cash is paid and the purchases figure from September, we can prepare Marcy's cash payments schedule for the three months ended December 31, 2004, as shown in Exhibit 8–13.

As you can see, the cash payments schedule is not nearly as complex as either the purchases budget or the cash receipts schedule. There are a couple of tricky parts, however, so let's examine the items included.

(a) *Purchases.* These are payments for the purchase of snowboards. Recall our assumption that payment for the purchase of merchandise is made in the month following purchase. The projected payment of $5,200 in October, then, is for purchases made in September, the payment of $6,300 in November will be for October purchases, and the $6,900 payment in December will be for November purchases.

Exhibit 8–13
Cash Payments Schedule for Marcy's Board Shop Inc.

	October	November	December	Total	
MARCY'S BOARD SHOP INC.					
Cash Payments Schedule					
For the Quarter Ended December 31, 2004					
Purchases	$5,200	$6,300	$6,900	$18,400	(a)
Selling and Admin. Expense:					
Salaries and Wages	2,500	3,000	2,750	8,250 ⎤	
Rent	500	500	500	1,500 ⎬ (b)	
Other Selling and Admin. Expense	800	1,000	900	2,700 ⎦	
Purchase of Display Case		240		240	(c)
Budgeted Cash Payments	$9,000	$11,040	$11,050	$31,090	(d)

 Discussion Question

8-20. In our assumptions about cash payments, we said that September purchases of merchandise totaled $5,200 so it is easy to see where the October payment originated. Where do you suppose the payment amounts ($6,300 and $6,900) originated for November and December?

(b) *Selling and Administrative Expense.* These are payments for the support costs Marcy's anticipates for each month of the budget period. The amounts come directly from the selling and administrative expense budget in Exhibit 8–9.

 Discussion Question

8-21. Look back at the selling and administrative expense budget in Exhibit 8–9. All the expense items included in that budget are included in the cash payments schedule *except* amortization. Why do you think amortization expense was included in the selling and administrative expense budget but excluded from the cash payments schedule?

(c) *Purchase of Display Case.* Evidently, Marcy's is planning to purchase a new display case for the showroom during the month of November. This purchase will be in addition to Marcy's property, plant, and equipment and will be important to us when we prepare the budgeted balance sheet and the budgeted cash flow statement. Incidentally, the planned purchase of this display case is what caused amortization expense in Exhibit 8–9 to increase by $4 in December.

(d) *Budgeted Cash Payments.* This figure is simply the sum of (a), (b), and (c). As the description indicates, it presents the total amount of cash Marcy's plans to pay out during the period covered by the schedule.

Building the Cash Budget

Now that we have prepared the cash receipts schedule and the cash payments schedule, we can prepare Marcy's cash budget for the quarter ended December 31, 2004. As was the case with the schedules, we must make some assumptions for the cash budget. First, we estimate that Marcy's Board Shop Inc. will have a cash balance of $2,170 on September 30, 2004. Second, Marcy's desires to maintain a cash balance of at least $1,900 at all times. If cash falls below $1,900, the company will borrow from a local bank. Finally, we ignore the interest Marcy's would be required to pay on any borrowings from the bank.

Using the assumption about Marcy's desired minimum cash balance, and the information from the cash receipts schedule and the cash payments schedule, we can prepare the company's cash budget for the quarter ending December 31, 2004, as shown in Exhibit 8–14.

Exhibit 8–14
Cash Budget for Marcy's Board Shop Inc.

MARCY'S BOARD SHOP INC.
Cash Budget
For the Quarter Ended December 31, 2004

		October	November	December	Total	
	Beginning Cash Balance	$ 2,170	$ 1,900	$ 2,230	$ 2,170	(a)
+	Cash Receipts	8,325	11,775	13,125	33,225	(b)
=	Cash Available	10,495	13,675	15,355	35,395	(c)
−	Cash Payments	9,000	11,040	11,050	31,090	(d)
=	Balance before Borrowing	1,495	2,635	4,305	4,305	(e)
+/−	Borrowing/(Repayment)	405	(405)	0	0	(f)
=	Ending Cash Balance	$ 1,900	$ 2,230	$ 4,305	$ 4,305	(g)

The cash budget itself is not as seemingly complicated as the purchases budget, the cash receipts schedule, or the cash payments schedule. There are, however, some potential pitfalls in your understanding of the way this budget is constructed, so we will take a few minutes and discuss the items included.

(a) *Beginning Cash Balance.* Like all balance sheet items, the beginning cash balance for any period is the ending cash balance for the previous period. As mentioned earlier, the ending cash balance for September will be $2,170. Therefore, October's beginning cash balance will be September's ending cash balance. The same pattern holds true for the other months presented. November's beginning balance is October's ending balance and December's beginning balance is November's ending balance. Note, however, that the beginning balance in the total column ($2,170) is the same as the beginning balance for October. Likewise, the ending balance in the total column ($4,305) is the same as the ending balance for December, because the total column represents the entire quarter. The beginning balance for the quarter is October's beginning balance and the ending balance for the quarter is December's ending balance.

(b) *Cash Receipts.* The cash receipts amounts are taken directly from the budgeted cash receipts line of the cash receipts schedule shown in Exhibit 8–12.

(c) *Cash Available.* This figure is simply the sum of (a) and (b). This amount represents the total cash Marcy's expects to be available before deducting any payments.

(d) *Cash Payments.* The cash payments amounts are taken directly from the budgeted cash payments line of the cash payments schedule shown in Exhibit 8–13.

(e) *Balance before Borrowing.* This amount is calculated by simply subtracting (d) from (c). It represents the anticipated ending cash balance before any adjustments for borrowing or loan payments.

(f) *Borrowing/(Repayment).* Marcy's wants to maintain a cash balance of at least $1,900. If the balance before borrowing drops too low, Marcy's will borrow enough money from the bank to bring the balance up to the desired ending cash balance of $1,900. As you can see, October's balance before borrowing is expected to be only $1,495. Therefore, Marcy's can anticipate the need to borrow $405 to bring the balance up to $1,900. So, if the balance before borrowing is less than the desired ending cash balance, as it will be in October, the amount that must be borrowed to bring the cash balance to the desired amount can be easily calculated. If, on the other hand, the expected balance before borrowing is greater than $1,900, as is the case in November and December, any amount in excess of the desired ending cash balance will be used to repay the loan ($405 in this instance).

(g) *Ending Cash Balance.* This figure is simply (e) plus the borrowing or less the repayment shown in (f). As we said earlier, this ending cash amount also becomes the next month's beginning cash balance.

Now the information from the cash budget and other budgets can be used to prepare the budgeted balance sheet.

Building the Budgeted Balance Sheet

We assume that you already know the basics of how a balance sheet is constructed, so, for our presentation of the budgeted balance sheet, we focus on how to determine the various asset, liability, and equity items and dollar amounts for these items.

Although some of the amounts needed to prepare the budgeted balance sheet are taken directly from the budgets already prepared, many amounts are not specifically included in any of those budgets. For example, we have not prepared a budget or schedule that shows the ending balances for accounts receivable, inventory, capital assets, accumulated amortization, accounts payable, notes payable, common stock, or retained earnings. For each of these items, we will present a brief discussion and a schedule to show how to calculate the amounts that should appear on the budgeted balance sheet. You will find as you examine each of these items that the budgeted ending balance is calculated by taking the beginning balance and adding or subtracting the changes that are expected to occur during the budget period. So, for each of these items, the beginning balance is our starting point. As discussed, the *beginning* balance of any balance sheet item is the prior month's *ending* balance. Therefore, all we need is the balance sheet for September 30 to determine the beginning balance for October. The balance sheet of September 30, 2004, for Marcy's Board Shop Inc. is shown in Exhibit 8–15.

Using the September 30, 2004, balance sheet in Exhibit 8–15 and information from the other budgets we have prepared so far, we can prepare a budgeted balance sheet for each of the three months included in our budget period, as shown in Exhibit 8–16.

The balance sheets presented in Exhibit 8–16 are much like the other balance sheets you have seen throughout your studies. The essential difference is not the format, but rather, the time frame. These are projected balance sheets whereas the others have presented past results. There is no total column for this budget, because the balance sheet is a financial snapshot of a business taken at the end of a

Exhibit 8–15
Balance Sheet as of
September 30, 2004,
for Marcy's Board
Shop Inc.

MARCY'S BOARD SHOP INC.
Balance Sheet
September 30, 2004

Assets
Current Assets

Cash		$ 2,170
Accounts Receivable, Net		4,650
Inventory		1,200
Total Current Assets		8,020

Capital Assets

Equipment		6,000
Less Accumulated Amortization		(1,200)
Capital Assets, Net		4,800
Total Assets		$12,820

Liabilities
Current Liabilities

Accounts Payable		$ 5,200
Total Liabilities		5,200

Shareholders' Equity

Common Stock		6,715
Retained Earnings		905
Total Shareholders' Equity		7,620
Total Liabilities and Shareholders' Equity		$12,820

period. Therefore, in a very real sense, the snapshot taken at the end of December is the total column.

As we have done with the other budgets prepared in this chapter, we will now take a few minutes and explain how the items on the budgeted balance sheet were determined.

(a) *Cash.* This amount is taken directly from the ending cash balance line of the cash budget shown in Exhibit 8–14. For example, the amount shown as the ending cash balance of $1,900 in the October column of the cash budget is shown as cash in the October column of the budgeted balance sheet.

(b) *Accounts Receivable.* To determine the ending accounts receivable balance for each month shown in Exhibit 8–16, we simply take the beginning accounts receivable balance, add budgeted credit sales for that month, and subtract budgeted collections for that month.

	October	November	December
Beginning Balance	$4,650	$ 5,325	$ 8,550
+ Credit sales	6,750	11,250	9,000
− Collections	(6,075)	(8,025)	(10,125)
Ending Balance	$5,325	$ 8,550	$ 7,425

The beginning accounts receivable balance of $4,650 for October is taken from the September 30, 2004, balance sheet shown in Exhibit 8–15. The cash receipts budget provides the rest of the information we need. The cash receipts budget shows the projected credit sales, and the total expected to be collected from credit sales. For October, the cash receipts budget shows credit sales of $6,750 and a total of $6,075 collected from credit sales. After adding the credit sales of $6,750 to the beginning balance of $4,650, we

Exhibit 8–16
Budgeted Balance
Sheet for Marcy's
Board Shop Inc.

MARCY'S BOARD SHOP INC.
Budgeted Balance Sheet
For the Quarter Ended December 31, 2004

	October	November	December	
Assets				
Current Assets				
Cash	$ 1,900	$ 2,230	$ 4,305	(a)
Accounts Receivable, Net	5,325	8,550	7,425	(b)
Inventory	3,000	2,400	3,600	(c)
Total Current Assets	10,225	13,180	15,330	
Capital Assets				
Equipment	6,000	6,240	6,240	(d)
Less Accumulated Amortization	(1,300)	(1,400)	(1,504)	(e)
Capital Assets, Net	4,700	4,840	4,736	
Total Assets	$14,925	$18,020	$20,066	
Liabilities				
Current Liabilities				
Accounts Payable	$ 6,300	$ 6,900	$ 7,200	(f)
Bank Loan Payable	405	0	0	(g)
Total Liabilities	6,705	6,900	7,200	
Shareholders' Equity				
Common Stock	6,715	6,715	6,715	(h)
Retained Earnings	1,505	4,405	6,151	(i)
Total Shareholders' Equity	8,220	11,120	12,866	
Total Liabilities and Shareholders' Equity	$14,925	$18,020	$20,066	

subtract the collections of $6,075 to arrive at the ending accounts receivable balance of $5,325. This amount is shown on the budgeted balance sheet for October. The ending accounts receivable amounts for other months are calculated the same way.

(c) *Inventory.* To determine the ending inventory balance for each month shown in Exhibit 8–16, we simply take the beginning inventory balance, add purchases made during the month, and subtract that month's cost of goods sold.

	October	November	December
Beginning Balance	$1,200	$3,000	$2,400
+ Purchases	6,300	6,900	7,200
− Cost of goods sold	(4,500)	(7,500)	(6,000)
Ending Balance	$3,000	$2,400	$3,600

The beginning inventory balance for October of $1,200 is taken from the September 30, 2004, balance sheet shown in Exhibit 8–15. By looking at the purchases budget in Exhibit 8–11 and the cost of goods sold budget in Exhibit 8–8, we find that expected purchases for October are $6,300 and cost of goods sold are expected be $4,500. After adding the purchases of $6,300 to the beginning balance of $1,200, we subtract the cost of goods sold of $4,500 to arrive at the ending inventory balance of $3,000. This amount is shown on the budgeted balance sheet for October. The ending inventory amounts for other months are calculated the same way.

(d) *Capital Assets.* To determine the ending balance in the equipment, we adjust the beginning balance by adding the cost of equipment purchased and subtracting the cost of any equipment sold. In our example, the only change in equipment is the $240 for the showcase the company is planning to buy in November. We add $240 to the $6,000 beginning balance to arrive at the budgeted ending balance of $6,240.

(e) *Accumulated Amortization.* To determine the ending balance for accumulated amortization, we adjust the beginning balance by adding the amortization for the period and subtracting the accumulated amortization associated with any assets that have been sold or scrapped. In our example, the company does not expect to sell or otherwise dispose of any equipment, so the only changes to accumulated amortization are increases relating to the budgeted monthly amortization. You might notice that the amount added to accumulated amortization in December is slightly higher than that for October and November. This is so because of the added amortization for the showcase the company expects to buy in November.

(f) *Accounts Payable.* To determine the ending accounts payable balance for each month shown in Exhibit 8–16, we simply take the beginning accounts payable balance, add budgeted purchases for that month, and subtract budgeted payments for that month.

	October	November	December
Beginning Balance	$5,200	$6,300	$6,900
+ Purchases	6,300	6,900	7,200
− Payments	(5,200)	(6,300)	(6,900)
Ending Balance	$6,300	$6,900	$7,200

The beginning accounts payable balance for October of $5,200 is taken from the September 30, 2004, balance sheet shown in Exhibit 8–15. By looking at the purchases budget in Exhibit 8–11 and the cash payments budget in Exhibit 8–13, we find that expected purchases for October are $6,300 and cash payments are expected be $5,200. After adding the purchases of $6,300 to the beginning balance of $5,200, we subtract the cash payments of $5,200 to arrive at the ending accounts payable balance of $6,300. This amount is shown on the budgeted balance sheet for October. The ending accounts payable amounts for other months are calculated the same way.

(g) *Bank Loan Payable.* To determine the ending bank loan payable balance for each month shown in Exhibit 8–16, we simply take the beginning bank loan payable balance, add the budgeted borrowing for that month, and subtract budgeted payments for that month.

	October	November	December
Beginning Balance	$ 0	$405	$0
+ Borrowing	405	0	0
− Repayments	0	(405)	0
Ending Balance	$405	$ 0	$0

The beginning bank loan payable balance for October would normally come from the September 30, 2004, balance sheet shown in Exhibit 8–15; however, in this example the beginning balance for bank loan payable on September 30, 2004, is zero, so bank loan payable does not appear. By looking at the cash budget in Exhibit 8–14, we find that borrowing of $405 is expected in October, a repayment of $405 is expected in November, and no activity is expected in December.

(h) *Share Capital.* In this example, no common stock transactions are expected during the budget period. Therefore, the beginning October balance for these items found on the September 30, 2004, balance sheet in Exhibit 8–15 remains unchanged during the budget period.

(i) *Retained Earnings.* To determine the ending retained earnings balance, we add the income for the period or, if the company has a loss, subtract the loss and deduct dividends, if they exist, from the beginning retained earnings balance.

	October	November	December
Beginning Balance	$ 905	$1,505	$4,405
+ Income/Loss	600	2,900	1,746
− Dividends	0	0	0
Ending Balance	$1,505	$4,405	$6,151

In our example, the $905 beginning balance of retained earnings is found on the September 30, 2004, balance sheet shown in Exhibit 8–15. To find the ending retained earnings that should appear on the budgeted balance sheet for October, we add the budgeted income for that month of $600 to the beginning retained earnings balance of $905. That figure becomes the beginning balance in November. To determine the November ending balance of retained earnings we simply add November's budgeted net income. December's ending balance would be calculated the same way. There are no dividends in our example so the dividend amount is zero for each month presented.

Budgeted Cash Flow Statement

Now that we have prepared all the other budgets, we can now prepare the budgeted cash flow statement. This statement must be the final budget prepared because, as you recall from your earlier study of this financial statement, it is a form of financial statement analysis. A cash flow statement prepared on historical results analyzes the income statement and the balance sheet to explain what caused cash to change from the beginning of a period to the end of the period. The budgeted cash flow statement does exactly the same thing, except that it analyzes the budgeted income statement and the budgeted balance sheet to explain what will cause the projected change in cash from the start to the end of the budget period.

A budgeted cash flow statement for Marcy's Board Shop Inc. is presented as Exhibit 8–17.

We will not do a line-by-line analysis of the presentation in Exhibit 8–17 because we have explained all the items elsewhere in this chapter as we have constructed the other budgets. It is worthwhile, however, for us to discuss what this budget reveals in overall terms.

In the normal course of business, a company can obtain cash from only three sources: borrowing, owner contributions, and profitable operations. Ultimately, the only source of cash for any company, including Marcy's Board Shop Inc., is the profitable operation of the business. If a company does not generate enough cash from operations to run the business, it must seek outside financing (borrowing and owner contributions).

The budgeted cash flow statement in Exhibit 8–17 reveals that for the three months covered by the budget, at least, Marcy's does not anticipate generating enough cash through operations to run the business and must, therefore, borrow the money. Three months is not a very long time, and all companies must obtain outside financing from time to time, but Marcy may not like what she sees when she looks at this budget. If she finds the prospects unacceptable, she may want to continue the budgeting process and make adjustments in how she plans to go about operating her business.

You will be delighted to know we are not going to do that for Marcy. We hope, however, that you have learned what a powerful tool the operating budget can be by going through the steps required to prepare one.

Exhibit 8–17
Budgeted Cash Flow
Statement for Marcy's
Board Shop Inc.

MARCY'S BOARD SHOP INC.
Budgeted Statement of Cash Flows
For the Quarter Ended December 31, 2004

	October	November	December
Cash Flows from Operating Activities:			
Receipts:			
Collections from Customers	$8,325	$11,775	$13,125
Payments:			
To suppliers for merchandise for resale	5,200	6,300	6,900
To suppliers for operating expenses	1,300	1,500	1,400
To employees	2,500	3,000	2,750
Total cash payments	9,000	10,800	11,050
Net cash inflow from operating activities	(675)	975	2,075
Cash Flows from Investing Activities:			
Cash paid for showcase		(240)	
Net cash inflow from investing activities	0	(240)	0
Cash Flows from Financing Activities:			
Proceeds from short-term borrowings	$405		
Repayment of short-term borrowings	0	(405)	
Net cash inflow from financing activities	$405	(405)	0
Net Increase/(Decrease) in Cash	(270)	330	2,075
Budgeted Beginning Cash Balance	2,170	1,900	2,230
Budgeted Ending Cash Balance	$1,900	$ 2,230	$ 4,305

USING (AND MISUSING) THE OPERATING BUDGET

We have seen that the operating budget can serve as a guide for the company to follow, assist a company in allocating its scarce resources, and foster communication and coordination among managers from different functional areas within the company. It can also establish performance standards, or benchmarks, against which the company can compare the actual results. This fourth application presents some serious challenges to managers, however. Misunderstanding how to set and use performance standards can lead to behaviour that is actually detrimental to the organization.

Once upon a time, someone figured out that the operating budget could be used as a means of controlling a company's activities. It is really a pretty simple concept. Once the operating budget is established for the year, you keep one eye on the budget and one eye on the actual results. The idea is that if you prepare a solid budget and then perform to meet that budget, you will naturally keep control of your operation. Before long, this way of using the operating budget had become quite common. As this practice became more popular, firms began evaluating the performance of their managers based on how they performed against the budget as well. This practice is known as the **performance to budget** evaluation. Salary increases, year-end bonuses, and promotions to senior management began to be dependent on a manager's ability to "meet or beat" the budget. By now, the operating budget had become the principal tool used to control costs. It was felt that if managers performed well against the budget, they were doing a good job of controlling the operations they managed, which makes sense, right? Wrong! Unfortunately, that is not what happens when the budget is used as the primary control device in a company. What happens is that using the budget for this purpose actually

performance to budget
A process of evaluating managers and employees based on how they perform against the budget.

encourages managers to make bad decisions and discourages them from making good decisions.

The Budget Performance Report

budget performance report
The evaluation instrument used to evaluate a manager's performance to budget.

As performance to budget became a popular way of measuring management performance, an instrument known as the **budget performance report** was developed to capture the information management thought was needed to perform the evaluation. A typical budget performance report has four columns as shown in Exhibit 8–18.

Exhibit 8–18
Budget Performance Report

(a)	(b)	(c)	(d)
Description	**Budget**	**Actual**	**Variance**
Salaries and Wages	$25,000	$23,000	$2,000 F
Office Rent	10,000	10,000	0
Office Supplies	1,000	1,200	200 U

As you can see, the report is not terribly complicated. In the description column (a), the items for which the manager being evaluated is responsible are listed. In the budget column (b), the budgeted amount for each of those items is listed. In the actual column (c), the amount actually spent during the period covered by the budget is listed. The difference between the amount budgeted and the actual amount is called a **variance.** The variances in our example appear in column (d). The letter *F* indicates a favourable variance and the letter *U* indicates an unfavourable variance.

variance The difference between the amount budgeted and the actual amount

 Discussion Question

8–22. What do the words *favourable* and *unfavourable* mean to you?

The major problem with the budget performance report is not the report itself but rather the way it is used. As an example, suppose that Brian Sedgwick is the sales manager at Pepperwood Furniture Company. Among other things, Brian is responsible for gas and oil expenditures for the fleet of delivery trucks his company owns. These trucks are used to deliver products to customers. Suppose further that Brian is responsible for establishing the budget for this item and he budgeted $50,000 for 2004. Now suppose that 2004 has ended and he spent $90,000 on gas and oil. Brian's budget performance report for this item would be as follows:

Description	Budget	Actual	Variance
Gas & Oil	$50,000	$90,000	$40,000 U

Now, what do you think might have caused this variance? Well, of the several possibilities, we will mention four.

1. Perhaps gas prices rose significantly. The budget was established based on what Brian *thought* gas and oil prices would be during the year. Perhaps OPEC reduced production of oil and forced the price of gas to rise.
2. Perhaps the budget Brian established was poorly done. Do not confuse this idea with the first possible explanation. In the first one, Brian did the best he could with the information he had—the information just turned out not to be reliable. This possibility comes from not taking the budgeting process seriously. Thus, for Brian, budgeting may mean filling out forms rather than being part of a real planning process.
3. Perhaps Brian was inefficient and wasted money. We would never want to forget this possibility. If he did waste money, he should be held accountable for his actions.
4. Perhaps business picked up significantly and the company had to make many more deliveries. This surely would have caused Brian to spend more money on gas and oil. Remember, the support costs in the budget are based on what is forecast to be sold.

Let's expand on the fourth possibility. Brian had an unfavourable variance caused by a good thing (greatly increased sales). This fact should help you understand that *unfavourable* in this context does not mean "bad," but rather "over budget."

Brian Sedgwick's performance evaluation will depend on his company's attitude about what performance to budget means. Unfortunately, in all too many companies today, the evaluation begins with the variance column. If there are unfavourable variances, regardless of cause, Brian's performance evaluation will not be good. He may not get his bonus, he may not get that raise he was anticipating, and he may not be promoted.

Before we talk about how to overcome the problem we just described, let's look at another example using the same essential facts. Brian budgeted $50,000 for gas and oil expenditures for 2004, but only spent $30,000. His budget performance report would be as follows:

Description	Budget	Actual	Variance
Gas & Oil	$50,000	$30,000	$20,000 F

We will not discuss what might have caused this variance, but with the exception of the poor budgeting possibility (which is the same in either case), the reasons are just the opposite of what caused the $40,000 unfavourable variance in our first example. If you think about the fourth possibility, then, this favourable variance could have been caused by a decline in the company's business. In other words, Brian has a favourable variance caused by a bad thing. That should help you understand that *favourable* in this context does not mean "good." It simply means "under budget."

What about Brian's performance evaluation? Once again, it depends greatly on how his company management views the performance to budget. In all too many companies, he would be rewarded in two ways. First, he would receive congratulations from everyone involved in the evaluation on what a great job he did of controlling gas and oil costs for the year. Second, his gas and oil budget for next year will be cut by $20,000. The reasoning is that if that's all he needed for this year, that's all he will need for next year, as well. This is called "use it or lose it" and is a practice that flourishes in many companies today.

If this is how Brian's company views the evaluation process, it is in his best interest to make sure he does not have actual expenditures that are too far under budget. If Brian is smart, he will make certain that his performance report on gas and oil costs looks something like the following:

Description	Budget	Actual	Variance
Gas & Oil	$50,000	$50,000	$0

This item will probably not be examined in any great detail during Brian's performance review, because the usual practice is to concentrate on the variance column. If no variance exists, it is assumed that the amount spent on the item was what should have been spent. This interpretation indicates efficient management: If managers are able to secure a large budget for a particular item, they will appear to be efficient simply by spending less than, or exactly, the amount budgeted.

In many companies, then, the focus is only on items with large variances. Further, when these variances are investigated, the analysis usually focuses on the actual performance column of the performance report. If a large, unfavourable variance exists, managers must explain why they spent more than the budget allowed. If a large, favourable variance exists, the item becomes a target for reducing costs next year, so the budget is cut.

What is bizarre about this method of using the budget performance report is that everybody knows budgets are established for the future. Everybody also knows that the future is to a great extent unknown to us. Yet, once the budget is established it becomes set in stone, so to speak, and any variance (favourable or unfavourable) between the budgeted cost and the actual cost is assumed to be because of the actual.

Are we suggesting that managers should be free to spend whatever amount they see fit on the cost items for which they are responsible? Absolutely not! This idea makes no sense, and it runs counter to everything we have said throughout this chapter, and indeed, throughout this book. Managers should be working every day to control costs and run their operations more efficiently. What we are saying is that this has very little to do with the operating budget. Cost control is an ongoing management process, of which the operating budget is only a part. Using the budget as the primary cost control device in a business is done in place of real control. Perhaps worse than that, using performance to budget as the evaluation instrument for managers encourages them to focus on the elimination of variances as their primary goal. As stated, because the budget is often considered to be set in stone, the only way to eliminate variances is to manipulate the actual performance to match the budget. This is what leads to silly budget games, such as the "use it or lose it" phenomenon we mentioned earlier.

If we lived in a perfect world where we could predict the future accurately, there would be no problem with the performance to budget evaluation technique. Unfortunately, we do not live in such a perfect world, and the future is largely unknown to us. When we prepare the operating budget we are attempting to predict the future. Differences are bound to exist between what we predict and what actually happens.

Earlier in the chapter we presented an exhibit that showed the interrelationship among all the budgets. We have reproduced that presentation as Exhibit 8–19.

As discussed during this interrelationship topic earlier in the chapter, a change in any one of the budgets has a ripple effect throughout all the other budgets. A little logic tells us that if there are variances in any one of the budgets there will also be a ripple effect throughout all the other budgets.

Perhaps more important as a cause of variances than the interrelationship among the budgets is the role of the sales forecast in the budgeting process. Note in Exhibit 8–19 that all the budgets included in the operating budget are dependent upon the sales forecast, which explains why we described the sales forecast as both the cornerstone and the keystone of the operating budget in our earlier discussions.

Exhibit 8–19
Interrelationship
among the Budgets

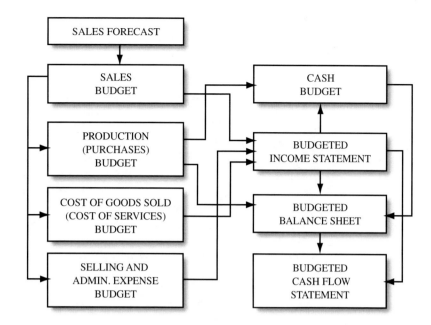

The sales forecast is so critical in the budgeting process that we will end this section by sharing three truths about the sales forecast and the operating budget:

Truth 1: If the sales forecast is inaccurate, the operating budget will be inaccurate. Do not confuse *inaccurate* with *bad*. A bad sales forecast comes from lack of effort and attention. An inaccurate sales forecast comes about when the actual results are different from the operating budget because the future did not turn out the way company management predicted.

Truth 2: The sales forecast will be inaccurate. Recall the items we discussed earlier in the chapter that affect a company's ability to forecast sales. The state of the general economy, actions of competitors, technological developments, and many other factors make an accurate sales forecast literally impossible.

Truth 3: The operating budget will be inaccurate. Once again, do not confuse inaccurate with bad. Inaccurate simply means that the actual results are going to be different from what was budgeted, meaning, of course, that variances will always exist.

Some approaches to the budget performance report help overcome the variances caused by actual sales being different from budgeted sales. The most popular of these is the flexible budget performance report, which is covered in more advanced management accounting courses. Note, however, that it does not eliminate the problem of using the budget in a way that was never intended, that is, as the primary control device in a business.

So, how do managers overcome the problems we have been discussing in this section? Well, they do it by using the budget as it was intended to be used—as a guide for the business. Just as prudent travelers would not hesitate to alter their plans during a trip as updated information becomes available, businesses should not hesitate to adjust their budgets when desirable or necessary. Further, when the period covered by the operating budget is over, an analysis should be performed to compare the actual results to the budget. The focus of this analysis, however, should be on how to improve the budgeting process rather than on the inevitable variances that have occurred.

SUMMARY

The operating budget is an integral part of the overall planning process for any company. Besides serving as a guide for the business throughout the period covered by the budget, the operating budget can assist management in the allocation of resources, foster communication and coordination among various segments of the company, and establish performance standards.

The operating budget is a set of estimated financial statements. These are the budgeted income statement, the budgeted balance sheet, and the budgeted cash flow statement. Besides the budgeted financial statements, the operating budget includes several other budgets prepared to support the budgeted financial statements. These are the sales budget, the production (or purchases) budget, the cost of goods sold (or cost of services) budget, the selling and administrative expense budget, and the cash budget (including the cash receipts schedule and the cash payments schedule).

There are several different approaches to the preparation of the operating budget. Perpetual, incremental, zero-based, top-down, bottom-up, imposed, and participative approaches to budgeting are just some that have developed over time. Each approach has certain advantages and certain disadvantages relative to the other approaches.

All the budgets included in the operating budget are dependent on the sales forecast. Indeed, the accuracy of the entire budget is dependent on the accuracy of the forecast. Many factors, including the state of the general economy, the condition of the company's industry, the actions of competitors, and technological developments all influence a company's ability to forecast its sales reasonably.

The operating budget was never meant to be used as the principal cost control device in business. Using the budget for this purpose actually encourages managers to make decisions that are detrimental to the business. If used properly, however, as a guide and coordination instrument, the operating budget can be of tremendous benefit for any company.

KEY TERMS

bottom-up budgeting, p. 280
budget performance report, p. 302
budgeted balance sheet, p. 275
budgeted cash flow statement, p. 275
budgeted income statement, p. 275
cash budget, p. 275
cash payments schedule, p. 293
cash receipts schedule, p. 291
continual budgeting, p. 278
cost of goods sold budget, p. 274
cost of services budget, p. 274
imposed budget, p. 280
incremental budgeting, p. 278
master budget, p. 269

master operating budget, p. 269
operating budget, p. 269
participative budget, p. 280
performance to budget, p. 301
perpetual budgeting, p. 278
production budget, p. 274
purchases budget, p. 274
sales budget, p. 273
sales forecast, p. 282
selling and administrative
    expense budget, p. 274
top-down budgeting, p. 279
variance, p. 302
zero-based budgeting, p. 279

REVIEW THE FACTS

1. What is the operating budget?
2. What is the master budget?
3. Which financial statements are part of the operating budget?
4. What is the difference between the financial statements included in the operating budget and other financial statements you have learned about in a financial accounting course?
5. List the main benefits of budgeting.
6. What is the basic difference between the production budget and the purchases budget?
7. What are two advantages of perpetual budgeting?
8. What is a disadvantage of perpetual budgeting?
9. What is incremental budgeting?
10. What problem is associated with incremental budgeting?
11. What is zero-based budgeting?
12. Describe the differences between top-down and bottom-up budgeting.
13. Describe the differences between an imposed budget and a participative budget.
14. Why is the sales forecast often called the cornerstone of budgeting?
15. Why is the sales forecast often called the keystone of budgeting?
16. List three factors that should be considered when preparing the sales forecast.
17. Why does the number of units budgeted to be purchased differ from the number of units budgeted to be sold?

18. When preparing the purchases budget, what two factors should be considered when determining the budgeted ending inventory?
19. What is presented on the cash receipts schedule?
20. For a particular budget period, why doesn't the budgeted cash collections from customers equal budgeted sales?
21. What is the basic difference between a budgeted balance sheet and a historical balance sheet?
22. In the normal course of business, what are the three sources from which a company can obtain cash?
23. What is a *performance to budget* evaluation?

Apply What You Have Learned

LO 3 & 4: Determine Order of Operating Budget Preparation

1. During the budgeting process, not all budgets are prepared at the same time. Following are several operating budgets.

1. _____ Cash budget
2. _____ Budgeted financial statements
3. _____ Purchases budget
4. _____ Sales budget
5. _____ Administrative expense budget
6. _____ Selling expense budget

REQUIRED:
Indicate a logical sequence for the preparation of the master budget.

LO 3: Indicate Advantages and Disadvantages of Top-Down, Bottom-Up Approaches

2. The operating budget can be prepared using either the top-down or bottom-up approach. Following in random order are several advantages and disadvantages of each approach.

Top-down Bottom-up	Advantage Disadvantage	
1. _____	_____	Budgeting process forces managers at various levels to think about future activities.
2. _____	_____	Top manager is more knowledgeable.
3. _____	_____	Employees at various levels must take time from their schedules to work on the budget.
4. _____	_____	Employees will be more eager to work toward goals they helped set.
5. _____	_____	Employees feel more like part of the company team.
6. _____	_____	Top manager is more aware of company goals.
7. _____	_____	Employees may try to pad the budget.
8. _____	_____	Employees are less accepting of budgeted goals if they had no part in setting them.
9. _____	_____	Top manager lacks detailed knowledge required to prepare budgets.

REQUIRED:
For each of these items, indicate whether it is associated with the top-down (T) or bottom-up (approach B), and whether it is an advantage (A) or disadvantage (D).

LO 3:   Indicate Budgeting Approaches

3. Following are approaches to budgeting, with a partial definition of those items in scrambled order.

    a. Perpetual budgeting   **d.** Top-down budgeting
    b. Incremental budgeting   **e.** Bottom-up budgeting
    c. Zero-based budgeting

    1. _____ Lower-level managers and employees initially prepare the budget.
    2. _____ Each item on the budget must be justified each year.
    3. _____ The budget is updated every month.
    4. _____ Lower-level managers generally do not participate in budget preparation.
    5. _____ Uses the prior year's budget to build the new budget.

REQUIRED:
For each partial definition, identify the budgeting approach to which it refers.

LO 5:   Prepare a Sales Budget

4. For 2005, Apex Computer Game Company expects to sell 6,000 games in the first quarter, 7,000 games in the second quarter, 9,000 games in the third quarter, and 12,000 games in the fourth quarter. Each game sells for $11.

REQUIRED:
Prepare the 2005 sales budget for Apex Computer Game Company.

LO 5:   Prepare a Sales Budget

5. For 2005, Monarch Barber Supply Company expects to sell 100 hair dryers in the first quarter, 90 hair dryers in the second quarter, 130 hair dryers in the third quarter, and 150 hair dryers in the fourth quarter. Each hair dryer sells for $67.

REQUIRED:
Prepare the 2005 sales budget for hair dryers for Monarch Barber Supply Company.

LO 5:   Prepare a Sales Budget

6. For 2005, Taub Yo Yo Company expects to sell 20,000 units in January, 25,000 units in February, and 30,000 units in March. Each unit sells for $1.20.

REQUIRED:
Prepare the sales budget for Taub Yo Yo Company for the first quarter of 2005.

LO 5: Prepare a Sales Budget

7. The Golden Bird Cage Company intends to sell 11,500 bird cages during 2004. The budgeted selling price per cage is $88. The following sales forecast is available.

	Units
First quarter	2,500
Second quarter	2,100
Third quarter	3,800
Fourth quarter	3,100

REQUIRED:
Prepare the 2004 sales budget for the Golden Bird Cage Company.

LO 5: Prepare a Sales Budget

8. Easy-Glide Strollers Inc. intends to sell 73,000 baby strollers in the first quarter of 2004. The budgeted selling price per stroller is $59. The following sales forecast is available.

	Units
January	22,500
February	22,500
March	28,000

REQUIRED:
Prepare the sales budget for Easy-Glide Strollers Inc. for the first quarter of 2004.

LO 5: Prepare a Purchases Budget

9. Only Caps Inc. plans to sell the following quantity of baseball caps during the first four months of 2004.

	Units
January	200
February	250
March	300
April	320

The company pays $6 for each hat, which it sells for $15.

At the beginning of January, the company plans to have 40 hats on hand, and hopes to maintain an ending inventory equal to 20% of the next month's sales.

REQUIRED:
Prepare a purchases budget for the first quarter of 2004 for Only Caps Inc. Remember, the first quarter is January, February, and March. April sales are only provided to help compute the ending inventory for March.

LO 5: Prepare a Sales Budget and Cost of Goods Sold Budget

10. Refer to the information in problem 9.

REQUIRED:
a. Prepare a sales budget for the first quarter of 2004 for Only Caps Inc.
b. Prepare a cost of goods sold budget for the first quarter of 2004 for Only Caps Inc.

LO 5:   Prepare a Purchases Budget

11. Anahi's Art Supplies plans to sell the following quantities of model AB222 airbrush during the first four months of 2005.

	Units
January	40
February	26
March	22
April	20

Anahi's pays $44 for each airbrush and sells them for $65.

At the beginning of January, Anahi's Art Supplies plans to have six airbrushes on hand, and hopes to maintain an ending inventory equal to 15% of the next month's sales.

REQUIRED:

Prepare a purchases budget for the first quarter of 2005 for Anahi's Art Supplies. Remember, the first quarter is January, February, and March. April sales are only provided to help compute the ending inventory for March.

LO 5:   Prepare a Sales Budget and Cost of Goods Sold Budget

12. Refer to the information in problem 11.

REQUIRED:

a. Prepare a sales budget for the first quarter of 2005 for Anahi's Art Supplies.
b. Prepare a cost of goods sold budget for the first quarter of 2005 for Anahi's Art Supplies.

LO 5:   Prepare a Sales Budget, Cost of Goods Sold Budget, and Purchases Budget

13. Diaz Lumber Inc. plans to sell the following quantities of BC Grade 1/2-inch plywood during the first four months of 2005.

January	220 sheets
February	250 sheets
March	200 sheets
April	300 sheets

Diaz pays $7 for each sheet of plywood and sells them for $12.

At the beginning of January, Diaz plans to have 66 sheets of plywood on hand, and hopes to maintain an ending inventory equal to 30% of the next month's sales.

REQUIRED:

a. Prepare a sales budget for the first quarter of 2005 for Diaz Lumber Inc.
b. Prepare a cost of goods sold budget for the first quarter of 2005 for Diaz Lumber Inc.
c. Prepare a purchases budget for the first quarter of 2005 for Diaz Lumber Inc.

LO 5: Prepare a Budgeted Income Statement Using Information Provided in Other Budgets

14. Smith Manufacturing Ltd. has prepared the following budgeted information for January 2004.

SMITH MANUFACTURING LTD.
Sales Budget
For January 31, 2004

Budgeted Sales in Units	3,300
× Budgeted Sales Price	$ 200
= Budgeted Sales Dollars	$660,000

SMITH MANUFACTURING LTD.
Cost of Goods Sold Budget
For January 31, 2004

Budgeted Sales in Units	3,300
× Budgeted Cost Per Unit	$ 110
= Budgeted COGS	$363,000

SMITH MANUFACTURING LTD.
Selling and Administrative Expense Budget
For January 31, 2004

Salaries and Wages	$101,500
Rent	64,000
Amortization	53,200
Other	2,300
Budgeted S & A Expense	$221,000

REQUIRED:

Prepare a budgeted income statement for January 2004 for Smith Manufacturing Ltd.

LO 5: Prepare a Budgeted Income Statement Using Information Provided in Other Budgets

15. Chaplain Sales Company has prepared the following budgeted information for March 2005.

CHAPLAIN SALES COMPANY
Sales Budget
For March 31, 2005

Budgeted Sales in Units	110,000
× Budgeted Sales Price	$ 4.95
= Budgeted Sales Dollars	$544,500

CHAPLAIN SALES COMPANY
Cost of Goods Sold Budget
For March 31, 2005

Budgeted Sales in Units	110,000
× Budgeted Cost Per Unit	$ 3.35
= Budgeted COGS	$368,500

CHAPLAIN SALES COMPANY
Selling and Administrative Expense Budget
For March 31, 2005

Sales Salaries	$ 51,500
Sales Commission	11,000
Other Salaries and Wages	35,000
Store Rent	24,000
Other Expenses	10,500
Budgeted S & A Expense	$132,000

REQUIRED:

Prepare a budgeted income statement for March 2005 for Chaplain Sales Company.

LO 5: Prepare a Budgeted Income Statement Using Information Provided in Other Budgets

16. Longoz Company has prepared the following budgeted information for December 2005.

LONGOZ COMPANY
Sales Budget
For December 31, 2005

	Budgeted Sales in Units	10,000
×	Budgeted Sales Price	$ 12.00
=	Budgeted Sales Dollars	$120,000

LONGOZ COMPANY
Cost of Goods Sold Budget
For December 31, 2005

	Budgeted Sales in Units	10,000
×	Budgeted Cost Per Unit	$ 8.00
=	Budgeted COGS	$80,000

LONGOZ COMPANY
Selling and Administrative Expense Budget
For December 31, 2005

Sales Salaries	$18,500
Sales Commission	3,000
Store Rent	9,000
Other Expenses	1,500
Budgeted S & A Expense	$32,000

REQUIRED:

Prepare a budgeted income statement for December 2005 for Longoz Company.

LO 5: Prepare a Budgeted Income Statement

17. For the first quarter of 2004, Philip's Sales Corporation has budgeted sales of $390,000 and budgeted cost of goods sold of $280,000. In addition, the budget for the first quarter of 2004 includes wages and salaries of $42,000, rent of $9,000, utilities of $2,000, maintenance of $1,000, and other expenses of $3,000.

REQUIRED:

Prepare a budgeted income statement for the first quarter of 2004 for Philip's Sales Corporation.

LO 5: Prepare a Budgeted Income Statement

18. For January 2005, Chung Manufacturing Inc. has budgeted sales of $1,200,000 and budgeted cost of goods sold of $980,000. In addition, the budget for January 2005 includes sales salaries of $98,000, administrative salaries of $54,000, rent of $24,000, utilities of $8,000, and other expenses of $9,000.

REQUIRED:

Prepare a budgeted income statement for January 2005 for Chung Manufacturing Inc.

LO 5: Prepare a Budgeted Income Statement

19. For the year 2004, Martin Sales Corporation has budgeted sales of $3,500,000 and budgeted cost of goods sold of $2,800,000. In addition, the budget for 2004 includes sales salaries of $220,000, administrative salaries of $130,000, amortization of $180,000, utilities of $38,000, and other expenses of $22,000.

REQUIRED:

Prepare a budgeted income statement for 2004 for Martin Sales Corporation.

LO 5: Prepare a Budgeted Income Statement for One Quarter

20. The following budgets were prepared for Gary's Jean Store Ltd.

GARY'S JEAN STORE LTD.
Sales Budget
For the Quarter Ended June 30, 2005

	April	May	June	Total
Budgeted Sales in Units	300	350	400	1,050
× Budgeted Sales Price	$ 27	$ 27	$ 27	$ 27
= Budgeted Sales Dollars	$8,100	$9,450	$10,800	$28,350

GARY'S JEAN STORE LTD.
Cost of Goods Sold Budget
For the Quarter Ended June 30, 2005

	April	May	June	Total
Budgeted Sales in Units	300	350	400	1,050
× Budgeted Cost Per Unit	$ 14	$ 14	$ 14	$ 14
= Budgeted Cost of Goods Sold	$4,200	$ 4,900	$5,600	$14,700

GARY'S JEAN STORE LTD.
Selling and Administrative Expense Budget
For the Quarter Ended June 30, 2005

	April	May	June	Total
Salaries and Wages	$1,800	$2,200	$1,900	$ 5,900
Rent	500	500	500	1,500
Amortization	100	100	100	300
Other	600	900	800	2,300
Budgeted Sales Dollars	$3,000	$3,700	$3,300	$10,000

REQUIRED:

Prepare a budgeted income statement for the second quarter of 2005 for Gary's Jean Store Ltd.

LO 5: Prepare a Budgeted Income Statement for One Quarter

21. Franklin Cart Company manufactures small carts that are designed to be pulled behind a small tractor or riding lawn mower. The following budgets were prepared for Franklin Cart Company.

FRANKLIN CART COMPANY
Sales Budget
For the Quarter Ended March 31, 2005

	Jan	Feb	Mar	Total
Budgeted Sales in Units	1,300	1,450	1,700	4,450
× Budgeted Sales Price	$ 186	$ 186	$ 186	$ 186
= Budgeted Sales Dollars	$241,800	$269,700	$316,200	$827,700

FRANKLIN CART COMPANY
Cost of Goods Sold Budget
For the Quarter Ended March 31, 2005

	Jan	Feb	Mar	Total
Budgeted Sales in Units	1,300	1,450	1,700	4,450
× Budgeted Cost Per Unit	$ 154	$ 154	$ 154	$ 154
= Budgeted COGS	$200,200	$223,300	$261,800	$685,300

FRANKLIN CART COMPANY
Selling and Administrative Expense Budget
For the Quarter Ended March 31, 2005

	Jan	Feb	Mar	Total
Salaries and Wages	$21,950	$22,200	$23,600	$67,750
Rent	4,000	4,500	4,500	13,000
Amortization	3,200	3,200	3,200	9,600
Other	2,300	2,500	2,800	7,600
Budgeted S & A Expense	$31,450	$32,400	$34,100	$97,950

REQUIRED:

Prepare a budgeted income statement for the first quarter of 2005 for Franklin Cart Company.

LO 5: Prepare a Budgeted Income Statement for One Quarter

22. The following budgets were prepared for Byrne Manufacturing Inc.

BYRNE MANUFACTURING INC.
Sales Budget
For the Quarter Ended September 30, 2004

	July	Aug	Sept	Total
Budgeted Unit Sales	900	1,100	1,300	3,300
× Budgeted Sales Price	$ 225	$ 225	$ 225	$ 225
= Budgeted Sales Dollars	$202,500	$247,500	$292,500	$742,500

BYRNE MANUFACTURING INC.
Cost of Goods Sold Budget
For the Quarter Ended September 30, 2004

	July	Aug	Sept	Total
Budgeted Unit Sales	900	1,100	1,300	3,300
× Budgeted Cost Per Unit	$ 204	$ 204	$ 204	$ 204
= Budgeted COGS	$183,600	$224,400	$265,200	$673,200

BYRNE MANUFACTURING INC.
Selling and Administrative Expense Budget
For the Quarter Ended September 30, 2004

	July	Aug	Sept	Total
Salaries and Wages	$ 4,800	$ 5,200	$ 5,800	$15,800
Rent	2,400	2,400	2,400	7,200
Amortization	1,150	1,150	1,150	3,450
Other	1,800	2,000	2,200	6,000
Budgeted S & A Expense	$10,150	$10,750	$11,550	$32,450

REQUIRED:

Prepare a budgeted income statement for the third quarter of 2004 for Byrne Manufacturing Inc.

LO 5: Prepare a Cash Receipts Schedule for One Quarter

23. The Deacon Company is preparing a cash receipts schedule for the first quarter of 2005. Sales for November and December of 2004 are expected to be $180,000 and $200,000, respectively. Budgeted sales for the first quarter of 2005 are presented here.

THE DEACON COMPANY
Sales Budget
For the Quarter Ended March 31, 2005

	Jan	Feb	Mar	Total
Budgeted Sales	$220,000	$240,000	$260,000	$720,000

Twenty percent of sales are for cash, the remaining 80% are on account. Ten percent of the sales on account are collected in the month of the sale, 60% in the month following the sale, and the remaining 30% in the second month following the sale. There are no uncollectible accounts receivable.

REQUIRED:

Prepare a cash receipts schedule for the first quarter of 2005.

LO 5: Prepare a Cash Receipts Schedule for One Quarter

24. Alda Distributors Inc. is preparing a cash receipts schedule for the first quarter of 2005. Sales for November and December of 2004 are expected to be $300,000 and $310,000, respectively. Budgeted sales for the first quarter of 2005 are presented here.

ALDA DISTRIBUTORS INC.
Sales Budget
For the Quarter Ended March 31, 2005

	Jan	Feb	Mar	Total
Budgeted Sales	$220,000	$290,000	$340,000	$850,000

Ten percent of sales are for cash, the remaining 90% are on account. Twenty percent of the sales on account are collected in the month of the sale, 70% in the month following the sale, and the remaining 10% in the second month following the sale. There are no uncollectible accounts receivable.

REQUIRED:
Prepare a cash receipts schedule for the first quarter of 2005.

LO 5: Prepare a Cash Receipts Schedule for One Quarter

25. The law firm of Smith and Wong is preparing a cash receipts schedule for the first quarter of 2005. Revenues for November and December of 2004 are expected to be $30,000 and $50,000, respectively. Budgeted revenues for the first quarter of 2005 are presented here.

SMITH AND WONG
Sales Budget
For the Quarter Ended March 31, 2005

	Jan	Feb	Mar	Total
Budgeted Revenues	$20,000	$25,000	$40,000	$85,000

Thirty-two percent of the revenues are collected in the first month, 45% in the second month, and the remaining 23% in the third month. There are no uncollectible accounts receivable.

REQUIRED:
Prepare a cash receipts schedule for the first quarter of 2005.

LO 5: Prepare a Cash Receipts Schedule for One Quarter

26. The Phillips Company is preparing a cash receipts schedule for the first quarter of 2004. Sales for November and December of 2003 are expected to be $33,000 and $55,000, respectively. Budgeted sales for the first quarter of 2004 are presented here.

THE PHILLIPS COMPANY
Sales Budget
For the Quarter Ended March 31, 2004

	Jan	Feb	Mar	Total
Budgeted Sales	$20,000	$30,000	$45,000	$95,000

Fifteen percent of sales are for cash; the remaining 85% are on account. Twenty percent of the sales on account are collected in the month of the sale, 50% in the month following the sale, and 30% in the second month following the sale. There are no uncollectible accounts receivable.

REQUIRED:
Prepare a cash receipts schedule for the first quarter of 2004.

LO 5: Prepare a Cash Receipts Schedule for One Quarter

27. The London Company is preparing a cash receipts schedule for the first quarter of 2004. Sales for November and December of 2003 are expected to be $40,000 and $80,000, respectively. Budgeted sales for the first quarter of 2004 are presented here.

THE LONDON COMPANY
Sales Budget
For the Quarter Ended March 31, 2004

	Jan	Feb	Mar	Total
Budgeted Sales	$30,000	$40,000	$50,000	$120,000

Ten percent of sales are for cash; the remaining 90% are on account. Fifteen percent of the sales on account are collected in the month of the sale, 60% in the month following the sale, and 25% in the second month following the sale. There are no uncollectible accounts receivable.

REQUIRED:
Prepare a cash receipts schedule for the first quarter of 2004.

LO 5: Prepare a Cash Receipts Schedule for One Quarter

28. NorAlta Distributors Inc. is preparing a cash receipts schedule for the first quarter of 2005. Sales on account for November and December of 2004 are expected to be $500,000 and $750,000, respectively. Budgeted sales for the first quarter of 2005 are presented here.

NORALTA DISTRIBUTORS INC.
Sales Budget
For the Quarter Ended March 31, 2005

	Jan	Feb	Mar	Total
Budgeted Cash Sales	$ 40,000	$ 45,000	$ 55,000	$ 140,000
Budgeted Sales on				
Account	400,000	450,000	550,000	1,400,000
Total Sales	$440,000	$495,000	$605,000	$1,540,000

Expected collection pattern for sales on account:

15% in the month of sale
60% in the month following the sale
25% in the second month following the sale
0% uncollectible

REQUIRED:
Prepare a cash receipts schedule for the first quarter of 2005.

LO 5: Prepare a Cash Receipts Schedule for One Quarter

29. The Steinman Company is preparing a cash receipts schedule for the first quarter of 2004. Sales on account for November and December of 2003 are expected to be $200,000 and $400,000, respectively. Budgeted sales for the first quarter of 2004 are presented here.

The Steinman Company
Sales Budget
For the Quarter Ended March 31, 2004

	Jan	Feb	Mar	Total
Budgeted Cash Sales	$ 20,000	$ 25,000	$ 27,000	$ 72,000
Budgeted Sales on				
Account	180,000	210,000	250,000	640,000
Total Sales	$200,000	$235,000	$277,000	$712,000

Expected collection pattern for sales on account:

    10% in the month of sale
    70% in the month following the sale
    20% in the second month following the sale
    0% uncollectible

REQUIRED:
Prepare a cash receipts schedule for the first quarter of 2004.

LO 5: Prepare a Cash Receipts Schedule for One Quarter

30. The Lowensohn Company is preparing a cash receipts schedule for the first quarter of 2005. Sales on account for November and December of 2004 are expected to be $320,000 and $550,000, respectively. Budgeted sales for the first quarter of 2005 are presented here.

THE LOWENSOHN COMPANY
Sales Budget
For the Quarter Ended March 31, 2005

	Jan	Feb	Mar	Total
Budgeted Cash Sales	$120,000	$150,000	$125,000	$395,000
Budgeted Sales on				
Account	180,000	225,000	190,000	595,000
Total Sales	$300,000	$375,000	315,000	$990,000

Expected collection pattern for sales on account:

    30% in the month of sale
    50% in the month following the sale
    20% in the second month following the sale
    0% uncollectible

REQUIRED:
Prepare a cash receipts schedule for the first quarter of 2005.

LO 5: Prepare a Cash Receipts Schedule for One Quarter

31. The S.R. Jackson Company is preparing a cash receipts schedule for the second quarter of 2004. Sales on account for February and March of 2004 are expected to be $50,000 and $60,000, respectively. Budgeted sales for the second quarter of 2004 are presented here.

THE S.R. JACKSON COMPANY
Sales Budget
For the Quarter Ended June 30, 2004

	April	May	June	Total
Budgeted Cash Sales	$15,000	$20,000	$25,000	$ 60,000
Budgeted Sales on				
Account	30,000	40,000	50,000	120,000
Total Sales	$45,000	$60,000	$75,000	$180,000

Expected collection pattern for sales on account:

    25% in the month of sale
    50% in the month following the sale
    25% in the second month following the sale
    0% uncollectible

REQUIRED:

Prepare a cash receipts schedule for the second quarter of 2004.

LO 5: Prepare a Cash Receipts Schedule for One Quarter

32. The Hodson Company is preparing a cash receipts schedule for the third quarter of 2005. Sales on account for May and June of 2005 are expected to be $100,000 and $120,000, respectively. Budgeted sales for the third quarter of 2005 are presented here.

THE HODSON COMPANY
Sales Budget
For the Quarter Ended September 30, 2005

	July	Aug	Sept	Total
Budgeted Cash Sales	$ 8,000	$ 9,000	$ 11,000	$ 28,000
Budgeted Sales on				
Account	80,000	90,000	110,000	280,000
Total Sales	$88,000	$99,000	$121,000	$308,000

Expected collection pattern for sales on account:

    10% in the month of sale
    60% in the month following the sale
    30% in the second month following the sale
    0% uncollectible

REQUIRED:

Prepare a cash receipts schedule for the third quarter of 2005.

LO 5: Prepare a Cash Receipts Schedule for One Quarter

33. The Ogden Company is preparing a cash receipts schedule for the fourth quarter of 2004. Sales on account for August and September of 2004 are expected to be $200,000 and $220,000, respectively. Budgeted sales for the fourth quarter of 2004 are presented here.

THE OGDEN COMPANY
Sales Budget
For the Quarter Ended December 31, 2004

	Oct	Nov	Dec	Total
Budgeted Cash Sales	$ 42,000	$ 46,000	$ 60,000	$148,000
Budgeted Sales on				
Account	210,000	230,000	300,000	740,000
Total Sales	$252,000	$276,000	$360,000	$888,000

Expected collection pattern for sales on account:

    20% in the month of sale
    70% in the month following the sale
    10% in the second month following the sale
    0% uncollectible

REQUIRED:

Prepare a cash receipts schedule for the fourth quarter of 2004.

LO 5 Prepare a Cash Receipts Schedule for One Quarter

34. The law firm of Hendricks & Hendricks is preparing a cash receipts schedule for the first quarter of 2005. Service revenue for November and December of 2004 is expected to be $90,000 and $50,000, respectively. All billings are on account. There are no "cash sales." Budgeted service revenue for the first quarter of 2005 is presented here.

HENDRICKS & HENDRICKS
Service Revenue Budget
For the Quarter Ended March 31, 2005

	Jan	Feb	Mar	Total
Budgeted Service Revenue	$40,000	$50,000	$65,000	$155,000

Expected collection pattern:

   30% in the month of billing
   60% in the month following the billing
   10% in the second month following the billing
   0% uncollectible

REQUIRED:

Prepare a cash receipts schedule for the first quarter of 2005.

LO 5:   Prepare a Cash Receipts Schedule for One Quarter

35. The veterinary practice of Heath & Dale is preparing a cash receipts schedule for the first quarter of 2004. Service revenue for November and December of 2003 is expected to be $120,000 and $110,000, respectively. All billings are on account. There are no "cash sales." Budgeted service revenue for the first quarter of 2004 is presented here.

HEATH & DALE
Service Revenue Budget
For the Quarter Ended March 31, 2004

	Jan	Feb	Mar	Total
Budgeted Service Revenue	$120,000	$130,000	$140,000	$390,000

Expected collection pattern:

   20% in the month of billing
   60% in the month following the billing
   20% in the second month following the billing
   0% uncollectible

REQUIRED:

Prepare a cash receipts schedule for the first quarter of 2004.

LO 5: Prepare a Cash Payments Schedule for One Quarter

36. AllTrans Distributors Inc. has prepared the following budgets for the first quarter of 2005.

ALLTRANS DISTRIBUTORS INC.
Selling and Administrative Expense Budget
For the Quarter Ended March 31, 2005

	Jan	Feb	Mar	Total
Salaries and Wages	$1,700	$2,200	$1,900	$ 5,800
Rent	300	300	300	900
Amortization	200	200	200	600
Other	900	1,200	1,000	3,100
Total	$3,100	$3,900	$3,400	$10,400

ALLTRANS DISTRIBUTORS INC.
Purchases Budget
For the Quarter Ended March 31, 2005

	Jan	Feb	Mar	Total
Forecasted Unit Sales	50	60	70	180
+ Desired Ending Inventory	12	14	16	16
= Total Units Needed	62	74	86	196
− Beginning Inventory	(10)	(12)	(14)	(10)
= Units to Be Purchased	52	62	72	186
× Cost Per Unit	$ 220	$ 220	$ 220	$ 220
= Cost of Purchases	$11,440	$13,640	$15,840	$40,920

Selling and administrative expenses are paid in the month incurred and purchases are paid in the month following the purchase. Purchases for December 2004 are $10,500. No equipment purchases or additional expenditures are made during the quarter.

REQUIRED:

Prepare a cash payments schedule for the first quarter of 2005.

LO 5: Prepare a Cash Payments Schedule for One Quarter

37. Dixon Sales Company has prepared the following budgets for the second quarter of 2004.

DIXON SALES COMPANY
Selling and Administrative Expense Budget
For the Quarter Ended June 30, 2004

	April	May	June	Total
Salaries	$1,000	$1,200	$1,300	$3,500
Rent	200	200	200	600
Utilities	120	180	220	520
Amortization	80	80	80	240
Other	500	600	650	1,750
Total	$1,900	$2,260	$2,450	$6,610

DIXON SALES COMPANY
Purchases Budget
For the Quarter Ended June 30, 2004

	April	May	June	Total
Forecasted Unit Sales	70	80	90	240
+ Desired Ending Inventory	16	18	19	19
= Total Units Needed	86	98	109	259
− Beginning Inventory	(15)	(16)	(18)	(15)
= Units to Be Purchased	71	82	91	244
× Cost Per Unit	$ 100	$ 100	$ 100	$ 100
= Cost of Purchases	$7,100	$8,200	$9,100	$24,400

Selling and administrative expenses are paid in the month incurred and purchases are paid in the month following the purchase. Purchases for March 2004 are $6,800. No equipment purchases or additional expenditures are made during the quarter.

REQUIRED:
Prepare a cash payments schedule for the second quarter of 2004.

LO 5: Prepare a Cash Payments Schedule for One Month

38. The following budgeted information is available for the Top Coat Clothing Company for January 2005.

Salaries	$120,000
Rent	9,000
Utilities	1,200
Amortization	3,200
Other Expenses	1,500
Purchases	380,000

Selling and administrative expenses are paid in the month incurred and purchases are paid in the month following the purchase. Purchases for December 2004 are $350,000. No equipment purchases or additional expenditures are made during the month.

REQUIRED:
Prepare a cash payments schedule for January 2005.

LO 5: Prepare a Cash Payments Schedule for One Month

39. The following budgeted information is available for Western Feed Store in June 2004.

Salaries	$12,000
Rent	600
Electricity	140
Amortization	800
Other Expenses	700
Purchases	80,000

Selling and administrative expenses are paid in the month incurred and purchases are paid in the month following the purchase. Purchases for May 2004 are $75,000. No equipment purchases or additional expenditures are made during the month.

REQUIRED:

Prepare a cash payments schedule for June 2004.

LO 5: Prepare a Cash Budget for One Quarter

40. The following information is available for Lam Sales Company for the first quarter of 2005.

	Jan	Feb	Mar
Budgeted Receipts from Credit Sales	$5,000	$5,500	$5,800
Budgeted Cash Sales	1,200	1,250	1,300
Budgeted Cash Payments	6,300	7,185	6,520

Beginning cash balance for January 2005 is expected to be $1,500. The company intends to maintain a cash balance of at least $1,000. The company has made arrangements to borrow from a local bank if necessary.

REQUIRED:

Prepare a cash budget for the first quarter of 2005.

LO 5: Prepare a Cash Budget for One Quarter

41. The following information is available for Holter Distributors Inc. for the second quarter of 2004.

	April	May	June
Budgeted Receipts from Credit Sales	$500,000	$520,000	$550,000
Budgeted Cash Sales	100,000	105,000	112,000
Budgeted Cash Payments	670,000	615,000	627,000

Beginning cash balance for April 2004 is expected to be $90,000. The company intends to maintain a cash balance of at least $50,000. The company has made arrangements to borrow from a local bank if necessary.

REQUIRED:

Prepare a cash budget for the second quarter of 2004.

LO 5: Prepare a Cash Budget for One Quarter

42. The following information is available for Everetti Company for the first quarter of 2005.

	Jan	Feb	Mar
Budgeted Receipts from Credit Sales	$100,000	$110,000	$115,000
Budgeted Cash Sales	80,000	95,000	98,000
Budgeted Cash Payments	178,000	215,000	206,000

Beginning cash balance for January 2005 is expected to be $20,000. The company intends to maintain a cash balance of at least $15,000. The company has made arrangements to borrow from a local bank if necessary.

REQUIRED:

Prepare a cash budget for the first quarter of 2005.

LO 5: Prepare a Cash Budget for One Month

43. The following information is available for Rees Company for November 2004.

Budgeted Receipts from Credit Sales	$25,100
Budgeted Cash Sales	5,900
Budgeted Cash Payments	32,600

Beginning cash balance for November is expected to be $5,800. The company intends to maintain a cash balance of at least $5,000. The company has made arrangements to borrow from a local bank if necessary.

REQUIRED:
Prepare a cash budget for November 2004.

LO 5: Prepare a Cash Budget for One Month

44. The following information is available for Sinclair Company for October 2004.

Budgeted Receipts from Credit Sales	$300,000
Budgeted Cash Sales	80,000
Budgeted Cash Payments	410,000

Beginning cash balance for October is expected to be $60,000. The company intends to maintain a cash balance of at least $50,000. The company has made arrangements to borrow from a local bank if necessary.

REQUIRED:
Prepare a cash budget for October 2004.

LO 5: Prepare a Cash Budget for One Month

45. The following information is available for Romy Ltd. for July 2005.

Budgeted Receipts from Credit Sales	$500,000
Budgeted Cash Sales	40,000
Budgeted Cash Payments	577,000

Beginning cash balance for July is expected to be $95,000. The company intends to maintain a cash balance of at least $75,000. The company has made arrangements to borrow from a local bank if necessary.

REQUIRED:
Prepare a cash budget for July 2005.

LO 5: Prepare a Budgeted Balance Sheet and Budgeted Cash Flow Statement for Three Months

46. The following information is available for Brookes Printing Supply Ltd.

BROOKES PRINTING SUPPLY LTD.
Sales Budget
For the Quarter Ended September 30, 2004

	July	August	September
Budgeted Sales Dollars	$90,000	$80,000	$70,000

BROOKES PRINTING SUPPLY LTD.
Cost of Goods Sold Budget
For the Quarter Ended September 30, 2004

	July	August	September
Budgeted Cost of Goods Sold	$54,000	$48,000	$42,000

BROOKES PRINTING SUPPLY LTD.
Selling and Administrative Expense Budget
For the Quarter Ended September 30, 2004

	July	August	September
Salaries and Wages	$12,600	$12,000	$11,800
Rent	1,000	1,000	1,000
Amortization	1,800	1,800	1,800
Other	3,800	3,000	2,900
Total	$19,200	$17,800	$17,500

BROOKES PRINTING SUPPLY LTD.
Budgeted Income Statement
For the Quarter Ended September 30, 2004

	July	August	September
Sales	$90,000	$80,000	$70,000
Cost of Goods Sold	54,000	48,000	42,000
Gross Profit	36,000	32,000	28,000
Selling and Admin. Expense	19,200	17,800	17,500
Net Income	$16,800	$14,200	$10,500

BROOKES PRINTING SUPPLY LTD.
Purchases Budget
For the Quarter Ended September 30, 2004

	July	August	September
Cost of Purchases	$52,000	$46,000	$41,000

BROOKES PRINTING SUPPLY LTD.
Cash Receipts Schedule
For the Quarter Ended September 30, 2004

	July	August	September
Budgeted Receipts from Credit Sales	$78,000	$76,000	$68,000
Budgeted Cash Sales	9,000	8,000	7,000
Total Cash Receipts	$87,000	$84,000	$75,000

BROOKES PRINTING SUPPLY LTD.
Cash Payments Schedule
For the Quarter Ended September 30, 2004

	July	August	September
Purchases	$56,000	$52,000	$46,000
Selling and Admin. Expense:			
Salaries and Wages	12,600	12,000	11,800
Rent	1,000	1,000	1,000
Other	3,800	3,000	2,900
Budgeted Cash Payments	$73,400	$68,000	$61,700

BROOKES PRINTING SUPPLY LTD.
Cash Budget
For the Quarter Ended September 30, 2004

		July	August	September
	Beginning Cash Balance	$ 18,500	$ 32,100	$ 48,100
+	Cash Receipts	87,000	84,000	75,000
=	Cash Available	105,500	116,100	123,100
−	Cash Payments	(73,400)	(68,000)	(61,700)
=	Balance before Borrowing	32,100	48,100	61,400
+/−	Borrowing/(Repayment)	0	0	0
=	Ending Cash Balance	$ 32,100	$ 48,100	$ 61,400

BROOKES PRINTING SUPPLY LTD.
Balance Sheet
June 30, 2004

Assets	
Current Assets	
Cash	$ 18,500
Accounts Receivable	20,000
Inventory	16,000
Total Current Assets	54,500
Capital Assets	
Equipment	108,000
Less Accumulated Amortization	(43,200)
Equipment, Net	64,800
Total Assets	$119,300
Liabilities	
Current Liabilities	
Accounts Payable	$ 56,000
Total Liabilities	56,000
Shareholders' Equity	
Common Stock	11,000
Retained Earnings	52,300
Total Shareholders' Equity	63,300
Total Liabilities and Shareholders' Equity	$119,300

REQUIRED:

a. Prepare budgeted balance sheets for July, August, and September of 2004.

b. Prepare budgeted cash flow statements for July, August, and September of 2004.

LO 5:   Determine Missing Budget Information

47. Following is a partial performance report.

Description	Budget	Actual	Variance
Wages	$5,000	$ 5,200	$?
Store Rent	6,000	?	200 F
Utilities Expense	?	1,200	50 U

REQUIRED:

Provide the missing information.

LO 5: Determine Budget Variances

48. Following is a partial performance report.

Description	Budget	Actual	Variance
Sales	$25,000	$22,000	$?
Cost of Goods Sold	20,000	17,600	?
Gross Profit	5,000	4,400	?

REQUIRED:

Calculate the variances for this information and indicate whether they are favourable (F) or unfavourable (U).

LO 5: Determine Budget Variances

49. Following is a partial performance report.

Description	Budget	Actual	Variance
Rent Revenue	$15,000	$14,000	$?
Interest Expense	15,000	14,000	?

REQUIRED:

Calculate the variances for this information and indicate whether they are favourable (F) or unfavourable (U).

LO 6: Discuss Variances

50. Robin Wince owns a small chain of frame shops. All the frames and other merchandise the company sells is purchased by the company's central purchasing department. A partial performance report showing the direct costs for one of Robin's stores appears as follows:.

	Budget	Actual	Variance
Sales	$200,000	$200,000	$ 0
Cost of Goods Sold	120,000	110,000	10,000 F
Selling and Admin. Expense	40,000	50,000	10,000 U
Income	$ 40,000	$ 40,000	$ 0

REQUIRED:

Robin is concerned even though the variance in income is zero. Because the total variance is zero, the store manager believes that there is no problem. Do you agree with the manager? Why?

LO 6: Prepare a Memo Regarding Variances

51. Matt Light owns the Zap Record Shop. He is in the process of examining the following performance report.

	Budget	Actual	Variance
Sales	$100,000	$120,000	$20,000 F
Cost of Goods Sold	60,000	72,000	12,000U
Selling and Admin. Expense	10,000	9,000	1,000 F
Income	$ 30,000	$ 39,000	$ 9,000 F

Matt is very pleased that the company had favourable variances for sales and income. However, he finds the sizable unfavourable variance for cost of goods sold very disturbing. He is preparing himself for a serious discussion with the purchasing agent who is responsible for purchasing the merchandise sold.

REQUIRED:

Assume that Matt Light has asked you for assistance in preparing for the meeting with the purchasing agent. Prepare a memo to Matt that provides him with any information you think would be helpful.

9

Standard Costing

"Many people have condemned standard costing, saying it is irrelevant to the current just-in-time based, fast-paced business environment. Yet surveys consistently show that most industrial companies still use it. Apparently, these companies have successfully adapted their standard costing systems to their particular business environments"[1]

In Chapter 1, we commented on the fact that many of the techniques used in management accounting were developed in the early part of the 19th century. Standard costing was one such technique. **Standard costing** is the process of setting performance goals that benchmark desirable performance and then use these cost goals to evaluate performance. As these goals are being set, employees are planning how production facility resources will be acquired and used. Then, once operations begin, employees strive to control costs so the goals can be met. The goals also provide management with a basis for performance evaluation when actual results are compared to goals.

Although standard costing began in manufacturing companies, it is applicable to all sectors of the economy, including service and not-for-profit companies.

As the quotation above indicates, standard costing is still as relevant today as it was 50 years ago, but users have to make sure their costing system is responsive to the needs of companies operating in the new economy. ∎

---

[1]David Johnsen and Parvez Sopariwala, "Standard Costing is Alive and Well at Parker Brass," *Management Accounting Quarterly, Winter 2000*. From Management Accounting Quarterly's web site, www.mamag.com (accessed August 21, 2002).

LEARNING OBJECTIVES

After completing your work on this chapter, you should be able to do the following:

1. Describe standard costing and indicate why standard costing is important.
2. Explain the concept of management by exception.
3. Contrast ideal and practical standards.
4. Identify and discuss the weaknesses of standard costing.
5. Compare standard costing, actual costing, and normal costing.
6. Determine standards for a manufacturing company.
7. Calculate standard cost variances for direct material, direct labour, variable manufacturing overhead, and fixed manufacturing overhead.
8. Describe the meaning of standard cost variances for direct material, direct labour, variable manufacturing overhead, and fixed manufacturing overhead.

WHY IS STANDARD COSTING USED?

standard costing   The process of setting cost performance goals that benchmark acceptable performance and then using these cost goals to evaluate performance.

standard   A preestablished benchmark for desirable performance.

standard cost system   A system in which cost standards are set after careful analysis and then used to evaluate actual performance.

In today's competitive environment, business success depends in large part on good planning, as discussed in Chapter 8. Standard costing is often a key planning tool. When a company uses standard costing, it establishes performance standards for the coming year. A **standard** is a preestablished benchmark for desirable performance. A **standard cost system** is one in which a company, after careful analysis, sets cost standards and then uses them to evaluate actual performance.

Standard costing is used to bolster business success. In general, the use of standard costing encourages planning, establishes performance targets, and provides a basis for evaluating actual performance.

Planning is a critical part of any standard cost system. Managers and other employees work to gather information and investigate ways of achieving acceptable performance at the lowest cost. With this information, standards are established. For example, standards are created for the amount and cost of direct material, and for the number of direct labour hours and their cost. The process of planning provides benefits to the company because, once employees have established standards during the planning process, they know what needs to be done and how to do it most efficiently.

Once standards have been set, they can be used as performance targets. Managers and employees are encouraged to act so that actual results meet the expectations established by the standards. For example, if the production cost standard (the cost goal) for a pair of skates made by Inline Skate Company is $34, employees are encouraged to make the skates for $34 or less. In an ideal situation, every employee would work to make the highest-quality skates for less than the $34 standard cost.

variance   The difference between actual performance and the standard.

unfavourable variance   The difference between actual performance and standard performance when the actual performance falls below the standard.

To determine whether and where problems exist, managers compare actual results to the standards. A **variance** is the difference between actual performance and the standard. Variances can be used to help determine where managers should focus their attention.

Actual performance that falls below standard results is an **unfavourable variance.** Essentially, an unfavourable variance reflects a situation in which the cost of actual performance is higher than planned performance. For example, if the standard direct labour time to manufacture a desk is 12 minutes and it actually takes 15 minutes, the three-minute difference constitutes an unfavourable variance of three minutes. Because it is more costly to the company when three minutes of additional labour is used than was planned, an unfavourable variance is an indication that a problem may exist and management attention is needed.

When actual performance exceeds the expectations established by the standard, a **favourable variance** results. In our desk example, if it actually takes 11 minutes to make the desk instead of the standard 12 minutes, the difference constitutes a favourable variance of one minute because cost to the company is reduced if labour time is one minute less than planned.

It might seem that a favourable variance indicates that management attention is not needed, but such is not always the case. Managers should review all variances, favourable and unfavourable, and use judgment and additional information to prioritize problem-solving efforts. For example, if a purchasing agent is able to buy direct material for less than the standard price, a favourable variance will occur. If the lower price is the result of purchasing substandard material, the "favourable" variance may not actually be to the company's benefit at all. Another reason to look into the cause of favourable variances is to learn how performance was improved. If the favourable variance is the result of improved performance, management may be able to learn how to make similar performance improvements in other areas of the company.

Items that have no variance should also be investigated. As discussed in Chapter 8, the absence of a variance should not be construed as meaning that everything is as it should be with that particular item. Managers must also remember that the cause of a variance may be the standard and not the performance. Standard setting is not an exact science. Standards must be reviewed often and changed as circumstances warrant.

It is most helpful if managers are able to review related standard cost variances together. For this purpose, a performance report is often prepared that summarizes variances for a particular operation of the company and shows where attention is needed. The process of focusing management attention on areas where actual performance deviates from the preestablished standards is called **management by exception.**

Under management by exception, managers first tend to problems associated with large variances. Then, once the large problems have been addressed, managers can turn to areas associated with lesser variances. Finally, as time permits, items where no variances exist are examined.

favourable variance
The difference between actual performance and standard performance when the actual performance exceeds the standard.

management by exception
The process of focusing management attention on areas where actual performance deviates from the preestablished standards.

STANDARDS—A CLOSER LOOK

Most companies set cost standards once each year. Even if variances occur, it is generally unwise to casually adjust standards during the year, because managers might be too quick to adjust them to eliminate unfavourable variance instead of working to improve performance. Also, if standards are often adjusted, performance becomes difficult to track. Performance that resulted in an unfavourable variance one month might result in a favourable variance the next month once the standard has been changed. Standards should be altered only if conditions change so significantly that the established standards lose their effectiveness as performance targets.

Cost and Quantity Standards

Performance standards can be set for almost any business activity. For example, standards can be set for the number of product returns, or for the amount of employee turnover. In practice, however, standards are used most often to help control costs.

Two things can cause cost to increase: the quantity used and the price paid. It is better to establish both a quantity standard and a separate price standard for each material used in production. For example, to say the direct material for product X should cost $3 per unit is not as helpful in controlling cost as saying that it should take 1.5 kilograms of material at $2 per kilogram to make product X. Establishing a quantity and price standard provides performance targets for the amount of material used in production and a separate target for finding the material at the best purchase price.

Although it is also helpful to establish quantity and price standards for direct labour, we generally do not refer to labour in terms of "quantity" and "price." Instead we use the equivalent terms "hours" and "rate." The quantity standard for labour is the number of hours, and the price standard is the rate.

Ideal versus Practical Standards

During the planning process, managers and other employees work to set standards that will both help provide performance targets and provide a basis for performance evaluation. If we were setting a price standard for the purchase of gasoline, for example, we could set a cost goal of $0.30 per litre, $3.00 per litre, or any price in between. The object would be to select a standard that would challenge employees to find gasoline at the best price. If the standard is set at $0.30 per litre, it is unlikely that employees will even try to achieve this impossible standard. On the other hand, if the standard is set at $3.00 per litre, employees will be able to achieve the standard so easily that it will offer no incentive to find low-cost gasoline. Generally it is best to select a standard that offers a challenging, yet achievable, performance goal.

ideal standard A standard that is attainable only under perfect conditions.

Ideal Standards   A standard that is attainable only under perfect conditions is called an **ideal standard.** Under ideal standards, there is no room for substandard performance of any kind. In a manufacturing setting, for instance, ideal standards assume that the factory operates in a perfect world with no machine breakdowns, no waste of direct material for any reason, and no employee rest breaks. In the real world, ideal standards are nearly impossible to achieve. Such standards may frustrate employees because, no matter how hard they try, they will never be able to meet them. In time, employees may throw up their hands and stop trying to meet the standards altogether.

practical standard A standard that allows for normal, recurring inefficiencies.

Practical Standards   A standard that allows for normal, recurring inefficiencies is called a **practical standard.** For example, in manufacturing, a practical standard for the quantity of direct material would allow for waste due to expected defects in the material. For labour, a practical standard would provide for employees working at a normal pace with adequate rest periods. When compared to ideal standards, practical standards are more realistic and less likely to result in unreasonable unfavourable variances. In addition, when practical standards are used, an unfavourable variance indicates that a true problem exists. Accordingly, most companies use practical standards.

Setting Standards

Often, standards are based on past performance. For example, if material Y was purchased for $4.45 per kilogram last year, it is likely it can be purchased for about $4.45 the next year; but using last year's actual amounts as next year's standards is overly simplistic. When setting standards, it is best to use historical information, and then incorporate any anticipated changes in efficiency or price.

Often, it is best to use a team approach to evaluate each standard. Whether formal or informal, a team approach for gathering input from various knowledgeable employees will result in better, more appropriate standards. For example, when setting direct material standards for a manufacturer, a team approach would likely be better than a single employee setting the standards based solely on his or her own limited knowledge. The team might include an accountant, production-line workers, production supervisors, purchasing agents, and others who are knowledgeable about the quality, use, sources, and prices of direct material. Then, the historical information provided by the accountants, information about usage and quality requirements provided by production personnel, and information about sourcing and pricing from the purchasing agent can be analyzed. Once the team has examined all this information, appropriate direct material standards can be set.

Once reasonable standards have been established, actual performance has been measured and compared to the standards, and a system to provide performance reports has been put in place, standard costing can be a valuable management tool. A flowchart of how standard costing works is shown in Exhibit 9–1. Managers can then encourage employees to strive to meet the performance goals established by the standards, and can use performance reports and management by exception to help direct their attention to troubled areas. Unfortunately, standard costing is not the answer to all management's problems. When managers rely too heavily on standard costing, serious problems occur.

Exhibit 9–1
The Standard Costing
Process

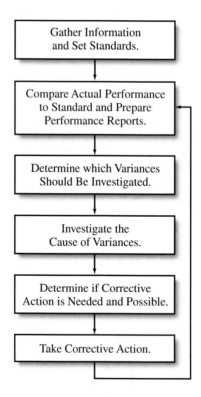

Problems with Standard Costing

To use standard costing as an effective management tool, managers must be aware of its drawbacks. The first problems may occur when standards are being set. Employees with expertise are often consulted to help establish an appropriate standard. Most of these employees are keenly aware that the standard will be used later to evaluate their performance. With lax standards, employees will not have to work as hard to meet the goals set by the standard, and unfavourable variances will be less likely. With stringent standards, employees will have to work much harder to meet targeted goals. Accordingly, employees often try to ensure that the standards adopted by the company are lax, resulting in suboptimal performance goals.

Another problem with standard costing stems from relying on historical information to set standards. If past performance was less than optimal, the new standards will call for performance that is less than optimal. The inefficiency of the past may be built into the new standards. Sometimes employees and lower-level managers deliberately manipulate actual performance so it appears that less stringent standards should be maintained. This way, employees are less likely to face the consequences of unfavourable performance variances in the future.

Still another serious problem associated with standard costing is that managers tend to manage everything "by the numbers." When a standard cost system is well established, managers often focus almost entirely on significant, unfavourable variances and overlook serious problems that do not give rise to unfavourable variances. For example, a manager may try desperately to reduce an unfavourable direct material variance while completely overlooking a significant product quality problem. Why? The product quality problem does not result in a variance; therefore, a manager whose attention is directed solely by management by exception would have no "exception" to direct him or her to the quality problem. Managers may get so engrossed in chasing down problems associated with unfavourable variance that they waste company time and resources as they try to rectify insignificant unfavourable variances.

In addition, managers who use management by exception may spend so much time on unfavourable variances that they fail to recognize employees who are responsible for favourable variances. By failing to recognize employees who do a good job, managers lose the benefit of positive reinforcement as a management tool.

Still another problem is that managers lose sight of the overall business operation as they focus on the multitude of details that have resulted in unfavourable variances. In time, managers focus so much on unfavourable variance details that they cannot see the forest for the trees. The overall performance of the company may suffer because managers are managing details while ignoring the big picture.

A summary of the problems associated with standard costing is presented in Exhibit 9–2. Take some time to become familiar with these problems.

Exhibit 9–2
Summary of Standard Costing Problems

> **Problems with Standard Costing**
>
> 1. Employees who help set standards try to avoid unfavourable variances by setting lax standards.
> 2. Reliance on historical information may perpetuate past inefficiencies in current standards.
> 3. Managers manage "by the numbers" and overlook significant problems that do not result in an unfavourable variance or waste time on insignificant unfavourable variances.
> 4. Managers focus so much on unfavourable variances that they fail to recognize employees who are doing a good job.
> 5. Managers focus so much on variances that they fail to see the big picture.

Who Uses Standard Costing?

Almost any business entity can use standard costing regardless of whether it is a for-profit or a not-for-profit organization. Service, merchandising, and manufacturing firms may use standard costing, although it is most often used by manufacturers. When it is appropriate to establish standards of performance for purposes of planning and control, standard costing can be used. For example, a tire store might establish a standard for the amount of time it should take to change a set of tires. An oil change centre might establish a standard for the amount of time it should take to change the oil and service an automobile. An airline catering company could develop standards for the quantity and price of each food item, the labour hours and labour rate to prepare each item, and a standard for the amount of overhead cost associated with the preparation of each item it sells.

In a manufacturing environment, a standard cost system is used to budget the cost of producing each individual unit of product. In effect, standard costing is like preparing a budget for a single unit of production. Managers estimate the cost of direct material, direct labour, variable manufacturing overhead, and fixed manufacturing overhead required to produce each item.

In Chapter 3 we discussed two types of cost systems. In an *actual cost system* we compute actual direct material, direct labour, and manufacturing overhead costs. In a *normal cost system* we compute actual direct material and actual direct labour costs, and use a predetermined rate for manufacturing overhead. Standard costing goes one step further. In a standard cost system, estimated amounts are used for direct material, direct labour, and manufacturing overhead. Exhibit 9–3 compares the three cost systems.

In the sections that follow, we discuss the details of how standard costing is used in manufacturing.

Exhibit 9–3
Comparison of Actual, Normal, and Standard Cost Systems

Cost Classification	Actual Cost System	Normal Cost System	Standard Cost System
Direct Material	Actual	Actual	Estimated
Direct Labour	Actual	Actual	Estimated
Manufacturing Overhead	Actual	Estimated	Estimated

 A User's View

Randy Hopkins is the owner-manager of Arbutus Service Centre, an automotive repair business located in Vancouver. The business has developed successfully over the past 20 years and, in addition to Randy and his assistant manager, Arbutus now employs six full-time mechanics. Randy's first love is working on cars, but over time he has had to develop a strong acumen for how to run a business. He has to ensure that he is running an efficient operation and that he is able to price his services to cover his costs and provide a return on his investment.

Randy has developed a standard costing system for his company. His most significant cost item is the salaries paid to his mechanics. In an effort to promote efficiency and to control this cost, he developed charge-out rates for his mechanics, based on their experience and ability, and he developed standards for routine services.

"In our business, it's a little harder to develop a precise standard, because you never know what you are going to find once you start working on a car. A simple oil change could lead to more complicated work if you find problems. But I have to have some way of monitoring my costs. By setting standards, I can pinpoint problems in our routine service work."

A User's View (continued)

Randy's accounting system provides management reports that compare operating results against a budget and to previous years. He is always conscious of the "three Cs" of management—customers, competitors, and costs. "We have built our client base by providing excellent work at competitive prices. A lot of my customers have been with me since the start. But I am well aware that our industry is very competitive, and if we don't perform we will lose customers. Because of this competitiveness, I have to manage my costs as effectively as possible in order to be profitable."

Basic Standard Costing for a Manufacturer

Standard costing is often used by manufacturing companies. Standards are set for direct material, direct labour, variable manufacturing overhead, and fixed manufacturing overhead. We will walk through the most commonly used standards and variances using Tree Top Mail Box Company as an example. Tree Top is a small company that makes a single product.

Tree Top Mail Box Company was founded by three college friends, Ali, Maria, and Bill. They started the company to earn spending money while they attended college. The trio had done some market research and determined that they could sell decorative wooden mail boxes for $10 each. They each planned to work about 60 hours per month for $10 per hour. Any remaining profits would be left in the company to be divided equally at the end of their venture.

The three entrepreneurs rented a garage to house the small company for $200 per month plus utilities. They purchased equipment, a table saw and drill press, for $900. The estimated useful life of the equipment is three years.

Exhibit 9–4
Tree Top's October 2004 Income Statement

Tree Top Mail Box Company
Income Statement
For the Month Ended October 31, 2004

Sales (300 mail boxes at $10 each)		$3,000
Less Expenses		
Direct Material	$ 600	
Direct Labour (180 hours at $10 per hour)	1,800	
Rent	200	
Utilities (all variable)	40	
Miscellaneous Variable Cost	30	
Amortization	25	2,695
Net Income		$ 305

In October, Tree Top's first month of operation, the company was able to sell every mail box produced. By the end of October, the three students had made and sold 300 boxes. As shown on the income statement in Exhibit 9–4, the company's profits for October totaled $305.

Discussion Questions

9–1. How did Ali, Maria, and Bill calculate the amortization expense of $25 per month?

9–2. Can you tell from Exhibit 9–4 whether the three Tree Top employees met their business goals in the month of October? Why or why not?

Ali, Maria, and Bill were thrilled that their equity in the company had grown by $305 in the first month. They felt that information for October's business activity could be used to develop a standard cost system to help manage their company.

SETTING DIRECT MATERIAL STANDARDS

As stated, setting direct material standards involves two important considerations: the quantity of material and the price paid. We now discuss each of these in some detail.

Direct Material Quantity Standard

direct material quantity standard The amount of direct material it should take to manufacture a single unit of product.

The amount of direct material it should take to make a single unit of production is called the **direct material quantity standard.** A bill of materials is often used to help establish the direct material quantity standard. A **bill of materials** is a listing of the quantity and description of each item of direct material used to manufacture an individual product. The bill of material for the 7ULTRA-A CB radio made by Cobra Electronics Corporation included just under 300 items, as shown in Exhibit 9–5.

bill of materials A listing of the quantity and description of each item of direct material used to manufacture an individual product.

Each item of direct material, from the speaker to the smallest resistor, is listed. With input from engineering, production, and other personnel, a bill of materials can be prepared and direct material quantity standards can be set. For Tree Top Mail Box Company, the bill of materials would be quite simple. Basically it involves only one direct material—wood.

To determine the direct material quantity standard for Tree Top Mail Box Company using practical standards, Ali measured the wood included in a single mail box. He determined that each mail box was made of five metres of 1 cm × 10 cm of pine. Then he examined the scrap wood from the prior week's production and estimated that the amount of wood to make a single mail box should be increased by 30 percent to allow for scrap due to knots and other expected defects in the wood. Accordingly, Tree Top adopted a practical direct material quantity standard of 6.5 metres (5 metres × 1.30% = 6.5 metres) per mail box.

Direct Material Price Standard

direct material price standard The anticipated cost for each item of direct material used in the manufacture of a product.

In addition to the amount of direct material used, the price per measure of direct material will affect the total cost of direct material. The **direct material price standard** is the anticipated cost for each item of direct material used in the manufacture of a product. For the plastic used to make golf balls, the direct material price standard would be the cost per kilogram of plastic. For wire used in a CD player, the direct material price standard would be the cost per metre of wire. Notice that

Exhibit 9–5

Bill of Materials for 7ULTRA-A CB Radio. © Cobra Electronics Corporation, Chicago, IL. Reprinted by permission.

BILL OF MATERIAL FOR 7ULTRA-A

COVER ASS'Y	
SPEAKER 8 OHM 0.3W 66MM P-250	
(+)TAPPING SCREW(BH)T3X6-2S (+)BH ZN-PLAT	SPK MTG:3
(+)TAPTITE SCREW(BH)T3X6 (+)BH BLK	UPPER.BOTTOM+ MAIN BODY:8
COVER UPPER ABS 94HB BLK	
COVER BOTTOM ABS 94HB BLK	
HOLDER(SPK)SPC 16X8XT1.2	SPK MTG:3
CUSHION 25X25XT5 RUBB.SP0.BLK STIC	
FELT &65XT0.3 FELT BLK	
FELT 10X110XT0.3 FELT STIC	
FELT 10X100XT0.3 FELT BLK	AIR VENT
ESCUTCHEON ASS'Y	
(+)MACHINE SCREW(FH)M2.6X4 (+)FH ZN-PLAT	
NUT M7 BSBM	
E.S.C ABS94 L153-S9001 BLK(7ULTRA-A)	
LENS ACRYL CLEAR	
KNOB(VOL.SQ) ABS 94HB BLK	95/08/18
KNOB(DOWN) ABS 94HB BLACK	95/08/18
KNOB(UP)ABS 94HB BLACK	
SPRING(COIL) SWP-3 &0.2	
FRONT BODY ASS'Y	
TRANSISTOR KTC2078(TO-220AB)	Q704
I.C KIA7217AP	IC401
P.C.B SUB 54X27X1.6	
JACK EARPHONE DHJ-3T	
CONNECTOR CH-239(A) SW-1229	
CONNECTOR SCN-16-4 PCB(R)	
MICA (FOR T.R 2SC2078)	
BUSHING(FOR T.R 2SC2078)	
VR10KB:15SK 161V	VR2
VR 50KA:RK16311116B153A	VR1
POWER CORD ASS'Y	
(+)MACHINE SCREW(BH)M3X10 (+)BH ZN-PLAT	TR:2
(+)TAPPING SCREW(BH)T3X6-2S (+)BH ZN-PLAT	M.P+MAIN BODY:4 HEAT SINK:1
NUT M3-1S SS41 ZN-PLAT	
WASHER SPRING M3 ZN-PLAT	TR:2
RIVET BLIND &3.2 ALB	NAME PLATE MTG:2
BODY MAIN EGI T1.0 US COATING	
HOLDER(ANT MTG)SPTE 29X35XT0.3 NI-PLAT	
CORD STOPPER P.P BLK	
ESD PROTECTOR CUP T0.05 (TRC-499)	
HEAT SINK ALP3 T2	IC MTG
HEAT SINK ALP3 T2	
SHIELD HOUSHING SPTE T0.3	
NAME PLATE ALP3 40X20XT0.4 (7ULTRA-A)	
MIC ASS'Y	
DISK CERAMIC 0.001UF DD330F102Z 50V	C959
MIC CONDENSER KUC4023-010010	
CURD CURLED 3CON 1SH 300MM BLK(KSK-23059)	
CONNECTOR PLUG SW-1461	
WIRE 1007 AWG 24 11/0.16 WHT	MIC(-)---SW
SW PUSH SPS-9522	
(-)SECURING SCREW M6X8 (P:1) ABS BLK	ACCESSORY
(+)TAPPING SCREW(PH)T3X8-2S (+)PH ZN-PLAT	ACCESSORY
(+)TAPPING SCREW(TH)T5X12-1S (+)TH ZN-PLAT	ACCESSORY
(+)WOOD SCREW (R+FH)2.7X18-1S (+)R+FH NI-PLAT	COVER MTG:3
WASHER 7X25X1.5T BLK RUBBER	ACCESSORY
WASHER(LOCK"B"TYPE) M3 "B"ZN-PLAT	ACCESSORY
ZN-PLAT	ACCESSORY
(+)PLUS SCREW(PH)3X10(+)PH ZN-PLAT	HOLDER MTG
COVER BOTTOM ABS 94HB BLK	
COVER UPPER(MIC)ABS 94HB BLK	
BRACKET (MIC)SPC 58X41XT1 CR-PLAT	
BRACKET(SET)SPC T1.5 BLK-SPRAY PICA	
HOLDER(MIC)PC BLK	
PLATE WEIGHT SPC 36X24XT3 ZN-PLAT	
KNOB(LEVER)ABS 94HB GRAY	
WIRE CLAMP (CORD)NYLON	
HOLDER(MIC) RUBB.(UL)BLK	
BOX MIC SW1S 222(W)X70(D)X52(H)	
POLYBAG P.P 100X100XT0.05	ACCESSORY
POLYBAG P.P 100X200XT0.05	
MAIN PCB AUTO ASS'Y	
FILM RESISTOR 100 1/ 8W 5% ST	R410.513.707.709
FILM RESISTOR 1K 1/ 8W 5% ST	R413.414.901
FILM RESISTOR 10K 1/ 8W 5% ST	R399.411.431. 502.508.515.964
FILM RESISTOR 100K 1/ 8W 5% ST	R404
FILM RESISTOR 1.2K 1/ 8W 5% ST	R518
FILM RESISTOR 150 1/ 8W 5% ST	R951-957
FILM RESISTOR 150K 1/ 8W 5% ST	R701
FILM RESISTOR 180 1/ 8W 5% ST	R962
FILM RESISTOR 1.8K 1/ 8W 5% ST	R420
FILM RESISTOR 22 1/ 8W 5% ST	R511
FILM RESISTOR 2.2K 1/ 8W 5% ST	R401.402.403.408.963
FILM RESISTOR 22K 1/ 8W 5% ST	R967
FILM RESISTOR 2.2 1/ 8W 5% ST	R711
FILM RESISTOR 270 1/ 8W 5% ST	R501
FILM RESISTOR 2.7K 1/ 8W 5% ST	R426.959
FILM RESISTOR 27K 1/ 8W 5% ST	R430
FILM RESISTOR 270K 1/ 8W 5% ST	R428.516
FILM RESISTOR 3.3K 1/ 8W 5% ST	R407.708
FILM RESISTOR 390 1/ 8W 5% ST	R510.702
FILM RESISTOR 3.9K 1/ 8W 5% ST	R406
FILM RESISTOR 47 1/ 8W 5% ST	R425.902
FILM RESISTOR 470 1/ 8W 5% ST	R512
FILM RESISTOR 4.7K 1/ 8W 5% ST	R503.703.704. 705.960
FILM RESISTOR 47K 1/ 8W 5% ST	R961
FILM RESISTOR 470K 1/ 8W 5% ST	R400
FILM RESISTOR 560 1/ 8W 5% ST	R504
FILM RESISTOR 5.6K 1/ 8W 5% ST	R405.409
FILM RESISTOR 68 1/ 8W 5% ST	R706
FILM RESISTOR 6.8K 1/ 8W 5% ST	R517
FILM RESISTOR 15K 1/ 8W 2% ST	R412
AXIAL CERAMIC 0.001UF UP050B102MK 50V	C404.426.427. 950.953.954
AXIAL CERAMIC 0.01UF EP050Y103MN 16V	C402.425.501. 504.508.518.520.
AXIAL CERAMIC 0.0022UF EP050X222MN 16V	C410
AXIAL CERAMIC 0.022UF RH050F 223Z 50V	C406.408.521.705.905
AXIAL CERAMIC 220PF UP050B221K 50V	C413.716
DIODE ZENER 1N5239B 9.1V 0.5W (DO-35)	D504
DIODE ZENER 1N5231B 5.1V 0.5W (DO-35)	D501
DIODE 1N4148(R.L)	D405.502.503.902.903
DIODE RECTIFIER 1N4004T/R 400V 1A (DO-41)	D404.701
COIL AXIAL 2.2UH:LAL03TB2R2M	RFC704
COIL AXIAL 6.8UH:LAL03TB6R8K	RFC509.706
COIL AXIAL 0.39UH:LAL02TBR39K	RFC701
MAIN PCB MANUAL ASSY	
METAL OXIDE RESISTOR15 2W 5% ST	R427
FILM RESISTOR 10 1/ 2W 5% ST MINI	R999
FILM RESISTOR 4.7K 1/ 2W 5% ST MINI	R712
RESISTOR SEMIFIXED 10KB RVM083H H 8DIA	RV1
RESISTOR SEMIFIXED 2K RVM083H	RV2
ELECT CAPACITOR 0.1UF 50V 20% 5X11	C403.956
ELECT CAPACITOR 10UF 16V 20% 5X11	C417.503.902
ELECT CAPACITOR 100UF 16V 20% 8X11	C424
ELECT CAPACITOR 10UF 16V 20% 4X7	C411
ELECT CAPACITOR 1000UF 16V 20% 12X16	C423
ELECT CAPACITOR 2.2UF 50V 20% 5X11	C707
ELECT CAPACITOR 220UF 16V 20% 10X12	C422.514
ELECT CAPACITOR 3.3UF 50V 20% 5X11	C416.421
ELECT CAPACITOR 33UF 16V 20% 5X11	C407.412.415
ELECT CAPACITOR 47UF 16V 20% 6X11	C430.515
ELECT CAPACITOR 470UF 16V 20% 10X12	C502.510
DISK CERAMIC 0.01UF HIK(B)F 103 50V	C721.722.723
DISK CERAMIC 0.022UF F 223Z 50V	C711.714
DISK CERAMIC 0.047UF X 473M 50V	C414.418
AXIAL CERAMIC 0.047UF SA105E473MAA 50V	C405
NPO100D 50V	
DISK CERAMIC 100PF NPO101K 50V	C712.718.999
DISK CERAMIC 12PF NPO120K 50V	C513.903
DISK CERAMIC 150PF SL 151K 50V	C715
DISK CERAMIC 270PF SL 271K 50V	C420
DISK CERAMIC 330PF SL 331K 50V	C717
DISK CERAMIC 39PF NPO390K 50V	C704
DISK CERAMIC 4PF NPO040D 50V	C706
DISK CERAMIC 470PF SL 471K 50V	C713
DISK CERAMIC 5PF NPO050D 50V	C506
DISK CERAMIC 82PF NPO820K 50V	C708
DIP TANTALUM 1UF 489D105X0025A125V	C957.958
DIP TRIMMER 20PF 6DIA CVN	CT1
TRANSISTOR KTC3194(O)	Q701.702
TRANSISTOR KTC3198(GR)	Q400.401.505.507
TRANSISTOR KTA1266(GR)	Q402.501.502. 503.506
TRANSISTOR KTC1006 (TO-92L)	Q703
I.C C5122A1P	IC501
DIODE GE 1N60	D402.403
CRYSTAL HC18U 10.240M 30PM	X1
FILTER CERAMIC LTU455HT	CF2
FILTER CERAMIC SK107M4-AC-20	CF1
TRASNFORMER CHOKE EI-19	CH1
TRANSFORMER POWER EI-24	T1
COIL RF CHOKE 0.8UH SPRING	RFC401
COIL SPRING 5X0.6X13.5T:R	RFC709
COIL SPRING 3.4X0.55X8.5T:R	RFC705
COIL RF CHOKE 10UH 10%	RFC707
COIL IFT 455KHZ-A	L902
COIL IFT 455KHZ-B	L903
COIL 27MHZ RX ANT	L901
COIL VCO	L501
COIL RF PRE AMP A TX27MHZ	L701.702
P.C.B MAIN 150 X121.5X1.6 94HB1/0	
MAIN PCB SMD ASS'Y	
F AMP MODULE ASS'Y	
CHIP RESISTOR 0 1/10W 5% T 2012	R200.219
CHIP RESISTOR 100 1/10W 5% T 2012	R203
CHIP RESISTOR 1K 1/10W 5% T 2012	R209
CHIP RESISTOR 10K 1/10W 5% T 2012	R207
CHIP RESISTOR 12K 1/10W 5% T 2012	R211
CHIP RESISTOR 15K 1/10W 5% T 2012	R218
CHIP RESISTOR 150K 1/10W 5% T 2012	R205
CHIP RESISTOR 1.8K 1/10W 5% T 2012	R206
CHIP RESISTOR 220 1/10W 5% T 2012	R212
CHIP RESISTOR 22K 1/10W 5% T 2012	R213
CHIP RESISTOR 3.3K 1/10W 5% T 2012	R210
CHIP RESISTOR 33K 1/10W 5% T 2012	R217
CHIP RESISTOR 3.9K 1/10W 5% T 2012	R202
CHIP RESISTOR 470 1/10W 5% T 2012	R204.208
CHIP RESISTOR 47K 1/10W 5% T 2012	R214.216
CHIP RESISTOR 560 1/10W 5% T 2012	R201
CHIP RESISTOR 82K 1/10W 5% T 2012	R215
ELECT CAPACITOR 1UF 50V 20% 4X7	C209
ELECT CAPACITOR 10UF 16V 20% 4X7	C204
CHIP CERAMIC 0.001UF CM21 X7R102K 50V AT	C206
CHIP CERAMIC 0.01UF CM21 X7R103K 50V AT	C201.203
CHIP CERAMIC 0.047UF CM21 X7R473K 50V AT	C202.205.207.208
TRANSISTOR KTA1504SY(SOT-23)	Q204
TRANSISTOR KTC3880SY(SOT-23)	Q201.202.203
DIODE GE 1N60	D201
P.C.B IF MODULE 44X16.88X1.6 94HB1/1	
VCO MODULE ASS'Y	
CHIP RESISTOR 0 1/10W 5% T 2012	R600.609
CHIP RESISTOR 10K 1/10W 5% T 2012	R606.607
CHIP RESISTOR 120K 1/10W 5% T 2012	R603
CHIP RESISTOR 22K 1/10W 5% T 2012	R608
CHIP RESISTOR 220K 1/10W 5% T 2012	R604
CHIP RESISTOR 2.7K 1/10W 5% T 2012	R605
CHIP RESISTOR 47 1/10W 5% T 2012	R601
CHIP RESISTOR 820 1/10W 5% T 2012	R602
CHIP CERAMIC 0.01UF CM21 X7R103K 50V AT	C601.610.611
CHIP CERAMIC 120PF CM21 CG 121J 50V AT	C608
CHIP CERAMIC 18PF CM21 CG 180J 50V AT	C602
CHIP CERAMIC 22PF CM21 CG 220J 50V AT	C603
CHIP CERAMIC 220PF CM21 CG 221J 50V AT	C607
CHIP CERAMIC 27PF CM21CG 270J 50V AT	C609
CHIP CERAMIC 33PF CM21 CG 330J 50V AT	C606
CHIP CERAMIC 47PF CM21 CG 470J 50V AT	C605
TRANSISTOR KTC3875SY	Q602
TRANSISTOR KTC3880SY(SOT-23)	Q601.603
DIODE VARICAP LV2209	D601
P.C.B VCO MODULE 30.7 X16.88X1.6 94HB1/1	
LOW PASS FILTER MODU	
CHIP CERAMIC 220PF CM21 CG 221J 50V AT	C801.805
CHIP CERAMIC 470PF CM21 CG 471J 50V AT	C802.803
COIL SPRING 3.4X0.55X6.5T:R	L802
COIL SPRING 3.4X0.55X7.5T:R	L803
COIL SPRING 3.4X0.55X8.5T:R	L804
P.C.B LPF MODULE 15.39X40.5 X1.6 94HB1/1	
4.5T SPRIN.COIL ASSY	L801
COIL SPRING 3.4X0.55X4.5T:R	
CORE 1108-KA-058 M9DTH3.7X6	
RF AMP H/H MODULE	
CHIP RESISTOR 0 1/10W 5% T 2012	
CHIP RESISTOR 100 1/10W 5% T 2012	R107
CHIP RESISTOR 10K 1/10W 5% T 2012	R106.108
CHIP RESISTOR 18 1/10W 5% T 2012	R104
CHIP RESISTOR 330 1/10W 5% T 2012	R103
CHIP RESISTOR 33K 1/10W 5% T 2012	R105
CHIP RESISTOR 470 1/10W 5% T 2012	R109.110
CHIP CERAMIC 0.01UF CM21 X7R103K 50V AT	C112
CHIP CERAMIC 150PF CM21 CG 151J 50V AT	C109
CHIP CERAMIC 220PF CM21 CG 221J 50V AT	C108
CHIP CERAMIC 33PF CM21 CG 330J 50V AT	C102
CHIP CERAMIC 47PF CM21 CG 470J 50V AT	C104
CHIP CERAMIC 680PF CM21 CG 681J 50V AT	C114
TRANSISTOR KTC3880SY (SOT-23)	Q102.103
DIODE SI CHIP KDS226 (SOT-23)	D101
P.C.B RF MODULE 39.25X16.88X1.6 94HB1/1	
6.5T SPRIN.COIL ASSY	L102.104
COIL SPRING 3.4X0.55X6.5T:R	
CORE 1108-KA-058 M9DTH3.7X6	
PACKING ASS'Y	
BOX TRAY SW1S 222(W)X127(D)X52(H)	
BOX INNER SW1S 224(W)X220(D)X54(H)	
BOX OUT DW1E 355(W)X238(D)X206(H)	
POLYBAG P.P 200X300XT0.05	SET:1 MANUAL:1
MANUAL OWNER'S MANUAL OWNER'S	
CARD REGISTRATION ARTPAPER 158X342	
CARD BOARD	
CB RULE	
SCHEMATIC DIAGRAM WOODFREEPAPER 420X297	
CARD INFORMATION WOODFREEPAPER 98.5X150	
LABEL CAUTION	
LABEL FCC POLYESTER 67X10XT0.05	
SUB PCB ASS'Y	
FILM RESISTOR 10K 1/ 8W 5% ST	R950
LED LAMP SLB55VR3 RED 3 V 60MW	LED1
LED DISPLAY UL-G233G-13 GRN	
SW TACT SAT-1102-2	SW3.4
SUB MATERIAL ASS'Y	
TUBE UL/CSA KEIT-30 AWG 12 (2&) CLEAR VINYL	
TUBE UL/CSA KEIT-30 AWG 2 (6.5&) CLEAR VINYL	
TUBE HIS 11M/M	
TUBE EMPIRE 1&	
PE SCOTCH 15M/M (0.015X20M)	
TAPE PACKING OPP (0.05X50M)	
TAPE PACKING O.P.P.(0.05X25M) IVORY	
SOLDER BAR 63:37	
SOLDER ROSIN CO.WIRE60:40 0.04"-0.05"	
FLUX ROSIN	
THINNER FOR FLUX	
SILICON GREASE YG-6111 OR XG-6111	
STAVILIZER MATERIAL	
BOND #201	
COMPOUND #1200 500GR	

the direct material price standard reflects a price per measure of direct material (that is, per metre of wire), *not* per unit of production (such as, per CD player).

Because purchasing agents are generally knowledgeable about the price paid for direct material, they are likely to be key players in determining direct material price standards. Purchasing agents would also gather historical direct material price information, making necessary adjustments for any anticipated price changes.

As indicated, Tree Top uses pine wood. The direct material price standard is expressed as an amount per metre of this wood. Tree Top Mail Box Company has no purchasing agent, so Ali shopped around and found that good-quality pine wood could be purchased for $0.30 per metre. Also, Ali determined that no price increases were expected during the year. Accordingly, Tree Top established a standard price per metre of wood of $0.30 per metre.

Although only a single direct material is used to make Tree Top's mail boxes, most products require the use of many different raw materials. Separate standards must be established for each direct material used in production. If production required the use of material A, material B, and material C, separate quantity and price standards must be prepared for each.

Once a manufacturer knows the direct material quantity standard and the direct material price standard, the standard cost for direct material per unit of production can be determined. For Tree Top, the standard cost for direct material of $1.95 is calculated by multiplying the standard quantity of 6.5 metres by the standard price of $0.30, as shown.

$$\begin{array}{ccccc}
\text{Standard} & & \text{Standard} & & \text{Standard Direct} \\
\text{Quantity} & \times & \text{Price} & = & \text{Material Cost} \\
& & & & \text{Per Unit} \\
\\
\text{6.5 Metres} & \times & \$0.30 & = & \$1.95
\end{array}$$

SETTING DIRECT LABOUR STANDARDS

As with direct material, setting direct labour standards involves two important considerations: the number of direct labour hours and the wage rate per hour.

Direct Labour Efficiency Standard

direct labour efficiency standard The estimated number of direct labour hours required to produce a single unit of product.

The estimated number of direct labour hours required to produce a single unit of product is called the **direct labour efficiency standard.** When the direct labour force works efficiently, labour hours are kept to a minimum. Conversely, too many hours of direct labour relative to production would indicate labour inefficiency. The standard for the number of direct labour hours could be called the direct labour quantity standard, or the direct labour hours standard, but neither of these terms sounds quite right, which explains why this standard has come to be known as the direct labour efficiency standard.

The production supervisors and other production employees are often key players in establishing direct labour efficiency standards. Historical information about direct labour and production volumes are used to help establish an appropriate standard for the number of direct labour hours per unit of production. Also, information from industrial engineers, such as the results of time-and-motion studies, may be helpful in determining the amount of direct labour time it should take to efficiently produce a unit of product.

Tree Top's founders wanted to select a standard that would help encourage them to make as many mail boxes as possible, but allow them to work at a quick, yet reasonable pace. After reviewing their activities for October, the three agreed that the standard hours allowed for a single unit of production should be 0.6 hours (36 minutes). This time, then, became Tree Top's labour efficiency standard.

Direct Labour Rate Standard

direct labour rate standard The planned hourly wage paid to production workers.

The **direct labour rate standard** is the planned hourly wage paid to production workers. The personnel manager is often a key player in determining the direct labour rate standard. Sometimes direct labour rates are established through collective bargaining or other employment agreements. Other times a less formal procedure is used to set hourly pay rates. In either case, historical information coupled with information regarding anticipated pay rate changes establishes the direct labour rate standard. Often, companies compute an expected average hourly direct labour rate, which is used as the factory-wide direct labour rate standard. For Tree Top, Ali, Maria, and Bill agreed that, based on their original plan, the direct labour rate standard of $10 per hour should be used.

Once a company knows the direct labour efficiency standard and the direct labour rate standard, the standard labour cost per unit of production can be determined. In the case of Tree Top, based on the direct labour efficiency standard of 0.6 hours and the direct labour rate standard of $10 per direct labour hour, the standard labour cost to make a single mail box is $6, shown as follows:

Direct Labour Efficiency Standard		Direct Labour Rate Standard (Per Hour)		Standard Direct Labour Cost Per Unit
0.6 Hours	×	$10 Per Hour	=	$6

SETTING VARIABLE MANUFACTURING OVERHEAD STANDARDS

Recall that manufacturing overhead includes all production costs that are not part of direct materials or direct labour. Manufacturing overhead includes costs of operating the factory such as the cost of rent, insurance, amortization, supplies, taxes, raw materials handling, and so forth. Recall also that costs can be classified as either fixed or variable. Fixed costs are those that remain constant in total, even as activity changes. Variable costs, in contrast, increase in total as activity changes. Therefore, variable manufacturing overhead would include those manufacturing overhead costs that increase in total as production increases.

In Chapter 3, we saw that manufacturing overhead was often allocated to production based on direct labour hours, direct labour cost, machine hours, or some other allocation base. In this section, we illustrate how a standard cost system works when manufacturing overhead is allocated using direct labour hours as the allocation base. Although the specific calculations would be somewhat different, standard costing can be used for other allocation bases as well.

To set standards for variable manufacturing overhead, managers must first estimate variable manufacturing overhead costs. Once they estimate total variable manufacturing overhead, they can then determine a cost per direct labour hour, or per unit of some other allocation base.

For Tree Top Mail Box Company, variable manufacturing overhead cost includes utilities and miscellaneous variable cost as shown on October's income statement presented in Exhibit 9–4. The miscellaneous variable cost includes the cost of indirect material such as glue, small nails, and wood stain. Based on October's results, Ali, Maria, and Bill estimated that variable manufacturing overhead cost would be about $63. The $63 includes $33 for utilities and $30 for miscellaneous variable cost. Tree Top planned to allocate this variable overhead cost to production based on direct labour hours.

The Standard Variable Manufacturing Overhead Rate

standard variable manufacturing overhead rate The rate used to apply variable manufacturing overhead to units of manufactured product.

The rate used to apply variable manufacturing overhead to units of product is known as the **standard variable manufacturing overhead rate.** As stated, Ali, Maria, and Bill expected to work about 60 hours each, or a total of 180 direct labour hours per month. Based on the planned variable manufacturing overhead cost of $63 and 180 estimated direct labour hours, we compute a standard variable overhead rate of $0.35 by dividing the $63 budgeted variable manufacturing overhead by the 180 estimated direct labour hours, as follows:

$$
\begin{array}{ccc}
\text{Budgeted Variable} & \text{Budgeted} & \text{Standard} \\
\text{Manufacturing} \div & \text{Direct Labour} = & \text{Variable Manufacturing} \\
\text{Overhead} & \text{Hours} & \text{Overhead Rate} \\
\\
\$63 \quad\quad \div & 180 \text{ Hours} = & \$0.35 \text{ Per Hour}
\end{array}
$$

When the variable manufacturing overhead allocation is based on direct labour hours, once the direct labour efficiency standard and the standard variable manufacturing overhead rate per direct labour hour have been determined, the standard variable manufacturing overhead cost per unit can be determined. The standard variable manufacturing overhead cost to build a single unit of production is calculated by multiplying the direct labour efficiency standard (the estimated direct labour hours per unit) by the standard variable manufacturing overhead rate. For Tree Top, standard cost per unit for variable manufacturing overhead is $0.21, determined as follows:

$$
\begin{array}{ccc}
\text{Standard} & \text{Standard} & \text{Standard Variable} \\
\text{Direct Labour} \times & \text{Variable Manufacturing} = & \text{Mfg Overhead} \\
\text{Hours Allowed} & \text{Overhead Rate} & \text{Cost Per Unit} \\
\\
0.6 \text{ Hours} \quad \times & \$0.35 \text{ Per Hour} \quad = & \$0.21
\end{array}
$$

SETTING FIXED MANUFACTURING OVERHEAD STANDARDS

Unlike variable manufacturing overhead cost, which changes in total as production increases or decreases, fixed manufacturing overhead cost remains constant in total regardless of how many units are produced.

To set the fixed manufacturing overhead standards, manufacturers must first estimate the total cost of fixed manufacturing overhead. For Tree Top Mail Box Company, this amount consists of rent of $200 per month and monthly amortization of $25 for the equipment used to make the mail boxes. Fixed manufacturing overhead then totals $225 per month ($200 + $25 = $225).

Standard Fixed Manufacturing Overhead Rate

standard fixed manufacturing overhead rate The rate used to apply fixed manufacturing overhead to units of manufactured product.

As with variable manufacturing overhead, fixed manufacturing overhead can be allocated to production based on units of production, direct labour hours, direct labour dollars, machine hours, or some other allocation base. The rate used to apply fixed manufacturing overhead to units of product is known as the **standard fixed manufacturing overhead rate.**

Our illustration assumes that fixed manufacturing overhead is allocated to production based on direct labour hours. In such a case, the standard fixed manufacturing overhead rate is determined by dividing the total estimated fixed manufacturing overhead cost by the total estimated direct labour hours. In the case of Tree Top Mail Box Company, the standard fixed manufacturing overhead rate of $1.25 per direct labour hour is calculated by dividing the budgeted fixed manufacturing overhead cost of $225 by the budgeted direct labour hours of 180 as shown here:

$$
\begin{array}{ccc}
\text{Budgeted} & \text{Budgeted} & \text{Standard} \\
\text{Fixed Mfg} \div & \text{Direct Labour} = & \text{Fixed Mfg} \\
\text{Overhead} & \text{Hours} & \text{Overhead Rate} \\
\\
\$225 \quad \div & 180 \text{ Hours} = & \$1.25
\end{array}
$$

We calculate the standard fixed manufacturing overhead cost to build a single unit of product by multiplying the direct labour efficiency standard per unit by the standard fixed manufacturing overhead rate. For Tree Top, standard cost per unit for fixed manufacturing overhead is $0.75, determined as follows:

Standard Direct Labour Hours Allowed	×	Standard Fixed Mfg Overhead Rate	=	Standard Fixed Mfg Overhead Cost Per Unit
0.6 Hours	×	$1.25 Per Hour	=	$0.75

Total Standard Cost Per Unit   Once standards have been set for direct material, direct labour, variable manufacturing overhead, and fixed manufacturing overhead, the total standard cost per unit can be calculated. This amount reflects how much it *should* cost to produce a unit of product. The standard cost per unit represents a useful estimate that can be helpful for planning and setting selling prices. For Tree Top, the total standard cost per mail box is $8.91 as shown in Exhibit 9–6.

Exhibit 9–6
Total Standard Cost Per Mail Box Built

Standard Direct Material Cost Per Mail Box	$1.95
Standard Direct Labour Cost Per Mail Box	6.00
Standard Variable Manufacturing Overhead Cost Per Mail Box	0.21
Standard Fixed Manufacturing Overhead Cost Per Mail Box	0.75
Total Standard Cost Per Mail Box	$8.91

As you might imagine, the *actual* cost of producing an item is almost never exactly the same as the *standard* cost. When actual cost exceeds standard cost, management should take steps to determine the cause of the variance, and, if necessary, take corrective action.

Actual total production cost that exceeds the standard may indicate that a general problem exists, but it provides almost no information that can help managers focus on the true cause of the problem. Managers need access to information that can be used to isolate and address specific cost problems.

The next sections show how managers use standard costing to isolate specific problems for each production cost category.

VARIANCE ANALYSIS

Standard costs can help control costs by serving as benchmarks to compare with actual production costs. To use standard costing as a control device, managers compare *standard costs* to *actual costs* to see whether a variance exists. Instead of calculating a single variance for total production cost, they make variances specific enough to isolate a particular production process problem. In this section we examine how detailed standard costs variances are calculated for direct material, direct labour, variable manufacturing overhead, and fixed manufacturing overhead. We will walk through the calculations for each standard cost variance using Tree Top Mail Box Company as an example.

Exhibit 9–7
Tree Top's November
2004 Income Statement

TREE TOP MAIL BOX COMPANY		
Income Statement		
For the Month Ended November 30, 2004		
Sales (225 mail boxes at $10 each)		$2,250
Less Expenses		
Direct Material (1,640 metres of wood)	$ 477	
Direct Labour (162 hours at $10.50 per hour)	1,701	
Rent	200	
Utilities (all variable)	50	
Miscellaneous Variable Costs	90	
Amortization	25	2,543
Net Income (Loss)		$ (293)

Unfortunately for Tree Top, November was not nearly as successful as October. The company produced and sold only 225 mail boxes in spite of demand for many more. The income statement for the month of November appears in Exhibit 9–7.

November's loss disturbed Ali, Maria, and Bill because they had spent nearly as much time at the shop as in October, but produced far fewer mail boxes. The question is, what changes should Tree Top make to get the company back on track? We can answer this question once we have calculated the variances and examined their causes.

To calculate standard cost variances, we use the standard costs discussed in the preceding sections, and compare them with Tree Top's actual performance. Actual performance data are obtained from various sources, including company reports and files. In our Tree Top Mail Box Company example, we have included the key details in November's income statement, presented in Exhibit 9–7.

Direct Materials Variances

Direct material variances can be used to answer three important questions. (1) Did the company use more or less direct material than it should have, based on the standards set? (2) Did the company pay more or less than it should have when the direct material was purchased from the supplier based on the standards set? (3) What was the cost impact of these quantity and price differences?

Direct Material Quantity Variance

direct material quantity variance A measure of the over- or underconsumption of direct material for the number of units actually manufactured.

direct material usage variance Another name for the *direct material quantity variance.*

The **direct material quantity variance,** sometimes called the **direct material usage variance,** is a measure of the overconsumption or underconsumption of direct material for the number of units actually manufactured. It informs management whether too much or too little direct material is used in the manufacturing process based on the standards. The direct material quantity variance is the difference between the standard quantity and the actual quantity of direct materials used. We follow three steps to calculate the direct material quantity variances. First, we calculate the standard quantity of direct material allowed for actual production. Second, we calculate the variance in units of direct material. Finally, we calculate the variance in dollars.

Step 1: Calculate the standard quantity of direct material allowed for actual production.

The standard quantity of direct material allowed is the amount needed for actual production, according to the standard. It is the amount *allowed* for *actual* production. To calculate this amount, we determine how much direct material should have been used according to the standard to make the units actually produced.

Recall that Tree Top produced 225 mail boxes in November. To determine the quantity of the wood that *should* have been used to make 225 mail boxes, we multiply the direct material quantity standard (6.5 metres per unit) by the number of mail boxes produced (225). For Tree Top, the standard quantity of direct material allowed for the actual production of 225 mail boxes is 1,462.5 metres, as shown here:

Standard Quantity Per Unit	×	Number of Units Produced	=	Standard Quantity of Direct Material Allowed
6.5 Metres	×	225 Units	=	1,462.5 Metres

We see from the calculations that 1,462.5 metres of wood is the standard direct material quantity allowed for the units produced—the direct material quantity that *should* have been used based on the number of units *actually* produced.

Step 2: Calculate the direct material quantity variance in units of direct material.

We calculate the direct material quantity variance in units of direct material by subtracting the actual quantity of direct material used from the standard quantity of direct material allowed. For Tree Top Mail Box Company, the direct material quantity variance in metres is determined by comparing the quantity of wood it *should* have taken to make the 225 mail boxes (determined in step 1) to the quantity of wood it *actually* took to make the mail boxes (the actual quantity).

 Discussion Question

9–3. If the actual amount of wood used was more than the standard quantity of wood, do you think the direct material quantity variance would be favourable or unfavourable? Explain your reasoning.

To use standard costing, a manufacturer must maintain a record of the quantity of direct material used in production. In the case of Tree Top, this information is found in the income statement as presented in Exhibit 9–7. A review of that income statement shows that the actual quantity of direct material Tree Top used to make the 225 mail boxes in November was 1,640 metres of wood. Often the quantity of material used in production differs from the quantity of material purchased. For this calculation it is important to remember to use the quantity of material used, not the quantity purchased.

Tree Top's direct material quantity variance is calculated by finding the difference between the standard quantity of direct material allowed and the quantity of direct material used in production. In this case the variance is 177.5 unfavourable, as calculated here:

Standard Quantity Allowed for Production	–	Actual Quantity Used	=	Quantity Variance in Metres
1,462.5 Metres	–	1,640 Metres	=	177.5 Unfavourable

We can see from the presentation that Ali, Maria, and Bill used 177.5 more metres of wood than the standard allowed to make the 225 mail boxes. Does this overuse of direct material really matter? Even if the direct material quantity variance in metres is 177.5 unfavourable, it *may* represent an insignificant dollar amount. To evaluate whether this variance is worthy of attention, we need to assign a dollar amount.

Step 3: Calculate the direct material quantity variance in dollars.

To avoid contaminating the quantity variance with problems relating to the actual price paid for material, the dollar amount assigned to the direct material quantity variance is based on the standard direct material price, not the actual price. Tree Top's direct material quantity variance in dollars is $53.25. This amount is calculated by multiplying the direct material quantity variance (177.5 metres) by the direct material standard price of $0.30, as follows:

Quantity Variance in Units of Direct Material (metres)		Standard Price Per Unit of Direct Material (metres)		Quantity Variance in Dollars
177.5 Unfavourable	×	$0.30	=	$53.25 Unfavourable

The direct materials quantity variance in dollars provides valuable information about the cost of using too much direct material to make the mail boxes. Now that a dollar amount has been assigned to the variance, we can evaluate its importance and devote the amount of management attention that is appropriate.

 Discussion Questions

9–4. Based on Tree Top Mail Box Company's quantity variance, do you think that Ali, Maria, and Bill need to examine reasons for using so much wood? Explain your reasoning.

9–5. If the dollar amount of a variance is insignificant, does the variance information help Tree Top's management team determine where it should focus attention? Explain.

9–6. If there had been no variance, would this mean Tree Top used the appropriate amount of wood to build its mail boxes in November? Explain your reasoning.

We assume that only one direct material is used to make the mail boxes for Tree Top. In practice most products require several different direct materials, ranging from one to thousands, and a separate material quantity variance is computed for each direct material used. The logic and computations, however, are similar to those presented here.

Once the direct material quantity variance has been calculated, management can assess the situation and, if necessary, take corrective action. Generally, a quantity variance should be discussed with the individuals who are responsible for the amount of direct material used. The focus of the discussion should be on finding and eliminating the cause of the variance. In many companies, the person responsible for direct material consumption is the production supervisor, who would attempt to determine the cause of the variance and take steps to eliminate it.

Direct Material Price Variance

direct material price variance A measure of the difference between the amount the company planned to pay for direct material purchased and the amount it actually paid for the direct material.

The **direct material price variance** is a measure of the difference between the amount the company *planned* to pay for direct material and the amount it *actually* paid. This variance provides an indication of whether the price paid to suppliers for direct material compares favourably to the standard price. To find the direct material price variance we use a two-step process. First, we determine the amount that should have been paid for the direct material. Second, we calculate the dollar amount of the direct material variance.

Step 1: Determine the amount that should have been paid for the direct material purchased according to the standard price.

According to the detailed information on November's income statement, Tree Top Mail Box Company purchased 1,640 metres of wood. How much should the company have paid for the 1,640 metres of wood if it had been able to purchase it at the standard price? We determine this amount by multiplying the actual quantity of direct material purchased by the standard price. Often the quantity of material purchased differs from the quantity of material used in production. Which amount should we use? For this calculation remember to use the quantity of material purchased, not the quantity used in production.

Actual Quantity Purchased	×	Direct Material Standard Price	=	Quantity Purchased Priced at Standard
1,640 Metres	×	$0.30	=	$492

Our calculations show that, based on the standard price of $0.30 per metre, the 1,640 metres of wood purchased should have cost $492.

Step 2: Calculate the dollar amount of the direct material price variance.

We calculate the dollar amount of the direct material price variance by subtracting the actual cost of direct material from the standard cost of the direct material purchased (determined in step 1). According to the detailed information on November's income statement, Tree Top purchased the 1,640 metres of wood for $477. By comparing the standard cost of $492 to the actual cost of $477, we determine that the price variance is $15 favourable.

Quantity Purchased Priced at Standard	−	Actual Direct Material Cost	=	Direct Material Price Variance
$492	−	$477	=	$15 Favourable

To review the calculations for the direct material price variance in dollars, we compare the amount the wood purchased *should* have cost, $492, to what the wood *actually* cost, $477, to determine the direct material price variance.

When a product requires the use of multiple direct materials, a separate material price variance is computed for each direct material used. The logic and computations, however, are similar to those presented here.

Once the direct material price variance has been calculated, management can assess the situation and, if necessary, take corrective action. In most manufacturing companies, direct material is purchased by purchasing agents working in the company's purchasing department. Therefore, direct material price variances are brought to the attention of the purchasing agent responsible for buying the particular direct material so that the price can be evaluated and corrective action taken when necessary.

In the case of Tree Top, the actual price paid for the wood was lower than the standard price, resulting in a favourable direct material price variance. It may seem that a favourable variance would not warrant investigation, but this is not always the case.

A significant favourable variance is worth examining for several reasons. First, repeated favourable variances may be an indication that the standard is too lax. Second, management should investigate the variance to see whether the techniques used to achieve the favourable variance can be used by other areas of the company to help reduce cost. Third, a favourable variance may have occurred because of a trade-off of some other value. For example, it might be achieved by purchasing direct material of a substandard quality.

Bill purchased the wood for Tree Top from the lumber company at a discounted price. The lumber company was able to offer the discount because another customer had refused the wood and the lumber company was overstocked. As it turned out, the wood had an unusually high number of knots and other blemishes. The substandard wood, then, may have caused the use of more direct material and direct labour than would have otherwise been required for production.

 ## Discussion Questions

9-7. How might the purchase of wood at a discount affect the direct material quantity variance?

9-8. If there had been no variance, would this mean Tree Top paid what it should have for the wood used to build its mail boxes in November? Explain your reasoning.

Direct Labour Variances

Direct labour variances help managers answer three key questions. (1) Did it take more or fewer direct labour hours than it should have taken for the company to manufacture its products based on the standards set? (2) Was the company's hourly direct labour rate more or less than it should have been based on the standards set? (3) What was the cost impact of these differences in the number of direct labour hours and the hourly labour rate?

It may be helpful to consider some parallels between direct material and direct labour. Instead of using "quantities" and "prices" terms as for direct material, we use "hours" and "rates" with direct labour. In reality, only the descriptive words change; the meanings stay the same. The "quantity" of direct material is similar to the "hours" of direct labour. Likewise, the "price" per measure of direct material is similar to the "rate" per hour of direct labour. Because of these similarities, the steps and calculations of standard cost variances for direct labour are comparable to direct material variances.

direct labour efficiency variance A measure of the difference between the planned number of direct labour hours and the actual number of direct labour hours for the units actually manufactured.

Direct Labour Efficiency Variance

The **direct labour efficiency variance** is a measure of the overconsumption or underconsumption of direct labour for the number of units actually manufactured. In other words, the direct labour efficiency variance informs management whether too much or too little direct labour is used in the manufacturing process based on the standards. This variance is comparable to the direct material quantity variance.

Both are used to evaluate the quantity of something used. In the case of the direct material quantity variance, the focus is on the quantity of direct material used. In the case of the direct labour efficiency variance, the focus is on the quantity of direct labour hours used.

We use three steps to calculate this variance. First, we find the standard number of direct labour hours allowed for production. Second, we determine the variance in hours. Finally, we calculate the variance in dollars.

Step 1: Calculate the standard number of direct labour hours allowed for actual production.

In this first step we determine the amount of direct labour time it *should* have taken to make all the units that were *actually* made during the period. According to the direct labour efficiency standard for Tree Top, it should have taken 0.6 hours (36 minutes) to make each mail box. Because 225 mail boxes were made in November, the total amount of direct labour hours should have been 135 hours ($225 \times 0.6 = 135$).

Step 2: Calculate the direct labour efficiency variance in hours.

We compute the direct labour efficiency variance in hours by subtracting the standard direct labour hours allowed from the actual number of direct labour hours worked. According to information taken from Tree Top's November income statement presented in Exhibit 9–7, the actual number of direct labour hours used in November was 162. By comparing the standard hours allowed for the 225 mail boxes, 135 hours, to the actual direct labour hours, 162 hours, we see that the direct labour efficiency variance in hours is 27 hours unfavourable.

Standard Direct Labour Hours Allowed		Actual Direct Labour Hours		Efficiency Variance in Hours
135 Hours	−	162 Hours	=	27 Hours Unfavourable

The variance between the standard and actual number of hours worked indicates that Tree Top's employees did not work very efficiently. If they had, they would have completed the 225 mail boxes in 135 hours, or maybe even less.

To grasp the true magnitude of the 27-hour unfavourable variance, we must assign a dollar amount.

Step 3: Calculate the direct labour efficiency variance in dollars.

To avoid contaminating the efficiency variance with problems relating to the actual labour rate, we calculate the direct labour efficiency variance in dollars by multiplying the variance in hours by the standard direct labour rate, not the actual labour rate. In the case of Tree Top, we multiply the 27-hour unfavourable direct labour efficiency variance by the standard direct labour rate of $10, shown as follows:

Direct Labour Efficiency Variance in Hours		Standard Direct Labour Rate		Direct Labour Efficiency Variance in Dollars
27 Hours	×	$10	=	$270 Unfavourable

Once the direct labour efficiency variance has been calculated, management can assess the variance and, if necessary, take corrective action. The factory manager would probably ask the production supervisor or production-line employees to help determine why the unfavourable variance occurred. Once the cause of the problem is found, corrective action can be taken.

Tree Top determined that substandard wood caused the unfavourable direct labour efficiency variance. To make mail boxes of sufficient quality, Ali, Maria, and

Bill needed extra time to cut the knots and other blemishes from the wood. The solution to the variance problem is to purchase only good-quality wood in the future.

Direct Labour Rate Variance

direct labour rate variance
A measure of the difference between the actual wage rate paid to employees and the direct labour rate standard.

The **direct labour rate variance** is a measure of the difference between the actual wage rate paid to employees and the direct labour rate standard. This variance shows the effect of unanticipated wage rate changes. The direct labour rate standard for the company is $10 per hour. As you will note by looking at the November income statement in Exhibit 9–7, each of the three owners received a $0.50 per hour raise during November. So, for Tree Top, the direct labour rate variance will indicate added cost caused by the pay raises. We use a two-step process to calculate the direct labour rate variance. First, we find the amount the company should have paid for direct labour for the hours worked. Second, we determine the dollar amount of the direct labour rate variance.

Step 1: Determine the amount that should have been paid for the actual direct labour hours worked according to the direct labour rate standard.

In this step we determine how much the company should have paid for the direct labour hours actually worked, based on the direct labour rate standard. For Tree Top, the actual direct labour hours totaled 162 for November. By multiplying the 162 actual direct labour hours by the direct labour rate standard of $10, we determine that the company should have paid $1,620.

Actual Direct Labour Hours	×	Direct Labour Rate Standard	=	Actual Direct Labour Hours at the Standard Rate
162 Hours	×	$10	=	$1,620

Once we determine what the company should have paid according to the standard, we can compare it to the amount actually paid to determine the direct labour rate variance.

Step 2: Calculate the dollar amount of the direct labour rate variance.

We compute the dollar amount of the direct labour rate variance by subtracting the actual cost of direct labour from the standard cost of the direct labour actually worked. The direct labour rate variance compares the amount the actual direct labour hours should have cost to the actual cost. In the case of Tree Top, we find that the actual direct labour cost for November was $1,701, as shown on the November income statement in Exhibit 9–7. Tree Top's labour hours at standard should have cost $1,620. When we compare actual labour cost ($1,701) to standard cost ($1,620), we find an unfavourable direct labour rate variance of $81, calculated as follows:

Actual Direct Labour Hours at the Standard Rate	−	Actual Direct Labour Cost	=	Direct Labour Rate Variance
$1,620	−	$1,701	=	$81 Unfavourable

The calculated variance is unfavourable because the actual labour cost is higher than the cost based on the standard rate. This $81 unfavourable variance provides useful information to Ali, Maria, and Bill about the effect of their $0.50 per hour raise.

Discussion Questions

9-9. What effect did the $0.50 per hour pay raise have on November's profits?

9-10. In light of the financial problems that occurred in November, do you think Tree Top's owners should roll back the wage rate to $10 per hour? Explain your reasoning.

As with other variances, once the direct labour rate variance has been calculated, management can assess the variance and, if necessary, take corrective action. Direct labour rate variances are caused by labour rate changes that are unanticipated. Generally, when labour rates are contractually set or a result of collective bargaining with labour unions, labour rate changes are not unexpected. Accordingly, these labour rates are factored into the labour rate standard. A labour rate variance can be caused by an unexpected rate change of some kind, or perhaps an unanticipated change in the makeup of the labour force. For example, if the company retains more experienced workers and has fewer new workers, an unfavourable rate variance is likely because new employees generally begin their employment at a lower hourly wage than experienced employees.

In the case of Tree Top Mail Box Company, the November income statement shows that Ali, Maria, and Bill gave themselves an unplanned $0.50 per hour raise. Although no corrective action will likely be taken, the trio now knows how the raise affected profits.

The direct labour variances reveal that Ali, Maria, and Bill had two important problems in November regarding direct labour cost. First, it took 27 extra hours to make the 225 mail boxes. The extra 27 hours increased labour cost by $270. Second, the hourly wage paid to Ali, Maria, and Bill was higher than the planned $10 standard wage rate. This higher wage rate increased labour cost by $81. The total effect of these two direct labour problems is $351 unfavourable.

Manufacturing Overhead Variances

Manufacturing overhead variances help managers answer two vital questions. (1) Did the company spend more or less on overhead items than it should have, based on the standards that were set? (2) Did the company utilize its production facility efficiently?

In this section we look at four different manufacturing overhead variances, two that deal with variable manufacturing overhead and two with fixed manufacturing overhead.

Variable Manufacturing Overhead Efficiency Variance

variable manufacturing overhead efficiency variance A measure of the variable manufacturing overhead cost attributable to the difference between the planned and actual amount of the allocation base.

The **variable manufacturing overhead efficiency variance** is a measure of the variable manufacturing overhead cost attributable to the difference between the planned and actual amount of the allocation base. The allocation base that is selected should be the driver that best reflects the usage of variable overhead costs. In the past, it was thought that direct labour hours or direct labour costs were the best allocation bases. As production facilities have become more automated, other bases, such as machine hours, are now used. For demonstration purposes, we will use direct labour hours as the allocation base.

As items are produced, the production facility consumes electricity for light, air conditioning, and machinery operations. Workers also use supplies and other production resources that all are part of manufacturing overhead. Thus, as production increases, workers work longer and they use more production resources. How much more? The variable manufacturing overhead efficiency variance helps answer this question.

An unfavourable variable manufacturing overhead efficiency variance is a measure of the variable manufacturing overhead cost associated with the extra hours worked by direct labour. A direct relationship exists between the direct labour efficiency variance and the variable manufacturing overhead efficiency variance. Accordingly, if the direct labour efficiency variance is unfavourable, the variable manufacturing overhead efficiency variance will also be unfavourable. Likewise, if the direct labour efficiency variance is favourable, the variable manufacturing overhead efficiency variance will also be favourable.

The first two steps for calculating the variable manufacturing overhead efficiency variance are the same as those for determining the direct labour efficiency variance. These steps are to find the standard number of direct labour hours allowed for actual production and then to calculate the direct labour efficiency variance in hours.

Assuming the direct labour efficiency variance has been calculated, we review the information learned from those calculations before moving to the third step of the calculations, which is determining the variable manufacturing overhead efficiency variance in dollars.

Recall that our calculation showed that Tree Top used an extra 27 direct labour hours to make the 225 mail boxes in November. The extra 27 direct labour hours not only increased direct labour cost, but it also increased other costs. While Ali, Maria, and Bill worked the extra 27 hours, they consumed electricity, supplies, and other factory resources. In sum, the inefficiency of the workforce increased variable manufacturing overhead cost. Had they not worked the extra 27 hours, Tree Top's owners would have saved not only the labour cost, but also the factory resources they consumed as they worked the extra time.

Step 3: Calculate the variable manufacturing overhead efficiency variance in dollars.

To calculate the variable manufacturing overhead efficiency variance in dollars, multiply the direct labour efficiency variance in hours by the standard variable manufacturing overhead rate.

For Tree Top, the direct labour efficiency variance in hours we calculated earlier is 27 hours. We multiply this amount by the standard variable manufacturing overhead rate we calculated earlier of $0.35. This results in an unfavourable variable manufacturing overhead efficiency variance of $9.45 as shown here:

Direct Labour Efficiency Variance in Hours		Standard Variable Mfg Overhead Rate		Variable Mfg Overhead Efficiency Variance
27 Hours	×	$0.35	=	$9.45 Unfavourable

Now that the $9.45 variance has been calculated, management can assess the variance and take corrective action if necessary. Because the variable manufacturing overhead efficiency variance is based on direct labour efficiency, improving the direct labour efficiency variance will solve the variable overhead efficiency variance problem.

Tree Top's variable manufacturing overhead efficiency variance is so small that it may warrant no management attention. Even so, as Ali, Maria, and Bill work to bring the direct labour efficiency variance under control, the variable manufacturing overhead variance will also improve.

 ## Discussion Questions

9–11. If variable manufacturing overhead is allocated to production based on direct labour hours, will an unfavourable variable manufacturing overhead efficiency variance always accompany an unfavourable direct labour efficiency variance? Explain your reasoning.

9–12. If the direct labour efficiency variance is zero, will the variable manufacturing overhead efficiency variance also be zero? Explain your reasoning.

Variable Manufacturing Overhead Spending Variance

variable manufacturing overhead spending variance The difference between how much was actually spent on variable manufacturing overhead and the amount that should have been spent based on the actual direct labour hours worked.

The **variable manufacturing overhead spending variance** is the difference between what was actually spent on variable manufacturing overhead and what should have been spent, based on the actual direct labour hours worked. The question this variance answers is, based on the actual number of direct labour hours worked, is variable manufacturing overhead cost in line? In the case of Tree Top, given that production took 162 direct labour hours, was variable manufacturing overhead more or less than it should have been for that many direct labour hours? To find the answer, we must first determine the standard variable manufacturing overhead for the actual number of hours worked and then calculate the overhead spending variance in dollars. Let's look at the first step in this process.

Step 1: Determine the standard variable manufacturing overhead for the actual number of hours worked.

To determine the standard variable manufacturing overhead for the actual hours worked, we multiply the standard variable manufacturing overhead rate by the actual number of direct labour hours. This calculation shows us the amount that should have been spent for variable manufacturing overhead based on the actual labour hours worked. Based on Tree Top's standard variable manufacturing overhead rate of $0.35 per hour, the standard variable manufacturing overhead cost for the 162 actual direct labour hours is $56.70 as shown here:

Actual Direct Labour Hours	×	Standard Variable Mfg Overhead Rate	=	Standard Variable Mfg Overhead for Actual Direct Labour Hours
162 Hours	×	$0.35	=	$56.70

Now that we know how much Tree Top's variable manufacturing overhead should have been, we can compare it to the actual variable manufacturing overhead amount to determine the amount of the variance.

Step 2: Calculate the variable manufacturing overhead spending variance.

We calculate the variable manufacturing overhead spending variance by comparing standard variable manufacturing overhead for the actual number of hours worked (determined in step 1) to the amount actually spent for variable manufacturing overhead. This calculation compares *actual* variable manufacturing overhead cost to what it *should* have been for the actual hours worked. In the case of Tree Top, the actual amount spent for variable manufacturing overhead in November was $140. By comparing this amount to the standard of $56.70, we determine that the variable manufacturing overhead spending variance is $83.30 unfavourable as shown here:

Standard Variable Mfg Overhead Cost for Actual Direct Labour Hours		Actual Variable Mfg Overhead Cost		Variable Mfg Overhead Spending Variance
$56.70	−	$140.00	=	$83.30 Unfavourable

 ## Discussion Questions

9–13. What are some possible reasons why Tree Top Mail Box Company's variable manufacturing overhead spending was much higher than it should have been based on the standards?

9–14. If there had been no variance, would this mean Tree Top paid what it should have for variable manufacturing overhead in November? Explain your reasoning.

As managers assess the variable manufacturing overhead spending variance, they should keep in mind that it is a result of many different overhead expenditures. In practice, most companies break down the variable manufacturing overhead spending variance into separate variances for each variable manufacturing overhead item. For example, a manufacturer would have separate variance calculations for electricity, water, telephone, cleaning supplies, maintenance supplies, and so forth. The logic and calculations for each variance, however, would be similar to what we have presented here.

For Tree Top Mail Box Company, the trouble with variable manufacturing overhead cost is a combination of an unfavourable efficiency variance of $9.45 and an unfavourable spending variance of $83.30. Although the unfavourable efficiency variance will require little or no attention, the spending variance is sizable and should be investigated. Each component of variable manufacturing overhead should be reviewed to see whether overhead spending can be reduced.

Fixed Manufacturing Overhead Budget Variance

fixed manufacturing overhead budget variance
The difference between the actual amount of total fixed manufacturing overhead cost and the budgeted fixed manufacturing overhead cost.

The **fixed manufacturing overhead budget variance** is a measure of how actual total fixed manufacturing overhead compares to budgeted fixed manufacturing overhead. For example, if a company expects fixed manufacturing overhead cost to be $200,000 per month, the budget variance indicates whether the actual fixed manufacturing overhead is more or less than the $200,000.

We take only one step to compute the fixed manufacturing overhead budget variance. The dollar amount is calculated simply by subtracting actual fixed manufacturing overhead cost from the budgeted fixed manufacturing overhead. For Tree Top, the fixed manufacturing overhead budget variance for November is zero, because actual fixed manufacturing overhead cost exactly equals the amount budgeted, shown as follows:

Budget Fixed Mfg Overhead Cost		Actual Fixed Mfg Overhead Cost		Fixed Mfg Overhead Budget Variance
$225	−	$225	=	$0

The company has only two fixed overhead items, rent and amortization, so the fact that actual cost equaled budgeted cost is not surprising. If Tree Top purchased additional production equipment resulting in higher amortization cost, an unfavourable variance could occur.

Fixed manufacturing overhead costs are generally associated with long-term commitments for specific production resources. Examples of fixed overhead include the cost of amortization on production equipment, rent, insurance, and property taxes. Unlike other production costs, fixed overhead is less likely to be affected by the routine decisions that managers and employees make daily. Therefore, the variation between the amount budgeted and the actual fixed manufacturing overhead incurred is just as likely to be caused by a flawed budget as it is by spending decisions made during the budgeted period. For example, if a company budgets $50,000 for property taxes but the taxes are actually $51,000, the $1,000 variance that results is caused by a flawed budget, not by uncontrolled spending. Accordingly, fixed manufacturing overhead budget variances should be closely scrutinized to determine whether the required corrective action is to improve the budgeting process or to modify spending during the period.

Like variable manufacturing overhead, fixed manufacturing overhead comprises many different items. In practice, separate budget variances are calculated for each fixed manufacturing overhead item.

Fixed Manufacturing Overhead Volume Variance

fixed manufacturing overhead volume variance
A measure of the utilization of production capacity. This variance is caused by manufacturing more or less product during a particular production period than planned.

The last standard cost variance we discuss is the **fixed manufacturing overhead volume variance,** which measures utilization of production capacity. A variance is caused by the manufacture of more or less product during a particular production period than planned. When a manufacturer invests in expensive production machinery, it does so in anticipation of producing a given amount of product. If the company expects to produce only a small amount of product, it invests in inexpensive, low-volume equipment. If, however, the company expects to produce a large volume of product, it usually acquires more costly, high-volume equipment. If expensive, high-volume equipment is purchased but actual production is low, then it is likely that the company spent too much on production capacity. The fixed manufacturing overhead volume variance focuses on this relationship between production capacity and the actual volume produced.

When Ali, Maria, and Bill formed their manufacturing company, they could have set up shop to produce a very small number of mail boxes using hand tools; or they could have chosen to invest heavily in a building and automated equipment, thereby greatly increasing their production capacity. They chose to rent a small garage and invest a small amount in power tools that gave them a capacity to produce about 300 mail boxes per month. If they produce more than 300 mail boxes, that's great, but if they produce fewer, they are underutilizing their capacity to produce. In November, they produced only 225 mail boxes. Tree Top Mail Box Company, then, underutilized its capacity to produce by 75 mail boxes. Is this a big problem? To evaluate the magnitude of the problem we need to assign a dollar amount to the underutilization.

In the case of Tree Top Mail Box Company, the monthly fixed cost of $225 provides a capacity to produce 300 mail boxes. We follow three steps to calculate the fixed manufacturing overhead volume variance. First, we find the difference between expected and actual production. Second, we determine the standard number of direct labour hours associated with the production. Finally, we calculate the dollar amount of the fixed manufacturing overhead volume variance. We examine these steps in detail next.

Step 1: Calculate the difference between expected (budgeted) production and actual production.

The budgeted production for Tree Top is 300 mail boxes per month. Tree Top's actual production was less than its budgeted production by 75 mail boxes, shown as follows:

Plant Production Capacity	–	Actual Number of Units Produced	=	Under- Or Overproduction in Units
300 Units	–	225 Units	=	75 Units Under

As you will see, when fixed manufacturing overhead is allocated to production based on direct labour hours, the direct labour efficiency standard, with the standard fixed manufacturing overhead rate per direct labour hour, is used to calculate the dollar amount of the fixed manufacturing overhead volume variance.

Step 2: Determine the standard number of direct labour hours associated with the under- or overproduction.

We determine the standard number of direct labour hours associated with the under- or overproduction by multiplying the under- or overproduction by the direct labour efficiency standard. In the case of Tree Top, the direct labour efficiency standard is 0.6 hours per unit. Accordingly, the standard direct labour hours associated with the underproduction of 75 mail boxes is 45 hours (75 units × 0.6 hours per unit), shown as follows:

Amount of Under- or Overproduction	×	Direct Labour Efficiency Standard	=	Standard Number of Hours Associated with Production
75 Units	×	0.6 Hours Per Unit	=	45 Hours

Now that we know the number of standard hours associated with the over- or underproduction, we can assign a dollar amount based on the standard fixed manufacturing overhead rate per hour.

Step 3: Calculate the dollar amount of the fixed manufacturing overhead volume variance.

The dollar amount of the fixed manufacturing volume variance is calculated by multiplying the standard number of direct labour hours associated with the under- or overproduction by the standard fixed manufacturing overhead rate per direct labour hour. In the case of Tree Top, the fixed manufacturing overhead volume variance is $56.25, calculated as follows:

Standard Direct Labour Hours for Under- or Overproduction	×	Standard Fixed Mfg Overhead Rate	=	Fixed Mfg Overhead Volume Variance
45 Hours	×	$1.25	=	$56.25 Unfavourable

Once the fixed manufacturing overhead volume variance has been calculated, management can attempt to determine what caused it. In the case of Tree Top, the variance resulted primarily from inefficiencies caused by substandard direct material. Surprisingly, however, fixed manufacturing overhead volume variances are often caused by marketing and sales activities, rather than by the production department. In general, production occurs in response to sales demand. If the product is selling poorly, production volume will be low because little product is needed to fulfill demand. Conversely, if sales demand is high, production volume is likely to be high to meet demand.

USING STANDARD COST VARIANCES TO MANAGE BY EXCEPTION

Once all the standard cost variances have been calculated, the accounting department prepares a performance report that lists each variance. Then managers can use management by exception to address the problems associated with the unfavourable variances, beginning with the largest. A performance report is presented in Exhibit 9–8 for Tree Top Mail Box Company.

As the Tree Top Mail Box Company example shows, sometimes relationships among standard cost variances can occur that help explain the cause of some variances. Also, managers must develop the skill to review the variances and then seek out their causes and possible remedies. Even though managers can use standard costing to spot pressing issues, they must be careful of its shortcomings. Standard costing is one management tool, but not the only tool.

Revenue variances can also be analyzed by management to provide a more complete picture of the company's operations. Revenue variances are discussed in most advanced management accounting textbooks.

Exhibit 9–8
Tree Top's November
Performance Report

TREE TOP MAIL BOX COMPANY
Performance Report
For November 2004

Variance	Amount	Favorable/ Unfavorable
Direct material quantity variance	$ 53.25	Unfavourable
Direct material price variance	15.00	Favourable
Direct labour efficiency variance	270.00	Unfavourable
Direct labour rate variance	81.00	Unfavourable
Variable mfg overhead efficiency variance	9.45	Unfavourable
Variable mfg overhead spending variance	83.30	Unfavourable
Fixed mfg overhead budget variance	0	——
Fixed mfg overhead volume variance	56.25	Unfavourable
Total	$538.25	Unfavourable

SUMMARY

In the process of operating businesses, managers must focus their valuable time on areas that need to be improved. One area that requires constant attention is controlling the costs of operations. A process designed to help managers focus on cost items that need attention is standard costing, which sets cost performance goals and then uses these cost goals to evaluate performance.

Differences between the costs incurred by actual performance and what the costs should have been, based on the standards, are called variances. A favourable variance results when the cost of actual performance is lower than planned performance. An unfavourable variance results when the cost of actual performance is higher than planned performance. Managers can investigate all variances from standard, or they can focus their attention only on significant variances. Focusing only on significant variances is known as management by exception.

In establishing performance standards, managers can use either ideal standards, which can be attained only under perfect conditions, or practical standards, which allow for normal working conditions.

Although a standard costing system can be extremely helpful to managers, it has several potential problems. These include employees setting lax standards to avoid unfavourable variances, relying on historical information that may perpetuate past inefficiencies, and managing "by the numbers" thus overlooking significant problems that do not result in variances.

A standard cost system in a manufacturing environment uses estimates for the cost of direct materials, direct labour, and manufacturing overhead. This system is in contrast to both an actual cost system, which uses the actual cost for direct materials, direct labour, and manufacturing overhead, and a normal cost system, which uses actual costs for direct materials and direct labour, and estimates for manufacturing overhead.

The standards used in a manufacturing type company generally include a direct material quantity standard, a direct material price standard, a direct labour efficiency standard, a direct labour rate standard, a standard variable manufacturing overhead rate, and a standard fixed manufacturing overhead rate.

To use standard costing as a control device, managers compare standard costs to actual costs to see whether a variance exists. Then they investigate variances, as appropriate, which is known as variance analysis. The variances most commonly used are the direct material quantity variance, the direct material price variance, the direct labour efficiency variance, the direct labour rate variance, the variable manufacturing overhead efficiency variance, the variable manufacturing overhead spending variance, the fixed manufacturing overhead budget variance, and the fixed manufacturing overhead volume variance.

APPENDIX—RECORDING PRODUCT COST USING STANDARD COSTING

This appendix is intended to provide an overview of the accounting entries to record product costs using standard costing.

LEARNING OBJECTIVES

After completing your work in this appendix, you should be able to do the following:

1. Record the purchase of direct material and the direct material price variance.
2. Record the use of direct material and the direct material quantity variance.
3. Record the use of direct labour and the direct labour rate and efficiency variances.
4. Record actual variable manufacturing overhead cost incurred.
5. Record the application of variable manufacturing overhead to production.

6. Close the variable manufacturing overhead accounts and record the variable overhead variances.
7. Record actual fixed manufacturing overhead cost incurred.
8. Record the application of fixed manufacturing overhead to production.
9. Close the fixed manufacturing overhead accounts and record the variable overhead variances.
10. Close the standard cost variances to cost of goods sold.

The following accounts will be used for the entries in this appendix:

1. Cash
2. Raw materials inventory
3. Work-in-process inventory
4. Direct materials price variance
5. Direct materials quantity variance
6. Direct labour efficiency variance
7. Direct labour rate variance
8. Variable manufacturing overhead efficiency variance
9. Variable manufacturing overhead spending variance
10. Fixed manufacturing overhead budget variance
11. Fixed manufacturing overhead volume variance
12. Variable manufacturing overhead incurred
13. Variable manufacturing overhead applied
14. Fixed manufacturing overhead incurred
15. Fixed manufacturing overhead applied
16. Accumulated amortization
17. Accounts payable
18. Cost of goods sold

Recall that debits increase assets, expenses, and losses, while credits increase liabilities, equity, revenues, and gains. Also, you will learn that if a variance is favourable, the variance account is credited and if a variance is unfavourable, the variance account is debited.

When standard costing is used, direct materials, work-in-process, and finished goods inventories are maintained at standard cost. The standard cost variances account for the difference between the standard cost maintained in inventory and actual costs.

Purchase of Direct Material

The following table presents the information needed to make the direct materials purchases entry for Tree Top Mail Box Company:

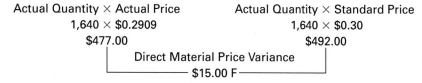

Actual Quantity × Actual Price	Actual Quantity × Standard Price
1,640 × \$0.2909	1,640 × \$0.30
\$477.00	\$492.00
Direct Material Price Variance	
\$15.00 F	

To record the purchase of raw material, raw materials inventory is debited for the actual quantity multiplied by the standard price. For Tree Top, the amount is \$492. The amount credited to accounts payable or cash is the actual purchase price of the material. For Tree Top, the amount is \$477. The difference between the amount debited to direct material and the amount credited to accounts payable is taken to the direct materials price variance account. If a credit to the variance account is required to balance the entry, the variance is favourable. Conversely, if a debit is required the variance is unfavourable. For Tree Top, the variance is $15 favourable so the direct material price variance account will be credited.

The entry for Tree Top appears as follows:

Raw materials inventory	492.00	
Accounts payable		477.00
Direct materials price variance		15.00

Use of Direct Material

The following table presents the information needed to make the entry for the direct materials used by Tree Top Mail Box Company:

Actual Quantity × Standard Price	Standard Quantity × Standard Price
1,640 × $0.30	225 × 6.5 metres × $0.30
$492.00	1,462.5 metres × $0.30
	$438.75

Quantity Variance
$53.25 U

To record the use of direct material, work-in-process inventory is debited for the standard quantity of material allowed for production multiplied by the standard price. For Tree Top, the amount is $438.75. The amount credited to raw materials is the actual quantity of material multiplied by the standard price. For Tree Top, the amount is $492.00. The difference between the amount debited to work in process and the amount credited to raw materials is taken to the direct material quantity variance account. If a credit to the variance account is required to balance the entry, the variance is favourable. Conversely, if a debit is required, the variance is unfavourable. For Tree Top, the variance is $53.25 unfavourable so the direct material quantity variance account will be debited.

The entry for Tree Top appears as follows:

Work-in-process inventory	438.75	
Direct materials quantity variance	53.25	
Raw materials inventory		492.00

Recording Direct Labour

The following tables present the information needed to make the entry to record direct labour for Tree Top Mail Box Company:

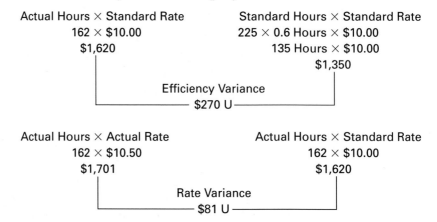

Actual Hours × Standard Rate	Standard Hours × Standard Rate
162 × $10.00	225 × 0.6 Hours × $10.00
$1,620	135 Hours × $10.00
	$1,350

Efficiency Variance
$270 U

Actual Hours × Actual Rate	Actual Hours × Standard Rate
162 × $10.50	162 × $10.00
$1,701	$1,620

Rate Variance
$81 U

To record direct labour cost, work-in-process inventory is debited for the standard hours allowed for production multiplied by the standard direct labour rate. For Tree Top, the amount is $1,350. Cash or wages payable is credited for the actual amount of wages paid to employees. For Tree Top, the amount is $1,701. The difference between the amount debited to work in process and the amount credited to cash is equal to the direct labour efficiency and rate variances. If the variance is favourable, the variance account is credited. Conversely, if the variance is unfavourable, the variance account is debited. For Tree Top, the efficiency variance and the rate variance are unfavourable so both of these variance accounts will be debited.

The entry for Tree Top appears as follows:

Work-in-process inventory	1,350.00	
Direct labour efficiency variance	270.00	
Direct labour rate variance	81.00	
Cash		1,701.00

Recording Variable Manufacturing Overhead

The following tables present the information needed to make the entries for variable manufacturing overhead for Tree Top Mail Box Company:

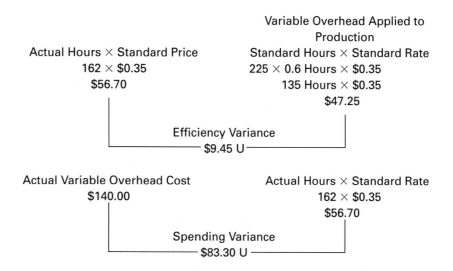

The variable manufacturing overhead incurred account is debited for the actual cost of variable manufacturing overhead. For Tree Top, the amount is $140. Depending on whether the item was purchased on account or for cash, accounts payable or cash would be credited. We assume the items were purchased for cash.

The entry for Tree Top appears as follows:

Variable manufacturing overhead incurred	140.00	
Cash		140.00

Work-in-process inventory is debited and variable manufacturing overhead applied is credited for the standard direct labour hours allowed for production multiplied by the standard variable overhead application rate. For Tree Top, the amount is $47.25.

The entry for Tree Top appears as follows:

Work-in-process inventory	47.25	
Variable manufacturing overhead applied		47.25

The difference between the balance of the variable manufacturing overhead incurred account and the variable manufacturing overhead applied account is equal to the variable overhead efficiency and spending variances. These variance accounts are established when the variable manufacturing overhead incurred and the variable manufacturing overhead applied accounts are closed. This closing procedure is generally done only at year end. For demonstration purposes, we will assume that Tree

Top has elected to close the overhead accounts to establish the variable overhead efficiency and spending variances at the end of November. As with the variance previously discussed, if the variance is favourable, the variance account is credited. Conversely, if the variance is unfavourable, the variance account is debited. For Tree Top, both the efficiency variance and the spending variance are unfavourable so the variance accounts will be debited as shown in the following entry.

Variable manufacturing overhead applied	47.25	
Variable manufacturing overhead efficiency variance	9.45	
Variable manufacturing overhead spending variance	83.30	
Variable manufacturing overhead incurred		140.00

Recording Fixed Manufacturing Overhead

The following tables present the information needed to make the entries for fixed manufacturing overhead for Tree Top Mail Box Company:

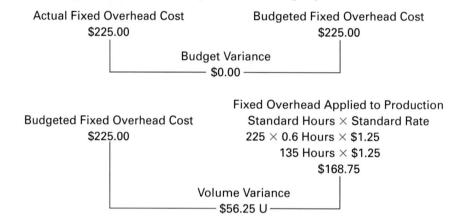

The fixed manufacturing overhead incurred account is debited for the actual cost of fixed manufacturing overhead. For Tree Top, the $225 actual fixed manufacturing overhead consists of $200 for rent and $25 for amortization. Cash should be credited for the amount of rent paid and accumulated amortization should be credited for the depreciation.

The entry for Tree Top appears as follows:

Fixed manufacturing overhead incurred	225.00	
Cash		200.00
Accumulated amortization		25.00

Work-in-process inventory is debited and fixed manufacturing overhead applied is credited for the standard direct labour hours allowed for production multiplied by the standard fixed overhead application rate. For Tree Top, the amount is $168.75.

The entry for Tree Top appears as follows:

Work-in-process inventory	168.75	
Fixed manufacturing overhead applied		168.75

The difference between the balance of the fixed manufacturing overhead incurred account and the fixed manufacturing overhead applied account is equal to the fixed overhead budget and volume spending variances. These variance accounts are established when the fixed manufacturing overhead incurred and the fixed manufacturing overhead applied accounts are closed. As with variable overhead, this closing procedure is generally done only at year end. For demonstration purposes, we will assume that Tree Top has elected to close the fixed manufacturing overhead accounts at the end of November. Once more, if the variance is favourable, the variance account is credited. Conversely, if the variance is unfavourable, the variance account is debited. Although entries for zero variances are not generally made in practice, we will show an entry for the budget variance for this demonstration. The volume variance will appear as a debit because it is an unfavourable variance.

The entry for Tree Top appears as follows:

Fixed manufacturing overhead applied	168.75	
Fixed manufacturing overhead budget variance	0	
Fixed manufacturing overhead volume variance	56.25	
Fixed manufacturing overhead incurred		225.00

Closing the Variance Accounts

The variance accounts are monitored during the year but generally no accounting entries are made to dispense with the amounts until the end of the year. For demonstration purposes, we will assume that Tree Top has elected to close the variance accounts at the end of November.

In most cases an accounting entry is made to close the standard cost variances to cost of goods sold. Because the amount of the variances is generally relatively small and most product cost ends up in cost of goods sold by year end, closing the variance accounts to cost of goods sold is adequate for most companies.

Tree Top's entry to close the standard cost variances to cost of goods sold follows:

Cost of goods sold	538.25	
Direct material price variance	15.00	
Direct material quantity variance		53.25
Direct labour efficiency variance		270.00
Direct labour rate variance		81.00
Variable manufacturing overhead efficiency variance		9.45
Variable manufacturing overhead spending variance		83.30
Fixed manufacturing overhead budget variance		0
Fixed manufacturing overhead volume variance		56.25

APPENDIX SUMMARY

When standard costing is used, direct materials, work-in-process, and finished goods inventories are maintained at standard cost. The standard cost variances account for the difference between the standard cost maintained in inventory and actual costs. If a variance is favourable, the variance account is credited. Conversely, if a variance is unfavourable, the variance account is debited.

To record the purchase of raw material, raw materials inventory is debited for the actual quantity multiplied by the standard price. The amount credited to accounts payable or cash is the actual purchase price of the material. The difference between the amount debited to direct material and the amount credited to accounts payable is taken to the Direct Materials Price Variance account.

To record the use of direct material, work-in-process inventory is debited for the standard quantity of material allowed for production multiplied by the standard price. The amount credited to raw materials is the actual quantity of material multiplied by the standard price. The difference between the amount debited to work in process and the amount credited to raw materials is taken to the Direct Material Quantity Variance account.

Work-in-process inventory is debited for the standard hours allowed for production multiplied by the standard direct labour rate. Cash or wages payable is credited for the actual amount of wages paid to employees. The difference between the amount debited to work in process and the amount credited to cash is equal to the direct labour efficiency and rate variances.

The Variable Manufacturing Overhead Incurred account is debited for the actual cost of variable manufacturing overhead. Work-in-process inventory is debited and variable manufacturing overhead applied is credited for the standard direct labour hours allowed for production multiplied by the standard variable overhead application rate. The difference between the balance of the Variable Manufacturing Overhead Incurred account and the Variable Manufacturing Overhead Applied account is equal to the variable overhead efficiency and spending variances. At year end, these variance accounts are established when the Variable Manufacturing Overhead Incurred and the Variable Manufacturing Overhead Applied accounts are closed.

The Fixed Manufacturing Overhead Incurred account is debited for the actual cost of fixed manufacturing overhead. Work-in-process inventory is debited and fixed manufacturing overhead applied is credited for the standard direct labour hours allowed for production multiplied by the standard fixed overhead application rate. The difference between the balance of the Fixed Manufacturing Overhead Incurred account and the Fixed Manufacturing Overhead Applied account is equal to the fixed overhead budget and volume spending variances. At year end, these variance accounts are established when the Fixed Manufacturing Overhead Incurred and the Fixed Manufacturing Overhead Applied accounts are closed.

The variance accounts are generally closed to cost of goods sold at year end. Because the amount of variances is generally relatively small and most product cost ends up in cost of goods sold by year end, closing the variance accounts to cost of goods sold is adequate for most companies.

KEY TERMS

bill of materials, p. 338
direct labour efficiency standard, p. 340
direct labour efficiency variance, p. 348
direct labour rate standard, p. 340
direct labour rate variance, p. 350
direct material price standard, p. 338
direct material price variance, p. 347
direct material quantity standard, p. 338
direct material quantity variance, p. 344
direct material usage variance, p. 344
favourable variance, p. 332
fixed manufacturing overhead
  budget variance, p. 354
fixed manufacturing overhead
  volume variance, p. 355
ideal standard, p. 333

management by exception, p. 332
practical standard, p. 333
standard, p. 331
standard cost system, p. 331
standard costing, p. 331
standard fixed manufacturing
  overhead rate, p. 342
standard variable manufacturing
  overhead rate, p. 341
unfavourable variance, p. 331
variable manufacturing overhead
  efficiency variance, p. 351
variable manufacturing overhead
  spending variance, p. 353
variance, p. 331

REVIEW THE FACTS

1. What is standard costing?
2. What is a standard?
3. What is a variance?
4. Describe management by exception.
5. How often do most companies set cost standards?
6. What are the two things that can cause cost to increase?
7. What is the difference between an ideal standard and a practical standard?
8. Briefly describe five problems with standard costing.
9. What is a bill of material?
10. What are the two direct material standards?
11. What are the two direct labour standards?
12. How can standard costs be used to control cost?
13. What is measured by the direct material quantity variance?
14. What is measured by the direct material price variance?
15. What is measured by the direct labour efficiency variance?
16. What is measured by the direct labour rate variance?
17. What is measured by the variable manufacturing overhead efficiency variance?
18. What is measured by the variable manufacturing overhead spending variance?
19. What is measured by the fixed manufacturing overhead budget variance?
20. What is measured by the fixed manufacturing overhead volume variance?

APPLY WHAT YOU HAVE LEARNED

LO 7: Determine Direct Material Variances

1. Zhang Manufacturing Company purchased 4,000 kilograms of direct material at $5.20 per kilogram. It used 2,700 kilograms to make 5,000 finished units. The standard cost for direct material is $5.00 per kilogram and the quantity standard is 0.5 (one-half) kilogram per finished unit.

REQUIRED:
a. According to the appropriate standard, how much should the company have paid for the 4,000 kilograms of direct material purchased?
b. Determine the direct material price variance based on the amount of direct material purchased.
c. According to the appropriate standard, how many kilograms of direct material should have been used to make the 5,000 finished units?
d. Determine the direct material quantity variance in kilograms of direct material.
e. Determine the direct material quantity variance in dollars.
f. Appendix: Prepare the following journal entries:
   (1) Record the purchase of direct material.
   (2) Record the use of direct material.

LO 7: Determine Direct Material Variances

2. Carbonnell Manufacturing Company purchased 15,000 kilograms of direct material at $1.30 per kilogram. It used 14,700 kilograms to make 5,000 finished units. The standard cost for direct material is $1.35 per kilogram and the quantity standard is three kilograms per finished unit.

a. According to the appropriate standard, how much should the company have paid for the 15,000 kilograms of direct material purchased?
b. Determine the direct material price variance based on the amount of direct material purchased.
c. According to the appropriate standard, how many kilograms of direct material should have been used to make the 5,000 finished units?
d. Determine the direct material quantity variance in kilograms of direct material.
e. Determine the direct material quantity variance in dollars.
f. Appendix: Prepare the following journal entries:
   (1) Record the purchase of direct material.
   (2) Record the use of direct material.

LO 7: Determine Direct Material Variances

3. Smithstone Company purchased 2,500 square metres of direct material at $6.30 per square metre. It used 2,055 square metres of material to make 500 finished units. The standard cost for direct material is $6.15 per square metre and the quantity standard is four metres per finished unit.

REQUIRED:

a. According to the appropriate standard, how much should the company have paid for the 2,500 square metres of direct material purchased?
b. Determine the direct material price variance based on the amount of direct material purchased.
c. According to the appropriate standard, how many square metres of direct material should have been used to make the 500 finished units?
d. Determine the direct material quantity variance in square metres of direct material.
e. Determine the direct material quantity variance in dollars.
f. Appendix: Prepare the following journal entries:
   (1) Record the purchase of direct material.
   (2) Record the use of direct material.

LO 7: Determine Direct Material Variances

4. Econo Manufacturing purchased 20,000 square metres of direct material at $0.54 per square metre. It used 12,625 square metres to make 1,250 finished units. The standard cost for direct material is $0.55 per square metre and the quantity standard is 10 square metres per finished unit.

REQUIRED:

a. According to the appropriate standard, how much should the company have paid for the 20,000 square metres of direct material purchased?
b. Determine the direct material price variance based on the amount of direct material purchased.
c. According to the appropriate standard, how many square metres of direct material should have been used to make the 1,250 finished units?
d. Determine the direct material quantity variance in square metres of direct material.
e. Determine the direct material quantity variance in dollars.

LO 7:   Determine Direct Material Variances

5. The following information is presented for Scout Manufacturing Company.

   - Direct material price standard is $1.55 per litre.
   - Direct material quantity standard is 2.5 litres per finished unit.
   - Budgeted production is 1,000 finished units.
   - 4,000 litres of direct material were purchased for $6,000.
   - 2,800 litres of direct material were used in production.
   - 1,100 finished units of product were produced.

REQUIRED:
a. Determine the direct material price variance.
b. Determine the direct material quantity variance in dollars.

LO 7:   Determine Direct Material Variances

6. The following information is presented for Flowvalve Manufacturing Company.

   - Direct material price standard is $15 per kilogram.
   - Direct material quantity standard is 0.25 kilograms per finished unit.
   - Budgeted production is 20,000 finished units.
   - 6,000 kilograms of direct material were purchased for $91,320.
   - 4,650 kilograms of direct material were used in production.
   - 18,000 finished units of product were produced.

REQUIRED:
a. Determine the direct material price variance.
b. Determine the direct material quantity variance in dollars.

LO 7:   Determine Direct Material Variances

7. The following information is presented for Munter Manufacturing Corporation.

   - Direct material price standard is $3.25 per kilogram.
   - Direct material quantity standard is six kilograms per finished unit.
   - Budgeted production is 25,000 finished units.
   - 175,000 kilograms of direct material were purchased for $559,650.
   - 155,200 kilograms of direct material were used in production.
   - 25,600 finished units of product were produced.

REQUIRED:
a. Determine the direct material price variance.
b. Determine the direct material quantity variance in dollars.

LO 7:   Determine Direct Material Variances

8. Information from the Quincy Company is as follows:

Actual cost of 33,000 kilograms of direct material purchased	$97,350
Direct material used in production	30,575 kilograms
Actual production	2,980 units
Direct material price standard	$3.00 per kilogram
Direct material quantity standard per finished unit of production	10 kilograms
Budgeted production	3,000 units

REQUIRED:

a. Determine the direct material price variance.

b. Determine the direct material quantity variance in dollars.

LO 7: Determine Direct Material Variances

9. Information from Wayne Manufacturing Limited is as follows:

Actual cost of 10,000 kilograms of direct material purchased	$2,400
Direct material used in production	9,177 kilograms
Actual production	980 units
Direct material price standard	$0.25 per kilogram
Direct material quantity standard per finished unit of production	9 kilograms
Budgeted production	1,000 units

REQUIRED:

a. Determine the direct material price variance.

b. Determine the direct material quantity variance in dollars.

LO 7: Determine Direct Material Variances

10. Information from Myco Manufacturing Company is as follows:

Actual cost of 120,000 metres of direct material purchased	$427,200
Direct material used in production	111,100 metres
Actual production	3,200 units
Direct material price standard	$3.50 per metre
Direct material quantity standard per finished unit of production	35 metres
Budgeted production	3,500 units

REQUIRED:

a. Determine the direct material price variance.

b. Determine the direct material quantity variance in dollars.

LO 7: Determine Direct Labour Variances

11. The direct labour rate standard for Anderson Manufacturing Inc. is $12 per direct labour hour. The direct labour efficiency standard is two hours per finished unit. Last month, the company completed 8,000 units of product using 16,350 direct labour hours at an actual cost of $194,565.

REQUIRED:

a. According to the appropriate standard, how much should the company have paid for the 16,350 actual direct labour hours?

b. Determine the direct labour rate variance.

c. According to the appropriate standard, how many hours of direct labour should it have taken to produce the 8,000 units?

d. Determine the direct labour efficiency variance in hours.

e. Determine the direct labour efficiency variance in dollars.

f. Appendix: Prepare a journal entry to record the direct labour and the direct labour rate and efficiency variances.

LO 7: Determine Direct Labour Variances

12. The direct labour rate standard for Calspan Manufacturing is $18.50 per direct labour hour. The direct labour efficiency standard is six minutes, or 1/10 of an hour, per finished unit. Last month, the company completed 105,650 units of product using 10,400 direct labour hours at an actual cost of $191,360.

REQUIRED:

a. According to the appropriate standard, how much should the company have paid for the 10,400 actual direct labour hours?

b. Determine the direct labour rate variance.

c. According to the appropriate standard, how many hours of direct labour should it have taken to produce the 105,650 units?

d. Determine the direct labour efficiency variance in hours.

e. Determine the direct labour efficiency variance in dollars.

f. Appendix: Prepare a journal entry to record the direct labour and the direct labour rate and efficiency variances.

LO 7: Determine Direct Labour Variances

13. The direct labour rate standard for Port Hardy Manufacturing Inc. is $10 per direct labour hour. The direct labour efficiency standard is three hours per finished unit. Last month, the company completed 2,800 units of product using 8,620 direct labour hours at an actual cost of $88,355.

REQUIRED:

a. According to the appropriate standard, how much should the company have paid for the 8,620 actual direct labour hours?

b. Determine the direct labour rate variance.

c. According to the appropriate standard, how many hours of direct labour should it have taken to produce the 2,800 units?

d. Determine the direct labour efficiency variance in hours.

e. Determine the direct labour efficiency variance in dollars.

LO 7: Determine Direct Labour Variances

14. The direct labour rate standard for Sakura Manufacturing Inc. is $15.25 per direct labour hour. The direct labour efficiency standard is 30 minutes, or 1/2 of an hour, per finished unit. Last month, the company completed 27,800 units of product using 14,050 direct labour hours at an actual cost of $215,246.

REQUIRED:

a. Determine the direct labour rate variance.

b. Determine the direct labour efficiency variance in dollars.

c. Appendix: Prepare a journal entry to record the direct labour and the direct labour rate and efficiency variances.

LO 7: Determine Direct Labour Variances

15. The direct labour rate standard for Thibert Manufacturing Inc. is $10 per direct labour hour. The direct labour efficiency standard is 0.25 (one-quarter) hour per finished unit. Last month, the company completed 38,000 units of product using 9,280 direct labour hours at an actual cost of $97,904.

REQUIRED:

a. Determine the direct labour rate variance.

b. Determine the direct labour efficiency variance in dollars.

c. Appendix: Prepare a journal entry to record the direct labour and the direct labour rate and efficiency variances.

LO 7: Determine Direct Labour Variances

16. The following information is presented for Marathon Manufacturing Company.

- Direct labour rate standard is $11.55.
- Direct labour efficiency standard is 2.5 hours per finished unit.
- Budgeted production is 1,200 finished units.
- Production required 2,910 direct labour hours at a cost of $33,174.
- 1,150 finished units of product were produced.

REQUIRED:

a. Determine the direct labour rate variance.

b. Determine the direct labour efficiency variance in dollars.

LO 7: Determine Direct Labour Variances

17. The following information is presented for Trites Manufacturing Company.

- Direct labour rate standard is $12.
- Direct labour efficiency standard is two hours per finished unit.
- Budgeted production is 2,200 finished units.
- Production required 4,560 direct labour hours at a cost of $54,036.
- 2,250 finished units of product were produced.

REQUIRED:

a. Determine the direct labour rate variance.

b. Determine the direct labour efficiency variance in dollars.

LO 7: Determine Direct Labour Variances

18. The following information is presented for the Green Manufacturing Company.

- Direct labour rate standard is $24.
- Direct labour efficiency standard is three hours per finished unit.
- Budgeted production is 775 finished units.
- Production required 2,375 direct labour hours at a cost of $57,475.
- 810 finished units of product were produced.

REQUIRED:

a. Determine the direct labour rate variance.

b. Determine the direct labour efficiency variance in dollars.

LO 7: Determine Direct Labour Variances

19. Information from Spin Manufacturing Company is presented as follows:

Actual number of direct labour hours	275
Actual direct labour cost	$4,620
Actual number of units produced	800 units
Direct labour rate standard	$16.10
Direct labour efficiency standard	0.3 hours per unit
Budgeted production	850 units

REQUIRED:

a. Determine the direct labour rate variance.

b. Determine the direct labour efficiency variance in dollars.

LO 7:   Determine Direct Labour Variances

20. Information from Oak Manufacturing Inc. is as follows:

Actual number of direct labour hours	1,275
Actual direct labour cost	$16,065
Actual number of units produced	1,255 units
Direct labour rate standard	$12
Direct labour efficiency standard	1 hour per unit
Budgeted production	1,200 units

REQUIRED:

a. Determine the direct labour rate variance.

b. Determine the direct labour efficiency variance in dollars.

LO 7:   Determine Direct Labour Variances

21. Information from Future Electronics Manufacturing Inc. is as follows:

Actual number of direct labour hours	12,830
Actual direct labour cost	$292,524
Actual number of units produced	2,040 units
Direct labour rate standard	$23.10
Direct labour efficiency standard	6 hours per unit
Budgeted production	2,000 units

REQUIRED:

a. Determine the direct labour rate variance.

b. Determine the direct labour efficiency variance in dollars.

LO 7:   Determine Direct Material and Direct Labour Variances

22. Information from Atlantic Company is presented as follows:

Actual cost of 30,000 kilograms of direct material purchased	$97,500
Direct material used in production	28,100 kilograms
Actual number of direct labour hours	12,850
Actual direct labour cost	$165,765
Actual production	2,500 units
Direct material price standard	$3.30 per kilogram
Direct material quantity standard per finished unit of production	11 kilograms
Direct labour rate standard	$13
Direct labour efficiency standard	5 hours per unit
Budgeted production	2,400 units

REQUIRED:

a. Determine the direct material price variance.

b. Determine the direct material quantity variance in dollars.

c. Determine the direct labour rate variance.

d. Determine the direct labour efficiency variance in dollars.

LO 7:   Determine Direct Material and Direct Labour Variances

23. Information from Progressive Company is presented as follows:

Actual cost of 9,000 kilograms of direct material purchased	$2,200
Direct material used in production	7,800 kilograms
Actual number of direct labour hours	980
Actual direct labour cost	$14,945
Actual production	240 units
Direct material price standard	$0.25 per kilogram
Direct material quantity standard per finished unit of production	30 kilograms
Direct labour rate standard	$15
Direct labour efficiency standard	4 hours per unit
Budgeted production	250 units

REQUIRED:

a. Determine the direct material price variance.
b. Determine the direct material quantity variance in dollars.
c. Determine the direct labour rate variance.
d. Determine the direct labour efficiency variance in dollars.

LO 7:   Determine Direct Material and Direct Labour Variances

24. Information from Packard Company is presented as follows:

Actual cost of 1,000 kilograms of direct material purchased	$10,300
Direct material used in production	830 kilograms
Actual number of direct labour hours	1,220
Actual direct labour cost	$13,176
Actual production	400 units
Direct material price standard	$10 per kilogram
Direct material quantity standard per finished unit of production	2 kilograms
Direct labour rate standard	$11
Direct labour efficiency standard	3 hours per unit
Budgeted production	450 units

REQUIRED:

a. Determine the direct material price variance.
b. Determine the direct material quantity variance in dollars.
c. Determine the direct labour rate variance.
d. Determine the direct labour efficiency variance in dollars.

LO 7:   Determine Variable Manufacturing Overhead Variances

25. Clifford Manufacturing Inc. applies variable manufacturing overhead to production on the basis of $15 per direct labour hour. The labour efficiency standard is five hours per finished unit. Last month the company produced 12,000 units and used 62,000 direct labour hours. Actual variable overhead cost incurred totaled $920,000.

REQUIRED:

a. Determine the variable manufacturing overhead spending variance.
b. According to the appropriate standard, how many direct labour hours should it have taken to produce the 12,000 units?

c. Determine the direct labour efficiency variance in hours.

d. Determine the variable manufacturing overhead efficiency variance in dollars.

LO 7: Determine Variable Manufacturing Overhead Variances

26. Knapp Manufacturing Ltd. applies variable manufacturing overhead to production on the basis of $5 per direct labour hour. The labour efficiency standard is two hours per finished unit. Last month the company produced 11,000 units and used 22,400 direct labour hours. Actual variable overhead cost incurred totaled $111,700.

REQUIRED:

a. Determine the variable manufacturing overhead spending variance.

b. According to the appropriate standard, how many direct labour hours should it have taken to produce the 11,000 units?

c. Determine the direct labour efficiency variance in hours.

d. Determine the variable manufacturing overhead efficiency variance in dollars.

LO 7: Determine Variable Manufacturing Overhead Variances

27. Martinuk Marine Manufacturing Inc. applies variable manufacturing overhead to production on the basis of $6 per direct labour hour. The labour efficiency standard is three hours per finished unit. Last month the company produced 15,000 units and used 45,650 direct labour hours. Actual variable overhead cost incurred totaled $277,800.

REQUIRED:

a. Determine the variable manufacturing overhead spending variance.

b. According to the appropriate standard, how many direct labour hours should it have taken to produce the 15,000 units?

c. Determine the direct labour efficiency variance in hours.

d. Determine the variable manufacturing overhead efficiency variance in dollars.

e. Appendix: Prepare the following journal entries:

  (1) Record the actual variable manufacturing overhead. (Use "various accounts" for the credit side of the entry.)

  (2) Record the variable manufacturing overhead applied to production.

  (3) Close the variable manufacturing overhead accounts and establish the variable overhead variance accounts.

  (4) Close the variance accounts to cost of goods sold.

LO 7: Determine Variable Manufacturing Overhead Variances

28. Alpine Manufacturing Ltd. applies variable manufacturing overhead to production on the basis of $13 per direct labour hour. The labour efficiency standard is four hours per finished unit. Last month the company produced 3,000 units and used 11,700 direct labour hours. Actual variable overhead cost incurred totaled $157,200.

REQUIRED:

a. Determine the variable manufacturing overhead spending variance.

b. Determine the variable manufacturing overhead efficiency variance in dollars.

c. Appendix: Prepare the following journal entries:

  (1) Record the actual variable manufacturing overhead. (Use "various accounts" for the credit side of the entry.)

  (2) Record the variable manufacturing overhead applied to production.

(3) Close the variable manufacturing overhead accounts and establish the variable overhead variance accounts.

(4) Close the variance accounts to cost of goods sold.

LO 7: Determine Variable Manufacturing Overhead Variances

29. Adler Manufacturing Company applies variable manufacturing overhead to production on the basis of $22 per direct labour hour. The labour efficiency standard is 0.5 hours per finished unit. Last month the company produced 14,500 units and used 7,300 direct labour hours. Actual variable overhead cost incurred totaled $162,000.

REQUIRED:

a. Determine the variable manufacturing overhead spending variance.

b. Determine the variable manufacturing overhead efficiency variance in dollars.

LO 7: Determine Variable Manufacturing Overhead Variances

30. The following information is presented for Nielson Manufacturing Company.

- Standard variable manufacturing overhead rate is $3.50 per direct labour hour.
- Direct labour efficiency standard is three hours per finished unit.
- Budgeted production is 810 finished units.
- Production required 2,370 direct labour hours.
- Variable manufacturing overhead cost was $8,500.
- 775 finished units of product were produced.

REQUIRED:

a. Determine the variable manufacturing overhead spending variance.

b. Determine the variable manufacturing overhead efficiency variance in dollars.

LO 7: Determine Variable Manufacturing Overhead Variances

31. The following information is presented for Collingsworth Manufacturing Company.

- Standard variable manufacturing overhead rate is $7.00 per direct labour hour.
- Direct labour efficiency standard is six hours per finished unit.
- Budgeted production is 500 finished units.
- Production required 3,400 direct labour hours.
- Variable manufacturing overhead cost was $23,600.
- 550 finished units of product were produced.

REQUIRED:

a. Determine the variable manufacturing overhead spending variance.

b. Determine the variable manufacturing overhead efficiency variance in dollars.

LO 7: Determine Variable Manufacturing Overhead Variances

32. The following information is presented for Kemp Manufacturing Company.

- Standard variable manufacturing overhead rate is $2 per direct labour hour.
- Direct labour efficiency standard is four hours per finished unit.

- Budgeted production is 1,500 finished units.
- Production required 6,100 direct labour hours.
- Variable manufacturing overhead cost was $12,325.
- 1,550 finished units of product were produced.

REQUIRED:
a. Determine the variable manufacturing overhead spending variance.
b. Determine the variable manufacturing overhead efficiency variance in dollars.

LO 7:   Determine Variable Manufacturing Overhead Variances

33. Information from Systek Manufacturing Company is as follows:

Actual number of direct labour hours	12,000
Actual variable manufacturing overhead cost	$145,965
Actual number of units produced	2,440 units
Standard variable manufacturing overhead rate	$12.10 per direct labour hour
Direct labour efficiency standard	5 hours
Budgeted production	2,500 units

REQUIRED:
a. Determine the variable manufacturing overhead spending variance.
b. Determine the variable manufacturing overhead efficiency variance in dollars.

LO 7:   Determine Variable Manufacturing Overhead Variances

34. Information from Altos Manufacturing Company is as follows:

Actual number of direct labour hours	12,330
Actual variable manufacturing overhead cost	$74,490
Actual number of units produced	12,540 units
Standard variable manufacturing overhead rate	$6 per direct labour hour
Direct labour efficiency standard	1 hour
Budgeted production	12,000 units

REQUIRED:
a. Determine the variable manufacturing overhead spending variance.
b. Determine the variable manufacturing overhead efficiency variance in dollars.

LO 7:   Determine Variable Manufacturing Overhead Variances

35. Information from Portage Manufacturing Company is as follows:

Actual number of direct labour hours	175,000
Actual variable manufacturing overhead cost	$2,400,000
Actual number of units produced	21,740 units
Standard variable manufacturing overhead rate	$14 per direct labour hour
Direct labour efficiency standard	8 hours
Budgeted production	20,000 units

REQUIRED:
a. Determine the variable manufacturing overhead spending variance.
b. Determine the variable manufacturing overhead efficiency variance in dollars.

LO 7:   Determine Fixed Manufacturing Overhead Variances

36. Hill Manufacturing Company applies fixed manufacturing overhead at the rate of $5.50 per direct labour hour. Fixed manufacturing overhead is budgeted to be $330,000 per month. The direct labour efficiency standard is five hours per finished unit. Although budgeted production for the month was 12,000, the company only produced 11,800 units. Production required actual direct labour hours of 60,000, and actual fixed manufacturing overhead cost incurred was $325,000.

REQUIRED:
a. Determine the fixed overhead budget variance.
b. What is the difference between the planned number of units and the number of units actually produced?
c. Determine the fixed manufacturing overhead volume variance.
d. Appendix: Prepare the following journal entries:
  (1) Record the actual fixed manufacturing overhead. (Use "various accounts" for the credit side of the entry.)
  (2) Record the fixed manufacturing overhead applied to production.
  (3) Close the fixed manufacturing overhead accounts and establish the fixed overhead variance accounts.
  (4) Close the variance accounts to cost of goods sold.

LO 7:   Determine Fixed Manufacturing Overhead Variances

37. Johnson Manufacturing Company applies fixed manufacturing overhead at the rate of $4.60 per direct labour hour. Fixed manufacturing overhead is budgeted to be $910,800 per month. The direct labour efficiency standard is three hours per finished unit. Although budgeted production for the month was 66,000, the company produced 67,800 units. Production required actual direct labour hours of 203,000, and actual fixed manufacturing overhead cost incurred was $920,000.

REQUIRED:
a. Determine the fixed manufacturing overhead budget variance.
b. What is the difference between the planned number of units and the number of units actually produced?
c. Determine the fixed manufacturing overhead volume variance.
d. Appendix: Prepare the following journal entries:
  (1) Record the actual fixed manufacturing overhead. (Use "various accounts" for the credit side of the entry.)
  (2) Record the fixed manufacturing overhead applied to production.
  (3) Close the fixed manufacturing overhead accounts and establish the fixed overhead variance accounts.
  (4) Close the variance accounts to cost of goods sold.

LO 7:   Determine Fixed Manufacturing Overhead Variances

38. Quesnell Manufacturing Limited applies fixed manufacturing overhead at the rate of $7 per direct labour hour. Fixed manufacturing overhead is budgeted to be $336,000 per month. The direct labour efficiency standard is three hours per finished unit. Although budgeted production for the month was 16,000, the company only produced 15,500 units. Production required actual direct labour hours of 60,000, and actual fixed manufacturing overhead cost incurred was $344,000.

REQUIRED:

a. Determine the fixed manufacturing overhead budget variance.

b. Did the company produce as many units as it had planned? What is the difference between the planned number of units and the number of units actually produced?

c. Determine the fixed manufacturing overhead volume variance.

LO 7: Determine Fixed Manufacturing Overhead Variances

39. The following information is presented for Laurier Manufacturing Company.

- Standard fixed manufacturing overhead rate is $2 per direct labour hour.
- Direct labour efficiency standard is four hours per finished unit.
- Budgeted production is 2,500 finished units.
- Budgeted fixed manufacturing overhead is $20,000.
- Actual fixed manufacturing overhead cost was $10,750.
- 2,150 finished units of product were produced.

REQUIRED:

a. Determine the fixed manufacturing overhead budget variance.

b. Determine the fixed manufacturing overhead volume variance in dollars.

LO 7: Determine Fixed Manufacturing Overhead Variances

40. The following information is presented for Alexander Manufacturing Company.

- Standard fixed manufacturing overhead rate is $6.50 per direct labour hour.
- Direct labour efficiency standard is two hours per finished unit.
- Budgeted production is 5,000 finished units.
- Budgeted fixed manufacturing overhead is $65,000.
- Actual fixed manufacturing overhead cost was $66,100.
- 5,150 finished units of product were produced.

REQUIRED:

a. Determine the fixed manufacturing overhead budget variance.

b. Determine the fixed manufacturing overhead volume variance in dollars.

LO 7: Determine Fixed Manufacturing Overhead Variances

41. The following information is presented for Adcox Manufacturing Company.

- Standard fixed manufacturing overhead rate is $9.50 per direct labour hour.
- Direct labour efficiency standard is nine hours per finished unit.
- Budgeted production is 9,000 finished units.
- Budgeted fixed manufacturing overhead is $769,500.
- Actual fixed manufacturing overhead cost was $755,360.
- 8,500 finished units of product were produced.

REQUIRED:

a. Determine the fixed manufacturing overhead budget variance.

b. Determine the fixed manufacturing overhead volume variance in dollars.

LO 7:   Determine Fixed Manufacturing Overhead Variances

42. Information from Shilling Manufacturing Inc. is as follows:

Actual number of direct labour hours	12,200
Actual fixed manufacturing overhead cost	$145,900
Actual number of units produced	2,400 units
Standard fixed manufacturing overhead rate	$12 per direct labour hour
Direct labour efficiency standard	5 hours
Budgeted production	2,500 units
Budgeted fixed manufacturing overhead	$150,000

REQUIRED:
a. Determine the fixed manufacturing overhead budget variance.
b. Determine the fixed manufacturing overhead volume variance in dollars.

LO 7:   Determine Fixed Manufacturing Overhead Variances

43. Information from Jennings Manufacturing Company is as follows:

Actual number of direct labour hours	5,130
Actual fixed manufacturing overhead cost	$24,900
Actual number of units produced	5,400 units
Standard fixed manufacturing overhead rate	$5 per direct labour hour
Direct labour efficiency standard	1 hour
Budgeted production	5,000 units
Budgeted fixed manufacturing overhead	$25,000

REQUIRED:
a. Determine the fixed manufacturing overhead budget variance.
b. Determine the fixed manufacturing overhead volume variance in dollars.

LO 7:   Determine Fixed Manufacturing Overhead Variances

44. Information from Columbia Manufacturing Company is as follows:

Actual number of direct labour hours	5,200
Actual fixed manufacturing overhead cost	$88,960
Actual number of units produced	2,700 units
Standard fixed manufacturing overhead rate	$15 per direct labour hour
Direct labour efficiency standard	2 hours
Budgeted production	3,000 units
Budgeted fixed manufacturing overhead	$90,000

REQUIRED:
a. Determine the fixed manufacturing overhead budget variance.
b. Determine the fixed manufacturing overhead volume variance in dollars.

LO 7:   Determine Fixed Manufacturing Overhead Variances

45. Cook Manufacturing Company's budgeted production is 200,000 units per month. Budgeted monthly fixed manufacturing overhead is $2,400,000 and is applied to production at a rate of $4 per direct labour hour. The direct labour efficiency standard is three direct labour hours per unit of production. Last month it took 520,000 actual direct labour hours to produce 175,000 units. Actual fixed manufacturing overhead for the month was $2,435,000.

REQUIRED:
a. Determine the fixed manufacturing overhead budget variance.
b. Determine the fixed manufacturing overhead volume variance.

LO 7: Determine Budgeted Production and Fixed Manufacturing Overhead Variances

46. Mast Manufacturing Company applies fixed manufacturing overhead at the rate of $20 per direct labour hour. Fixed manufacturing overhead is budgeted to be $4,000,000 per month. The direct labour efficiency standard is two hours per finished unit. Last month the company produced 89,000 units using 180,000 direct labour hours and incurring fixed manufacturing overhead cost of $4,100,000.

REQUIRED:
a. Determine the fixed manufacturing overhead budget variance.
b. Did the company produce as many units as it had planned? What is the difference between the planned number of units and the number of units actually produced?
c. Determine the fixed manufacturing overhead volume variance.

LO 7: Determine Budgeted Production and Fixed Manufacturing Overhead Variances

47. Clark Manufacturing Company applies fixed manufacturing overhead at the rate of $10 per direct labour hour. Fixed manufacturing overhead is budgeted to be $418,000 per month. The direct labour efficiency standard is four hours per finished unit. Last month the company produced 9,800 units using 36,500 direct labour hours and incurring fixed manufacturing overhead cost of $410,000.

REQUIRED:
a. Determine the fixed manufacturing overhead budget variance.
b. Did the company produce as many units as it had planned? What is the difference between the planned number of units and the number of units actually produced?
c. Determine the fixed manufacturing overhead volume variance.

LO 7: Determine Budgeted Production and Fixed Manufacturing Overhead Variances

48. Sappinere Manufacturing Inc. applies fixed manufacturing overhead at the rate of $15 per direct labour hour. Fixed manufacturing overhead is budgeted to be $247,500 per month. The direct labour efficiency standard is six hours per finished unit. Last month the company produced 2,500 units using 15,500 direct labour hours and incurring fixed manufacturing overhead cost of $230,000.

REQUIRED:

a. Determine the fixed manufacturing overhead budget variance.
b. Did the company produce as many units as it had planned? What is the difference between the planned number of units and the number of units actually produced?
c. Determine the fixed manufacturing overhead volume variance.

LO 7: Determine Budgeted Fixed Manufacturing Overhead and Fixed Manufacturing Overhead Variances

49. Information from Nasland Manufacturing Company is as follows:

Actual number of direct labour hours	32,500
Actual fixed manufacturing overhead cost	$428,000
Actual number of units produced	8,000 units
Standard fixed manufacturing overhead rate	$12 per direct labour hour
Direct labour efficiency standard	4 hours
Budgeted production	9,000 units
Budgeted fixed manufacturing overhead	$?

REQUIRED:

a. Determine the fixed manufacturing overhead budget variance.
b. Determine the fixed manufacturing overhead volume variance in dollars.

LO 7: Determine Fixed Manufacturing Overhead Variances

50. Information from Gordon Manufacturing Company is as follows:

Actual number of direct labour hours	13,000
Actual fixed manufacturing overhead cost	$50,000
Actual number of units produced	2,120 units
Standard fixed manufacturing overhead rate	$4 per direct labour hour
Direct labour efficiency standard	6 hours
Budgeted production	2,000 units
Budgeted fixed manufacturing overhead	$?

REQUIRED:

a. Determine the fixed manufacturing overhead budget variance.
b. Determine the fixed manufacturing overhead volume variance in dollars.

LO 7: Determine Fixed Manufacturing Overhead Variances

51. Information from Bradley Manufacturing Limited is as follows:

Actual number of direct labour hours	27,000
Actual fixed manufacturing overhead cost	$260,000
Actual number of units produced	3,250 units
Standard fixed manufacturing overhead rate	$9 per direct labour hour
Direct labour efficiency standard	8 hours
Budgeted production	3,500 units
Budgeted fixed manufacturing overhead	$?

REQUIRED:

a. Determine the fixed manufacturing overhead budget variance.
b. Determine the fixed manufacturing overhead volume variance in dollars.

LO 7: Determine Direct Material, Direct Labour, Variable Manufacturing Overhead, and Fixed Manufacturing Overhead Variances

52. Information from Bleinham Company is as follows:

Actual costs and amounts

Actual production	3,800 units
Actual cost of 23,000 kilograms of direct material purchased	$89,700
Actual amount of direct material used	22,950
Actual direct labour cost	$23,205
Actual direct labour hours	1,950 kilograms
Actual variable overhead cost	$12,000
Actual fixed overhead cost	$18,000

Standards and other budgeted amounts

Budgeted production	4,000 units
Direct material price standard	$3.85 per kilogram
Direct material quantity standard	6 kilograms per unit
Direct labour rate standard	$11 per hour
Direct labour efficiency standard per unit	0.5 hours
Standard variable manufacturing overhead rate	$5.50 per direct labour hour
Standard fixed manufacturing overhead rate	$10 per direct labour hour
Budgeted fixed manufacturing overhead	$20,000

REQUIRED:
Determine the following variances:
  a. Direct material price variance
  b. Direct material quantity variance in dollars
  c. Direct labour rate variance
  d. Direct labour efficiency variance in dollars
  e. Variable manufacturing overhead spending variance
  f. Variable manufacturing overhead efficiency variance in dollars
  g. Fixed manufacturing overhead budget variance
  h. Fixed manufacturing overhead volume variance in dollars

LO 7: Determine Direct Material, Direct Labour, Variable Manufacturing Overhead, and Fixed Manufacturing Overhead Variances

53. Information from Kay Manufacturing Inc. is as follows:

Actual costs and amounts

Actual production	6,300 units
Actual cost of 20,000 kilograms of direct material purchased	$40,000
Actual amount of direct material used	19,100 kilograms
Actual direct labour cost	$386,100
Actual direct labour hours	26,000 hours
Actual variable overhead cost	$165,000
Actual fixed overhead cost	$310,000

Standards and other budgeted amounts

Budgeted production	6,000	units
Direct material price standard	$2.10	per kilogram
Direct material quantity standard	3	kilograms per unit
Direct labour rate standard	$15	per hour
Direct labour efficiency standard per unit	4	hours
Standard variable mfg. overhead rate	$6.50	per direct labour hour
Standard fixed mfg. overhead rate	$12.75	per direct labour hour
Budgeted fixed manufacturing overhead	$306,000	

REQUIRED:

Determine the following variances:
  a. Direct material price variance
  b. Direct material quantity variance in dollars
  c. Direct labour rate variance
  d. Direct labour efficiency variance in dollars
  e. Variable manufacturing overhead spending variance
  f. Variable manufacturing overhead efficiency variance in dollars
  g. Fixed manufacturing overhead budget variance
  h. Fixed manufacturing overhead volume variance in dollars

LO 7: Determine Direct Material, Direct Labour, Variable Manufacturing Overhead, and Fixed Manufacturing Overhead Variances

54. Information from Collins Company is as follows:

Actual costs and amounts

Actual production	2,300	units
Actual cost of 16,000 kilograms of direct material purchased	$19,360	
Actual amount of direct material used	12,000	kilograms
Actual direct labour cost	$46,410	
Actual direct labour hours	4,750	hours
Actual variable overhead cost	$29,100	
Actual fixed overhead cost	$50,125	

Standards and other budgeted amounts

Budgeted production	3,000	units
Direct material price standard	$1.10	per kilogram
Direct material quantity standard	5	kilograms per unit
Direct labour rate standard	$12	per hour
Direct labour efficiency standard per unit	2	hours
Standard variable manufacturing overhead rate	$6	per direct labour hour
Standard fixed manufacturing overhead rate	$8	per direct labour hour
Budgeted fixed manufacturing overhead	$48,000	

REQUIRED:

Determine the following variances:

  a. Direct material price variance
  b. Direct material quantity variance in dollars
  c. Direct labour rate variance
  d. Direct labour efficiency variance in dollars
  e. Variable manufacturing overhead spending variance
  f. Variable manufacturing overhead efficiency variance in dollars
  g. Fixed manufacturing overhead budget variance
  h. Fixed manufacturing overhead volume variance in dollars

10

Evaluating Performance

$\mathcal{J}$ohnson & Johnson is a large multinational corporation. This manufacturer of health care products, with sales of more than $32,000,000,000, has over 100,000 employees, and operates in Canada and 53 other countries around the world.

How does a company of this size manage all of its operations? It would be almost impossible for the senior management of the company to manage so many employees and operating units. Consequently, Johnson & Johnson decentralized.

"Since the company's founding more than 100 years ago, Johnson & Johnson's organization structure has evolved into one unlike any other company of similar size. Johnson & Johnson is comprised of 37 global affiliates with 198 operating units—each of which is highly autonomous and accountable for its individual performance. This unique organization structure allows us to effectively support our business strategy of remaining the world's most comprehensive and broadly based health care company. It helps each of our affiliates and autonomous operating units focus on that part of our broadly based business where their accountability and expertise lie."[1]

Johnson & Johnson is an extreme example of how management responsibility must be delegated to subordinate managers as a company grows in size. This chapter will focus on how companies evaluate the performance of these managers. ■

---

[1] From the Johnson & Johnson web site's "Learn About Our Unique Organization Structure" section at www.jnj.com/careers/learn.html (accessed August 23, 2002).

LEARNING OBJECTIVES

After completing your work on this chapter, you should be able to do the following:

1. Describe centralized and decentralized management styles.
2. Describe the different types of business segments and the problems associated with determining segment costs.
3. Prepare a segment income statement.
4. Describe and calculate the return on investment.
5. Describe and calculate residual income.
6. Describe and calculate transfer prices.
7. Describe nonfinancial performance measures.

BUSINESS SEGMENTS

business segment A part of a company managed by a particular individual or a part of a company about which separate information is needed.

To help make businesses more manageable, their owners often divide them into parts. A **business segment** represents a part of a company managed by a particular individual, or a part of a company about which separate information is needed, perhaps to evaluate management performance or to help managers make better management decisions.

Companies can be segmented by geographic area or location, business function, product, product line, or department. Examples of business segments include the Latin American subsidiary of the Molson Companies, an individual The Bay department store, a Proctor and Gamble manufacturing factory, and the Faculty of Commerce at the University of Alberta. A segment can be described as a department, a division, an area, a region, a product line, or some other designation.

segment reports Reports that provide information pertaining to a particular business segment.

Obtaining detailed information about business segments is a vital part of the management decision process. Managers need information that relates to their business segment. Reports that provide information pertaining to a particular business segment are called **segment reports.** Segment reports should not be clouded by data that relate to other segments or by general information pertaining to the company as a whole. For example, if you were the manager of the Hard Rock Cafe in Toronto, and responsible for enhancing the restaurant's profits, you would benefit by having information about your particular restaurant. Although it might be somewhat helpful to know the overall profitability of the entire restaurant chain, specific information about the Toronto Hard Rock would be much more useful. You might want to know detailed sales information by product, by server, and by time of day. You would also want a comprehensive listing of your restaurant's expenses. Reports that include only revenues and expenses for your restaurant would help you to find opportunities to increase profits.

 Discussion Question

10–1. If you were the manager of the Fairmont Chateau Whistler, what information would you want to help maximize the performance of the hotel?

Segment Information

Depending on the needs of management and the availability of information, segment reports may be simple and include little detail, or they may be quite elaborate and include an abundance of detailed segment information. For example, it is possible for segment reports to consist simply of a listing of the segment's sales by product; or, segment reports may include sales, expenses, and other information. The extent of the information included in segment reports depends on management's need to know, balanced with the cost of providing the information.

THE SEGMENT INCOME STATEMENT

segment income statement
An income statement prepared for a business segment.

An income statement prepared for a business segment is called a **segment income statement.** When a segment income statement is prepared, either the functional income statement or the contribution income statement format can be used. Recall from our discussions in Chapter 5 that the functional income statement separates costs into product and period costs. The contribution income statement classifies costs by behaviour, either variable or fixed. We know that a variable cost is one that changes in total based on some activity, whereas a fixed cost is one that remains unchanged regardless of the level of activity. To be sure you remember these two income statement formats, we reproduce them in Exhibit 10–1.

Exhibit 10–1
Functional and Contribution Income Statement Formats

Functional Format	Contribution Income Format
Sales	Sales
− Cost of Goods Sold (Product Cost)	− All Variable Costs (Product and Period)
= Gross Profit	= Contribution Margin
− Selling and Admin. Expense (Period Cost)	− All Fixed Costs (Product and Period)
= Net Income	= Net Income

segment margin The amount of income that pertains to a particular segment.

To prepare a segment income statement, we gather revenue and expense information that pertains to the particular segment and then arrange it in the appropriate income statement format. The amount of income that pertains to a particular segment is called the **segment margin.** Because the contribution income format is particularly well-suited for our work in this chapter, we use that format in all our remaining presentations. A segment income statement for the Calgary office of William Moving Company appears in Exhibit 10–2.

Exhibit 10–2
Segment Income Statement for the Calgary Office

WILLIAM MOVING COMPANY
CALGARY OFFICE
Segment Income Statement
For the Year Ended December 31, 2004

Sales	$1,200,000
Variable costs	800,000
Contribution margin	400,000
Fixed costs for Calgary office	300,000
Segment margin	$ 100,000

It is important that the segment income statement for the Calgary office of William Moving Company include all the appropriate information for the Calgary office, and no more. Often, this is easier said than done. Generally, revenue can easily be traced to individual business segments; therefore, obtaining detailed revenue information by segment is not too difficult. Unfortunately, however, the same cannot always be said for cost information.

It is often difficult (if not impossible) to obtain cost information that includes all the costs for a particular segment and excludes costs associated with other segments. There are several reasons for this. First, it may be difficult to identify all the costs that relate to the segment. For example, say that the Eastern Division of Trans-Canada Distributing Inc. has three copiers. Certainly the cost of these copiers should be included in any evaluation of the Eastern Division. These three copiers, however, are just three of the 27 copiers owned by Trans-Canada Distributing Inc. (the other 24 copiers are in other segments). The problem is that all 27 copiers were purchased by the central company purchasing department, and Eastern Division has no record of the cost of its three copiers.

 Discussion Question

10–2. What are three other costs that relate directly to the Eastern Division, but for which the division probably does not have information?

The second reason it may be difficult to identify costs to particular segments is that costs are often mixed together in the accounting process. An example of this might be advertising purchased by Trans-Canada Distributing, Inc., which benefits not only the Eastern Division, but also the three other divisions of the company. The exact amount that should be charged to the Eastern Division is virtually impossible to determine accurately.

 Discussion Question

10–3. What are three other costs that benefit the Eastern Division but benefit at least one other division as well?

To help manage a business segment, we should include all the costs associated with the segment on cost reports prepared for it. It is equally important that costs that do not pertain to the segment be excluded from the segment's cost reports. In the case of variable costs, this is fairly straightforward. Variable costs can be traced directly to the business segments to which they pertain and then be included on the appropriate segment reports.

Fixed costs are more difficult to trace to individual business segments and therefore present more of a challenge. One problem with tracing fixed costs to business segments is that some fixed costs pertain to a single business segment whereas others benefit several segments or perhaps the company as a whole. Fixed costs that arise to support a single segment are called **direct fixed costs** or **traceable fixed costs.** These fixed costs can be *traced* to an individual business segment. Direct fixed costs should be included on the cost reports for the segment to which

direct fixed cost Fixed cost incurred to support a single business segment.

traceable fixed cost Another name for *direct fixed cost.*

common fixed cost Fixed cost incurred to support more than one business segment or the company as a whole.

indirect fixed cost Another name for *common fixed cost.*

they pertain. Fixed costs that arise to support more than one segment or the company as a whole are called **common fixed costs** or **indirect fixed costs.**

This discussion of direct and indirect costs should not seem entirely new. It is a subject we covered in some depth in Chapter 2 when we discussed the concept of a cost object. As you recall, a cost object is any activity or item for which a separate cost measurement is desired. A cost that can be traced directly to a cost object is a direct cost, whereas a cost that is incurred to support multiple cost objects is an indirect cost. In our present discussion, the cost object is the business segment.

Because common fixed costs benefit several segments or the company in general, segment managers often have little control over these costs. A simple question can be asked to determine whether a cost is a common cost or a direct cost:

Would the cost continue if the segment were to disappear?

If the cost will continue even if the segment disappeared, the cost is a common fixed cost. If, on the other hand, the cost would disappear if the segment disappears, the cost is a direct fixed cost. There are very few, if any, common variable costs; thus, in virtually all instances, the common costs we must consider are fixed.

For many years there has been debate as to whether cost reports prepared for an individual segment should include some allocated amount of common fixed costs. Proponents of allocation maintain that common fixed costs benefit the entire company and therefore each segment should be charged for its "fair share" of the common cost. Further, they argue that it is impossible to determine true segment profitability if common costs are excluded. Opponents of allocation argue just the opposite. They maintain that because segment managers have little or no authority to exercise control over common fixed costs, these costs should not be included in segment reports. These folks believe it is unfair to charge a manager's department for costs that are out of his or her control. In addition, common fixed costs are generally distributed to various business segments based on an arbitrary allocation scheme and can make a segment appear to be unprofitable when, in fact, that segment is contributing to the overall profitability of the company. Managers may attempt to "control" the common fixed costs allocated to their segment by manipulating the allocation base.

 Discussion Question

10–4. Assume for a moment that you are a segment manager at Proctor and Gamble. How would you react to a charge made to your department for a portion of the cost of the fleet of corporate aircraft, even though you have never even seen one of the planes?

Both the proponents and opponents of common fixed cost allocation to business segments feel strongly about their positions. There seems to be little question, however, that the practice of including common fixed costs in segment reports is losing popularity. This fact is not surprising when we consider that the main purpose of management accounting is to influence managers to act to benefit the company. It seems clear that including common fixed costs in segment reports can lead managers toward behaviour that is counterproductive. Restricting a segment cost report to costs over which a manager has control makes it a more useful tool for supporting sound business decisions.

The Pitfall of Allocating Common Fixed Costs— A Closer Look

When common fixed costs are allocated to segments, segment information may be misleading and result in disastrous business decisions. As an example, consider the segmented income statement for Cloverdale Feed Stores presented in Exhibit 10–3.

Exhibit 10–3
Cloverdale Feed Stores
Segment Income
Statement

CLOVERDALE FEED STORES
Segment Income Statement
For the Year Ended December 31, 2005

	Company Total	North Store	South Store	Central Store
Sales	$500,000	$105,000	$225,000	$170,000
Variable costs	332,950	73,750	141,000	118,200
Contribution margin	167,050	31,250	84,000	51,800
Direct fixed costs	75,000	20,000	32,000	23,000
Segment margin	92,050	11,250	52,000	28,800
Common fixed costs	60,000	12,600*	27,000**	20,400***
Net income	$ 32,050	($ 1,350)	$ 25,000	$ 8,400

* $105,000/$500,000 = 21\%; 21\% \times $60,000 = $12,600$

** $225,000/$500,000 = 45\%; 45\% \times $60,000 = $27,000$

*** $170,000/$500,000 = 34\%; 34\% \times $60,000 = $20,400$

As you can see from Exhibit 10–3, the $60,000 common fixed cost has been allocated to the business segments based on relative sales volume, which means that because the South Store provided 45 percent of the company's sales ($225,000/$500,000 = 45%), this store is allocated 45 percent of the common fixed cost ($60,000 × 45% = $27,000). Of the common fixed cost, 34 percent was allocated to the Central Store based on its percentage of sales, and 21 percent was allocated to the North Store. As you can see, it appears that the North Store is unprofitable. Based on the information in Exhibit 10–3, it seems that profits could be increased if the unprofitable North Store is closed. By closing the North Store it appears that the $1,350 loss would be eliminated. Let's look at the results had the North Store been eliminated. The segment income statement for Cloverdale Feed Stores without the North Store is presented in Exhibit 10–4.

As the exhibit shows, when the North Store is eliminated, Cloverdale's net income actually *declines* from $32,050 to $20,800. On the surface this seems to make no sense, because the results in Exhibit 10–3 showed the North Store with a net loss for the year of $1,350. So, how did eliminating the North Store cause profits to drop by $11,250 ($32,050 − $20,800)? The answer lies in the practice of allocating common fixed cost. Notice in Exhibit 10–4 that the common fixed cost of $60,000 did not change when the North Store was removed, because the common fixed cost is for items that are necessary to operate the company even if there are fewer stores. For example, even if the North Store closes, common costs for such items as accounting, finance, and the cost of operating the home office would continue. Therefore, the $60,000 common fixed cost would have to be distributed to the two remaining stores. Again, this configuration is done based on relative sales values.

CLOVERDALE FEED STORES
Segment Income Statement
For the Year Ended December 31, 2005

	Company Total	South Store	Central Store
Sales	$395,000	$225,000	$170,000
Variable costs	259,200	141,000	118,200
Contribution margin	135,800	84,000	51,800
Direct fixed costs	55,000	32,000	23,000
Segment margin	80,800	52,000	28,800
Common fixed costs	60,000	34,200*	25,800**
Net income	$ 20,800	$ 17,800	$ 3,000

* $225,000/$395,000 = 57% (rounded); 57% × $60,000 = $34,200
** $170,000/$395,000 = 43% (rounded); 43% × $60,000 = $25,800

In truth, the North Store is contributing to Cloverdale's overall profitability. When the North Store is eliminated, so is its segment margin. It is not a coincidence that the $11,250 decline in profits without the North Store is exactly equal to the North Store's segment margin in Exhibit 10–3. If the North Store is eliminated, its segment margin disappears, but the common fixed cost remains and must be allocated to the remaining segments.

To avoid such misleading information and the poor decisions that can result, many companies have stopped the practice of allocating common fixed costs to segments. The segmented income statement for Cloverdale Feed Stores without the allocation of common fixed cost is shown in Exhibit 10–5.

Exhibit 10–5
Cloverdale Feed Stores
Segment Income
Statement without
Allocation of Common
Fixed Cost

CLOVERDALE FEED STORES
Segment Income Statement
For the Year Ended December 31, 2005

	Company Total	North Store	South Store	Central Store
Sales	$500,000	$105,000	$225,000	$170,000
Variable costs	332,950	73,750	141,000	118,200
Contribution margin	167,050	31,250	84,000	51,800
Direct fixed costs	75,000	20,000	32,000	23,000
Segment margin	92,050	$ 11,250	$ 52,000	$ 28,800
Common fixed costs	60,000			
Net income	$ 32,050			

As shown in Exhibit 10–5, when common fixed costs are not allocated, the segment margin becomes the "bottom line" for each segment. This amount is a better indicator of segment profit performance because it considers direct costs, costs over which the segment manager has control.

To provide useful information to help evaluate segment performance and to help segment managers make informed decisions, all direct costs that pertain to a particular segment must be included in the management reports for that segment. If a direct cost is excluded, it is unlikely that the segment manager will work to reduce that cost. For example, assume that a leased photocopier is used exclusively by the finance department of a major corporation. Assume further that the rent for the photocopier, plus the rent for all the other photocopiers used by the company, is included in a monthly bill from Acme PhotoCopy Equipment Inc. If the rent cost included on this single bill is not distributed (charged) to user departments, the cost for each department is understated by the amount of the rent. If this happens, the rent for the photocopier would be excluded from the information used to help evaluate the finance department's performance. Therefore, it is unlikely that the finance department manager would work to reduce the rental cost by switching to a less expensive photocopier. In fact, once the manager finds that the cost of the photocopier is not charged to the department, he or she might even upgrade to an overly elaborate photocopier knowing that the department will not be penalized for such an expenditure. Thus, it is important to include all costs associated with a business segment in the segment's cost reports.

SERVICE DEPARTMENT COST ALLOCATION

service department A business segment responsible for secondary (support) functions. Service departments provide service to the main business operations and to other service departments.

The main operation of a merchandiser is selling products. For a manufacturer, the main operation is manufacturing and selling products. For a service business, the main operation is providing services to customers. In addition to any company's main business operation, however, secondary support operations also occur. Most companies, whether merchandisers, manufacturers, or service type businesses, also have accounting departments, a human resources department, and other departments that provide support to the various functions of the company. Further, telephone service must be provided, and a facility (building) within which to operate. The business segments that handle these and other secondary operations are called **service departments.** These departments provide necessary services to the main business operations and other service departments.

 Discussion Question

10–5. Besides the ones listed in the previous paragraph, what are five other service departments you think would be common to most companies?

The cost of operating a service department can be substantial. This cost is allocated to the departments that use the services provided. In other words, if a particular department receives benefit from a service department, that department should be charged for the cost of the service.

Determining the amount of service department cost to charge various user departments is not an exact science. For some kinds of service cost, a direct correlation can be found between the amount of service provided to a department and the cost charged to that department. In these instances, the manager of the user department rarely disputes the charge. For other types of service cost, however, no direct cause and effect can be found. In that event, the cost charged to departments for services is based on an allocation method that may or may not be accurate or even fair. This allocation is much like that of common fixed cost to segments, as discussed earlier. The allocation of service department cost when no correlation can be found between the service and the cost can actually cloud management's vision about the performance of a department.

As was the case with the allocation of fixed common cost to segments, certain managers believe that service department costs should be allocated whereas others believe the practice should be stopped. As usual, both sides hold strongly to their views. Although some companies have stopped allocating service department cost, the majority of companies still maintain this practice. The responsibility of department managers is to be vigilant in making certain that the costs charged to their departments reasonably reflect the amount of service received. Examples of service departments and possible allocation bases are shown in Exhibit 10–6.

Exhibit 10–6
Representative Service Departments and Possible Allocation Bases

Service Department	Allocation Basis
Human Resources	• Number of employees
Communications	• Number of phones • Number of lines • Long-distance charges • Number of computers with e-mail access

Photocopy Machine or Copy Centre	• Quantity of services used:
	  • Number of single-sided copies
	  • Number of double-sided copies
	  • Number of bindings

Employee Cafeteria	• Number of employees • Number of meals served
Finance Department	• Amount of capital invested
Building Occupancy	• Square metres of building occupied
Computer Operations	• Computer mainframe time • Number of personal computers • Number of reports generated
Computer Programming	• Hours of programming
Office Services	• Area in square metres of office occupied • Number of offices
Engineering Department	• Number of engineering changes • Hours of engineering services
Maintenance	• Area in square metres of building occupied • Hours of maintenance
Aircraft Operations	• Number of "passenger miles" • Number of hours flown • Weight of load and distance flown

ACTIVITY-BASED SERVICE DEPARTMENT COST ALLOCATION

Activity-based costing is a topic we covered in Chapter 3 when we discussed alternative ways to allocate manufacturing overhead to units of product produced.

Activity-based costing can also be a valuable tool for allocating service department cost to other departments. When possible, the allocation base used to allocate cost should be an activity that causes the cost. As stated in Chapter 3, an activity that causes cost to occur is called a *cost driver*. The two major benefits to using cost drivers to allocate service department cost are (1) this cost allocation method tends to be more fair and accurate, and (2) in attempting to control the cost allocated to their departments, managers will work to reduce the allocation base—the cost driver. Because the cost driver is also the cost cause, reducing the cost driver will actually reduce the amount paid by the company for goods and services. For example, when the cost driver used to allocate basic phone service is the number of phone lines, a reduction in the number of phone lines will not only reduce the allocation of phone cost, but it will also reduce the amount the company spends for phone service. This reduction results in true cost savings for the company.

 Discussion Question

10–6. Refer to the list of five service departments you made in response to Discussion Question 10–5. What is a possible allocation base for each of the departments you listed?

It is important to know about service department cost allocation for several reasons. First, as a department manager, you will need to know how to control service department costs allocated to your department. Second, you should be able to discriminate between costs that are arbitrarily allocated to your department and those that are equitable. Third, as a high-level manager, you should be able to recognize when an allocation method should be modified or replaced, because it does not result in information that provides incentives for managers to act in fulfillment of company goals.

Sometimes the allocation method can cause managers to do counterproductive things, especially when activity-based costing is not used to allocate costs. For example, consider what happened to a major corporation when it changed the allocation base it used to distribute the cost of office space. From a charge for all the square metres the departments occupied, the firm changed to a charge for only the square metres of the enclosed office space occupied by the departments. Top managers felt that departments should not be charged for halls, elevator waiting areas, or other common areas but only for the office space dedicated entirely to the department's use. Some managers recognized that their department's allocation for office space could be cut if they were to reduce the square metres used for enclosed offices. Accordingly, they demolished several offices occupied by department secretaries and provided them with desks and work space in the "common" area. The result was an increase in the amount of common space, and a marked decrease in the amount of square metres used for enclosed offices. Because the departments were only charged for enclosed office space, their office space cost allocation was reduced.

The change worked to the detriment of the company as a whole, however, because managers were rewarded for remodeling their offices even though the cost of the remodeling was unnecessary. Interestingly, only managers who had a working knowledge of how service department costs were allocated knew how to take advantage of the situation.

Discussion Question

10–7. Do you think the cost previously described should even be allocated? If not, explain your reasoning. If yes, what would you suggest to the company to overcome the dysfunctional management behaviour described?

Reducing the service cost allocated to a particular department is not a difficult task to accomplish. First, the department manager must determine what allocation base is being used. Second, the manager must reduce the amount of the allocation base consumed by the department. If the allocation base used is a cost driver, the actual cost involved will decrease. If the allocation base is arbitrary and unrelated to the actual cost, the amount allocated to the department will decrease, but the actual cost to the company will continue and simply be shifted to some other manager's department.

As an example of how to control service department cost allocation, assume that the cost of photocopies is allocated based on the number of copies made. A reduction in the number of copies made will reduce the copy cost allocated to the user department. An attempt to reduce the number of copies would include a review of department procedures to ensure that only necessary copies are made. It might also include a review of alternative technologies such as e-mail to find ways to reduce the need for photocopies. This same logic can be used to control the cost allocation for telephone use, which is often allocated to departments based on the number of phone lines used. To reduce the cost allocation, unnecessary telephones are eliminated.

In each of these two examples, because the allocation base is a cost driver, a reduction in the base would not only cause a reduction in the cost allocated to the department but would also cause a true reduction in cost to the company.

APPROACHES TO SEGMENT MANAGEMENT

The strategy used to manage business segments varies from company to company. Some companies prefer that top management make all but the most routine decisions, whereas other companies prefer that lower-level managers make most or all of the decisions within their area. When almost all decisions are made by the top managers and little is left to the discretion of lower-level managers, the company is said to have a centralized management style. Conversely, if management decisions are made at the lowest possible management level, the company is said to have a decentralized management style. These management styles have both advantages and disadvantages.

Centralized Management

centralized management
A management style in which top managers make most management decisions.

When a **centralized management** style is used, top management makes most management decisions. Middle- and lower-level managers are responsible only for routine decisions and supervisory functions. This management style ensures that the wishes of top management are incorporated into each management decision. Top managers often have the most experience, which could lead to wise business decisions. A centralized management style has certain disadvantages: (1) Top managers must spend their valuable time making routine, low-level business decisions. (2) Top managers may not have an intimate familiarity with the various routine aspects of the business. (3) Lower-level employees have little opportunity to gain experience in decision making.

Decentralized Management

decentralized management
A management style in which lower-level managers are responsible for decisions that relate to their segment of the company.

When a **decentralized management** style is used, lower-level managers are responsible for management decisions that relate to their segment of the business. When a highly decentralized management style is used, decisions are made at the lowest possible level in the organization.

A decentralized management style has several advantages. It helps spread the decision-making responsibilities among the various management levels of the company and allows lower-level managers greater control over their business segments. Another benefit is that a decentralized management style provides an opportunity for lower-level managers to sharpen their decision-making skills, thus providing the company with experienced managers to progress through the ranks to top management positions. Decentralization also means that decisions are made by the managers who are most familiar with the problems and opportunities occurring in the routine operations of the company. Top managers may be somewhat removed from the intimacies of the daily routine business operations and therefore would be hard pressed to make well-informed decisions. Another advantage is that it relieves top managers of the responsibility of routine decisions and allows them to focus on strategic decisions and the overall goals of the organization.

A disadvantage of decentralized management is that decisions may not entirely reflect the views of top managers. Also, decisions are made by managers who may be less experienced than the top managers.

 Discussion Questions

10–8. If you were the chief executive officer of your company, would you prefer a centralized or decentralized management style? Why?

10–9. If you were a lower-level manager in your company, would you prefer a centralized or decentralized management style? Why?

10–10. What similarities do you see between our discussion here of centralized and decentralized management and our discussion in Chapter 8 of top-down and bottom-up budgeting?

EVALUATION OF BUSINESS SEGMENTS

To evaluate the performance of business segments, we must first determine just what constitutes good performance. To establish whether a manager is doing a good job, for example, we must first have some idea of just what a "good job" means. To evaluate segment performance, a standard must be developed that establishes just what constitutes "good performance."

The performance of a business segment can be evaluated based on a number of criteria. The most logical evaluation criteria match the scope of responsibility and authority afforded the segment's manager. That is, if a particular segment's manager has the responsibility and authority only to control costs, the segment performance should be evaluated based on criteria that focus on cost control. Conversely, if the segment manager has the responsibility to generate revenue and also to control costs, the segment's performance should be evaluated based on criteria that focus on profits. Segments may be categorized based on the criteria used for their evaluation. The most popular segment categories are revenue centres, cost centres, profit centres, and investment centres.

Revenue Centres

revenue centre A business segment in which the manager has responsibility and authority to act to increase revenues but has little or no control over costs and the amount invested in the segment.

A **revenue centre** is a business segment whose manager has responsibility and authority to act to increase revenues but has little control over costs and the amount invested in the segment. The performance of a revenue centre is evaluated based on the amount of revenue generated by the segment, and the manager is evaluated based on his or her ability to generate sales revenue.

An example of a business segment properly designated a revenue centre is a sales office whose segment manager has little or no control over costs. The results of the manager's actions would affect sales revenue but have minimal effect on cost.

Cost Centres

cost centre A business segment where the manager has responsibility and authority to act to decrease or at least control costs but has little or no control over the revenues generated or the amount invested in the segment.

A **cost centre** is a business segment whose manager has responsibility and authority to decrease or at least control costs while keeping output high. Generally, cost centre managers are not responsible for generating revenue, nor do they have control over the amount invested in the segment. The performance of a cost centre is evaluated based on the amount of cost incurred by the segment and the manager is evaluated based on his or her ability to control these costs.

Business segments that provide service to the company or customers but do not contribute directly to revenues are good candidates to be designated as cost centres. Examples of cost centres include the accounting department of a company, a repair department that handles warranty repair work, an assembly department, and an inspection facility in a manufacturing factory.

Profit Centres

profit centre A business segment in which the manager has the responsibility and authority to act to increase revenue and decrease or at least control costs, but has little or no control over the amount invested in the segment.

A **profit centre** is a business segment whose manager has the responsibility and authority to act to increase revenue and decrease or at least control costs but does not have control over the amount invested in the segment. The performance of a profit centre is evaluated based on the amount of profits it generates. The manager of a profit centre is evaluated based on his or her ability to increase revenue and control expenses, because profits are increased by increasing revenue and/or decreasing expenses.

Examples of profit centres could include individual stores in a department store chain, a college bookstore, and the information technology division of a consulting practice.

Measuring Performance of Revenue, Cost, and Profit Centres

The most commonly used method of evaluating the performance of revenue centres, cost centres, and profit centres is performance to budget. The sales goals established during the budgeting process can be used as a basis for evaluating the performance of revenue centres. If, for example, actual sales are higher than budgeted sales, this would be a favourable indication. If, on the other hand, actual sales are lower than budgeted sales, this would be an unfavourable indication. For a cost centre, the goals established during the budgeting process for output and cost can be used as a basis for evaluating cost centre performance. Actual production that exceeds budgeted production, for example, would be a favourable indication. Costs per unit of output that are lower than budgeted would also be a favourable indication. Obviously, favourable performance would be indicated by high output and low cost relative to output volume. For a profit centre, the profit goals established during the budgeting process can be compared to actual profits to evaluate profit centre performance. Favourable performance would be indicated by actual profits that meet or exceed budgeted profits.

It is often argued that having managers strive to meet budgeted performance targets is so simplistic that it leads to suboptimal performance. Managers may simply strive to meet the expectations established by the budget instead of trying to maximize sales. Another potential problem is that managers who are evaluated based on performance to budget can make themselves look good by negotiating relatively low budgeted sales and relatively high budgeted costs. Then when the actual sales are higher than budget, and the actual costs are lower than budgeted, the manager appears to have performed well. This information may seem familiar to you. Other chapters in the text included brief discussions of the problems associated with performance to budget as a way to measure managers' performance—a subject addressed in Chapter 8 when we presented the operating budget and again in Chapter 9 in the presentation of standard costing. Everything about the potential for counterproductive behaviour inherent in the performance to budget evaluation technique applies to measuring the performance of revenue centres, cost centres, and profit centres.

If we move away from performance to budget as a means of evaluating revenue centre managers, however, what do we put in its place? This topic has been a topic of debate for some time in management accounting circles. The answer, we suspect, is not to drop performance to budget as a performance measure entirely. Rather, it should be supplemented with other types of measures, some of which are presented near the end of this chapter. For now, just remember that a company runs a real risk of encouraging silly management behaviour if it relies too heavily on performance to budget as a means of evaluating its managers.

 A User's View

Alan Raffan is the vice-president of finance for AFM Hospitality Inc. The company acts as the franchise holder for several different international hotel chains in addition to managing hotels for a variety of clients. Alan explains how the company's hotel managers are evaluated:

"One part of our business is to manage hotels for absentee owners. Part of our management fee for running a hotel is based on the net income the hotel generates. The hotel is managed as a profit centre, and the manager is evaluated on his or her ability to provide net income in excess of a budgeted amount. In turn, the manager evaluates the performance of each of the hotel's major operating departments, such as Rooms, or Food and Beverage. Thus, the hotel manager has to pay attention to the results of the operating departments and take corrective action to address problems as they arise. Since the hotel managers receive a bonus if their results are favourable compared to budget, they are motivated to ensure that their departments run smoothly and to control their costs. We find this system motivates the managers to make decisions that are in the best interests of the company."

Investment Centres

Does earning a profit of $100,000 constitute good performance? Before we can tell just how good it is, we should also consider the amount of investment required. Surely, almost any business segment can be profitable if there is an unlimited amount to invest in assets and technology. In business, the hope is to keep the profit high and the amount invested low.

investment centre A business segment that is evaluated based on the amount of profit generated relative to the amount invested in the segment.

An **investment centre** is a business segment that is evaluated on the amount of profit generated relative to the amount invested in the segment. An investment centre manager should strive to maximize profit while minimizing the amount of investment used to earn the profit. Reducing the investment in a given segment allows the freed-up funds to be used by other segments. If the funds are not needed by the company elsewhere, financing can be reduced.

If a segment manager has responsibility and authority for revenues, costs, and capital investment in the segment, it should probably be designated an investment centre. Examples of business segments that might be designated investment centres are individual stores in a department store chain, a college bookstore, and an operating division of a manufacturing company. Note that some of these examples are the same as those given for segments designated as profit centres in our earlier discussion, because the classification of a business segment as a revenue centre, profit centre, cost centre, or investment centre depends not only on the operation of the segment but also, and as importantly, on the responsibility and authority afforded the segment's manager. If a manager's responsibility includes the generation of revenue, cost control, and control of the amount invested in the segment, then the business segment she or he manages should be designated an investment centre.

As stated earlier, an investment centre should be evaluated not only on the income generated by the segment, but also on the amount of investment required to earn the income. Obviously the higher the net income, the better, and the lower the investment required to generate that net income, the better. To evaluate the performance of an investment centre we must be able to quantify the relationship between income earned and the investment required. For example, if you are about to invest in a savings account, it might be beneficial to know that a $5,245 deposit will earn interest of $183.57 in one year's time. Without knowing the percentage interest rate of return, however, the amounts have little meaning when evaluating the performance of the savings account. In business, the percentage return on an amount invested is called the return on investment.

RETURN ON INVESTMENT

In 1903, Pierre Du Pont and two cousins, Alfred and Coleman, formed the E.I. Du Pont de Nemours Powder Company by combining several gunpowder companies they had purchased from other Du Pont family members. When the cousins purchased the companies, they paid for them by issuing bonds equal in value to the expected future earnings potential of the companies acquired to form the new business. Pierre and his cousins could realize a profit only when the income from the new company exceeded the projected income of the companies they had purchased. Therefore, if income did not increase, there would only be enough profits to pay the bonds, leaving no profit for the cousins. This transaction is an early example of a leveraged buyout.

Knowing only the *amount* of income was not enough to monitor the success of the new organization. Accordingly, Pierre Du Pont devised the return on investment model to calculate the percentage return on the cousins' investment. The return on investment could be used to assess whether the returns of the individual segments of the Du Pont Company exceeded the rate used to calculate the purchase price and interest payments on the bonds. Of course, the hope was that each of the segments of the Du Pont Company would have a return on investment that exceeded the rate used to determine the purchase price. The company went on to become the Du Pont chemical company we know today, of which DuPont Canada Inc. is a part.

 Discussion Question

10–11. What similarities do you see between our discussion here of return on investment and our discussion in Chapter 7 of capital expenditures?

return on investment (ROI)
The percentage return generated by an investment in a business or a business segment.

Since its inception, Du Pont's return on investment model has been a popular method of evaluating investment centres. **Return on investment (ROI)** is the percentage return generated by an investment in a business or business segment. The ROI is calculated by dividing the amount of income by the amount invested. For example, assume that the Ontario Division of Delta Corporation generated a segment margin of $896,750 for 2004 and the amount invested in the division was $10,550,000. This information is interesting, but it is probably more meaningful to know the percentage return that the investment generated. The ROI for Delta Corporation is 8.5 percent, determined as follows:

$$\frac{\text{Segment Income}}{\text{Investment in the Segment}} = \text{Return on Investment}$$

$$\frac{\$896,750}{\$10,550,000} = 8.5\%$$

After we determine the ROI for the division, the next question is, is the ROI adequate? If a company uses ROI as the measurement criterion for evaluating segment performance, it must establish a required rate for the ROI. The required rate of return that companies normally use is the weighted-average cost of capital rate, as discussed in Chapter 7 concerning capital expenditures. Once established, the required ROI rate is used as a benchmark to evaluate the performance of the various investment centres in the company. A segment with an ROI that equals or exceeds the company's required rate will be viewed favourably, whereas a segment with an ROI that is lower than the required rate will be viewed as deficient. If we assume that the required rate for the ROI for Delta Corporation is 8 percent, then the Ontario Division's performance is certainly adequate.

 Discussion Question

10–12. What similarities do you see between our discussion here of the ROI calculation and our discussion in Chapter 7 of the internal rate of return?

In evaluating segment performance, we can rank segments by their return on investment. For example, if the Western Division of Delta Corporation has income of $857,500 with an investment on $9,800,000, how does the performance of the Western Division compare to that of the Ontario Division? The return on investment of both divisions is presented as Exhibit 10–7.

Exhibit 10–7
Return on Investment for Both Divisions of Delta Corporation

Ontario Division	Western Division
$\dfrac{\text{Segment Income}}{\text{Investment in the Segment}} = \text{ROI}$	$\dfrac{\text{Segment Income}}{\text{Investment in the Segment}} = \text{ROI}$
$\dfrac{\$896,750}{\$10,550,00} = 8.5\%$	$\dfrac{\$857,500}{\$9,800,000} = 8.75\%$

Based on the ROI, the performance of the Western Division is superior to that of the Ontario Division because its ROI is greater. In this case, the Western Division's manager may be rewarded because of that division's better performance. As you might imagine, the use of ROI tends to encourage competition among segment managers, who strive to enhance performance evaluation by choosing investments that will work to increase their segment's ROI.

For the ROI to increase, the ROI of any new investment must exceed the segment's current ROI. If a new investment promises an ROI that is equal to the segment's current ROI, the segment's ROI will remain unchanged. However, if the new investment's ROI is less than the segment's current ROI, the segment's ROI will decrease. For example, assume that the manager of the Ontario Division is contemplating a new investment in the hope of improving his or her performance evaluation. An investment opportunity is available that promises additional income of $123,750 and requires an additional investment of $1,500,000. The ROI for this new investment opportunity is 8.25 percent calculated as follows:

$$\frac{\text{New Investment Income}}{\text{Investment in the New Project}} = \text{ROI}$$

$$\frac{\$123,750}{\$1,500,000} = 8.25\%$$

Based on the company's required rate of return of 8 percent, it seems that the project should be accepted. Will the manager of the Ontario Division accept the project because it exceeds the company's required ROI and would benefit the company as a whole? Unfortunately, the answer is probably no. The manager of the Ontario Division may not select this project because it would work to reduce the *segment's* current ROI, as shown in Exhibit 10–8.

Although the Ontario Division's ROI would still be well above the required ROI rate of 8 percent, the new investment would reduce the division's ROI from 8.5 percent to approximately 8.47 percent.

When ROI is used as the segment performance measure, the evaluation is usually based not only on how the segment's ROI compares to the company's required rate, but also on how the segment's ROI compares to the ROI of other segments. Therefore, managers will only select projects that will enhance their current ROI. Unfortunately this often works to the detriment of the company as a whole, because projects that meet the company's required ROI rate are rejected simply because they will not increase the segment's ROI. Fortunately, another

Exhibit 10–8

Effect of New Project on Ontario Division's Segment ROI

Ontario Division *Without* the New Investment Opportunity	Ontario Division *With* the New Investment Opportunity
$\dfrac{\text{Segment Income}}{\text{Investment in the Segment}} = \text{ROI}$	$\dfrac{\text{Segment Income}}{\text{Investment in the Segment}} = \text{ROI}$
$\dfrac{\$896,750}{\$10,550,000} = 8.5\%$	$\dfrac{\$896,750 + \$123,750}{\$10,550,000 + \$1,500,000} = \text{ROI}$
	$\dfrac{\$1,020,500}{\$12,050,000} = 8.47\%$

evaluation technique encourages managers to accept projects that have an ROI exceeding the company's required ROI rate. This evaluation technique is called residual income.

RESIDUAL INCOME

residual income The amount by which a segment's actual income exceeds the income needed to meet a company's required rate of return.

economic value added (EVA®) Another name sometimes used for *residual income.*

Residual income (sometimes called **economic value added,** or **EVA**®[2]) is a technique used to evaluate investment centres by focusing on the amount by which a segment's actual income exceeds the income needed to meet the company's required rate of return. As an example, let us take another look at Delta Corporation. Recall that the investment in the Ontario Division of Delta Corporation is $10,550,000 and that the company's required rate of return is 8 percent. With that said, the Ontario Division must earn $844,000 ($10,550,000 × 8%) just to equal the 8 percent required rate of return. This required earnings amount represents the dollar amount of earnings the segment must earn to equal the required rate of return for the company. Any earnings in excess of the required earnings (in this case $844,000) will constitute the segment's residual income. For the Ontario Division, the $896,750 actual income exceeds the $844,000 required income by $52,750. Therefore, the residual income for the Ontario Division is $52,750, calculated as follows:

Actual Income	$896,750
Less Required Income ($10,550,000 × 8%)	($844,000)
Equals Residual Income	$ 52,750

This is not to say that the Ontario Division only earned $52,750. Rather, the Ontario Division's income exceeded the company's required earnings by $52,750.

If the division's actual income were less than the income required to meet the company's required rate of return, the residual income amount would be a negative number. In our example, the positive residual income amount indicates that the segment's actual earnings exceed the company's required rate of return. In the unlikely event that residual income is zero, it would indicate that the actual income for the segment exactly equals the company's required rate of return.

---

[2]EVA® was popularized and trademarked by Stern, Steven & Co. in the United States.

Discussion Question

10–13. What similarities do you see between our discussion here of the residual income calculation and our discussion in Chapter 7 of net present value?

We now calculate the residual income for the Western Division so we can evaluate the relative performance of the two divisions. Using the amounts previously presented for the Western Division, we calculate residual income as $73,500:

Actual Income	$857,500
Less Required Income ($9,800,000 × 8%)	($784,000)
Equals Residual Income	$ 73,500

Notice that the residual income of the Western Division exceeds that of the Ontario Division. Accordingly, the performance of the Western Division would obviously be viewed more favourably than that of the Ontario Division. In an attempt to improve the Ontario Division's relative performance, managers would strive to increase revenue, decrease expenses, or seek new, high-return investment opportunities.

When ROI is used to evaluate potential investment opportunities, managers invest only in projects with an anticipated return that exceeds the segment's current ROI. Projects that exceed the company's required rate of return but did not exceed the segment's current ROI would likely be rejected. Look again at the investment opportunity proposed for the Ontario Division. Recall that the project would require an investment of $1,500,000 with anticipated additional income of $123,750. Therefore, the total investment of the Ontario Division would increase to $12,050,000 ($10,550,000 + $1,500,000), while total segment income would increase to $1,020,500 ($896,750 + $123,750).

If residual income were used to evaluate segment performance, management of the Ontario Division would tend to accept the proposed project if it worked to increase residual income. Look again at the residual income for the Ontario Division both with and without the proposed investment opportunity. The data are presented in Exhibit 10–9.

Exhibit 10–9
Residual Income for Ontario Division with and without Proposed Investment

Ontario Division *Without* the New Investment Opportunity		Ontario Division *With* the New Investment Opportunity	
Actual Income	$896,750	Actual Income	$1,020,000
Required Income		Required Income	
$10,550,000 × 8% =	$844,000	$12,050,000 × 8% =	$ 964,000
Residual Income	$ 52,750	Residual Income	$ 56,000

As you can see, the investment opportunity for the Ontario Division would increase residual income. Therefore, management of the Ontario Division would tend to favour the investment. Notice that the residual income method, unlike ROI, prompts managers to accept projects with return rates that exceed the company's required rate of return even if the project's rate of return falls short of the segment's current ROI.

TRANSFER PRICING

transfer pricing The set of rules an organization uses to allocate jointly earned contribution margin among responsibility centres.

Situations arise in decentralized companies when responsibility centres transfer goods or services between or among themselves. If the divisions are treated as profit or investment centres, the price of the transfer becomes important since it will affect performance evaluation. **Transfer pricing** is the set of rules an organization uses to allocate jointly earned contribution margin among responsibility centres.

Assume Crossman Electronics Inc. is a small manufacturer of subassembly parts for a DVD player. Crossman has two divisions. The first division is the Component Division, which produces the component parts for DVD players. The second division is the Assembly Division, which assembles the components into subassemblies. The Component Division supplies all of the components required by the Assembly Division and also sells to external customers. The Assembly Division sells directly to DVD manufacturers. Both divisions are evaluated as profit centres.

What price should the Component Division charge for the components transferred to the Assembly Division? As the manager of the Component Division, you would want to receive the same price as if you sold the components to an external customer, since you are being evaluated on your division's profitability. Now, assume you are the manager of the Assembly Division. You know that the cost to the Component Division to manufacture the components is much less than the price charged to external customers. You would argue for a price less than the normal selling price because both divisions are a part of the same company. You too are being evaluated on your division's profitability, so you want to keep the cost as low as possible.

Both managers make a good case. What is the correct answer? It depends on the situation. For example, is the Component Division producing at capacity? If so, and it could sell the components to an external customer, the Component Division should be entitled to the market value for the item. If the Component Division is not producing at capacity, the situation changes. As discussed in previous chapters, the only costs that are relevant to the decision are the costs that will change if the Component Division provides the product for the Assembly Division. In most cases, the only costs that will change are the variable costs, since the fixed costs are not likely to change over the relevant range. Thus, depending on the situation, an appropriate transfer price could be anything from the variable cost to the fair market value (the selling price to external customers) of the item.

The general rule for transfer pricing is:

$$\text{Transfer Price} = \text{Variable costs to produce} + \frac{\text{The opportunity cost per unit}}{\text{to the supplying division}}$$

Transfer pricing policies will vary from company to company. Keeping in mind the general transfer pricing rule, organizations choose from among three different approaches:

market-based transfer prices Transfer prices based on the price in the external market, when an external market exists for goods or services transferred between responsibility centres.

1. Market-based transfer prices
2. Cost-based transfer prices
3. Negotiated transfer prices

Market-Based Transfer Prices

If an external market exists for the transferred good or service, then market prices are the most appropriate basis for transferring the good or service between responsibility centres.

Cost-Based Transfer Prices   When the transferred good or service does not have a defined market price, responsibility centre managers often determine transfer prices on the basis of cost. Some common transfer prices are: variable cost; full cost (variable cost plus fixed costs); and full cost plus a markup for profit for the transferring centre.

Negotiated Transfer Prices   If there is no external market for the good or service, some companies prefer to let the mangers of the supplying and receiving responsibility centres negotiate transfer prices between themselves.

For many companies, transfer pricing is an important element of performance evaluation. In companies with international operations, the transfer pricing policy may affect the overall profitability of a company due to different tax rates and duties in different countries. Our purpose here is to introduce to you to the basics of transfer pricing. Transfer pricing is covered in more detail in advanced management accounting courses.

An Example of Transfer Pricing

Edwards Bicycle Manufacturing Inc. makes mountain bikes. The company is divided into two divisions. The Frames Division manufactures the bicycle frame. The frame is then either transferred to the Assembly Division where the bicycle is assembled or the frame is sold to other manufacturers. The company treats both divisions as profit centres.

The company's managers are trying to determine the appropriate price for transferring the frame from the Frames Division to the Assembly Division. The following information is available:

Final selling price of the bicycle:	$550.00
Variable costs in the Frames Division	$180.00
Variable costs in the Assembly Division	$225.00
External selling price (market price) of the bicycle frame	$300.00

If we assume that the Frames Division of Edwards Bicycle Manufacturing Inc. is not operating at full capacity, the appropriate transfer price, according to the general rule for transfer pricing, would be:

$$\text{Transfer Price} = \text{Variable costs to produce} + \text{The opportunity cost per unit to the supplying division}$$
$$= \$180.00 + \$0.00$$
$$= \$180.00$$

Since the company has excess capacity, the Frames Division is not losing any contribution margin, and therefore profit, by transferring the frames to the Assembly Division. Thus, only the variable cost to produce the frame is relevant in determining the transfer price.

If the Frame Division was operating at capacity, the calculation would be somewhat different:

$$\text{Transfer Price} = \text{Variable costs to produce} + \text{The opportunity cost per unit to the supplying division}$$
$$= \$180.00 + (\text{The external selling price of the bicycle frame} - \text{The variable cost of the bicycle frame})$$
$$= \$180.00 + (\$300.00 - \$180.00)$$
$$= \$300.00$$

As you can see, when the division is at full capacity, the transfer price should be equal to the market price of the item being transferred. Why? If you are the Frames Division manager, you are being evaluated based on your ability to generate profit. Would you be willing to forego the opportunity to sell a frame to an outside buyer for $300.00 and earn a contribution margin of $120.00 just so that you could transfer the frame to the Assembly Division and earn a contribution margin of zero? Each unit that is transferred at less than market price reduces the Frames Division's contribution margin and net income in this situation.

However, if the Frames Division is not at full capacity, the Frames Division manager is indifferent about transferring units to the Assembly Division, as long as the external market is satisfied. Any transfer price in excess of variable cost will be acceptable.

In many situations like this one, the managers of the two divisions will negotiate a transfer price. The Assembly Division manager would be happy to pay less than market price for the frame, while the Frames Division manager would be happy to receive any price in excess of variable cost. Thus, a compromise price between the two extremes is logical when the supplying division is not at full capacity.

In this case, the transfer price is used to create a selling price for the Frames Division and a cost for the Assembly Division. This transfer price is then used to evaluate the performance of the division. Remember that the overall contribution margin to the company is not normally affected by the transfer price. The transfer price merely allocates the contribution margin among the contributing divisions. In our example, Edwards Bicycle Manufacturing Inc. would generate the following contribution margin from selling one bicycle:

Selling Price		$550.00
Variable Costs—Frames Division	$180.00	
Variable Costs—Assembly Division	225.00	
Total Variable Costs		405.00
Contribution Margin		$145.00

The transfer price will effectively allocate the $145.00 between the two divisions. At full capacity, the divisions would receive the following contribution:

	Frame Division		Assembly Division	
Selling Price		$300.00		$550.00
Transferred-In Cost	$ 0.00		$300.00	
Variable Cost	180.00		225.00	
Total Variable Costs		180.00		525.00
Contribution Margin		$120.00		$ 25.00

NONFINANCIAL PERFORMANCE MEASURES

In the past, normal business practice has focused almost exclusively on financial amounts to measure success. Success has been gauged by how much revenue can be generated, how much costs can be reduced, or how much profit can be earned. Recently, however, many companies have begun to also consider nonfinancial performance measures in evaluating business performance. Many managers are finding out that tracking the various flows of dollars and cents alone cannot ensure business success. Intense competition has prompted businesses to take a second look at nonfinancial performance measures in the hope that better performance on these will ultimately lead to greater financial rewards.

Quality

Today, many companies are calling for continuous quality improvement in every area of business. Today's quality-conscious companies are not only producing higher-quality products, but also demanding high-quality performance throughout every aspect of business. To remain competitive, companies must produce the high-quality products their customers have come to expect. Thus, they have begun to monitor product quality in a number of ways. Production reports are no longer limited to data pertaining to numbers of units and unit cost. Information about the number of defective products and the amount of rework is now prepared and used as a basis for measuring segment success. Product quality is also monitored by tabulating the amount and nature of customer complaints. Product warranty repair costs and the number of repairs or service calls are also useful tools in evaluating product quality.

The trend in business today is to establish extremely high goals for quality. For FedEx, 100 percent on-time deliveries is the goal. Imagine, not 90 percent or 95 percent, but 100 percent on-time deliveries. This goal may seem impossible to achieve, but FedEx has mobilized the company to achieve high-quality performance in every aspect of the delivery process. From delivery truck maintenance to the package tracking system, quality is the hallmark of the company.

The Costs of Quality

Companies have come to recognize the costs associated with quality and the significance of them. Quality costs are generally divided into four areas:

prevention cost Cost incurred to avoid poor-quality goods or services in the first place.

appraisal cost Cost incurred to detect poor-quality goods or services.

internal failure cost Cost incurred to correct defective goods or services before delivery to the customer.

external failure cost Cost incurred to correct problems after a good or service has been delivered to the customer.

1. **Prevention costs.** Costs incurred to *avoid* poor-quality goods or services in the first place. Generally speaking, these are costs companies incur to train personnel to produce an appropriate product the first time.
2. **Appraisal costs.** Costs incurred to *detect* poor-quality goods or services. For example, manufacturing companies employ inspectors to test and check products at various stages of production.
3. **Internal failure costs.** Costs incurred to correct defective goods or services *before* delivery to the customer. For example, if an inspector detects a problem with a product at the final inspection stage, any costs to repair the defect would be considered an internal failure cost.
4. **External failure costs.** Costs incurred to correct problems *after* a good or service has been delivered to the customer. An example would be costs incurred to fix a faulty product that is covered by a warranty. There is also a further cost associated with external failure. If a good or service fails after it is in the marketplace, the reputation of the producer may be damaged, which could affect future sales.

Companies recognize that costs become more significant as the goods or services being produced move farther along in the process. Thus, spending more time and resources in prevention and appraisal will reduce the costs incurred in internal and external failures.

Companies today take the issue of quality very seriously. In fact, many manufacturers want to ensure that their customers know how important quality is in their facility, so they adhere to the guidelines of the **International Organization for Standardization (ISO)**. The ISO is made up of approximately 130 national standards institutes from countries large and small. ISO develops voluntary standards, over almost the entire range of technology, that add value to all types of business operations. Two common certifications are ISO 9000 and ISO 14000, which are families of standards for management systems and related supporting standards.

International Organization for Standardization (ISO) The organization that develops voluntary quality and procedural standards, and certifies companies that meet these standards.

Companies that adhere to the ISO standards can be certified; ISO certification assures customers that a company has strict standards of quality control.

Quality has become increasingly important for companies. Customers want assurance that the good or service they purchase are of the highest quality for the price paid. By implementing appropriate training and appraisal procedures, or by adhering to ISO standards, companies provide their customers with quality assurance.

 Discussion Question

10–14. What, if any, are the potentially negative financial effects of focusing on quality?

Customer Satisfaction

In today's competitive business environment, customer satisfaction is often viewed as the most critical ingredient in achieving and maintaining success. Even if customer satisfaction is important, how can it be evaluated to measure segment performance? There are several ways. First, customer complaints can be monitored. At IBM, for example, detailed records are kept regarding each customer complaint. In addition to a simple count of the number of complaints, IBM records the nature and severity of each and follows up every complaint to ensure that the customer's needs have been reasonably met.

To satisfy customers, you must first know what customers want. Surveys can be used to identify what is important to customers and to help determine whether they are satisfied with products and services. For example, buyers of General Motors automobiles are surveyed each time their cars are serviced. This survey accomplishes at least two important things. First, it provides information that can be used to evaluate the performance of the service facilities. Second, it can alert the company to an unhappy customer so that reasonable action can be taken to remedy each customer complaint.

 Discussion Question

10–15. What, if any, are the potentially negative financial effects of focusing on customer satisfaction?

Employee Morale

An increasing number of companies are targeting company morale as an almost certain road to higher profits. It stands to reason that employees who are happy with their jobs are more likely to work hard to benefit both themselves and the company. Without question, low morale leads to high turnover, which in turn leads to the enormous cost of hiring and training employees. It follows, then, that managers should work to keep employee morale high. Measuring employee morale can be challenging, but some useful indicators of employee morale are the amount of absenteeism, the rate of employee turnover, and recruiting success rates.

Discussion Question

10–16. What, if any, are the potentially negative financial effects of focusing on employee morale?

Employee Safety

In today's business world, it is critical that employees be provided with a safe work environment. DuPont Canada Inc., for example, has invested a great deal of money in promoting safety in the workplace. Employees are routinely reminded of the importance of safety through company-provided posters, safety seminars, and safety awareness contests. The information DuPont provides to its people is not limited to safety on the job but also extends to automobile and home safety.

DuPont Canada Inc. is not alone in its campaign to promote safety. Many companies are using employee safety information to evaluate segment performance. Some measures that indicate the level of employee safety include the number of hours worked between injury accidents, the number of hours worked per injury accident, and the number of employees injured or killed in a given time period. Managers can be evaluated based on the number of safety seminars or other safety programs they hold per year.

Discussion Question

10–17. What, if any, are the potentially negative financial effects of focusing on employee safety?

Efficiency

In today's competitive environment, customers demand high-quality products at the lowest possible price. Accordingly, efficiency has become one of the cornerstones of success for many companies. Efficiency is the measure of output achieved versus the amount of resources required. To increase production efficiency relative to material, companies are attempting to produce the maximum number of units with the minimum amount of wasted material. This efficiency can be measured by the amount of scrap or the amount of material used per unit produced. For labour, efficiency can be measured by the relationship of production output to the direct labour required.

Many manufacturers are making major commitments to improve general factory efficiency. To be successful, these efforts must be supported by everyone from production-line workers to the chief executive officer. It is particularly important that top management be supportive. Typically, efficiency drives extend far beyond making minor changes and rallying the troops to work a little faster. Rather, they encompass major reorganizations of labour, new factory layouts, and innovative work flow philosophies. Many of the concepts that contribute to increased factory efficiency are part of the just-in-time philosophy.

10–18. What, if any, are the potentially negative financial effects of focusing on efficiency?

The Balanced Scorecard

balanced scorecard A business-strategy model that views a company from four different perspectives—the financial perspective, the customer's perspective, the internal processes perspective, and the learning and growth perspective—to measure a company's financial and nonfinancial performance.

A formal process has been developed to ensure that the nonfinancial performance measures discussed above are incorporated effectively into a company's management system. The **balanced scorecard** is a business-strategy model that views a company from four different perspectives: the financial perspective, the customer's perspective, the internal processes perspective, and the learning and growth perspective. Objectives are developed for each perspective, and performance measures are set to assess whether the objectives are met. Companies using the model recognize that achieving financial performance objectives alone is not enough to assure their long-term success; evaluating their nonfinancial performance is vital. The balanced scorecard is discussed in much more detail in advanced management accounting texts.

JUST-IN-TIME PHILOSOPHY

just-in-time (JIT) A philosophy that eliminates all unnecessary inventory and limits the use of company resources until they are absolutely needed to fulfill customer demand.

The **just-in-time (JIT)** philosophy involves eliminating all unnecessary inventory and limiting the use of company resources until they are absolutely needed to fulfill customer demand. Expenditures are made only to fulfill the immediate customer demand. Products are "pulled" through the system. That is, products are made in response to the *pull* from customer demand, rather than to a *push* to have inventory to fill orders that may or may not materialize.

Often, JIT is described as a method of eliminating or greatly reducing inventory by delaying the purchase of raw material until it is needed for production. This narrow view is greatly flawed and prompts many managers to reject the whole JIT idea. Limiting the use of company resources until they are needed for production cannot be achieved by simply adopting a mind-set that purchases will be delayed until the last possible minute. Instead, the JIT philosophy focuses on delaying expenditures for inventory and reducing inventory levels to near zero by creating very efficient production processes that require only a minimal amount of inventory to successfully manufacture high-quality products.

One key component of JIT is that manufacturers must be able to depend on their suppliers for 100 percent on-time deliveries of 100 percent defect-free material. For JIT to work, manufacturers must develop close relationships with suppliers who can provide absolutely on-time deliveries and absolutely consistent high quality. When JIT is implemented, manufacturers defer quality inspections to suppliers and insist upon parts and components that are free of defects. **Zero defects** is a term that is often used to describe the concept of products that are completely free of imperfections. In a JIT environment, zero defects becomes the norm.

zero defects Describes the concept of products that are completely free of imperfections.

As part of the program to develop close relationships with their suppliers, firms greatly reduce that number of suppliers. By working with a core of carefully selected suppliers, the manufacturer is able to make substantial purchase commitments that help compensate suppliers for the added effort required to meet the manufacturer's demands. Also, the financial benefits they gain from receiving on-time deliveries of consistently high-quality products make it possible for manufacturers to justify paying a premium price for the goods they purchase.

In a JIT environment, setup times must be reduced to the lowest possible levels. As mentioned in Chapter 3, **setup time** is the time it takes to prepare manufacturing equipment for the production of a particular product. One major problem with long setup times is that while production equipment is being set up, it cannot be used to produce anything. The trouble does not end there, however. If setup time is substantial, fewer and longer production runs must be made to justify the substantial setup effort. It makes no sense to go through a long setup process to produce only a few units. The result of long production runs is higher inventory levels. This method is in direct conflict with the JIT philosophy. Conversely, if setup time is very short, running a short production run to produce fewer units of product is more feasible. With shorter production runs making fewer units, inventories can be reduced.

setup time The time it takes to prepare manufacturing equipment for the production of particular products.

In JIT environments, setup time is now measured and average setup times are used to evaluate the performance of segment managers. In factories using just-in-time production, setup time is reduced from hours or days to minutes.

Another focus of the JIT philosophy is reduced throughput time. **Throughput time** is the time between the entrance of a unit of production into the production process and the time it emerges as a finished product. It is an important measure of factory efficiency because the amount of money invested in work-in-process inventory can be lowered by reducing the time products are in the production process. In addition to reducing inventories, shorter throughput time frees production equipment so it can be used to make other products. Throughput time can thus be measured and used as a basis for evaluating performance.

throughput time The time that passes from the time a unit of product enters the production process until it emerges as a finished product.

Another hallmark of the JIT philosophy is reduction in lead time. **Lead time** is the time between the receipt of an order and the completion of a product ready for shipment. Decreasing setup and throughput times can greatly reduce lead time. Many manufacturers that have adopted JIT have reduced lead time from months or years, to days or even hours. Lead time can be measured and used as a basis for evaluating factory performance.

lead time The time that passes from the time an order is received until the product is complete and ready for shipment.

In a further effort to increase efficiency, managers are working to reduce unscheduled downtime. **Unscheduled downtime** is the amount of time production equipment is out of service due to unscheduled repairs and maintenance. To keep this factor low, managers implement routine maintenance programs that not only keep unscheduled downtime to a minimum but also keep machinery running at peak performance. Companies are now tracking unscheduled downtime and using the information to evaluate factory performance.

unscheduled downtime The amount of time production equipment is out of service due to unscheduled repairs and maintenance.

By now, you may be wondering just how these JIT production improvements can be achieved. They do not come cheaply or easily. A great deal of time and money must be spent to achieve the added efficiency that comes with a JIT production environment. Some key factors are improved factory layout and product flow, mechanized procedures for machine setup, convenient storage and labeling of machine parts used in the setup process, and a formal factory maintenance program.

The production facility layout should be designed so that raw materials enter the production process with little or no need to be transported to work stations. For example, when a new Saturn automobile in made, the truck that transports the seats to the factory is literally connected to the production building, and the seats are fed to the production line, in the proper order, through conveyors in the truck to conveyers in the factory. The days of buying a bunch of seats of various colours and styles to be stored in a warehouse are gone at Saturn. Gone too are the days when materials handling personnel picked through massive inventories of seats to find the colour and style they needed only to transport the selected seats to the production line. By cooperating with a seat manufacturer and a transportation company, Saturn can depend on the seats not only arriving on time but being received in the correct order by colour and style with zero defects. A backup plan for shipment delays is the responsibility of the supplier and transportation company.

In addition to facilitating efficient handling of raw material, a JIT environment should also strive to streamline the movement of material from one production process to the next. For example, the Dunlop Golf Ball Factory in South Carolina has eliminated the use of hopper carts to transport golf balls from the painting process to the packaging process. This decision was achieved by changing the factory layout so that golf balls travel by conveyor from one process to the next. This production improvement saves time and eliminates the need for handling the golf balls between processes. An added feature of this change was the elimination of inspection stations between the painting department and the packaging department, as the golf balls were no longer subject to blemishes caused by rough treatment in the hopper carts. The production change worked to greatly increase factory efficiency and improve product quality.

Each manufacturing environment is unique. Managers and factory workers cooperate to continually reinvent the production environment. Old production techniques and strategies must be set aside in favour of new standards of production excellence, efficiency, and product quality. Company management and production personnel must work together to achieve the world-class production excellence required in today's competitive business environment. It takes a team effort characterized by an innovative spirit and a willingness to invest in grand-scale changes.

SUMMARY

As companies grow and the products and services they provide become more diversified, it becomes virtually impossible for one person to perform all management functions. More managers are required to operate and control the various facets of what we call management. A natural outgrowth of a company's evolution is the creation of business segments. A segment is any part of a company about which separate information is required to evaluate performance.

When a company is segmented, it will employ either a centralized management style or a decentralized management style. In a centralized company, upper management makes most of the important business decisions. In a decentralized company, lower-level managers are responsible for virtually all decisions that relate to their segment of the company.

Determining what costs should be charged to a particular business segment and the amount of those costs is sometimes very difficult. Some costs associated with operating a business segment are directly incurred by that segment. Others, however, are incurred to support more than one segment. These common costs must be allocated in some way to the segments receiving the benefit of the costs.

The four most commonly used designations of business segments are revenue centres, cost centres, profit centres, and investment centres. Revenue and cost centres are usually evaluated based on performance to budget. Profit centres are also evaluated on the basis of actual net income compared to budgeted net income. Using net income to evaluate performance can cause some problems, particularly when goods or services are transferred between segments. In this case, companies must determine an appropriate transfer price for these goods or services. The most common choices are market-based transfer prices, cost-based transfer prices, and negotiated transfer prices.

The performance of investment centres is most often evaluated using the return on investment (ROI) technique or the residual income approach, sometimes called economic value added (EVA®).

Although performance to budget and either return on investment or residual income (EVA®) are still commonly used to evaluate business segment performance, other nonfinancial measures have become popular in recent years. Many companies now follow a balanced scorecard approach, and emphasize product quality, customer satisfaction, employee morale, and training, in addition to financial measures, to better measure and improve company performance.

KEY TERMS

appraisal cost, p. 406
balanced scorecard, p. 409
business segment, p. 385
centralized management, p. 394
common fixed cost, p. 388
cost-based transfer prices, p. 404
cost centre, p. 396
decentralized management, p. 395
direct fixed cost, p. 387
economic value add (EVA®), p. 401
external failure cost, p. 406
indirect fixed cost, p. 388
internal failure cost, p. 406
International Organization for
  Standardization (ISO), p. 406
investment centre, p. 398
just-in-time (JIT), p. 409
lead time, p. 410

market-based transfer prices, p. 403
negotiated transfer prices, p. 404
prevention cost, p. 406
profit centre, p. 396
residual income, p. 401
return on investment (ROI), p. 399
revenue centre, p. 396
segment income statement, p. 386
segment margin, p. 386
segment reports, p. 385
service department, p. 391
setup time, p. 410
throughput time, p. 410
traceable fixed cost, p. 387
transfer pricing, p. 403
unscheduled downtime, p. 410
zero defects, p. 409

REVIEW THE FACTS

1. Describe a business segment.
2. What is the difference between direct fixed cost and common fixed cost?
3. What is a service department?
4. Why is it important to know about service department cost allocation?
5. Describe the difference between centralized and decentralized management.
6. Describe a revenue centre.
7. Describe a cost centre.
8. What is the difference between a profit centre and an investment centre?
9. Why is residual income sometimes preferred to return on investment?
10. What is transfer pricing?
11. What is the general guideline for determining a transfer price?
12. List five nonfinancial performance measures.
13. What are the four costs of quality?
14. What is ISO certification? What does it signify?
15. What is the balanced scorecard approach to performance evaluation?
16. What are the four perspectives of the balanced scorecard approach?
17. What is meant by the just-in-time philosophy?
18. How can companies achieve the very low inventory levels embraced by the just-in-time philosophy?

APPLY WHAT YOU HAVE LEARNED

LO 2 & 3: Prepare a Segment Income Statement with and without the Allocation of Common Fixed Costs to Segments

1. Mission Estates Sales Company has two divisions. The following information is available for the year ended December 31, 2004.

   The sales for Mission Estates are $300,000 for the Eastern Division and $200,000 for the Western Division. Variable costs for the Eastern Division are $250,000, whereas variable costs for the Western Division are $170,000. Direct fixed costs of the Eastern Division are $20,000, and direct fixed costs of the Western Division are $15,000. Mission Estates Sales Company allocates common fixed costs to segments based on relative sales. Common fixed costs for the company are $25,000.

REQUIRED:

a. Prepare a segment income statement for the company that distributes common fixed costs to segments based on relative sales. Your answer should include a column for the total company and columns for each segment.

b. Do you think it is wise to evaluate the performance of a business segment based on income that includes an allocation for common fixed costs? Why or why not?

c. Prepare a segment income statement for the company that does not distribute common fixed cost to segments. Your answer should include a column for the total company and columns for each segment.

LO 2 & 3: Prepare a Segment Income Statement with and without the Allocation of Common Fixed Costs to Segments

2. Woodbridge Sales Company has two divisions. The following information is available for the year ended December 31, 2005.

   The sales for the company are $30,000 for the North Division and $90,000 for the South Division. Variable costs for the North Division are $18,000, while variable costs for the South Division are $54,000. Direct fixed costs of the North Division are $5,000, and direct fixed costs of the South Division are $15,000. The company allocates common fixed costs to segments based on relative sales. Common fixed costs for the company are $10,000.

REQUIRED:

a. Prepare a segment income statement for the company that distributes common fixed costs to segments based on relative sales. Your answer should include a column for the total company and columns for each segment.

b. Do you think it is wise to evaluate the performance of a business segment based on income that includes an allocation for common fixed costs? Why or why not?

c. Prepare a segment income statement for the company that does not distribute common fixed cost to segments. Your answer should include a column for the total company and columns for each segment.

LO 2 & 3: Prepare a Segment Income Statement with and without the Allocation of Common Fixed Costs to Segments

3. Leung Sales Company has two divisions. The following information is available for the year ended December 31, 2004.

The sales for the company are $200,000 for the Central Division and $400,000 for the South Division. Variable costs for the Central Division are $150,000, whereas variable costs for the South Division are $300,000. Direct fixed costs of the Central Division are $19,000, and direct fixed costs of the South Division are $54,000. The company allocates common fixed costs to segments based on relative sales. Common fixed costs for the company are $27,000.

REQUIRED:

a. Prepare a segment income statement for the company that distributes common fixed costs to segments based on relative sales. Your answer should include a column for the total company and columns for each segment.

b. Do you think it is wise to evaluate the performance of a business segment based on income that includes an allocation for common fixed costs? Why or why not?

c. Prepare a segment income statement for the company that does not distribute common fixed cost to segments. Your answer should include a column for the total company and columns for each segment.

LO 2 & 3: Prepare a Segment Income Statement with and without the Allocation of Common Fixed Costs to Segments

4. Peppermill Corporation has three divisions. The following information is available for the year ended December 31, 2005.

The sales for the company are $200,000 for the Central Division, $400,000 for the South Division, and $600,000 for the West Division. Variable costs for the Central Division are $150,000, variable costs for the South Division are $300,000, and variable costs for the West Division are $450,000. Direct fixed costs of the Central Division are $20,000, direct fixed costs of the South Division are $54,000, and direct fixed costs of the West Division are $100,000. The company allocates common fixed costs to segments based on relative sales. Common fixed costs for the company are $102,000.

REQUIRED:

a. Prepare a segment income statement for the company that distributes common fixed costs to segments based on relative sales. Your answer should include a column for the total company and columns for each segment.

b. Based on your answer for part a, which segment seems to have generated the least profit?

c. Prepare a segment income statement for the company that does not distribute common fixed cost to segments. Your answer should include a column for the total company and columns for each segment.

d. Based on your answer for part c, which segment seems to have generated the most profit?

LO 2 & 3:   Prepare a Segment Income Statement with and without the Allocation of Common Fixed Costs to Segments

5. Camrose Sales Company has three divisions. The following information is available for the year ended December 31, 2005.

   The sales for the company are $100,000 for Division A, $200,000 for Division B, and $300,000 for Division C. Variable costs for Division A are $50,000, variable costs for Division B are $100,000, and variable costs for Division C are $150,000. Direct fixed costs of Division A are $20,000, direct fixed costs of Division B are $30,000, and direct fixed costs of Division C are $60,000. The company allocates common fixed costs to segments based on relative sales. Common fixed costs for the company are $186,000.

REQUIRED:

a. Prepare a segment income statement for the company that distributes common fixed costs to segments based on relative sales. Your answer should include a column for the total company and columns for each segment.

b. Based on your answer for part a, which segment seems to have generated the least profit?

c. Prepare a segment income statement for the company that does not distribute common fixed cost to segments. Your answer should include a column for the total company and columns for each segment.

d. Based on your answer for part c, which segment seems to have generated the most profit?

LO 2 & 3:   Prepare a Segment Income Statement with and without the Allocation of Common Fixed Costs to Segments

6. Porter Sales Company has three divisions. The following information is available for the year ended December 31, 2004.

   The sales for the company are $100,000 for Division 101, $100,000 for Division 202, and $200,000 for Division 303. Variable costs for Division 101 are $50,000, variable costs for Division 202 are $60,000, and variable costs for Division 303 are $110,000. Direct fixed costs of Division 101 are $20,000, direct fixed costs of Division 202 are $30,000, and direct fixed costs of Division 303 are $50,000. The company allocates common fixed costs to segments based on relative sales. Common fixed costs for the company are $40,000.

REQUIRED:

a. Prepare a segment income statement for the company that distributes common fixed costs to segments based on relative sales. Your answer should include a column for the total company and columns for each segment.

b. Based on your answer for part a, does it appear that one of the segments is a cause for concern?

c. Prepare a segment income statement for the company that does not distribute common fixed cost to segments. Your answer should include a column for the total company and columns for each segment.

d. Based on your answer for part c, does it still seem that one of the segments is a cause for concern?

LO 2: Analyze Segment Cost and Prepare a Memo

7. The following segment income statement has been prepared for Robertson Sales Company.

ROBERTSON SALES COMPANY
Segment Income Statement
For the Year Ended December 31, 2005

	Company Total	Medical Division	Industrial Division	Consumer Division
Sales	$750,000	$337,500	$157,500	$255,000
Variable cost	499,425	211,500	110,625	177,300
Contribution margin	250,575	126,000	46,875	77,700
Direct fixed cost	112,500	48,000	30,000	34,500
Segment margin	138,075	78,000	16,875	43,200
Common fixed cost	90,000	40,500 [*]	18,900 [**]	30,600 [***]
Net income	$ 48,075	$ 37,500	($ 2,025)	$ 12,600

[*] $337,500/$750,000 = 45\%; 45\% \times \$90,000 = \$40,500$

[**] $157,500/$750,000 = 21\%; 21\% \times \$90,000 = \$18,900$

[***] $255,000/$750,000 = 34\%; 34\% \times \$90,000 = \$30,600$

The company President, Bob Robertson, is calling a management meeting to explore the idea of closing or selling the Industrial Division. Many managers are complaining that the division is "dragging the company down."

Assume that, in preparation for the meeting, Mr. Robertson has contacted you and asked that you explore the situation.

REQUIRED:

Based on the information presented for Robertson Sales Company, prepare a memo to Mr. Robertson that includes a brief summary of the problem and a proposed solution.

LO 2: Identify the Area of Responsibility Associated with Different Types of Business Segments

8. Following are some popular segment classifications followed by three areas of management responsibility.

Segment Classification

Revenue centre	_____	_____	_____
Cost centre	_____	_____	_____
Profit centre	_____	_____	_____
Investment centre	_____	_____	_____

R—Revenue
C—Cost
I—Amount invested

REQUIRED:

In the blank spaces provided, match the area of responsibility—revenue (R), cost (C), and amount invested (I)—to the appropriate segment classification. Although not all the blank spaces will be used, some segment classifications will have more than one area of responsibility.

LO 4: Determine Return on Investment

9. The Chemical Division of SaskChem Incorporated generated a segment margin of $220,680 for the year 2004, and the amount invested in the division was $1,226,000.

REQUIRED:
Determine the return on investment for the Chemical Division.

LO 4: Determine Return on Investment

10. The Southern Division of Benson Sales Company generated a segment margin of $790,020 for the year 2005, and the amount invested in the division was $4,158,000.

REQUIRED:
Determine the return on investment for the Southern Division.

LO 4: Determine Return on Investment

11. The Automotive Division of Bascom Company generated a segment margin of $1,916,800 for the year 2004, and the amount invested in the division was $11,980,000.

REQUIRED:
Determine the return on investment for the Automotive Division.

LO 4: Determine Return on Investment

12. Alcad Farm Products Corp. generated income of $558,620 for the year 2003, and the amount invested in the division was $3,286,000.

REQUIRED:
Determine the return on investment for Alcad Farm Products Corp.

LO 2 & 4: Determine and Interpret Return on Investment

13. The following information is available for the three divisions of Pompano Company.

Amount invested in each division	
Division A	$3,255,000
Division B	$2,145,000
Division C	$3,587,000

Segment margin of each division	
Division A	$553,350
Division B	$407,550
Division C	$573,920

The required rate of return for the company is 16%.

REQUIRED:
a. Determine the return on investment for each division.
b. Rank the three divisions assuming they are considered profit centres.
c. Rank the three divisions assuming they are considered investment centres and performance is evaluated based on return on investment.
d. Why do the rankings for parts b and c differ?

LO 2 & 4: Determine and Interpret Return on Investment

14. The following information is available for the three divisions of Stevens Company.

Amount invested in each division

Division 101	$1,225,000
Division 202	$2,445,000
Division 303	$3,697,000

Segment margin of each division

Division 101	$198,450
Division 202	$371,640
Division 303	$569,338

The required rate of return for the company is 15%.

REQUIRED:

a. Determine the return on investment for each division.
b. Rank the three divisions assuming they are considered profit centres.
c. Rank the three divisions assuming they are considered investment centres and performance is evaluated based on return on investment.
d. Why do the rankings for parts b and c differ?

LO 2 & 4: Determine and Interpret Return on Investment

15. The following information is available for the three divisions of Reed Incorporated.

Amount invested in each division

North Division	$7,225,000
South Division	$5,105,000
Central Division	$4,322,000

Segment margin of each division

North Division	$1,336,625
South Division	$898,480
Central Division	$816,858

The required rate of return for the company is 14%.

REQUIRED:

a. Determine the return on investment for each division.
b. Rank the three divisions assuming they are considered profit centres.
c. Rank the three divisions assuming they are considered investment centres.
d. Why do the rankings for parts b and c differ?

LO 5: Determine Residual Income

16. The Eastern Division of Port McNeil Ltd. generated a segment margin of $1,836,800 for the year 2005, and the amount invested in the division was $12,780,000.

The company's required rate of return is 14%.

REQUIRED:

Determine the residual income for the Eastern Division.

LO 5: Determine Residual Income

17. Division A of Emry Company generated a segment margin of $522,567 for the year 2003, and the amount invested in the division was $2,778,450.

The company's required rate of return is 18%.

REQUIRED:

Determine the residual income for Division A.

LO 5: Determine Residual Income

18. Central Division of Craft Company generated a segment margin of $244,765 for the year 2005, and the amount invested in the division was $1,335,500.

The company's required rate of return is 17%.

REQUIRED:

Determine the residual income for the Central Division.

LO 2, 4, & 5: Determine and Interpret Return on Investment and Residual Income

19. The following information is available for the three divisions of Top Company.

Amount invested in each division	
Division D	$7,555,000
Division E	$5,995,000
Division F	$3,082,000

Segment margin of each division	
Division D	$1,133,250
Division E	$911,240
Division F	$493,120

The required rate of return for the company is 14%.

REQUIRED:

a. Determine the return on investment for each division.
b. Determine the residual income for each division.
c. Rank the three divisions assuming they are considered profit centres.
d. Rank the three divisions assuming they are considered investment centres and performance is evaluated based on return on investment.
e. Rank the three divisions assuming they are considered investment centres and performance is evaluated based on residual income.
f. Why do some of the rankings for parts c, d, and e differ?

LO 2, 4, & 5: Determine and Interpret Return on Investment and Residual Income

20. The following information is available for the three divisions of Lowen Company.

Amount invested in each division	
Division 1	$1,155,000
Division 2	$3,988,000
Division 3	$3,080,000

Segment margin of each division

Division 1	$196,350
Division 2	$634,092
Division 3	$492,800

The required rate of return for the company is 15%.

REQUIRED:

a. Determine the return on investment for each division.
b. Determine the residual income for each division.
c. Rank the three divisions assuming they are considered profit centres.
d. Rank the three divisions assuming they are considered investment centres and performance is evaluated based on return on investment.
e. Rank the three divisions assuming they are considered investment centres and performance is evaluated based on residual income.
f. Why do some of the rankings for parts c, d, and e differ?

LO 2, 4, & 5: Determine and Interpret Return on Investment and Residual Income

21. The following information is available for the three divisions of Gill Incorporated.

Amount invested in each division

Division H	$5,188,000
Division I	$2,588,000
Division J	$6,386,000

Segment margin of each division

Division H	$933,840
Division I	$491,720
Division J	$1,136,708

The required rate of return for the company is 16%.

REQUIRED:

a. Determine the return on investment for each division.
b. Determine the residual income for each division.
c. Rank the three divisions assuming they are considered profit centres.
d. Rank the three divisions assuming they are considered investment centres and performance is evaluated based on return on investment.
e. Rank the three divisions assuming they are considered investment centres and performance is evaluated based on residual income.
f. Why do some of the rankings for parts c, d, and e differ?

LO 2 & 4: Determine and Interpret Return on Investment

22. The following information is available for the three divisions of Global Logistics Inc.

Amount invested in each division

Automotive Division	$1,235,000
Industrial Division	$2,005,000
Consumer Division	$6,022,000

Segment margin of each division

Automotive Division	$202,540
Industrial Division	$332,830
Consumer Division	$963,520

The required rate of return for the company is 14%.

The company uses return on investment to evaluate segment performance.

The company is considering acquiring an automotive parts manufacturing company that is expected to provide income of $36,450. The acquisition would require an investment of $225,000. Although the prospective acquisition would fit nicely into the Automotive Division's operation, the Automotive Division's manager has voiced considerable reservations. He believes it would not be in the company's best interest to acquire the new segment.

The manager of the Industrial Division agrees with the Automotive Division manager. Oddly enough, the Consumer Division manager not only thinks the acquisition is a good idea, but has volunteered to accept it in her division.

REQUIRED:

a. Determine the return on investment for each division.
b. Do you feel that it is in the company's best interest to acquire the automotive parts manufacturer? Explain your answer.
c. Why are the Automotive and Industrial Division managers reluctant to recommend the acquisition?
d. Why would the Consumer Division manager volunteer to accept the proposed acquisition into her division?

LO 2 & 5:   Determine and Interpret Residual Income

23. Refer to the information in problem 22.

REQUIRED:

Explain how each of the managers' feelings about the acceptability of the proposed acquisition would differ if the company used residual income to evaluate segment performance instead of return on investment.

LO 2 & 6:   Determine Transfer Prices

24. Pacific Salmon Fisheries Inc. is a fish processing facility located in Vancouver. It has two divisions, the Processing Division and the Canning Division. The Processing Division purchases salmon from independent fishing boats and processes the raw salmon. The Canning Division cans salmon and sells it to large supermarket chains for $1.00 per can. Each can contains 500 grams of salmon.

The Processing Division pays the fishing boat operators approximately $0.50 per kilogram for raw salmon. Unfortunately, the yield from the raw fish is only approximately 50%. That is, only 50% of the salmon can be processed for canning. The rest of the salmon is considered to be waste and has no value. The Processing Division also incurs variable costs of $0.10 per can and fixed costs of $0.05 per can.

The Canning Division is able to can all of the salmon it receives. There is no waste in this division. The Canning Division incurs variable costs of $0.20 per can and fixed costs of $0.05 per can.

The Processing Division could sell its processed salmon to other canneries for $0.43 per can, and the Canning Division could buy processed salmon from other processors for $0.45 per can.

The managers of Pacific Salmon Fisheries Inc. are considering making the two divisions profit centres. Before they do, they want to determine what an appropriate transfer price might be.

REQUIRED:

a. What is the contribution margin per can of salmon to the company as a whole?
b. Assume that Pacific Salmon Fisheries Inc. is not running at full capacity in either division. Using the general transfer price guideline, what should the transfer price be to transfer the processed salmon from the Processing Division to the Canning Division?
c. Assume that Pacific Salmon Fisheries Inc. is running at full capacity in the Processing Division. Using the general transfer price guideline, what should the transfer price be to transfer the processed salmon from the Processing Division to the Canning Division?

LO 2 & 6: Interpret Transfer Prices

25. Refer to the information in problem 24.

REQUIRED:

Assume the role of the manager of the Processing Division. Suppose Pacific Salmon Fisheries Inc. has set the transfer price between your division and the Canning Division at $0.43 per can. Would you be more inclined to sell your product to the Canning Division or to other canneries? Would the decision that is best for your division be in the best interests of the company? What impact would your decision have on the company as a whole?

LO 2 & 6: Determine Transfer Prices

26. Blue Lake Mines Inc. is a mining company in Northern Ontario. The company is decentralized into two divisions, which are both treated as profit centres. The Mining Division is responsible for extracting the ore from the ground. The Processing Division takes the ore and processes it into a finished product. The finished product is known as zalium. The ore, known as myla, is the main ingredient in zalium. It takes two kilograms of myla to make one kilogram of zalium. The divisions have the following cost structures:

Mining Division

Annual production	500,000 kilograms
Variable cost per kilogram of myla	$2.00
Fixed cost per kilogram of myla	$1.00

Processing Division

Annual production	250,000 kilograms
Variable cost per kilogram of zalium	$5.00
Fixed cost per kilogram of zalium	$2.00

The Processing Division can sell all of its production to external customers for $16.00 per kilogram. The Mining Division can sell all of its output to external customers for $5.00 per kilogram.

REQUIRED:

a. Assume that Blue Lake Mines Inc. transfers all of the extracted ore from the Mining Division to the Processing Division. What is the net income to Blue Lake Mines Inc., assuming the company sells 250,000 kilograms of zalium?

b. Assume that Blue Lake Mines Inc. is not running at full capacity in either division. Using the general transfer price guideline, what should the transfer price be to transfer the myla from the Mining Division to the Processing Division?

c. Assume that Blue Lake Mines Inc. is running at full capacity in the Mining Division. Using the general transfer price guideline, what should the transfer price be to transfer the myla from the Mining Division to the Processing Division?

LO 2 & 6:   Interpret Transfer Prices

27. Refer to the information in problem 26. Suppose Blue Lake Mines Inc. has set a transfer price of $4.00 per kilogram of myla for transfers between the Mining Division and the Processing Division.

REQUIRED:

a. Determine the contribution margin for each division.

b. As the manager of the Mining Division, are you satisfied with this transfer pricing arrangement? Why or why not?

LO 7:   Use a Balanced Scorecard to Focus on Long-Term Success

28. Alpha Sports Limited operates a chain of sporting goods stores in Canada. In the past, the senior management of Alpha has treated each store as a profit centre and has evaluated store performance based on net income. However, while most of the stores have been profitable, senior management has become concerned that store managers focus too much on profitability and do not focus on other important factors that affect long-term success. Senior management points to high turnover of employees and a decline in market share as examples of trends that are not positive.

REQUIRED:

a. How does evaluating store managers on financial performance force them to focus on the short-term? Give an example.

b. In general terms, explain how a balanced scorecard approach to performance evaluation might help Alpha Sports Limited to better motivate store managers to focus on long-term success for the company. Include a discussion of the negative trends in your response.

Glossary of Accounting Terms

accounting rate of return The rate of return for a capital project based on the anticipated increase in accounting operating income due to the project, relative to the amount of capital investment required. (p. 239)

activity-based costing Allocating cost to products based on the activities that caused the cost to happen. (p. 71)

activity-based management (ABM) The process of using activity-based costing information to make decisions that increase profits while satisfying customers' needs. (p. 88)

administrative cost All costs incurred by a company that are not product costs or selling costs. Includes the cost of accounting, finance, employee relations, and executive functions. (p. 21)

allocation base An amount associated with cost objects that can be used to proportionately distribute manufacturing overhead costs to each cost object. (p. 69)

annuity A stream of equal periodic cash flows. (p. 244)

appraisal cost Cost incurred to detect poor-quality goods or services. (p. 406)

balanced scorecard A business-strategy model that views a company from four different perspectives—the financial perspective, the customer's perspective, the internal processes perspective, and the learning and growth perspective—to measure a company's financial and nonfinancial performance. (p. 409)

bill of materials A listing of the quantity and description of each item of direct material used to manufacture an individual product. (p. 338)

bottom-up budgeting A budget initially prepared by lower-level managers and employees. (p. 280)

breakeven Occurs when a company generates neither a profit nor a loss. (p. 156)

break-even point The sales required to achieve breakeven. This can be expressed either in sales dollars or in the number of units sold. (p. 156)

budget performance report The evaluation instrument used to evaluate a manager's performance to budget. (p. 302)

budgeted balance sheet A presentation of estimated assets, liabilities, and owners' (or shareholders') equity at the end of the budgeted period. (p. 275)

budgeted cash flow statement A statement of a company's expected sources and uses of cash during the period covered by the operating budget. (p. 275)

budgeted income statement Shows the expected net income for the period covered by the operating budget. (p. 275)

business segment A part of a company managed by a particular individual or a part of a company about which separate information is needed. (p. 385)

capital assets Long-lived expensive items such as land, buildings, machinery, and equipment. (p. 223)

capital budget The budget that outlines how a company intends to allocate its scarce resources over a five-year, ten-year, or even longer time period. (p. 222)

capital budgeting The planning and decision process for making investments in capital projects. (p. 219)

capital investments Business expenditures in acquiring expensive assets that will be used for more than one year. (p. 219)

capital projects Another name for *capital investments.* (p. 219)

capital rationing A term describing the allocation of the limited amount of money a company has to invest in capital projects and operations. (p. 229)

cash budget Shows whether the expected amount of cash generated by operating activities will be sufficient to pay anticipated expenses during the period covered by the operating budget. (p. 275)

cash payments schedule Presents the amount of cash a company expects to pay out during the budget period. (p. 293)

cash receipts schedule Presents the amount of cash a company expects to collect during the budget period. (p. 291)

centralized management A management style in which top managers make most management decisions. (p. 394)

common cost Another name for *indirect cost.* (p. 19)

common fixed cost Fixed cost incurred to support more than one business segment or the company as a whole. (p. 388)

compound interest Interest calculated on the original principal amount invested plus all previously earned interest. (p. 243)

continual budgeting Another name for *perpetual budgeting.* (p. 278)

contribution income statement An income statement that classifies cost by behaviour (fixed cost and variable cost). (p. 152)

contribution margin The amount remaining after all variable costs have been deducted from sales revenue. (p. 153)

contribution margin ratio The contribution margin expressed as a percentage of sales. (p. 155)

controller A company's chief accountant, who is responsible for the preparation of accounting reports for both external and internal decision makers. (p. 5)

cost The resources forfeited to receive some goods or services. (p. 18)

cost accounting A narrow application of management accounting dealing specifically with procedures designed to determine how much a particular item (usually a unit of manufactured product) costs. (p. 2)

cost-based transfer prices Transfer prices based on the cost of a good or service when an external market does not exist for goods or services transferred between responsibility centres. (p. 404)

cost behaviour The reaction of costs to changes in levels of business activity. (p. 119)

cost centre A business segment where the manager has responsibility and authority to act to decrease or at least control costs but has little or no control over the revenues generated or the amount invested in the segment. (p. 396)

cost driver A cost cause that is used as a cost allocation base. (p. 71)

cost object Any activity or item for which a separate cost measurement is desired. (p. 19)

cost of capital The cost of obtaining financing from all available financing sources. (p. 225)

cost of capital rate Another name for *cost of capital.* (p. 225)

cost of debt capital The interest a company pays to its creditors. (p. 225)

cost of equity capital What equity investors give up when they invest in one company rather than another. (p. 226)

cost of goods sold budget Calculates the total cost of all the product a manufacturing or merchandising company estimates it will sell during the period covered by the budget. (p. 274)

cost of services budget Calculates the total cost of all the services a service type business estimates it will provide during the period covered by the budget. (p. 274)

cost pool   An accumulation of the costs associated with a specific cost object. (p. 69)

cost-volume-profit (CVP) analysis   The analysis of the relationship between cost and volume and the effect of these relationships on profit. (p. 155)

decentralized management   A management style in which lower-level managers are responsible for decisions that relate to their segment of the company. (p. 395)

direct cost   A cost that can be easily traced to an individual cost object. (p. 18)

direct fixed cost   Fixed cost incurred to support a single business segment. (p. 387)

direct labour cost   The cost of all production labour that can be traced directly to a unit of manufactured product. (p. 25)

direct labour efficiency standard   The estimated number of direct labour hours required to produce a single unit of product. (p. 340)

direct labour efficiency variance   A measure of the difference between the planned number of direct labour hours and the actual number of direct labour hours for the units actually manufactured. (p. 348)

direct labour hours   The time spent by production workers as they transform raw materials into units of finished products. (p. 27)

direct labour rate standard   The planned hourly wage paid to production workers. (p. 340)

direct labour rate variance   A measure of the difference between the actual wage rate paid to employees and the direct labour rate standard. (p. 350)

direct material   The raw material that becomes a part of the final product and can be easily traced to the individual units produced. (p. 26)

direct material price standard   The anticipated cost for each item of direct material used in the manufacture of a product. (p. 338)

direct material price variance   A measure of the difference between the amount the company planned to pay for direct material purchased and the amount it actually paid for the direct material. (p. 347)

direct material quantity standard   The amount of direct material it should take to manufacture a single unit of product. (p. 338)

direct material quantity variance   A measure of the over- or underconsumption of direct material for the number of units actually manufactured. (p. 344)

direct material usage variance   Another name for the *direct material quantity variance.* (p. 344)

direct materials cost   The cost of all raw materials that can be traced directly to a unit of manufactured product. (p. 25)

discounting cash flows   Determining the present value of cash to be received in the future. (p. 231)

economic value added (EVA®)   Another name sometimes used for *residual income.* (p. 401)

engineering approach   A method used to separate a mixed cost into its fixed and variable components using experts who are familiar with the technical aspects of the activity and associated cost. (p. 126)

equivalent units   The number of units that would have been completed if all production efforts resulted in only completed units. (p. 91)

external failure cost   Cost incurred to correct problems after a good or service has been delivered to the customer. (p. 406)

factory burden   Another name for *manufacturing overhead cost.* (p. 28)

factory overhead   Another name for *manufacturing overhead cost.* (p. 28)

favourable variance   The difference between actual performance and standard performance when the actual performance exceeds standard. (p. 332)

finished goods inventory   Products that have been completed and are ready to sell. (p. 26)

fixed cost   A cost that remains constant in total regardless of the level of activity. (p. 119)

fixed manufacturing overhead budget variance   The difference between the actual amount of total fixed manufacturing overhead cost and the budgeted fixed manufacturing overhead cost. (p. 354)

fixed manufacturing overhead volume variance   A measure of the utilization of production capacity. This variance is caused by manufacturing more or less product during a particular production period than planned. (p. 355)

functional income statement   An income statement that classifies cost by function (product cost and period cost). (p. 152)

future value   The value of a payment, or series of payments, at some future point in time calculated at some interest rate. (p. 243)

high-low method A method used to separate a mixed cost into its fixed and variable components using the mathematical differences between the highest and lowest levels of activity and cost. (p. 133)

hurdle rate Another name for *cost of capital.* (p. 225)

hybrid firms Companies that generate revenue from providing services and selling products. (p. 38)

ideal standard A standard that is attainable only under perfect conditions. (p. 333)

imposed budget A budget in which upper management sets figures for all operating activities that the rest of the company rarely, if ever, can negotiate. (p. 280)

incremental budgeting The process of using the prior year's budget or the company's actual results to build the new operating budget. (p. 278)

indirect cost A cost that supports more than one cost object. (p. 19)

indirect fixed cost Another name for *common fixed cost.* (p. 388)

indirect labour The labour incurred in support of multiple cost objects. (p. 28)

indirect materials Materials consumed in support of multiple cost objects. (p. 28)

Industrial Revolution A term used to describe the transition in North America from an agricultural-based economy to a manufacturing-based economy. (p. 7)

internal failure cost Cost incurred to correct defective goods or services before delivery to the customer. (p. 406)

internal rate of return (IRR) The calculated expected percentage return promised by a proposed capital project. (p. 236)

International Organization for Standardization (ISO) The organization that develops voluntary quality and procedural standards, and certifies companies that meet these standards. (p. 406)

inventoriable cost Another name for *product cost.* (p. 20)

investment centre A business segment that is evaluated based on the amount of profit generated relative to the amount invested in the segment. (p. 398)

job cost sheet A document that tracks the costs of products, and organizes and summarizes the cost information for each job. (p. 76)

job order costing A costing method that accumulates cost by a single unit, or batch of units. (p. 74)

just-in-time (JIT) A philosophy that eliminates all unnecessary inventory and limits the use of company resources until they are absolutely needed to fulfill customer demand. (p. 409)

labour time ticket A document used to track the amount of time each employee works on a particular production job or a particular task in the factory. (p. 82)

lead time The time that passes from the time an order is received until the product is complete and ready for shipment. (p. 410)

least-squares method Another name for *regression analysis.* (p. 135)

linear regression analysis Another name for *regression analysis.* (p. 135)

management accounting The branch of accounting designed to provide information to internal economic decision makers (managers). (p. 2)

management by exception The process of focusing management attention on areas where actual performance deviates from the preestablished standards. (p. 332)

managerial accounting Another name for *management accounting.* (p. 2)

manufacturing overhead All activities involved in the manufacture of products besides direct materials or direct labour. (p. 28)

manufacturing overhead allocation The process of assigning or allotting an amount of manufacturing overhead cost to each unit of product produced based on some reasonable basis of distribution. (p. 69)

manufacturing overhead cost All costs associated with the operation of the manufacturing facility besides direct materials cost and direct labour cost. It is composed entirely of indirect manufacturing cost—that incurred to support multiple cost objects. (p. 25)

market-based transfer prices Transfer prices based on the price in the external market, when an external market exists for goods or services transferred between responsibility centres. (p. 403)

master budget Another name for *operating budget.* (p. 269)

master operating budget Another name for *operating budget.* (p. 269)

material stores   Another name for *raw materials inventory*. (p. 25)

materials requisition   A formal request for material to be transferred from the raw materials storage area to production. (p. 79)

mission statement   A summary of the main goals of the organization. (p. 221)

mixed cost   An individual cost that has both a fixed cost and a variable cost component. It also describes a company's total cost structure. (p. 125)

negotiated transfer prices   Transfer prices based on a price negotiated between the supplying and receiving responsibility centre managers when an external market does not exist for goods or services transferred between responsibility centres. (p. 404)

net cash flows   Cash inflow less cash outflow. (p. 230)

net present value (NPV)   The present value of all cash inflows associated with a proposed capital project minus the present value of all cash outflows associated with the proposed capital project. (p. 232)

normal cost system   System in which product cost reflects actual direct material cost, actual direct labour cost, and estimated overhead costs. (p. 85)

operating budget   A budget for a specific period, usually one to five years, that establishes who is responsible for the day-to-day operation of a business during that time. (p. 222, 269)

opportunity cost   The benefit foregone (given up) because one alternative is chosen over another. (p. 197)

organizational goals   The core beliefs and values of the company. They outline why the organization exists and are a combination of financial and nonfinancial goals. (p. 220)

outsourcing   Buying services, products, or components of products instead of producing them. (p. 194)

overhead   In a manufacturing company, another name for *manufacturing overhead cost*; in a service type business, the indirect service cost. (p. 28)

participative budget   A budget in which managers and employees at many levels of the company are involved in setting the performance standards and preparing the budget. (p. 280)

payback period method   A capital budgeting technique that measures the length of time a capital project must generate positive cash flows that equal the original investment in the project. (p. 238)

performance to budget   A process of evaluating managers and employees based on how they perform against the budget. (p. 301)

period cost   All costs incurred by a company that are not considered product cost. Includes selling and administrative cost. (p. 20)

perpetual budgeting   The budgeting approach of updating the budget every month. (p. 278)

practical standard   A standard that allows for normal, recurring inefficiencies. (p. 333)

predetermined overhead application rate   An overhead allocation rate calculated using estimated annual manufacturing overhead cost and the annual estimated amount for the allocation base. (p. 85)

present value   The amount future cash flows are worth today based on an appropriate interest rate (p. 246)

prevention cost   Cost incurred to avoid poor-quality goods or services in the first place. (p. 406)

process costing   A method of allocating manufacturing cost to products to determine an average cost per unit. (p. 74)

product cost   The cost of the various products a company sells. (p. 20)

production budget   Details the cost and number of units that must be produced by a manufacturer to meet the sales forecast and the desired ending inventory. (p. 274)

profit centre   A business segment in which the manager has the responsibility and authority to act to increase revenue and decrease or at least control costs, but has little or no control over the amount invested in the segment. (p. 396)

profitability index   A method used to rank acceptable proposed capital projects. (p. 235)

purchase order   A formal document used to order material from a vendor. (p. 77)

purchase requisition   A request form that lists the quantity and description of the materials needed. (p. 71)

purchases budget   Details the cost and number of units that must be purchased by a merchandiser to meet the sales forecast and the desired ending inventory. (p. 274)

purchasing department   A specialized department that purchases all the goods required by a company. (p. 77)

qualitative factors   Factors that cannot be measured by numbers—they must be described in words. (p. 187)

quantitative factors   Factors that can be measured by numbers. (p. 187)

raw materials inventory   Materials that have been purchased but have not yet entered the production process. (p. 25)

real rate of return   Another name for *internal rate of return.* (p. 236)

receiving report   A document that indicates the quantity of each item received. (p. 78)

regression analysis   A method used to separate a mixed cost into its fixed and variable components using complex mathematical formulas. (p. 135)

relevant cost   A dollar inflow or outflow that pertains to a particular management decision in that it has a bearing on which decision alternative is preferable. (p. 186)

relevant costing   The process of determining which dollar inflows and outflows pertain to a particular management decision. (p. 186)

relevant net cash flows   Future net cash flows that differ between or among the alternatives being considered. (p. 230)

relevant range   The range of activity within which cost behaviour assumptions are valid. (p. 124)

required rate of return   Another name for *cost of capital.* (p. 225)

residual income   The amount by which a segment's actual income exceeds the income needed to meet a company's required rate of return. (p. 401)

return on investment (ROI)   The percentage return generated by an investment in a business or a business segment. (p. 399)

revenue centre   A business segment in which the manager has responsibility and authority to act to increase revenues but has little or no control over costs and the amount invested in the segment. (p. 396)

sales budget   Details the expected sales revenue from a company's primary operating activities during a certain time period. (p. 273)

sales forecast   The prediction of sales for the period covered by the operating budget. (p. 282)

scatter graphing   A method used to separate a mixed cost into its fixed and variable components by plotting historical activity and cost data to see how a cost relates to various levels of activity. (p. 127)

scientific management   A management philosophy based on the notion that factories were run by machines—some mechanical and some human. Scientific management experts believed they could improve production efficiency by establishing standards of performance for workers. (p. 7)

segment income statement   An income statement prepared for a business segment. (p. 386)

segment margin   The amount of income that pertains to a particular segment. (p. 386)

segment reports   Reports that provide information pertaining to a particular business segment. (p. 385)

selling and administrative expense budget   Calculates all costs required to support a company's forecasted sales other than the cost of product or services. (p. 274)

selling cost   The cost of locating customers, attracting customers, convincing customers to buy, and the cost of necessary paperwork to document and record sales. (p. 20)

sensitivity analysis   A technique used to determine the effect on cost-volume-profit when changes are made in the selling price, cost structure (variable and/or fixed), and volume used in the CVP calculations. Also called "what if" analysis. (p. 162)

service department   A business segment responsible for secondary (support) functions. Service departments provide service to the main business operations and to other service departments. (p. 391)

setup time   The time it takes to prepare manufacturing equipment for the production of particular products. (p. 410)

simple interest   Interest calculated on the original principal amount invested only. (p. 243)

The Society of Management Accountants of Canada (CMA-Canada)   A professional association of management accountants comparable to the professional association of financial accountants (Canadian Institute of Chartered Accountants). (p. 8)

special order   An order that is outside a company's normal scope of business activity. (p. 192)

standard   A preestablished benchmark for desirable performance. (p. 331)

standard cost system   A system in which cost standards are set after careful analysis and then used to evaluate actual performance. (p. 331)

standard costing   The process of setting cost performance goals that benchmark acceptable performance and then using these cost goals to evaluate performance. (p. 331)

standard fixed manufacturing overhead rate   The rate used to apply fixed manufacturing overhead to units of manufactured product. (p. 342)

standard variable manufacturing overhead rate   The rate used to apply variable manufacturing overhead to units of manufactured product. (p. 341)

strategic plan   A long-range plan that sets forth the actions a company will take to attain its organizational goals. (p. 221)

sunk cost   A past cost that cannot be changed by current or future actions. (p. 186)

throughput time   The time that passes from the time a unit of product enters the production process until it emerges as a finished product. (p. 410)

time-adjusted rate of return   Another name for *internal rate of return.* (p. 236)

time value of money   The increase in the value of cash over time due to investment income. (p. 192, 231)

top-down budgeting   A budget prepared by top managers in a company. (p. 279)

traceable fixed cost   Another name for *direct fixed cost.* (p. 387)

transfer pricing   The set of rules an organization uses to allocate jointly earned contribution margin among responsibility centres. (p. 403)

treasurer   The corporate officer who is responsible for cash and credit management and for planning activities, such as investment in long-lived property, plant, and equipment. (p. 5)

unfavourable variance   The difference between actual performance and standard performance when the actual performance falls below standard. (p. 331)

unscheduled downtime   The amount of time production equipment is out of service due to unscheduled repairs and maintenance. (p. 410)

value engineering   The process of systematically evaluating activities in an effort to reduce costs while satisfying customers' needs. (p. 89)

variable cost   A cost that changes in total proportionately with changes in the level of activity. (p. 120)

variable manufacturing overhead efficiency variance   A measure of the variable manufacturing overhead cost attributable to the difference between the planned and actual amount of the allocation base. (p. 351)

variable manufacturing overhead spending variance   The difference between how much was actually spent on variable manufacturing overhead and the amount that should have been spent based on the actual direct labour hours worked. (p. 353)

variance   The difference between actual performance and the budgeted or standard amount (p. 302); also the difference between actual performance and the standard. (p. 331)

weighted-average cost of capital   The combined cost of debt financing and equity financing. (p. 225)

work-in-process inventory   Products that have entered the production process but have not yet been completed. (p. 25)

zero-based budgeting   A process of budgeting in which managers start from scratch, or zero, when preparing a new budget. (p. 279)

zero defects   Describes the concept of products that are completely free of imperfections. (p. 409)

Index